MILE HIGH CITY

An Illustrated History of Denver

by Thomas J. Noel

Pioneer Fountain
in Civic Center.
Credit: Denver
Metro Convention
& Visitors Bureau

PRINTED BY A. B. Hirschfeld Press, Denver, CO USA

LIBRARY OF CONGRESS CATALOG CARD NUMBER: 97-71126

ISBN: 1-886483-10-8

PUBLISHED BY Heritage Media Corporation, Denver, CO and Encinitas, CA

PRODUCED IN COOPERATION WITH Historic Denver, Inc.
Kathleen Brooker, *Historic Denver President*
John Castellano, *Historic Denver Board Chairperson 1995-1997*
Cal Cleworth Chair, *Historic Denver Publications Committee*
Joan Prusse Co-Chair, *Historic Denver Preservation Committee*

AUTHOR Tom Noel
PHOTO EDITOR Tom Noel
PRODUCTION EDITOR Lori M. Parks
ART DIRECTOR Ann Hoff Scott, Visual Antics
PUBLISHER C. E. Parks

PROJECT MANAGER Ray Spagnuolo

PARTNERS IN DENVER SALES COORDINATORS
Pamela Bjerke
Janet Melody
Marion Nold
Martin P. Page
Jan Warriner

PARTNERS IN DENVER EDITORIAL COORDINATOR Betsy Lelja

PARTNERS IN DENVER CONTRIBUTING WRITERS
Brad Dunevitz
Rosemary Fetter
Peggy G. Hazelwood
Aaron Makinen
Tom Noel
Janet Raasch
MaryJo Reiger
Sonia Weiss

Denver civic center from capitol. *Credit: photo by Ron Ruhoff*

Acknowledgments

HISTORIC DENVER, INC. MADE THIS PROJECT possible in many ways. Thanks to president Kathleen Brooker and Dottie Ambler, John Castellano, Cal Cleworth, Kelly Ferris, Kim Grant, Leigh Grinstead, Hal Logan, Julia Secor, and others.

At the Colorado History Museum, my gratitude goes to the library staff, especially manuscripts curator Stan Oliner and photo curator Eric Paddock. A tip of the hat to the CHS's David F. Halaas, Jim Hartmann, Rebecca Lintz, Andy Masich and Peg Ekstrand as well as Dale Heckendorn and the State Historic Preservation Office crew.

The Denver Public Library's Western History Department, led by manager Eleanor Gehres, with a skilled staff including Bruce Hanson, Philip Panum, Kathey Swan, Barbara Walton, Kay Wisnea, and the late Augie Mastroguiseppe, guided me expertly through DPL's immense treasury.

Rich Grant of the Denver Metro Convention & Visitors Bureau generously allowed use of illustrations from the bureau's slide library. At the Denver Urban Renewal Authority, Sue Powers and Mary Ann LeClair were equally generous. Thanks also librarians at the Colorado State Archives, The Colorado College, Colorado State University, the Carnegie Local History Branch in Boulder, the Colorado Springs Public Library, *The Denver Post*, the Greeley History Museum, Joanne Dodds and the Pueblo Regional Library, the Amon Carter Museum in Fort Worth, the Library of Congress, the National Archives, and the Beinecke Library at Yale University.

Other collaborators were Jack Murphy of the Denver Museum of Natural History, Dick Conn and Lewis Sharp of the Denver Art Museum, Rick Daley and Wendy Tucciarone of the Denver Botanical Gardens, and Gully Sanford of the Denver Center for the Performing Arts, Debbie Ellerman of Lakewood's Heritage Center and Lakewood Planning Director Frank Gray; Bob McQuarrie and Lorena Donahue of the Littleton History Museum; Boulder's Carnegie Library Staff; the Aurora History Museum and Aurora planner Kate Kienast; and Lois Lindstrom and Marcetta Lutz of the Arvada Historical Society and David Burger of the Arvada Center. Photographers James Baca, Glenn Cuerden, Michael Gamer, Jim Milmoe, Eric Paddock, Rhoda Pollock, Ron Ruhoff, Martin Weiker, Roger Whitacre and artist Barbara Froula kindly allowed reproduction of their art.

Denver Mayor Wellington Webb graciously allowed interviews and otherwise expedited this project. Thanks also to Dennis Gallagher, Andrew Hudson and Dana Crawford. The people at Heritage Media Corp., especially Chuck and Lori Parks, Ann Scott, Ray Spagnuolo, and others have made this book a pleasant and rewarding experience from an author's perspective.

My colleagues and students at the University of Colorado at Denver have been of tremendous assistance. CU-Denver graduate students helped with research, writing and editing, especially Owen Chariton, Dan Corson, Janet Cunningham, Barbara Gibson, Eric Hammersmark, Bill Convery, Rosemary Fetter, Steve Hart, Marcie Morin, and Kevin Rucker. Thanks also to Bill Bessesen, Margaret Coel, and Steve Leonard who has taught me much Denver history. Readers wanting more detail and fuller documentation should consult the book, *Denver: Mining Camp to Metropolis*. Sumiko, my wife, once again served as a silent partner who made this work possible in many ways.

—T.J.N., *Denver, May 6, 1997*

CONTENTS

LEFT: Denver from City Park Golf Course.

Credit: photo by Ron Ruhoff

FOREWORD

WILLIAM SHAKESPEARE KNEW THAT THE PAST holds valuable lessons for those willing to explore it. We ignore the past at our peril; each time we lose a piece of our history, we lose a piece of our identity. Historic Denver strives to protect the historic places that helped to shape our city's past, because they are vital parts of our city's future.

Since its formation in 1970, Historic Denver, Inc. has worked to preserve Denver's unique architectural character through education and advocacy programs. HDI's community-based board and over 1500 members and volunteers promote and preserve historic buildings, neighborhoods, and cultural landscapes.

Working side by side with business and civic leaders, this citizen organization has developed and delivered educational programs about Denver's rich history; restored and interpreted the Molly Brown House Museum for the enjoyment of 40,000 visitors and natives each year; undertaken key projects such as the creation of Ninth Street Historic Park on the Auraria campus; managed Four Mile Historic Park on behalf of the City of Denver; saved Five Points' Justina Ford House, now home of Thomas Hornsby Ferril, Colorado's notable poet laureate; established an easement program to protect landmarks in perpetuity; initiated the oldest and most successful annual house tour in Denver; and spearheaded creation of the Lower Downtown Historic District, now home to a true urban renaissance.

Educating the public has always been an important element of Historic Denver's mission to enlist Coloradans in the ongoing effort to preserve and revitalize the special places that make this a great place to live and work. That heritage is really the centerpiece of our quality of life, as the readers and supporters of this book know. One of the best ways to educate is through publishing. HDI is proud to continue a long tradition with this outstanding offer from Heritage Media Corporation.

The publication of *Mile High City: An Illustrated History of Denver* is a celebration of generations of enterprise which created a city of real character. It's been a pleasure to recognize the achievements of long time supporters and welcome new partners in these pages.

Kathleen Brooker

—Kathleen Brooker, President, Historic Denver, Inc.

PREFACE

UNLIKE SAN FRANCISCO, WHICH THE SPANISH founded as a mission, and Salt Lake City, which the Mormons started as a communal religious utopia, Denver originated as a place to make money. From the beginning, the town aspired to be the supply hub: the business, manufacturing, service, and political center for surrounding mines, farms, and ranches.

Not until the early 1900s did Denver overcome the frontier rawness with governmental efforts aimed at sound planning, environmental improvements, and the public good. Instead of just holding the door open for private interests, the city focused on erecting grand public places and on the general welfare. Ironically, it took a slick city boss, Mayor Robert W. Speer, to impose such City Beautiful era reforms.

That dream of the progressive age was revived at the end of the twentieth century by mayors Federico Peña and Wellington Webb. They emphasized public projects, including parks, paths, public buildings, schools, libraries, and historic preservation to promote a sense of pride and of place. In the surrounding suburbs, which now contain more than three-fourths of the metropolitan population, privatism prevails. Despite generally wealthier populations and richer tax bases, most suburbs have been stingy with public amenities, while private golf courses, country clubs, three-car garage subdivisions, and upscale shopping havens proliferate.

Denver's history remains an ongoing struggle between those interested in private profits and those pursuing the public good, a tug of war between givers and takers. On some happy occasions, the two parties have worked together, blending private gain and public good. This narrative overview, along with the sketches of prominent businesses and institutions, attempts to celebrate those who have contributed to the city, those who have worked to create a benevolent public-private partnership.

The motivation of the city's founders was captured in a song written for the town's first Christmas party in 1858. The ode was produced by a Pennsylvania newspaperman, A. O. McGrew, better known to history as "Wheelbarrow" McGrew, after he arrived in Denver pushing all of his possessions in a wheelbarrow. Supposedly McGrew reached the promised land and pushed his wheelbarrow into the auriferous waters of the South Platte. He expected the river to gold plate his vehicle while he took a nap.

After waking up to the reality that was Denver, McGrew wrote the following:

A Hit at the Times

Way out upon the Platte, near Pike's Peak we were told,
There by a little digging we could get a pile of gold,
So we bundled up our duds, resolved at least to try
And tempt old Madame Fortune, root hog, or die.

So we traveled across the country, and we got upon
*   the ground,*
But cold weather was ahead, the first thing we found.
We built our shanties on the ground, resolved in
*   spring to try*
To gather up the dust and slugs, root hog, or die.
Speculation is the fashion even at this early stage,
And corner lots and big hotels appear to be the rage,
The emigration's bound to come, and to greet them
*   we will try,*
Big pig, little pig, root hog, or die.

Let shouts resound, the cup pass around, and we all
*   came for gold;*
The politicians are all gas, the speculators sold;
The scads are all we want, and to get them we will try,
Big pig, little pig, root hog, or die.

Surveyors now are at their work, laying off the towns,
And some will be of low degree, and some of high renown.
They don't care a jot nor a title who do buy
The corner lots, or any lots, root hog, or die....

The Arapaho Camp

PALEFACES POURING INTO COLORADO IN 1858-59 were greeted — in English — by the Arapaho camped along the base of what that tribe called "the shining mountains." Chiefs Little Raven and Left Hand welcomed "the spider people" with a generosity that they later regretted.

Long before Denver began, the Arapaho had been camping along Cherry Creek near its junction with the South Platte. They named the creek for its wild choke cherry bushes. French traders and trappers, whom the Arapaho also befriended, baptized the Platte River with their word for shallow or flat.

The Arapaho fondness for Cherry Creek led the St. Louis fur trader, Auguste P. Chouteau, to host a trading camp on the creek in 1815. Forty-five mountain men attended the rendezvous to trade directly with the Indians. Another St. Louis fur trader, Louis Vasquez, built a cottonwood-log fort in 1832 near the confluence of the South Platte and Clear Creek, which was originally called Vasquez Creek in his honor. At this short-lived fort, in what is now suburban Adams County, Vasquez traded with the Arapaho and other tribes for buffalo robes, beaver pelts and wild horses. Louis also built the better-known and longer-lived adobe Fort Vasquez about 40 miles downstream on the South Platte at Platteville, now reconstructed and operated as a museum by the Colorado Historical Society.

Of the tribe on the site of Denver, little but the name remains. The name "Arapaho" may be derived from the Pawnee word meaning "buyer" or "trader." The Arapaho called themselves "bison path people" or "our people." The earliest known use of the name Arapaho comes from John Bradbury, the English naturalist, who wrote of "Arapahays" robbing fur traders around 1810.

During the 1840s and 1850s, as many as 1,500 Arapaho camped on the future site of Denver. This small tribe of Plains Indians with their light skin and prominent noses, were also known as the "Tattooed People." After scratching their breasts with a yucca leaf needle, they rubbed wood ashes into the wound to make an indelible chest tattoo.

The Arapaho, part of the Algonquin family, once lived in the Great Lakes area. They had been pushed west by other tribes, who were retreating from advancing whites. After crossing the Missouri River, the tribe split. The northern Arapaho headed for what would become Wyoming, the Southern Arapaho for Colorado. Around 1750, the Arapaho reached the eastern edge of the Rocky Mountains. The Utes, Colorado's ancient mountain tribe, resisted Arapaho expeditions into the high country. So it was in eastern Colorado that the Southern Arapaho would make their last stand.

As one of the smaller plains tribes, the Arapaho found it wise to befriend rather than to fight larger tribes such as the Sioux and the Cheyenne. The Arapaho did take on the Utes, a small tribe with a different language and roots. The Utes, a Shoshonean people, are physically shorter, darker and stockier than the Plains Indians. The Arapaho claimed that the "ugliness" of the Utes led them to raid Arapaho villages and kidnap Arapaho women in hopes of improving the tribe's appearance.

The Arapaho called whites "spider people." Too late the Arapaho realized the significance of the web of roads, survey lines and fences with which palefaces were measuring and seizing the land. At first, the Indians welcomed the pale-faced gold seekers trespassing on the area given to the Arapaho by the 1851 Fort Laramie Treaty. That treaty promised to the Arapaho and their allies, the Southern Cheyenne, the territory between the Platte and the Arkansas rivers at the eastern base of the Rockies. Seven years later that treaty promise was undone by the discovery of gold in the sands of Cherry Creek and the South Platte.

....

OPPOSITE PAGE: Native Americans camped at the base of the Shining Mountains originally welcomed the gold-crazed "Spider People" to Colorado. Credit: *The Colorado College Library*

A tattered assortment of mountain men, prospectors, town promoters and gamblers rushed to the frontier crossroads at the eastern base of the Rocky Mountains, confident that the creator had endowed a future metropolis with unlimited riches of the earth. The Arapaho chief, Little Raven, entertained newcomers in his own handsomely- decorated tepee and visited them in their strange square houses.

The Blue Brothers

Arapaho acceptance of the argonauts flooding into Denver after 1858 is well illustrated by the saga of the Blue brothers. The Blues and a few others made the mistake of leaving the Platte River Road for a short-cut into Denver. When Daniel and his two brothers ran

out of food and water, they survived only by cannibalism. An Arapaho found Daniel, the sole survivor, and took him into his tepee to nurse the lost, starving goldseeker back to physical and mental health. The Arapaho then took Blue to Denver, where he reported in his statement of May 12, 1859:

"Alexander, my eldest brother, died, and at his own last request, we used a portion of his body as food on the spot, and with the balance resumed our journey towards the gold regions. We succeeded in traveling but ten miles, when my younger brother, Charles, gave out, and we were obliged to stop. For ten days we subsisted on what remained of our brother's body, when Charles expired from the same cause as the

ABOVE: Little Raven's tepee, like that of other Arapaho, was decorated with paintings depicting his exploits. His tepee faced east toward the rising sun with its back to stormy west winds. *Credit: Tom Noel Collection*

others. I also consumed the greater portion of his remains, when I was found by an Arapaho Indian, and carried to his lodge, treated with great kindness, and a day and a half thereafter brought to…Denver City."

General William Larimer

Townsfolk raised a collection to send Daniel Blue back to Illinois to tell his family the terrible truth. Unlike Blue, most '59ers arrived safely at the frontier crossroads that proclaimed itself to be Denver City. General William Larimer founded the upstart "city" by crossing cottonwood sticks at the center of a square mile town plat on November 22, 1858. Larimer chose the east side of Cherry Creek because it was on higher ground and on the more accessible side of the Cherry Creek and South Platte River trails. Larimer named the newborn metropolis for James W. Denver, governor of Kansas Territory, to help ensure that it would be chosen as the county seat of what was then Arapahoe County, Kansas Territory.

In a letter to the wife and nine children whom he had left behind in Kansas, Larimer boasted that: "It is well the Pilgrims landed upon Plymouth Rock and settled up that country before they saw this one or that would now remain unsettled. Everyone will soon be flocking to Denver for the most picturesque country in the world, with fine air, good water, and everything to make man happy and live to a good old age."

Larimer fancied calling himself "General" after capturing that title in the Pennsylvania State Militia. The "general" did not discover gold or found the first town at the confluence of Cherry Creek and the South Platte. He had merely followed the Russell party, which first discovered gold and platted the original settlement — Auraria — on November 1, 1858. William Green Russell and his group of Georgians headed back to the South to join the Confederate Army.

Larimer, the claim jumper, proclaimed himself Denver's founding father. Without false (or true) modesty, Larimer boasted "I am Denver City."

Arapahoe County & Arapahoe City

Larimer and other leaders named the huge surrounding area, stretching from the Front Range of the Rockies to the Kansas border, for its rightful owners — the Arapaho. Arapahoe County, Kansas Territory also contained an early town called Arapahoe.

It originated in the autumn of 1858 when Marshall Cook's party of soldiers pushed a few miles beyond Auraria to the base of Table Mountain and founded on November 29, 1858, a winter camp they called Arapahoe City. They were joined by the Arapaho Chief Left Hand (Niwot), who spoke English well. He

ABOVE: General William Larimer founded Denver on November 22, 1858, and wrote home to his family: "We are bound to have a territory if not a state, and the capital will be Denver City." Credit: *Colorado Historical Society*

Albert Bierstadt,
one of the first
notable artists to
portray Colorado,
came with the 1859
Gold Rush and stayed
to paint romantic
landscapes such
as this one, "Indian
Encampment."
*Credit: Denver
Art Museum*

Cowboys and Indians, mythical all-American heroes, played very real roles as an Arapaho camp evolved into the biggest
of all Rocky Mountain cowtowns. Alexander P. Proctor's sculptures in Civic Center Park give city hall historical perspective.
Credit: photo by Michael Gamer

told Cook that he hoped "to clear up the mystery of how their white intruders obtained their bread by the sweat of their brow, while the redman alone procured his meat by the chase."

Mexican Diggings

Arapahoe, like many other would-be "cities," quickly shriveled and died. So did Mexican Diggings on the South Platte River about where Overland Park now stands in Denver. This 1857 gold camp of pioneer Mexican miners was dismissed by Anglo "discoverers" a year later. These Yankee newcomers ignored the camp's original name and its Hispanic origins.

Mexican Diggings is mentioned by Jerome Smiley in his *History of Denver*. Smiley reported that John Simpson Smith, a mountain man who married into the Cheyenne tribe, was already there when Denver's "founders" arrived. As Smiley put it, "Smith, in company with some Mexicans had, in the summer of 1857, discovered and taken out considerable gold at a place on the Platte River, about three miles above the mouth of Cherry Creek. The spot thus became known in the local annals, as 'the Mexican Diggings' — or, by some, as 'the Spanish Diggings.'"

Uncle Dick Wootton, another pioneer of 1858, pointed out in his autobiography, that "the old Spanish mine on the Platte River...probably brought gold hunters to the point originally." These 1857 digs along the banks of the South Platte near today's South Santa Fe Drive and West Alameda Avenue, pre-dated both the October 30, 1858, founding of Auraria by the Russell brothers and the November 22, 1858, founding of Denver City by General William H. Larimer, Jr., and company.

Like the Arapaho camp, Mexican Diggings has largely disappeared from historical records. The Mexican pioneers and their original gold strike have been overlooked by English-speaking settlers. Not only were these Hispanic roots buried, the City of Denver passed ordinances outlawing construction with adobe bricks. By restricting the size of bricks to $8\frac{1}{4}$ x $4\frac{1}{4}$ x $2\frac{1}{4}$ inches and requiring that all bricks be kiln-fired, Denver kept adobe-dwelling Mexicans from feeling at home.

Besides Mexican Diggings, another early rival — Auraria — was absorbed by Denver City. General Larimer's colleague, Richard E. Whitsitt, the first president of the Denver City Town Company, proclaimed Denver's victory over the Russells' town of Auraria in a May 16, 1859 letter to Daniel Witter: "Them Southern desperados from Georgia that located their city on the west side of Cherry Creek have reached the end of their rope. They have lied about our town-site and traduced its obvious merits wherever they had a chance to wag a tongue or write a letter. But their doom is sealed already and Denver is the city of the present and the future."

The rival towns on Cherry Creek were finally brought together by an outside threat from Golden City, which aspired to become the territorial capital and economic hub. "Countermeasures of consolidation and more congenial relationships between Denver and Auraria are not only our alternative," Larimer reported, "but an absolute necessity for the survival of all." Auraria was absorbed in a moonlight ceremony on the Larimer Street bridge over Cherry Creek on April 6, 1860. Denver had gobbled up its first great rival.

General Larimer had predicted as much in a November 18, 1858, letter to the mayor of Leavenworth, Kansas Territory: "Denver City is situated at the mouth of Cherry Creek where it forms its confluence with the South Platte. This is the point where the Santa Fe and New Mexico Road crosses to Fort

Laramie and Fort Bridger, also the great leading road from the Missouri River; in short, it is the center of all the great leading thoroughfares and is bound to be a great city."

Despite the bluster of town founders, Denver City was a long shot. It lay hundreds of miles from Santa Fe, Omaha, Salt Lake City, or any other sizable city. Not until the struggling hamlet actually became a city did Denverites feel secure enough to drop the word "city" from the town's official title.

Realizing that his town had to have connections to the outside world to survive, Larimer bribed the Leavenworth and Pike's Peak Stage Company with 53 town lots to make Denver its Rocky Mountain headquarters. The first stagecoaches, traveling in pairs for safety, arrived May 7, 1859.

....

Little Raven, with his granddaughter on his lap, is seated next to William Bent, one of the few Indian agents to sympathize with the Arapaho and Cheyenne.
Credit: Colorado Historical Society

The hallmark of any viable western city was a newspaper and William Byers wasted no time establishing his *Rocky Mountain News*. Diplomatically, he located his press in the middle of Cherry Creek, straddling the line between the rival cities of Denver and Auraria so as not to impede sales to either community.

The Arapaho shook their heads when Byers and other whites began building Denver City, a town of shacks and shanties in and around the sandy creek bottoms. Sooner or later, the Arapaho warned, the creek would rise and sweep away anything in its path. Byers and other town builders just laughed — and kept on building. When the editor and his newspaper office were washed away in the flood of 1864, he barely escaped with his life. The *News* managed to keep above water after that by retreating to higher ground in Denver City.

Little Raven

In the May 7, 1859, *Rocky Mountain News*, Byers reported that: "Little Raven, the head chief of the Arapaho nation…is highly spoken of by those who know him… Little Raven said he likes all the whites that he had anything to do with, and was glad to see so many here." Little Raven and the Arapaho, the *News* claimed, "are desirous of being instructed in agriculture, manufactures and the arts of peace to live in quiet with the whites and the surrounding tribes of Indians."

The Arapaho watched as some 100,000 gold seekers swarmed into Colorado Territory. Some Indians suggested that the East must now be empty of whites and perhaps the Arapaho should go there.

The argonauts' welcome wore thin and there seemed to be some confusion as to who was visiting whom. Byers' *News*, on May 14, 1859, reported: "Our city and vicinity has been visited recently by great numbers of the native population...coming in large numbers, erecting their lodges in our midst, they spend a few days and then move on to other hunting grounds." The same article recounted cordial visits from both Little Raven and Left Hand before the Arapaho bands departed "on a Buffalo hunt." Other

Indian lands were seized by hordes of miners such as this 1860 crew which used hydraulic mining and sluices in Gregory Gulch, a golden mother lode that quickly evolved into Central City. *Credit: Mazzulla Collection, Amon Carter Museum.*

newspaper accounts described in lurid detail the Arapaho war dances at their camp in Denver, long nights of dancing, singing, and celebrating the capture of Ute scalps.

Arapaho continued to camp in Denver during the early 1860s. Albert D. Richardson, in his book, *Beyond the Mississippi*, described his visit to an Arapaho village between Blake Street and the South Platte. There, in his words, "barbarism had thus far maintained its ground against the advancement of (nominal) civilization." Influenced perhaps by the cigar Little Raven gave him, Richardson called him "the nearest approximation I ever met to the Ideal Indian. He had a fine manly form and a human, trustworthy face." However, he quite accurately predicted that the Arapaho encampment would be crowded out before long.

....

Indians may have lost battles and land to the whites, but their own records tended to show them victorious. The Cheyenne Ledger Book, captured after the tribe's defeat at Summit Springs on the Colorado Plains in 1869, portrayed White Bird firing at a dismounted calvary bugler, wounding him in the right cheek and finishing him off with a sabor through the head. Credit: *Colorado Historical Society*

William McGaa

The land, of course, belonged to the Native Americans, as recognized by the 1851 Fort Laramie Treaty. This inconvenience led General Larimer to confer with William McGaa, a mountain man who had long camped on the banks of Cherry Creek. The story of William McGaa demonstrates how boosters banished less edifying characters in order to polish the city's reputation.

For starters, McGaa was condemned as a "squaw man" for living with Indian women. The Arapaho freely shared their women with whites (whites, however, charged for the sexual favors of their prostitutes).

McGaa claimed to be married into various Indian tribes and was willing, on behalf of his wives' relatives, to convey the land to Larimer and other town-founders. To reward the Indians, McGaa supposedly asked that streets be named after his "wives" — Wewatta, Wazee and Champa (Sioux for chokecherry.) McGaa further requested that a major street be named for himself and another for his ancestral castle in Scotland, Glenarm Place.

One of McGaa's wives, according to Jerome Smiley, was a handsome high-cheeked, half-breed who wore fine, frilly, flower-bedecked Victorian dresses and dressed her black hair in stylish curls. Smiley thought less highly of McGaa himself: "McGaa had promised more than he could perform, was a troublesome customer to manage, and a hard man to browbeat." When McGaa refused to improve his Denver City lots, his rights to them were revoked.

McGaa, according to *Reminiscences of General William H. Larimer and of His Son William H.H. Larimer*, boasted of being the son of the Lord Mayor of London. McGaa was Denver's first great storyteller according to the younger Larimer, who fancied McGaa's tale of why the Arapaho had fled the "Bad Lands" when they became "entirely destitute and barren of every living thing, both vegetable and animal." Furthermore the bad lands were "inhabited by a race of tiny people not more than eighteen inches high." McGaa claimed to have seen not only the Lilliputian Indians but "the ruins of villages and towns…in perfect state of petrification.

He said he saw large pine trees with the limbs and branches turned to stone, and among them deer that were petrified in the very act of running and looked as natural as the living."

Perhaps McGaa, in a drunken fantasy, had imagined leprechauns on the High Plains. Or perhaps he was retelling some Arapaho folktale which belittled their enemies. The petrified towns are possibly inspired by abandoned Anasazi sites in western Colorado.

McGaa is mentioned in John White's book, *Sketches from America*, after White reported that "by some lucky chance" he found McGaa in Denver one Sunday "in a state approaching sobriety." White began an interview, but McGaa kept "throwing such longing looks toward the bar" that White finally obliged him.

Following the custom of the day, the bartender set in front of McGaa an empty tumbler, a tumbler of water and a whiskey bottle. McGaa, White reported, "did not trouble the water at all." The furry-tongued McGaa poured forth tales of the great city he had founded, showing, White assured his British readers, "what manner of man in reality are [James Fenimore] Cooper's idealized 'Pathfinders.'" McGaa, the original resident of Denver, claimed to have fathered the first partly white child born here and built the first cabin.

This town founder became an embarrassment to respectable pioneers. In 1866, the Denver City Council renamed McGaa Street as Holladay Street, in honor of the man who brought the Holladay Stage line to town. McGaa, the unworthy tosspot, was banished from the ranks of the founding fathers. His presence — and that of his half-Indian children — in the Denver Pantheon of pioneer heroes might sully the reputations of other noble white male founders, whom future generations were expected to celebrate.

McGaa Street fared no better as Holladay Street. By 1880, this thoroughfare accommodated the most notorious red light district in the Rockies. At the request of the Holladay family, the name was changed in 1887 to Market Street — a fitting name for a street where an estimated 1,000 prostitutes marketed their wares in brothel windows with signs such as, "Men Taken in and Done for." Reputable businesses and residents on Market above Twenty-Third Street and below Cherry Creek demanded that those parts of Market be called Walnut Street, which they are to this day.

The Sand Creek Massacre

General Larimer left before Indian wars troubled early Denver. Like many other boosters, Larimer's loyalties were transferable. When Denverites failed to elect him mayor or territorial representative and President Abraham Lincoln refused to appoint him territorial governor, Larimer soured on his promised land. He returned to Kansas, denouncing Denver's "lack of comforts."

Friendly relations deteriorated when many Arapaho refused to sign the Fort Wise Treaty of 1861 which

No known photographs or Indian ledger books portray the Sand Creek Massacre, where peaceful Arapaho and Cheyenne faced a deadly apparition that may have looked like this. Credit: *Colorado Springs Pioneer Museum*

After losing their land, the Arapaho also faced an attack on their culture. Young Arapaho men, like these, were "educated" to ignore their tribal heritage and become "civilized Christians."
Credit: *Denver Public Library*

expelled them from their homeland in the Cherry Creek and South Platte valleys. Indian agent William Bent, a founder of Bent's Fort, resigned rather than participate in this treaty which confined the Arapaho to a much smaller, more arid tract of southeastern Colorado north of the Arkansas River around an intermittent stream called Sand Creek.

Albert G. Boone, a grandson of Daniel Boone, succeeded Bent and negotiated the Treaty of Fort Wise, sometimes called Boone's Treaty. Little Raven, along with three other Arapaho chiefs — Storm, Shave-Head and Big Mouth, signed the treaty although other Arapaho refused. Boone reported that some Southern Arapaho on the Sand Creek reservation were "an indolent community" who are "great lovers of whiskey [and] very licentious, they worship the Sun Earth and smoke and swear by the pipe." Unusually close friendship with the whites had left the Arapaho ravaged by alcoholism and diseases.

The 1862 Indian census counted 720 Northern Arapaho and 1,500 Southern Arapaho. Many of the southerners had left Sand Creek because they were never given the promised agricultural tools and training, or even enough water to farm. Facing starvation, they hunted buffalo and other game — on and off the reservation.

When they could not find wild game the Arapaho sometimes pursued the white man's cows. At the Van Wormer ranch 35 miles east of Denver, the Arapaho stole several head of cattle, horses, and some of the rancher's personal goods. This was the beginning of a number of incidents involving either the Arapaho or their allies, the Cheyenne.

The most famous incident was the "Hungate Massacre" in 1864, again at the Van Wormer ranch where Ward Hungate was the ranch manager. Amid the burned ruins of the ranch, a rescue party found two little girls with their throats cut so severely that they were nearly decapitated. Mrs. Hungate had been raped, stabbed and scalped. Her husband had been shot numerous times, then horribly mutilated and scalped by rampaging Arapaho.

To further inflame public sentiment, the scalped and badly mutilated bodies of the Hungates were taken to Denver and put on public display. No better recruiting device could have been found for a local populace who already hated the Indians. Colonel John M. Chivington was in charge of the pursuit of the renegades. Although the Arapaho and Cheyenne were promised protection at a camp called Sand Creek, a few months later Chivington and his men massacred about 150 Indians, mostly women and children. One woman, Kohiss, escaped with a baby at her breast. The babe on her back and a third child in her arms were killed. She lived on the Arapaho reservation in Oklahoma until the age of 104, showing battle scars and re-telling the sad story of Sand Creek.

Little Raven's Lament

After the battle, Chivington spent another week pursuing Little Raven and his band, but could not find them. Following Sand Creek, the surviving Arapaho were shoved out of Colorado and onto reservations in Wyoming and Oklahoma. Bemoaned Little Raven:

> It will be a very hard thing to leave the country that God gave us…That fool band of soldiers cleared out our lodges, and killed our women and children…There, at Sand Creek…Left Hand, White Antelope and many chiefs lie there, and our horses were taken from us there…Our friends are buried there, and we hate to leave these grounds…

Arapaho no longer camped along the creek and river where they had welcomed the first Denverites. A few names survive as reminders of the Arapaho's prouder days in Colorado. Much of modern metropolitan Denver lies within Arapahoe County, which was named for its earlier residents — a friendly tribe of Plains Indians who were soon swept rudely away.

After Sand Creek, Little Raven still steered his people toward peaceful coexistence with the whites. He represented the Arapaho at the 1865 Treaty of the Little Arkansas and the 1867 Medicine Lodge Treaty, where one newspaper wrote him off as a "fat, tire-

some old man." Little Raven persistently argued that the Arapaho were peaceful and that disturbances were caused by other tribes. Invited to tour the east, he visited Boston, New York and Washington. He returned after a visit to the White House to tell his people that they did not need to raise corn after all. The Great White Father had a heap of money to help Indians and he could always mint or print more. Little Raven remained the principal chief of the Southern Arapaho until he died in 1889 of natural causes, on his tribe's Oklahoma reservation.

In 1994 Little Raven Street opened between the 2100 block of 15th Street and Elitch Gardens on the banks of the Platte River, belatedly commemorating the hospitable Arapaho chief. On June 7, 1996, Tsistsis-Hinono'ei (Cheyenne/Arapaho) Park was dedicated at 9300 E. Iowa Avenue in Aurora with a stone monument at the entrance to the park reading "Dedicated to the Arapaho and Cheyenne Nations." Wildflowers frame this park which contains ceremonial Indian circles, red sandstone slabs inscribed with Indian memories and an abstract lodge pole and I-beam sculpture by an Indian artist. Belatedly, the Mile High City is celebrating the Arapaho camp in which it was born.

Jim Beckwourth, a mulatto mountain man, was one of the few Denverites to defend the Arapaho and Cheyenne. Disgusted with the slaughter of peaceful old men, women and children at Sand Creek, he left Denver to live with the Crow tribe in Montana. Credit: Massachusetts Historical Society

....

After seeing the Arapaho and Cheyenne crushed and removed from Colorado, Chief Ouray of the Utes smoked this peace pipe with the palefaces. Partly because of his efforts, the Utes are the only tribe with reservations in Colorado today. Credit: Colorado Historical Society

THE GOLDEN GAMBLE

AGES BEFORE THE ARAPAHO ARRIVED, GOLD settled at the confluence of Cherry Creek and the South Platte River. Over a span of hundreds of millions of years, the heavy yellow metal bubbled up in hot, volcanic forms that injected it into cracks and faults of rocks.

Erosion of the Rockies, and of an ancestral range that existed some 250 million years ago, created the High Plains. The same glaciers and streams that melted the mountains also washed out some of the gold into placer deposits whose discovery gave birth to Denver.

William Greeneberry "Green" Russell, a veteran of both the Georgia and the California gold rushes, scrutinized the Colorado Rockies carefully. He suspected the three-mile-high barrier to America's westward expansion might become a goal one day. He reckoned that the Rockies hid mineral treasures. His discovery of a few ounces of gold in the summer of 1858 proved his suspicion correct and triggered a mass migration to Colorado. An estimated 100,000 people rushed into Colorado between 1858 and 1860. Only one out of three found Colorado worthwhile, because in 1860 the census taker found only 34,277 residents.

Russell and his party founded the first permanent settlement in what is now metro Denver. They named their town Auraria — from the Latin word for gold — after their hometown in the Georgia gold fields. Auraria merged with Denver City, its rival on the opposite bank of Cherry Creek, on April 6, 1860. Afterwards, Auraria became known as West Denver.

Denver's Puppy Days

Denver City was a long shot. Most of the Gold Rush settlements would become ghost towns. In the struggle to become the county seat, the state capital and the regional metropolis, there would be many losers and only one winner. While other Coloradans gambled on gold, Denverites mined the miners, relieving them of whatever wealth they might find up in the hills. Denverites gambled with cards and dice, with mining stock and real estate and railroads. They bet on everything from dog fights to snowfall. During the slow winter months, city fathers amused themselves with card games. They used town lots as poker chips and whole blocks of downtown Denver changed hands in an evening.

Demas Barnes, an argonaut crossing the plains, marveled at Denver's site and its construction. "Why [Denver] was ever located here for is more than I can decipher," he wrote home on June 25, 1866. "Ten thousand carcasses of poor overworked animals mark the highway over seven hundred miles of parching, treeless plain."

Despite the barren High Plains and the dead animals, Barnes explained that gold fever made Denver a magnet: "It is almost impossible not to partake of the general enthusiasm, for you hear gold discussed morning, noon, all night, and far into the next day. It is not a myth. You see it — you select specimens for your cabinet...you hold the pure golden nuggets in your hands, your eyes dilate, your mouth waters..."

Gold gave birth to Denver and bankrolled the reckless rush to construct a great city. Almost from the beginning Denver built for permanence in brick and stone — unlike so many other now-vanished Colorado towns of frame and canvas. "Denver," as Barnes put it in a letter of June 27, 1865, "is a square, proud, prompt little place...There being no wood, brick becomes a necessity for building purposes...It has fine brick stores, four churches, a good seminary, two theaters, two banks, plenty of gambling shops, a fine U.S. mint [which] has actually coined the vast amount of four thousand dollars in a whole year!"

Denver had few visible means of support, and little reason to become a city. It lacked the navigable water-

---

OPPOSITE PAGE: Gold panning paid off although cynics said gold bubbled up from the fires of hell to provoke greed and evil. Indians agreed, calling gold the excrement of the gods. *Credit: Tom Noel Collection*

William Greeneberry "Green" Russell led the Georgians
and Cherokee Indians who first found gold in Cherry Creek
and the South Platte River in 1858. The Russell Party also
founded Auraria, the area's oldest permanent settlement,
before returning South to join the Confederate Army.
Credit: Colorado Historical Society

After gambling on gold in them thar hills,
many fortune seekers tried less strenuous
games of chance in Denver's gambling "hells,"
such as the Progressive Hall, featured
in the February 7, 1866 issue of *Harper's Magazine*.
Credit: Colorado Historical Society

In a town founded on a gamble for gold,
games of chance with cards and dice became
a favorite pastime, as shown in this scene from
Frank Leslie's Illustrated Newspaper, Jan. 9, 1864.
Credit: Colorado Historical Society

ways that usually determine the location of cities, and other settlements were closer to the mines which were Colorado's livelihood. In the decade after the Gold Rush, Denver faced the same fires, floods, Indian wars and ore-processing difficulties that left Colorado Territory littered with dead towns. Yet an English visitor, Miss Rose Kingsley, reported in her book *South by West* that the mile-high town was "one of the most successful of all the new cities of the West."

Kingsley best described Denver's precarious and isolated existence. After seeing the baby town in 1871, she marveled: "It looked just as if it had been dropped out of the clouds accidentally, by someone who meant to carry it further on, but got tired, and let it fall anywhere."

The People's Government

To govern this accidental city the People's Government was formed in September, 1860, in Apollo Hall, a saloon in what is now Larimer Square. City fathers wrestled with law and order, taxes and the homeless. At the request of Denver merchants, the first law enacted on October 8, 1860, was "an Ordinance prohibiting Gambling & the selling of Liquor or Merchandise on the Streets or from Wagons or Tents." This ordinance suggests that two-year-old "Denver City," the hub of the Colorado Gold Rush, bustled with boozers and losers.

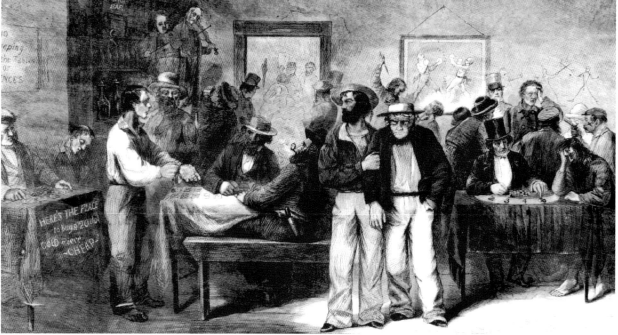

Owen Goldrick, Denver's first school teacher, also helped open the Denver City & Auraria Reading Room & Lending Library to uplift the grubby little village of gold diggers. *Credit: Tom Noel Collection*

The People's Government selected "Noisy Tom" Pollock as marshal, partly because of his commanding voice. Pollock, who had arrived from New Mexico in 1858, opened Denver's first blacksmith shop on January 10, 1859. Three months later he erected the two-story Pollock House at 11th and Market streets, a site now on the Auraria Campus. Pollock received 50 cents for every criminal he caught and his pioneer hotel soon bulged with prisoners.

Pollock earned his star in a shootout by killing George Steele, a swaggering, murderous gambler. Pollock administered doses of "lead-poisoning" and "rope-burn" to weed out Denver's numerous "bummers." He repeatedly reappears in the People's Government ledger, asking for help in housing prisoners. When the town failed to build a jail, Pollock resigned.

The People's Government struggled to raise funds not only for a jail, but for a courthouse, and a public school. Voters balked. After one disastrous election on November 10, 1860, Denver "indefinitely postponed" plans to collect taxes and began asking for voluntary donations. By May 14, 1861, the new city had spent $8,739 and incurred a debt of $6,463. To solve the budget quandary, the People's Government took to taxing the town's ubiquitous saloons.

Another revenue-raising scheme, proposed on Nov. 22, 1860, aimed to "establish a course of Lyceum

One of the great mass migrations in American history, the 1858-59 Pike's Peak Gold Rush lured some 100,000 fortune seekers to Colorado. More than half of them soon went back to their former homes, bitterly blasting Colorado as a "bust." **Credit: Tom Noel Collection**

Criminals, as well as gamblers, flocked to Denver City, which lay 700 miles from the nearest jail. Denver vigilantes headed by "Judge Lynch" generally labeled the corpse with the crime. *Credit: Tom Noel Collection*

Lectures, with proceeds for the City Poor Fund." This pioneer effort to simultaneously promote culture and care for the homeless never materialized.

On Dec. 11, 1860, the People's Government authorized a "Literary and Historical Society of the City of Denver" which was also asked to be "one of the overseers of the poor." This society was still-born. Its mission fell to the state, which did not organize the Colorado Historical Society (CHS) until 1879. The Denver Public Library did not finally open its doors until 1889. Not until 1990 did the Colorado Historical Society open the first Denver History Museum in the old Byers-Evans House.

The clash between community and private interests began early. In a resolution to outlaw private structures erected in the public streets and in the bed of Cherry Creek, the pioneer city officials noted that "Such posession [sic] by individuals of public property is an infringement upon the rights of the community and of individual owners of property in the vicinity."

The People's Government was replaced on November 19, 1861, by today's city government, which was officially authorized by the new Territorial Government of Colorado. All that is left of the People's Government is a slender, mud-stained ledger recording the pioneer struggle to govern often reluctant citizens — a battle that continues today.

William N. Byers

A prime mover behind the People's Government was William Newton Byers. Byers fought to bring stagecoach service to the isolated town and endeavored to make Denver the steamboat capital of the Rockies. The greatest Denver booster of all, Byers was born on an Ohio farm but he did not stay put long. He headed west to Iowa and then to Omaha, the great jumping-off place and home base for the Union Pacific Railroad. Byers had helped lay out Omaha, which became the largest town between St. Louis and San Francisco. He served on its first city council, and represented it in the Nebraska Territorial Legislature. Succumbing to gold fever, he abandoned Omaha in 1859 for the Cherry Creek Gold Rush settlements. He wrote one of seventeen 1859 guidebooks to the new promised land, selling himself as well as thousands of others on the golden gamble called Denver City.

Byers published Denver's first newspaper, the *Rocky Mountain News*, on April 23, 1859. The *News* puffed Denver as the pre-ordained metropolis of the Rockies, even imagining river traffic for the high, dry city on the shallow South Platte. In early issues of the *News* aimed at Omaha and other cities filled with investors, capital, and potential immigrants, Byers called Denver the steamboat hub of the Rockies. Noting that water traffic made major cities of New Orleans, St. Louis, and other river towns, Byers launched a "shipping news" department. On September 10, 1859 the *News* announced in its "Boat Departures" column: "'Ute' and 'Cheyenne' for mouth of the Platte. Scow 'Arapahoe' for New Orleans. All laden with passengers and freight."

Subsequent announcements for the benefit of eastern investors and the national press proclaimed ships sailing from Denver to Pittsburgh and New York. Despite such heroic efforts by the "Rocky Mountain Liar," as critics termed the *Rocky Mountain News*, the South Platte never became a mighty Mississippi clogged with steamboats whistling for a landing on Denver's waterfront.

Byers also used the *News* to promote agriculture. He offered free seeds to anyone stopping by his office, and publicized agricultural experiments. In the first issue of the News, Byers warned in his editorial, "Farming vs. Gold Digging" that farmers "taken off with the Cherry Creek yellow fever" would do better "to raise stock and produce for the mines." All Colorado needed to make the Great American Desert bloom, Byers asserted, were a few good farmers and a little water. Of course, cynics scoffed, a few good people and a little water could turn hell into heaven.

As Byers' career illustrates, newspapers were the primary tool of boosterism in western frontier towns. Lord Bryce, the English ambassador who captured Yankee eccentricities in his classic, *The American Commonwealth*, put it well: "Many a place has lived on its 'boom' until it found something more solid to live on; and to a stranger who asked in a small Far Western town how such a city could 'keep up four

newspapers,' it was well answered that it took four newspapers to keep up such a city."

Footloose frontier hordes troubled city builders like Byers. He urged the miners swarming into, over, and often out of Colorado to settle. In the *News*, March 14, 1861, he blasted the "folly of being eternally on the tramp, without stopping long enough in any place to learn its resources or to earn a livelihood…If the time thus spent in running over the country were judiciously employed in prospecting or making preparation for farming, a class that is now not far removed from a public nuisance would soon develop rich mines [and] open up valuable ranches and farms."

Newspapers attracted newcomers and capital to upstart towns such as Denver. Byers became the spokesman for Denver and outlasted dozens of ink-stained competitors. He was the voice of the city and might well have been elected mayor or governor or senator — except for an indiscretion with a woman who was not his wife.

Hattie Sancomb, a pretty divorcee from Kansas, grew very fond of the handsome, nobly-bearded Byers. He found their affair easier to slip into than to get out of. When he tried in 1876 to cool her ardor, she drew a pearl handled pistol and fired. She missed, damaging only his reputation. From behind a lace curtain of her parlor window, Mrs. Libby Byers saw her husband ambushed in the street and rushed out to rescue him. Denver buzzed with a delicious scandal concerning its most prominent citizen. Subsequently, Byers sold his newspaper and abandoned his political aspirations. Yet he stuck with Denver — and his wife stuck with him. He helped to organize a Chamber of Commerce and tirelessly promoted Denver as the queen city of the Rockies.

Born in a gold rush, Denver got a fast start. By 1865, it had emerged as the capital of Colorado Territory. Denverites had out-politicked Golden and Colorado City, both of which briefly served as the capital. In an 1881 election, Colorado Springs and Pueblo failed to muster enough votes; Denver became the permanent political hub. Denver legislators helped arrange lesser prizes for Boulder, Cañon City, Colorado Springs and

Pueblo. The latter received the state mental hospital and Colorado Springs the state home for the deaf and dumb, as it was originally called. Cañon City was awarded the state penitentiary — a coveted prize, since convicts provided cheap or free labor. Boulder got last prize — the state university. Many people then (and some now) reckoned that faculty and students were a rowdy, disruptive lot, given to dissipation and idleness.

Historical Consciousness

Nineteenth-century Coloradans were history conscious. They prided themselves on being the first to see, to name, to settle, and to build. As early as 1872, Denverites held pioneer picnics for their founding mothers and fathers. In 1879, the State Historical and Natural History Society was created. The state legislature gave the society $500 to collect, preserve and exhibit Colorado's heritage before "the men who have been the actors, and the material for collections will be quite beyond our reach."

In 1900, the historians and natural historians parted company and settled in different homes. The historical society built a Greek temple of Colorado Yule marble across Fourteenth Street from the State Capitol. The Denver Museum of Natural History constructed its museum at the east end of City Park.

Colorado did not produce any literary giants to immortalize the frontier era — no Washington Irving, James Fenimore Cooper, Mark Twain, Willa Cather or Mari Sandoz. Travelers such as Isabella Bird, Helen Hunt Jackson, Richard Townsend, Louis Simonin and Oscar Wilde left lively, literary accounts, but not until the 20th century would Coloradans such as Hal Borland, David Lavender, Marshall Sprague and Frank Waters do literary justice to the settlement of mountain and plain. Not until the poet Thomas Hornsby Ferril (1896-1988) began celebrating Colorado's mountains and rivers, its mining camps and its Mile High City, could Colorado claim a literary giant.

Historians have been luckier. LeRoy Hafen, Frank Hall, Jerome C. Smiley and Wilbur Fisk Stone all compiled multi-volume state histories. Smiley also completed a monumental, 978-page *History of Denver* detailing the rise of people and places in a magical mile high setting. Since 1908, the Colorado Historical Society has issued a magazine celebrating local history, starting with *The Trail* in 1908 and evolving into today's glossy, color quarterly, *Colorado Heritage*.

Artistic Endeavors

Denverites emphasized the edifying. They ignored the fact that their city government, as well as the territorial government, had been conceived, born and raised in saloon halls. Saloons also housed the first theaters, art exhibits, dance, music, theater and even libraries. By 1910, Denver had 410 saloons which offered a wide variety of goods and services, of arts and amusements, as well as nickel beers and free lunches.

Bar art attested to early cultural aspirations. Original art today is often confined to museums, corporate board rooms and the homes of the wealthy. In 19th-century Denver, much original saloon art was public art. Charles Stobie, a western artist, lived above the Gallup & Stanbury Saloon (which still stands at 1445 Larimer Street) and exhibited his work downstairs in the bar. Editor Byers appraised Stobie's work as "the most excellent and beautiful work in oil painting we have seen executed in this country." Stobie's works, like the paintings Charles Russell once swapped for drinks in the Mint Saloon, now command much higher prices. Denver has lost most of its bar art with the reckless demolition of it 19th-century architectural heritage. Two exceptions are the landscapes on the old high back booths at the Punch Bowl Tavern, 2052 Stout Street, and the Windsor Hotel bar mural which survives in the Oxford Hotel dining room.

Colorado artists and art lovers organized the Artists Club in 1893 to promote the visual arts. During the 1920s, this club reorganized as the Denver Art Museum. Anne Evans, a leading benefactor and an artist herself, helped to establish what is still the Denver Art Museum's strongest collection, its American Indian material. Ironically, she was the daughter of territorial

Ed Chase's Palace Theatre, a notorious early-day amusement parlor, specialized in "leg art." In 1997,
the old Palace site at 15th and Blake in lower downtown became home to an overscaled new high-rise, the Palace Lofts.
Credit: *Colorado Historical Society, photo by Joseph P. Sturtevant*

governor John Evans, who was removed from office after the massacre of about 150 Indians, primarily old men, women and children, at Sand Creek. Anne Evans and the art museum prized the artifacts that were disregarded by many pioneers as the trinkets and trappings of savages. In their rush to culture, the pioneer generation overlooked the Indian culture and artifacts now showcased at the Denver Art Museum, Colorado History Museum and Denver Museum of Natural History.

Performing Arts

Colorado's performing arts were also born in barrooms. Apollo Hall on Denver's Larimer Street staged Colorado's first theatrical performances in 1859. Saloonkeeper Libeus Barney, who adored Shakespeare, reported that 400 people squeezed into his hall,

demonstrating "the appreciation of art in this semi-barbarous region." In early saloon-theaters, enthusiastic audiences customarily treated their favorite actors and actresses to libations between acts. This custom, as historian Smiley noted, "often resulted in lowering the standard of artistic effects of the closing scenes of the drama."

The Occidental Hall on Blake Street featured Colorado's "favorite balladist" to "delight all with operatic and sentimental, as well as comic songs." At other times, this Blake Street bar advertised a reading room with the latest newspapers and free stationery, offering readers a haven two decades before the Denver Public Library was founded in 1889. The Occidental, during its long career as a pioneer performing arts center, ballyhooed a German violinist and Miss Lulu ("the California Prima Donna,") trapeze performances by "Professor" Wilson and a musical machine "which makes as much music as a dozen brass bands." The most notorious theater was Ed Chase's Palace at 15th and Blake streets (the Palace Lofts now occupy the site.) This saloon, gambling hall and theater was notorious for its "leg art" and laughing ladies of easy virtue.

Such artistic efforts helped make Denver a cultural as well as a commercial capital for Colorado. Farmers from the eastern plains, ranchers from the San Luis Valley and the Western Slope, and miners from the mountains have long relied on Denver as an amusement center. Although high-brow critics have rolled their eyes and aimed snide comments at Denver's "cowtown culture," it has entertained Coloradans with western humor, sentimental nostalgia, and treatment of regional topics.

The Tabor Grand Opera House

In Europe and America, grand opera houses reigned as the ultimate palaces of culture. Visitors to Colorado marveled at finding opera houses in small mining towns such as Central City as early as the 1870s. Denver, of course, erected the grandest opera house of all — the Tabor Grand at 16th and Curtis streets. To erect the most lavish building Denver has ever seen, silver magnate Horace Austin Warner Tabor went shopping for an architect in Chicago. He came back with Willoughby and Frank Edbrooke. After touring opera houses in eastern cities to find what was most fashionable and functional, the Edbrookes designed an $800,000 palace for opera.

"Denver," Tabor declared, "was not building as good buildings as it ought to and I thought that I would do something towards setting them a good example." The Tabor Grand wore a high Victorian facade of golden-pressed brick trimmed in Manitou limestone under a slate roof from Maine. It sported asymmetrical Queen Anne towers, a Second Empire mansard roof, and steep chateauesque roofs on its towers and dormers. Denverites were flabbergasted. Some called it "oriental luxury" while the journalist

Eugene Field pronounced the edifice's eclectic style to be "modified Egyptian Mooresque."

Marble steps led to the large marble rotunda with two immense mirrors in which Denver's socialites could admire themselves. The main hall's magnificent chandelier glittered with hundreds of crystal pendants. Patrons often came early to watch the lighting of the chandelier 65 feet above the parquet floor. Above the 144-jet gas chandelier, fleecy pink clouds floated in the twilight sky of the dome. Plush silk curtains, tapestries, 1,500 crimson velvet opera chairs, and six eight-person opera boxes adorned the opera house. The Tabor Grand Saloon, the finest bar in town, featured its own ladies orchestra.

Augusta Tabor begged her husband to take her to the Tabor Grand for the opening night. He refused, but a heavily veiled Mrs. Elizabeth "Baby Doe" McCourt Doe was there in Horace's box, which was draped with a plaque of silver from the Matchless mine inscribed "TABOR." Denver historian Louisa Ward Arps claimed in her fine book, *Denver in Slices*, that after Tabor married Baby Doe, his mistress, their two baby girls used the opera house box as a 16-square-foot playpen.

Prophetically, the main curtain of the Tabor Grand bore a line from Charles Kingsley's poem, "Old and New: A Parable:"

> So fleet the works of men,
> Back to the earth again
> Ancient and holy things
> Fade like a dream.

Within a generation, the Tabor Grand stooped to 10 cent movies. Clumsily remodeled and renamed the Colorado Theater, it suffered numerous "improvements." One of the last desecrations, a gamble to compete with a newfangled invention of the 1950s, was converting part of the enormous mezzanine into a miniature theater called "Tabor's Television Room." Following this defilement, Tabor's ancient and holy dream was demolished in 1964 to build a modern Federal Reserve Bank, a prison-like edifice where worn-out paper money is shredded.

The Tabor Grand Opera House (1880-1964) at 16th & Curtis streets reigned over the Queen City. As the most splendiferous erection of silver magnate H.A.W. Tabor, this towering palace of brick and marble anchored Denver's once extensive Curtis Street Theater District. The Tabor and two dozen other Curtis Street theaters are gone, leaving only the Denver Center for Performing Arts at 14th and Curtis as a souvenir of when Curtis Street was Denver's answer to New York City's Broadway. *Credit: Colorado Historical Society, photo by William Henry Jackson*

In 1957, the Tabor Grand
Opera House featured
a smashing new movie,
Oklahoma. Even popular,
cheery musicals could not
save Denver's most exquisite
theater, razed seven years
later to build a far less grand
Federal Reserve Bank.
Credit: Tom Noel Collection

Colorado's ace mining man (Horace Tabor), a hard-working pioneer wife (Augusta Tabor), and the most beautiful woman in Colorado (Baby Doe) became a sensational love triangle and inspired the great American opera, *The Ballad of Baby Doe*.
Credit: Colorado Historical Society & Betty Moynihan

With picks and pans, prospectors prowled the creeks tumbling out of the Rockies, hoping to strike paydirt.

Credit: Harrison Mills Drawing, Tom Noel Collection.

Bankrupt Banks

The Federal Reserve Bank System was established in 1913 to prevent economic crashes like the one that undid Horace Tabor. The federal reserve bank came too late to save Denver's shaky 19th-century banks. These money houses floundered in the 1890s when the big gamble on mining became a colossal bust. Half of Denver's 18 banks closed in July of 1893.

The federal government's remedy for the Depression, repealing the Sherman Silver Purchase Act, was worse than the disease as far as Coloradans were concerned. Without the federal subsidy, the price of silver tumbled from over $1 an ounce to half that. Silver mining, Colorado's number one industry, collapsed.

Bankers became much more cautious, much more wary of borrowers infected with gold and silver fever. Colorado National Bank, one of the survivors, learned the truth of the old joke: a mine is a hole in the ground owned by a liar. After the crash of 1893, the Colorado National foreclosed on several hundred

After placer miners exhausted surface gold, goldseekers sank shafts deep into the earth for lode mines such as Nevadaville's Hubert Mine. *Credit: Colorado Historical Society, photo by Harry H. Buchwalter.*

stock and mines, had become "assets" of gullible bankers who bankrolled the golden gamble.

The golden — and especially the silver — gamble had become a painful lesson. Much more money was sunk into most mines than was ever taken out. Even if the golden gamble began to look like a bust, it had given Denver a fast start, attracting capital from the East and Europe to build up Colorado and its capital city.

Although mining faltered, Denver had gained a grand opera house, fine residential neighborhoods, and an impressive collection of handsome stone and brick buildings downtown. Denverites pushed onward to eclipse Santa Fe, Cheyenne and Salt Lake City, and to build a bigger city than Montanans, Dakotans, Kansans and Nebraskans. By 1890 Denver had become the undisputed regional metropolis of the Rockies — thanks largely to a spiderweb of steel.

Jefferson Randolph "Soapy" Smith, one of Denver's slickest gamblers, also fleeced greenhorns with phony mining stock sales. *Credit: Denver Public Library.*

mining companies. Slowly the bankers got around to assessing their collection of mines. W.F. Berger of Berger and Sayre, mining engineers, personally investigated some 200 claims and 30 mining companies. He reported for mine after mine; *"stock is probably worthless"* and "lots of work has been done but it has not produced a cent."

Piles of handsomely printed stock certificates for gold and silver mines impressed this author while he was investigating Colorado National Bank's vaults in 1985 with the grandson of Colorado National Bank's founder, the late Harold B. Kountze. Among the confiscated collateral was a metal tube-like contraption with an elaborately inscribed scroll from Thomas H. Edwards of Denver's Chlorination and Cyanide Supply Company. It explained how the apparatus could be used for "extracting gold, silver, copper and platinum from their respective or mixed ores." Such magical devices, along with all the dubious mining

To bankroll Colorado mining, corporations issued stock. Despite the fancy certificates, mines rarely paid off as promised, inspiring Mark Twain to define a mine as "a hole in the ground owned by a liar." *Credit: Tom Noel Collection*

Rail City

THE TOWN CONCEIVED, BORN AND RAISED IN A mining boom began to look like a bust during the 1860s. Between 1860 and 1870, the town gained only 10 additional residents. The U.S. Census of 1870 counted 4,759 residents, not the predicted 100,000.

Editor Bill Byers fumed about what he called "go-backers" in the *Rocky Mountain News*: "Because they cannot shovel out nuggets like they have been accustomed to dig potatoes, they raise the cry that it is all a humbug and take the back track for home where it is to be hoped that they will ever after remain."

Denver's doldrums, as Byers pointed out, could only be relieved by railroad connections. The town's isolated position 600 miles from the nearest urban centers along the Missouri River retarded growth.

Another champion of the railroad was former territorial governor William Gilpin, Colorado's greatest orator, or, according to arch rival Byers, the state's biggest windbag. Gilpin proclaimed in 1869 that Denver was "preeminently cosmopolitan," for it lay at the crossroads where "the vast area of the Pacific fits itself to the basin of the Atlantic."

Of course, Gilpin generally saw the center of universe as wherever he happened to be. Denver, as he elaborated in his 1873 book, *Mission of the North American People*, lay along the isothermal zodiac that ran through Athens, Rome, Paris, London and New York. Through Denver the "condensed commerce of mankind" was destined to flow.

John Evans

Governor Gilpin's rhetoric not withstanding, Denver lay in the middle of nowhere, 600 miles from "the states" and the nearest sizeable city. Denver's rail hopes soared when President Abraham Lincoln appointed John Evans to replace William Gilpin as territorial governor in 1862. Evans, who was born to a Quaker family on an Ohio farm in 1814, gravitated to the Ohio Valley boom town of Cincinnati. There he graduated from Lynn Medical College and moved west to Indianapolis, where in 1845 he spearheaded the establishment of one of America's early insane asylums.

In 1847, Evans moved to the boom town of Chicago where he taught at Rush Medical College. He also began investing in Chicago real estate and railroads. Business interests led him into politics and he became a Chicago city councilman and early supporter of Abraham Lincoln. Evans proved to be a sharp businessman. He helped found the Chicago suburb of Evanston and its academic claim to fame — Northwestern University. He also helped promote the railroads that made Chicago the rail hub of America.

If anyone could bend the rails of transcontinental lines into Denver, it would be the new territorial governor. President Lincoln had appointed Evans a commissioner of the Union Pacific Railway, a position Evans would use to Denver's advantage. Governor Evans found a close friend and ally in editor Byers, who had feuded with Governor Gilpin. These two, more than anyone else, were responsible for making Denver the metropolis of the Rockies.

If Byers was Denver's number one booster, Governor Evans became the city's number one builder. He erected railroads, churches, a university, and a fine home at Fourteenth and Arapahoe streets that attracted other home builders to Denver's first fancy residential address — 14th Street.

Some, including Mrs. Evans, wondered why the wealthy and respected Dr. Evans left the comforts of Chicago for the Colorado wilderness where he found Denver "really the only tolerable place."

Certainly Evans, who had assets of $1.3 million according to the 1870 census, did not come West for the salary of $2,500 a year as territorial governor.

OPPOSITE PAGE: Without a railroad in the 1860s, Denver stagnated. The Occidental Billiard Hall and Reading Rooms on sleepy Blake Street promised patrons newspapers from Chicago that were "only a week old." Not until the rail age, would Denver become an up-to-date, wide-awake city. Credit: *Colorado Historical Society, photo by William G. Chamberlain*

Perhaps Evans was motivated by the missionary idealism that led him to found Colorado Seminary in 1864. This pioneer college evolved into what is now the University of Denver on Evans Avenue. Evans also gave $100 toward the construction of any new house of worship. Churches, Evans felt, could civilize the raw, saloon-filled frontier crossroads which Isabella Bird found to be a spree city where "men go to spend the savings of months of hard work in the maddest dissipation."

Although Governor Evans assured Denverites that he would capture the iron horse, the hamlet of Golden organized Colorado's first railroad. Golden lay 15 miles to the west of Denver at the mouth of Clear Creek Canyon, Colorado's richest mineral stream of the pioneer era. Golden promoters William A.H. Loveland and Henry M. Teller organized the Colorado Central in 1864. Working with Boston capitalists who had created the Golden City Town Company in 1859, Loveland and Teller hoped to make their town the rail hub of Colorado.

Loveland and Teller's "Golden Crowd" also hoped to politically railroad the "Denver Crowd" led by Evans and Byers. After the first session of the territorial legislature found Colorado City (the predecessor town of Colorado Springs) uncomfortably crude in 1861, Golden seduced the legislators by offering them free accommodations in Loveland's Hall in downtown Golden, as well as free firewood and iced libations. Not until 1867 did equally generous offers coax the legislators to move to Denver, where they have remained.

While Golden City courted the lawmakers, backers of Golden's railroad courted the mining camps up Clear Creek Canyon. Central City, Black Hawk, Idaho Springs, Georgetown and other Clear Creek communities generally shared a mistrust of big, bad Denver. Many Coloradans considered the Mile High City a parasitical supply-and-spree town that drained wealth from its hard-working hinterlands. The Central City *Colorado Times* cheered Golden's efforts to build the Colorado Central up Clear Creek Canyon as "good news for mining districts, for there is but little of the Denver egotism about the Golden folks. We can hope for advantages from Golden City that Denver in her exclusiveness would never grant. Denver is like the snake, which perishing from the cold, was taken by the countryman out of pity into his bosom, but which

....

John Evans, although forced to resign as Territorial Governor after the Sand Creek Massacre, stayed in Denver to the end of his life. He became Denver's great pioneer railroad builder and, with his son William Gray Evans, also helped to construct the Denver Tramway Company's extensive street railway system.

Credit: Tom Noel Collection

upon being revived by his warmth, as a return for his kindness, bit him. So Denver in her selfishness would have the mines of Colorado — the very bowels of their existence — shift for themselves."

Despite these editorial jabs, Denver rushed into the railroad race. Making molehills out of the mountains west of Denver, Byers wrote of the two-mile-high mountain wall: "the country is fully described when we say hilly; but few elevations attaining the prominence of mountains, the valleys and slopes are rich in grasses, prolific in fruits and abounding with inexhaustible forests of pine, fir, and cedar timber, presenting a most vivid contrast to the barren and desert plains [of Wyoming]."

Union Pacific engineer Grenville M. Dodge came to a different conclusion about the "hilly" land west of Denver. He knew better after surveying a possible Berthoud Pass rail route in September 1866, when he and his men were nearly buried by a sudden blizzard. Only paper railroads, like paper steamboats, reached Denver in the 1860s.

Dodge and the Union Pacific decided that a route through Wyoming would be much faster and cheaper to build. Cruelly, the transcontinental railroad bypassed

"The Queen City of the Mountains and Plains" in favor of Cheyenne and the gentler hills of Wyoming. "Denver," crowed the *Cheyenne Daily Leader* "was too far from Cheyenne ever to amount to much." Other rivals added: "Denver would soon be too dead to bury."

Many Denver pioneers began moving to Cheyenne, reckoning that the Union Pacific town would be the rail hub of the Rockies. As Denver's population dwindled, civic leaders such as Byers and Evans grew alarmed. They joined with bankers David Moffat and Luther and Charles Kountze, and entrepreneur Walter Scott Cheesman to rescue the city with a lifeline of steel. Evans, relieved of his governorship after the Sand Creek Massacre, stayed in Denver although his dismissal also killed his hope that the governorship might lead to the U.S. Senate. Free of political responsibilities, Evans devoted his considerable abilities, experience, and energy to railroading the Rockies.

The Denver Pacific

To rescue the fading Colorado capital, Evans, Byers and the Board of Trade persuaded voters to approve

Denver, South Park & Pacific locomotive # 28, "Denver", was one of a fleet of narrow gauge coal
burners that brought the riches of the hinterland into the Mile High City. *Credit: Colorado Historical Society*

bond support for constructing the Denver Pacific Railroad. Citizens also donated labor to help grade the tracks and even cut trees and made railroad ties for the 106-mile line between Denver and Cheyenne.

Denverites celebrated the arrival of the Denver Pacific on June 24, 1870. At last, Denver lay on the nation's railroad maps. The steel lifeline kept the town from blowing away, anchoring it for a railroad boom. Once the Denver Pacific arrived, other railroads built to Denver. After these iron horses galloped into town during the 1870s, gold, silver, coal and other pay dirt began to pay off. The reborn town constructed a spider web of rails to tap a vast Rocky Mountain hinterland of mining, farming and ranching communities. Denver became the node of a railroad network stretching from Montana to New Mexico, from Utah to Kansas.

In subsequent years, dozens of other railroads steamed into Denver making it the rail hub of the Rockies. By 1900, 100 trains a day snorted in and out of Denver's Union Station.

This rail network enabled Denver to establish its metropolitan sway over Coloradans. Gold and silver ores mined in the mountains rode the rails into Denver's smelters. The giant Argo, Globe and Grant smelters became Denver's biggest employers by the 1890s. Acrid, black smelter smoke hung over the city, signaling its emergence as an industrial center.

After finishing the Denver Pacific, John Evans presided over the Denver, South Park and Pacific (DSP&P). This narrow gauge line, incorporated in 1872, followed the South Platte River into the Rockies. The DSP&P first stopped at Morrison, a scenic town located in the red sandstone foothills. There Evans joined the Scottish stonemason George Morrison in establishing the Morrison Stone, Lime and Townsite Company.

The South Park line crawled up South Platte Canyon and over Kenosha Pass to tap South Park's

Denver's early rival, Golden City, housed the Colorado Territorial Legislature from 1862 to 1867. Golden's Colorado Central Railroad aimed to make the Jefferson County seat the Rocky Mountain rail hub. Golden lost the ironhorse race and the state capital to Denver, but cherishes its proud past. Pioneer cabins were restored in 1996 along Clear Creek in Twelfth Street Historic Park. A facelift of Washington Avenue (Main Street) has resurrected many 1870s storefronts, including Loveland Hall and the nearby Astor House, and Golden's Welcome Arch. Commemorating Golden's glory days of narrow gauge railroading up Clear Creek Canyon to the silver city of Georgetown and to gold rich Central City, Golden's Colorado Railroad Museum displays an awesome collection of rolling stock and railroadiana.

Credit: Photos by Tom Noel

To court ladies, railroads offered wildflower excursions such as this 1910 frolic and deflowering of a mountain meadow. The Colorado Midland Railroad observation car shown here is on exhibit at the Colorado Railroad Museum in Golden. *Credit: Denver Public Library photo by Louis C. McClure*

goldfields. A spur line climbed over Boreas Pass to reach Breckenridge and Summit County's mineral riches. The main line went through Fairplay and down Trout Creek Pass to the Arkansas River. From the Arkansas, a branch ran north to tap Leadville's silver mines. The main line resumed its quest for the Pacific by digging the Alpine Tunnel, the first transportation bore under the Continental Divide. In 1883 the DSP&P ran out of steam in a mountain valley near Gunnison, 200 miles southwest of Denver. Like the Denver Pacific and all of Colorado's other "Pacific" railroads, the DSP&P never came within 1,000 miles of that ocean. Nevertheless, the South Park served the Mile High City well. To feed the city's building boom, that road brought in Platte Valley lumber and granite, Morrison sandstone and lime, South Park gold ores, and Gunnison County coal.

Evans' last great rail dream was the Denver & New

By 1890, Denver's Union Station hosted a hundred trains a day. Day and night, train whistles and snorting steam engines reminded residents that Denver had railroaded the Rockies. *Credit: Tom Noel Collection*

1878. Miniature Railway Station, Lakeside Park, White City, Denver, Colorado.

Railroads shaped the Mile High City in many ways. Lakeside Amusement Park in North Denver, which still delights visitors, built this replica of Union Station for youngsters waiting to board the miniature train. Credit: Tom Noel Collection

Street railways, as horsedrawn streetcars were first called, enabled city dwellers to suburbanize. Denver's first line, opened in 1871, ran from Auraria to Curtis Park. It was in that elegant new suburb wrapped around Denver's first city park, that Mayor Wolfe Londoner built his crested Italianate residence at 2222 Champa Street. Credit: Colorado Historical Society

Orleans Railroad, later renamed the Denver, Texas and Gulf. He established this standard gauge line in 1881 hoping to give Denver a port on the Gulf of Mexico. On the way to Galveston, the road nourished the towns of Parker, Franktown and Elizabeth. The latter town is named for Evans' sister-in-law, Elizabeth G. Hubbard and is in Elbert County, which is named for Evans' son-in-law — and Colorado territorial governor (1873-74) — Samuel H. Elbert. Elizabeth and Elbert County would remain sleepy rural areas until the 1990s, when Elbert became one of the fastest growing counties in the country and a booming hotspot on Denver's suburban frontier.

The Denver Tramway Company

Railroads caused Denver's population boom, and street railways enabled Denver to grow physically outward onto the surrounding prairies. Just as John Evans had established railroads, he helped start the streetcar line which did much to shape Denver's growth.

In 1886, John Evans and his son William Gray Evans incorporated the Denver Tramway Company (DTC) with William Byers, hotel keeper Henry C. Brown and businessman and library builder Roger Woodbury. The DTC secured an exclusive city franchise to build

Winter and summer, Denver's Union Station bustled with the clanging and screeching, the huffing and puffing of rail traffic. *Credit: Winter view by Clark Blickensderfer, summer view by Roger Whitacre*

Cheerful yellow streetcars of the Denver Tramway Company took Denverites to work, play, shopping and home until trolley service ended in 1950. *Credit: photo by Dick Kindig*

electric streetcar lines, thereby dooming the horse railways that built Denver's first streetcar lines in the 1870s. By 1900, the DTC had driven rival cable car and horse railways out of business and monopolized Denver streetcar service. The Tramway installed a city-wide network of overhead electric trolleys for lines that reached every neighborhood in Denver. The DTC shot out East Colfax Avenue to Park Hill, Montclair and Aurora, out West 13th Avenue to Lakewood and Golden. One of the busiest lines went south on Broadway to Englewood and Littleton. Another DTC line headed west on 32nd Avenue to Wheat Ridge and Arvada. The Washington Avenue line served Globeville and Adams County.

The Denver Tramway Company became one of the city's biggest employers and an essential part of many peoples' lives. Most, lacking horse and carriages, took streetcars to work, to shop and to play. Special tramway cars were rented out for weddings and honeymoons, while Funeral Cars A and B took many Denverites on their final rides — to Riverside and Fairmount cemeteries.

The rapidly expanding DTC built a huge power plant at the confluence of the South Platte and Cherry Creek (today's Forney Transportation Museum.) After the death of John Evans, his son demolished the family house at

14th and Arapahoe to construct the Tramway headquarters in 1912. The complex included an office tower, classrooms to train streetcar conductors to be courteous and efficient, and car barns and shops.

John Evans' railroads and streetcars transformed Denver into a fast growing city on rails. Evans capitalized on that growth. In 1872, to house his offices, he built the two-story Evans Block at 15th and Arapahoe, a block from his home. In 1888, Evans constructed the eight-story, $100,000 Railroad Building at 1515 Larimer Street with a handsome facade of Morrison sandstone.

Growing alarmed at the unbridled, chaotic growth he had helped unleash, John Evans in 1894 proposed a park and parkway system to bring some badly-needed greenery and visual relief to the urban hodgepodge. The city rejected the Evans plan, claiming it would be too expensive to acquire, build and water these parks and parkways. Evans' critics claimed that the parks were simply a scheme to increase ridership on his streetcars. Of the Evans masterplan, only Park Avenue and improvements to City Park were implemented. Evans' final dream for Denver would have to await another generation of progressive era reformers more interested in city beautification.

Evans made money on his railroads and streetcars, fleecing eastern and European capitalists in typical Gilded Age style. Although Indians and stockholders had good reason to think otherwise, most Denverites praised Evans for building up Denver in both the private and the public sectors. To the Indians, Governor Evans was an enemy and his railroads were deadly. The "iron snake" brought thousands of white settlers and army troops, as well as hide hunters who almost exterminated the buffalo. Evans was also criticized by stockholders who lost money on his railroads, while the governor and other inside investors made money through the construction companies.

Both Indians and investors might well agree with Henry David Thoreau's conclusion that: "We do not ride on the railroad; it rides upon us." As Harry Kelsey, Evans biographer, puts it, the man did not neglect his

personal interests, while building a city that is his greatest monument.

The 1893 Depression

John Evans' death in 1897 came at the end of Denver's golden age, which ended abruptly with the Depression of 1893. The Evans family squeaked through the 1890s crash — many other capitalists were not so lucky. The silver mining tycoon Horace Tabor lost his opera house, his Capitol Hill mansion and other assets. He rented a room for his family in the Windsor Hotel, where he died bankrupt in 1899.

Denver's response to the Depression was to diversify. Whereas the city had relied on supplying and smelting for the mining industry, it shifted to other businesses to weather the Depression. A boom town is easy to boost; reviving a dwindling city is much harder. After 1893 Denver's population began to decline for the first time since the mid-1860s. An estimated 10,000 people left the city after the 1893 crash. Even the president of the Chamber of Commerce, mining magnate John F. Campion, admitted that "public spirit is as dead as Lot's wife after she was turned to a pillar of salt."

To cheer up a depressed Denver, boosters proposed a municipal carnival inspired by Mardi Gras in New Orleans. Denver's Festival of Mountain and Plain consisted of three days of parades and exhibits showcasing Colorado's agricultural, industrial, mineral and mercantile enterprises for tourists and local customers.

At the first festival in 1895, impoverished businessmen and their wives marched in their finery, pretending to be rich as Midas. The parade became an annual event, not abandoned until 1912 when Denver finally seemed to be back on its feet.

Although the mining industry recovered with the 1890s Cripple Creek gold boom, mining would decline steadily during the 1900s. The rail network however, survived, allowing Coloradans to tap other sources of wealth.

Women's Touch

While their husbands scrambled to find economic solutions to the terrible 1893 depression, women worried about the victims. A few handed out food to every beggar who knocked on the door and tried to find yard or house work for the unemployed. As the number of destitute increased, however, kind individuals could no longer handle the problem. They banded together to organize charitable institutions. Elizabeth Byers, wife of the newspaperman, had organized the Ladies Union Aid Society in 1860 to assist the hungry, sick, homeless and destitute. Margaret Gray Evans, wife of the governor, helped Mrs. Byers reorganize the Union Aid Society in 1872 as the Ladies Relief Society. This society also strove to provide food, shelter and clothing for the needy and in 1873 founded the Old Ladies Home, which still pursues its original mission in handsomely restored quarters at 4115 West 38th Avenue now known as The Argyle.

A growing number of private and church charities combined in 1887 to create the Charity Organization Society, an umbrella group to coordinate fund-raising for all social services. The Charity Organization Society evolved into the United Way. This Denver idea, spearheaded by women such as Frances Weisbart Jacobs, of consolidating fund raising for charity has since been adopted by many other cities.

Since 1873, the Old Ladies Home founded by pioneer philanthropists Elizabeth Byers and Margaret Gray Evans has made the residents' golden years comfortable and dignified.
Credit: Tom Noel Collection

The Byers-Evans House Museum exhibits tell the story of Denver and the two pioneer families who did so much to build the city. Exquisitely restored by the Colorado Historical Society, this Victorian show home at 1410 Bannock Street behind the Denver Art Museum is the sole survivor of an elegant downtown residential district. *Credit: photo by Tom Noel*

Elizabeth Sumner Byers stuck with her rambling journalist husband, and devoted herself to improving the rough-hewn frontier town. In January, 1860, she formed the Ladies Union Aid Society to find homes for deserted children, tend the sick and dying, and gather food, clothing and money for the needy.
Credit: Denver Public Library

Hundreds of now forgotten Catholic nuns gave their lives to hospitals, orphanages, schools and other institutions working to help all Denverites, especially those at the bottom of society. Doing heavenly work, the Sisters of Charity from Leavenworth arrived in Denver in 1872 to establish St. Joseph's Hospital. When asked about the questionable location on Market Street, Denver's red light district, Sister Superior Johanna Brunner replied "We'll take the question out of

Most of the nuns who founded and staffed many early Denver hospitals, schools, orphanages and old age homes are forgotten. One of the few remembered today is Mother Frances Cabrini, an Italian immigrant who became the first U.S resident to be canonized a saint. She founded Denver's Mount Carmel School, Queen of Heaven Orphanage, and Mother Cabrini Shrine, visible from I-70 on the south shoulder of Lookout Mountain. *Credit: Denver Catholic Register photo by James Baca.*

By 1900, many more people came to Denver in search of health than mineral wealth. Charitable Jews concerned about tuberculosis, the deadliest of all diseases until cures were found in the 1930s, built National Jewish Hospital in East Denver and the Jewish Consumptive's Relief Society Sanatorium on the West Side. Both survive, although much of the property along West Colfax Avenue was sold off for the JCRS Shopping Center.
Credit: Tom Noel Collection

the neighborhood." By setting up homes for orphans, working girls, and former prostitutes, the good sisters did much to lift up Denver's daughters. The sisters moved their hospital in 1876 to its current site on Franklin Street, where they still operate St. Joseph as the oldest and one of the best private hospitals in the state.

Frances Wisebart Jacobs, the wife of a Jewish merchant, made the Hebrew Benevolent Ladies Aid Society a godsend to Denver's down and out. Jacobs also led in organizing the Charity Organization Society, which more effectively appealed to the city's fat cats for funding which it then distributed to appropriate agencies. Jacobs helped to start a hospital for poor tuberculars, which opened its doors in 1892 with the slogan "None may enter who can pay — none can pay who enter." Originally called Frances Jacobs Hospital, it is now National Jewish Center for Immunology and Respiratory Medicine at East Colfax Avenue and Colorado Boulevard.

While aiding others, Jacobs neglected herself. In 1892, while nursing patients in a slummy section of town, she collapsed. Despite doctor's orders to rest

Tuberculosis, the world's deadliest disease until the mid 1900s, led many to try Colorado's climate cure. To capture the dry, sunny "champagne" air, lung disease patients and other health seekers summered in tent colonies such as this one in Boulder's Chautaugua Park.
Credit: Carnegie Branch Library for Local History, Boulder Historical Society Collection

and recover, she was soon out tending the sick again, exacerbating her own health problems. She died a few months later at the age of 49. Denver's "Mother of Charities" is one of the few women and non-politicians enshrined in stained glass at the Colorado State Capitol. Certainly she did more for the poor and sick than the much richer men who surround her in the Capitol rotunda windows.

Not only Denver residents, but the poor, disabled and homeless from elsewhere rode or stole rides on the rails into Denver. Mining, which had given birth to the city and promised to make many rich, left many sick and impoverished instead. Thanks to compassionate Denver women, the poor profited from Denver's willingness to cope with social problems.

Agriculture

If Coloradans could not dig gold and silver, why not dig for crops? From the beginning, editor Byers promoted agriculture to give Denver economic roots that would survive mining busts. He personally filed an 1863 homestead claim along the South Platte River around Alameda Avenue. Here he built a frame house, 18 by 32 feet, with two doors and seven windows according to Federal Land Office Records. Byers had 35 acres under cultivation, a stable, a granary, an ice house, irrigation ditches, an orchard and a vineyard. All are gone today, although commemorated by a street name, Byers Place.

Byers experimented with various crops himself and urged others to do likewise, offering free seeds to anyone who would drop by his office. He also planted a lot of seeds in the pages of his paper, propagating agricultural possibilities and publicizing everything from the largest squash to the sweetest cherries.

Byers and Territorial Governor John Evans founded the Colorado Agricultural Society in 1863 and bought 40 acres east of Denver, in what is now City Park, as a fairground. The farm fair helped to showcase new crops, encourage experiments and reward diligent and creative farmers. The Colorado Agricultural Society held annual festivals that helped make Denver the major market city for Colorado's ranchers and farmers. Denverites launched a determined crusade to produce as many goods and services as possible. Railroads hauled wheat and sugar beets, cattle, sheep and hogs into Denver, which emerged as a major food processing and distribution point. The aromas of stockyards, canneries, breweries and flour mills replaced acrid, dark smelter smoke, as agricultural riches of the earth became more important to Denver than gold, silver and other precious minerals.

Denver was surrounded by ranches and farms that fed the hungry, fast-growing city. Agricultural success stories abounded, although they never captured the popular fancy like silver and gold. John Kernan Mullen, a young Irish immigrant, left school at age 14 to work in a flour mill and wound up with a multi-million dollar milling empire. Mullen's Colorado Milling & Elevator and Hungarian Flour empires owned wheat fields, grain elevators and flour mills throughout the Rockies.

Others helped make the city a center for processing food and leather goods. Henry Perky invented a machine to produce America's first shredded wheat in his downtown Denver factory. Jesse Shwayder and his brothers opened a Denver trunk-manufacturing company that, under the trade name Samsonite, grew into what is now a worldwide giant. Charles Gates, an out-of-work mining engineer, and his brother John invented the world's first V-belt. The Gates hired Buffalo Bill to ballyhoo their belts, tires and hoses, originally made of leather before Gates switched to rubber. Gates rode his rubber accessories for horseless carriages into prominence and wealth with the auto age.

To work Colorado's fields, farms, and food processing factories, railroads brought in thousands of newcomers between the 1870s and the 1920s. Many of these were immigrants fleeing war-torn Europe, hoping for a new start in America's highest state and its mile high metropolis.

Ranches, farms and dairies surrounding Denver fed the hungry, fast-growing metropolis. Women owned and operated a good many of these operations, which paid off with the help of cats who kept rodents out of the livestock feed. *Credit: Colorado State University Archives*

Immigrants

IN 1868, A 24-YEAR-OLD GERMAN STOWAWAY landed in Denver, where he came to appreciate the frontier virtue of not questioning a man's past. Orphaned at age 15, this youngster was running away from personal tragedies and long, compulsory and often deadly military service in the Prussian army. Like some 50,000 other foreign-born immigrants reaching Denver before the 1920s, Adolph Kuhrs wanted a chance to start anew in a new world.

Kuhrs changed the spelling of his name to Coors and established what would become the world's largest single-site brewery. America attracted 55,000 Germans — and almost 500,000 immigrants — the year Coors arrived in Denver. Germans were the most numerous of many immigrants coming to Colorado between the 1860s and the 1920s, when the United States began officially restricting immigration and the Ku Klux Klan began unofficially making foreigners feel unwelcome.

On his 1880s visit to Denver, Oscar Wilde characterized it as one of the few cities in the world where few of the adult residents were native born. From the beginning, Denver has been a city of newcomers. More people have been residents by choice than by accident of birth. Many Denverites, including the pioneer generation, came from New York, Ohio, Illinois and Missouri. In more recent times, many have also come from Texas and California.

Distance from the Atlantic and Pacific shores may have been the main reason the foreign born were always a minority. Denver never had the teeming immigrant neighborhoods of New York, Boston, Philadelphia or San Francisco. Between 1880 and 1920, during the high tide of immigration to the U.S., only one-fourth to one-fifth of Denver's residents were foreign-born. Among the immigrants in 19th-century Denver, Germans, Irish, English, Swedes, Scots and Italians were most numerous.

Germans

Of Denver's immigrants, the most prominent, prosperous and populous were the Germans. In 1870, according to the census calculations of historian Stephen J. Leonard, Germans in Denver had more large fortunes (above $4,000) than the English, Irish, Swedes and Scots combined, although the latter groups consolidated had a far greater population. Typically Germans arrived with more money and earned and saved more after settling in the Mile High City.

Among the German movers and shakers were brewers Adolph Coors and Adolph and Philip Zang; Charles Kountze and William Berger of Colorado National Bank, developer Walter von Richthofen, capitalist William Barth, pickle and cannery czar Max Kuner, hardware dealer George Tritch, carpenter and contractor Frank Kirchof, and Mayor Wolfe Londoner. Second generation Germans included William Byers of the *Rocky Mountain News* and Robert S. Roeschlaub, Denver's great pioneer architect.

One German immigrant, Charles Boettcher, developed the mightiest and most successfully diversified financial empire in the Rockies. Rather than sink his money into one industry, such as mining, Boettcher concentrated on hardware and mining supplies. Moving into agriculture even before mining began to flounder, Boettcher fathered the Great Western Sugar Company. To construct his sugar beet plants he organized the Ideal Cement Company.

Boettcher and other German-born immigrants were joined by Germans from Russia. The Volga-Deutsche, as they were sometimes called, had been enlisted by Catherine the Great to settle in Russia's Volga Valley. After the German-born czarina died, other Russian rulers were less kind to these Teutons, forcing them to join the Russian military and to otherwise become more Russian. Subsequently thousands fled Russia. Many settled on the Great Plains of North America,

OPPOSITE PAGE: Successful immigrants often employed their countrymen, whom they trusted and understood. Adolph Coors (in white hat with a vest watch behind his son Adolph Coors, Jr.) posed around 1900 with the German workers who helped make Coors the best-known brand in the Rockies. Credit: *Denver Public Library*

including eastern Colorado's South Platte Valley.

All sorts of Germans, unified by a common language, joined together to form ethnic clubs. As early as 1865, Germans organized a local branch of the German Turnverein, an international organization dedicated to German culture, exercise and sociability. "The German Temple of Art," as historian William B. Vickers called it, built the largest hall in town, a popular place for calisthenics, games, dances, balls, concerts and political rallies. At the Turnverein, now Colorado's oldest ethnic club, Teutons could read German language newspapers, magazines and books, hear German opera and music, and enjoy the Denver Mäennerchor, a singing group founded in 1872.

While other ethnic groups suffered varying degrees of harassment in Denver, the well-organized Germans had enough political clout to discourage discrimination and encourage deference. Such was the case in 1874, when a policeman tried to arrest a patron in the Turnverein for drinking beer after midnight. Germans ejected the officer and shot off a letter to city hall: "We want it clearly understood that we want no policemen in our hall in any official capacity." Shortly thereafter Mayor Francis Chase promised to comply with this request.

Germans took a keen interest in public education, persuading the Colorado legislature to pass a law in 1877 requiring the teaching of German and of gymnastics in the public schools. The active German element led Colorado to print its laws, from 1877 to 1889, in German, as well as in English and Spanish. Of the several German newspapers published in Denver, the longest lived was the *Colorado Herald*, which championed German causes until it became a casualty of World War II.

By 1880, a third of Denver's 48 saloons were owned by German or Austrian born immigrants. Inside these beer halls, customers spoke and sang in German, read German newspapers and magazines, consumed sauerkraut and strudel, and quaffed beer. Denver establishments such as the Bavarian House, Deutsches House, the Edelweiss, Germania Hall, Heidelberg Cafe, Mozart

Wholesome, if not angelic, women were used to promote beer as a healthy, All-American product.
Credit: Adolph Coors Brewing Co.

Hall, Saxonia Hall and Walhalla Hall offered not only "Dutch |Deutsche or German| lunches," but the customs and culture of the old country.

Baron Walter von Richthofen, one of the most exuberant Germans, told his countrymen that "Denver is called the 'parlor city' on account of its cleanliness and beauty…It is the center of science, art, intelligence, and refinement of the West." Frederick Steinhauer, a founder of the Denver Turnverein and a member of the territorial legislature, wrote to German newspapers extolling Colorado as "a better place for a young man to secure his living and independence."

Germans built many of the city's first fine churches. Jewish Germans erected Temple Emanuel; German Catholics built St. Elizabeth's. German Congregationalists, German Methodists, the German Reformed Church and German Baptists all constructed substantial early houses of worship, while German Lutherans filled two congregations.

Coloradans benefitted from the Teutonic interest in music and culture. In 1873, the Kaltenbach family ordered a $1,000 orchestrion from Germany. When the elaborate instrument arrived a year later, the Kaltenbachs renamed their tavern Orchestrion Hall. It took a week to assemble and tune the 11-foot-high machine and attach the reeds, horns, drums and xylophone. To celebrate the instrument's debut, hundreds crowded into the hall. "No one," an observer recalled, "had ever supposed there were so many Germans in the region and |all| were amazed that the beer held out through the long night." As Germans drank and sang along, the largest musical apparatus in the Rockies ground out "Die Wacht am Rhein," George Schweitzer's "Yodel Hi Lee Hi Loo," and Ludwig von Beethoven's "Moonlight Sonata."

Teutons also gave the Queen City one of its first annual festivals. When the city's German brewers cleaned out

GREETINGS 19

their beer fermenting vats in May, they made dark syrupy bock beer from the residue. Editor Byers reported on May 21, 1874, that all nationalities joined in the spring beer fest as large wagons, decorated with flags and laden with kegs of beer, rumbled through the streets to the saloons. Otto Hienrich's Saloon at 16th and Larimer set the record for Bock Beer Day in 1874, serving some 3,000 glasses of beer, 50 loaves of bread and 125 pounds of meat.

Although Germans had a happier life in 19th-century Denver than most ethnic groups, the 20th century changed that. The swelling prohibition movement tended to blame all evil on drink. Breweries and saloons,

according to nativists, were un-American bastions where people spoke German and plotted against the established order. Countering the attack of the "temperentzlers," Germans formed the Citizens Protective Union, which defended the saloon as "the poor man's club house." Saloons served as lodging halls and restaurants for many immigrants, places where they could cash checks, borrow money and receive credit, find jobs, and meet with their countrymen. Politically, saloons were often the place for registering and organizing new voters, havens for both front hall rallies and backroom deals.

Xenophobes hoping to crack down on foreigners and their "un-American" activities joined Prohibitionists

Germans, as Colorado's single largest foreign-born group until World War I, gave much to Colorado's cultural life. This wagon load of Teutons is ballyhooing a performance at the Denver Auditorium by the German Singing Societies, along with a gymnastic exhibition from the German Turnvereins. *Credit: Colorado Historical Society*

Germans lost their jobs, and were physically and verbally abused. The Denver Public School District became one of the first in the country to outlaw German language classes. Restaurants renamed sauerkraut "liberty cabbage" and hamburgers became "liberty steaks." "Patriotic" places put up signs such as: "There are two places to talk German. In hell and in Germany. Go there to speak it."

After the double-barreled blow of Prohibition and World War I, this group that had contributed so much to Denver's cultural, educational and social life never fully reemerged as a distinctive ethnic community.

Irish

Throughout the 19th century, the Irish comprised Denver's second largest immigrant group. The Irish born represented less than three percent of the city's population, but were highly visible with their saloons, clubs, churches and political presence. In a predominantly non-Irish city, Irishmen served as city councilmen, and occasionally as mayor, although the first Irish Catholic governor, Stephen L.R. McNichols, would not be elected until 1957, three years before John F. Kennedy's election as president.

Despite prejudice against them and the highest arrest record for any ethnic group, the Irish seemed irrepressible. Their political clout revolved around saloonkeepers, policemen and politicians, three groups attracting large numbers of gregarious, power-seeking Irishmen. Early day police chiefs David J. Cook and James B. Veatch were one time saloonkeepers, as was the pioneer marshal, "Noisy Tom" Pollock.

The Irish proved to be one of the most prolific immigrant groups. Unlike Scandinavians, Italians, Chinese, and most other groups, both sexes of Irish came. Irish girls were in great demand as domestics and factory workers. Starving times in Ireland due to the potato famine led many families, however reluctantly, to send daughters as well as sons to America, their only hope for a decent life. With as many women as men in the new country, the Irish tended to marry each other and raise large families. Many

Baron Walter von Richthofen, like most Germans, came to Denver with money. He developed the east Denver neighborhood of Montclair, where his castle still stands at East 12th Avenue and Olive Street.
Credit: Colorado Historical Society

to vote for statewide prohibition. The dry spell began for Coloradans on New Year's Day, 1916. Many Germans lost their jobs in the liquor business. The Zang Brewery, Neef Brothers Brewery and dozens of distributors and bottlers closed their doors along with some 400 Denver saloons.

An even heavier blow came to the Teutonic community with the outbreak of World War I. Germans became the target of a widespread hate campaigns. Regardless of their professed and proven patriotism,

Irish girls raised on famine-stricken potato farms in the old country found Colorado's wheat farms far more fertile.

Credit: Greeley Museum

other immigrants came to make their fortunes and then return to their homelands and their sweethearts.

Denver's Irish, like the Germans, experienced little trouble melting into the mainstream. "No Irish Need Apply" signs stayed back on the Eastern Seaboard for several reasons. The presence of Indians, Hispanics, Asians and Blacks at the bottom of society pushed the English-speaking, white Irish up a few notches in western cities. If people could assert their superiority by treating red, brown, yellow and black people as inferior, they were less likely to discriminate against whites, even if they were Irish.

Like the Germans, the Irish were generally acculturated by the time they reached Denver. Unlike the impoverished, Gaelic speaking, just-off-the boat Irish who flooded into Boston, they usually arrived in Denver with job skills and other assets, often including a wife

and family. Most had spent time in Boston, New York, or elsewhere in North America, learning American English, American ways and accumulating some capital. Many came via Canada, a large source of 19th-century Denver immigrants. Most Canadians were of British, Scottish, Irish or French extraction. Colorado's great mineral rushes and the booming city of Denver attracted many Canadians who might otherwise have settled in the colder and poorer Canadian West.

Most Irish came to Colorado as miners or as "terriers," as the Irish railroad construction crews called themselves. Like the railroads themselves, many Irish made Denver their headquarters, settling into the working class neighborhoods of northeast and northwest Denver. St. Leo's church in Auraria and St. Patrick's in North Denver were rallying points, as were Irish saloons. Irish born men ran 10 percent of Denver's bars.

That same year, according to the *Denver Times*, October 18, 1873, one Irishmen supposedly wrote home to his brother, "Dear Patrick come! A dollar a day for ditching, no hanging for stalign, Irish Petaties a dollar a bushel, and whiskey the same!"

Denver's Irish organized local chapters of the Ancient Order of Hibernians, the Daughters of Erin,

This 1890s photo captures a cheerful dish wiper in the Bauer residence at 780 S. Pennsylvania St. in Denver.
Credit: photo by Felix Bauer

....

Poverty drove many of Ireland's daughters to America, where they often found work as domestic servants. This unidentified Colorado nanny used a shoe-shaped carriage to entertain her charge. Credit: Greeley Museum.

Late into the night, strains of "My Wild Irish Rose," "Wearing of the Green," "Danny Boy," and "Where the River Shannon Flows" drifted out of tavern doors.

The Irish fraternized not only in groggeries, but in numerous ethnic clubs. Denver's Fenian Brotherhood organized as early as 1865 to celebrate July 4th, a holiday whose anti-English overtones delighted the Irish.

the Irish Progressive Society, the Land League, a Ladies Land League, the St. Patrick's Mutual Benevolent Association, and the Shamrock Athletic Club. John K. Mullen, Denver's wealthiest Irishman and a major employer of his countryman, presided over the St. Joseph's Total Abstinence Society, an effort to reform the city's hard-drinking Celts.

The *Rocky Mountain Celt*, the short-lived *Western Irishman*, and the *Colorado Catholic* further promoted Irish solidarity. Well-organized Irishmen elected one of their own, Robert Morris, as mayor of Denver in 1881. He defeated George Tritch, a favorite of the larger and wealthier German community. This election, noted J. K. Mullen, "united the Irishmen as they have never been united before." Although more than 75 percent of Denver's Irish were registered as Democrats, they crossed party lines en masse to elect their countryman, a Republican. Morris rewarded his constituency by sanctioning the city's first St. Patrick's Day parade in 1883.

Mayor Robert W. Speer made the parade an official city function in 1906, a practice continued until World War I. Anti-Catholic, anti-immigrant, and anti-liquor interests help suppress St. Patrick's Day parades until the 1960s when the parade was revived. Since then Denver's Irish parade has become one of America's

John Kernan Mullen, Denver's most successful Irish immigrant, made millions in flour milling and became a legendary philanthropist. "Myself and my wife," he explained, "came here when there were no old people, we were all young and because of this we consider ourselves pioneers...we wanted, before we passed away to leave something." Mullen gave the city such monuments as St. Cajetan's Church, Mullen School, and the Mullen Home for the Aged, and contributed heavily to Immaculate Conception Cathedral and the University of Denver. Credit: Denver Public Library

RIGHT: Among J.K. Mullen's gifts to Denver is "The Broncho Buster" in Civic Center. Credit: *photo by Tom Noel*

Kit Carson and his horse top downtown's Pioneer Fountain at the northwest corner of Colfax Avenue and Broadway. Sculptor Frederick MacMonnies originally crowned the fountain with an Indian but infuriated Denverites insisted he replace the "savage" with the famed mountain man and Indian scout.
Credit: photo by Tom Noel

The Irish gave Denver its St. Patrick's Day Parade. Celebrated on the Saturday before March 17th, this extravaganza welcomes floats and demonstrations from every ethnic group to the delight of thousands of spectators. *Credit: Photos by Tom Noel*

largest, partly by welcoming any and all celebrants — even gays and Englishmen.

English

Although the English were Denver's third largest foreign born group after the Germans and the Irish, they were not as visible, blending into the dominant Anglo society. Behind the scenes, the British rein- forced an Anglophilic culture underwritten by an esti- mated £50 million which Britons invested in Colorado before World War I.

Unlike non-English-speaking peoples, English- born Denverites saw less need to organize ethnically. They, like U.S. born Anglo-Americans, generally assumed they were the prevalent culture. Not only the language but English capital prevailed, bankrolling Colorado mining, railroads and ranching. By 1890, 25 British mining firms were digging for Colorado paydirt.

Railroads, which were first developed in England, began criss-crossing Colorado with considerable financial support from the British Isles. The Denver & Rio Grande Railroad, for instance, was a favorite of British investors. Dr. William A. Bell, a London society

The Denver Club, founded with the help of English and Scottish investors, was an Anglophilic club that frowned on Germans, Irish, Italians, Jews, Scandinavians and other "foreigners." Founded in 1880, this gentlemen's club helped funnel millions of English pounds into Colorado investments. *Credit: Tom Noel Collection*

doctor, became interested in the D&RG, invested, and promoted it among his patients. His son, Dr. William A. Bell, Jr., became so intrigued with this narrow gauge "toy" railroad that he came to America, where he wound up as the road's vice president. Young Bell wrote a book, *New Tracks in North America* (London: 1870) explaining and promoting Colorado railroads to English readers and capitalists.

Ranching also appealed to the English, who had no trouble imagining the rewards of roast beef, milk and fresh cream. The Scottish investor James Duff steered English investors into the Colorado Ranch Company and other agricultural schemes such as the High Line Canal, an 88-mile-long diversion of South Platte Water to turn south and east Denver into profitable agricultural land. The Highline Canal,

or "English Ditch," completed in 1882 at a cost of $550,000, nourished the development of both Denver and its eastern suburb, Aurora.

Duff spearheaded the creation and activities of The Colorado Mortgage and Investment Company, which shaped Denver as well as surrounding farms and ranches. That firm erected the Windsor, Denver's first fine hotel, and the adjacent office block, the Barclay. Duff and other Britons helped build the Denver Club and erected fine residences, both personal and speculative, throughout the city.

The immensity of the prairies surrounding Denver astonished Englishmen such as Richard B. Townshend. In his book, *A Tenderfoot in Colorado*, Townshend describes the ranch life that lured many Englishmen, or at least their capital, to the former "Great American

St. John's in the Wilderness, a grand English Gothic
Cathedral, graces a beautifully landscaped block of
Capitol Hill. Exquisite stained glass and fine carvings
distinguish this Episcopal edifice. A particularly seductive
Eve in the Garden of Eden window distracted worshippers,
necessitating the addition of a rose bush for modesty's sake.
Credit: *Above photo from* Denver Public Library

Credit: *photo by* Tom Noel

Desert." Like many other Englishmen, Townshend came with capital and letters of introduction, which gave him access to governors and bankers, as well as to the best clubs and families.

By the 1880s, the St. George's Association and the Albion Club were organizing cricket matches in Denver. Englishmen also belonged to the Denver Club, the Denver Athletic Club, the University Club and the Denver Country Club — all exclusive enclaves more or less pursuing standards based on Britain's private clubs.

Although Englishman G. W. Stevens pronounced the Queen City of the Plains "more plain than Queenly," he and his countrymen did much to transform the raw western crossroads into a handsome and prosperous metropolis with solid Victorian churches, office buildings, hotels, clubs and mansions. Unlike Colorado Springs, Denver did not call itself "Little London." Yet visitors staying at the Brown Place, Oxford and Windsor hotels, admiring St. John's Episcopal Cathedral, and touring Capitol

Denver's small but proud Scottish community donated this statue of the poet Robert Burns to City Park.

Credit: photo by Tom Noel

Hill's elegant Queen Anne and English Revival style mansion districts might conclude that the English set the city's standards.

Swedes

Swedish immigrants were the fourth most common foreign-born group in Denver according to the 1900 census. Danes and Norwegians also came, but in far smaller numbers. Denver in 1890 had the eighth largest Swedish population among U.S. cities. By 1900, the city had eight Swedish societies, led by the Skandia Benevolent Association founded in 1876.

Most Swedes were bachelors who came to make money and then return to their homes in the Midwest or the old country. Swedes clustered around their churches, such as the lovely sandstone Swedish Evangelical Lutheran Church and graveyard at Ryssby, northwest of Boulder. Denver Swedes congregated at Augustana Lutheran Church, the Swedish Baptist Church, and in the Methodist Episcopal Chapel in the basement of Trinity United Methodist Church. The Swedish Evangelical Lutheran Church served Northwest Denver, where many worked in the smelters — the hardest, hottest, most dangerous work in town.

Prominent Swedes included Edgar M. Wahlberg, born in Denver to immigrants. After working his way through the University of Denver's Iliff School of Theology, Reverend Wahlberg took on a bankrupt urban parish, Grace Methodist Church. He transformed Grace into one of the most successful, reform-minded churches in Colorado, which set the pace in helping Denver's poor cope with the Great Depression. His church opened an employment agency, shoe shop, barbershop, and food, clothing and fuel distribution center. Wahlberg's legendary Denver career led the United Nations to recruit him for relief work in Europe at the end of World War II. Returning to Denver, he worked for the War on Poverty. Wahlberg spent his life among the working classes, fighting the discrimination and poverty that led his father, a tailor, to complain, "I should have stayed in Sweden. Things were better there."

Scots

Although not as numerous as the English or the Irish, the Scots had a Denver population of 1,000 by 1890. One of them, James Duff, was the most influential foreign investor in Colorado, brokering deals for English, Irish and Scottish investors. The Scots organized a Caledonian Club and St. Andrews Society. William J. Palmer and Dr. William A. Bell of the Denver & Rio Grande Railroad laid out North Denver's Scottish Village, a tiny neighborhood of short curving streets with Scottish names that is an unusual exception to Denver's ubiquitous street grid. Although some Scots-Irish settled in that area known as Highlands, they were soon outnumbered by Irish, Italian and Hispanic residents. Like the English, the Scots assimilated into the dominant Anglo culture and made less of their ethnicity than most other groups. One of the few traces left of Denver's Scottish pioneers is a bronze statue of Robert Burns installed in City Park in 1904 by the Colorado Caledonian Club with the inscription:

"A poet, peasant born,
Who more of fame's immortal dower
Upon his country brings
Than all her kings."

Italians

Only a sprinkling of Italians settled in Denver before 1880, when the census taker found a scanty 86.

Siro Mangini, a pioneer Italian entrepreneur, opened Christopher Columbus Hall to welcome his countrymen to Denver. Credit: Tom Noel Collection

In the following decades the railroads, mining companies and other industries recruited Italian labor and the 1890 census listed an Italian population of 999. By 1920, their population had climbed to over 3,000 and the North Denver neighborhood of Highland became known as "Little Italy."

One of the first Italian couples to arrive in the early 1870s was Mary Anne and Angelo Capelli. They opened a fruit stand and diner on Wazee Street near Union Station, saving enough capital to build the Highland House on Fifteenth and Platte streets. The Capellis treated both their countrymen and non-Italians to pasta dinners on Columbus Day, when they draped their business with American and Italian flags to celebrate Italian-American solidarity.

Like the Capellis, many Italians started out in the Bottoms, the slummy area bordering the Platte River and the railroad tracks. In this dumpy flood plain, these former peasant farmers found water and good soil. Soon the river bottoms were checkerboarded with Italian vegetable patches. These urban farmers hawked their produce downtown from fruit, vegetable and flower stands. Some saved enough to buy a horse and wagon. After putting a canvas roof on the wagon and hanging a scale on the outside, Italians began infiltrating Denver neighborhoods and even suburbs with their street song of "Vegetable Man! Vegetable Man! Nice ripe tomatoes! Fresh pascal celery! Just picked strawberries!"

As the Mile High City grew, many of these farmers graduated to larger businesses, opening pasta factories and restaurants, groceries and wholesale produce companies. To this day Denver's large wholesale produce firms are clustered around the Denargo Market in the Platte bottomlands and many are run by descendants of Italian pioneers.

The Italians who came to Colorado tended to be poor and were derided for their dark complexions, Catholicism, foreign language, different food and homemade wine. Denverites called them macaroni eaters, wops (without official papers), and Dagos (originally "Diegos" a derogatory term for Hispanics who were confused with Italians). Many lived in tents, shacks

Italian produce stands perfumed lower downtown as recently as 1937 when an unknown photographer captured this scene on 15th between Larimer and Market streets. *Credit*: D*enver Public Library*

Italians built Mount Carmel Church as the soul of North Denver's "Little Italy,"
an area still flavored with Italian restaurants and bakeries. *Credit: Tom Noel Collection*

and shanties along the South Platte River bottoms and worked the toughest and poorest paying jobs — building railroads, digging coal, tending truck farms and toiling in smelters.

Mother Frances Xavier Cabrini, the Italian nun who became the first U.S. citizen to be canonized a saint, visited Colorado in 1902 and reported: "Here the hardest work is reserved for the Italian worker...they merely look upon him as an ingenious machine for work...I saw these dear fellows of ours engaged on construction of railways in the most intricate mountain gorges...Poor miners work uninterruptedly year in and year out, until old age and incapacity creep over them, or at least until some day a landslide or explosion or an accident of some kind ends the life of the poor worker, who does not even need a grave, being buried in the one in which he has lived all his life."

To give Italian immigrants "the holy joys which in our own country the poor peasant has on Sundays at least," Mother Cabrini helped erect Our Lady of Mount Carmel Church in North Denver's Little Italy. This dignified Romanesque church, with its ornate Italian interior, still stands at 36th and Navajo Street. One of the twin copper-capped towers houses the 1,000-pound bell known as "Maria del Carmelina."

With the help of Mother Cabrini's church, as well as a school and orphanage, Denver's Italian community prospered, moving out of the river bottoms to North Denver and, still later, out to suburban Adams and Jefferson counties. Hard-working, first-generation immigrants sacrificed themselves to feed, cloth and educate their children, who often became professional and white collar workers. In a once condescending city, Italians slowly earned respect — and even admiration for making it — often the hard way.

Denver historian Stephen J. Leonard, in his detailed study of early Denver immigrants, concludes that most groups, with the exception of the Chinese, fared better in Denver than in many larger eastern cities. Yet the Depression of 1893 and the rise of the anti-immigrant American Protective Association darkened that dream for many by 1900. Many immigrants, especially the Chinese and Scandinavians, were among the thousands who left Denver during the 1890s. When the economy and immigration perked up again after 1900, a new wave of immigrants came from central and eastern Europe, followed by blacks from the South and East and Hispanics from southern Colorado and New and Old Mexico.

OPPOSITE PAGE: Kolorado's Ku Klux Klan briefly controlled the Highest State during the 1920s, when Klansmen served as mayor of Denver and governor. The Klan, shown here marching down 16th Street in 1926, attacked Denver's foreign-born immigrants as "un-American." Credit: Tom Noel Collection

A Sparkling Jewel on the Bosom of the Desert

"THE MOST MARVELOUS GROWTH OF MODERN times is the city of Denver, Colorado…In 1858 there were only a few tents and huts on the spot where the city now stands. Less than fifty people were there through the winter of 1858-59, drawn thither by the discovery of gold. A barren waste was all that met the vision in every direction…What do we see now where these pioneers pitched their tents? The largest, richest, and most beautiful city of its age on earth — a sparkling costly jewel on the bosom of the 'desert.'"

— *William M. Thayer, Marvels of the New West* (1890)

Colorado's gold and silver rushes led to another stampede — the rush to respectability. The instant city and its overnight millionaires demanded elegance. Between the 1858 Gold Rush and the 1893 Silver Crash, Coloradans exported paydirt and imported culture. Denverites strove to show the world that the Highest State was no cultural lowland. The jewel on the bosom of the desert, wanted to sparkle.

Denver soon glittered with the riches of the earth. Not only Colorado's gold and silver, but the state's mining magnates gravitated to Denver. Wealth and the wealthy from Central City, Leadville, Aspen, the San Juans and Cripple Creek flowed into Denver. In the Mile High City, the *nouveau riches* used cultural trappings to separate themselves from less successful gold grubbers. Peacocks in the front yard, servants in the kitchen, and children in private schools helped the successful flaunt their new status. Inspired by a sincere interest in culture as well as the use of culture to define an aristocracy, Coloradans rushed to respectability.

The rush began during the golden territorial era and peaked during the Silver Age that followed Colorado statehood in 1876. By 1890, Denver boasted mansion-studded neighborhoods, stately churches and schools, the Tabor Grand Opera House, and private clubs such as the Denver Club and the Denver Athletic Club, where the wealthy and their offspring could mingle and frolic.

Mansions capped Capitol Hill where mining millionaires built their multi-story masonry piles. After Fairmount Cemetery sprouted in southeast Denver and Mount Olivet northwest of town in 1890, millionaires' rows also graced those new cemetery parks, where movers and shakers built their final mansions — palatial mausoleums of granite and marble.

By 1892, Denver had a *Blue Book* to showcase its society types. Compiler Agnes Hill described her social register as "a list of householders having sufficient money and position to be available either as good customers for merchant, florist or caterer, or to grace a feast, adorn a dance or add to the interest of the occasion where a city gathers her beauty and her chivalry and her financial power."

Originally a dull metal crowned the Colorado Capitol until 1908, when the mining industry gilded the dome with gold leaf. Credit: Denver Public Library

Society families insisted on more elegant schools for their offspring. During the 1880s, Robert S. Roeschlaub began designing dignified educational edifices for the Denver school district. Some of his notable schools are still standing, including Emerson (1884) at East 14th Avenue and Ogden Street, Dora Moore at East 9th Avenue and Corona Street, and University Hall

---

The State Capitol gave its name to the stately residential enclave east of Broadway. Many fine houses and apartment houses still dignify Capitol Hill, including the Grafton Apartments at East 17th Avenue and Ogden Street, seen here on one of Denver's few foggy days. Credit: photo by Michael Gamer

Prominent residents erected elaborate monuments and mausoleums at Fairmount Cemetery, Colorado's largest city of the dead. A fine French Gothic chapel, left, is the centerpiece of this cemetery park opened in 1890. Many tombstones taught lessons in family values, typified by the Bethell monument, below, of a mother teaching her son to read.
Credit: Tom Noel Collection

ABOVE: Mount Prospect Cemetery, the original 1860 boneyard, was vacated to create what is now Cheesman Park and the Denver Botanic Gardens. *Photo courtesy of* The Denver Post

The large granite mausoleum of Dr. John Galen Locke, Grand Dragon of the Kolorado Ku Klux Klan, is featured
on Historic Denver's tombstone tour with professors Tom Noel and Dennis Gallagher. *Credit: Tom Noel Collection*

Molly and J.J. Brown moved into this Queen Anne
dwelling, left, at 1340 Pennsylvania Street, guarded by
sphinx-like stone lions, far left. The ostentatious interior
includes a dining room, above, with tromp d'oeil ceiling.
Credit: Photos courtesy of Historic Denver, Inc.

Molly Brown, who left
school at 13 to work in a
cigar factory, epitomized
the rush to respectability,
after her husband struck
paydirt in Leadville.
Credit: Colorado
Historical Society.

(1890) and Chamberlain Observatory (1889) for the
University of Denver.

Roeschlaub's contemporary, William Lang, specialized in designing stone palaces for Denver's elite. He
built castle-like Romanesque palaces, bulging with
turrets and towers. Lang also designed more modest
middle class Queen Anne style homes, such as the
Molly Brown House.

Molly Brown

The often — and variously — told tale of Margaret
Tobin Brown epitomized the rush to respectability.
Different people see different persons in this Irish
Catholic girl of modest origins and wondrous
achievements.

Actress Debbie Reynolds, who portrayed Molly in
the film, The Unsinkable Molly Brown, praised her as "a
female ahead of her time. Today she would be called
a feminist, an independent woman who believed in
growth and self expression. She was going to learn to
read 'n write — to go 'n see — to be what she had
to be — even to make mistakes."

Less kind critics, such as The Denver Post reporter
Polly Pry, derided Molly as a social-climbing fraud. Polly
ridiculed her dress, deriding her as Colorado's largest
fur-bearing mammal. Snubbed by Denver's high society,
Molly found acceptance on the east coast and in Europe.

Molly started out as Maggie. Born July 18, 1867, she
was raised in a one-bedroom shack in Hannibal, Missouri, along the Mississippi River bottoms. This bright,

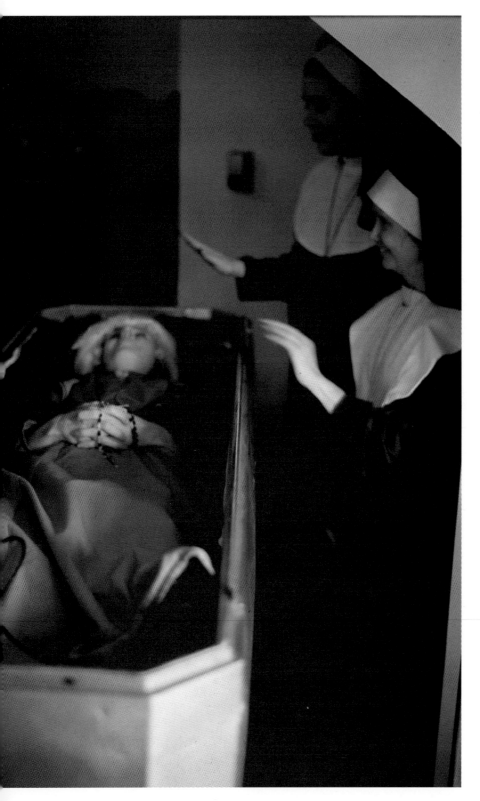

Historic Denver hosts an array of social and educational galas in the house, including a mock wake for Molly's mother, Johanna Tobin, left. Staged for the general public around March 17, this reenactment, above, includes Victorian deathways and Irish folkways.
Credit: *Photos courtesy of Historic Denver, Inc.*

ambitious girl left school at age 13 to work in a cigar factory. She saved her money and at 19 fled Hannibal for America's great boom town of the 1880s — Leadville, Colorado. In the two-mile-high Magic City, the red-haired, green-eyed, buxom young woman found work sewing drapes — and a wealthy, handsome husband, Leadville mine manager James Joseph Brown.

After the Silver Crash of 1893, Brown's resourceful gold mining of the Little Jonny Mine made the Browns rich. Like the Boettchers, the Campions, the Tabors and many other mining millionaires, the Browns moved to Denver's swanky Capitol Hill neighborhood.

Molly's efforts to conquer Denver society were hampered by the fact that her roots were all too evident. She shared her Denver home with her aging father, John Tobin, an Irish-born day laborer, and her Irish-born mummsie, Johanna, who smoked a pipe. Perhaps to escape her humble ancestors, Molly began to travel a great deal. She joined European grand tours, and in 1912 decided to return with high society on the most fashionable of vessels, the *Titanic*.

Molly did not sink on the *Titanic* — where she heroically saved other panic-stricken passengers. After she

died in 1932, her house was converted to a home for wayward girls. Then it became an even more cramped boarding house for single gentlemen. By 1969 some were talking about demolishing the house for a modern office building, but the possibility of losing one of Denver's greatest landmarks jolted the city's historical consciousness. Ann Love, wife of Governor John Love, and others distressed about the proposed demolition, incorporated a private, nonprofit organization called Historic Denver, Inc. (HDI) on December 11, 1970. HDI raised $80,000 to buy the house and has poured in $500,000 and 250,000 hours of volunteer time.

Molly would be tickled pink to know that the restoration of her house inspired a renaissance in the Capitol Hill neighborhood. She was Denver's pioneer preservationist: when the cottage of poet and journalist Eugene Field faced demolition in 1927, Molly bought it and moved it to Washington Park to serve as a branch of the Denver Public Library.

Like Field's Cottage, Molly's own home has been fully restored. It is a beautiful, picture-perfect house of the aspiring 19th-century middle class, from the statue of the Nubian slave at the door to the polar bear rug in the parlor. Since the 1970s, it has also become the town's most popular house tour, attracting some 40,000 visitors a year.

Molly Brown House Director Leigh Fletcher Grinstead reports: "We hope to introduce a new generation of Coloradans to the fascinating ups and downs of Molly Brown. She is a great role model for girls especially. She was an early feminist, suffragist, preservationist and philanthropist. She overcame her humble origins with lifelong learning. She studied music, opera, French, German, Italian, Spanish and literature to make herself a polished lady."

Henry C. Brown & His Palace

Although unrelated to Henry C. Brown, Molly Brown did enjoy his hotel. Like the Tabor Grand Opera House, that grand hotel signified Denver's arrival as a city of significance. Any city hoping to make it out West

When the Brown Palace Hotel, above left, opened in 1892, it dominated a skyline, but is now dwarfed by 40- and 50-story highrises. The nine-story atrium lobby, right, remains a glorious place for high tea.
Credit: Tom Noel Collection

aspired to build a great hotel. Elegant accommodations would help to lure the rich and the famous, to attract newcomers and investors. Denver's grand hotel of the 1870s — the American House — and of the 1880s — the Windsor — are long gone, but the Brown Palace has been in business every day since its grand opening in 1892.

Denver's palace began as the dream of an itinerant carpenter — Henry C. Brown. This Ohio orphan ran away at age 16 from the farmer to whom he was apprenticed. He headed West, working as a carpenter in St. Louis, as a contractor in San Francisco, and as a lumberman in Oregon. By the time he landed in Denver in 1860, Brown was a budding carpenter-contractor-developer.

He homesteaded Capitol Hill, erecting a claim cabin at 12th and Sherman. From there he wheel-barrowed his tools down to Denver, where he constructed various buildings, including one for the *Denver Tribune*, which he owned and operated after the journalists defaulted. By the mid-1880s Brown was worth $250,000.

Brown boasted that his homestead, bordered by Broadway on the west and Logan on the east between East 20th and 8th avenues, would one day be the Queen City's elite residential neighborhood. But Brown's Bluff housed mostly prairie dogs. To enhance his real estate, Brown donated a site for the state capitol and built the first Capitol Hill mansion at 17th and Broadway. Looking somewhat like a triple-decker Mississippi River steamboat, Brown's showhome launched a building boom on the four streets he named for his favorite Civil War heroes — President Lincoln and Generals Sherman, Grant and Logan. In 1879 Brown sold his mansion to Horace Tabor, the silver magnate from Leadville, who fancied the ostentatious 20-room house perched on a prominent corner. Nowadays, the site houses the 52-story Norwest Bank complex.

Brown reckoned that a grand hotel just across Broadway from his house would pull Denver eastward toward Capitol Hill. After British investors failed to build the hotel they promised, he undertook the project himself. He engaged Denver's finest architect,

Frank E. Edbrooke, and spent $2 million to make this hotel Denver's showplace. To erect the building's steel skeleton, Brown and Edbrooke hired Denver's Lane Bridge and Iron Works. Edbrooke then wrapped the steel frame in a skin of red sandstone with carved ornamentation. Some of the stone figures that once swarmed over the facade have been scraped off, probably after loose chunks of sandstone began bombarding pedestrians. A carved Colorado bestiary of wildlife in inset medallions still enlivens the seventh floor. The grand stone cornice inscribed "The H. C. Brown Hotel" has been pared off the Broadway facade, but the arched entry is still flanked by the stone monogram, HCB, and a bust of Brown.

The Brown Palace introduced visitors to the wonders of the age — steel frame construction and indoor plumbing, elevators and electricity. A city within a city, the Brown had its own power plant and two artesian wells, various shops and services and even a basement crematorium so guests would never have to check out. Gawking at such a palace gave Coloradans a peek at the latest gadgets and interior decor, at new fashions in food, dress and amusements.

Private Clubs

Characters such as Henry C. Brown and Horace Tabor epitomized the graduation of the *nouveau riches* from mining rushes to cultural rushes. Besides a grand hotel and a grand opera house, they and their colleagues established private clubs where they could socialize and talk business. First and foremost of these was the Denver Club. Founded in 1880, this private men's club included noteworthies such as David Moffat, Walter Cheesman, James Grant and Nathaniel Hill. This club, as historian Christine Whitacre points out, "represented an effort by the city's economic leaders to boost Denver's reputation within the national business community and to lure new investment capital to the West." Indeed, one of the club founders was James Duff, a Scotsman who represented the London-based Colorado Mortgage & Investment Company, which sunk millions of pounds into Colorado.

The Denver Club dominated Denver's club scene for almost 100 years. Decline set in after the club demolished its grand old mansion at 17th and Glenarm in 1953 to build a high-rise office building with the club in the top three floors.

"If only we had kept that old mansion," lamented former club president Richard H. Shaw in 1992, "we'd probably have a five year waiting list today." Instead the club is struggling to stay alive in a lackluster edifice overshadowed by many newer, taller towers.

Wealthy young men of the 1880s also flocked to the Denver Athletic Club, which promoted sports of all sorts. Founded in 1884, the DAC grew rapidly, claiming 1,000 members by 1892, when it completed the $250,000 red brick and sandstone clubhouse at 1325 Glenarm Place. In 1890, the DAC introduced football to Denver as the Club humiliated the University of Colorado, 34 to 0. The DAC team continued to whip collegians until 1906, when it dropped the game after newspapers reported that it was paying "amateurs" recruited from top college teams.

The DAC also rode the bicycle craze of the 1890s after development of the safety bicycle and pneumatic tire led to safer, more comfortable machines than the original "bonebreakers." Denver's generally flat terrain and dry, sunny climate made it ideal for cyclists. The DAC bicycle division captain promised that an "enjoyable and health-giving run with the Bicycle Division" would do wonders for working men: "His mind will be relieved of the cares and anxieties of his business affairs, his digestive organs improved, his appetite strengthened, his nerves relaxed, his brain cleared up…He will be in a much better humor, better condition to attend to his duties, will be enabled to accomplish more work with better results."

Society maidens and matrons followed Denver's dashing young sports into the DAC. Women soon transformed the DAC into a haven for fine dining, dancing and socializing. DAC athletes grumbled that the gym was often closed for banquets, balls and bridge parties. Despite recent additions that fall stylistically short of Varian and Sterner's fine original landmark, the DAC remains energetic on its full block site between 13th and 14th streets, Glenarm to Tremont places.

Sporting men also founded the Denver Country Club in 1901, converting a wheat field straddling Cherry Creek between Downing Street and University Boulevard into a golf course for the upper crust. Crawford Hill took to the greens with lawyer Henry Wolcott, brother of U.S. Senator Edward O. Wolcott, and James Duff of the Denver Club. As at the DAC, women followed men into the DCC and soon joined men in golf, tennis, swimming and ice skating.

Chamber of Commerce

Denver's power elite had broad ambitions. They regarded all of Colorado as their hinterland, as manifested in the Chamber of Commerce's founding goal "to promote general prosperity in all the varied interest of Colorado and Denver." With imperialistic aspirations, Denver boosters claimed to speak for the whole state. The chamber manned many fronts: it proposed creation of the Denver Museum of Natural History and housed the original collection on its shelves in the old, chamber building that stood at Fourteenth and Lawrence streets. Looking to the future as well as the past, the chamber anticipated Denver's emergence as an international port of entry. Overlooking the fact that Denver lay hundreds of miles from any national border, boosters persistently lobbied Washington to designate Denver an official port of entry. Washington succumbed in 1882 and awarded Denver a customs house. Ever since, Denver has aspired to be an international hub for transportation and business.

By 1890 Denver's population had soared to 106,713 — behind San Francisco and Omaha, but larger than Los Angeles or any town in Texas. After Colorado men approved full woman's suffrage in 1893, Denver became the largest city in the world where women could vote. Carolyn Nichols Churchill, editor of Denver's *Queen Bee* proclaimed Denver not only politically enlightened but also a pure, curative atmosphere for asthmatics, tuberculars and other

William Henry Jackson, the most famous of all western photographers, captured tourist-thrilling scenarios such as this view of the Durango to Silverton line for the Denver & Rio Grande Railroad. *Credit: Colorado Historical Society*

invalids. Colorado's climate cure might turn even the proverbial 98-pound weakling into a robust mountain man — or mountain woman.

The Switzerland of America

Denver's boosters energetically promoted a relatively recession-proof business — tourism. Railroads joined the crusade. Setting a tone for many subsequent railroad appeals, the Kansas Pacific's 1873 booklet, *Colorado: Its Resorts and Attractions for the Pleasure Seeker, Tourist and Invalid* proclaimed: "Denver, the political capital and commercial center, an aristocratic little burg, romantically situated at the foot of the 'Shining Mountains' is without doubt one of the most beautiful cities of the world…Many persons on first arriving in Denver have started from their hotels to walk to the mountains before breakfast."

The Denver & Rio Grande, which had carried farm crops and gold and silver ores, adopted the slogan "The Scenic Line of the World" and began catering to sightseers. The D&RG hired photographer William Henry Jackson to produce seductive images for calendars, postcards and booklets which were mass produced for national distribution. The D&RG's in-house "Literary Department" cranked out poetry and fiction, as well as travel books and brochures. Other railroads also pushed tourism, generating an endless supply of publicity to lure sightseers and pleasure seekers to the highest state.

Coloradans looked to the world's pace-setting tourist destination, Switzerland, as a model. As Colorado had comparable climate and Alpine scenery, boosters decided to market the highest state as "The Switzerland of America." Samuel Bowles, in his 1869 guide to Colorado entitled *The Switzerland of America*, marveled: "I who have seen the Alps from Berne join in the judgment that no grand mountain view exists that surpasses this as seen from the high roll of the prairie just out of Denver."

Emma Abbott Gauge reaffirmed the theme in her 1900 book, *Western Wanderings & Summer Sauntering*

through Picturesque Colorado: "The Alps have long since become the synonym for grandeur, but they cannot rival these grand old Rockies, with their sublime magnificence."

Winter sports, a key to Switzerland's hardy tourist industry, inspired Coloradans to capitalize on their "white gold." Soon after 1900, the Denver Mountain Parks Department, the Colorado Mountain Club and the Denver Chamber of Commerce began promoting skiing and erected warming huts and ski lifts. The first mass market publication to push winter tourism in Colorado, the Union Pacific's 1925 brochure, *Colorado Mountain Playground*, promoted ski areas and "tobagganing, skiing, skating and snow shoe trips."

Skiing received a big push from the Denver & Rio Grande Railroad, which has been running special ski trains to Winter Park ever since that Denver Mountain Park opened in 1940.
Credit: photo by Tom Noel

Winter and summer, railroads brought tourists into Denver, and street railways carried them to various attractions in and about the Mile High City. By the 1890s, sightseers could board "Seeing Denver" streetcar excursions at the Brown Palace Hotel. For 25 cents, rubberneckers were promised 25 miles of sightseeing aboard the open cars which "Seeing Denver" leased from the Denver Tramway Company.

Jollier tourists were even taught Gus Brohm's "Seeing Denver" song:

"There's a city out west and it outshines the rest
Where the sun shines the whole year round
With its air fresh and light, breath to your delight
Just jump on a car and take in the sights with me
Seeing Denver is my delight either by day or by night"

Nocturnal tourism became a thrust of the Chamber of Commerce's "City of Lights" campaign. Although hardly an original idea — many other cities also had big, bright ideas for light bulbs — Denverites illuminated their town energetically. The Curtis Street Theater District shone most radiantly. The 1910 Chamber of Commerce Building at 1726 Champa Street, the 1910 Denver Gas and Electric Building at Fifteenth and Champa streets and the 1908 Municipal Auditorium at 14th and Curtis were all outlined in electric light bulbs. A related tradition, the Christmas lighting of Civic Center, began about the same time. Denver's nocturnal sparkle could be seen for miles around, beckoning all to the city's shops, theaters, restaurants and night clubs.

Boosters fancied bright lights and tourism, which not only brought in visitors and their dollars but also pumped up civic pride. By 1940, tourists constituted Colorado's third largest source of income, after agriculture and manufacturing.

Making the Great American Desert Bloom

The Denver Chamber of Commerce touted the South Platte Valley, the former "Great American Desert," as a Garden of Eden. Twenty thousand people began farming in Colorado between 1910 and 1920. Cattle sales doubled, and sheep sales increased by 600 percent between 1900 and 1920. As both farm products and ranch livestock rode the rails to market, railroads readily promoted Colorado as an agricultural paradise.

Denverites embraced their country cousins, knowing that cattle and sheep, hogs and chickens, winter wheat and other grains flowed into Denver for food processing, storage and wholesaling. In the Queen City, Colorado's farm bounty was transformed into beer and bread, into canned and bottled foods, into hamburger and steaks.

Cheerfully blazing with electric light, the old Denver Gas & Electric Company Building at 15th and Champa streets is still illuminated to delight nocturnal downtowners. *Credit: Tom Noel Collection.*

Cattle drives on the Goodnight-Loving Trail brought fresh beef from Texas up the Front Range of the Rockies to Denver. This 1860s outfit is nooning near Pueblo. *Credit: Pueblo Regional Library*

Westerners grew up on beef, as well as gold and silver. After many investors found mines to be bottomless holes that swallowed money, easterners and Englishmen began to sink their teeth — and capital — into cattle.

Europeans accustomed to plodding old world farmers marveled at the wild adolescents who herded American cattle. The "cow servant," sniffed Lady Rose Pender in A *Lady's Experiences in the Wild West in 1883* (London: 1888), is "a strange creature, quite unlike any of his fellow men, and all he does must be done with swagger and noise…utterly devoid of manners or good feeling."

Kinder accounts of cowboys came from Dr. William A. Bell, Jr. the son of an English society doctor. The good doctors, father and son, persuaded their wealthy London patients to invest in their American toy —

the Denver and Rio Grande Railroad — and in Colorado cattle ranching. Ultimately young Dr. Willie Bell moved to Colorado Springs as vice president of the D&RG. When mining traffic sank, the D&RG began transporting cattle.

On his 1868 visit to Colorado with a railroad survey crew, Dr. Bell was astonished to find cattle grazing on the open prairie. Although "they had been out all winter, without shelter or hay" as Bell noted in *New Tracks in North America* (London: 1870), they, like buffalo, emerged in the spring fat and juicy.

Bell and others found they could buy wild Texas longhorns for $5 or $10 and raise them free on the open range, where naturally-cured gramma and buffalo grasses served as fodder year around. Fattened cattle could be sold for $30 to $50 a head at stockyards in Denver, Kansas City or Chicago.

© BY W.S.BOWMAN NO 29-C. BONNIE McCARROL THROWN FROM SILV

Promoters in the 1870s and 1880s promised 30 to 40 percent annual profits in the western cattle industry. One of the propagandists, Baron Water von Richthofen, dabbled in cattle and wrote *Cattle-Raising on the Plains of North America* (N.Y.:1885), a book proclaiming that "this former Great American Desert is the largest and richest grass and pasture region in the world, and it will probably soon become the most important beef-producing country of the globe."

Despite the baron's claim that "profit of 25 percent per annum is the minimum the cattle business will

yield," he himself failed in the cattle industry. So did many others during the blizzards of 1885-86 and the subsequent federal crackdown on unrestrained use of public lands by cow punchers.

Baron von Richthofen's book, however, sold well, and he built his Colorado castle as a show home for his new suburban town — Montclair. There the German adventurer constructed the Molkerei (milk house) on East 12th Avenue between Oneida and Newport streets and promised tuberculosis victims a sure cure. They could drink fresh milk from cows stabled below,

Cowboy garb and yee-hawing have marked Denver's National Western Stock Show every January since 1905, a celebration of the city's cowtown heritage with rodeos, livestock exhibits and auctions at the Denver Union Stockyards.

Credit: photo by Tom Noel

then lie out on the decks of the Molkerei in Colorado's salubrious sunshine, breathing champagne air that only the angels had sipped before.

Best of all, the "lungers" could inhale, through grates in the milkhouse floor, the barnyard effluvium rising from the cattle stabled below. These pungent fumes were a sure cure for lung disorders, according to the Baron von Richthofen. Nowadays, the dairy cows are gone but the Molkerei and the Richthofen Castle linger as centerpieces of the Montclair Historic District in what is now a sedate East Denver neighborhood.

The cattle industry changed not only the West but all of America. Cheap western beef transformed the American diet. Before the 1880s, few Americans could

afford fresh beef. But cowpokes, feed lots, stockyards, meat processing and refrigeration changed all that. Fresh beef in refrigerated railroad cars flooded eastern grocery stores. Americans became beefeaters. Steak and hamburgers became the all-American meals.

Nothing, not even beef, sweetened Denver's economy in the early 1900s like sugar beets. After the federal government placed the Dingly Tariff on sugar and other imports from foreign countries in 1897, the Denver Chamber of Commerce began preaching the glories of these big, ugly tubulars. The chamber distributed seeds to anyone who would try growing them, offering $50 cash prizes for the sweetest beets. Such booster campaigns helped sugar beets become the number one crop in Colorado by the 1920s. By then agriculture had eclipsed mining as Colorado's premier industry. Denver started out as a mining supply and ore processing center, but its role as an agricultural hub sustained the city after 1900 as mining lost its glitter.

Denver Needed Dandelions

Despite the boasting of the Chamber of Commerce and promoters such as the Baron von Richthofen, Denver remained a dusty, drab looking place.

Another Capitol Hill resident, Dr. Frederick G. Bancroft, a pioneer physician, came up with a solution. Why not introduce dandelions to the Great American Desert?

Like other English romantics fond of natural gardens, he celebrated the dandelion as "a tramp with a golden crown." His granddaughter, the late Caroline Bancroft, delighted in telling the story: "When grandfather arrived, he was aghast. Colorado was so dusty, barren and ugly. He declared that Denver needed a dandelion."

Dandelions are not the only thing Dr. Bancroft gave Denver. He helped found the Colorado Historical Society and the Denver Medical Society. He first researched Market Street's *Nymphs du Pave* and called public attention to local outbreaks of sexually transmitted diseases.

A wonderful, old-fashioned kind of doctor, Bancroft was legendary for eating and drinking double portions of red meat and red wine. This was followed, presumably, by brandy and cigars. He weighed over 250 pounds, and may have told his patients that they were underweight.

Dr. Bancroft even knew the dandelion's Latin name: *Taraxacum officinale*. It is a stemless herb of the Composite Family, with leaves in spear-shaped rosettes, and flat solitary bright yellow disc flowers. In some eyes, the dandelion is just another of the scourges with which Euro-Americans cursed Native Americans in their Garden of Eden. Europeans cultivated dandelions for salad "greens," and developed special strains with very large, curly leaves. The root has medicinal uses and the flower can be used to make wine.

The dandelion has one of the world's most exotic, delicate and perfectly shaped seed heads — a perfect globe of silvery, lacy ecstacy. The dandelion seeds rapidly, is perfectly hardy, and will grow — like the proverbial weed — in almost any kind of soil. Despite the dandelion's merits, *The Denver Post*, ever vigilant in weeding out public enemies, took an unflinching stand against them.

"It is conceded through the world that Denver lawns are the most beautiful and perfect existing anywhere on earth," explained a front page story, April 29, 1926. "But the dandelion pest is sweeping over the city and unless immediate steps are taken our lawns will be seriously marred, so let everybody get busy now — don't wait. There is only one way to exterminate the dandelion — human labor — just bend your backs and dig them out."

The *Post* offered "to furnish men and women who know how to clear lawns of this nuisance." All unemployed persons were urged "to come to our office and let us register you as willing to work on lawns, destroying the dandelions, at $3 for eight hours work. There are a number of very deserving people who are not employed at the present time who will be glad to get jobs of this kind…let no guilty dandelion escape! They mar your own property and harm your neighbor's property. Join in this dandelion crusade for the mutual benefit of all citizens."

Dandelions backfired as beautification in a city of avid gardeners — including many former midwestern farmers — or their offspring. These folks relished their grassy lawns, their vegetable patches, their shrubs and border gardens, and their street trees. Indeed Denver's avid gardeners have led some to suggest that the garden hose should be on the city seal. For such citizenry, dandelions are not to be abided. Denver, the jewel on the bosom of the desert, would have to look elsewhere for City Beautiful solutions.

THE CITY BEAUTIFUL

DENVER ROARED PAST URBAN RIVALS TO BECOME the biggest city in the Rockies, but chaotic speculation and growth left many scars. Not a single park or public square graced downtown Denver. Little sense of order or aesthetics prevailed as the boomtown became a dusty, drab midwestern city.

A few enlightened pioneers envisioned city-wide beautification as early as the 1890s. After visiting the Chicago World's Fair in 1893 and seeing how a swamp on Lake Michigan had been transformed into a beautiful neoclassical showplace, John Evans returned to Denver inspired to improve the Mile High City. The aging ex-governor and businessman proposed a park and parkway plan, but he was too old and tired to push the plan past penny-pinching city officials. Of the Evans plan, only Park Avenue and City Park materialized. Greater city beautification awaited an idealistic but ruthlessly realistic politician.

"The Speer That Made Denver Famous"

As the economy slowly recovered, the city's political fortunes also improved with the election of Denver's most powerful mayor. Robert W. Speer proved to be incredibly energetic in transforming a raw, young city into what he called the "Paris of America."

Speer came to Denver from Pennsylvania in 1878 at the age of 23. Like thousands of others, he arrived with lungs raw and bleeding from tuberculosis, under doctor's orders to seek out a dry, sunny, curative atmosphere. Colorado's salubrious climate transformed the puny Pennsylvanian. He gained weight, a strong handshake, and a broad grin.

Renewed, Speer jumped into the favorite sport of Denver's wheelers and dealers — real estate. He served as secretary of Horace Tabor's Lookout Mountain Development Company. Belatedly, Speer realized that the anticipated boom in Lookout Mountain luxury homes might not come for decades. He shrewdly switched to an upscale real estate market closer to home, joining John A. Ferguson, Frederick R. Ross, and others in developing a fashionable residential area on the northern edge of the Denver Country Club. In this still affluent neighborhood between First and Fourth avenues, from Downing Street to University Boulevard, Speer garnered his reward — his large home still stands at 300 Humboldt Street. Critics sniped that he built Speer Boulevard as a fancy driveway for himself and his Country Club chums.

Speer seemed to be everywhere. On the board of directors of the Festival of Mountain & Plain, he ballyhooed this fair to lift Denver's spirits

Robert W. Speer brought together the business community and idealistic reformers to capitalize on the civic consciousness of the Progressive era. Mayor Speer, who came to Denver as a youth struggling with tuberculosis, reflected in 1909: "Denver has been kind to most of us by giving to some health, to some wealth, to some happiness, and to some a combination of all. We can pay a part of this debt by making our city more attractive." *Credit: Colorado Historical Society*

OPPOSITE PAGE: A variety of performers have graced the Greek Theater in Civic Center. Credit: *photo by Glenn Cuerden*

Elegant artistic statements, such as these gates to the
Country Club neighborhood, encouraged private citizens to
build grand, beautifully landscaped residential neighborhoods.
Mayor Speer, who lived in the Country Club area, used public
parks and parkways to pump up civic pride.
Credit: Denver Public Library.

Denver's long tradition of Christmas decorations and lighting
began around 1907 on 16th Street and Civic Center,
where live reindeer also delighted the children. "Denver,"
boasted the Municipal Facts Magazine, was "America's
foremost Christmas City… the unique fortress of the beneficent
St. Nicholas." Credit: Denver Department of Parks & Recreation

and showcase Colorado's assets after the 1893
Depression struck. As a staunch booster, he became
a stalwart member of the Chamber of Commerce.
Fellow upbuilders liked Speer's "go-ahead-ativeness."
They elected him president of the Denver Real Estate
Exchange and named him a director of the Denver
Manufacturers Bureau.

Speer also went to work for the Democratic Party.
After he was elected city clerk in 1884, he moved through
appointments as Denver postmaster, Fire and Police
Board commissioner, and president of the Board of

Civic Center sparkles on
winter nights with the
Christmas lighting of the
City and County Building.
This colorful tradition
began in 1919 when city
electrician John Malpiede
whimsically replaced
the white lights around
Civic Center with globes
of red and green.
Credit: photo by Ron Ruhoff

City Beautiful planners converted the slummy heart of Denver into a spacious office park for government buildings — Civic Center — with the arching facade of City and County Building at the west end. *Credit: Colorado Historical Society*

At the north end of Civic Center, the wading pool with sculptor Robert Garrison's cherubs and sea lion fountains is a popular summertime place to chill out. *Credit: photo by Michael Gamer*

Public Works. He became the city's craftiest politician. "I am a boss," Speer once confessed. "I want to be a good one."

"Red tape and restricting laws," Speer said on another occasion, "will not make a crooked politician straight but will make a straight politician useless. Personally, I believe in the concentration of all administrative powers in the hands of one official. It fixes the responsibility for good or bad government."

At the east end of Civic Center, the Colorado State Capitol has been the backdrop for free Symphony in the Parks performances. *Credit: Roger Whitacre*

In 1904, Speer successfully ran for mayor after he and other city shapers drafted a new city charter and persuaded voters to approve it. The so-called "Speer Charter" gave Denver one of the country's most powerful mayoral offices. Speer seized that office to which he was reelected in 1908 and 1916.

The new mayor changed the color of Denver from brown to green. In 1905, he inaugurated a tree-planting program that ultimately gave away 110,000 shade trees to residents who promised to plant and care for them. Speer established the office of the city forester to help transform a patch of the Great American Desert into an oasis of trees, shrubs and lawns.

Speer shared his vision in a January 7, 1907, pep talk to the city council: "We are in a plastic state. As the twig is bent so the tree will grow…Denver can be made one of the ordinary cities of the country, or she can be made the Paris of America. It will cost money, but this investment will pay ten dollars for every one spent. Let us start [with Civic Center] plaza near the business center — have statues, trees, and flowers — where

Two Years Ago Cherry Creek Looked Like This

The eyesore known as Cherry Creek Drive was transformed into an orderly, landscaped Speer Boulevard with retaining walls to discipline temperamental Cherry Creek. Credit: Tom Noel Collection

Between Speer Boulevard and West High School, Sunken Gardens Park once contained a large pond, exquisite flower beds and a picnic pavilion. Credit: Tom Noel Collection

our people and tourists may gather each evening under the most artistic electric lighting — near the spray from grand fountains and listen to the finest music in the land…Then build not an ordinary, but an extraordinary drive or Appian Way into the mountains…Take these forward steps, and you will never turn back — our future greatness will be assured."

The City Beautiful Plan

Mayor Speer could be found in his office evenings and on weekend mornings pondering plans for new parks and public buildings. In the heart of the city, Speer proposed a gracefully landscaped Civic Center. Between the State Capitol on the east and a projected new City and County Building on the west, he had

Creekfront Park with its Indian art and water wall opened at Larimer Street and Speer Boulevard in 1992. Credit: photo by Tom Noel

Reviving City Beautiful dreams, the city enhanced Cherry Creek during the 1980s with a paved path for walkers, joggers, skaters and bicyclists. Credit: *photo by Tom Noel*

some of the nation's foremost city planners design grounds, monuments, a central library, fountains and an outdoor Greek theater. This park-like heart was step one of a four-part plan for transforming Denver into a City Beautiful.

The second step, a network of tree-lined parkways, led from downtown to outlying residential neighborhoods. "Shaded drives," as Speer noted, "in this climate and land of bright sunshine, are appreciated more than in most cities." During Denver's hot, dry summers,

On the west side of Ferril Lake, the City Park Pavilion overlooks the recently restored electric fountain illuminated on summer evenings. *Credit: Tom Noel Collection*

At the east end of City Park, the Museum of Natural History overlooks a large wading pool. *Credit: Tom Noel Collection*

Fortunately, Mayor Speer had a better idea. Striving to preserve and enhance Denver's meager waterways, he walled the creek and began landscaping it with trailing vines, shrubbery and trees. Small triangular parks were created along Speer Boulevard where the diagonal boulevard intersected downtown streets. Two larger tracts were acquired for Sunken Gardens Park in front

Credit: photo by James Baca

Credit for Below: Tom Noel Collection

parkways are at least 10 degrees cooler than unshaded streets. Speer Boulevard, the pace-setter parkway, also resolved the problem of what to do with dumpy, dangerous Cherry Creek.

Denver's City Beautiful era is epitomized by the transformation of Cherry Creek, where the 1858 gold strike gave birth to the town. Jerome Smiley, in the closing pages of his 978-page *History of Denver* (1901), urged the Mile High City to begin "municipal works that would vastly contribute toward making Denver the City Beautiful." Smiley argued that the first target should be "the avoidable and blighting blemish — to use a mild term — caused by the presence of the wretched Cherry Creek." He recommended that the creek "be diverted to Sand Creek, and its water passed around the city to discharge into the Platte River several miles below [the city limits]." Then the city could install "a trunk sewer in the creek's bed, that sandy and miserable waste."

Framed by monolithic red sandstone slabs and landscaped with native junipers, this outdoor theater hosts popular Easter sunrise services, Colorado Symphony Orchestra performances, and pop stars ranging from the Beatles to Denver songbird Judy Collins, shown here at Red Rocks in 1992.

Most awesome of Denver Mountain Parks, the Red Rocks Natural Amphitheater, right, opened in 1941. *Credit Tom Noel Collection*

of West High School and Alamo Placita Park at First Avenue. To honor the man who turned the town eyesore into the scenic centerpiece of a grand boulevard, the city council in 1910 renamed Cherry Creek Drive as Speer Boulevard.

Denverites have picnicked in and around the Cheesman Pavilion in Cheesman Park ever since the family of real estate mogul Walter S. Chessman donated funding for the park in 1907. *Credit: Tom Noel Collection*

Speer Boulevard led to Washington Park via the Downing-Marion Street Parkway. East Sixth, Seventh, Seventeenth and Monaco Parkways extended the plan into East Denver. Most of the parkway plan has been implemented, although subsequent mayors have failed to complete a few remaining segments such as a proposed South Platte River Parkway.

The third step in Denver's City Beautiful evolution was the establishment of large neighborhood parks to serve as mini-civic centers. These major parks became centerpieces for public buildings — schools, branch libraries, firehouses, churches and other community hubs. Sloan's Lake, Washington and City parks are legacies of this plan.

The fourth step in Speer's City Beautiful plan was the creation of the Denver Mountain Parks. This last and most ambitious scheme of Denver's Progressive-era boosters carried the dream of public playgrounds and

Providing free, wholesome recreation for youngsters such as these in the Lincoln Park Pool in 1912 was a successful City Beautiful era formula for preventing juvenile delinquency. *Credit: Tom Noel Collection*

open space beyond the boundaries of the City and County of Denver into Clear Creek, Douglas, Grand and Jefferson counties. These Denver Mountain Parks later came to include the Winter Park Ski Area and the Red Rocks Outdoor Amphitheater.

Some 13,500 acres of mountain parks survive, reflecting Denver's dreams of enhancing not only the city itself, but the entire metropolis. Thanks to this park system, Denver is one of the few cities in America that boasts its own ski area, its own outdoor amphitheater and its own buffalo herd.

The Park System

Speer doubled the city's park space from 573 to 1,184 acres. At City Park, where the zoo consisted of a few chained and caged animals, Speer installed zoological gardens. Behind protective moats, monkeys, sea lions, bears and other beasts could cavort in natural looking environments. In City Park Lake, an electric fountain with nine colored lights and 25 water jets provided visual accompaniment to the free concerts of the Denver Municipal Band. On the east side of Big Lake (renamed Ferril Lake in 1996 for poet Thomas

Among the youngsters posing at the Curtis Park pool in 1940 is a 14-year-old diving champion, seated at the edge of the board, Viola Salazar. *Credit: Tom Noel Collection*

Colorado sculptor Mabel Landrum Torrey designed the Wynken, Blynken & Nod Fountain in Washington Park.
Credit: Tom Noel Collection

....

Hornsby Ferril), City Hall worked with Denver philanthropists such as the Boettcher, Gates, and Phipps families to construct the Denver Museum of Natural History, Colorado's largest museum to this day.

Realizing the special magic of water in a semi-arid region, Mayor Speer built the south lake of Washington Park, Sunken Gardens Lake, and added Berkeley, Sloan's and Rocky Mountain lakes to the park system. When city dwellers reached their new parks, they found plenty to do. The city provided bathhouses and bathing beaches at Berkeley, City, Sloan's Lake and Washington parks. Visitors found fish in the well-stocked waters as well as sailboats, canoes and paddle boats. In winter, the lakes were converted to ice skating rinks.

Whereas the private sector built clubs and amenities for privileged individuals, the Speer administration built public tennis courts, swimming pools, ball fields, playing fields and graciously landscaped parks and parkways for all citizens. Recreational opportunities, as Progressive era reformers argued, should not just be for the rich.

Robert and Kate Speer never had children, but made all of Denver's children their own. Their favorite statues were the Children's Fountain in City Park and

Wynken, Blynken and Nod in Washington Park. Playgrounds were constructed in every corner of the city, including the poorest neighborhoods, which needed them most. "Three years ago," reported the *American City Magazine* for May 1910, "Denver did not know that a good playground for children was...something else than a vacant space where children, unsupervised, had the opportunity to fight it out. Today Denver is one of the leading cities in the playground movement."

The late Denver historian Louisa Ward Arps cherished a favorite story about Mayor Speer's fondness for chil-

One of Denver's first playgrounds delighted these youngsters in Curtis Park. By providing supervised play and recreation in poorer urban neighborhoods, the city eliminated many potential gang problems. *Credit: Tom Noel Collection*

....

dren: "When Boss Speer heard via the grapevine that the telephone company was planning to tear down Cedric Kaub's tree house on Gaylord Street, he became furious. Speer sent one of his men out to assure the Kaubs that no one would touch Cedric's tree house. No one did."

Speer used his skill and experience as a real estate developer to the city's advantage. When the city attorney ruled that Denver had no power to acquire land west of the city limits at Sheridan Boulevard, Speer bought the land as a private citizen and sold what is now Inspiration Point Park and its million-dollar view to the city for the price he paid for it — $8,000.

Denver's greatest asset, as the mayor realized, was its view of the snow-capped Rocky Mountains. Even lifelong Denverites can still round a corner or reach the top of a hill and thrill at the panorama framed between

Pikes Peak and Longs Peak. While the mountains had not been growing higher, buildings and billboards had. Realizing the threat, the Speer administration urged that telegraph and telephone cables be buried underground, worked out a compromise 12-story building height limit, and tried to ban billboards. Speer also worked with the Denver Chamber of Commerce to fight another threat to the mountain view: Denver passed its first smoke abatement ordinance in 1916. This pioneer effort began the fight against air pollution that still sullies Denver's reputation and mountain views.

Denver's Only National Political Convention

To boost Denver as a convention city, the mayor campaigned for a $500,000 municipal auditorium — the largest in America except for Madison Square Garden in New York. Speer and the Chamber of Commerce raised $100,000 to celebrate the 1908 grand opening of the auditorium with Denver's first and only national political convention. This Democratic Party lovefest focused national attention on the Mile High City.

"Whiskers are in evidence everywhere," snickered the *New York Times* on July 7, 1908: "Homespun suits are to be seen, also the 'biled' [boiled] shirt." The *Times* called it a "hayseed" convention, and journalist William Allen White agreed. He compared "this gathering of the 'peepul', this uprising of the oppressed" to "the great barbaric yap of which Walt Whitman speaks."

For the convention, the city draped downtown with red, white and blue bunting. Brass bands greeted each state delegation as it arrived at Union Station. Thousands donned "I live in Denver — Ask Me" buttons and showed delegates around town. Others brought a trainload of

This souvenir postcard commemorated Denver's only national political convention, which opened the city's new auditorium.

Credit: Tom Noel Collection

6463. The Welcome Arch and 17th .... Street at Union Depot, Denver, Colorado

snow down from the mountains and dumped it in front of the auditorium so delegates could cool off with a snowball fight. A band of Arapaho Indians circled downtown on a streetcar, letting out war whoops whenever they spotted a delegate.

At Union Station, arrivals encountered the city's new Welcome Arch. This 70-ton bronze-coated, steel gateway supported a huge "WELCOME" sign, illuminated by 2,194 light bulbs. Mayor Speer dedicated the arch on July 4, 1906, declaring that it "is to stand here for ages as an expression of love, good wishes and kind feelings of our citizens to the stranger who enters our gates."

The Welcome Arch in front of Union Station was changed to read "Mizpah" on the downtown side, shown here, shortly after this photo was taken. Boosters belatedly realized they should not "Welcome" visitors to depart, only to arrive. *Credit: Denver Public Library, photo by Louis C. McClure*

Although Denverites told visitors that the word on the sign was an "Indian word" for "Howdy, Pardner," *Mizpah* is really a Hebrew parting salutation found in Genesis 31:49. *Credit: Denver Public Library photo by Louis C. McClure*

Initially the arch also said "WELCOME" on the downtown side, but the Chamber belatedly realized that departing visitors should not be "WELCOME" to leave. Red-faced Chamber officials replaced that side of the sign with the word "MIZPAH." Denverites simply told visitors that it was an "Indian word" for "Howdy, Pardner."

Actually, *Mizpah* is the Hebrew parting salutation found in Genesis 31:49: "The Lord watch between me and thee, when we are absent one from another." Despite the Mizpah misinterpretation, *The Denver Post* assured arriving Democrats, "We can read and write, lots of us, and we don't know a woman in Denver who carries more than one revolver when she comes downtown shopping." Damon Runyon, ace reporter for the *Rocky Mountain News*, concluded: "Miss Denver, a sassy cre-

ation of red, white and blue, appliqued with green and edged in purple mountains, stood waiting to receive all visitors and conventioneers with open arms."

A *Chicago Tribune* reporter found many delegates in Denver's saloons and wondered "just what effect altitude and alcohol together have on Democrats." The *Tribune* and conservative mossbacks scoffed at the Democratic presidential pick, William Jennings Bryan. Despite strong support from Colorado and other western states, the "boy orator" from Nebraska was defeated that fall of 1908 in his third and last presidential race.

Denver in the Progressive Era

Denverites of the Progressive era aspired to make Denver not only the biggest and richest city in the region, but the most attractive. The Mile High City achieved that goal thanks in large part to Mayor Speer. Although hardly handsome himself, the pudgy, balding politico gave Denver some of America's finest parks, parkways and public buildings. The city's schools, libraries, and even its fire stations were built as noble, neoclassical-style monuments. Among the new public amenities was a municipal bathhouse with free soap and towels for the unwashed masses. Street urchins lined up outside the bathhouse, now a designated Denver landmark at 20th and Curtis streets, in winter as well as summer.

Speer passed a pioneer gun control bill in 1911, making it a felony punishable by a $1,000 fine and a penitentiary sentence to carry concealed weapons. Civility, as well as cleanliness and beauty, became a civic goal. Denver's violent, dirty, and raw frontier hangovers were minimized and its progress maximized.

Speer walked to work one nippy day in 1918, fed the sparrows on his office window ledge as usual, and then was stricken by influenza. He became one of the millions killed by the worldwide flu epidemic which ultimately caused more deaths than World War I. More than 10,000 people jammed the Municipal Auditorium to say good-bye to the city's most loved, most controversial, and most effective mayor.

His widow Kate Thrush Speer donated much of her husband's small estate of $40,000 to pay for the bronze eagle and chiming clock atop her husband's dying dream — the City and County Building finally completed in 1932 at the west end of Civic Center. Kate remained in their house at 300 Humboldt Street until her death in the 1950s. Her most prized possession was a model of the Wynken, Blynken and Nod statue she and Robert had erected for the children of Denver in Washington Park.

One of the eulogies for Mayor Speer came from the prince of the Progressive era muckrakers, Lincoln Steffens. In his autobiography (1931), Steffens described a tour of Europe's model cities with American city shapers, including Denver's mayor:

"We saw...London and Paris, Brussels, Frankfort, Munich, Vienna and Switzerland. We saw the good things to copy that Mayor Speer sought for Denver. He was

Judge Benjamin Barr Lindsey gave Denver the nation's first juvenile court system. A militant reformer, he also exposed some of the ugly corruption that tarnished the City Beautiful era. Although a giant among reformers, he was a tiny man (with moustache at left) not much larger than many of the troubled youths he strove to help. Credit: *Colorado Historical Society*

Denver, that honest, able man; his eyes were Denver's eyes; his ambition was his city's…When we came to Düsseldorf, `the best-governed city in Europe,' he looked like a painter seeing a paintable landscape."

Admittedly, Speer used some ugly tactics to achieve a City Beautiful. Judge Benjamin Barr Lindsey in his classic exposé *The Beast* (1910), paints a dark picture of the Speer era. According to Lindsey, Speer was first elected mayor in 1904 with the help of 10,000 illegal votes. In 1916, however, all parties admitted that he was honestly elected for his last term. Although Speer eventually cleaned up his act, it is true that he achieved so much because he operated both above and below the table. Certainly he relished dealing with the city's power brokers in the proverbial smoke-filled back room.

During the Great Depression of the 1930s, Mayor Benjamin F. Stapleton and his manager of Parks, George Cranmer, used New Deal funding and manpower to further implement the City Beautiful dream. During Stapleton's administration, the city finished Civic Center, extended and improved the park and parkway system, and added to the Denver Mountain Parks system. Thanks to the Progressive era propensity for long-range masterplanning, New Deal employment programs such as the CCC and WPA found plenty of civic projects awaiting a work force which completed many City Beautiful era dreams.

Buffalo Bill

Lookout Mountain, one of the earliest and best-known Denver Mountain Parks, gained special significance when Denver laid to rest there the remains of William Frederick "Buffalo Bill" Cody. This Western icon outperformed all the others; he taught the world to think of Americans as cowboys and Indians. Thanks largely to him, generations of children grew up playing a game which often started with a squabble to see who would play the greatest cowboy of all — Buffalo Bill.

Americans, starved for national heroes, seized upon living persons to recast into mythical role models. Such was the fate of Buffalo Bill. During his lifetime,

he became the star of stage plays, movies, 557 dime novels and his own Wild West Show.

Heroes of one generation, of course, become the next generation's target practice. Buffalo Bill stayed in the saddle longer than most, although his debunking began in the 1920s. During the 1960s his long curly hair, grandiose goatee, and buckskin fringes made him a hairy role model for hippies.

Western historians of the 1990s have found Buffalo Bill beneath contempt. In the newest, most politically correct western history textbook, Richard White's *It's Your Misfortune and None of My Own*, the greatest mythic westerner of all is given only one sentence in 644 pages of tiny type. Buffalo Bill has been written off as a white male chauvinist fraud, a violent bigot who slaughtered animals and Native Americans.

A buffalo herd resides in Genesee, Denver's first mountain park, delighting motorists on I-70 which now bisects the park with an underpass for the municipal mammals. To make more room for exotic species at the Denver Zoo in 1917, most of the large elk and buffalo herds were shipped to Genesee.
Credit: *Metro Denver Convention & Visitors Bureau*

Western history without Buffalo Bill would have astonished early 20th-century Americans. Cody's career began when he ran away from home at age 13 to join the Colorado Gold Rush. A year later he became a Pony Express rider who boasted that he covered 322 miles in 21 hours and 40 minutes using 21 horses. In one of his alleged autobiographies, *Life & Adventures of Buffalo Bill* (1917), Cody says railroad construction crews nicknamed him after he fed them buffalo steaks. Bill killed, according to his own count, 4,280 buffalo.

Although portrayed as an enemy of the Indians, Buffalo Bill (shown with Sitting Bull) offered profitable and rewarding work in his Wild West Show to Indians eager to relive the good old days. Trying to avoid the 1890 Wounded Knee disaster which killed Sitting Bull, Cody left his show to hurry to the Black Hills because "I was an old friend of the chief and [might] induce the old fox to abandon his plans for a general war." *Credit: Buffalo Bill Museum, Lookout Mountain*

After Buffalo Bill's 1917 burial atop Lookout Mountain, folks in Cody, Wyoming threatened to steal the corpse. To keep the body — and the tourists who would come to the grave-side shrine and museum — the Colorado National Guard defended the tomb with this tank. *Credit: Buffalo Bill Memorial Museum*

Cody also hunted Indians. He slew Yellow Hand, a Cheyenne leader, in 1876 and boasted: "Jerking his war-bonnet off, I scientifically scalped him in about five seconds…As the soldiers came up, I swung the Indian chieftain's top-knot and bonnet in the air, and shouted: `The first scalp for Custer!'"

Despite Cody's fame as an Indian fighter, he later befriended many former foes. Ironically, the Indians who he helped put on reservations found some of their better paying and more gratifying jobs with Cody, travelling the U. S. and Europe as performers with the Wild West Show.

Fred Bonfils and Harry Tammen, founders of *The Denver Post*, reckoned Buffalo Bill the greatest west-erner of all and smelled money. Tammen loaned Cody $20,000 and later foreclosed on the bankrupt, aging showman. Tammen made Cody the star of the *Post's* Sells-Floto Circus, although the creaky, bewigged hero had to be lifted onto his horse. Cody moved into his sister's house, a Queen Anne dwelling at 2932 Lafayette Street, now a designated Denver landmark. There on January 10, 1917, the Sir Galahad of the Plains crossed over the Great Divide.

Some 25,000 people viewed the corpse as it lay in state inside the gold-domed Colorado State Capitol. Another 25,000 joined the funeral procession to the top of Lookout Mountain. *The Denver Post's* huge, $100,000 equestrian statue never materialized, but a museum and grave-side shrine did. Cody's hefty wife Lulu, who died in 1921, was buried atop her rambling husband to pin him down for eternity. Millions of pilgrims have climbed the mountain to visit the grave of the poor farm boy who grew up to be America's most celebrated Westerner. Thus Lookout Mountain, one of the first Denver mountain parks established to pre-serve a natural area, also became a shrine to a hero who had done much to transform the wilderness.

While Buffalo Bill, as usual, stole the show, the more important point of the Lookout Mountain story was to celebrate Denver's unique and enlightened approach to its mountainous hinterland. Jacques Benedict, who designed many mountain park structures, pointed out in his article "The Denver Park System," for the November 1914, issue of *The National Architect*: "Surely there is nothing being created in other cities quite so unique, so distinctive as the Mountain Park Idea, and the future fame of Denver will rest on the fact that with small means and great sacrifice, this smaller city chose rather to advertise, not her commercial supremacy, but her generosity, her belief in the broad spaces, and the distant vistas which make progres-sive citizens…"

DENVER'S UPS AND DOWNS

URING THE 1920S, DENVER FLEW INTO THE AIR
age with construction of Denver Municipal Airport.
Mayor Benjamin Franklin Stapleton encountered
shrill opposition led by *The Denver Post*, which ridiculed "Stapleton's Folly" and dubbed the proposed
Sand Creek site in northeast Denver "Simpleton's
Sand Dunes." Why build an airport so far away from
downtown when there were better, closer sites? If
God meant for men to fly, he would have given them
wings. This boondoggle, fumed the *Post*, had been
conceived to allow the mayor to squander municipal
money buying out landowners, most notably the
mayor's crony, H. Brown Canon of Windsor Farm
Dairy, at inflated prices.

"Rattlesnake Hollow," as other cynics called the site
at East 32nd Avenue and Quebec Street, was blasted
as a taxpayer subsidy for a few rich kids who liked to
play with airplanes. Sure enough, the power elite,
whose offspring flocked to the new sport of aviation,
endorsed the plan. Denver's first families swamped
the grand opening celebration, October 17-20, 1929 —
one week before the stock market crash. The city paid

$143,013 for the 640-acre site and another $287,000
to build the airport with four gravel runways, one
hangar, a tiny terminal and a wind sock.

Three days of dedication festivities drew crowds
estimated at 15,000 to 20,000. Rubberneckers watched
the climbs and dives, the loops and rolls of airplanes
overhead. Sightseers thronged around Boeing's "Levi-
athan of the Air," a 14-passenger bi-plane equipped
with Pullman sleepers, a kitchen and a dining room.

Coloradans celebrated "The West's best airport…a
model for further airport development…a great center on America's aerial map…large enough and level
enough to meet all future needs of long distance
passenger flying."

To feed the flyers, "Mom" Williams opened her
Skyline Buffet next door to the terminal. Mom, the original airport concessionaire, was replaced in the 1960s

by Sky Chef, which opened one of Denver's fanciest
restaurants. Shrimp boat dinners and ice cream sun-
daes made Sky Chef famous, as did its orchestra and
after-dinner dancing. Denverites held their children's
birthday parties at the airport, toasting the air age
future of their offspring.

Mayor Stapleton, a penny-pincher, installed devices
wherever he thought the city could grab some spare
change to help pay for the new airport. Coin-operated
turnstiles guarded the stairway to the observation

CHAPTER 7

**Stapleton Airport, left,
remained a sleepy place
during the 1930s, 1940s,
and 1950s, despite promo-
tional efforts from airlines
such as Frontier, which hired
actor Jimmy Stewart to boost
business. *Left Credit: Colorado
Historical Society, Above
Credit: Tom Noel Collection***

**OPPOSITE PAGE: Friendly stewardesses made air travel more congenial and glamorous, helping Stapleton International
Airport to become the fifth busiest in the U.S. and the seventh busiest in the world by 1980. *Credit: Tom Noel Collection***

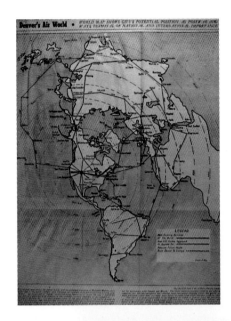

UPPER LEFT:
In 1953, *The Denver Post*
produced this air age
map showing Denver as
the center of attention,
a bit of boosterism
helping to explain why
America's 25th largest
city felt compelled to
build America's largest
(53 square miles),
state-of-the-art
airport in the 1990s.
Map Credit:
The Denver Post

Stapleton International
Airport, upper right,
was replaced by Denver
International Airport, right.
Upper Right Credit:
Tom Noel Collection
Right Credit:
photo by Ron Ruhoff

The Civilian Conservation
Corps hired jobless city
kids during the Great
Depression to work on
outdoor projects. This
CCC team helped build
a scenic foothills drive,
the Rampart Range Road,
from Denver to Colorado
Springs. Hand crafts-
manship, displayed here
in a cattle underpass,
distinguished CCC work.
Credit: photo by
Allen S. Dakan

deck. Catch-penny vending machines sold everything from combs to flight insurance. Pay toilets captured as much as $45,000 a year until 1974, when the Women's Coalition to End Pay Toilets sued the city. Women protested that men had an unfair advantage with free urinals. After pondering how to meter urinals, Mayor William H. "King Solomon" McNichols, Jr. had half the locks removed on the women's stalls.

The bathroom battle ended in somewhat shorter lines in front of women's toilets. Feminist eyebrows were further raised by the "baggage bunnies" — teenage girls attired in culottes and polka-dot ties. These youngsters were told to convince travelers that "Denver really does have something special about it."

Baggage bunnies and free women's toilets may have helped airport usage take off after World War II, finally catching up with the pie-in-the-sky rhetoric of its 1929 dedication. To honor the mayor who had

braved considerable opposition to build it, Denver Municipal was renamed Stapleton Airport on August 25, 1944.

The Great Depression

Denver's new airport and activity elsewhere around the city slowed down in the 1930s as the Great Depression struck Colorado. By 1933, the worst year of the Depression, one out of every four Denver adults was out of work.

Following Franklin D. Roosevelt's election in 1932, the federal government began experimenting with solutions to the nation-wide economic chaos. Some of these federal programs not only provided jobs, but improved the city and its hinterlands.

One of Roosevelt's pet projects, the Civilian Conservation Corps (CCC) hired young men for federal service and housed them in government barracks

at such places as Fort Logan and Morrison. They worked to improve the outdoors, building trails, campgrounds and other amenities in Denver's Mountain Parks, including a unique outdoor amphitheater at Red Rocks.

This theater was the dream of George Cranmer, a wealthy ex-stockbroker, who had liquidated his firm a year before the market crash. He had long been fascinated by the large rocks jutting up at the base of the mountains west of Denver. While traveling in Sicily, he saw the Greek outdoor theater at Taormina and envisioned a Denver counterpart.

Mayor Stapleton in 1935 appointed Cranmer as manager of Improvements and Parks, giving him a chance to realize his Red Rocks dream. Stapleton regarded Denver's Red Rocks Mountain Park as a giant rock garden. Cranmer, conversely, wanted to make a giant outdoor theater by levelling the boulder-strewn area between two massive outcroppings for seating. He convinced CCC officials to proceed quietly with plans to clear the area. Workers took several days to

set all the dynamite charges. Then they blew up all the baby boulders at once — pulverizing Stapleton's rock garden. Denver architect Burnham Hoyt designed the stage and seating in harmony with the natural setting, making the theater an architectural as well as an acoustical triumph.

Another New Deal agency, the Works Progress Administration (WPA), put Denver's unemployed to work repairing schools, fixing gutters, planting trees, killing rats and filling chuckholes. Larger WPA projects included installation of sewers, reinforcing the banks of the South Platte River and Cherry Creek, and constructing West Alameda Avenue Parkway to Red Rocks Park.

The WPA hired women to make clothing, stuff dolls, prepare school lunches and run nurseries. It supported weavers who repaired old Indian and Hispanic textiles at the Denver Art Museum. At the Colorado Historical Society, researchers gathered historical data and compiled an excellent state guidebook: *Colorado: A Guide to the Highest State.*

LEFT: Civilian Conservation Corps labor filled Denver's Red Rocks Amphitheater. Designed by architect Burnham Hoyt, this outdoor arena incorporates natural stone formations and native junipers into what New York's Museum of Modern Art and the American Institute of Architecture called "Colorado's finest 20th Century building."
Credit: *Denver Metro Convention & Visitors Bureau*

New Deal programs hired unemployed historians and artists to make dioramas that are still among the most popular exhibits at the Colorado History Museum.
Credit: *Tom Noel Collection*

Many Denver artists ate because of WPA's art program, which paid them $35 a week to decorate schools and government buildings. Allen Tupper True, an 1899 graduate of Denver's Manual Training High School, locally known for his murals in the Colorado National Bank Building and in the Telephone Building, also did murals for the WPA. A Treasury Department grant supported Gladys Caldwell while she chiseled two of Denver's largest statues, the mountain sheep guarding the 18th Street entrance to the Post Office (now the Byron White Federal Courthouse).

....

RIGHT: Of many Colorado muralists, the most talented and prolific was Allen Tupper True. For the Colorado Telephone Building at 14th and Curtis streets, True adorned the entry court with murals depicting the history of communications.
Credit: photo by Tom Noel

BELOW: For the Colorado National Bank lobby at 17th and Champa streets, True produced a magnificent large mural series entitled "Indian Memories" *Credit: Colorado National Bank*

Showing support for World War II, young ranchers and miners marched with this mule to the Colorado State Capitol.

Credit: Mazzulla Collection, Amon Carter Museum

Despite Denver's isolated inland location, wartime fears included that of an enemy bombing.
Credit: Tom Noel Collection

The WPA spent more than $42 million in Colorado — $5 million more than the state produced in gold during the same period. By 1937 over 1,500 WPA workers were remodeling the Agnes Phipps Tuberculosis Sanatarium at East Sixth Avenue and Quebec Street into an Army Air Corps Technical School that evolved into Lowry Air Force Base. When the WPA ceased operating in 1943, Denver's unemployed no longer worried about jobs. They knew the United States military wanted them. America was at war.

BELOW: Among many Denver firms fighting the Cold War was Eaton Metals, a fabricator of water tanks, gas pumps, underground tanks and tanker trucks. When the Cold War introduced the threat of nuclear bombing to Denver, Eaton made underground missile silos and this Radi-Gard Radiation Fallout Shelter to shield families from nuclear holocaust. *Credit: Eaton Metal Products*

The Rocky Mountain Arsenal sprouted during World War II on what had been an asparagus farm. Used to make toxic weapons and pesticides until the 1980s, it became the most hazardous spot in the metropolis until a 1990s cleanup began to convert it into a wildlife refuge.

Credit: photo by Tom Noel

The Cold War

The Denver Chamber of Commerce, which helped locate sites for Fort Logan in the 1880s, for Lowry Air Force Base in the 1930s, and for the Federal Center in the 1940s, continued to boost the Mile High City as a military town after World War II. Pointing out that the east and west coasts were far more vulnerable to enemy bombs and missiles, Coloradans promoted the Rocky Mountain West as an unassailable bastion for military installations.

The Pentagon concurred. The Air Force Academy arrived in 1958, followed by the North American Air Defense Command. Both complexes are in Colorado Springs, but Denverites regarded the Springs as just another jewel in their Rocky Mountain Empire. The Cold War likewise increased business at Denver's Lowry Air Force Training Base, as well as at Buckley Field and Fitzsimons Army Hospital. Denver lobbied effectively for two other major military installations — the Rocky Mountain Arsenal and Rocky Flats.

Whereas the United States' active involvement in World War I lasted only a few months, World War II involved Americans for four years. Wartime industry and military installations transformed Denver.

The wartime ordinance plant on West Sixth Avenue epitomized the transformation. After the war it became a huge Federal Center for numerous agencies and thousands of employees who make Denver the largest federal office center outside of Washington, D.C. Stable well-paying federal jobs with good benefits brought many newcomers to Denver during and after the war.

Bicyclists crusaded for smooth roads which paved the way for automobilists. *Credit: Denver Public Library*

At Rocky Flats, plutonium triggers were manufactured while the Arsenal produced toxic materials for chemical warfare. Both sites were regarded as heaven-sent boosts for the local economy. With the end of the Cold War in the 1990s, Lowry Air Force Base closed and was converted to civilian housing and educational purposes. Coloradans also began the long, costly cleanup of Rocky Flats and the Rocky Mountain Arsenal.

The Cold War also fueled an explosion in the number of defense contractors. Ball Brothers Research Corporation, Martin Marietta Aerospace Corporation, and other firms set up Denver area plants employing tens of thousands in the Highest State, which portrayed itself as the fortress of America.

Denver's growing role as the largest government employee center outside of Washington sparked a post-World War II boom comparable to the initial 1870–1893 bonanza days. This new boom put Denver on an economic roller coaster ride that reached it zenith in the early 1980s before the inevitable, scary downward plunge.

Automobiles first appeared on Denver streets in 1900 and would transform the city during the 20th century.
Credit: Colorado Springs Pioneer Museum

By the 1950s, cars clogged downtown's 16th Street.
Credit: *The Denver Post*

The Oil Boom

Oil and the automobile age reshaped the Mile High City. Denver's emergence as an oil hub rivaling Houston and Dallas was not accidental. As early as the 1950s, the Denver Chamber of Commerce began sponsoring an "Oil Progress Luncheon." Hundreds of oil and gas men, with their lackeys and lawyers, were treated to a display of Colorado's climatic and recreational advantages. They were assured of Colorado's favorable tax laws for oil companies, including minimal

Denver's oil boom is reflected in the towering spires of the Conoco Refinery on the city's northeastern skyline.
Credit: photo by Michael Gamer

Many Coloradans who fancied "wheel estates" settled into mobile homes such as the Aspen Terrace at 960 South Jason Street.

Credit: photo by Eric Paddock

land use costs and no severance taxes. The chamber also advertised Colorado's advantages in petroleum trade journals such as the publications of Petroleum Information, a large Denver clearinghouse and information center for the oil and gas industry.

Major oil companies as well as wildcatters flowed to Denver to open new headquarters or branch offices. The city's new royalty were oil kings and queens, including Colorado's first two billionaires — oil men Philip Anschutz and Marvin Davis.

During the 1990s a new peripheral beltway, C-470, generated explosive growth in suburban Douglas and Jefferson counties.

Credit: Tom Noel Collection

Among the oil magnates were a few givers as well as a horde of takers. Frederick R. Mayer, for instance, sold his contract oil-drilling firm, Exeter, Inc., in 1980 — just before the oil crash. With proceeds estimated at $75 million, Mayer moved into the airy pinnacle of the Norwest Tower and dedicated his time and money to making Denver a home for the arts. He became the principal supporter of the Denver Art Museum. Of Frederick and Jan Mayer, DAM Director Lewis Sharp said in 1997: "Before you can ask, they come and ask what the museum needs." Often working anonymously, the Mayers donated to an encyclopedia of needy causes. For instance, they helped the Denver Public Schools set up a successful School of the Arts to show deprived youngsters that the arts can pay off and provide fulfilling lifelong vocations or avocations. Honoring the memory of Anne Evans, the Mayers bought and restored her mountain cabin on Upper Bear Creek. Like Anne Evans, this couple shared their love for art with all Coloradans.

While some oil tycoons sank money into community, most were preoccupied with extracting black gold. Colorado crude oil production soared from five million barrels in 1945 to 47 million by 1970. During

The oil boom fueled suburban growth, epitomized by a huge new office park, the Denver Tech Center. The DTC clustered around the I-25 and C-470 interchange emerged as a business district rivaling downtown.
Credit: Tom Noel Collection

the 1970s, oil and energy companies bankrolled a gusher of downtown high rises, topped by the 44-story Anaconda Tower and its swanky Petroleum Club (reorganized as the Top of the Rockies Club in 1996).

In the early 1980s, Denver continued to be the nesting place of the construction crane. Philip Anschutz and others erected the 56-story Republic Plaza (1984), which boasted almost as much prime office space as did all of downtown in 1950. Republic Plaza topped the 54-story City Center Tower (1983) and the 52-story United Bank Tower (1984) with its curved pinnacle (the Mayers' office) that led locals to dub it the cash register building.

The curved top of the cash register building represented the peak of the boom, which soon turned to bust. Indeed, United Banks of Denver, which built the tower, soon disappeared into the economic maelstrom, becoming just another acquisition of Norwest Banks of Minneapolis. Every aspect of life in Denver was affected by the boom and bust cycle — from high-rise banks on 17th Street to the wildlife at the zoo.

The Denver Zoo

Whereas the original mining boom inspired Coloradans to rush to respectability, the second great boom era led them to greatly improve and expand their cultural facilities in a quest to make Denver a World Class City. Typical of Denver's aspirations was a boom and bust campaign to give the city one of America's best zoos.

Denver opened a zoo in 1896 at City Park after William Jennings Bryan — a black bear cub, not the presidential candidate — became a troublesome pet for Denver Mayor Thomas S. McMurray. The mayor gave "Billy" to Alexander J. Graham, the keeper of City Park, whose house at 2080 York Street is now a designated Denver landmark. After Billy gobbled up his chickens, Graham built the first cages of what became the Denver Zoo.

The oil boom of the 1970s and early 1980s gave Denver a new skyline dominated by the 52-story Norwest Bank Tower (center) with its curved top. *The Denver Post* building (right) overlooks the Civic Center Historic District.
Credit: *Denver Metro Convention & Visitors Bureau*

In 1917 Denver Parks City Zoo constructed Bear Mountain to resemble a cliff dwelling like those at Mesa Verde National Park. Originally a home for monkeys, it was changed to a habitat for sea lions — a species less likely to escape. *Credit: Denver Public Library.*

Besides the frisky bears, the 1896 "zoo" consisted of native wild fowl at Duck Lake. Prairie dogs and antelope also occupied the bleak 320-acre tract set aside as City Park at the eastern edge of town. A large collection of Chinese pheasants became the zoo's main attraction until many of them became liberated on the eastern plains, where they have proliferated to the delight of hunters.

Not all zoo animals were appreciated. After the 1905 importation of red squirrels, the furry acrobats reproduced quickly and took over the zoo. These egg-eating rodents next invaded City Park's Duck Lake and

reduced the population of native and imported birds from 83 to 12. The city, egged on by the Audubon Society, planned to shoot the squirrels. Animal lovers and naturalists such as Enos Mills loudly protested these public executions. The city spared the squirrels, banishing the ones that could be caught to the Denver Mountain Parks. Liberated squirrels multiplied all too rapidly throughout the Mile High metropolis.

Denver's zoo consisted of a sad collection of caged and chained creatures until Robert W. Speer became mayor in 1904. His famous 1906 appeal to civic pride and civic benefactors, his "Give While Your Live" speech,

The Denver Zoological Gardens in City Park offers naturalistic settings such as Bear Mountain, where bruins can frolic on trees or shower in a miniature waterfall and pool. Completed in 1918, this artificial mountain replaced small crowded bear cages.
Credit: Denver Metro Convention & Visitors Bureau

envisioned, among many other improvements, a great zoo: "Our animals in City Park need new homes. Prison bars can be done away with…Concrete rocks, waterfalls, trees, etc., with a moat in front would make animals even in captivity feel at home."

Speer had the city's landscape architect, Saco R. DeBoer, draw plans for improving the zoo. The mayor appointed Denver native, Victor H. Borcherdt, zoo director. Borcherdt designed and built Bear Mountain, the high point in the zoo's history — and topography. Completed in 1918, this artificial hill 43 feet high and 185 feet long cost $50,000. It was a natural habitat built of tinted and textured concrete cast from formations on Dinosaur Mountain on the north side of Morrison. Barless bear pits are surrounded by hidden moats, native plants and a natural looking stream.

The protruding south tip of Bear Mountain was constructed to resemble a cliff dwelling like those at Mesa Verde National Park. This, Borcherdt reckoned, would make a perfect home for the zoo's monkeys. The first monkey arriving in 1917 was named Woodrow Wilson, in the presidential tradition of Billy Bryan, the bear who started the zoo. Woodrow soon had plenty of company. But the monkeys kept escaping from their moated cliff dwelling, and it was converted to a sea lion habitat. After being placed on the National Register of Historic Places in 1986, Bear Mountain received a $250,000 restoration that rebuilt, among other things, concrete trees worn to stubs by climbing, scratching and rubbing bruins.

Bear Mountain put Denver in the forefront of American zoos. The St. Louis Zoo crew, one of the world's best, saw Bear Mountain and promptly hired Borcherdt. After his departure and Mayor Speer's death, the Denver Zoo went into a long hibernation. The Albuquerque Zoo used New Deal funding to improve its facilities as did Pueblo's City Park Zoo. Even Cheyenne Mountain Zoo in Colorado Springs drew Denverites. Although many New Deal funds and labor programs were available, Denver made only one notable addition to its zoo between 1918 and the 1950s: Monkey Island was installed in 1937 with the help of the WPA. The island, soon ruled by a spider monkey named Cleopatra, became a hit with those wanting to watch their distant ancestors.

In winter the zoo puts up its "wild lights," featuring electric light animals. *Credit: Denver Metro Convention & Visitors Bureau.*

Rocky Mountain bighorn sheep have their own artificial cliffs to climb at the Denver Zoo. *Credit: Denver Metro Convention & Visitors Bureau.*

Denver's youngest mayor, James R. "Quigg" Newton, far left, took office in 1947 to reform and expand city government. He installed a Career Service Authority to eliminate most patronage appointments, set up a professional Planning Department, hired the city's first traffic engineer, and established a Committee on Human Relations to improve the lives of ethnic minorities. Fifty years later in 1997, Newton, left, remained an active citizen still pursuing more honest and effective municipal government. As mayor, Newton greatly improved and expanded health care, bringing in renowned cellular scientist and public health specialist, Dr. Florence Rena Sabin, below, as manager of Health and Charities. Dr. Sabin's effective programs to improve the lives of all residents led to her selection as Colorado's first representative in Statuary Hall at the National Capitol.

The zoo desperately needed attention. Tight-fisted Mayor Stapleton had put the zoo on a starvation diet. Little had been constructed — or even well maintained when James "Quigg" Newton became mayor in 1947. Among many other reforms, Newton hired Saco R. DeBoer to masterplan a rebirth for the long neglected zoo. To fund restoration and additions, Newton oversaw creation of a private fund-raising and management support arm, the Denver Zoological Foundation.

Mayor Newton, planner DeBoer and Helen Johnson, chair of the Denver Zoological Foundation, began a major overhaul of the zoo. They started with a 1950 rehabilitation of Monkey Island, followed by construction of a Children's Zoo (1951), a Pachyderm Habitat (1959), a Feline House (1964), a Giraffe House (1966), an Animal Hospital (1969), and the Johnson Bird World (1975) on the site of the old Singing Pavilion birdhouse. The new aviary allows visitors to walk through several habitats with free-flying birds in a building covered outside with vines in which native birds nest. The Mountain Sheep Habitat echoes Bear Mountain, but lacks the exquisite detailing. Northern Shores (1987) houses sea lions and other Arctic wildlife, which included Klondike and Snow, polar bear cubs rejected by their mother and raised by the zoo staff.

Pete Smythe, a favorite Denver media man, operated the City park trains in the 1940s. The recorded voice of this familiar long-time radio celebrity now also greets travelers on the Denver International Airport train.

Courtesy: Peter D. Smythe, credit: Tom Noel Collection

Wolf Pack Woods (1988) was followed by Tropical Discovery (1993). The zoo's most ambitious undertaking since Bear Mountain, Tropical Discovery is an $11.5 million exhibit topped by a huge glass pyramid soaring over the ruins of a pre-Columbian temple, invaded by plants and animals. Primate Panorama opened in 1996 on the site of the old Children's Zoo.

Some 1.6 million visitors annually come to see more than 3,100 animals representing 640 species from all over the globe. Clayton Freiheit, director since 1970, has added hundreds of new species, including many rare and endangered ones, and planted more than 500 trees in the 76-acre zoological park. At last Denver has a world class zoo.

Flush Times

The oil boom and federal spending made Denver flush, and air travel put the isolated, provincial Mile

High City within a few hours of New York, Chicago and Los Angeles. By making itself the regional air travel hub, as well as the rail center, Denver attracted the federal government and business, both of which opened numerous new offices in Denver. Some firms, such as Johns Manville, Anaconda, and American Express, even left New York to establish headquarters in Metro Denver. Between the 1950s and the 1980s, downtown Denver erupted with new skyscrapers. Suburban subdivisions, shopping malls, and office parks flooded the High Plains in all directions. Ranch houses replaced ranches and prairie dog villages in suburban Adams, Arapahoe, Boulder, Douglas and Jefferson counties.

More Ups and Downs

The crash came in the mid 1980s as the price of oil slid from $34 a barrel in 1981 to $9 a barrel in 1986. Once again unemployment and office vacancy rates soared. In 1985 and 1986, a downtown Denver overbuilt during the energy boom of the 1970s and early 1980s had the highest office vacancy rate in the nation — 30 percent. Republic Plaza, the tallest of 10 new office towers sprouting skyward between 1978 and 1983, stood strangely quiet, a 56-story ghost.

In March 1987, downtown office space, which once commanded as much as $40 per square foot, was auctioned off for prices closer to $5 per square foot. A 2,348-square-foot office on the 13th floor of the once-proud Denver Club Building leased for 10 cents a square foot.

During the 1990s, Denver continued its economic roller coaster ride. The 1980s nose dive ended in an abrupt upturn. Newcomers attracted by the relatively cheap housing prices, high vacancy rates, and Colorado's climate and recreational advantages turned the economy around. By the mid-1990s Denver had emerged as one of the healthiest and fastest

Within an hour's drive of Denver, campers find solitude in the Indian Peak's Wilderness area. Credit: *photo by Tom Noel*

growing cities in America. On the suburban outskirts, Douglas County became the fastest growing county in the country.

In a November 1996 article for *National Geographic* on "Colorado's Front Range," Michael E. Long found that "a robust economy and swift access to mountains, canyons, trails, trout streams, and ski slopes have lured hordes of new suburbanites to the Front Range, all seeking their slice of the West's open spaces and blue skies." Newcomers and oldtimers alike found that the new boom darkened skies with air pollution and hemmed in Colorado open spaces.

Whereas Denver's ups and downs once rode the gold, silver, and oil markets, the next bust may be a Los Angeles-style exodus from a community where the quality of life is diminished by air pollution, traffic congestion, limited water supplies and too many people. While suburban frontiers were wrestling with tremendous growth, the core city underwent an even more remarkable renaissance that made Denver the envy of many other urban centers.

ABOVE: River rafting became Colorado's fastest-growing sport during the 1990s.
Credit: *photo by Byron Hetzler*

The frozen majesty of Rocky Mountain National Park lures snowshoers to Bear Lake.
Credit: *photo by Tom Noel*

URBAN RENAISSANCE

A CARDBOARD SIGN ON THE OAK DOOR OF ONE Larimer Street saloon read, "Open During Destruction." As neighboring buildings fell, men shook on their barstools. A few went out to watch the devastation. It was 1969 and the Denver Urban Renewal Authority was demolishing a busted downtown, hoping to generate a new boom.

From bar doors, flophouse windows, and old sandstone sidewalks, Denver's down and out watched bleary-eyed. At first, the lead wrecking ball bounced off defiant buildings. Then sprinkles of dust came down, followed by showers of stone trim. Finally bricks and chunks of granite tumbled from wooden skeletons.

Whole walls fell and daylight invaded naked rooms where yesterday's movers and shakers had puffed their cigars, sipped brandy, and risked fortunes to make Denver the Queen City of the mountains and plains.

Denver grew up fast and recklessly. With each new boom, the town tore down buildings to replace with bigger ones. Jerome Smiley noted this propensity for trashing the past in his 1901 *History of Denver*:

During the 1960s and 1970s, much of downtown was demolished for "progress" and parking lots. For the Cooper Building at 17th and Curtis, DURA prescribed dynamite.
***Credit:** photo by Roger Whitacre*

LEFT: Old Denver City had deteriorated into skid row by the 1930s and was largely demolished 40 years later by the Denver Urban Renewal Authority. Larimer Street, shown here in 1958, then housed a dozen flophouses and 37 bars. Credit: *The Denver Post*

Neoclassical structures celebrated the imperial glory that was Greece and the grandeur that was Rome. Architecturally ambitious Denver, which dominated its own Rocky Mountain Empire, also fancied the Neoclassical style in the early 1900s. This temple-like office building on Welton Street, like many other aging downtown edifices, was leveled by the wrecking ball.
Credit: photos by Roger Whitacre

"Although Denver is but little more than forty years old, nearly all the buildings that constituted the pioneer town have disappeared." In the central business district Smiley calculated that, "many of the present buildings are the third structures erected on their sites; and in some instances present buildings are of the fourth series."

During the post-World War II boom, Denver experienced a demolition derby like the 19th-century building boom. In addition to private developers razing sites, a public agency, the Denver Urban Renewal Authority (DURA), systematically leveled much of the urban core. Block after block of downtown disappeared under a rising sea of black asphalt parking lots.

At first, city leaders accepted urban renewal's standard nation-wide prescription for deteriorating core cities. Only after the demolition of much of old

138

After most of old downtown was demolished,
a new urban core of steel, concrete and glass arose
during the 1970s and 1980s. *Credit: Glenn Cuerden*

Proposed demolition of the Daniels & Fisher Tower, Denver's best known landmark, alarmed citizens who encouraged the city to create the Denver Landmark Preservation Commission in 1967. *Credit: The Denver Post, cartoon by Pat Oliphant*

After narrowly escaping the wrecking ball, the restored D&F Tower became the centerpiece of Skyline Park with its sunken gardens and waterfalls. *Credit: Denver Metro Convention & Visitors Bureau*

Denver, Auraria, and the South Platte Valley bottoms, did city officials begin to wonder. Was it wise to erase urban neighborhoods and replace them with housing subdivisions and shopping mall replicas of suburbia?

Agony about the losses gave birth to Denver's historic preservation movement. Although Charleston, Savannah, San Antonio, Santa Fe, New Orleans and a few other cities had pushed preservation for decades, Denverites did not grow alarmed until much of downtown had been erased by DURA.

Auraria: Where Denver Began

Between 1969 and 1974, DURA leveled much of the city's oldest neighborhood, Auraria. Bounded by the South Platte River, Cherry Creek and West Colfax Avenue, this pioneer residential area had evolved into a mix of factories, shops, bars, and a heavily Hispanic residential community. DURA demolished much of this "blighted" area for construction of the Auraria Higher Education Center (AHEC).

This new campus opened in 1977 as an experiment in shared facilities for the Community College of Denver, Metropolitan State College of Denver, and the University of Colorado at Denver. The governor and the legislature liked the AHEC idea of a compact, no-frills campus that would give lower income and working people, especially minorities, greater access to higher education.

Auraria, spawned by the 1858 gold strike and named from the Latin word for gold, was Denver's oldest neighborhood. During the 1970s the Denver Urban Renewal Authority demolished 38 blocks for the Auraria Higher Education Center that opened in 1976. On this campus shared by the University of Colorado at Denver, Metropolitan State College of Denver, and the Community College of Denver, Franciscan monks once taught Aurarians at the now-demolished St. Elizabeth's School. *Credit: Tom Noel Collection*

Night, day and weekend courses; inexpensive tuition; and the convenient downtown location soon gave Auraria the largest campus enrollment in the state — more than 32,000 students. The centerpiece of the campus was a block of 19th-century houses restored by Historic Denver, Inc. Rechristened Ninth Street Historic Park, this block of homes borders a grassed-in street that retains its old granite curbs and red sandstone sidewalks. Spires and towers of other recycled landmarks — the Tivoli Brewery, St. Elizabeth's Church,

St. Cajetan's Church and the Emmanuel Sherith-Israel Chapel also distinguish the campus.

Central Business District

Across Cherry Creek from Auraria, DURA's Skyline Urban Renewal project condemned as "Skid Row" 30 blocks of the old Central Business District bounded by Speer Boulevard, Curtis Street, 20th Street and the alley between Larimer and Market streets. Only a few landmarks and the 1400 block of Larimer Street escaped the bulldozer. From 1969 to the mid 1970s, wrecking crews worked days, nights and weekends.

After downtown was flattened, the Skyline site remained forlorn flats of seedy, weedy parking lots for a decade. Slowly, new towers rose from the asphalt sea. The last Skyline development — the Tabor Center — did not open on the site of the demolished Tabor Block until 1984. In defense of DURA, Director J. Robert Cameron pointed out that the completed project gave Denver an impressive new skyline and that developers had to reserve 40 percent of their sites for open space. The new downtown, he asserted, was more spacious and gracious.

The most popular campus in the state is enhanced by landmarks such as the Emmanuel Sherith Israel Chapel, below, and Ninth Street Historic Park, right.

Credit: photo by Tom Noel

Credit: photo by Michael Gamer

Dana Crawford, right, organized Larimer Square Associates, which included Denver's former U.S. Representative Patricia Schroeder. The associates transformed the 1400 block of Larimer Street into shops, restaurants, offices, and a setting for public celebrations such as Oktoberfest, which delighted spectators. *Above Credit: The Denver Post, photo by Duane Howell*
Left Credit: Denver Metro Convention & Visitors Bureau

The Denver Landmark Preservation Commission

Some found downtown's disappearance distressing. Oldtimers grew confused and alienated with the loss of familiar landmarks and destinations. For long-time residents, it sometimes seemed that a trip downtown was like a trip to a foreign city.

One Denver native, Helen Millett Arndt, decided to act. Educated at Denver's Kent School for Girls and Columbia University, she became, in 1959, the first woman appointed to the Denver Planning Board since Anne Evans sat on Mayor Speer's Art Commission, the board's ancestor.

Arndt feared that "Denver had grown so fast after 1946 that it had lost its sense of quality, its identity." She and other concerned citizens began pushing for the creation of a local landmark commission like those in New York, Boston and other cities.

"Mayor Tom Currigan was leery," Arndt recalled, "but a remarkable lot of Denver citizens of all ages, from 90 to about 10, stood up and said they didn't like to see their city torn apart." In 1967, the city created

Women spearheaded the historic preservation movement. Dana Crawford shown here at the 1965 birth of her Larimer Square restoration, recalls: "I first went down to Larimer Street looking for antiques at Goodwill, Salvation Army, the second-hand stores, and pawn shops. I couldn't help but notice that some of the buildings there were fine antiques." Dana helped found Historic Denver as well as Larimer Square. Hal Haney, HD's first chairman, recalls the organizational meeting: "I suggested that the group call itself the Molly Brown House Foundation, but Dana suggested that we not limit ourselves to one house and proposed the name Historic Denver." Credit: *The Denver Post,* photo by Duane Howell

Poet Thomas Hornsby Ferril, a human landmark as well as a landmark commissioner, introduced the white-haired poet Carl Sandburg to some Denver goats and to his wife Helen (pictured with black hat). Sandburg repaid Ferril with these words: "He's terrifically and beautifully American. He is a poet, wit, historian, man of books and human affairs." *Credit: Denver Public Library*

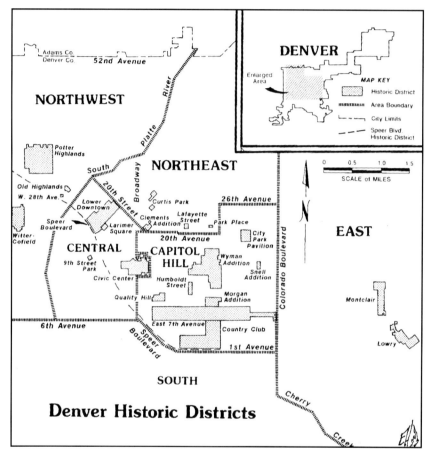

Denver Historic Districts

The Mayan Theater at 110 Broadway, one of six U.S. theaters designed inside and out with motifs of the famous Meso-American tribe, narrowly escaped demolition with a 1984 landmark designation. Credit: *watercolor by Barbara Froula*

the Denver Landmark Preservation Commission with ordinance power to hold public hearings on proposed landmarks and recommend those eligible for their historic, architectural or geographic merits to the City Council. Landmark designation meant that after the council's approval, any application for a building permit to alter or demolish would be sent to the DLPC for review. By ordinance, the DLPC can delay incompatible alterations or demolition of an individual landmark, gaining time to seek a happier solution. In the case of buildings within a historic district, the commission can deny inappropriate exterior alterations or demolition.

Denver Historic Districts. Credit: *map drawn by Eric Hammersmark*

During its first 30 years, the commission gained designation for some 300 individual landmarks and 30 historic districts. Such protection of Denver's special places pleased residents proud of their neighborhoods but fearing high rises, billboards and commercial intrusions. Landmark status also protects solar access, mountain views and open space. The success of Denver's landmark program has proven the wisdom of Helen Arndt's observation that "where an older generation will see nothing but obsolete and worn-out buildings, a younger generation may see an opportunity for a new kind of space."

Arndt found formidable allies in such disparate personalities as historian Louisa Ward Arps, former city councilman Philip Milstein, and Colorado's poet laureate, Thomas Hornsby Ferril. After joining the landmark commission, Ferril proposed "funeral rites whenever one of Denver's historic buildings is about to be destroyed." Ferril denounced DURA's "bureaucratic demolitionists" who "shattered landmark after landmark into shards of oblivion."

Individual landmarks vary from the traditional Governor's Mansion to the radically-modern Boettcher Conservatory at the Denver Botanic Gardens. Designation revived the otherwise doomed Elitch, Mayan, and Paramount Theaters and Denver's two grand old hotels — the Brown Palace and the Oxford. It has kept many historic church spires pointing heavenward even in downtown's skyscraper canyons.

Historic districts range from the commercial block of Larimer Square to much of Denver's parkway network, from linear City Ditch to Potter Highlands, a Northwest Denver neighborhood of 667 buildings. This tree-shaded haven of red flagstone walks has large Queen Anne and Italianate homes bristling with trim as well as more sedate classic cottages, masonry terraces and foursquares. The largest historic district, East Seventh Avenue Parkway, stretches from Logan Street to Colorado Boulevard, roughly between East Sixth and Eighth avenues. Little-known residential neighborhoods protected by historic districts include Witter Cofield in Northwest Denver, Montclair

in East Denver, and Lafayette Street and East Park Place in north central Denver. Historic district designation became a successful way to fight blight in once-deteriorating neighborhoods such as Auraria, Lower Downtown, Five Points, Capitol Hill and Highlands.

Historic Denver, Inc.

Whenever citizens rallied to save historic buildings and neighborhoods, they could count on staunch support and technical assistance from Historic Denver, Inc (HDI). Like the landmark commission, this private preservation group was formed to protect Denver's disappearing architectural heritage. HDI incorporated on December 11, 1970, to rescue the Molly Brown House from demolition. By 1971, HDI had 1,500 members and 200 volunteers who converted Molly's place at 1340 Pennsylvania Street to a popular house museum.

Dr. Justina Warren Ford delivered about 7,000 babies during more than 50 years of practice in Denver. As one of the few licensed obstetricians who would make house calls, she was popular with Denver's blacks, Hispanics, and Asians, many of whom either distrusted or could not afford hospital delivery rooms. Credit: Denver Public Library

The founding mothers and fathers of Historic Denver, Inc., included Helen Arndt, Jean Catherwood, Larimer Square developer Dana Crawford, Denver Post columnist Joanne L. Ditmer, attorney Don Etter, architect Alan Fisher, Don Holland, The Denver Post editor Bill Hornby, Christine Kosewick, Colorado first lady Anne Love, Bob Sheets and architect Edward D. White, Jr. They all served on the first Historic Denver board chaired by Harold L. "Hal" Haney, with E. James "Jim" Judd as president, Barbara Norgren as secretary, and Kenneth D. Watson as executive director. To fund activities, HDI in 1971 began staging ice cream socials at the Molly Brown House, its annual "Night In Old Denver" street fair, and in 1974 began annual house tours and summertime cemetery tours with dining afterwards amid the tombstones.

Fostering awareness of the Mile High City's rich past, HDI in 1973 kicked off a publications program with Richard R. Brettell's *Historic Denver: The Architects and the Architecture, 1858-1893*. Both the hardback first edition and paperback reprint (1979) quickly sold out, as readers devoured the first serious look at the city's architectural history. Inspired in part by Brettell's work, HDI joined with the Junior League and the Denver Planning Office to conduct the city's first architectural survey. Volunteers scoured all 73 Denver neighborhoods block by block, discovering many treasures among some 25,000 pre-1910 structures recorded in the *Historic Building Inventory: City & County of Denver* (1974, revised, 1981).

Christine Whitacre, a pioneer editor of HDI's monthly newspaper, *Historic Denver News*, also became the compiler of HDI's *Restoration Resource Guide* (1981) and author of *Molly Brown: Denver's Unsinkable Lady* (1984). Barbara Norgren and Tom Noel collaborated on *Denver: The City Beautiful and Its Architects, 1893-1941* (1987). This lavishly illustrated, 287 page work, including biographical sketches of 67 major Denver architects, sold out and was reprinted in softcover (1993).

HDI celebrated Colorado's centennial and the U.S. bicentennial in 1976 by turning over Ninth Historic Street Park, resplendent after a $1 million restoration, to the Auraria Higher Education Center. Some of the same higher education bureaucrats who opposed saving "dinky little old houses" promptly began squabbling for space in the restored Victorians. These charming houses were reincarnated for about $20 a square foot, while the bland new campus buildings cost around $30 per square foot.

After finishing Ninth Street, HDI created the Historic Paramount Foundation in 1981 and began a $1.5 million campaign to buy and restore the endangered Paramount Theater, sole survivor of downtown's movie palaces. When the house of Dr. Justina Ford, a pioneer black physician, faced demolition in 1983, HDI moved it to 3901 California Street for restoration as the Black American West Museum.

Museum founder Paul Stewart started out as a barber who collected tales from his customers. "When I was cutting hair and hearing a good story I would reach back and turn on a tape recorder," Stewart recalls. "Folks dropped in with stories, artifacts, photos. I put up displays in the barber shop as conversation pieces. I got so much stuff that I ran out of room."

By the 1970s, Stewart gave up barbering to devote more time to his museum. His interviews, artifacts, books, sheet music, and memorabilia soon outgrew the barber shop storefront and two other locations before Historic Denver helped him relocate in the Justina Ford House. There Colorado's black heritage is preserved and showcased in a house that itself is a reminder of the physician who delivered and cared for thousands of babies in the core city. Dr. Ford lived in the house until her death in 1952. Late in life, after being admitted to the Denver General Hospital staff and receiving

Thanks to Paul Stewart's Black American West Museum and his many public appearances, the role of Colorado's pioneer African-American cowboys, miners, railroaders, and business and professional people has been documented and publicized. Credit: photo by Tom Noel

The Denver Theater,
like all movie palaces
on Sixteenth Street
save the Paramount, was
demolished. The wrecking
crew got this final 1986
view of the grandiose
interior, which allowed
Coloradans to escape
everyday life for fantasy
motion picture worlds.
Credit: *photo by
Glenn Cuerden*

Across Sixteenth Street from the demolished Denver Theater, the Paramount survives and sometimes brings
back thrillers such as these 1956 flicks. *Credit: Denver Public Library*

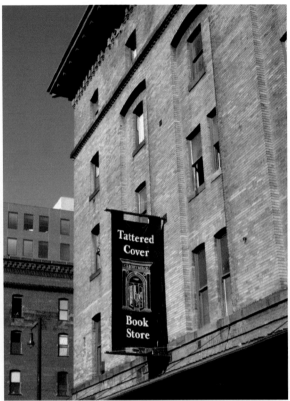

Denver's LoDo Historic District recycled stout masonry buildings for new uses, including the Tattered Cover, which the *New York Times* pronounced "the best general book store in the United States." *Credit: photos by Tom Noel*

night council meetings, alumni and council persons shared memories, songs and affection for schools worthy of protection.

HDI moved into Union Station in 1983 during a campaign to designate Lower Downtown as a historic district before demolitions reduced it to surface parking for the Central Business District. HDI also started a revolving preservation loan fund for what *The Denver Post* columnist Dick Kreck nicknamed LoDo. Designation came in 1988 for the area between Larimer and Wynkoop streets from Cherry Creek to 20th Street.

Historic district designation triggered LoDo's rebirth as a popular area for bars, art galleries and night clubs. LoDo's renaissance attracted Coors Field, million dollar lofts, a half dozen brew pubs, and youthful night owls from throughout the metropolis. By the 1990s, the poorest and most disreputable part of 1970s Denver had become one of the hottest real estate and entertainment districts in the Rockies.

Historic Denverites staged a wake in 1989 for a lost landmark, the Central Bank. That Neoclassical gem, the only known commercial work of renowned Denver Beaux Arts architect Jacques Benedict, was replaced by a parking lot despite widespread protest and the efforts of Mayor Federico Peña. The mayor was a staunch preservationist whose intervention had saved the Mayan Theater at 110 Broadway, one of two remaining Pre-Columbian Deco movie houses in the United States.

Thomas Hornsby Ferril, Colorado poet laureate, HDI member, and landmark commissioner, died in 1989 in the Five Points house where he had lived since 1900. His daughter, Anne Ferril Folsom, donated the landmarked dwelling at 2123 Downing Street to Historic Denver, Inc. HDI restored the house and transferred it in 1996 to the Colorado Center for the Book. With seminars, poetry readings, and tours, the center perpetuates the work of the poet-preservationist and lends space and ears to up-and-coming poets.

The Masons abandoned their Scottish Rite Consistory and El Jebel Shrine Temple at 18th and Sherman streets in 1994, leaving the exotic Moorish temple prey to nearby office tower occupants hungry for parking

a Human Relations Award in 1951, she said: "I fought like a tiger against the barriers of race and sex."

The oldest structure in Denver, the Four Mile House (1859) at 715 S. Forest Street, became the next project of HDI, which helped restore and interpret the Cherry Creek Roadhouse as a living history farm, before turning it over to the City of Denver Parks and Recreation Department.

In 1987 HDI started "Preservation in the Schools". Youngsters practiced preservation by helping to prepare landmark nominations for schools of outstanding historic and architectural merit. The younger generation proved adept at persuading landmark commissioners and city council persons to award their schools the brass landmark plaques. At memorable Monday

Credit: *photo by Tom Noel*

Coloradans have fallen in love with Coors Field, the new, old-timey-looking ball park built in 1995 for the Colorado Rockies. During their first season in the ball park, the Rockies astonished everyone by making the National League Playoffs. Despite poor pitching, the team's home run hitters earned the Rockies acclaim as "the Blake Street Bombers" in a dozen sports bars that sprang up on Blake Street.

....

facilities. HDI orchestrated landmark designation and helped find a new owner in The Eulipions, a theater group who had outgrown their Five Points hall.

FAR LEFT AND LEFT:
Credit: *Denver Metro Convention & Visitors Bureau*

Bill West has restored a half dozen Curtis Park dwellings, including his own Italianate-style cottage.

Credit: photo by Tom Noel

In 1996, downtown Cleveland, Ohio, celebrated the opening of its Rock and Roll Museum, a typically daring design from one of the world's best known living architects, Ieoh M. Pei. That same summer Denver allowed the Adams Mark Hotel to demolish Pei's famed hyperbolic paraboloid on the Sixteenth Street Mall, despite protest led by HDI and the American Institute of Architects.

To promote greater public awareness and appreciation of Denver's architectural heritage, HDI has launched a series of neighborhood guidebooks. University of Colorado at Denver architectural history professor Diane Wilk, who first proposed this illustrated pocket guide book series, wrote A *Guide to Denver's Architectural Styles and Terms* (1996) and *The Wyman Historic District* (1996). Jack A. Murphy, curator of geology at the Denver Museum of Natural History, authored *Geology Tour of Denver's Buildings and Monuments* (1996) and *Geological Tour of Capitol Hill* (1997). Nancy Widmann prepared *The East Seventh Avenue*

Historic District (1997). Leigh Fletcher Grinstead, director of the Molly Brown House, wrote *Molly Brown's Capitol Hill Walking Tour* (1996). LoDo loft dweller Barbara Gibson, who spearheaded installation of historic markers in LoDo, produced *The Lower Downtown Historic District* (1996) guide.

Kathleen Brooker, HDI president since 1992, reports that: "HDI is looking forward to the millennium, confident that we have saved much of the best. We are a private organization dependent on our members' generosity, public contributions, grants, and income from the Molly Brown House Museum, tours, book sales, and special events. Historic Denver, Inc. is a citizen organization. Our purpose is to preserve Denver's significant historic fabric, its distinctive architecture, and its cultural landscapes as tangible refections of our heritage and the foundation of our quality of life. We and our 1,500 members hope to revitalize the past to give Denver a brighter future."

The Rebirth of Curtis Park

HDI turned to one of the city's oldest and most endangered neighborhoods, Curtis Park. HDI established a revolving loan fund for restoring homes, conducted house tours, and gave volunteer time and money to aid residents restoring antique houses. HDI relocated three doomed cottages to vacant lots in the 2800 block of Glenarm Place, and reinstalled flagstone sidewalks and street trees.

Sandra Dallas Atchison, an HDI officer and activist, first called attention to Curtis Park in one of her books, *Cherry Creek Gothic* (1970): "Few people are aware that within walking distance of downtown Denver lies a Victorian neighborhood almost completely intact…in a semi-slum trance waiting to be torn down or perhaps discovered by someone with the imagination to clean it up and turn it into one of the finest Victorian restorations in the country."

After reading this, some people took a closer look at the so-called "ghetto" and "slum" between Larimer and Welton, 23rd and Downing streets. Among them was Prof. William A. "Bill" West, the bachelor who fathered the Curtis Park renaissance and taught Victorian literature at CU-Denver. His interest in all things Victorian led him to Curtis Park and to write a book, Curtis Park (1980), with photography by Don Etter. He championed the Curtis Park Historic District for successful National Register and Denver landmark designations.

West bought his first Curtis Park house in 1976 for $15,000 and later purchased and restored the Italianate cottage at 2826 Curtis Street and the Queen Anne at 2418 Stout. These ornate red brick houses with red sandstone trim are picturesque reminders of the time when Curtis Park attracted such notable residents as Mayor Wolfe Londoner and department store czar John Jay Joslin.

Curtis Park is the pioneer suburb in a city that has become a huge conglutination of suburbs. Suburbanization did not begin in the 20th century with the automobile, but with the city's first light rail line in 1871. That horse-drawn contraption ran up Larimer Street, then along 16th Street, and out Stout Street to the elegant streetcar suburb named for its developer, Samuel Curtis. Curtis donated land at 30th and Curtis in 1868 for Denver's first city park.

By the 1880s, Denver's growing suburban tide swept beyond Curtis Park to more fashionable Capitol Hill and, still later, to the Denver Country Club. Westerners wanting more elbow room kept moving farther away from the core city and county. By the 1990s homebuilders were pushing beyond Arapahoe, Adams, Boulder, and Jefferson counties into an outer ring of suburban counties — Park, Clear Creek, Larimer, Weld, Douglas and Elbert, some of the fastest growing counties in the country.

Curtis Park is a key not only to Denver's growth pattern, but to its ethnic history. At first the neighborhood filled with Germans, the city's single largest foreign-born group before World War I. Not until the early 20th century did Curtis Park and adjacent Five Points become a haven for Blacks, Hispanics and Asians.

Denver's grand residential suburb of the 1870s became one of its poorest urban neighborhoods. Most of the newcomers could not afford to tear down the old and build anew. They retained the Italianate and Queen Anne houses built in the 1870s and 1880s. During the 1960s, as Blacks began moving into Park Hill many Hispanics moved into Curtis Park. During the 1970s, whites interested in inexpensive, architecturally exquisite antique homes re-discovered Curtis Park. Today it is about one-half Hispanic, one-fourth black, and one-fourth white.

"This neighborhood is rich in the diversity of its residents and its architecture," Bill West said while tweaking his exuberant Victorian moustache. "As a place where renters have a chance at becoming first-time home owners, Curtis Park, as in the 1870s, is once again Denver's urban frontier."

Credit: **Denver Public Library**

Denver's African American community has a proud history originating with pioneer miners, cowboys and railroaders. Blacks have been blessed with able leaders, ranging from Barney Ford in the pioneer era to Wellington Webb, who became Denver's first black mayor in 1992. Blacks have remained a small minority, comprising about five percent of the 1990 metro population.

Since the early 1900s, the black community has centered on Five Points, so-named for the intersection of 26th Avenue, 27th Street and Welton Street. During the 1930s Depression a leader emerged to help Five Points, whose residents were often the last people to be hired and the first to be fired. Benjamin Franklin Hooper, "The Unofficial Mayor of Five Points," helped the black community through many of its 20th century's ups and downs.

The Young Women's Christian Association promoted not only physical and spiritual fitness but equality and opportunity for all women. Credit: *Colorado Historical Society*

....

For decades, Hooper's club at 2625-33 Welton was a hot spot for jazz, barbecue, craps and dancing. The two-story, red brick complex labeled Deluxe Recreation Parlor and Ex-Servicemen's Club was no longer deluxe by the 1970s. The old oak backbar held trophies and plaques honoring Benjamin Franklin Hooper as the "Unofficial Mayor of Five Points."

Two homemade cardboard signs on the backbar read "No Profanity" and "No Profanity Please." Although the afternoon crowd was spirited, it was not profane. Of course, Hooper's place was primarily noc-

turnal. Benny, a short, slight, plainly-dressed man moved fast as a cat, attending to customers.

Hooper was born at 2226 Welton Street on May 2, 1893, one of seven children of a janitor. He quit Ebert School after the sixth grade, bellhopped at the old St. James Hotel downtown, and served in World War I. Army pay seemed like a fortune to Benny, who saved it for the day he returned to Denver.

"Those days," Benny said in 1973, "colored people couldn't stay in the downtown hotels, so I used my army money to open the Ex-Serviceman's Club for colored soldiers. I started out in a little place down on 23rd and Arapahoe. But Mayor Stapleton came by, put his arm around my shoulder, and asked me 'Benny, why don't you get a new location?'"

In a predominately white town, finding a new location for a black club was not easy. Some residents felt threatened by a growing black population, and took the usual step of using real estate covenants to restrict "colored" people to certain neighborhoods. Mayor Stapleton steered Hooper to 2625 Welton in the heart of Five Points. The mayor protected Benny in his new location and Benny became a devout Democrat: "I even started working on other negroes who said they would never leave the party of Abraham Lincoln. But then Mayor Stapleton and President and Mrs. Roosevelt started helping our people."

Hooper, the first black drafted in Denver for World War I, wanted colored soldiers to be part of Denver's Veterans Day Parade. As blacks were not allowed to march with weapons, Benny had wooden guns carved and painted to look like real ones. "So they let us march. We had all our shoes spit-polished, every man looked great. We got downtown and they told us we had to go last, even though we were the best dressed unit!"

During the relatively flush 1920s, Benny added a bar, billiard room and a basement jazz joint to his Ex-Servicemen's Club. Veteran *Rocky Mountain News* reporter Alberta Pike found it "a swell place" where "business is good. The noisy black-and-tan crowd is the sporting, fun-loving, easy-going element...Benny at the front counter gives you a shrewd once-over from

The Denver Urban Renewal Authority has reformed. Since the 1980s, DURA has been restoring rather than razing structures, including the Denver Dry Goods Store at 16th and California streets. After removing paint, DURA repaired the brick walls and stone and metal cornice for a department store reborn as luxury lofts above the two stories of retail and third story offices. Credit: DURA

enormous soft brown eyes...At Benny's you are likely to find almost the entire personnel of the White Elephant ball club, the team of colored boys that pretty regularly cleans up the other clubs in the City League."

During the 1930s, Benny opened the Casino Dance Hall next door to the Ex-Serviceman's Club. The Casino evolved into a two-story hall with balcony seating for 1,000, a 40-foot-long bar, and a huge hardwood dance floor. This largest and most luxurious of all the Five Points jazz clubs, was dressed up for Christmas, Easter and other holidays. Benny donated the hall to churches, charities, and civic groups, including the NAACP, Zion Baptist Church, the YMCA and the YWCA.

During the good years, the Casino swung to the music of Brook Benton, James Brown, Ray Charles, Fats Domino, George Morrison, Muddy Waters and other musical legends. During the grim years, Hooper cooked up a scheme to get people through starving times. "I ran bread lines through the pool hall. And The Denver Post dropped off those jack rabbits that gun clubs and sportsman would shoot in the Post's annual rabbit hunts. We gave those critters away so the poor could make rabbit stew."

When Benny was born in 1893, the town had a black community of less than 4,000. By the time he died in 1984, the population was more than 40,000. Seeing Denver's black citizenry grow, prosper and become better integrated was bittersweet for him. Making it in Denver often meant leaving Five Points. "Now people have moved all the way out to the airport," Benny said shaking his head in the 1970s. "But once colored town was just Five Points."

The neighboring Curtis Park restoration and construction of the Welton Street light rail line has led some to begin fixing up "the Points." In 1997 Hooper's old casino, closed since his death, reopened after a $500,000 facelift, once again looking sleek and inviting.

The Sixteenth Street
Pedestrian Mall opened
in 1982 with a free mall
shuttle bus, re-energized
the Central Business
District. *Credit: Denver
Metro Convention
& Visitors Center*

Riding Back to the Future

Two transportation developments have helped revive Five Points, Auraria and the core city by strengthening their connections to the rest of the Mile High metropolis. Both were initiated by the Regional Transportation District (RTD), which in 1974 replaced the old Denver Tramway Company as metro Denver's public transit agency.

RTD's Sixteenth Street Mall shuttle, which began operating on October 7, 1982, made downtown more accessible. This mile-long bus and pedestrian corridor links LoDo with Civic Center via the retail and residential loft-lined 16th Street strip. The Sixteenth Street Mall is also a central stop on RTD's light rail service. Inaugurated in 1994, the light rail line runs from a large park and ride station at I-25 and Broadway to the Auraria Campus to another Park and Ride Station in Five Points. A second line is expected to open to Littleton and suburban Arapahoe County by the year 2,000. Other branches are planned for Denver International Airport and the Denver Tech Center. Light rail should help clear up both traffic and air pollution. Denver does not have to go the way of Los Angeles, tied up in a Gordian knot of freeways that are no longer free.

Denverites may well ride out of the 20th century in rail cars like those that carried their great-grandparents into it. And those riding the rails into Denver's core city will find that the urban renaissance has preserved for the 21st century some of Denver's rich 19th-century heritage.

Denver's new light rail system runs roughly the same route of the first streetcar line of 1871 — from Auraria, shown here, to Five Points.
Credit: photo by Tom Noel

IMAGINE A GREAT CITY

O N SEPTEMBER 14, 1958, A MEXICAN FAMILY reached Denver with their life savings of $500. Gonzalo G. Silva brought his wife and nine children with him from Chihuahua. Like thousands since 1858, they came to Denver looking for a new and better life.

Gonzalo liked the vacant one-story hall at 2010 Larimer which had once been the jewelry store of a Japanese immigrant, H. T. Osumi. "We thought $500 would be plenty to open a restaurant," Gonzalo's son Manuel Silva recalled years later. "But Public Service wanted a $350 deposit and the phone company wanted $35. And in this part of town it is hard to get credit. So we just sat here with no heat, light, or phone.

"Finally Mariano Galindo of La Popular Bakery next door came over and asked us what was happening. Then he borrowed $300 from the St. Cajetan Credit Union and gave it to us. Tomas Molino of Molino Foods also loaned us money. So we opened a restaurant here and within a year we paid Mariano and Tomas back."

The Silvas served only Mexican food and made nearly everything from scratch. Gonzalo Silva prospered and returned to Mexico. His son Manuel took over the restaurant in 1974. Manuel Silva can still be found cooking in back or cashiering in front of the dining room on Larimer Street. La Casa De Manuel is the third oldest of more than 115 Mexican restaurants listed in the current metro phone book. For 40 years this tiny cantina has survived despite Manuel's 90-day demolition lease. "That means," Manuel explained, "that the owner can tear it down after he give me a 90-day notice to vacate."

To dress up his little cantina, Manuel hired Jose Castillo, a waiter at the Brown Palace Hotel, to paint murals. Most of these depict life in old Mexico. One wall panel, however, shows Spanish explorers overlooking the virgin site of Denver, a sagebrush flat at the confluence of the South Platte and Cherry Creek.

This mural in a humble cafe reflects what many books do not — that Hispanics were in Colorado before 1858. Along with Mexican Diggings on the future site of

CHAPTER 9

Since 1958, Manuel Silva has produced tasty, inexpensive meals at La Casa de Manuel, 2010 Larimer Street, the granddaddy of some 115 Mexican restaurants that now spice metropolitan Denver. *Credit: photo by Roger Whitacre*

OPPOSITE PAGE: Hispanic construction workers such as this spirited crew have done the hard work of city building, including the glistening metallic high rise that went into this hole (above left) at 17th and Larimer streets. *Credit: photo by Roger Whitacre*

Denver, much of Colorado's Hispanic history has been lost. Robbed of their history, they have been treated as newcomers and second-class citizens. It mattered little to the Yankee newcomers that Colorado once belonged to Spain, that part of it later belonged to Mexico and that Spanish-speaking settlements in Colorado predated the founding of Denver.

They scoffed at "Mexican mud" buildings of adobe that 20th century Coloradans have come to regard as a practical and aesthetic building material. They derided as "lazy Mexicans" the people who have done — and still do — most of the hardest work in Colorado, toiling on farms and in factories, on ranches and railroads, and in mines, restaurant kitchens and on construction crews.

When the Silvas moved to Denver in the 1950s, officials guessed that the city contained around 30,000 Spanish-Americans. The 1960 federal census, the first to count Hispanics separately, recorded 43,147 Spanish-Americans in Denver. By 1990 the number had risen to 107,382 — 23 percent of the core city population. Within the six-county metro area, Hispanics comprise roughly 13 percent of the residents.

A 1950 study by the Denver Area Welfare Council, "The Spanish-American Population of Denver," reported that the average Spanish-American family made only $1,840 a year. Black families earned $1,930 and whites averaged over $3,000. The council estimated that 60 percent of Hispanics lived in substandard housing, that 90 percent of them dropped out of school, that 50 percent sought help from social welfare agencies, and that they constituted over a third of the city's jail inmates. Their infant mortality rate was six times greater than that for whites.

The Spanish-surnamed have become the largest — and fastest growing — major ethnic group in Colorado. Their income and home ownership has risen dramatically since the 1950s. Once the credit unions of Catholic churches such as St. Cajetan's and Our Lady of Guadalupe were the financial anchors of the community, as they were for the Silvas. Small businesses such as La Casa de Manuel that originally catered to Mexicans

have become popular with many others. The surging number and growing status of Hispanos helped in 1983 to elect the city's first Hispanic mayor.

Mayor Federico Peña

Federico Peña, born in Laredo, Texas, in 1947, arrived in Denver in 1973 as a young attorney wearing his long hair in a ponytail. He worked for the Mexican American Legal Defense Fund, then moved to a private law practice. In 1979 Peña successfully ran for the Colorado House of Representatives, where he became minority (Democratic) leader during his second term.

Federico Peña, mayor of Denver from 1984 to 1992, subsequently went to Washington as Secretary of Transportation for President William J. Clinton, then later became Secretary of Energy. *Credit: Tom Noel Collection*

Even though Peña's ponytail disappeared, he seemed an unlikely echo of Mayor Robert W. Speer, who had done more for Denver than all other mayors before him put together. But once again, a visionary mayor used a

Denver dazzles visitors with exuberant municipal floral displays, such as these plantings in Washington Park. *Credit: Denver Metro Convention & Visitors Bureau*

period of slower economic times to rebuild and greatly expand the city's infrastructure and public stature.

"Imagine a Great City" was Peña's campaign slogan. Not since Speer had a mayor promised so much and been so serious about delivering it. Cynics who thought "Imagine a Great City" was just an election gimmick were in for a surprise.

Critics blasted the short, wiry Mexican-American as "Feddy" and his allies as "the Dreamers." Despite all the criticism and jokes, Feddy and the Dreamers made many of their dreams come true. Denver gained a new airport, a major league baseball team, a grand new central library, a convention center, and restoration of Speer-era parks, parkways and public buildings.

Mayor Peña moved Denver with an unusual power base, which included white liberals, minorities and labor. He also was the first mayor to solicit support from fringe groups such as gays and historic preservationists, who both found in Peña their first city hall champion. These diverse backers, combined with new-found allies

As this 1978 Colfax Avenue march suggests, gays came out of the closet during the 1970s. In the 1980s they helped to elect Federico Peña, the first Denver mayor to recognize gay interests. *Credit: photo by Glenn Cuerden*

in the business and booster community, enabled Peña to do more than just imagine a great city.

During two terms as mayor, from 1983 to 1991, Peña persuaded Denverites to reinvest billions in their city — even though the city was then in the worst recession since the 1930s. In the spring of 1989, voters approved a $3 billion airport. Two months later residents approved a $242 million bond issue to rebuild streets, provide infrastructure for redevelopment of the South

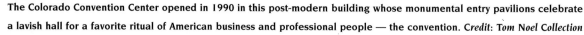

The Colorado Convention Center opened in 1990 in this post-modern building whose monumental entry pavilions celebrate a lavish hall for a favorite ritual of American business and professional people — the convention. Credit: Tom Noel Collection

Platte Valley, improve parks, plant 30,000 trees, expand the National Western Stock Show Grounds, update Denver General Hospital, and restore Civic Center Park and the City and County Building.

In 1990 Denver completed the $126 million Colorado Convention Center, with almost a million square feet on a 25-acre site between Cherry Creek and the Central Business District. That same year, the electorate approved a $200 million bond issue for the Denver Public Schools. Another $95 million bond issue won overwhelming support to enlarge the central library and restore or expand many branch libraries.

Voters narrowly approved a 0.1 percent sales tax to build a new baseball stadium for the Colorado Rockies. Many oldtimers and fiscal conservatives became horrified as Denver's gross bonded indebtedness climbed over $1 billion.

Naysayers such as *Rocky Mountain News* columnist Gene Amole complained that "Feddy and the Dreamers" were on a ruinous spending spree and "charging it on our credit card." A majority of voters, however, proved willing, as Mayor Peña put it, to "invest in Denver's future."

The Greater Denver Chamber of Commerce

Mayor Peña found an ally in the Denver Chamber of Commerce. That 103-year-old relic was rejuvenated

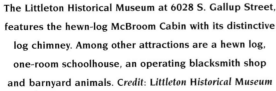

The Littleton Historical Museum at 6028 S. Gallup Street, features the hewn-log McBroom Cabin with its distinctive log chimney. Among other attractions are a hewn log, one-room schoolhouse, an operating blacksmith shop and barnyard animals. Credit: Littleton Historical Museum

in 1987 by a fresh chief executive officer, Richard C. D. Fleming. The flamboyant and omni-present Fleming

transformed the old Denver Chamber into the "Greater Denver Chamber of Commerce" by including representatives of suburban counties. Fleming elaborated in a 1992 interview:

"The world sees Denver as you see it from an airplane — without artificial boundaries. We should treat it that way and deal together with the common problems of air pollution, economic development, transportation and water. We need to market Denver as a six-county metropolis and let prospects see all the

One of Colorado's most exquisite cultural gems is the Central City Opera House. Erected by miners in 1878, it reopened in 1932 starring Lillian Gish as Camille. The drama and elegance of re-opening night was captured in this watercolor by Boulder artist Muriel Sibell Wolle. The interior, restored with the help of SCFD and State Historical Gaming Funds, recaptures the golden aspirations of mining towns during America's Gilded Age. Dividends from Colorado's first major historic preser–vation project included the renaissance of the neighboring Teller House with its legendary saloon. Credit: Central City Opera House Association

The Colorado Railroad Museum in Golden has a collection of standard and narrow gauge rolling stock, including live steam trains. *Credit: Colorado Railroad Museum, photo by Rick Cooley*

In the fast growing mountain suburb of Evergreen, the Hiwan Homestead House narrowly escaped demolition to become a crackerjack museum. *Credit: Hiwan Homestead*

alternatives. That's a lot better than having each county try to build itself up by running down the others."

John Lay, the current Chamber president, points to two successful metro-wide agencies — the Metropolitan Sewage District and the Regional Transportation

District. The Metropolitan Sewage District, organized by state law in 1961, encompassed 20 different municipalities and in 1988 gained voter approval for a $97 million bond issue to expand sewers and treatment plants in what environmentalists call a model program. Sewage was recycled as sludge to enrich soil. This agency, recently reorganized as the Metropolitan Wastewater District, is the pacesetter for metro cooperation, perhaps because local governments are not so territorial about their sewage.

The Regional Transportation District (RTD) is more controversial, although it too has been mostly a success story. After the antiquated Denver Tramway Company went out of business in 1970, the legislature approved the establishment of RTD in 1974.

Initially, RTD aspired to be one of the largest transportation districts in the country, embracing seven metro counties. Residents of Douglas and Weld counties, as well as eastern Adams and Arapahoe, however, removed themselves from the RTD tax district. Remaining voters in Adams, Arapahoe, Boulder, Denver, and Jefferson counties approved a 0.5 percent sales tax to finance RTD.

After this vote of confidence, RTD revitalized bus service and expanded it to the suburbs, buying seven suburban bus lines in the process. A free Sixteenth Street Mall shuttle bus, express buses, numerous park-and-ride stations, and a light rail system enabled RTD to capture national attention as a pace-setting public transit agency.

Culture Comes to a Cowtown

Major cultural institutions also received considerable boosts during the Peña era. Denver's renaissance stemmed from a unique tax that has become a model for other cities struggling to sustain their cultural assets. The Scientific & Cultural Facilities Tax District (SCFD), approved in 1988 by voters in Adams, Arapahoe, Boulder, Denver, Douglas and Jefferson counties, is a 0.1 percent sales tax which garnered $13 million in 1989 for various facilities.

Most of the funding goes to the major institutions: the Denver Art Museum, the Denver Botanic Gardens, the Denver Center for the Performing Arts, the Denver Museum of Natural History, and the Denver Zoological Gardens. The SCFD tax, renewed by voters for another decade in 1994, also generates increasing monies for some 200 other organizations, ranging from the Littleton Historical Museum to the Central City Opera House Association, from the Colorado Railroad Museum in Golden to the Hiwan Homestead Museum in Evergreen. Hunger Artists are fed funding and so is Dinosaur Ridge, with its awesome hogback trails following the footprints of the giant creatures that once roamed a swampy Colorado.

A 1996 study by Deloitte & Touche found that the cultural facilities outdrew the Denver Broncos, Denver Nuggets and Colorado Rockies combined. Groups funded by the Denver metro area's Scientific and Cultural Facilities District attracted more than 7.1 million visitors in 1995. Among the most popular destinations are four big Denver institutions devoted, respectively, to art, horticulture, natural history and the performing arts.

Denver Art Museum

In 1971, the Denver Art Museum (DAM) found a permanent home within its Civic Center castle, a dramatic design by Gio Ponti of Milan and James Sudler of Denver. The DAM had earlier struggled to find gallery space in nooks and crannies of the City and County Building. Besides European, American, Asian, Latin American and African collections, the museum has one of the world's finest collections of Native American materials. The DAM claims to be the first museum in America to have established a separate Native American collection. Here Indian artistic creations have been prized not as curious relics of barbarians, but as artifacts of under-appreciated native cultures.

Since its 1893 birth at the Denver Artists Club, the DAM has championed local and regional arts as well as masterpieces from around the world. Lewis Sharp, who moved from the Metropolitan Museum in New York City to become director of the DAM in 1989,

Denver Art Museum as seen from the sea lion fountain in Civic Center Park. Credit: *photo by Ron Ruhoff*

LEFT: Denver youngsters played in Mount Calvary, the Catholic section of the old City Cemetery, before it became the Denver Botanic Gardens in the 1950s.
Credit: *Denver Public Library*

BELOW: Water features grace the Denver Botanic Gardens with Boettcher Conservatory in the background.
Credit: *Denver Botanic Gardens, photo by Ron Ruhoff*

RIGHT: Thanks to nocturnal lighting of Boettcher Conservatory and the Blossom of Lights winter exhibition, the Gardens bloom even on chilly December nights.
Credit: *Denver Botanic Gardens*

expanded the museum along Acoma Street and converted that street to an "Avenue of The Arts." Public sculpture, a parking lot trimmed with metallic pop art, and street and sidewalk art have been installed, making Acoma a glitzy entry for the DAM, the Denver Public Library, the Colorado History Museum and Civic Center.

D e n v e r   B o t a n i c   G a r d e n s

Denver and the South Platte Valley were classified as "the Great American Desert" by Major Stephen H. Long, who led the first scientific investigation of the area in 1820. The "desert" theory, along with others, can best be explored at the Denver Botanic Gardens.

The Denver Museum of Natural History is crawling with dinosaurs, coyotes, moose and other wildlife dioramas.
Credit: Denver Museum of Natural History
Credit for Below: photo by Ron Ruhoff

On the northeast bank of Cherry Creek, the Denver Center for the Performing Arts offers music, dance and theater galore.

Credit: photo by Ron Ruhoff

The Gardens sprouted in the 1940s, thanks to a coalition of socialites and plant lovers who first tended gardens in City Park. In the 1950s the city acquired the Catholic portion of the old City Cemetery on the east edge of Cheesman Park for $80,000. As part of the deal, the city agreed to remove the remaining 6,000 corpses to Mount Olivet Cemetery. Crews worked rapidly at night to transplant most of the remains, yet expansion of the Botanic Gardens unearths a skeleton every now and then. The well-fertilized gardens have expanded in recent decades to cover more of the former boneyard with alpine, cutting, herb, High

Plains, Japanese, vegetable, and water gardens. DBG's large domed Boettcher Conservatory shelters an extensive garden of tropical plants.

In 1973, DBG acquired 750 acres at Chatfield Reservoir on the South Platte River in suburban Jefferson County. At this relatively undeveloped site where Deer Creek flows into the reservoir, DBG opened its Chatfield Arboretum Visitors Center in 1982. There the DBG also focuses on natural vegetation, offering tours and interpretive programs for anyone interested in the greening of "The Great American Desert."

The Denver Museum of Natural History

Founded in 1900 on a hill at the east end of City Park, the Denver Museum of Natural History has become the largest and most popular museum in the Rockies. The original temple-like edifice designed by Frederick J. Sterner at 2001 Colorado Boulevard is now buried under precast concrete and glass additions. This museum has more than doubled its space in recent decades, adding the Gates Planetarium and the IMAX Theater. The Museum's famed wildlife dioramas and dinosaur exhibits continue to be major draws as do blockbuster exhibits such as Ramses II, Aztec and The Imperial Tombs of China. Some 100 exhibits range from Colorado building stones to butterflies, from a lifesize diorama of a Cheyenne camp to the cavernous Coors Mineral Hall with its replicas of treasure filled mines and caverns. "Prehistoric Journey" features animated replicas of the monsters as well as actual dinosaur fossils, helping to attract some 1.8 million visitors a year to what has become America's fifth largest natural history venue.

Denver Center for the Performing Arts

Soaring glass canopies shelter the concrete acrobatics of the Denver Center for the Performing Arts. The DCPA complex at 14th and Curtis streets is an echo of Denver's old Curtis Street "Great White Way." All of the old Curtis Street theaters, including the fabu-

lous Tabor Grand Opera House, have been demolished.

Their descendant, the DCPA, boasts four theaters, a television studio, voice research laboratories, and the largest professional resident theater company between Chicago and the West Coast. This four-block

Watercolor by
Barbara Froula

complex and park is the second largest performing arts complex in the country, after Lincoln Center in New York City.

The DCPA's cornerstone is Mayor Speer's 1908 Denver Municipal Auditorium. Along with weekend and evening concerts, the auditorium has hosted everything from the 1908 Democratic National Convention to auto shows, with flags flying from its domes and light bulbs outlining its pediments, cornice and corners. The auditorium received a facelift in the early 1990s when the Temple Hoyne Buell Theater was built into it. Named for the Denver architect and developer whose fortune posthumously helped fund it, this state-of-the-art theater is a 2,834-seat reincarnation of the municipal auditorium's old theater and basketball and wrestling arena. Colorado quartzite lines the walls and the proscenium arch, while the seating is accented with snazzy blue and purple neon ribbons. The Buell is home to the Colorado Ballet and DCPA's Best of Broadway touring presentations.

Boettcher Concert Hall hosts the Colorado Symphony and Opera Colorado. In this $13 million hall, the 2,600 seats are arranged in asymmetrical banks in a 360-degree surround, so that 80 percent of the audience sits within 65 feet of the 2,400-square-foot stage.

Denver's "most remarkable musical story of the past decade," as Denver Post critic Jeff Bradley put it, "has been the resurgence of the Colorado Symphony Orchestra, brought back to life by its own musicians after the debt-laden Denver Symphony Orchestra folded in the spring of 1989. Adopting a new name and a user-friendly approach, the 78-member CSO quickly expanded its budget from an initial $2 million to nearly $7 million in 1995 and appointed Marin Alsop, the country's most prominent woman conductor, as its first music director."

The DCPA's Helen Bonfils Theater Complex contains four theaters with production space and rehearsal rooms. The Denver Center Theater Company

The Winter Park Ski train offers easy escape to the snowy Rockies, where Denverites can find solitude in cross country skiing. *Credit: photo by Bryon Hetzler*

is the largest professional resident ensemble between Chicago and the West Coast.

"The World's Greatest Airport"

Mayor Peña's greatest achievement — Denver International Airport — lies at the end of Peña Boulevard. DIA replaced crowded Stapleton International Airport, which by the mid-1980s had become the seventh largest airport in the world. It was the fourth busiest in the nation after Chicago, Atlanta, and Dallas-Fort Worth.

Air age activity was the key to many of Denver's dreams of prosperity and national prominence. The ski business, for instance, relied on airborne customers to become one of Colorado's largest and steadiest growth industries. Unlike gold and silver, coal and oil, and other nonrenewable riches of the earth, snow reappears annually. It also can be artificially increased by cloud seeding and snow-making machinery. By the 1990s Colorado attracted some 10 million skiers a year. Ski Country USA, the booster association headquartered in Denver, puffed the state's 55 ski areas, including Vail, the largest ski area in North America.

Two-thirds of Colorado ski visitors arrive by air, mostly through Denver's airport. Just as Denver once thrived as the supply town for mountain mining towns, it flourishes as the hub city for Ski Country USA. Thanks to the ski boom, Colorado's tourist industry became a year-round bonanza.

Denver became and remains the regional metropolis because of its role as the trade and travel hub of the region, yet Denver's rank among cities nationally has fallen. Since 1900, the Mile High City has been surpassed in population by once smaller Dallas, Houston, Los Angeles, Phoenix, San Diego and Seattle.

Denver's air-age dream has been to attract newcomers with the West's grandest airport, a marvel that would make it a "world-class city." More specifically airport boosters hoped that the new facility would enable Denver to at least catch up with Dallas, whose new airport made it the air hub of the inland western United States. Like Denver's slow-starting

professional football team, the Broncos, Denver's new airport finally began to worry the Texans. *The Dallas Times Herald* editorialized in 1989: "The Denver Airport — a huge project with 45 [sic: 53] square miles and five runways — emphasizes all the more that DFW [Dallas-Fort Worth International Airport] must be vigilant in protecting its position. Currently DFW is expected to be the second busiest airport in the year 2000, behind Chicago's O'Hare. Denver is likely to be third."

The Dallas-Fort Worth Airport, the last major aviation hub to be built in the U.S. before DIA, inspired Denver's DIA fantasy. After its 1973 opening, DFW went from 9 to 43 carriers and soared ahead of Stapleton to become the world's fourth busiest airport in terms of passengers served. The new airport, along with the oil boom, propelled a 25 percent growth in the Dallas-Fort Worth area during the 1970s. The DFW success story was not lost on Denver, which, during the mid-1980s oil bust, had become the national champion in empty office space and business bankruptcies.

While Denver was envying Dallas, it got a poke in the backside from Salt Lake City. The Utah capital emerged as a rival after Delta Airlines acquired Western Airlines in 1986 and made Salt Lake City its western hub. This new threat was publicized by full-page ads in national journals such as the *New York Times*. A 1986 ad showed a harried executive arriving late for a meeting with the apology: "Sorry I'm late but I had to fly through Denver." Next time he would fly through Salt Lake City. Mayor Peña and the Greater Denver Chamber of Commerce retaliated with a $200,000 campaign to sing Stapleton's praises.

Boosters of the Beehive State stung Coloradans again in 1987 by creating a new Utah license plate. Instead of the corny old beehive of activity representing Mormon industry, the new plate was snow white and featured a skier and the slogan "Utah! Greatest Snow on Earth."

Salt was rubbed deeper into Denver's thin skin in 1995 when Salt Lake City captured the 2002 International Winter Olympic Games. A month later, in July, Salt Lake also captured a $241 million federal grant

to build a light rail system, while Denver's proposal for federal aid to expand its existing light rail to the southwestern suburbs was rejected until 1997.

Salt Lake celebrated with ads claiming its airport was closer to ski areas and cheaper. Although Salt Lake City has only a third of Denver's population and Utah only a third the number of Colorado skiers, the Mile High City faces aggressive competition from the City of the Saints.

When Denver opened what boosters claimed was "the World's Largest State-of-the-Art Airport" in 1994,

the city boasted it had built the planet's greatest inland port. The terminal's billowing white sails are held aloft by masts with loudspeakers hidden in the crow's nests. The Denver architects responsible for the airport, Curt Fentress and Jim Bradburn, constructed its terminal roof of translucent, teflon-coated fiberglass. Sunlight streams into the airport by day, and by night DIA is visible from 100 miles away. Its snowy white tents echo the white-capped Rockies and commemorate the Arapaho and Cheyenne tepees pitched there long ago.

Stapleton Airport terminal, 1983. *Credit: photo by Ron Ruhoff*

NEXT PAGE: Like snowy peaks, the tent top of DIA's Jeppesen Terminal glow in the sunset. *Credit: photo by Ron Ruhoff*

MILE HIGH METROPOLIS

I N 1991, WELLINGTON WEBB PULLED OFF ONE of the biggest upsets in Colorado political history. The former state legislator and city auditor had less than 7 percent support in opinion polls asking who should replace the retiring mayor, Federico Peña. After running short on campaign money to buy ads, Webb walked all 73 Denver neighborhoods to court voters personally. He won the election with 58 percent of the vote.

Wellington Edward Webb was born Feb. 7, 1941, in Chicago, where his father, Wellington Marion Webb, was captain of the club car on the deluxe passenger train called the City of Denver. Asthma bedeviled young Wellington, so the family took him to Denver when he was five. Like thousands of other families, the Webbs came for Colorado's climate cure. In Webb's case, it worked. The sickly youngster grew into a giant of a man, standing 6' 4" in size 12 sneakers.

Webb became a basketball star at Denver's Manual High School and received a scholarship to the University of Northern Colorado in Greeley, where he earned a master's degree in education. He taught high school and coached basketball at Adams City High School, then taught African-American History part time at the University of Colorado at Denver.

After being elected mayor, Webb said: "Denver is still a friendly city. Most people still look you in the eye. My election and that of Mayor Peña shows that Denverites give everyone a chance, regardless of their skin color. My goal is to keep this a friendly, safe, tolerant and exciting city."

Oh, Give Me A Home

Mayor Webb presided over a prosperous city as well. But even the flush times have a downside. For example, the 1990s boom has been a curse to the homeless, who traditionally squatted in the South Platte River bottoms. Arapaho Indians had camped along the river, later followed by busted prospectors, broken down cowboys, homeless homesteaders, poor immigrants and downsized capitalists.

For decades squatters were allowed this unofficial reservation. Ancient hobo paths along the river bottoms, however, are evolving into cafe and condo lined trails for strollers, in-line skaters, joggers and cyclists. These newcomers do not want to be disturbed by the sight of begging indigents.

Nor are leisured indigents welcome in Denver's old skid row — it is now trendy LoDo with million dollar lofts, Coors Field and upscale restaurants selling $25 cigars. The homeless were also chased out of their nests under the bridges over Cherry Creek after Denver Country Clubbers complained about vagrants following the creek into their golf course.

Like this resident of a South Platte River sewer, Denver's homeless have squatted along the river and Cherry Creek. Credit: photo by Tom Noel

OPPOSITE PAGE: Wellington Webb, who walked all 73 Denver neighborhoods during his successful mayoral campaigns, poses with first lady Wilma Webb in front of East High School. During Mayor Webb's terms, the core city gained population for the first time since the 1970s, zooming past the 500,000 mark in 1997. Credit: Rocky Mountain News, photo by Steve Groer

On freezing winter nights, a softhearted priest, Rev. Charles B. Woodrich, lets vagrants sleep on the golden oak pews in the majestic marble sanctuary of Holy Ghost Catholic Church. Credit: *Fentress Bradburn & Associates, photo by Merrick Hadrich-Blessing*

On an average day in the metro area, some 3,300 people are homeless. Not all of them want help from the Catholic Worker House, Central Presbyterian Church, Denver Rescue Mission, First Baptist Church, Sacred Heart Shelter, the Salvation Army's Crossroads Shelter, Samaritan House or other overnight shelters. Many preferred the riverbank, until they were evicted early in 1997 as part of a $40 million campaign to transform the riverfront into upscale housing, offices, parks, and even an aquarium.

Despite this removal, the homeless generally have found a big friend at city hall. Mayor Webb agonized over the removal, vowing to relocate the riverside homeless — and even their pets — into comfortable quarters.

In 1995, when the corpse of a vagrant was found in Civic Center, most people and all but one politician,

RIGHT: Although Father "Woody" burned lots of incense to hide the smell, some parishioners complained about housing the homeless in the church. The solution came when the Catholic Archdiocese of Denver sold some of the land around Holy Ghost, along with the air rights, to the developers of the 1999 Broadway high rise, which towers over the church. Credit: *photo by Glenn Cuerden*

....

BELOW: With $2.4 million from the Holy Ghost deal, the Archdiocese of Denver built the Samaritan House in 1987 for homeless men, women and families. Credit: *photo by Tom Noel*

looked the other way. Mayor Webb, however, called the press to publicize the plight of the homeless. On December 19, 1996, the mayor hosted a candlelight memorial service at City Hall for the 43 homeless people who died in Denver in 1996. "I wanted," he explained, "to dignify their tragic deaths."

Rapids built into the rejuvenated South Platte River drown out urban sounds and delight kayakers and rafters. *Credit: Denver Metro Convention & Visitor's Bureau.*

"Neighborhoods don't step forward to welcome the homeless," the mayor observed. "It's always `Not in My Back Yard.' So we've put these people in our own backyard down here at City Hall." Webb's administration offered the city-owned office building across 14th Street from City Hall to the Colorado Coalition

for the Homeless. The coalition revamped it in 1996 as 100 single-room apartments.

"I toured the Forum Apartments before the homeless moved in," Mayor Webb recalled. "It has security, a shower and a kitchen in every unit. Now, when I walk into City Hall I no longer see a vacant, deteriorating building but one filled with people. It looks just like any other apartment or condo." Nor has it deterred upscale loft and restaurant development in the adjacent Golden Triangle neighborhood bounded by Broadway, Speer Boulevard and West Colfax Avenue.

What motivates his honor?

"I don't help the homeless because they vote. They don't. In fact, they are a political liability. Helping them alienates some voters — who want the poor to just disappear.

"I learned to be kind to all kinds of people from my parents, my grandmother, and my great, compassionate wife. I also learned from my first real job, working at Fort Logan Mental Health Center. For three and a half years, I taught gym classes for emotionally disturbed kids. Many of our homeless remind me of those kids."

The mayor was raised to practice Christian kindness. "My folks wouldn't let us five kids go out on Saturday night unless we went to church on Sunday — no matter how tired we were. If we fell asleep in church, we had to sleep with our eyes open!

"I've learned to take chances on people. In 1991, when I was at 7 percent in the polls, the people of Denver took a chance on me. I want to gamble on

ABOVE: Most spectacular among Denver's new riverside attractions is Elitch Gardens, Denver's grand old amusement park, it moved from Northwest Denver to this central Platte Valley site in 1995. Riding into their own fantasy worlds, youngsters for more than a century have fancied Elitch's old fashioned carousel. Thanks to Elitch's tower, ferris wheel and famed rollercoaster, Mr. Twister, downtown Denver has one of America's dizzier skylines. *Credits: Carousel: photo by Tom Noel, Rollercoaster: Denver Metro Convention & Visitors Bureau*

LEFT: Turning the Platte River bottoms into an urban oasis of parks, residences, amusements and work places has been a major thrust of Denver Mayor Wellington Webb. *Credit: Denver Metro Convention & Visitors Bureau*

people, to create opportunities. There is a lot of talent in any pool of people — the homeless too.

"Denver is one big family. We need each other and we need to care for everyone. When I spent the night in the Samaritan Shelter, I was struck by the diverse backgrounds of the homeless. You can't stereotype them as comic strip hobos, bums and winos. Most distressing are the homeless mothers with children. Kids under 17 make up almost a third of that population. If we ever turn our back on the homeless, no matter how far we have advanced otherwise, we have become a backward society."

The Denver Public Library

Mayor Webb, who once worked as a shelver in the Denver Public Library, took a special interest in Denver's grand new public library on the south side of Civic Center.

The library serves the entire state and region through its special collections and inter-library loan programs. With a dramatic 1995 addition designed by Michael Graves, one of America's foremost postmodernists, the central library offers a 4.2 million-item collection. It is the eighth largest public library in the nation, second only to Boston in per capita circulation. Over half of all Denverites have library cards.

The Denver Public Library's Western History Department houses a priceless collection of architectural drawings, art, diaries, 6,000 maps, 2,500 manuscripts, newspapers, menus, 500,000 photographs, posters, postcards, theater programs, as well as books, including many rare and some unique items. Nationally, DPL stacks up well against the great private research libraries and other public libraries.

The Colorado Historical Society

The Colorado Historical Society (CHS) also has a notable collection of printed materials as well as thousands of artifacts. Among its treasures are some priceless Depression-era WPA dioramas. One of these, a large scale model of Denver in 1860, enables visitors to see how far Denver has come since its golden origins at the confluence of Cherry Creek and the South Platte River.

The CHS's State Historic Preservation Office oversees a gambling bonanza that has amounted to more than $50 million since limited stakes gambling began

The exterior of the Denver Public Library also uses shapes and colors to define interior departments. *Credit: photo by Rhoda Pollack*

The Colorado Historical Society has reincarnated the Byers-Evans House behind the Denver Art Museum as a Denver History Museum. *Credit: Metro Denver Convention & Visitors Bureau*

Colorado Historical Society treasures, exhibited at the Colorado History Museum at 1300 Broadway, include this Ute Indian pack for a papoose. *Credit: Colorado Historical Society*

in three Colorado towns in 1991. Voters approved gaming with the proviso that it be taxed to fund historic preservation projects. This fortune, which annually averages about $10 million, is distributed statewide.

Within the metro area, the State Historical Fund has made many preservation dreams come true. Restorations range from Mayor Speer's old Municipal Auditorium to the J.S. Brown Mercantile's reincarnation as the Wynkoop Brewing Company, the first of some two dozen brewpubs to spring up in the metro area since 1990. Gaming funds also helped the Platte Valley Trolley transport people from Confluence Park to the Children's Museum and Mile High Stadium. The Golda Meir House, where the first female prime minister of Israel spent her Denver years, has been reincarnated as meeting rooms and a museum on the Auraria Campus. At Fort Logan, the fund facilitated restoration of the Field Officer's Quarters where young Dwight David Eisenhower lived while courting a Denver girl, Mamie Dowd. Other State Historical Fund projects aided main street restorations in Boulder, Castle Rock, Golden and Littleton. By preserving past achievements, these towns hoped to create a stronger sense of place among both longtime residents and newcomers pouring into the fast-growing metropolis.

New Denverites

Denver has always been a city of newcomers. One historian, Lyle W. Dorsett, referred to Denver as a "turnstile town." Studies tracing individuals through Denver City directories and the federal census records suggest that people came to and left

Denver even more often that the American average of a move every five years. Each new boom and bust cycle in mining, oil or high tech industries washed thousands of people into and out of the Mile High City.

Nineteenth-century Denverites came in the greatest numbers from New York, Ohio, Illinois, Missouri and the Midwest. By the 1990s, Californians comprised a quarter of the newcomers. In 1994, the peak year for California arrivals, 33,522 Golden Staters applied for Colorado driver's licenses (in the same year only 9,975 Coloradans requested California driving privileges.)

After Californians, the most numerous recent immigrants have come from Texas, Illinois, New York and Kansas. Now, as throughout Denver's history, native-born whites have formed the bulk of the immi-

gration to Denver. Heavy in-migration led the Greater Denver Chamber of Commerce to predict a metro area population in the year 2000 of 2,196,035. By the year 2020, the sprawling metropolis will include Clear Creek and Gilpin counties, according to planners, and an estimated population of 2.8 million.

Denver's awesome mountain setting and salubrious climate attract many newcomers. The city, and especially the suburbs, are communities of strangers whose strongest bond may be the diseases known as Broncomania, Rockies fever and Avalanche fever. Although the National Football League's Denver Broncos have been around since 1960, and the National League Colorado Rockies since 1993, it was the Colorado Avalanche of the National Hockey League, who arrived in 1995, that brought the city its

Fresh home brew made the Wynkoop Brewing Company an inspirational prototype for dozens of brewpubs and micro-breweries that have tapped into the beer business in 1990s Colorado. Credit: *photo by Tim Murphy*

ABOVE AND NEXT PAGE: Aurora's Plains Conservation Center preserves a patch of undeveloped prairie, along with an old sod house and conestoga wagon. *Credit: photo by Tom Noel*

only major professional sports championship — the Stanley Cup.

Denverites differ from other Americans in several ways. They boast one of the highest per capita education levels in the country. Although 19th-century Denver was an industrial city with many smelters and manufacturers, the modern city relies more on a service economy and high tech businesses such as telecommunications that require a well-educated labor force. The city's educational resources include the Health Sciences Center and a general campus of the University of Colorado, Metropolitan State College of Denver and the Community College of Denver. Regis University is a Jesuit college which opened its Northwest Denver campus in 1887. The University of Denver, founded in 1864, is the city's oldest institution of higher education.

Denver is characterized by single family residences and a high rate of home ownership — even the poorest citizens often live in single-family, detached houses which they own. The American dream of home ownership has become reality for many in the Mile High City.

Automobility

Denverites are unusually mobile. They boast one of the highest per capita licensed motor vehicle ownership rates in the world with more auto registrations than adult residents. Cars are basic to the Colorado lifestyle, but Coloradans pay a price for their mobility. Roads have scarred the state, as have parking lots galore. Automobile exhaust is the chief cause of the brown cloud — highly visible and unhealthy pollution that darkens a city that once puffed itself as America's health spa.

This automobile metropolis retains its greatest asset — easy escape. Within an hour's drive to the east lay prairie ghost towns and the exquisite solitude of the High Plains. An hour's drive to the west takes Denverites to campgrounds, hiking trails, mountain lakes, ski resorts and wilderness areas snuggled against the Continental Divide.

Denver has grown into a metropolis sprawling across six Front Range counties and spilling into another outer ring of counties — Clear Creek, Gilpin, Weld, Larimer, Elbert and Park. In 1996, the metro area passed the two million mark in population. Many newcomers settled in the Denver suburbs of Aurora, Lakewood, Arvada, Westminster or Boulder, which have grown into Colorado's third, fourth, sixth, ninth and tenth largest cities.

Aurora

Explosive growth transformed a tiny farm town into Colorado's third largest city with a population over 250,000. Aurora originated in 1891 with the founding of Fletcher. City father Donald K. Fletcher failed financially during the Panic of 1893 and fled Colorado, leaving folks in Fletcher saddled with bonded indebtedness for a failed water scheme. Irate residents renamed their village for Aurora, goddess of the dawn. She remained a sleepy country hamlet until the establishment of Stapleton Airport, Fitzsimons Hospital, Lowry Air Base, and Buckley Air Base.

Aurora boomed after World War II, becoming Colorado's fastest growing town, zooming from 3,437 in 1940 to 222,103 in 1990. During the 1970s, Aurora began an aggressive annexation program that has given it an area of 138 square miles, larger than Miami, Buffalo and San Francisco combined. With new assets such as a huge park at Aurora Reservoir, a dozen designated landmarks and the Aurora History Museum, Aurora promotes itself as "The Gateway to the Rockies."

Indeed, the Rockies can be seen better from Aurora because, unlike Denver, it has outlawed large billboards and passed height restrictions. Gazing into the metro future, Aurora Mayor Paul Tauer predicts "a twin-city relationship like Minneapolis-St. Paul, with Aurora in the role of Minneapolis and Denver playing St. Paul."

Lakewood

Lakewood was platted in 1889 by William A.H. Loveland, his wife Miranda, and Charles Welch as a 13-block country town strung out along West Colfax Avenue. It has become Colorado's fourth largest city with a 1990 population of 126,481. Epitomizing the anti-urban sentiment of many suburbanites, Lakewoodites have been leery of urbanization. Clinging to the notions of a country hamlet, they refused to incorporate until

May Bonfils Stanton, above, used her *Denver Post* fortune to construct this Carrara marble palace, left, inspired by the Petit Trianon at Versailles. Lakewood's grandest mansion was demolished after her death in 1962 for what is now a modern municipal complex and museum. *Credit: Lakewood Heritage Center*

In Lakewood, the country estate of *The Denver Post* heiress May Bonfils Stanton has evolved into a municipal center and museum complex. That tiny farm town once known for its turkey farms has mushroomed into Colorado's fourth largest city. Credits: *photos by Michael Gamer*

1969. Residents fancied ranch houses and spacious lawns. Many prefer to identify with the rural ideals and the rugged independence of the mountains to the west rather than with the monster metropolis of which they are a reluctant part.

The federal government, whose activities make or break western towns, destined Lakewood to grow when it established a munitions plant in 1940 on the Downing-Hayden Ranch, stretching from West Sixth to West Alameda avenues, between Kipling and Union

The Arvada Center for the Arts & Humanities houses exhibits and stage plays that attract visitors from throughout the metropolis.
Credit: Arvada Center

streets. This $35 million World War II facility was guarded by concrete watchtowers fenced off by 15 miles of chain link. Although topped by barbed wire, the fence did not keep out coyotes looking for the turkeys once raised on the many poultry farms thereabouts.

West Sixth Avenue was converted to Denver's first freeway to expedite access to the wartime industries. After World War II ended in 1945, the ordinance plant was converted to the Denver Federal Center, which has evolved into the largest compound of federal agencies outside Washington, D.C. Some 30 agencies provide stable, well-paid jobs and enviable benefits for almost 10,000 employees, of whom only 317 can be accommodated in a bomb shelter, to keep the government humming in a post nuclear-war world.

Lakewood has taken steps to engender community pride, launching Lakewood on Parade Day in 1977. Another community asset is Belmar Park and Lakewood's Heritage Center on what was May Bonfils Stanton's estate at the corner of West Alameda Avenue and South Wadsworth Boulevard. The original 750-acre grounds surrounded a $1 million, Carrara marble mansion. May Bonfils Stanton, heiress of *The Denver Post* fortune, declared that "the 20th century does not exist." She slept in a bed once owned by Marie Antoinette, sat in a crested chair that had supported Queen Victoria, and owned a piano played by Frederic Chopin.

After her death at Belmar in 1962, the mansion was demolished. Where formal gardens, lily ponds, game parks and an exquisite Italian-style villa once stood, development began in 1964 with the construction of the Villa Italia Shopping Center. The Irongate Office Complex ultimately arose near Belmar's grand entry gate, which still stands. The rest of the grounds have gone to housing subdivisions and Lakewood's municipal government center, with a city hall, the 127-acre Belmar Park and Lakewood's Heritage Center.

The Heritage Center has grown from a tiny museum in the old calf barn to a complex of structures ranging from the 1869 Ralston schoolhouse to a 1930s-style ranch house, the Hallack-Webber residence. Lakewood also enacted a special ordinance to protect treasures such as the 36-foot-high neon sign of a cowboy and a palamino horse on top of Davies Chuck Wagon Diner on West Colfax Avenue. Lane's Tavern, another legendary hangout, has been reconstructed at the Heritage Center.

By the year 2000, Jefferson County probably will be more populous than Denver County. To deal with growth, Lakewood's 1996 masterplan focused on the 21st century while preserving and celebrating the town's 20th-century history. Lakewood's Heritage Center Director Deborah Ellerman reported in 1997 that, "Our heritage center will focus on this community's rich agricultural history, on the commercialization of West Colfax Avenue and on family histories. By building understanding and appreciation for Lakewood's 20th-century history through preservation and interpretation, we hope to create a stronger sense of place, a greater sense of community in the 21st century."

Arvada

North of Lakewood on the west side of the metro area is Arvada, with a large, active and ambitious Arvada Center for the Arts and Humanities, a lively historical society, and a downtown historic district. It is Colorado's sixth largest city, with a population of more than 100,000.

Arvada traces its origins to the 1850 gold strike on Ralston Creek, but settlement did not come until Benjamin Franklin Wadsworth staked out the town on Ralston Creek near its junction with Clear Creek in 1870. Wadsworth donated land for churches, helped organize a public school, dug the Wadsworth water ditch, and converted part of his home to the post office. His wife, the first postmistress, named the town for the biblical figure Arva, leader of the Arvadites who settled in what today is Lebanon.

Eugene E. Benjamin enhanced the town's role as a farm hub in 1925 by opening the Arvada Flour Mill, which crowned the skyline and touted the town in sacks labeled Arva-Pride. Hoping to make the town shine further, the chamber of commerce erected a large electric "ARVADA" on the water tank. Both landmarks have been preserved.

Arvadans in 1973 approved a $7 million bond issue to create not only parks and open space, but also the Arvada Center for the Arts and Humanities. It opened in 1976 in a grassy south-facing hillside park. The spa-cious brick complex housed a 2,000-seat amphithe-ater, a 500-seat theater, and 1,500 square feet of gallery space, as well as studios, meeting halls, and a museum. It outshone any other Denver suburban showcase for the visual arts, humanities, and per-forming arts, attracting nationally prominent artists and exhibitions.

Westminster

Westminster traces its name to Westminster University, a Presbyterian school founded in 1892 on the highest point in Adams County. The "Princeton of the West" erected a magnificent red sand stone edifice, prominently situated at West 88th Avenue and Lowell Boulevard.

Even earlier, Edgar Bowles homesteaded the area in 1871 and built the big red brick home at 3924 W. 72nd Avenue that was restored in 1988 as the Westminster Historical Society museum. Bowles raised majestic

OPPOSITE PAGE AND BELOW: From a sleepy rural stop at Westminster University on the Denver & Interurban Railroad, Westminster has evolved into Colorado's ninth largest city. Credit: *Denver Public Library, photos by Louis C. McClure*

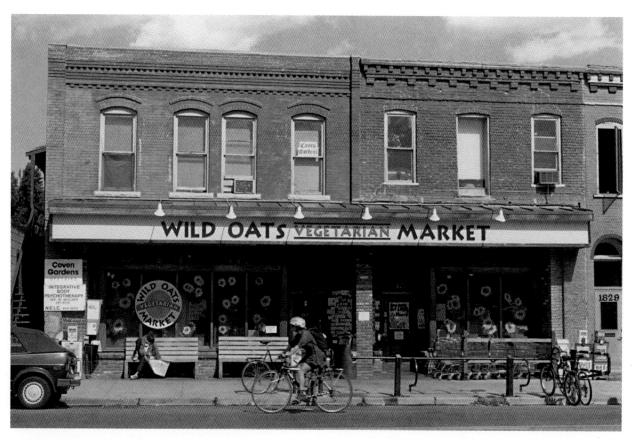

stable horses that put Westminster on the map. He also became a member of the first school board, promoted organization of the first church in Westminster and oversaw Westminster's incorporation as a town in 1911. To coax the Denver Interurban rail line to Westminster, Bowles gave land to construct a depot for a commuter train from Denver. With fast regular train service, Westminster began to blossom as a suburban town. Population climbed from 235 in 1920 to 1,686 in 1950. Growth accelerated with the 1952 completion of the Denver-Boulder Turnpike. Two Westminster exits feed what is now a city of more than 83,000.

Westminster's boom was not shared by its university, which in 1915 decided to become an all-male school. After losing many students to the military during World War I, Westminster University closed. Although resurrected in the 1920s as Belleview College, a seminary for the fundamentalist Pillar of Fire Church, it never became "the Princeton of the West."

Westminster celebrated its arrival as the state's ninth largest city with a new City Hall in 1988. Borrowing a world-famous symbol from Westminster, England, the town erected its own 136-foot-high clock tower. This architectural allusion to Big Ben is only half as tall as the London landmark, but its bells outnumber Big Ben's 14 to one. While many suburban governments erected penny-pinching, nondescript public buildings, this tower has given Westminster pride, identity, and an echo of both distant Big Ben and the nearby towers of Westminster University.

Boulder

Deadwood Diggings, as Boulder was called before formation of the Boulder City Town Company, has become Colorado's tenth largest city. Shunning such status, Boulder has struggled to keep its population under 100,000 and has led the state in fighting growth. This town created greenbelts and tightly restricted

building permits to insulate itself against creeping metropolitan sprawl.

Besides capitalizing on its role as an educational center, the university town developed cultural and recreational amenities. By protecting its spectacular natural setting, respecting its older neighborhoods, and restoring its main street as the Pearl Street Mall, the town used its past to cushion residents against the shock of rapid growth.

Gold strikes first attracted settlers to Boulder, but coal, tungsten and oil later became more important. The University of Colorado, which opened its doors in 1876, has developed first rate science and engineering programs that attracted major federal scientific centers such as the National Center for Atmospheric Research and the National Bureau of Standards as well as high-tech enterprises such as IBM and Storage Tek.

Frederick Law Olmsted, Jr., America's leading city planner and landscape architect, gave Boulder a

dream to which it has clung with his 1910 work, *The Improvement of Boulder, Colorado*: "The main lookout of citizens is not how to make money as quickly as possible so as to go somewhere else to enjoy life, but how to get as much satisfaction out of life as they can in a very agreeable locality."

Boulder became a model of growth management during the 1970s, enacting a one percent sales tax to buy a huge carpet of greenspace. The town also limited motor vehicle noise to 80 decibels, building heights to 55 feet, and new housing permits to a two percent annual increase.

Ironically, the town, renowned for planning, originated in a plan gone awry. Townfounder Captain Thomas A. Aikins and 10 other gold seekers struck out in 1858 for the Cherry Creek diggings. After stumbling across Boulder Creek, Aiken named it for its many boulders. Aikins and others founded "Boulder City" on February 10, 1859. They platted a two-mile long town in the

On Denver's suburban fringe, prairie dogs have surrendered their villages to subdivisions and shopping malls.
Credit: photo by Tom Noel

....

mouth of Boulder Canyon, offering 4,000 home sites at $1,000 each. These lots, measuring 50 by 140 feet, were larger than the 25 by 125 feet standard parcels in Denver and elsewhere. The community's early interest in elbow room was reflected in the initial town plat's generous assignment of almost half the land to roads, alleys, parks and public space.

Some disagreed with Boulder's growth control tactics. Amos Bixby, a boomer and editor of the *Boulder Valley News*, wrote in 1880, "Early in the affairs of the Town Company, two parties arose — one in favor of holding the lots high, in order to make a 'big thing' for themselves; the other in favor of giving away alternate lots to those who would build on them, or doing most anything to induce population and capital. Unfortunately, the high-priced party prevailed, but the lots were not taken at $1,000 each...It was the hope and reasonable expectation, of the advocates of the liberal

policy, to have centered here the men of money and enterprise...and thus to have made Boulder what Denver afterward became, the leading town of the territory."

Metro Overview

From airplane windows, observers see a Mile High metropolis of residential subdivisions that surround shopping center nuclei. These retail centers are the financial as well as the geographical hubs for many metro communities because they are sustained by sales tax revenues. This economic reality drives each community to offer tax breaks and concessions on landscaping, parking and other requirements to subsidize proliferation of ever newer shopping malls, discount stores and strip shopping centers.

Consequently the metropolis is littered with half-empty old strip mall stores, huge ugly boxes of short-lived discount stores, and elderly, struggling shopping malls. The Colorado legislature has neglected the issue of regional or statewide planning that might rationalize metro growth and end the wasteful, cutthroat competition for retail sales taxes. The Denver Regional Council of Governments was created to resolve such problems, but it has been a weak advisory body.

Political entities proliferate to join the competition for new retail outlets and sales tax revenues. Metro Denver has more than 300 special jurisdictions, including some 65 cites and towns. This governmental maze makes administration and planning difficult, confuses taxpayers about who taxes and who serves them, and leads to wasteful duplication of services. Each community, no matter how tiny and poor, is forced into uneven and bitter competition to annex more land and capture more retail business.

An example of the problem is the blue collar town of Federal Heights caught in between two much larger and more aggressive Adams County neighbors. Westminster and Thornton used tax breaks and other ploys to persuade giant Kmart and King Soopers stores to move out of Federal Heights, leaving that town with giant empty stores — and a loss of 30 percent of its sales tax revenues.

Whenever a new state-of-the-art shopping mall opens on the outer edge of suburbia, it generates new traffic problems and cancerous growth. It also takes business away from struggling older core city and suburban retail centers. Retail malls and residential subdivisions now sprawl over the Front Range from Fort Collins to Colorado Springs. If every metro city and county built out to its current comprehensive plan for growth, according to a 1997 study by Alan Katz of *The Denver Post*, Denver's urbanized area would swell to 1,150 square miles — an area larger than Long Beach, Los Angeles, Oakland, San Diego, San Jose and San Francisco combined.

Neither the legislature, nor the governor, nor local officials have dealt with sprawl, although planners have long pointed to the Oregon model for effective, politically possible, growth management. Oregon's pathbreaking 1973 law forced all counties, cities, and towns to rezone their turf to meet strict state guidelines aimed at controlling suburban sprawl, reducing pollution, and preserving rural lands, small towns, open space, and scenic landscapes.

The Denver Water Department

Limited water resources may force Coloradans to deal with the issue of unbridled growth. For the giant green oasis at the base of the Rockies lies in what early explorers called the Great American Desert. The semi-arid Denver area is characterized by an average precipitation of only 14 inches a year. Even that figure is misleading, as Denver's moisture has fluctuated between 7 and 23 inches a year.

Many metro communities depend on the indispensable product of the Denver Water Department. The DWD, an agency of the City & County of Denver since 1918, uses a vast network of trans-montane diversions, reservoirs and pipes to capture flow from the Colorado River, which carries more water than the South Platte, Arkansas and Rio Grande rivers combined.

Without water diversions, Denver might go the way of Colorado's first great civilization — the Anasazi, the prehistoric Indian culture commemorat-

ed at Mesa Verde National Park in southwestern Colorado. If Denver experienced an extended dry spell such as the 25-year drought that apparently chased prehistoric Indians out of their Mesa Verde cliff dwellings, the Mile High Metropolis could evaporate. A mass exodus might leave the canyons of 17th Street as ghostly as those silent stone cities in the canyons of Mesa Verde.

Like other westerners, Denverites are generally optimistic and energetic. Why fret about drought, smog, sprawl and other problems, when it is possible to escape to the mountains for the weekend? As the metropolis zoomed past the two million mark in 1996, its residents remained determined to find a way to keep their lawns green and to boost the Mile High City higher. Like the Arapaho camped long ago along Cherry Creek and the South Platte River, Denverites look up to the shining mountains and expect sunny tomorrows.

......

As one muralist has suggested, Denver might outgrow its water supplies and become an abandoned ruin, the fate of Mesa Verde's prehistoric cliff dwellers. *Credit: Tom Noel Collection*

Partners *in* Denver

Denver

PROFILES OF BUSINESSES THAT HAVE CONTRIBUTED TO THE BEAUTY, STRUCTURE, ECONOMIC BAS

PARTNERS IN DENVER TABLE OF CONTENTS

Partners in Denver

DENVER'S REAL ESTATE AND CONSTRUCTION INDUSTRY SHAPES TOMORROW'S SKYLINE, PROVIDING

Building a Greater Denver

Working and Living Space for Its People.

THE D.C. BURNS REALTY & TRUST COMPANY

In 1899, horse-pulled buggies dominated Larimer Street, home-town star Douglas Fairbanks performed at the Tabor Grand before it sold, $57 million dollars in pay dirt had already been plucked from Colorado's hills, and one thousand building permits were issued. As the Mile High City prepared for the turn of the century, Daniel Cochran Burns, a lawyer, loan man and budding philanthropist, opened a realty office — then called The United Securities Realty Company — on Glenarm Place.

The Kittredge Building, at 16th and Glenarm Place, was The D.C. Burns Realty & Trust Company's first home in 1899. The beautiful building is still in use today.

Venture capital was plentiful then. Building projects like the new Federal Mint and the St. Joseph's Hospital addition were under way. It was a grand time for making grand profits, but amid the luxurious Capitol Hill mansions, starvation wages ran rampant.

Prices were low, but salaries were a mere pittance. Eggs sold for fifteen cents a dozen, three cents would get a shirt laundered, and ten dollars was a high monthly wage for a housemaid. The families of the working class just dreamt of owning their own home. D.C. understood that $1,500.00 to $5,000.00 dwellings were a crying need. He built and sold houses at 10% down (long before the FHA was conceived in 1935) and almost unheard of low monthly terms; specializing, even then, in sub-dividing property for development.

Then the Great Depression gripped the nation. Local government, charities, churches, and volunteers were challenged with providing relief to tens of thousands of unemployed, homeless, and starving Denverites. Skilled carpenters and laborers hung up their tools. There was no work. Land development was the downfall of many realtors from 1929 to 1934. Fortunately, D.C. had established himself on a scale large enough that he could still make money while liquidating his holdings as needed, carrying the firm through the Great Depression's lean years.

His first low-cost homes were known as the Barnum Tract, built on the property subdivided by P.T. Barnum. As the years went by, D.C.'s liberal business policy paid off. There are many costlier Burns-built structures still standing as enduring landmarks around Denver. One is The Graystone at Delaware and 14th. Other developments remembered by old-timers are the Burns Hill Addition, Burns Sunset Heights,

This photo of the Burns Brentwood subdivision (circa 1946-1952), near Federal Boulevard and Evans Avenue, depicts a humble vignette of early suburbia, set against the backdrop of the snowy foothills.

Burnsdale, and Burns Montclair. Many of these stable, low-cost homes are still loved and lived in by Denverites.

D.C.'s creed — to provide a home for the working man — has been carried on for decades by his nephew, Franklin L. Burns. Franklin, a Denver native, joined the firm — which had become known as The D. C. Burns Realty & Trust Company of 1536 Welton — as a salesman in 1938. At that time, the average single family home sold for $3,424.00. Franklin was a visionary. Reportedly working from the trunk of his

Built in beautiful Cherry Hills Vista by the Burns
Construction Co., Denver's largest residential builder

SHOW HOUSE
*Beautifully decorated
and furnished*

OPEN TODAY
AND EVERY DAY
2:00-9:00
2995 So. York

Admission 25¢
per person

Net Proceeds go to
American
Cancer Society
HELP
FIGHT CANCER

Built by BURNS CONSTRUCTION CO.

BURNS
REALTY & TRUST CO.

The D.C. Burns Realty &
Trust Company found itself
in the national spotlight
when *Life* magazine ran
this ad showcasing Burns'
'Operation Trade Secrets'
home in 1953. The home is
at 2995 South York Street.

car, he gathered a tiny group of home builders, and the seeds were planted for the Home Builders Association of Metro Denver.

D. C. Burns died in 1939, one decade after the stock market crashed. Thousands of Denverites were still out of work. The company had moved to the Burns Vault Building at 26th and Acoma. Franklin became Vice President of the firm, and at the age of 28, he was President. Fifty years from the turn of the century, The D. C. Burns Realty & Trust Company had sold more than five thousand homes; one thousand of them built by the firm. With no indoor plumbing, the homes offered a privy out back.

To honor the founder and perpetuate his name, Franklin deeded property at Colorado Boulevard and Alameda Avenue to the City and County of Denver, with the stipulation that it be used for a park. In ensuing years, Franklin won a battle with the City to keep it a park, which today, is dotted with numerous abstract sculptures. Aurora's Burns United Methodist Church pays homage to Franklin's mother, Florilla Burns.

Like his predecessor, Franklin proved to be a trend-setter in his own right. Since their first $1,250.00 home in 1939, Burns Construction Company prospered, partly through the assistance and advice of the Federal Housing Administration and the Veterans Administration. Franklin was among the first to offer homes financed by the Federal Housing Authority. The firm spent years building housing for the enlisted men and women stationed at Lowry Air Force Base and Fitzsimons (a World War I relic) Army Hospital complex. The city of Aurora went from a sleepy 'tumbleweed' suburb into a sprawling community during this rapid build-out, providing housing to thousands of soldiers during World War II.

Burns continued to frontier Denver's 'subdivision' movement. Prior to the Burns Brentwood subdivision, near Federal Boulevard and West Evans Avenue, the plan of buying a large farm, putting in utility mains and streets, and securing city annexation was uncommon. Gunnison Heights, Cherry Hills Vista, and Burns Aurora soon followed Burns Brentwood.

As a young World War II veteran himself, a DU graduate, and the grandson of two real estate men, Franklin was sympathetic to the plight of veterans returning to civilian life in Denver. After the war, Franklin designed and patented his "Handyman House." Burns Construction would 'frame out' new, low-cost houses, add indoor plumbing, and sell them to GIs who could complete the finish work themselves.

Nearly 300 veterans found the homes of their dreams in Brentwood, a development that was conceived while Franklin was home for a one-week furlough from the Army. Acreage was reserved for shopping (the Brentwood Shopping Center), a new Catholic parish (Church of All Saints), and a Denver public high school (Abraham Lincoln High School).

Veterans who were not 'handy' cherished Brentwood's city locale, desirable suburban setting, and a quality-constructed Burns home with such modern conveniences as an automatic home laundry with Bendix® washers built in.

In 1949, Burns Construction completed over 500 homes in the City of Denver — the most homes that had ever been completed in one year, by any builder, in the State of Colorado.

Burns' business savvy recognized the need to assure the sale of these homes. He built a sales organization that was competent and dedicated to serving the public. Burns also realized that no company could grow in stature unless it stood behind its product; so, in honor of the company's 50th anniversary, he introduced a written 'Homeowner's Construction Warranty.' The D.C. Burns Realty & Trust Company Warranty, a simple pledge to the home buyer that Burns Realty was proud to stand behind Burns Better-Built Bungalows, set the precedent for today's homeowner warranties. The burgeoning company launched an aggressive advertising campaign, and 'Burns Better-Built Bungalows' became a sign of the times.

The Duke and Duchess of Denver Development, Franklin and Joy Burns, relax in the gorgeous Penthouse Suite of Denver's World Trade Center — the company's headquarters since 1986. The city they helped build, and continue to help thrive, stretches out across the horizon.

The D.C. Burns Realty & Trust Company received national attention in 1953 when *Life* magazine featured a Burns home from the Cherry Hills Vista subdivision in the National Association of Home Builders' 'Operation Trade Secrets Home.' The NAHB spearheaded the idea to incorporate all new ideas, or 'trade secrets,' used by builders in every part of the country. These secret ideas were put into working plans for a house that combined the most logical use of materials and designs, with the most livability, for the least cost.

The result? A modern, uncluttered dream home that represented the last word in convenience, comfort, economy, distinctive use of materials and functional ideas. The house of (trade) secrets, at 2995 South York, had an unequalled view of the Rockies, with unlimited furniture arrangements possible in each room. Bedroom doors led onto an enclosed patio, while complete bath plus a powder room added a 'dream house' touch. An overflow crowd of 4,500 home-seekers saw the home. It became so popular that the very same model sprang up in fourteen states.

Burns' residential home building and selling branched out in many areas. By 1955, Burns Enterprises' highly diversified holdings consisted of nearly 70 legal entities which included housing developments, construction companies, investment companies, an insurance agency, an electrical equipment company, a rental company, and a savings and loan association.

But it wasn't all work and no play for Franklin, a divorcee and father of two sons. In 1958, Franklin found love the second time around when he met Texas businesswoman Joy Steelman Colwick at the Cherry Hills Country Club. It was love at first sight, and the two wed in 1960. Joy went on to blaze her own trail as a premiere Denver civitan and business leader.

The Burnses implemented a real estate acquisition and investment program for the firm during home building's peaks and valleys in 1960's and 1970's. In 1965 and 1966, less than 6,000 building permits for single-family homes were issued in the metro area, but in 1973, 19,000 permits were written. Commercial real estate also skyrocketed.

In 1976, The National Home Builders' Housing Hall of Fame was initiated to honor those whose outstanding achievements made possible the housing of millions of American families. Franklin was the first home builder inducted into the Housing Hall of Fame in 1977, recognized for his achievements in the industry during the 1940s. He was inducted again, honorarily, in 1984. Franklin's face and many accomplishments are memorialized by bronze plaques on permanent display at the National Housing Center in Washington, D.C.

All together, The D. C. Burns Realty and Trust Company has developed more than 14,000 residential and commercial projects valued at more than $129 million. These include Green Mountain Plaza, the Boettcher School for the Handicapped, Southern Hills, and Cherry Hills Vista, as well as other sites located in Utah, Nevada, and Puerto Rico.

After resting on its laurels during the boom and bust cycle of the 1980's, the firm aggressively re-entered the commercial marketplace in the early 1990's. A new brokerage division actively marketed the firm's commercial listings for sales and leasing and to represent the firm's equity partners in Denver-area investments. Top-drawer professionals with years of Denver market experience were hired to make the plan work. Burns was successful in selling listing and existing assets, representing properties valued at more than $20 million, in order to implement new investment strategies for the coming millennium.

Franklin has been involved as Director and President of the Homebuilders Association of Metro Denver and as Secretary and Treasurer of the National Association of Homebuilders. A history of sound land use and urban development, coupled with Franklin's years of service with the Urban Land Institute, earned him ULI's highest honor- Emeritus Member- in 1986. He was a charter member of the Denver Urban Renewal Commission, served on the Denver Planning Commission and the governing boards for the Denver Symphony, Central City Opera, Mount Airy and Mercy Hospitals, and the 100 Club- which aids families of police officers and firefighters who have fallen in the line of duty. He has been a Director of the United Bank of Denver, and he holds an honorary Doctorate of Humane Letters from the University of Denver. Franklin is a major Republican Party benefactor, and is personal friends with numerous past Presidents and political dignitaries.

Joy was instrumental in the founding of Denver's Women's Bank, and was the first woman ever elected to Chair the University of Denver's Board of Trustees. She is a member of the Mayor's Business Leaders Council. She is past Chairwoman of the Denver Metro Convention & Visitors Bureau, and a member of the 9 Who Care Board of Governors.

Today, The D. C. Burns Realty and Trust Company owns large tracts of land in Douglas County, and continues to manage its properties from the gorgeous Penthouse Suite of Denver's World Trade Center — the business' home since 1986.

Franklin has semi-retired. Joy took the reins of Presidency in 1996, which she juggles with the Presidency of her hotel, The Burnsley.

The D. C. Burns Realty & Trust Company has successfully grappled with nearly a century of the dynamics of Denver's fluctuating marketplace. The significant contributions that the firm, its holdings, and the Burnses have made are an infinite legacy of benevolence, vision, performance, integrity, and success in the growth of the Queen City's suburbia and metropolis.

Representative of the many commercial properties that The D.C. Burns Realty & Trust Company manages today is the office building at 100 Inverness Terrace East.

Burns Realty continues to be a company to reckon with on the commercial real estate front. Its future will be guided by the same principles as its past- the reliability of a solid, ethical real estate firm that fosters goodwill and instills confidence in the people of our fair city.

AMES CONSTRUCTION INC.

Some of Denver's most famous interchanges represent the work of the Denver division of Ames Construction Inc., including the "Mousetrap" interchange of I-25 and I-70, the interchange of I-70 and Wadsworth, and an interchange under construction on E-470.

The roads and runways at Denver International Airport, the "mousetrap" interchange of I-25 and I-70, and the E-470 beltway are all familiar structures to those who live in or visit Denver.

All three of these massive projects represent the work of the Denver division of Ames Construction Inc. Ames has been located in the city since 1980 and employs between 400 and 500 people in Colorado, depending on the season and the division's work volume.

Ames Construction is a general contractor specializing in the heavy civil and highway segments of the construction industry. Typical projects involve self-performing earthwork, large-diameter piping, structural concrete and bridge construction work.

The company has also provided construction services for the new Cresson Mine at the historic Cripple Creek Mining District.

Ames Construction was founded in 1960 as a small local commercial earthwork contractor in Minnesota. Founder Richard J. Ames serves as the private company's president and secretary. Raymond G. Ames is vice-president and treasurer.

Ames also performs mine development and contract mining services for the metallic and non-metallic mining industry. The company possesses one of the largest contractor-owned fleets of earth-moving and mining equipment in the country.

In addition, Ames has performed major earthwork and piping contracts for many large power plants, water and wastewater treatment plants, and water supply and flood control dams and reservoirs throughout the midwestern and western United States.

Other notable Ames' projects in Denver and Colorado include the interchange of I-70 and Wadsworth, the interchange of I-76 and I-25, and a multi-level cantilevered pre-stressed concrete structure in Glenwood Canyon along the Colorado River.

Ames is headquartered in Burnsville, Minnesota, a southern suburb of Minneapolis. It maintains permanent regional offices in Denver, Phoenix and Salt Lake City, and a satellite office in Carlin, Nevada. In 1997,

the Denver division will occupy a new 15,000-square-foot office in the Gateway Industrial Park in Aurora, while maintaining its equipment and shop facilities at a site a few miles east of there.

Ames Construction has completed projects in 24 states and Uzbekistan, and has a subsidiary currently bidding on mining projects in Mexico. In 1996, the company employed 1,500 people and posted construction volume in excess of $200 million.

In all of its highway, mining and heavy industrial projects, Ames is committed to working in harmony with the environment. The company offers special expertise in the clean-up of hazardous waste.

In Denver, Ames supports a number of charities and community improvement projects. In 1992, the company established a scholarship at the engineering school of the University of Colorado in Boulder as a memorial to William "Bill" Smith, former director of aviation and director of public works for the City and County of Denver.

Ames Construction, founded more than 35 years ago, has succeeded by putting into practice the fundamental principles of a strong work ethic, the free enterprise system, and an uncompromising commitment to quality.

Mining

Ames Construction has been involved in some of the largest mining projects in the country, performing both construction-related work and contract mining. The company's scope of work includes all types of earthwork, process piping, concrete foundation and

In Colorado, Ames Construction has constructed leach pads and other mine development work for the new Cresson Mine, located in the Historic Cripple Creek Mining District.

....

MINING CLIENTS INCLUDE:

American Barrick Resources Corporation

Asarco

Atlas Gold Mining Inc.

BHP Copper

Brush Wellman, Inc.

Cyprus Amax Minerals Company

Independence Mining Company Inc.

Kennecott Corporation

Newmont Gold Company

North American Coal Corporation

Pegasus Gold Inc.

Phelps Dodge Mining Company

Placer Dome U.S., Inc.

Round Mountain Gold Corporation

miscellaneous steel and equipment erection.

Contract mining includes haul-road construction, pre-production stripping and ore mining. Recent projects include copper mine modernization, new gold mines and gold mine expansion.

In Colorado, Ames Construction has constructed leach pads and other mine development work for the new Cresson Mine, located 20 miles west of Colorado Springs in the historic Cripple Creek Mining District. This new open-pit heap-leach mine operation, which is owned by a joint venture of Cripple Creek and Victor Gold Mining Company, commenced operation in 1995.

Denver International Airport

When ground was broken for Denver International Airport in 1989, Ames Construction was the first major contractor on the site. Eventually, Ames was awarded seven prime contracts at DIA for grading, drainage and piping work — contracts that totaled $250 million. Over a seven-year period, Ames moved more than 108 million cubic yards of earthwork, installed more than 90 miles of large diameter pipe, and placed more than 80,000 cubic yards of concrete at Denver International Airport.

CARMEL COMPANIES

Denver residents fit a unique profile. They are younger than the national average, they are better educated and they lead a more active lifestyle. Attracted by the wealth of opportunities the city has to offer, Denver residents are likely to have moved here from another part of the country.

All of these characteristics define the kind of people who look to the apartment and condominium market to meet their need for high quality, well-managed housing — at a price they can afford.

Since 1965, Denver-based Carmel Companies has been directly involved in the development and management of more than 8,500 apartment units in 30 complexes in the United States. Carmel Companies, the largest owner and manager of apartment homes in the state, employs more than 300 people. The story of Carmel Companies' success is the story of Kal Zeff — the company's founder, president and owner.

Kal Zeff, a native of Israel, came to the United States to do graduate work in 1954 after obtaining his Bachelor of Science degree in engineering from the Israel Institute of Technology, which was located on Mount Carmel. He earned his Masters of Science degree from the University of Colorado in 1956. Prior to 1960, he served as a construction, structural and soil engineer for various firms in Israel and Denver.

In 1960, Zeff founded Geotek Consultants, a successful geotechnical (soil) engineering firm, which he sold in 1986. In 1965, in a venture capitalized by the earnings from his engineering business, Zeff formed the beginning of Carmel Companies when he built his first 40-unit apartment complex.

With only two employees, Zeff continued to develop additional apartment projects, including the Lancelot Apartments in 1967. With Stuart Ohlson as the architect, the Lancelot project was innovative for its time, employing cutting-edge technology to become the first mid-rise, pre-stressed, pre-cast concrete structure in the United States. The main structure was erected in less than a month and the project was completed at a cost of $10 per foot, an accomplishment that was recognized by an award from the concrete industry.

In the 1970s, Zeff continued to develop and manage apartments, including the 573-unit Spyglass Apartments in Denver and the 612-unit Willows Lakeshore Apartments in Lakewood.

Carmel Companies, founded in 1965 by Kal Zeff, is the largest owner and manager of apartment homes in Colorado.

Michael Zeff is president of Carmel Homes, a home-building division of Carmel Companies that was established in 1986.

Ron Zeff, executive vice president of Carmel Companies, is responsible for new apartment development and acquisitions.

The 612-unit Willows Lakeshore Apartments, developed by Carmel Companies in the 1970s, is located in Lakewood.

In the late 1970s and early 1980s, Zeff broadened the company's base by building townhomes and condominiums, meeting sharp market demand by building a few thousand units in a very short time. Using resourceful financing techniques, including warehousing his own mortgages during this high-interest-rate period, Zeff developed and sold more than 4,000 townhomes and condominiums in 10 different projects during this period.

With the completion of Cherry Tower in 1982, Carmel Companies entered the field of commercial development. Cherry Tower, a 16-story, 225,000-square-foot office building, is located at 950 South Cherry Street in southeast Denver. It was designed by architect Stuart Ohlson and houses the central offices of Carmel Companies on its eleventh floor. Owned and managed by Zeff, Cherry Tower has won awards for its unique design. The company also maintains an office in the San Francisco suburb of Burlingame, at 839 Mitten.

Lancelot Apartments, an early project designed by Stuart Ohlson and built in 1967, was awarded for its innovation by the concrete industry.

The mid-1980s proved to be a very exciting time for Carmel Companies. Zeff recognized the availability of weekly low-floater tax-free financing as a unique — although not entirely risk-free — opportunity to build apartment homes. This type of financing resulted in a

very low long-term interest rate, which increased the profitability of apartment community development. It was perceived as God's gift to developers.

Zeff acquired numerous parcels of land at this time and received several loan commitments, which he used to develop several thousand apartment homes in Denver, Lakewood and Arapahoe County — including Greenwood Point, Coventry Village, Central Park, The Village at Loretto Heights and The Hamptons.

With the completion of Cherry Tower in 1982, Carmel Companies entered the field of commercial development. Carmel Companies houses the central offices of Carmel Companies on the eleventh floor.

Capitalizing on a unique financing opportunity, Carmel Companies developed several thousand apartment homes during the mid-1980s — including The Village at Loretto Heights.

From 1988 to 1991, Denver suffered a severe economic contraction. Zeff kept the company on a steady plan that emphasized its strength and competitive advantage, including low interest rates. By not over-leveraging his properties and by continuing to reinvest in the properties without deferring maintenance, Carmel was able to keep its properties at a higher occupancy level than its competitors.

By forming Carmel Homes in 1986, Zeff was able to keep Carmel's construction team together by building homes through this slow period in multi-family development. In the latter part of 1991, with apartment occupancy and rental rates climbing once again, Zeff returned his attention to his first love — multi-family development.

In 1991, Carmel Companies began to develop the latest trends in apartment development, including massive clubhouses with elaborate facilities and apartment units with high ceilings, luxurious amenities and outstanding architectural design. During this time, Carmel Homes expanded with many successful projects.

Significant projects of the 1990s include The Villas at Homestead, The Covington, The Windsor, The Renaissance, The Bentley, The Waterford, Hanover Square Condominiums, Carmel Homes at Three

Lakes and Carmel Homes at Highlands Ranch. Out-of-state projects include The Plantation in Mississippi, Chesapeake Bay in the California market and Autumn Chase in Texas.

Carmel Companies also expanded its operations into both retail development and the energy field. Central Park Shopping Center is an Albertson's-anchored mall in southeast Denver. Zeff also formed CDM Oil & Gas, with wells in Colorado, Montana, Louisiana and Texas and a natural gas pipeline in northern Colorado. CDM Hydroelectric was formed to develop, own and manage a hydroelectric plant in Idaho.

In the 1990s, Carmel Companies'
luxurious apartment developments featured massive
clubhouses — like those at The Windsor (left)
and The Covington (above).

Zeff's sons have joined him in his endeavors. Michael Zeff is the president of Carmel Homes and Ron Zeff is the executive vice president of Carmel Companies. Ron Zeff, who was previously a partner with Trammell Crow Residential in San Francisco, is primarily responsible for new apartment development and acquisitions. He received his BA from the University of California at Berkeley and his MBA from the Stanford Graduate School of Business. Several joint ventures have been achieved through the efforts of this new generation.

Kal Zeff attributes his success to the tremendous vibrancy and economic expansion of the Denver area. Without question, the Zeff family's dedication to quality and its unique pride in long-term ownership have contributed to Carmel Companies' success and continue to point to a vibrant future.

THE HOUSING AUTHORITY OF THE CITY AND COUNTY OF DENVER

Introduction

The Housing Authority of the City and County of Denver (DHA) is the largest public housing authority in the Rocky Mountain region. DHA provides quality subsidized housing to more than 20,000 low-to moderate-income residents of Denver. Just as significant, the Denver Housing Authority is also one of the highest-performing housing authorities in the nation. In 1996, for the fourth consecutive year DHA was rated as a "High Performing Housing Authority" by the U.S. Department of Housing and Urban Development (HUD) for its management practices, occupancy rates, rent collection, housing maintenance, unit turnaround, and resident initiatives. DHA is ranked number two in the nation on performance among large public housing authorities with more than 4,000 units.

History

In 1937, under the New Deal, Congress passed the Wagner-Steagall Act. Attached to this bill was the Housing Act of 1937. The Act was designed to create jobs, as well as provide federal funding to build safe, decent, and sanitary housing and to clear out slums and blighted areas in urban and rural communities. An integral part of the New Deal, the Act led to the establishment of more than 3,400 housing and redevelopment agencies across the country.

In the summer of 1938, Denver's City Council passed an ordinance creating the Housing Authority of the City and County of Denver, and in September of that year, Mayor Stapleton swore in DHA's first board of commissioners. Over the next two decades, DHA built 13 row-type family projects containing approximately 3,240 units. DHA identified neighborhoods most in need of assisted housing. DHA's first family development, Las Casitas Homes, originally housed war-time workers employed by the Rocky Mountain Arsenal and employees of what is now the Denver Federal Center.

The federal government never designed or intended the public housing system to be a "way of life" or an "end destination" for economically disadvantaged families. The original intent of public housing was to provide temporary housing for families whose head-of-household had been discharged from the military, and families displaced due to manufacturing plant shut-downs, illness, divorce, or a death in the family. The housing gave families a safe, comfortable place to live while providing the opportunity for families to stabilize their income and move from federal subsidized housing.

The 1960s brought the realization that the federal government needed to become more involved with public housing through the establishment of housing

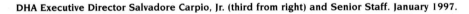

DHA Executive Director Salvadore Carpio, Jr. (third from right) and Senior Staff. January 1997.

standards. In 1964, the U.S. Department of Housing and Urban Development was created. HUD established uniform housing regulations and controlled the flow of federal dollars to public housing authorities across the nation. The Civil Rights Act of 1964, provide an avenue for cities and communities to better address the housing needs of the economically disadvantaged and other racial, age, and gender discrimination practices.

In 1965, DHA began diversifying its public housing stock by constructing the first of ten elderly high-rises for Denver's low income senior population. Over the next 15 years, in addition to completing the construction of 1,236 high-rise units, DHA constructed 792 dispersed housing units consisting of single-family homes, duplexes, four-plexes, and small cluster units located throughout the city.

DHA enthusiastically embraced the 1974 Fair Housing Act's Section 8 program, which was designed to give eligible residents greater freedom of choice in locating housing suitable to their needs. Under the Section 8 program, DHA issues certificates or vouchers to eligible Denver residents for subsidized housing with private-sector landlords whose rental properties meet the housing quality standards and who make their properties available to DHA clients. The program was welcomed by DHA as a vehicle to provide incentives to eligible families and create the opportunity for upward mobility for highly motivated public housing residents.

In the 1980s, DHA was able to continue to make housing improvements at a time when federal funding for public housing had been severely cut by its demonstrated well-managed community planning and budget management capabilities in all program areas. Through non federal funding, DHA was able to acquire, market, and sell the newly acquired properties to developers to create housing in and around downtown Denver as part of the City's downtown housing plan. Also, DHA continued to acquire homes that were in disrepair and becoming a blight on the neighborhoods throughout the city. Many of the homes were sold to first-time home buyers to help stabilize neighborhoods.

DHA Today

Today, through the DHA Comprehensive Grant Program, DHA uses its federal funds to renovate, rehabilitate, and modernize its public housing stock. By reducing density in family row-type developments and by changing unit configuration to improve livability in the high-rise apartments, DHA has brought up and maintained its properties to the highest established housing standards. From start to finish, DHA works closely with the residents and the community to ensure the physical improvements reflect

and add to Denver's distinctive neighborhoods and wealth of cultural diversity to positively "change the face of public housing."

As it continues to "change the face of public housing" DHA works closely with residents to increase opportunities to move to self-sufficiency. DHA coordinates with local community based organizations, the private sector, and other public agencies to provide early childhood education, summer youth employment programs, youth leadership, employment and training programs and home-ownership opportunities.

DHA Platte Valley Homes in Denver's Curtis Park Neighborhood Modernization. Energy-efficient lighting and open space. Summer 1996.

Much of DHA's success can be attributed to its management improvement program which utilizes improved and efficient management tools such as automated management information systems, a computerized maintenance tracking system, a customer-friendly application process, videotape of housing options, and other property management techniques to sustain DHA as a high-performing housing authority.

DHA has a strong financial base, with total assets in excess of $180 million dollars. In addition, DHA has established internal financial and management controls to ensure its assets are properly safeguarded. As a result, DHA is the only public housing authority in the nation that has been recognized by the Government Financial Officers Association for both its Comprehensive Budget "Distinguished Budget Presentation Award" and the Comprehensive Annual Financial Report "Certificate of Achievement in Excellence in Financial Reporting" every year since 1988.

The following public housing initiatives exemplify DHA's progressive and innovative low-income housing programs: successful implementation and completion of DHA's replacement housing program; the Urban Revitalization Demonstration Program at Quigg Newton Homes also known as HOPE VI; the Campus of Learners at the newly redeveloped North Lincoln Park Homes; and DHA's Designated Senior Housing.

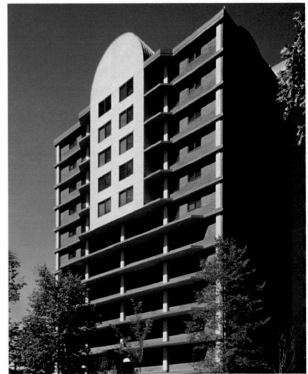

DHA Walsh Manor Senior Highrise in Southwest Denver.
Complete renovation interior and exterior, summer 1996.

Lastly, DHA continues to excel in the administration and management of the HUD Section 8 program. Since 1995, under the HUD-approved "lottery" application process for potential Section 8 residents, DHA has eliminated fraud and abuse in the distribution of Section 8 certificates and vouchers. In 1996, DHA received the Section 8 Administration Award and the Section 8 Innovation Award from the National Association of Housing and Redevelopment Organizations in recognition of its management practices.

DHA Dispersed Housing in Central Denver.
Single-family home, summer 1996.

DHA Vision for 2002

The mission of the Denver Housing Authority is to provide a variety of affordable housing opportunities for low- and moderate-income people, while supporting and promoting activities which enhance the quality of life for residents; operating in an environment of respect, openness, fairness and sensitivity; complying with legal and regulatory guidelines; and providing a professional work environment for employees. To accomplish this mission, DHA's vision

DHA Dispersed Home in Southwest Denver. Single-family home and handicapped accessible, summer 1996.

DHA Dispersed Single-Family Homes, Montbello Neighborhood in East Denver, summer 1996.

for the year 2002 will strive to reduce DHA reliance on existing HUD funding by identifying and securing new sources of operating revenues, cost reduction strategies, capital improvement and investment dollars to meet DHA capital needs.

Into the year 2002, as the largest housing authority in the Rocky Mountain region DHA will build its capacity in the development and acquisition of a variety of housing and mixed-use developments while seeking to stimulate and create housing opportunities for all sectors of Denver's housing market. This will include the development of market-rate housing in Denver for use as mixed-income housing utilizing market-rate rentals and Section 8 rentals.

Additionally, under this new vision, DHA will continue to promote, coordinate and encourage the opportunity for upward mobility and long term self-sufficiency of families.

In conclusion, DHA recognizes the challenges and opportunities for public housing in the City and County of Denver and across the nation. But, DHA under the established leadership of the board of commissioners, the mayor, the city, local community-based organizations, and local housing providers — DHA will build its capabilities to rise above the changing political, social and economic trends and

Vision 2002 Statement

DHA *through strong communications, revenue expansion, and property development, will enhance our residents' self-sufficiency, strengthen communities, improve our financial stability and increase Denver's affordable housing stock.*

continue to successfully provide affordable safe, decent, and sanitary housing for the working class of the City and County and Denver while also promoting ... **People Not Projects.**

ROCKY MOUNTAIN PRESTRESS, INC.

The United Bank Tower in Colorado Springs.

Constructing Denver's past and building the bustling city's future skyline takes on literal meaning for Rocky Mountain Prestress, Inc.

RMP, founded in 1958, manufactures and installs high-quality prestressed and precast concrete units

for the construction industry. A national leader, the firm's products are used for office and industrial buildings, highways and bridges, warehouses, institutional facilities and more.

An airborne traveler's first moments in Denver are on RMP's turf — the Denver International Airport. Virtually every structure at the world's third-largest airport has RMP's signature on it. Over 400 million pounds of concrete erected the airport's control tower, underground tunnel and parking facilities which, alone, account for more than 17,000 pieces of concrete and

4.5 million square feet. Even a DIA rental car outlet, its central plant, hangars, fire stations and exterior walls come courtesy of Rocky Mountain Prestress.

When the Colorado Rockies took over Coors Field in 1993, RMP made it possible for 50,249 people to jump to their collective feet when Dante Bichette swatted the first Rockies' home run at the spacious stadium. RMP manufactured and installed the triple-bleacher sections and designed their complex geometric shapes.

About 500 employees contribute to the company's award-winning talents that are featured predominantly in Colorado, but also stand tall in San Francisco and Honolulu. While claiming distinction as one of the nation's largest manufacturers and installers of precast and prestressed concrete, RMP is firmly committed to the construction needs of metro Denver and the Front Range.

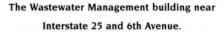

The Wastewater Management building near Interstate 25 and 6th Avenue.

The Jefferson County Justice Center in Golden.

Precasting is almost complete for
Denver International Airport's parking structures,
in the foreground.

Among its flagship projects in the state are the Colorado Convention Center; the Aurora Justice Center; the Jefferson County Government Center; Waste Water Management; Merrill Lynch at the Denver Meridian Campus; the Dominion Plaza and many more structures, including the parking structures and the exterior of Sak's 5th Avenue at the Cherry Creek Shopping Mall.

The organization has both architectural and structural manufacturing plants in Denver — two of the largest in the country — plus a manufacturing plant on the island of Guam. Because the city of Denver is at the nation's forefront of precast buildings per capita, RMP is often involved in up to 50 projects at a time. Rocky Mountain Prestress has aided the state's rapid growth by providing products for bridges throughout the Front Range, as well as for millions of square feet of offices and apartments.

The company's focus is twofold:

- structural products. These include the members that support a structure — floors, roofs, columns, beams, walls, stairs and specialty items like bridge girders.

The Aurora Municipal Justice Center's dome was precast
by Rocky Mountain Prestress.

RMP's quality shines in the
dome, rows, columns and
staircase at the Aurora
Municipal Justice Center.

- architectural products. RMP provides services and products to enhance a building's exterior facade and aesthetics through an unlimited array of colors, textures and detailing.

The Colorado Convention Center, located in
Downtown Denver.

Precasting, a method of producing concrete, is
conducted at the company's plants where the
pieces — some as heavy as 80 tons and measuring
160 feet in length — are hauled to and installed on
the job sites. Prestressed concrete is inherently fire-

proof, aesthetically pleasing, structurally sound
and less vulnerable to weather conditions, which
makes it a favorite building material in Denver,
Colorado Springs, Steamboat Springs, Vail, Aspen,
Grand Junction, Durango, Basalt, Ft. Morgan and
other towns that boast of Rocky Mountain Prestress'
products.

To accommodate each project's varying needs,
RMP provides a customized product through its cutting edge computer operations. Several of the industry's finest design engineers are employed at the
Denver-based facility, where a significant percentage
of detailing is performed via an in-house designed
CAD programming system. The industry's inherently
high-tech needs demand computer expertise for
designing and drafting products for specific projects.
The CAD system at Rocky Mountain Prestress allows
for creation of production drawings, scheduling and
material control, and assures the company's commitment to quality and safety.

A member of the Prestressed Concrete Institute
and the Colorado Prestressers Association, RMP's
community-minded approach includes donations to
a number of local civic organizations.

From storefront signage to the nation's largest airport, Rocky Mountain Prestress is shaping the future
of Denver with visionary solutions.

A parking structure at the Cherry Creek Shopping Center.

Concrete Coring Company

When a new entrance had to be built on C-470 to provide access to Park Meadows, someone had to saw and seal the expansion joints in the concrete before it could be opened to traffic.

When the old Stapleton Airport runway bridges over I-70 were demolished, someone had to even out the rough road surfaces that were left behind.

When the Tattered Cover bookstore in Cherry Creek North wanted to install a three-story stairway, someone had to cut through the building's concrete floors.

In all of these cases, that "someone" was Concrete Coring Company — the largest sawing and drilling company in Colorado. In addition, the family-owned company is one of only a handful of women-owned construction subcontractors in the state.

Concrete Coring Company, which was founded in 1968, provides a wide variety of construction services.

Concrete Coring Company offers joint sawing and sealing for almost any condition. Joint sawing and sealing is generally performed on highways to help relieve stress between the slabs of concrete, allowing them to move and keeping them from cracking.

The company also provides grinding and grooving services so that highways, parking lots and airport runways will conform to state and FAA standards.

Grinding evens out rough surfaces, allowing for safer and smoother travel. Grooving improves the safety and durability of paved surfaces by providing better traction and drainage.

The dust- and vibration-free coring of walls, floors and ceilings is also included in Concrete Coring Company's capabilities. The coring is done in a precise manner and ranges from one-inch to 36-inch diameter cores cut at various angles and up to one hundred feet deep.

Concrete Coring Company provides wall sawing that is dust- and vibration-free and can be done up to depths of 24 inches. Both coring and wall sawing can be performed through concrete, brick, block, stone and asphalt surfaces.

Another service that is available from Concrete Coring Company is slab sawing. Slab sawing can be done up to a 24-inch depth and can be performed with either an electric or gas saw. Decorative or pattern sawing is also available.

Concrete Coring Company maintains a fleet of "self-contained" service vehicles with on-board water and power sources. The company's long-term employees draw on a broad range of experience in coming up with creative solutions to difficult problems.

Concrete Coring Company is based in a remodeled home just north of downtown and has branches in Colorado Springs and Fort Collins. The company employs about 40 people and in 1995 posted sales of more than $4 million. The company contributes to Denver Children's Hospital and is a corporate circle partner of the Denver Zoo.

Since 1968, Concrete Coring Company has provided sawing and drilling services to the contractors and residents of Colorado and the surrounding region.

FAR LEFT: Concrete Coring Company, a woman-owned business, is the largest sawing and drilling company in Colorado.

BELOW: Concrete Coring Company offers a wide variety of construction services: joint sawing, sealing, grinding and grooving of surfaces plus coring of walls, floors and ceilings, wall sawing and slab sawing.

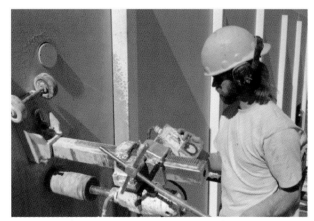

APARTMENT FINDERS INTERNATIONAL

It was 1970, and Denver was growing fast! The oil companies were expanding by leaps and bounds, and the Petroleum Club downtown was the place to see and be seen at lunch time.

It was also the time that Tom Luinstra brought his young family from Wichita, Kansas in search of new business opportunities. Tom had grown up in a family that owned rental property and had experienced first hand what property owners go through to fill vacant units. With all the growth taking place...and possibly inspired by his own family's apartment search in an unfamiliar environment...Tom realized residents moving to the Denver metropolitan area needed help in finding their new home, suited both to their needs and financial parameters.

Tom began to knock on apartment manager's doors, proposing they list their properties with Apartment Finders Int'l (AFI) a new company whose business is locating qualified prospects for vacant apartments.

He then purchased an old gas station building in a strategic location and set up his first three employees with notebooks filled with information and descriptions of each apartment complex he had contacted: prices, amenities, availability, etc. Tom began advertising, and Apartment Finders International was born!

In subsequent years, with the advent of computers, Tom developed his own software programs to replace all that handwork, so clients could phone or come in, delineate the specifics of location, amenities, and price and...Viola!...the computer sorted through hundreds of possibilities and produced introduction cards to the properties that fit a client's requests. Maps were marked to orient newcomers, and they were on their way to finding a new home. Today clients are still helped the old fashioned way (customer service) as well as with fax machines, E-mail and on-line through the internet. From high rises to garden apartments; condominiums to houses Apartment Finders Int'l has truly become Denver's "Specialist in Apartment Leasing."

> ### "Specialist in Apartment Leasing"

Meanwhile, too, the gas station building was outgrown and blossomed into the bright, beautiful, two-story red brick building Tom designed to welcome all those new clients.

Denver had "boom years" (and, sadly some "bust years," as well), but Apartment Finders had found that niche of filling an ongoing need with a very valuable service that could sustain it through all the city's changes. The service was quick, eased the pain of establishing a new home, and it was "Free."

The number of employees has grown from that original three to seventeen full-time employees with

Apartment Finders International began here, in what was originally, a gas station.

two metro Denver locations, and planned expansion into other areas of this burgeoning metro area.

The service today encompasses far more apartments (some 250,000 units) than even Tom could have envisioned on that day in 1970 when Denver opened up his dream of establishing a service business in Colorado. Many homeowners and condo owners have found AFI to be a boon to them, as well, in locating and qualifying good tenants to fill their vacant properties.

Since starting in 1970 Apartment Finders has help over half a million people find rentals in metro Denver. Apartment Finders Int'l truly does *"Rent Denver Free."*

In the intervening years, Tom became a Certified Property Manager through the Institute of Real Estate Management. Tom expanded AFI involvement in Denver's community by working with various Chambers of Commerce, the Denver and National Apartment Association, Bethesda Psyche-Health Center, Family Homestead, and many others. With the able support of his wife Carol, working with him in both business and family, Tom raised two sons, Jeff and Scott, who have now taken their place as contributing members of the Denver community.

Tom and Carol Luinstra

"Rent Denver Free"

Apartment Finders is readily found in every home and business in Denver by way of it's advertisement on the back cover of the U. S. West Phone Book. AFI will continue to make itself highly visible in this and many new and innovative ways, including the Internet.

Through whatever channel it flows in the future, the vision will remain the same that Tom imagined that day in 1970 when it all began…that a vital, growing city will always need a service to direct its new and mobile residents to that perfect home that fits their needs. This is a service that is continually fed by new residents, growing families, and those "moving up" or "moving on," so it looks to be a service that has a permanent place in Denver's future.

AFI has grown with Denver.

BROOKFIELD

The Brookfield group of commercial real estate companies owns and manages more office space in the heart of Downtown Denver than any other company — almost 2.4 million square feet.

In fact, nearly one out of every ten downtown employees works in a building owned and managed by Brookfield. This is more than the total population of many small cities!

Brookfield's downtown properties, both winners of the BOMA Office Building of the Year Award, include the landmark Republic Plaza and the twin-towered World Trade Center. Brookfield also manages and has a 50 percent interest in the Colorado State Bank Building.

Republic Plaza, Denver's tallest office building and a prominent local landmark, is the most expensive and technically advanced building ever built in the city.

BELOW: Republic Plaza and the World Trade Center both boast attractive plazas — together covering two city blocks — that soften the hard edges of "Wall Street West."

Republic Plaza and the World Trade Center both feature attractive plazas that serve as green spaces and gathering places for Downtown Denver workers, tourists, shoppers and residents.

On the south side of Republic Plaza, opening onto the city's Sixteenth Street Pedestrian Mall, is a sun-filled, attractively landscaped plaza featuring an array of small shops and restaurants. During the summer months, Brookfield sponsors a series of lunchtime concerts on this plaza for the enjoyment of the downtown community.

The plaza at the World Trade Center, also adjacent to the pedestrian mall, showcases a sculpture commemorating the Rotary Club's worldwide campaign to eradicate polio. As the City of Denver considers well-publicised initiatives to make "Wall Street West" more user friendly, Brookfield is already doing more than its part.

Republic Plaza is Denver's tallest office building and a prominent local landmark. The most expensive and technically advanced building ever built in the city, Republic Plaza was completed in 1984 — just as the city's oil economy went bust. Republic Plaza is 714 feet tall and includes 56 stories.

Designed by Skidmore, Owings & Merrill and built of Sardinian granite, Republic Plaza includes 1.2 million square feet of office space, including three retail levels devoted to shops and restaurants.

This elegant building is renowned for its spacious three-story marble lobby, double deck elevators, day porters, executive car wash, security and smart-building features — and downtown Denver's only full-service office building concierge.

In an ongoing effort to integrate the arts into the workplace, Republic Plaza's "Art in Public Places" program regularly features major art exhibits of Colorado and regional artists.

Under Brookfield's financially secure ownership, Republic Plaza today offers Denver's top companies, including many law, accounting, and investment firms, a prestige address with spectacular Rocky Mountain views. The building also continues to house many companies associated with the oil and gas industries.

The Plaza at the World Trade Center showcases
a sculpture that commemorates the Rotary Club's
worldwide campaign to eradicate polio.

The World Trade Center
provides a central location
for public and private
resources that support
the Denver business
community's efforts
to participate in the
global economy.

Denver's World Trade Center, also designed by Skidmore, Owings & Merrill, consists of two 28-story octagonal towers clad in gray reflective glass. The towers were built in 1979 and 1980. The World Trade Center offers many of the same tenant services and activities as the neighboring Republic Plaza.

The World Trade Center provides a convenient central location for a wide variety of public and private resources that support local businesses in their efforts to participate in the global economy. It is one of about 170 world trade centers operating worldwide under the aegis of the World Trade Centers Association in New York.

Established in 1988, Denver's World Trade Center was a collaborative effort of the Colorado Office of Economic Development, the Greater Denver Chamber of Commerce, the U.S. Department of Commerce, Metropolitan State College and the buildings' owner.

The two towers offer convenient on-site access to worldwide communications, library and reference services, international travel and tours, educational programs and seminars, language and translation services, and information about and participation in international trade missions and shows.

The Colorado World Trade Center Association, of which Brookfield is a founding member, is located in the World Trade Center. In the early 1990s, the World Trade Center also housed the local organizing arm for World Youth Day, which attracted more than 65,000 young people and world-wide media attention to Denver.

Throughout the year, Brookfield uses its "community" newsletter to inform the 7,500 citizens of Republic Plaza and The World Trade Center of facility-based programs like blood drives, safety seminars, recycling programs and carpools. Holiday food, clothing and toy drives benefit Denver's needy children and families.

In addition to its downtown properties, Brookfield owns two suburban buildings, Highland Place II and Academy Place.

From the massive office buildings that dominate the city's skyline to the human-scale plazas and activities that provide a sense of community for the men and women who work in them — Brookfield has made a long-term commitment to Downtown Denver.

CRESTMOOR DOWNS

Denver's Luxury Apartment "Address of Distinction"

It is said that success happens when preparation meets opportunity. That's an accurate description of what sparked the development of Crestmoor Downs, south-east Denver's award winning, 710 unit luxury apartment community.

In the late 1960s, Crestmoor Down's co-founder, Paul Swalm, was sick and tired of being sick and tired. Having worked for other people for most of his adult life, Swalm wanted to be his own boss.

Crestmoor Downs developers and majority owners Paul Swalm and Roland Wilson.

ABOVE: High-rises and town-homes provide luxury living for a variety of lifestyles.

RIGHT: Just one of the many amenities for Crestmoor Downs' active residents.

bricks and mortar, which is where architect and co-founder Roland Wilson came in.

It was Wilson who had the idea of putting the large number of parking spaces that would be required for the development underground. The result was a beautiful marriage of opposites: multiple mid-rise apartment buildings and townhomes surrounded, not by parking lots, but by acres of parks, ponds, trees and lush flower beds.

Open space was an idea ahead of its time for an urban community built in the 1970s. But it wasn't just green belts that put — and kept — Crestmoor Downs firmly ahead of the pack. Although now well into its third decade of being a place that Denverites are proud to call home, Crestmoor Downs was seemingly designed and located with the fast paced, active lifestyle of the 21st century in mind.

Every amenity is included. Crestmoor Downs features quiet apartments with spacious floor plans, generous closet space, on-site mini-storage units, indoor and covered parking, and modern kitchens

Opportunity presented itself to Swalm in the form of a run down driving range near Alameda Avenue and Monaco Parkway. While others saw little more than a patch of weeds, Swalm saw potential — a site for what was destined to become one of Denver's largest and most successful luxury apartment communities.

While Swalm had the vision and a real-estate background that gave him a good feel for the financial angles, he needed help translating the dream into

that open onto large patios or balconies that command beautiful views of the surrounding parks and the mountains beyond.

For the fitness minded, there are indoor and out-door swimming pools, tennis, racquetball, and volley-

ball courts, saunas, exercise rooms, and even a playground for children. For get-togethers with friends, there are party and game rooms as well as a community center that features a big-screen TV.

Crestmoor Downs accommodates business needs by providing corporate rentals, office facilities, conference rooms, a beauty shop, and transportation services.

Include the less tangible amenities, such as gorgeous mountain views and tranquil, shaded walkways around the ponds and fountains, and one has a good idea why referrals from satisfied residents have been the best source of new customers since the day the doors opened.

Still, it hasn't been just on-site features which have made Crestmoor Down's residents so loyal that many have made it their home since the community began. Location, location and location are still the first three rules of successful real-estate development. And as the city has grown around it, Crestmoor's location has proven to be ideal. Everything is close at hand; business at the dynamic Denver Tech Center or exciting Downtown, shopping at the fabulous Cherry Creek Mall. Even the new Denver International Airport can be accessed in no more than 15 to 30 minutes.

Yet, convenience and amenities still don't fully account for Crestmoor Down's ongoing appeal to the many busy doctors, business owners, media personalities, and countless others who have made Crestmoor Downs their home over the years. What these busy people are looking for is the most valuable of commodities: time. At Crestmoor they find even that. With a "high touch" approach to maintenance and service, Crestmoor residents have more time to devote to the things that make life in Colorado so special. None of a resident's time needs to be invested in mowing lawns, shoveling snow, or painting trim. All these needs, and more, are promptly taken care of by Crestmoor's skilled and professional staff.

With so much success behind it, has Crestmoor Downs taken to resting on its laurels? Hardly. Under the still attentive eyes of founders Swalm and Wilson and their top-notch management team, upgrades, renovations, and capital improvements are the order of the day. Everyday.

Crestmoor's ongoing commitment to excellence is confirmed by the accolades it has won from its peers. In a recent recognition program sponsored by the Apartment Association of Metro-Denver, Crestmoor Downs received the following "Tributes" awards: Grand Award for Large Community Built Before 1980, Best Floor Plan for One Bedroom Unit, Best Community Presentation Built Before 1980, and Best Clubhouse.

But what of the future? Crestmoor Downs' proud legacy will be continued. Anchored as it is, in one of the most livable neighborhoods of one of the nation's most dynamic cities, the Crestmoor management team is determined to keep up the pace. And do all that is necessary to enable Crestmoor Downs to continue to deserve its reputation as Denver's luxury apartment "Address of Distinction."

Beautiful gardens and tranquil lakes create an open space environment unparalleled in Denver.

LEFT:
Spectacular landscaping creates a sophisticated environment in an urban setting.

FREDERICK ROSS COMPANY

Now Into Its Second Century and Defining Real Estate Services for the 21st Century

Frederick Ross Company, Colorado's oldest, largest, and most diversified commercial real estate company, has achieved preeminence in the Front Range marketplace and is leading the redefinition of real estate services among major independent real estate companies across the nation.

The Ross organization offers uncommon breadth and depth of services: Leasing, sales, and tenant representation brokerage; consulting for private- and public-sector clients; real estate management for office, retail, and industrial properties; development management; and investments.

Perhaps more important, Ross has succeeded in a rarely achieved integration and cross-fertilization of expertise among these disciplines. This synergistic relationship of specialties has enabled Ross to acquire a national client base and to deliver the highest levels of expertise to such projects as corporate master plans and portfolio analysis.

At the threshold of the 21st Century, Ross is proudly local in history, culture, and community commitment, but its business is hardly local in scope.

In the mid 1990s, Ross assignments ranged from the seat of government in Washington, DC, to the seat of innovation in the Silicon Valley. Ross teams were planning headquarters facilities as far north as Minneapolis and master planning corporate real estate in Atlanta and Sao Paulo, Brazil.

John P. Box

At the same time, Ross investment teams were working the capital markets to sell portfolios of investment properties and to arrange real estate financings for leading high technology companies to free up their real estate capital for new technology projects.

For CEO Jack Box, "minding the store" in the 1990s was as likely to mean joining partner Rich McClintock at the ground breaking for a new Ross project as flying to London in his role as Chairman of ONCOR International, the world's largest full service commercial real estate organization.

That Frederick Ross Company welcomes the 21st century from a position of unprecedented strength and optimism is tribute to the ever-expanding vision of succeeding generations of leadership. Ross executives, professionals, and staff are justly proud of having carried the Ross name across the continent and across oceans.

Young Frederick Ross Goes West

Few who ventured West in the 1880s had a bigger stake in the decision than did young Frederick Ross. When doctors in his native Vermont gave him little hope of surviving New England's bitter weather, he literally bet his life on Denver's high and dry climate.

He formed Ross Investment Company and became a force in Denver real estate. He also served in many civic and charitable activities and the Ross Trust he created donated funds for the construction of four Denver branch libraries.

The Hackstaff Generations

On Ross's death in 1938, Cyrus Hackstaff assumed the chairmanship and, with a view toward his own succession, brought his sons, Robert and Allan, into the company. Cyrus Hackstaff's leadership took Ross through the postwar boom years of the 1950s and '60s. He turned Ross over to his sons in 1970, with Robert, succeeding his father as CEO, and Allan focusing on property management.

Robert Hackstaff saw his stewardship as the company's "second phase." He made Ross more client- and transaction-oriented in the 1970s and brought additional changes:

- Ross Investment Group (RIG) was created in 1981 as an independent affiliate to pursue development opportunities under Richard G. McClintock, who today heads Ross investments under the banner of Westfield Development Corporation.

- Ross Consulting Group was created under Rick A. Pederson in 1982 to provide financial, economic, and market analysis for private and public sector clients. Consulting's Research Services have become the state's unquestioned leader in market data and analysis.
- ONCOR International was founded by Ross and three other companies to serve clients with real estate in multiple cities. Today ONCOR's 45 companies cover 200 markets worldwide.

In 1980 Ross ownership changed from a family-owned enterprise to a more diverse structure when six Ross executives, including Jack Box and Rich McClintock, joined Bob Hackstaff as owners.

This ownership change just preceded the eight-year peak in OPEC oil prices and thecollapse of oil prices that would bring painful recession to Colorado and the U.S. "oil patch."

Difficult times were not yet on the horizon in 1984, when the British company EF International, which owned the Denver Tech Center, engaged Ross to purchase the 1,000-acre Meridian Office Park in southeast Denver for $100 million. The volume of business transacted through Ross led EFI to purchase a 50 percent ownership interest in Ross. When Peninsular & Orient Steam Navigation Company (P&O) acquired EFI and became Ross's partner, two of the seven Ross partners sold their interests.

The Ross Centennial:
Difficult Times and Recovery

As the oil bust brought deteriorating market conditions in 1988, Ross's centennial year, the company closed its DTC office and reduced total staff. With the Centennial also came a major leadership transition: Box and McClintock bought out their three partners, becoming 50 percent owners with P&O. The two men refocused the company on brokerage, eliminating asset management activities. They also established Ross Development Management Group under Cyrus A. "Rus" Hackstaff III to develop build-to-suit

Richard G. McClintock

projects for select clients.

Box and McClintock strengthened Ross's position in the Front Range in 1995 by acquiring 50 percent ownership in Colorado Springs' premier real estate firm, Palmer McAllister, headed by Gary Hollenbeck.

The year 1996 brought the change in Ross ownership that defined the company's leadership into the 21st Century. Box and McClintock bought out P&O's stake to acquire sole ownership of the 108-year-old firm irrefutable evidence of their confidence in Denver's future and of Ross's place in that future.

Box and McClintock:
Building a 21st Century Team

Colleagues portray Ross partners John P. Box and Richard G. McClintock as the ideal team. They are congenial, extremely knowledgeable, and service-oriented. They have in common a combination of "street" knowledge gained from their years as highly successful brokers and rare sophistication from having managed real estate transactions of all types, sizes, and degrees of complexity.

Both the qualities they have in common and those that are unique to each man have shaped Ross's strategy for the 21st Century. The two share a common business perspective and rarely disagree, giving Ross both momentum and stability under their leadership.

"I think it starts with a philosophy of business and a philosophy of personal life that we find the same," says McClintock. "It's a kind of kindred spirit that keeps us in synch." Business associates agree with this assessment, observing that each partner's distinctive strengths enhance the other's. "With Rich and I," says Box, "one plus one has always equaled three."

Jordon Perlmutter & Co.

Although Jordon Perlmutter & Co. was formed in 1983, its origin dates back to 1952 — the year when Jordon Perlmutter returned from the Coast Guard and decided to form a residential construction company with his cousin, Samuel Primack, under the name Perl-Mack. They were soon joined by a third partner, William J. Morrison, Jordon's brother-in-law.

Initially, Perl-Mack built and sold one house at a time — the partners building the houses during the day and changing into suits to sell them at night. In the mid-1950s, when the Veterans Administration introduced its program of home loans with no down payment, business took off. A new 800-square-foot home sold for $10,000.

On one particularly memorable Sunday in 1954, the young company sold all 44 homes in a Denver development, located at Sheridan Boulevard and First Avenue. The company then took orders for 15 more homes. Soon after, the company built a total of 112 homes at a site called Athmar Park. Buoyed by its success, Perl-Mack acquired and developed 550 acres in Adams County, which is still known as the Unincorporated Perl-Mack Area of Adams County.

Perl-Mack was now considered a major residential builder in the Denver metropolitan area. The company acquired 2000 acres and developed the totally planned community of Northglenn. Northglenn, which included 6000 single-family homes as well as apartments, churches, schools, fire and police departments, and industrial and commercial development, was acclaimed as the best-planned community in America by *Life Magazine* and the *National Association of Home Builders Journal*.

Development of Northglenn transformed Perl-Mack into one of the top ten builders in the United States and introduced the company to the development and construction of commercial real estate. Northglenn was followed by development of the Southglenn community in Arapahoe County and Montbello, a "City within a City," on land in northeast metropolitan Denver.

The company expanded to other fields of development that eventually supplanted its home-building activities. Commercial development resulted in the planning, development, construction and leasing of the Northglenn Regional Shopping Center in 1968 and the Southglenn Regional Shopping Center in 1974.

The early 1980s found the company active in development of commercial projects along the South Wadsworth Boulevard retail corridor extending from Quincy Avenue to Bowles Avenue. The crowning jewel of this activity was Southwest Plaza Shopping Center, containing 1.46 million square feet of retail space and anchored by five major department stores.

Following completion of Southwest Plaza in 1983, Perl-Mack was dissolved and a new entity formed under the name of Jordon Perlmutter & Co. when Jordon and his son Jay Perlmutter became partners. Jordon Perlmutter & Co., in association with other partners, immediately concentrated on further development along the South Wadsworth corridor between Quincy and Bowles Avenues.

At the north end of this area is the Southwest Autopark, which includes automobile dealerships for Ford, Saturn, Jeep-Eagle, Suzuki, Pontiac and Dodge. This development also includes a Price Club, a Wal-Mart and a PetsMart.

A little further south, Belleview Shores includes an impressive array of restaurants — including the Olive Garden, Black-eyed Pea, Applebee's, Tony Roma's, Grady's American Grill — and is also home to big box retailers like Office Max, Home Base, American Furniture Warehouse, Best Buy, Baby Superstore, Michael's and Linens 'N Things.

Next to Belleview Shores is Plaza On The Green, which is anchored by Cub Goods. Just down the road and directly across from Southwest Plaza is Bowles Crossing, which is home to Media Play, Gart Sports, Sears Homelife, Mervyn's, 'Lil Things, Pacific Linen and a Mann 12 Theatre.

Presently under construction is the Chanson Plaza Shopping Center, which will house a variety of stores including Barnes & Noble Book Store, Soundtrack, UMB Bank, Macaroni Grill and Gunther Toody's restaurant.

Today, Jordon Perlmutter & Co. is recognized for its professional and outstanding performance in not only development but in management of all types of real estate, from residential to commercial. Jordon Perlmutter and Jay Perlmutter have since been joined in the company by Jordon's son, Jonathan, and his son-in-law, Shell D. Cook. Many employees who were employed by Perl-Mack have moved to Jordon Perlmutter & Co. and a great number of them have been with the company for more than 30 years.

The company has ventured into other aspects of business and is currently developing, with a partner, The Great Mall of the Great Plains, a value-oriented regional mall located in the Kansas City suburb of Olathe that is scheduled to open in summer of 1997. The company has acquired land for future development in both the Denver metropolitan area and in Olathe.

In Denver, Jordon Perlmutter & Co. manages and leases a number of high-quality office buildings and

apartment complexes, including JP Plaza in lower downtown, where it maintains its corporate headquarters. The company employs about 100 people.

Jordon Perlmutter has been married to his wife, Essie, since 1953, and is the father of four children. He has been very active in community and charitable causes and has served on the boards of Rose Hospital and the Denver chapters of the Allied Jewish Federation and the Anti-Defamation League. He is a trustee of the University of Denver.

Jordon Perlmutter provided the leadership and guidance for development of Shalom Park, a place for the elderly, and served as president of the board of directors for Shalom Park from 1984 until 1996. Shalom Park stands as an example of outstanding achievement in construction of facilities for the elderly.

For three generations, the Perlmutter name has been synonymous with excellence in the field of real estate development. With this solid foundation behind it, the future of Jordon Perlmutter & Co. is bright.

Since the opening of Southwest Plaza, pictured here, Jordon Perlmutter & Co. has successfully developed a number of successful shopping centers along the South Wadsworth retail corridor.

Southwest Plaza opened for business in 1983 as the largest shopping complex between Chicago and the West Coast.

Lowry Redevelopment Authority

The closure of Lowry Air Force Base in September 1994 gave the cities of Denver and Aurora the unique opportunity to design a mixed-use, master-planned community in the heart of the metropolitan area.

The Lowry Redevelopment Authority (LRA) is the planner and developer of the 1,866-acre site. The project has become a national model for military base redevelopments as the LRA transforms the area into a mixed-use, master-planned community funded mostly by private sources.

Lowry community planning is guided by traditional planning concepts—to reestablish friendly neighborhoods and commercial districts that feature tree-lined streets, porches and nearby parks. Combined with a healthy dose of public and private schools and thriving businesses, Lowry will become one of the most advanced, self-sufficient communities in the country.

The idea is to replicate the best features of Denver's traditional neighborhoods into a new community where people can live, learn, work and play.

Lowry's reuse plan is fourfold:
- **"Live."** About 3,200 homes of varying costs will be built in three neighborhoods and around the golf course. Each home will be within walking distance of Lowry's parks, schools and businesses. Lowry's ideal location — adjacent to and surrounded by east Denver and west Aurora— is just 25 minutes from DIA, 15 minutes to downtown Denver and 10 minutes to the Cherry Creek shopping district.

  The Lowry Redevelopment Authority is philosophically committed to building a full range of housing, from entry level to custom homes. In compliance with federal guidelines, a small percentage of Lowry's residential development will be dedicated to affordable housing.
- **"Learn."** The Higher Education and Advanced Technology Center at Lowry offers technology-based classes and training. Part of the Colorado Community College and Occupational Education System, the high-tech campus offers certificates

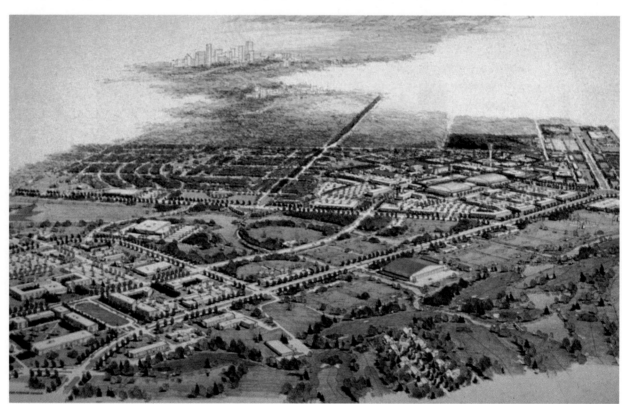

Lowry will be Denver's first urban, mixed-use, masterplanned community.

through post-graduate studies in numerous areas, including aeronautics, computer science, metrology and biotechnology.

The Stanley British Primary School and Montclair Academy are private institutions serving students in grades K-8. Two more private schools and a public elementary school are planned.

- **"Work."** Lowry's 165-acre business center is targeting four industries — telecommunications, biomedical technology, computer software development and financial services. The park-like setting will feature low-rise office buildings. Bonfils Blood Center has built a new state-of-the-art facility at Lowry where it collects, tests, stores and distributes more than 70 percent of the state's blood supply.

The Colorado Department of Public Health and Environment has built the new state laboratory at Lowry. The regional Defense Finance and Accounting Service and Air Reserve Personnel Center will employ some 3,000 of Lowry's potential work force of 7,000 people.

- **"Play."** Denver tops the country in park acreage per capita, and Lowry is no exception. About 800 acres of open space will feature two public 18-hole golf courses, 12 playing fields, seven baseball diamonds, water attractions, public trails, wildlife viewing, a public ice arena and a recreation center.

Golfers will enjoy one of the country's largest publicly owned facilities when the Colorado Golf Association makes the site their statewide headquarters. Outdoor enthusiasts will enjoy Lowry's trails that lead to public parks and connect with the regional park system, including the Highline Canal and Sand Creek trails.

The capstone of the Lowry redevelopment is a community-wide fiber optics network that will connect every home, school and business to the Internet, each other and the world. Lowry is one of the first master-planned communities in Colorado that is installing technology that allows users to teleconference with colleagues in Dallas, interact with a college professor in New York or telecommute to work in Boulder. Users can watch a football game while monitoring their baby's room via a surveillance camera that appears on the television screen, or program their furnace, air conditioning or lights from a remote telephone.

Lowry's central location makes it ideal for commercial and residential development.

Nationally, other cities and states interested in redeveloping closed military bases and urban areas already are viewing Lowry as a model. Its financing plan also appeals to financially conscious agencies. The LRA has issued $33 million in revenue bonds, plans to issue $34 million of tax increment bonds and has received $8.2 million in federal, state and local grants to finance demolition, infrastructure improvements, park development and construction of a public elementary school.

Lowry, when fully rebuilt, will be a self-sustaining community that will preserve its role as an economic generator for the region. Although the Air Force is gone, the economic force remains.

The historic headquarters building will be a centerpiece of the future Lowry business center.
Credit: Randy Brown

MELODY HOMES

A Colorado Company

Melody Homes has deep roots in Colorado. The company was founded in Boulder in 1953 by a Colorado native whose ancestors arrived here during the Gold Rush. Unlike some out-of-state builders who swoop down on Colorado to take advantage of hot markets, Melody Homes has built only along Colorado's Front Range. By being here for its past buyers, and providing homes for present and future families, Melody has not only survived and thrived during good times, it has weathered the building industry's cyclical highs and lows for 44 years.

The dining room has evolved over the years but remains the gathering place for the celebration of family traditions.

Now in its fifth decade, Melody has been synonymous with affordable, quality, single-family homes from the beginning. The company was founded to provide starter homes for returning Korean War veterans and other first-time buyers. Its first effort, built at Martin Acres in Boulder, was an all-brick 1,100 square foot model

Then 1950s.
credit: Sickles Photo Reporting/FPG Intl

Now 1990s.
In the 1990s, the family room has replaced the living room as the perfect place for family relaxation.

that sold for $12,995 and helped establish the company. In the 1950s one out of every five homes built in Boulder was a Melody Home. The company has also contributed significantly to the growth of other metro areas by developing neighborhoods in Arvada, Aurora, Colorado Springs, Fort Collins, Longmont, Brighton, Thornton, Westminster, and Arapahoe, Douglas, and Jefferson Counties.

Along the Front Range, Melody has built over 15,000 starter and move-up homes that feature more than 20 floor plans in ranch, two-story and multi-level styles priced from the low-$100s to the $180s. Through affordable quality and value, the company prides itself on designing homes to fit family's active lifestyles by taking advantage of superior schools, community services, employment centers and recreational facilities — all within easy highway access.

The company's 18-page, site-criteria checklist helps employees strictly select communities that yield neighborhood traits, creating a diverse mix of homes, families and memories. Because they build solely in Colorado, Melody's officials have expert knowledge about soil testing, site preparation and building techniques that are suited to the state's unique geography and climate. Melody prefers land that meshes with trees, creeks and wetlands, and provides a panoramic view of Colorado's trademark Rocky Mountains. In 1996, the company was designated a Green Builder, signifying its desire to provide more comfortable, healthier living while conserving natural resources, safeguarding the environment and producing savings to home buyers.

The firm's award-winning homes all offer an attached two-car garage and an unfinished basement for storage or future expansion. Depending on the floor plan, dramatic features include wrap-around windows, lofts, bridges and up to five bedrooms. Home buyers can specialize their homes from the Personal Touch Options package, which includes fireplace, three-car garage, jetted tub, radius drywall corners, bay window, oak flooring, upgraded cabinets, appliances and more.

A tribute to its fine craftsmanship and customer-oriented service is Melody's stalwart warranty — one year on materials and workmanship, two years on concealed mechanical systems and 10 years on structural components. Quality assurance and value are the primary concerns at Melody Homes, which was named the fastest-growing private company in metro Denver in 1993 by the Denver Business Journal. That year, the company's revenues jumped 88 percent from the previous year, thanks, in part, to Melody's Westgold Meadows and Arrowhead — the most active individual subdivisions in the area. All of the home builder's communities were listed in the top 10 that year.

In 1994, the company grew from 85 to 100 employees, computerized its sale offices, opened the Melody Mortgage Company for its customers' ease and convenience and launched a design center for home buyers to seek professional help when selecting interior materials. The company's association with value encouraged many of its customers in 1994 to move up to their second or third Melody home. Based on recorded closings, the company boasted the top two communities in the six-county Denver area.

Melody sold more new homes in the $100,000-$124,999 price category than any other builder in metro Denver in 1995. The following year's gross revenues again skyrocketed as the company opened three new neighborhoods and celebrated the success of Erie's Meadow Sweet Farm being tabbed the best-selling Boulder County community of single-family homes. Melody Homes caused such a frenzy in Erie that nearby residents camped out in tents to be the first to snatch up one of the best valued homes in the county.

The popularity of the company's products, noted for their light-filled, airy interiors and comfortable, functionable environments, is primarily determined by its dedication to satisfying customers. Melody compiles input from focus groups, buyers and non-buyers and gathers their advice on design, efficiency, ambiance, ease of maintenance, and preferred materials for floors, walls, cabinets and countertops. This adaptive nature instills innovative concepts to meet the needs of future clients and has been instrumental to the privately owned company's success in garnering several industry awards.

Since 1990, when Melody began competing for Major Achievement in Merchandising Excellence Awards, it's been a finalist for 39 of the prestigious accolades, winning 18 MAMEs for Best Home, Best Interior Design and Best Detached Home in their price categories, plus other MAME classifications. In 1993, the City of Westminster also honored the home builder with an award for excellence in design and development for its Arrowhead Community plan.

Perhaps its greatest achievement is the "Read to Win" incentive program that encourages elementary school students to read and report on books. Launched in 1993, the program has won several MAME Awards, including best single promotion by a homebuilder. Money from every Melody home closed is donated to the campaign to buy library books and upgrade computers for neighboring schools. Employees also donate to the community by volunteering to Habitat for Humanity and contributing resources and time to advance Wilderness on Wheels, an agency that makes fishing, trails and other natural wonders available to people in wheelchairs.

Melody Homes, synonymous with quality and value, dedicates countless time and effort into building communities and creating neighborhoods.

Neighborhoods and traditional two-stories are still a family favorite.

MOORE AND COMPANY

Moore and Company, independently owned and operated by the same family for more than 65 years, is one of Denver's most venerable real estate firms.

W. Max Moore,

Founder

William M. Moore,

President and CEO

In spite of its lengthy past, however, Moore and Company still considers itself an entrepreneurial firm — a firm with its eyes fixed firmly on the future. In fact, company president and CEO William M. Moore was a 1995 finalist for the Entrepreneur of the Year Award sponsored by *The Denver Business Journal*.

Moore and Company is in the process of systematically broadening its scope — from "real estate firm" to "complete center for real estate services and products." In 1995, the firm added Acacia Mortgage LLC to complement its established residential and commercial real estate capabilities. It also plans to add title and casualty insurance, and is considering development activities and commercial construction.

The non-franchise firm also plans to increase its geographic presence along the front range and expand into major recreational areas and the western slope. Moore and Company is currently represented in 20 offices located throughout all four quadrants of metropolitan Denver as well as in Boulder, Breckenridge, Conifer, Evergreen, Fairplay, Frisco, Loveland and Winter Park.

It is Moore and Company's mission to be associated with the top 20 percent of the real estate industry.

In fact, the company achieved sales volume that exceeded the $1-billion mark in 1994, 1995 and 1996. About 80 percent of the company's revenues come from residential sales, the remainder from commercial. The company's new corporate headquarters will be located in the Denver Tech Center.

"Nobody cares how much you know until they know how much you care" has been Moore and Company's corporate slogan for decades. The company puts a premium on hiring experienced sales associates with proven family, religious and community values who are prepared to work hard and provide exceptional client service. In 1996, the company has 480 residential sales associates and 40 commercial sales and leasing specialists.

Because of this unique culture, and a strong emphasis on continuing education, Moore and Company sales associates enjoy productivity rankings in the top ten percent of the largest 250 independent brokers in the nation. The company has more sales associates with the Graduate Realtor Institute and Certified Residential Specialist designations than any other real estate company in Colorado.

Nancy Striebing,

Director of Marketing

Peter Niederman, General

Sales Manager and COO

Moore and Company was founded in downtown Denver in 1931, during the Great Depression, by Colorado native and real estate legend W. Max Moore. The struggling young realtor sometimes had to take his commission in canned goods. With determination and hard work, however, the company flourished.

William Moore joined his father at the company in 1954. In 1970, Max Moore died and his son succeeded him as president and chief executive officer. Bill Moore, a University of Colorado graduate, is past president of the Denver Board of Realtors, the Colorado Association of Realtors, and the National Association of Realtors.

Steve Miller, President
Moore Commercial Company

Jerry Grasmick,
President Acacia Mortgage

Bill Moore's sister, Nancy Striebing, is director of marketing for Moore and Company. His son-in-law, Peter Niederman, is chief operating officer and general sales manager — ensuring the company a third generation of family ownership and operation.

In 1961, Bill Moore created a commercial real estate company. Today, Moore Commercial Company is the fastest growing commercial real estate firm in the state. The company has nine divisions: hospitality, industrial, international, investment, land, office, retail, property management and research.

Moore Commercial Company is the only metropolitan Denver member of New America Network, the largest commercial brokerage network in the world. In the 1990s, Moore Commercial Company merged with Denver Real Estate Services and Griffin Doyle & Associates. President of Moore Commercial Company is Steven Miller.

In 1995, Moore and Company became a major partner in a mortgage company, Acacia Mortgage LLC, which allowed the company to place financial service representatives in its major sales offices and provide clients with convenient "one-stop shopping." President and founder of Acacia Mortgage is Jerry Grasmick.

Moore and Company is extremely active in the corporate relocation business and has affiliated with the largest corporate relocation company in the world, PHH Homequity. The company's client list reads like a "who's who" of Denver business and industry.

Because of Moore and Company's emphasis on community values, the company supports its sales associates in their involvement in local causes. In addition, the company is a sponsor of "9 Cares — Colorado Shares" holiday program and "For Children Only," a non-profit organization supporting educational outreach for underprivileged children.

By stressing values and continuing education, Moore and Company has established a "family" of realtors that includes the best managers in the business, the top producing agents in the nation, and a support staff second to none.

Moore and Company, Denver's largest independently owned and operated real estate firm, will soon occupy new headquarters at the Denver Tech Center.

THE NEENAN COMPANY

The Neenan Company is the largest design/build firm in Colorado, having completed more than 500 industrial, office, medical and retail projects along the Front Range since its founding in 1973. The company employs 150 people and posted 1996 revenues of $100 million.

It is anticipated that revenues will increase to $250 million within five years as the company's target markets expand from the Front Range to the entire nation. Major projects of The Neenan Company include facilities for Boston Chicken, Gerry Baby Products,

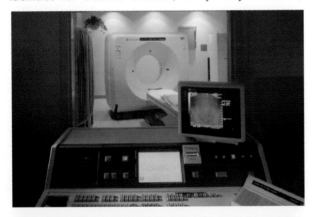

Hauser Chemical Research, Inc., Hunter Douglas, Up With People, Celestial Seasoning and CaseLogic.

The mission of The Neenan Company is to become a historically significant company. The Neenan Company has built a reputation as a leader in delivering complex, fast-track projects on time and under budget. With the ability to operate as the developer, contractor, design/builder or construction manager, the company assumes complete responsibility for delivering the successful completion of the project.

The Neenan Company offers a partnership approach and has a commitment to absolute customer satisfaction. True partnership between the owner, developer, financier, architect and contractor allows the entire development, design and construction process to be shaped around the needs of the owner or user.

The Neenan Company's emphasis on partnership and communication has resulted in an extraordinarily low rate of change orders — 1.6 percent as compared with an industry-wide rate of 12.4 percent. In addition, The Neenan Company has never been involved in a lawsuit.

Through this philosophy of partnership has evolved the term *Archistruction*™, which is a term The Neenan Company uses to describe its process. This revolutionary approach carries the design/build concept to a completely new level by combining development, finance, design and construction within one full-service company.

The intended outcome of the *Archistruction*™ process is to satisfy the owner while providing a single source of responsibility for the entire project with

an enforceable price. The company's commitment to this concept is based on integrity in their relationships, integrity in service and integrity in the quality of construction.

This process works because each person in the company is committed to open communication with the client and each other, constantly questioning and challenging ideas and processes in a productive manner. The relentless pursuit of improvement allows The Neenan Company to add value without adding cost. The company's people succeed by building and sustaining strong relationships with owners, subcontractors, architects and engineers. A sense of teamwork is fostered by focusing on the project's goals to ensure that the clients' expectations are met.

In addition to industrial and commercial projects, The Neenan Company also specializes in advanced and high technology facilities, where complex processes for the performance of special research and manufacturing take place. This industry requires rapid delivery of facilities; the company's unique approach allows activities to be performed concurrently and possibly shortened. The Neenan Company has extensive experience in Class 0.1 to Class 100,000 cleanroom build-outs, mechanical and electrical system upgrades, fab and support area shells, tool hook-up and cleanroom renovation and retrofit.

The Neenan Company has also dedicated a group of specialists for the design and construction of state-of-the-art facilities for the health care industry, including office buildings, clinics, ambulatory surgery cen-

ters, and imaging, diagnostic and treatment centers.

The company's own health care professionals work closely with the health care providers to offer ownership and financing alternatives and planning efficiencies for improved provider productivity and satisfaction with accessible, patient-focused, image enhancing designs that work.

The Neenan Company has successfully delivered projects that provide cost-effective proven building systems at a level of quality, completeness of service and overall coordination that is unmatched in the health care development, design and construction industry.

The Neenan Company pledges to meet and exceed its clients' expectations, to help all Neenan Company employees share in the company's success, to treat all individuals with dignity and respect and to insure personal satisfaction from a job well done. The impressive number of satisfied customers who keep returning to The Neenan Company for additional construction needs is proof positive that the company keeps its promises.

ABOVE: Central utilities plant for Quantum Peripherals in Louisville, CO. Equipment installation provided by Trautman & Shreve, Inc.

TOP: Quantum Peripherals in Louisville totals 188,000 square feet for Phases 1 and 2. This office, research and design facility has 30,000 square feet of Class 10, 100, 10,000 and 100,000 cleanroom space. Facility design, OZ Architecture. Cleanroom design by Anderson DeBartolo and Pan (ADP). The Neenan Company, general contractor.

"Initial budgets for the facility considerably exceeded our target, and your team continued to work relentlessly on value engineering considerations and building alternatives until we found a solution that worked. Your assistance in evaluating ownership and financing options was invaluable in helping us determine the best structure of ownership for our facility. Financing was a major hurdle and your guidance provided ... a very creative solution without which we might still be looking."

-Neil Puester, Optima Batteries, Inc.

"In a project (Ohmeda) of this size, with the complexity of the clients, time constraints, and extremely tight budget, one might wonder why the architect would write an unsolicited recommendation letter to the contractor. It is very simple. During many difficult periods of the project, many other contractors would have 'thrown in the towel' instead of problem solving to obtain a solution to the issue."

-Bob West, OZ Architecture, The Neenan Company

Palace Construction Co.

As an award-winning general contractor serving Denver and the Front Range since 1963, Palace Construction knows that listening turns business arrangements into partnerships. Listening eases the challenges and complexity of construction projects. It builds the bond of trust and fairness between clients and contractor. Listening assures careful attention to a client's time frame, budget and special needs. Most importantly, it assures full client satisfaction.

Palace Construction received a 1996 ACE Award from the Associated General Contractors of Colorado for its restoration of the Austin Building, located at Colfax and Josephine Streets. Eight months of refurbishing resulted in 18 units of affordable housing, and retail space. Exterior renovation was made possible through a grant from the Colorado Historical Society.
Credit: Dean Birinyi.

The Austin Building, built in 1904, is now owned and managed by the Northeast Denver Housing Center. Shown before (ABOVE) and after renovation (RIGHT)

Throughout its history, Palace Construction has worked closely with the Catholic Archdiocese of Denver on a wide variety of projects — most recently rehabilitation of the former Saint Thomas Seminary on Steele and Louisiana into the new Catholic Pastoral Center. In this photograph, the staff of Palace Construction is gathered on the front steps of the facility prior to its renovation. Designed by Owen Tryba Architects.
Credit: Philip Wegener Kantor.

In the beginning, Palace Construction operated from a 500-square-foot office. Insurance companies hired the company to perform small repairs on the homes of policy holders. As Palace grew, the company became an expert in the field of repairs and restorations, specializing in residential and commercial buildings suffering from fire and severe water damage. No matter how large or small the project, the company never forgot its keystone principle of building partnerships.

In the mid-1970s, Palace Construction adapted its expertise in repairing structures to the restoration of historic buildings. The company also provided tenant improvement services as well as the construction of new buildings. In the 1980s, the company began refurbishing multi-family apartment and town-home buildings and working closely with engineers on structural repairs caused by expansive soils. These repairs include re-leveling structures, sister walls and sub-floors.

In 1996, Palace Construction completed more than 500 projects ranging in size from a few hundred dollars to nearly $5 million. Several of these projects included full pre-construction services including value engineering and conceptual estimates to meet clients' needs. Project types varied from new construction of schools, senior housing and assisted care facilities, to tenant improvements of office and industrial space, to major structural repairs, fire and water restoration and historic renovations.

Today, as in the past, Palace Construction starts by listening to its clients' individual needs and then approaching each project with expertise, talent and enthusiasm. "It is the only way to do business," said company president Richard Carter. Palace Construction continues the traditions handed down from founder Lou Jahde, who now serves as chairman and chief executive officer.

As Palace Construction surveys Denver and the progress made by the city over the past decades, the company knows that the "built environment" affects people and their lives. In strict economic terms, it is

The 1921 Colorado State Office Building, once slated for the wrecking ball, required a $3.4 million renovation, with almost complete interior demolition. On time and under budget, this seven-month restoration included repairing stained glass, matching 70-year-old marble and replicating chandeliers.

The Balustrade, located in the historic Golden Triangle, offers 32 units of upscale residential space, featuring a loft-style Mediterranean-inspired exterior and high-end interior finishes. Balustrade was developed by Fullerton and Company. Designed by Michael Murphy Architects.

often less expensive to tear down a building and replace it with a new one; but as a community, a higher price is paid. Much of the city's heritage is lost. There is something about the character and charm of historic buildings — the skilled work of a craftsman's hands, the exquisite detail and beauty. It has been said that a man loses part of his soul when he loses contact with his past. For this reason, restoring historic buildings is important — keeping the tradition, the sense of belonging and the sense of order that is vital to any city's development.

In a rapidly changing world, with new technological breakthroughs occurring every day, Palace Construction has adapted to modern times, but one thing remains constant — the company's unwavering commitment to its clients. Now, as in the past, Palace Construction places the needs of its clients above all else. The company has taken the time to hear and understand their clients and work for and with them to achieve goals.

Today, Palace Construction is a full-service general contractor providing construction management, pre-construction services, new construction and design/build as well as renovations, insurance restoration and structural repairs. The company's historic routes have paved the way to handle today's new projects and those of the future.

Palace Construction is committed to rebuilding and restoring the many one-of-a-kind buildings that embody Denver's colorful past and to constructing new buildings that embrace the progress and spirit of Denver today.

Palace Construction served as general contractor for the 46,000-square-foot new Lawrence Elementary School in Arvada. The school was designed to reflect the history of the neighborhood it serves. Architecture by RNL Design. Credit: Ed LaCasse.

RAE & COMPANY

A city's architectural history can be the chart of its future. Like the theme of the old film "It's a Wonderful Life," it would be hard to imagine the fate of Denver's Capitol Hill district if Realtor Mary Rae had not played a major role galvanizing families and financiers to reinvest in its colorful history over the past two decades.

Without the commitment and activity of Rae and her firm—Rae & Company—many of the magnificent

....

Mary Rae, owner of Rae & Company.

old mansions would be long gone and several single-family neighborhoods would have had parts of blocks leveled for high-rise apartments or condos.

Always a core city resident, her own commitment to preservation was stimulated by the demolition of the Moffat mansion on Grant Street in 1972. It wasn't

the first to fall as one-by-one, many of the great homes, too expensive for most single families to maintain, were slated for the wrecking ball. Her indignation and resolve to "do something about these appalling cultural losses" was the catalyst that prompted her to leave a corporate job and take up real estate. With a gifted instinct for an old mansion's commercial possibilities, she bought and "recycled" into offices the Croke-Patterson Mansion on Pennsylvania Street to save it from becoming another historic city treasure lost to redevelopment.

From this early success and encouragement from others, she decided to form her own realty company with the singular objective of advocating a back-to-the-city residential movement that renovated and restored the amenities and charm of the city's Victorian-era homes. Since then, she and her associates have turned countless old mansions into charming offices and filled many older but modest residences with young families equally determined to make inner-city life and neighborhoods vital again.

Once, when a number of adjacent smaller residences in the 1100 Block of Denver's Gaylord Street were slated to be demolished for a new high rise, Rae provided an alternative for the property owner when the financing for the development fell through. She and her company arranged for the sale of all the properties to individual owners and closed them all on the same day. She similarly sold 13 derelict homes in the Pearl-Pennsylvania Street and 1st Avenue neighborhood when, they too, were scheduled for demolition.

Citing that there is a "craziness quotient" to her single-minded determination, she, on two occasions, arranged for the sale and physical move of historic buildings to new sites rather than see them destroyed. The first move was a 400-ton home from Race Street to a vacant lot on High Street, and the other a piecemeal move of a mansion from Pennsylvania Street to 10th Avenue and Emerson Street where the parts of the old structure were incorporated into a human-scale condominium project that stands there today as Brisbane Commons. On both occasions, the buildings got stuck during the move and a fascinated public watched the progress of her projects on television and in the daily newspapers.

Since the doors opened in 1975, Mary Rae & Company has been acknowledged as the principal catalyst for a movement of homeowners who have enthusiastically restored respectability to living in the core city and giving a tangible meaning to historic preservation.

One result of the activities and foresight of Rae & Company over the years has been a persuasive campaign to convince mortgage lenders in Denver that it's good business to finance and preserve homes in the inner city. When not doing office work, she often spends time with clients recommending expert craft people to do renovation work, or helping an owner get an historic landmark designation for a particularly unique and significant property.

Over the years, her firm has received countless awards from historic preservation organizations as well as awards for pioneering marketing and advertising that go beyond the ordinary to please her listing clients and attract buyers. The style and creativity of her graphic sales literature, use of flowers, line drawings, photography, balloons, banners and open house luncheons, and her exquisite and detailed personal touch with her clients and buyers have been copied but never equaled by competitors who have leaped on her "back to the city bandwagon."

Now in her third decade of business, Mary Rae's commitment to Denver's core neighborhoods continues unabated. Her repeat business tells the story of her imagination, enthusiasm and expertise. Children and grandchildren of some of her original clients return to her company to buy and sell property. She has sold many grand and modest old houses several times as family circumstances have changed over the years, but whose owners remain loyal to the flair and effectiveness of her marketing skills.

During the boom and bust cycle of Denver's economy from oil boom days of the 1970s, the decline of

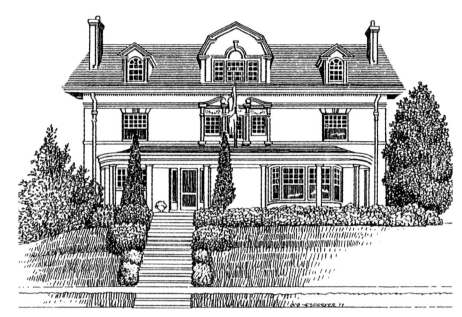

The French Consulate Mansion at 738 Pearl St.,

houses the offices of Mary Rae & Company

the 1980s and resurgence of the '90s, Mary Rae has kept to her persistent theme of the joys and benefits of city living. She has been vindicated by market forces that are now aggressively revitalizing residential units in Denver's downtown and core neighborhoods.

She rarely misses an opportunity to "sell the city" and relishes the support she still receives by mail and phone from grateful city residents. A securities broker wrote her, "You are one of the movers and shakers in all Denver History! There isn't a person among us who is not grateful to you for your pioneer spirit."

A century from now, historians will note the names of the early mining, manufacturing, publishing and other 19th century moguls who built the culture and splendor of the city's architectural heritage and they also will note the name of Mary Rae, one of the very important people who helped preserve that legacy.

Today, she and her firm continue to specialize in luxury and high-end properties that make the city the fashionable place to live.

RIDGE ERECTION COMPANY — RIDGE CRANE SERVICE, INC.

When the historic Masonic Temple in Downtown Denver was destroyed by a fire in 1984, Ridge Erection Company saved the building's exterior walls by bracing them — before the ashes from the fire had even cooled. Later, Ridge rebuilt the interior structure.

Ridge Erection Company, with more than 35 years of experience, is the oldest steel erector in the Rocky Mountain Region. The company has erected the structural steel frames that support many of Denver's most familiar and impressive buildings.

The company also uses its cranes to set fragile materials such as limestone, precast concrete and granite for building exteriors.

Located in Arvada, Ridge Erection Company serves clients along the Front Range, in mountain communities and in neighboring states. The company's work can been seen in roadways, bridges, high-rises, midrises, shopping malls, historical structures, civic centers, stadiums and hospitals.

One of the company's most recognizable projects is Republic Plaza, Denver's tallest building, for which Ridge Erection Company erected 1.2 million square feet of steel and decking work.

A large Ridge Crane lowers the tubular steel space frame that will form part of the skylight over the atrium of the Corporate Express headquarters.

On a smaller scale, the company has more recently been retained to strengthen the structural skeletons of historic buildings being remodeled into residential lofts in LoDo. Ridge has participated in a majority of the remodeling projects in Central City — including moving a historic cabin to a new site, completely intact.

Ridge Erection Company has erected structural steel for the Cherry Creek and Southwest Plaza shopping centers and for most of the bridges that constitute "The Mousetrap."

The company also built the complex moveable grandstands at the Denver Mile High Stadium, which adapt the facility for varying use as a football field, a baseball diamond or concert grounds. Pike's Peak Center for the Performing Arts in Colorado Springs, Fort Carson Army Hospital, Moby Gymnasium at Colorado State University in Fort Collins and the Village Hall at Beaver Creek are also Ridge projects.

Owning the only crane capable of navigating the site's difficult terrain, Ridge Erection Company was retained for the complex job of building the steel canopy over the stage at Red Rocks Amphitheater. This is one of the few sites where the company's structural work is actually on permanent display — not covered up by cladding materials.

In 1991, Ridge Erection Company attracted industry attention and was featured in *The Ironworker* magazine when it installed huge clear-span steel trusses — each one 415 feet long by 31 feet deep — for the American Airlines hangar at Tulsa Airport. It took three cranes working in concert to lift each truss.

Ridge also operates the state's largest crane rental and rigging company, Ridge Crane Service. Established in 1983, Ridge Crane Service boasts a fleet of 16 expertly operated cranes, ranging in size from 15 tons to 200 tons and offering up to 340 feet of boom.

The company's most recent acquisition — a 200-ton crane that cost $1.3 million — is the largest mobile crane in the State of Colorado.

Ridge Erection Company prides itself on being one of the few remaining unionized companies in its field.

Ridge Cranes are used to hoist signs at McNichols Arena and constructed the large video screen for the 1997 Stock Show.

UPPER LEFT: Ridge Erection Company has erected the structural steel frames that support many of Denver's most familiar and impressive buildings — including the new Corporate Express headquarters in Broomfield.

....

Company owner Steven "Gus" Price is a familiar figure in Denver's Labor Day Parade, walking alongside the company's 200-ton crane and tossing candies to the children who line the sidewalks.

Price prides himself on treating Ridge Erection Company's 60 employees like family. Many own stock in the company. As a result, turnover is exceptionally low and the average employee has been with the company more than 15 years. This wealth of experience is a strong selling point with the company's customers.

Ridge Erection Company was founded in 1960 by L. Rex Price. He was succeeded as president by his son, Gus Price, in 1985.

Price, who holds a business degree from the University of Colorado, is a director of the National Erectors Association — the organization's youngest director and the only one from west of the Mississippi. Price was instrumental in establishing an innovative captive insurance company, the Ironworking Contractors Insurance Program, that today helps manage the cost of workers compensation insurance in the industry.

Also essential to the operations of the company are Darrel Dugger, vice president and general field superintendent for Ridge Erection Company, and Dan

ABOVE: In an example of industrial erection, Ridge Erection Company hoists an extremely heavy component of a concrete batch plant for Mobile Premix.

....

Strange, operations manager for Ridge Crane Service.

Ridge Erection Company is a corporate sponsor of the Arvada Center for the Performing Arts, two local high-school scholarship funds, and the Alie Foundation — an organization that trains bloodhouds to find missing children.

In addition, the company has offered its services at less than market rate for projects like the Samaritan Center, sponsored by the Catholic Archdiocese, which provides housing for displaced families. The company also financially supports the charitable, civic, union and athletic activities of its individual employees.

Ridge Erection Company, a part of Denver's heritage, has provided the city with a skyline as durable as the mountains beyond.

Sanford Homes

As Tim Sanford thumbs through his album filled with photos, newspaper articles and ads from his 35 years building neighborhoods in Denver, a small history of this town unfolds. From the yellowing newspaper clipping that reported his first house built at Ridgewood Highlands in Littleton to today's beautiful street-scapes at Home Farm in Westminster, you can start to see the changes that have been a part of Denver's growth.

Generations of Denverites have come home to Sanford Homes. From that first neighborhood of 44 homes in Ridgewood Highlands, came Ridgewood. Then on a third parcel bought from Roy Romer, Ridgewood Village emerged. Moving from suburban Littleton to the southeastern suburbs, Hunter's Hill, Homestead and Homestead Farms; as well as Governor's Ranch in south Jeffco, Sanford Homes® continued to represent the area's finest traditional homes.

One of the truest signs of the quality of a neighborhood is how it matures. And Sanford® neighborhoods have become models for their livability and warmth. A look around any established Sanford® community reveals the fact that many people choose to update and modify their existing home rather than move from the neighborhood. This keeps communities and people together and helps build the strong environment that has helped Denver grow with quality.

In fact, the number of children who have grown up in Sanford Homes® over the last 35 years could fill

McNichols Arena. And their parents could fill most of Denver's high-rises.

Many current buyers of Sanford Homes® grew up in one.

As more people discover the wonders of living in the Mile High City, the need for distinctive homes continues to grow. And Sanford Homes® are leading the way with beautiful new communities at Home Farm in Westminster, The Reserve and The Glen at West Ridge in Highlands Ranch plus numerous other neighborhoods all around Denver.

Joined by their competitively priced affiliate, HighView Homes®, the members and managers pictured represent an average of 17 years in the construction of HighView® and Sanford Homes® neighborhoods.

Sanford Homes is proud to be a part of the quality growth of Denver, from a small town to the thriving city that it has become. They are proud to be building neighborhoods where our next generation of leaders will grow up—leading all of us in Denver to a bigger and better future.

THE

SANFORD HOME®

Sanford Homes® are traditional, practical homes that combine award winning architecture with the finest craftsmanship. These timeless designs are a fusion of proven traditional floor plans, historic elevations, and today's technology.

Homes that you can actually live in, featuring spacious family gathering areas, large secondary bedrooms, private dens, and luxurious master suites. Elegant formal rooms with coffered ceilings and crown moldings, convenient sunny kitchens with breakfast nooks, dramatic entries, and three car garages. Sanford Homes® are built for people who understand how important buying the right home in the right neighborhood is to their family.

We establish a buyer-builder partnership when you purchase a Sanford Home®, tailoring fine-tuned traditional plans into a practical home for you and your family.

Creating livable floor plans that feel right today and for years to come. Delivered on time and built with value you can see and touch.

Discover Sanford® today.

❶ Piney Creek-Aurora
From the $230s-300s • Parker Rd. and Orchard Rd.
Bev Teigen   680-3411

❷ The Reserve at Westridge Village
From the $190s-280s • Highlands Ranch Parkway
and Wildcat Reserve Parkway
Pat Rice and Cynthia Considine   791-1553

❸ Westridge Glen
From the $230s-350s • Highlands Ranch Parkway
and Desert Willow Road
Kay Jensen and Ellen Holliman   683-8199

❹ Home Farm-Westminster
From the $200s-300s • 124th and N. Huron
Dennis Helbig and Jeanne Zerr   450-2969

❺ High Woods-Highlands Ranch
Custom Homes from the $500s   771-7400
S. Broadway to Fairchild Drive   773-3399

SHAW CONSTRUCTION

Building Satisfaction through Performance

Shaw Construction, founded by George Shaw in 1962, has grown and flourished along with Colorado's expanding economy to become one of the state's top ten general contractors.

BOTTOM LEFT:
Shaw Construction built the Joan and Irving Harris Concert Hall in Aspen, which opened in 1993.

RIGHT:
Tenant finish accounts for a significant part of Shaw Construction's work along the Front Range, including 60,000 square feet of space for Arthur Andersen & Company in Denver.

During the 35 years since Shaw Construction was founded, its adherence to the motto "Building Satisfaction through Performance" has helped the company grow and flourish along with Colorado's expanding economy. In the 1990s, Shaw Construction became one of the state's top ten general contractors.

Shaw Construction offers new construction, renovation and tenant finish services throughout the state. It has built a vast array of projects such as office buildings, schools, hotels, restaurants, ski resort facilities, manufacturing facilities and luxurious private residences, ranging in cost from $10,000 to more than $30 million. With offices in Denver and Grand Junction, Shaw Construction posted 1996 revenues of $70 million. The company employs about 50 people — including project managers, superintendents, management and support staff.

Shaw Construction was founded in 1962 by George Shaw. Initially, the company consisted of George Shaw alone, operating out of his station wagon and building a few custom homes. Over time, Shaw diversified into commercial construction, which today accounts for most of the company's business. However, the company still builds a few larger custom homes for select clients. In 1996, for example, Shaw Construction completed a 18,000-square-foot log home in Evergreen and a 13,000-square-foot custom home in Telluride.

In 1983, Steve Meyer joined Shaw Construction and was assigned to the company's Grand Junction office. Meyer gradually acquired an ownership interest and succeeded George Shaw as president in 1995, thus providing Shaw Construction with its second generation of leadership.

Shaw Construction is proud of the fact that virtually all of its work is obtained through negotiation with its respective clients. Its team-managed construction philosophy includes a full spectrum of pre-construction services. The owner, architect and Shaw Construction strive to form a strong working team during the early stages of a project, which almost always results in significant economies of design, scheduling and budget. The company's clients appreciate the bottom-line value which this approach brings to the building process, from conceptual planning through final owner acceptance.

A long list of repeat customers is also a major source of pride to Shaw Construction. This list includes Aspen Ski Company, Coors Ceramics, Eagle County, Telluride Housing Authority, Telluride Ski Company, Winter Park and the YMCA of the Rockies. In fact, more than 95 percent of the company's clients and architects have chosen to work with Shaw Construction on two or more projects.

Because of its professionalism, ethical business practices and large volume of work over time, Shaw Construction has built strong and cooperative relationships with its many subcontractors and vendors. In recognition of this fact, the company has been honored by the Colorado Subcontractors' Association as Contractor of the Year.

Shaw Construction also won the Downtown Denver Improvement Award for its renovation of the Ideal Cement Building at 17th Street and Champa. The structure, originally built in 1906, was the first all-concrete building in Denver. In addition to office space, it currently houses Colorado Business Bank and the Broker Restaurant.

For its work in constructing the new terminal at Eagle County Airport, Shaw Construction received

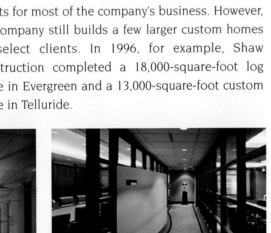

Shaw Construction's corporate philosophy is to be a long-term builder of significant high-quality projects throughout the state of Colorado for selected owners and experienced architects and to be a good community citizen in the markets in which it builds.

the 1996 National Excellence in Construction Award from the Associated Builders and Contractors. The $7.5 million building, which includes 4-1/2 acres of parking and concrete ramps for loading and unloading aircraft, was completed in just 5-1/2 months. The company has also been honored as an Accredited Quality Contractor by the Rocky Mountain Chapter of the ABC.

Shaw Construction has completed projects all along the Front Range, from Pueblo to Fort Collins. In the late 1980s, the company completed a $7.7 million renovation of McNichols Arena, adding considerable space on the west side, three restaurants, private boxes, restrooms, the Arena Club, and ticket and administrative offices.

The 15-story Boettcher DTC Building, which was completed in 11 months, holds the record as the company's tallest Denver project. Shaw Construction recently built a fine arts building and a gymnasium and will soon complete a multi-purpose building for Mullen High School. In addition, it has rebuilt almost the entire infrastructure of the Mullen campus.

Tenant finish accounts for a significant part of Shaw Construction's work along the Front Range. In a little more than two months during 1995, the company completed a $2 million project for Arthur Andersen & Company which consisted of 60,000 square feet of space on three floors of the Seventeenth Street Plaza Building. Most recently, Shaw renovated the 125,000-square-foot Public Market building in Aurora for ADT Security Systems. The $7.5 million project, which will house one of the largest call centers in the country, was completed in just four months.

Shaw Construction offers exceptional expertise in mountain construction, where it employs special construction techniques to meet with the harsh high-altitude climate and demanding building conditions. Most projects on the Western Slope are handled by the company's Grand Junction office.

Notable mountain projects are the world-famous Little Nell Hotel, renovation and addition to the Hotel Jerome, the Aspen Meadows and the Joan and Irving Harris Concert Hall — all in Aspen; the Eagle County Government Center and the American Airlines Terminal in Eagle; the Vail Athletic Club and the Crossroads Shopping Center in Vail; the Copper Mountain Restaurant (built at 11,000 feet during the short summer interval between snows); the Franz Klammer Lodge in Telluride; and base facilities at Aspen, Copper Mountain, Silver Creek, Keystone, Telluride and Winter Park.

In addition to normal steel/concrete commercial construction, Shaw Construction offers extensive wood-frame construction experience — perhaps more than any other contractor in Colorado. It has completed thousands of apartments and condominiums to date. These projects range from affordable housing in Denver, Telluride, Vail, Steamboat Springs and Frasier to the luxurious River Park Townhouses in Aspen.

For 35 years, Shaw Construction has achieved remarkable success by concentrating on its clients' goals, objectives and ambitions, and by doing everything possible to exceed their expectations.

Shaw Construction renovated the Public Market building in Aurora for ADT Security Systems. Behind the reception desk is a two-ton wall built of Chinese slate.

LEFT: Large logs and native rock re-create the look and feel of a traditional Western lodge at the Lazy Bones Ranch in Sedalia, Colorado.

For its work in constructing the new terminal at Eagle County Airport, Shaw Construction received the 1996 National Excellence in Construction Award from the Associated Builders and Contractors.

LaSalle Partners

Investment Management

Occupancy Services

Property and Transaction Services

LaSalle Partners is a global leader in commercial real estate, providing investment management, occupancy and property services to public and private institutions, corporations, professional organizations and individuals throughout the world. Guided by the interests of its clients, LaSalle works to identify, evaluate and execute real estate strategies that achieve our clients goals and financial objectives. With over 1,000 employees located in more than 75 offices throughout the United States, Latin America, Europe and Asia, LaSalle advises clients on over $15 billion of real estate assets and manages over 145.5 million square feet of property.

LaSalle established its Denver office in 1973. The initial focus in Denver was on the sale of investment real estate properties. Over the years, LaSalle has expanded its Denver expertise to include development, tenant representation, investment management, property management and facilities management. Today the firm manages and advises its clients on over 3 million square feet of office, retail and industrial properties in Colorado.

LaSalle has developed over 1.3 million square feet of high-profile office buildings in Colorado, including the 650,000 square foot Seventeenth Street Plaza in downtown Denver and the 550,000 square foot Denver Corporate Center in the Denver Technological Center. Recently, LaSalle has been retained by SunMicrosystems to be the Development Manager of a 500,000 to 1 million square foot corporate campus in the Denver area.

LaSalle's leasing experience has included negotiating anchor leases with Mobil, IBM, Manville, AT&T and J.D. Edwards for building owners throughout the Denver Metro area. In addition, the Tenant Representation Group has negotiated leases on behalf of clients such as Waste Management, Budget Rent A Car and Total Petroleum.

LaSalle Advisors, a subsidiary of LaSalle Partners, is a global real estate investment manager serving pension funds and other institutional investors. In Colorado, LaSalle Advisors represents a number of different clients, including the Public Employees' Retirement Association of Colorado, the Oregon Public Employee's Retirement Fund, Prudential U.K. and the California Public Employees' Retirement System.

....

Seventeenth Street Plaza is a high-profile, 650,000-square-foot downtown office building developed by LaSalle Partners.

ARKANSAS VALLEY SEED COMPANY

Like many of the small companies that you may drive by each day, there is a group of talented people who labor away, quietly, day in and day out, to provide the fodder and fuel for the growth of any great community. Arkansas Valley Seed Company, just off I-70 at Colorado Boulevard, is one such company. For more than 50 years, they have provided "growth" throughout the Denver region, and the fruits of their labor can be seen everywhere. From the native grasses along the highways to the turf grasses in the parks, from grasses

that grow at the high altitudes of our beautiful mountains to the waves of grain that flourish on the plains, from alfalfa and pasture grasses for livestock to the many vegetables that grace our tables, Arkansas Valley provides the seeds to enhance our quality of life.

Headquartered in Denver, Arkansas Valley Seed Company was founded in 1945 in Rocky Ford, Colorado, and is named for the Arkansas River Valley that courses through Colorado. The "Rabbit Ears" brand and logo are derived from the mountain pass in northwest Colorado. In addition to Denver and Rocky Ford, the company also has branches in Longmont Monte Vista and Rapid City.

The people at Arkansas Valley work with landscape architects, designers and contractors to encourage the right seed for the job conditions. They provide much of the seed for the stabilization and beautification of the many highway and reclamation projects in the area. Your favorite ski slopes may be reseeded each spring with seeds from Arkansas Valley. They provide seeds to forest management agencies to help maintain our marvelous mountains; especially right after a forest fire, to help control erosion. They provide seeds to ranchers and other governmental agencies to help maintain the delicate ecological balance on the great plains to the east and in the vast western deserts. Most of these seeds are species that are native to the area or adapted to the various unique conditions for which we are all collective custodians.

Arkansas Valley provides seed to the sod growers that produce the rolls of beautiful green grass for areas such as the diamond at Coors Field® and the home next door. They provide seed for major projects such as the huge Denver International Airport, the "Mouse Trap" and C470 at Ken Caryl Ranch. They provide seed to most golf courses; each requiring different state-of-the-art seeds for their greens, fairways and roughs. Arkansas Valley seeds also find their way into our school grounds and parks. They can even mix in a few wildflowers to brighten your day!

Arkansas Valley also provides quality seeds to the agricultural industry. You can taste their work in wondrous ways. Alfalfa and pasture grasses help raise prime beef and other livestock. Wheat seeds yield delicious breads and pastas. Vegetables seeds eventually ignite taste buds all across the country. Their malting barley varieties may end up in a tall glass of cold beer!

CONSOLIDATED ELECTRICAL DISTRIBUTORS

When Denver residents think about local landmarks — like Denver International Airport, Coors Field or the Adams Mark Hotel — chances are they think about elegant, award-winning exteriors.

When Consolidated Electrical Distributors and its clients think about these landmarks, however, they think about miles of electrical cable, circuit breakers, lighting fixtures, and countless switches and receptacles.

CED is the Denver metropolitan area's leading wholesale distributor of electrical products.

The company's amazing growth during the 1990s is directly linked to the heartiness of the area's economy and to CED's proven record of service to its clients. In addition to DIA, Coors Field and the Adams Mark Hotel, CED has been a major supplier to contractors working on projects that range from the house next door to the office buildings that comprise the downtown skyline.

CED distributes quality products of the world's most reputable electrical equipment manufacturers, including General Electric, Square D, Osram Sylvania, Cutler Hammer (Westinghouse Products) and Bussmann — to name a few.

The company can trace its history in the Denver area to Livran Electric Supply Company, which was established in 1950 by Ed Livran, Sr. Twenty years later, the company was purchased by privately owned Consolidated Electrical Distributors, Inc. With more than 400 locations nationwide, CED is one of the nation's largest distributors of electrical products.

In order to best meet the needs of its local market, CED Denver is granted exceptional operating autonomy. At the same time, CED Denver benefits from CED's vast purchasing power and widespread distribution network.

Since 1970, CED has been located in south Denver along Platte River Drive. In 1997, the company will occupy its new main distribution center off of Sixth Avenue near the I-25 interchange. To better serve its customers in the southeast part of the metropolitan area, CED will also open a satellite center near Centennial Airport. The company employs 70 people and maintains a fleet of nine trucks.

Consolidated Electrical Distributors offers a proven record of service, integrity and reliability to Denver-area electrical contractors.

CED is the Denver Metropolitan area's leading wholesale distributor of electrical products to Denver area contractors, employing 70 people and maintaining a fleet of nine trucks.

CAMAS Colorado, Inc.

The CAMAS name spells out what CAMAS Colorado, Inc. provides for its customers on the Colorado Front Range: Construction Aggregates, Materials And Services. That name has also become synonymous with the concept of responsible corporate stewardship of the Earth's resources.

CAMAS Colorado is made up of three divisions; each formed from a respected Denver area construction materials company.

Cooley Gravel Division

The Cooley Gravel Division was founded in 1925, as a family owned business. One of the region's largest producers, Cooley supplies to a wide range of customers, including ready-mixed concrete and asphalt producers, concrete pavement contractors, precast concrete product manufacturers, and private construction contractors.

Cooley Division has also earned an outstanding reputation as an innovator in mined land reclamation. Through visionary thinking and cooperative efforts with private, community, and government entities, sites previously mined by the company have been transformed into a public park and a luxury residential development (which became the location of a prestigious Parade of Homes show).

Flanagan Ready-Mix Division

Another family-owned business, the Flanagan Ready-Mix Division, has been handed down through two generations of Flanagans since it was founded in 1921. The company was acquired in 1992, adding considerable aggregates reserves and strategically placed ready-mixed concrete plants to CAMAS Colorado's resources. Expanded in 1994, with the acquisition of C&M Ready Mix, Flanagan is now the largest ready-mixed concrete producer in the Denver market.

Bituminous Roadways Division

Bituminous Roadways of Colorado was acquired and integrated into the CAMAS group in 1989. As one of the largest asphalt paving producers in the metro Denver area, the Bituminous Roadways Division of CAMAS is recognized as a leader in quality and workmanship. In fact, for several years in a row, a number of the company's paving projects have been named "Best in Colorado" by the Colorado Asphalt Pavement Association.

A Philosophy of Stewardship

CAMAS Colorado views protecting the environment as an integral part of its basic corporate philosophy. Success is gauged not only by dollars on the bottom line but also by striking a balance between profitability and responsible stewardship of the environment.

The commitment to stewardship shows up in many ways. It can be seen in a large number of mined land reclamation projects. It also shows up as sensitivity to surrounding communities. Noise and dust abatement, as well as minimization of visual impacts, are as vital a part of stewardship at CAMAS Colorado as maintaining wildlife habitat and replanting trees.

The award-winning South Platte Park Reclamation Project

That dedication to running a profitable business, while being a responsible corporate citizen, has earned accolades from many sources. In presenting The Governor's Environmental Award to Cooley Gravel's South Platte Park Reclamation Project, Colorado Governor Roy Romer said, "Cooley Gravel Company is to be commended on the positive impact of its responsible mining and land reclamation efforts." In 1996, Michael E. Hayes, President / CEO of CAMAS Inc., received the prestigious National Stone Association Award for Environmental Steward of the Year.

While honors and awards such as these are appreciated, the true rewards of CAMAS Colorado's stewardship efforts come in protecting, preserving and enhancing the beauty of Colorado while providing much needed resources for a growing country.

Stewardship Beyond the Bottom Line

CONTRACT DESIGN SERVICES

Contract Design Services has installed commercial floor coverings in every major building in Denver and the Denver Tech Center.

RIGHT: Although Contract Design Services specializes in carpet, it also carries the major manufacturers of resilient and ceramic tiles.

Contract Design Services, one of Colorado's top woman-owned companies, is owned by (left to right) Bonnie Bowman, President, Jo Ann Cardone, Vice-President and Sheryl Shariat, Vice-President Sales.

In spite of Denver's heady altitude, the city's movers and shakers have their feet planted firmly on the ground. More often than not, that "ground" is cushioned with floor coverings provided by Contract Design Services.

Contract Design Services, one of Colorado's top woman-owned companies, has installed commercial floor coverings in every major building in Denver and the Denver Tech Center — including all of the floor coverings for the newly remodeled Adams Mark Hotel. The privately owned company posted 1995 sales of $4.5 million and hit $6 million for 1996.

Contract Design Services offers its clients more than 100 lines of carpet. Although the company specializes in carpet, it also carries the major manufacturers of resilient and ceramic tiles. In fact, Contract Design Services installed 100,000 square feet of wood flooring at the new Park Meadows shopping center.

Contract Design Services provides its clients with a full range of services — including design, product specification, project coordination, installation and warranty service. If a product is flawed, the company will serve as the client's advocate with the mill. Because of its exceptional service, the company has been able to build its book of business primarily by word of mouth.

The company's more than 100 clients include many of the major contractors, property managers and architects in the metropolitan Denver area. In 1996, Contract Design Services installed more than 20,000 yards of carpet each month.

Contract Design Services employs a staff of 15 and maintains an exclusive relationship with a number of professional installation crews that total more than 40 individuals. In order to manage the logistics of installation, the company developed a proprietary software program that it is marketing to other companies.

Contract Design Services is a values-driven company that shares its success through a generous benefits package. It was one of the first companies in Denver to further the cause of "safe" commercial buildings by using only environmentally safe carpets and adhesives.

Contract Design Services was founded in Denver in 1982. In the mid-1980s, the company was purchased by employees Bonnie Bowman, who is president, and Sheryl Shariat, who is vice-president of sales. Jo Ann Cardone is also an owner and vice president. Named a WBE by the City and County of Denver in 1988, Contract Design Services emerged from the tumultuous 1980s debt-free and profitable.

Contract Design Services has donated thousands of yards of carpet and installation to worthy Denver organizations, including schools and shelters for battered women, abused children, and the homeless. The company has also donated to the Colorado AIDS Project and Habitat for Humanities/The House That Women Built.

Contract Design Services, a successful woman-owned company, is dedicated to giving the best possible service to its clients at all times.

THE KENTWOOD COMPANY

Since 1981, professionalism has been the hallmark of The Kentwood Company. A high-end residential real estate company, the firm has led the nation in productivity-per-agent for five consecutive years.

The Kentwood Company was established in 1981 by a small group of experienced real estate agents who wanted to create a high-end alternative to large, impersonal real estate organizations. In 1987, the partnership expanded, the sales force doubled, and the company emerged as the dominant residential brokerage in the southern sector of the Denver marketplace.

Kentwood's agents average more than 17 years of full-time service (the company hires no part-time agents) and are well-versed in current sales trends, real estate law, tax changes and financing alternatives. In 1996, the company averaged more than $10 million in sales per agent. The average listing price of a home sold by Kentwood is more than $360,000. A traditional brokerage that is committed to remaining manageable in size, Kentwood has 35 seasoned professional residential real estate agents, including agents with the best credential and reputation in the nation.

Kentwood is located in the Denver Tech Center, at the heart of burgeoning southeast suburban Denver. The company consistently sells more homes in this area than any other real estate firm, partly because it serves as exclusive marketing agent for several of the area's most prestigious new-home communities. The company supports its agents with 21 full-time staff people and experienced record sales in 1996 of more than $350 million.

Kentwood is the only company in the Denver market whose listings are featured in *Christie's Great Estates: The International Showcase for Distinctive Properties*, published three times per year by Christie's, the famous international auction house. In addition, the company is listed among "Real Estate's Top 300 Power Brokers" by National Relocation & Real Estate magazine.

Kentwood Relocation Services, established in 1991, works closely with corporations and their employees to coordinate successful moves — moves that control costs for the employer while satisfying

A high-end residential real estate company, The Kentwood Company has led the nation in productivity-per-agent for five consecutive years.

the unique needs of each family. In 1996, corporate relocation accounts for about 35 percent of the company's business.

In order to provide its clients with convenient access to financing, the company formed Colorado Express Mortgage Company in 1984. Colorado Express is a joint venture with Waterfield Mortgage Corporation, the largest privately held mortgage company in the country.

Kentwood is actively involved in the Denver community, lending support to many charities, including the Make-A-Wish Foundation, the Cancer League of Colorado and The Cherry Creek Schools Foundation. Individual agents fill leadership positions in their industry, communities and neighborhoods.

For Denver residents or corporate transfers, for home-buyers who love older homes in established neighborhoods or new homes in the finest planned communities, The Kentwood Company offers an unbeatable combination of experience, reputation and results.

The Kentwood Company consistently sells more homes in southeast suburban Denver than any other real estate firm, partly because it serves as exclusive marketing agent for several of the area's most prestigious new-home communities.

MATHIAS LOCK & KEY

Established in 1901, Mathias Lock & Key is the oldest locksmith company in the State of Colorado. For most of its existence, this woman-owned business has been under the ownership of one family.

Historically, Mathias Lock & Key has provided both commercial and residential security services. Today, however, more than 95 percent of the company's clients are commercial.

Mathias Lock & Key customers span the metropolitan area and include the most security-conscious of Denver's businesses — major banks, law firms and office buildings. The company also meets the specialized security needs of casinos in Black Hawk and Central City.

For its commercial clients, Mathias Lock & Key offers master key systems, high security hardware, Medeco high security locks, digital access, magnetic locks, ADA-compliant access and egress hardware and office furniture lock services. The company also sells and repairs commercial and residential safes.

Mathias Lock & Key credits much of its success to its 13 loyal and skilled employees — none of whom has left in the past 12 years.

Mathias Lock & Key can trace its roots to the Sorensen Novelty Works, founded by Oscar Sorensen in 1901. The small shop was located in the 1100 block of 18th Street.

Sorenson was a "tinker" who repaired locks, irons, electric trains, guns, small appliances, cash registers, mechanical toys and slot machines. He also sharpened knives, saws, skates, lawnmowers and hand tools. The company continued many of these services well into the 1970s. Sorenson sold the shop to Max Winkler, a blacksmith.

In 1917, John Mathias, who had started working for Winkler in 1907, bought the business and renamed it Mathias Novelty Works. Mathias added new services, including door hardware, master keying, door closer works, and safe and safe deposit box repair. As consumer demand for these newer services increased, the company's name evolved into Mathias Lock & Key.

In 1933, John Mathias hired his nephew as an apprentice. Steve Benoit gradually assumed full responsibility for operation of the company, which he purchased after John Mathias died in 1951. Steve Benoit Jr. joined the company in 1965 and became president when his father retired in 1981. His wife, Mary Benoit, was business manager.

In 1997, Mary Benoit is president of the company and Steve Benoit Jr. is chief executive officer. Their two sons, Benny and Michael, also work for Mathias Lock & Key, providing a fourth generation of family involvement. The company is located downtown on the corner of 18th and Welton — just four blocks from its original location.

Mathias Lock & Key supports a variety of professional, civic and community organizations, including the Denver Metro Chamber of Commerce and the Building Owners and Managers Association.

Steve Benoit was president of the Rocky Mountain Locksmith Association in 1986 and 1987. Mary Benoit was 1996-97 president of the Denver club of Zonta International, a worldwide organization dedicated to advancing the status of women.

For more than 95 years, Mathias Lock & Key has provided safety and peace of mind for the businesses and residents of Denver.

STAPLETON DEVELOPMENT CORPORATION

The citizens of Denver have always been men and women with vision. In the late nineteenth century, Denver took action to ensure that it would have a vital connection to the new railroad pushing its way across the nation. In the 1930s, Mayor Ben Stapleton and civic leaders created the Denver Municipal Airfield, later known as Stapleton International Airport, which guaranteed Colorado a link to cities throughout the nation and around the globe.

Denver exhibited that same vision in 1995 when it opened Denver International Airport as the most modern and efficient airport in the world. With the closure of Stapleton that same year, a significant chapter in Denver's history ended and a new chapter began, as the community formulated a new vision for Stapleton that would develop jobs, housing and open space on the 4,700 acres of the former airfield.

A key element of the Stapleton Development Plan proposed by the community, and agreed to by Mayor Webb and the Denver City Council, was the recommendation to create a non profit private sector organization that would bring a coordinated and timely business approach to development of the property according to the values and goals articulated by the community. That organization is the Stapleton Development Corporation, a master developer governed by a board of community leaders and aided by an advisory board of citizens.

In shaping Stapleton's future, the citizens called for a mixed-use development over thirty years of 10,000 housing units in pedestrian-friendly urban neighborhoods that enjoy mass transit and "telecommuter" links to employment centers of clean, sustainable, commercial development. The quality of life in those urban villages is to be enhanced by 1,700 acres of parks, nature areas and open space, as well as recreation amenities that include hiking, biking and equestrian trails along the Sand Creek corridor that crosses the Stapleton property. The open space and recreational elements of the new Stapleton are designed to reflect the "Colorado lifestyle" that is the envy of the nation and the magnet that draws

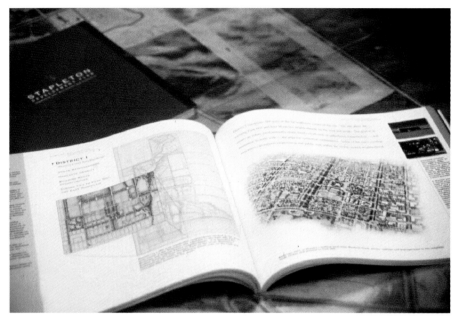

The Stapleton Development Plan

tourism and healthy new business development to communities across our state.

The commercial development at Stapleton will be in the range of 17 million to 20 million square feet of space, divided between a creative re-use of some existing hangars and other aviation facilities and new construction that meets the highest design standards. Among the first and most significant tenants to commit to "the new Stapleton" was United Airlines, which negotiated an agreement with the Stapleton Development Corporation and the City of Denver to invest in a $140 million expansion of its flight training facilities and create a corporate training campus at Stapleton. The expanded center will provide one hundred new jobs as it increases the training capability not only for United Airlines personnel, but personnel from airlines throughout the world. Overall, new development at Stapleton will involve a cumulative investment of more than $2.5 billion.

The Stapleton Development Corporation is committed to the successful transformation of the former airport into one of the most livable and successful communities in the nation, bringing new strength to our economy and Colorado's international reputation as one of the best places to live and work in the nation!

W. M. BROWN CONSTRUCTION

Brown Construction is a family- and woman-owned general contractor. (Left to right) Michael Brown is vice president. Roselle Brown is secretary and treasurer. Wayne Brown is executive project director. Mary Anderson is president.

An explosion-resistant manufacturing facility for O.E.A.

The Davis Pavilion at Denver Health Medical Center.

Brown Construction has built some of Denver's most recognizable public spaces.

W. M. Brown Construction, a family- and woman-owned general contractor, specializes in design-build commercial construction. The company offers exceptional expertise in concrete structures.

The company recently served as general contractor and construction manager for a specially designed explosion-resistant 160,000-square-foot manufacturing facility for O.E.A., the Arapahoe County-based manufacturer of automotive airbags.

Brown Construction is the only contractor in Colorado licensed by CON/STEEL, a designer of pre-cast tilt-up concrete buildings, whose system was used to construct the $12.6 million O.E.A. facility.

In addition, Brown Construction completed 26 different construction contracts at Denver International Airport. The company also built a three-story Comfort Inn near DIA, and intends to participate fully in the burgeoning construction market surrounding the successful new airport.

Brown Construction has also built some of Denver's most recognizable public spaces, like the green space that softens the terrain between the Cherry Creek Mall and Cherry Creek and the Gateway urban park along Speer Boulevard between Lawrence and Zuni. For several years, in preparation for Broncos season, the company has made structural repairs and facelift architectural upgrades at Mile High Stadium.

Brown Construction recently completed the Cultural Center parking lot that served the Denver Public Library and the Denver Art Museum. Tall standards surrounding the parking lot feature silk-screened banners designed by local school children. Children's poetry has been sand-blasted into the stones.

A portion of the cost of the school's involvement in this project was donated by Brown Construction. The company strongly believes that the construction trades should be presented as a worthwhile career goal to school-age children and undertakes a variety of projects that put this belief into action.

Other local projects include the pavilion at Denver Health Medical Center, the Buckley Office of Special Investigations for the Army Corps of Engineers and the Watkins Front Range Armory for the State of Colorado.

Brown Construction Company, located in the Denver suburb of Westminster, was founded in 1985. Wayne Brown, the company's executive project director, is a civil engineer who had retired in 1985 as president of a major local construction company. Roselle Brown, his spouse, is secretary and treasurer of the company. Michael Brown, a son, is vice president. Mary Anderson, a daughter, is president. At Brown Construction, the concept of "family" extends to include valued key personnel.

In 1997, the company will occupy its new 5,000-square-foot headquarters building in "old" Westminster. Employment ranges between 60 and 100 people, depending on the season. The entire Brown Construction "family" takes a personal interest in each project.

Mary Anderson is very involved in the construction industry. She has served as president of the Colorado Chapter of Women Construction Owners and Executives and sits on the national organization's board of directors; is a member of the Colorado Building Industry Council; and currently sits on the board of the Associated General Contractors of Colorado. She is also a representative on the State of Colorado Goals Committee for State Building Construction projects.

W.M. Brown is a diversified construction company that relies on teamwork to get the job done right the first time — completed on schedule, within budget and with quality.

Partners in Denver

INVESTMENT BANKING AND SECURITIES BROKERAGE, INSURANCE, SECURITIES AND DIVERSIFIED

BUSINESS AND FINANCE

HOLDING COMPANIES PROVIDE FINANCIAL FOUNDATION FOR A HOST OF DENVER ENTERPRISES.

Colorado-Lincoln Financial Group

Colorado-Lincoln Financial Group has served the needs of Colorado's business and community leaders for more than 30 years. Colorado-Lincoln Financial Group, together with its planning affiliate Professional Financial Planning, is recognized throughout the region as a leading financial services and planning firm, offering its clients solutions to a wide variety of personal and business needs.

Pamela Bruning
Regional CEO
Colorado-Lincoln
Financial Group

....

"Our clients appreciate our flexibility when it comes to fees. We're able to offer our services on a fee-only, hourly, commission or percent-of-assets basis — or whatever combination of these methods best meets the client's needs.

....

Colorado-Lincoln Financial Group differs from most insurance or investment companies in two very significant ways. Although the group is an affiliated company of Lincoln Life, it recognizes that no single company can provide all of the solutions to an individual's or a business' financial services and planning needs. Through strategic relationships, Colorado-Lincoln Financial Group provides access to the products and services of most major insurance and investment companies.

In addition, Colorado-Lincoln Financial Group and its associates emphasize a planning approach to finding solutions to its clients' financial problems. A comprehensive discovery process assists the firm's associates in getting to know their clients and building relationships with them. Solutions are recommended only after this process is complete.

Colorado-Lincoln Financial Group has significant experience and local expertise in several major areas:

Financial Planning
Investment advice is offered through Professional Financial Planning, a registered investment adviser.

For highly compensated professionals and business owners, the firm offers a detailed, documented plan that is developed over several meetings. Current and projected income, assets and inheritances are all considered in conjunction with applicable tax and revenue codes.

Inflation and asset-growth calculations are made to help clients develop an accurate assessment of their current situation in relationship to their agreed-upon plans. A plan of action is selected and implemented. This approach includes regularly scheduled reassessments to monitor progress.

Estate Planning Services
Qualified estate planning professionals examine a client's current estate situation and offer a written analysis that may include recommendations to reduce estate tax liabilities, to establish a gifting plan for heirs or charitable organizations, or to create wills or trusts to ensure that the estate owner's goals are successfully implemented following his or her death.

Business succession planning assistance is a rapidly growing sector of Colorado-Lincoln Financial Group's work, as owners pass control to successive generations or search for buyers for their closely held companies.

Asset Management
Many individuals, foundations and businesses look to Colorado-Lincoln Financial Group and its affiliates for assistance in monitoring current invest-

Jeffrey Guard
Colorado-Lincoln
Financial Group

"**The busy medical professional has special needs. In this day and age of consolidation and network practices, compensation arrangements are no longer simple. Combine the compensation trends with the time requirements of an active medical practice and you soon develop a situation where minimal attention is paid to the physician's personal financial situation. That's where I come in.**"

....

ments and for advice on appropriate investment vehicles. The most current investment management thinking is utilized in conjunction with sophisticated software to ensure that portfolio growth meets reasonable client expectations.

S m a l l   B u s i n e s s , E m p l o y e e   B e n e f i t s

An outgrowth of the firm's experience in dealing with the small business owner is its ability to provide access to an increasing number of products and services geared to meet the needs of companies with fewer than 200 employees. Cafeteria plans, 401(k) and retirement plans, health and disability insurance benefits and executive compensation programs are just a few of the benefits most often requested by clients.

E x p e r i e n c e d   P l a n n i n g P r o f e s s i o n a l s

Colorado-Lincoln Financial Group prides itself on the expertise and experience of its professionals but is also extremely comfortable working with the advisors of its clients. This consultative approach is reassuring to the client and draws upon the experience of existing advisors to make the best possible recommendations.

Located in the Denver Tech Center, Colorado-Lincoln Financial Group employs 15 people and uses sophisticated systems to support the activities of 50 planning associates and 450 brokers.

Colorado-Lincoln Financial Group is a sponsor of DECA, Habitat for Humanity and the Life Underwriters Charity, Inc. The company also sponsors a national high school debate competition — the Lincoln Life Lincoln-Douglas Debates.

Colorado-Lincoln Financial Group is an affiliate of Lincoln Life, the nation's 12th largest life insurer.

....

"**The last five years represent enormous changes in the amount of information that technology now enables us to sift, sort and filter through. We can examine numerous measures of risk and performance to evaluate current client portfolios or make recommendations. An experienced professional with the right tools can be of tremendous value to an individual responsible for investment decisions.**"

....

As part of a national organization, Colorado-Lincoln Financial Group can access a sophisticated national database when advising customers with interests in more than one state or region.

A. Raymond Benton
Colorado-Lincoln
Financial Group

....

THE REGISTERED PRODUCTS AND SERVICES OF LNC EQUITY SALES CORPORATION, A REGISTERED INVESTMENT ADVISER, INCLUDING ITS PROFESSIONAL FINANCIAL PLANNING DIVISION, ARE:

Mutual funds	Self-directed IRAs	Estate planning	Risk management
Stocks and bonds	Variable life and annuities	Tax planning	Education seminars
Limited partnerships	Securities brokerage	College funding	
Asset management	Financial planning	Investment advice	

The Advanced Planning Department At Colorado-Lincoln Financial Group

Many successful Colorado residents have worked hard all their lives, putting together a portfolio of assets or building a business. Many of these individuals and businesses have found the financial advice they need at Colorado-Lincoln Financial Group.

The advisers who work in the Advanced Planning department of Colorado-Lincoln Financial Group bring a well-rounded package of life and professional skills to the table when they sit down to help solve their clients' problems. They provide a continuing, independent source of financial advice for professionals, families, individuals and business owners. Financial advisory services are offered through Professional Financial Planning, a registered investment advisor.

The Advanced Planning department uses a comprehensive perspective to help wealthy clients accumulate and manage financial resources, working with them closely to develop integrated strategies in the areas of:

- investment supervision
- income tax management
- estate design and implementation
- insurance strategies
- financial planning
- retirement planning and
- business consultation.

Advanced Planning offers financial advisory services that include a balanced approach to portfolio design and management as well as comprehensive and modular planning. Business services include succession planning, retirement plan design and corporate feasibility studies. Representatives of Professional Financial Planning also assist charitable organizations and individuals with planned giving strategies.

A . Raymond Benton

A. Raymond Benton, who is enrolled to practice before the Internal Revenue Service, has been a certified financial planner and a registered investment adviser representative since 1984. He was recently named to serve on the Practice Standards Task Force of the Institute of Certified Financial Planners.

His client base includes individuals and businesses in Colorado, New Mexico, California, Iowa and Nevada.

In cooperation with a local law firm, Benton has presented a well-received series of estate planning programs. He has written advice columns for local newspapers and is co-host, with Jeffrey Guard, of "Real Money," a local radio program broadcast on KTLK 760 AM each Sunday morning at 10 a.m.

Benton received his undergraduate degree from Oklahoma State University and a graduate degree from Miami University in Oxford, Ohio. He also holds a Divinity degree from Chicago Theological Seminary, where his studies focused on social ethics and philosophy.

Jeffrey W. Guard

Jeffrey W. Guard has been a registered investment adviser representative in the Denver area since 1984. His father is a prominent local physician; consequently, Guard has developed special expertise in working with medical professionals.

He has clients in Colorado, California, Florida, Arizona, Nebraska, Kansas, Wyoming, New Mexico and Texas.

Guard is a regular speaker at local investment clubs and co-hosts, with colleague Ray Benton, a local radio program on financial management. He has also appeared as an expert commentator on local television. Guard has taught courses in financial planning at the high school and adult education levels.

A Denver native, Guard attended Western State College in Gunnison. He has worked closely with the Rocky Mountain Conference of the United Methodist Foundation to conduct planned giving and estate planning classes throughout that organization's three-state region.

UNION BANK & TRUST

On August 30, 1934, a new bank opened its doors in an elegant marble-floored building at the corner of 1st & Broadway. At the time, it was a bit of a drive or trolley ride south of downtown Denver. In attendance on that day, sharing in the celebration, was a charter customer by the name of A. M. "Miller" Jacobsen. As 1996 came to a close, Mr. Jacobsen and his wife Hilma were still customers of that bank — Union National Bank, which subsequently became Union Bank & Trust (UB&T) in 1972.

The historic headquarters of UB&T is a 6-story, granite, marble and brick structure standing majestically on the northeast corner at the intersection of 1st & Broadway. The area was a hotbed of banking activity serving residents and businesses in what was then known as South Denver.

Originally built in 1917, the structure has always served as a banking facility. The first institution to occupy the premises was the Fleming Brothers Bank. In 1921, another brother duo, the Bowens, purchased the Fleming's assets and changed the name to the Broadway Bank. But it was just a few months later when the Bowens sold to Gordon Hollis. He, in turn, applied for and received a National Charter for the Broadway National Bank, which was closed in December 1925. Horace Bennett took over the

impressive building and opened the South Broadway National Bank in 1926. In 1934, UB&T took over the deposits of that bank and opened its doors with capital and surplus totaling $112,500. The rest is history.

UB&T opened at the height of The Great Depression. It was a period characterized by frequent bank sales, foreclosures, repossessions and difficult economic times for everyone. Individuals and businesses in the area needed banking relationships built on understanding, trust, reliability, loyalty and friendship. Many came to UB&T for those reasons.

While UB&T has expanded into three branch locations in the Denver metro area, the fact that the institution still occupies its original 1st & Broadway home speaks volumes for a history of commitment and dedication to meeting customer needs. Still operated by local on-site management under the theme "Personal Attention, Professional Service," UB&T has provided financial support for local families and businesses, and is consequently part of the history and fabric that make up Denver today.

Banking relationships at UB&T are often measured in generations. Many of today's customers have followed parents, grandparents and other family members through the bank's doors. Few financial institutions have achieved a history of service and stability as that offered by UB&T. All symbolized by the stately structure at 100 Broadway.

BLUE CROSS AND BLUE SHIELD OF COLORADO

During the Great Depression, many Americans were unable to pay their hospital and doctor bills. This historic crisis led to the development of reimbursement-type health insurance — and the first Blue Cross and Blue Shield plans.

Before long, the nonprofit Blue Cross and Blue Shield plans had become the industry's strongest brand name — associated with quality care, outstanding doctors and hospitals, and dependability.

Sixty years later, the health-care system is facing another dramatic revolution — the revolution of managed care. This crisis is driven by the dynamics of maintaining high-quality health care; providing subscribers with choice, flexibility and access; and addressing the issues of cost and affordability.

Once again, Blue Cross and Blue Shield of Colorado — the major Colorado-based health insurance company — has positioned itself to meet the challenges of change. It is transforming itself from a health-care insurer to a total health-management company.

In 1997, Blue Cross and Blue Shield of Colorado, through its various subsidiaries, is a single-source provider of a wide range of benefit products — health insurance, life insurance, dental insurance and workers' compensation administration. The company's customers range from some of the state's largest employers to small businesses and individuals.

Blue Cross and Blue Shield of Colorado still offers the traditional indemnity-style health insurance plans that made it famous. However, the majority of the company's customers have chosen a new family of health-care plans called BlueAdvantage, which offers HMO, point-of-service and preferred provider organization options. There is also a BlueAdvantage for Seniors plan specially designed to substitute for Medicare.

BlueAdvantage features the largest state-wide network of primary care physicians in Colorado. Affiliation with the nationwide Blue Cross and Blue Shield network — HMO Blue USA — means that Colorado Blue Cross and Blue Shield HMO customers can receive health-care services — routine or emergency — across the country.

Other health-care plans offered by the company include Medicare supplements, national accounts,

the federal employees health benefits program, and individual PPO and indemnity plans.

In 1996, Blue Cross and Blue Shield of Colorado announced the advent of on-line health policy enrollment. Subscribers will be able to use a new Internet service called Healtheon to select an insurance plan, enroll family members and check on coverage.

Health Management Systems (HMS), the company's dental insurance program, offers employers a variety of choices — a traditional dental plan, a state-wide preferred provider plan, and a low-cost HMO-type plan.

Rocky Mountain Life, a subsidiary, offers a complete line of traditional group life and disability products. It has also developed a variety of voluntary products that enrich an employee's benefit package at minimal cost — group term life, accidental death and dismemberment, and short- and long-term disability.

Another subsidiary, Occupational Healthcare Management Services (OHMS), administers medical services and paperwork for self-insured workers' compensation programs. OHMS offers claims management and loss control services, a dedicated network of primary care physicians and specialists, individual medical case management, and customized cost-savings reports employers can use to track results.

Blue Cross and Blue Shield of Colorado can trace its roots in the state to 1938, when a group of community leaders, hospital executives and physicians formed the Colorado Hospital Services, which later became known as Blue Cross of Colorado, to offer affordable prepaid group hospitalization insurance.

Two years later, a group of 169 physicians formed the Colorado Medical Service, which later became Blue Shield of Colorado.

The two nonprofit organizations combined office space in 1958, but continued to operate independently. In 1974, the "Blues" occupied their current headquarters, a 13-story building on Broadway, just south of Downtown Denver and adjacent to the Historic Golden Triangle neighborhood.

The two companies merged in 1978, forming Blue Cross and Blue Shield of Colorado. In 1996, the com-

pany employed almost 1,000 Colorado residents and maintained offices in Colorado Springs, Durango and Grand Junction. It had 325,000 subscribers.

In January 1997, the company merged once again, this time with Blue Cross and Blue Shield of Nevada. Retaining the Blue Cross and Blue Shield of Colorado name, the merged company benefitted from expanded markets and a stronger financial base. This strength allowed it to continue offering a high level of service to customers in the two states, while also continuing its commitment to the community.

Faced with formidable competitive pressures and the need to raise capital, Blue Cross and Blue Shield of Colorado announced in 1996 that it would seek to convert from a not-for-profit entity to a for-profit stock company. The state approved a law making this change possible and the company submitted a conversion plan to state regulators for approval.

When conversion is complete, 100 percent of the value of the converted company will be transferred to two independent nonprofit foundations dedicated to addressing the health-care needs of Colorado — particularly Colorado children.

The 700 Broadway Building has been home to Blue Cross and Blue Shield of Colorado since 1974. The company employs 1,000 people in Colorado.

For nearly 60 years, Blue Cross and Blue Shield of Colorado has provided the state's residents with high-quality, affordable health-care plans and services.

By providing modern health-care management products and taking steps to ensure its financial stability, Blue Cross and Blue Shield of Colorado will continue this tradition well into the 21st Century.

Colorado National Bank

In 1862, Denver Township was only one year old, and the enterprising Kountze Brothers, Luther and Charles, were already staking their claim to their first "big idea" by opening a bank to provide financial support for this growing city.

On December 2, 1862, Luther Kountze opened the doors of Kountze Brothers bank in the corner storefront of Walter Scott Cheesman's building at 15th and Blake. *Rocky Mountain News* editor, Williams N. Byers,

declared that the bank "will pay the treasury notes, and first-class bank currencies. Mr. Kountze is a gentleman of high business character, substantial, straight forward and solvent for anything he may do."

Luther's first two years in Denver included Indian scares, the Cherry Creek flood and the Great Fire of 1863, which destroyed the Kountze Brothers' first office. The day after the fire, Luther set up shop in Tootle & Leach's mercantile house, a few doors down Blake Street from his old corner. Relying on his Omaha and eastern banking connection, Luther made loans to most to most of the town's leading entrepreneurs. With this capital infusion from Kountze Brothers, Denver rebuilt in brick and stone, recovering rapidly from what is still known as the "Great Fire."

Colorado National bank was born on June 7, 1866 when Luther and Charles Kountze received the territory's second national charter — Charter Number 1651 — from Comptroller of the Currency Freeman Clark. Luther served as president of CNB, just as he had

presided over Kountze Brothers. Charles remained cashier and much of the work fell to him, especially after Luther left for a year in Europe that same year. Charles became the president of CNB in 1874.

Charles welcomed a diverse range of customers as a precaution against the boom and bust mining economy. To promote a broader diversification emphasizing agriculture and industry, Charles joined other business leaders in forming the Denver Chamber of Commerce in 1884.

Growing with the city and the times, the bank moved to a four-story building at 17th and Larimer in 1882. As continued growth took place, there was a need for additional expansion, and construction was started on the bank at 17th and Champa streets, its present site, in 1914. The "bank that looks like a bank"opened its doors on September 4, 1915.

Inside the stately new bank building, Alan True, one of the nation's foremost painters, was commis-

sioned to create a series of murals that have now become a tribute to the history for the plains Indians. True made an extensive study of early Indian life and took nearly two years to paint the series which symbolizes the cycle of life as the Indians lived it from youth to death. The series was completed in 1923.

While many banks floundered in the 1920s, CNB prospered. Its capital stock was doubled to $1 million, still tightly held by the Kountzes, the Bergers and a few top bank officers. A Trust Department, established in 1924, became an important asset to the bank's capital formation. In 1930, a year after the great crash, CNB still showed undivided profits of $773,699.

Colorado National Bank continued to prosper with its commitment to sound, conservative banking practices, but with an eye to the future. In the late 1960s, CNB purchased a credit card franchise from Bank of America that later grew to become Rocky Mountain BankCard System, an innovator in credit, debit card, ATM (automated teller machine) and electronic banking. In 1982, Colorado National Bank led the development of PLUS SYSTEM, Inc., now an international ATM network.

Traditional banking was also taking a new turn as Colorado National Bankshares was incorporated on April 17, 1967. By this move, the bank, which could not operate branches, created a bank holding company that could acquire and establish subsidiaries. Over the next several years, the company grew to include bank offices throughout Colorado as well as a mortgage company, an insurance agency and a leasing company.

During the 1960s, the bank purchased and demolished the remaining buildings in the block bordered by 19th, 17th, Champa and Curtis streets. In 1975, the Colorado National Building provided room to grow for the bank and its 700 employees.

In November 1992, First Bank System in Minneapolis reach an agreement with Colorado National Bankshares to acquire the Colorado company. By July 1993, the acquisition was complete and CNB merged with two other Colorado financial institutions, Central Bank and Bank Western. The merger created a banking company with assets in excess of $8 billion and some 60 offices and more than 300 ATMs throughout the state of Colorado. With the merger, CNB became part of a company committed to providing banking convenience not only through the traditional branch system, but also through innovative on-line and electronic systems.

The new Colorado National Bank is now the largest financial service provider in the Rocky Mountain Region, with consumer, business and trust products and services and a continued commitment — that began in 1862 — to Colorado and its citizens.

In 1987, the bank celebrated its 125th anniversary by bringing together the old and the new.

A three-story expansion to the bank was completed in 1965. The Colorado National Building, next door to the bank, was completed in 1975.

COLORADO STATE BANK OF DENVER

With the passing of the gold mining boom in 1908, Denver had broadened its economic base and had established itself as the industrial and commercial center of the Rocky Mountain region. The population was nearing 200,000, and the city was enjoying a comfortable prosperity.

Into this setting came William A. McCutchen from Wichita Falls, Texas. An experienced financier and perceptive business man, he recognized the promising

In 1917, the bank hired Mary Heatwole who was one of the first female tellers in Colorado and who later rose to become a vice president, and first woman bank officer in the state.

potential of Denver and the opportunities present for a bank that would give knowledgeable, personalized financial service to the people of the city. It was McCutchen who organized and was the first president of the Colorado State and Savings Bank. The bank opened for business on October 2, 1908 on the first floor of the Majestic Building on the corner of Broadway and 16th Street.

Meanwhile in Ft. Collins, a former bank examiner for the state of Missouri, Benjamin F. Clark, was broadening his banking experience. In 1910 he came to Denver and purchased controlling interest in Colorado State and Savings Bank. The following year his son-in-law, Forrest L. Barkley also moved to Denver from Ft. Collins and joined the staff of the bank. The bank's name was officially changed to The Colorado State Bank of Denver in 1919.

FAR RIGHT:
Even during the depression, the soundness of Colorado State Bank was never in question. In 1932, it proceeded with an extensive interior remodeling program at its location in the Majestic Building at 16th and Broadway in Denver.

The skills and talents of Clark and Barkley guided the bank through a dynamic half-century of growth. Under their precise, aggressive leadership, the bank would play an important role in the financial success of many Denver firms and individuals. Mr. Clark "retired" at the age of 93, after many years of service.

In 1910 the horse and buggy era was drawing to a close; America's young automobile industry was steadily gaining strength. At that time, only finance companies and dealers made automobile loans. Colorado State Bank was one of the first banks in the nation to enter the field of auto financing in 1914.

With those early loans the bank gained a favorable reputation as a progressive, pioneering bank with a positive attitude towards its customers' needs...a reputation that would serve it well as it expanded its base of services and clients over the years.

The stock market crash on October 29, 1929, marked the end of the post-war prosperity and the beginning of America's greatest depression. The bank's soundness was never in question, however, and it proceeded with an extensive remodeling program in 1932.

In January 1934, Colorado State Bank was the first bank in Denver to be notified that its application for Federal Deposit Insurance had been approved. It had been one of only three banks in Denver to re-open

In 1971, Colorado State Bank constructed its own 26-story building across the street from where it opened for business. The bank has occupied one of these corners in Denver ever since its founding in 1908.

after the 1933 bank "holiday" without calling on government assistance of any kind.

The bank grew in size and scope during the lively, prosperous years following World War II. On its fortieth anniversary in 1948, the bank had 32 employees. Included in this number was Elwood M. Kullgren, son-in law of Forrest L. Barkley, who joined the bank staff in 1937.

On January 1949, Colorado State Bank introduced drive-up banking to Denver with the installation of a curb teller. It was only the third curb teller in the United States, with others in St. Louis, Missouri and Portsmouth, Virginia. The event made headlines in local and national publications.

The natural growth of Denver, in the 40's and 50's, especially the downtown area, resulted in steady growth for the bank. Its directors selected Elwood M. Kullgren as President of Colorado State Bank. Mr. Kullgren retired in 1997 after 60 years of service, most recently as Chairman of the Board and CEO. His son-in-law, John G, Wilkinson, has been with the bank since 1966 and its president since 1985. He succeeded Mr. Kullgren as Chairman and CEO Mr. Wilkinson represents the fourth generation of father-in-law to son-in-law management of the bank.

The bank thrived under its dynamic new leadership. It was becoming evident that increased space would soon be needed to efficiently and effectively serve bank customers. In November of 1966, Colorado State Bank's Officers and Directors made the decision to build a magnificent new building — one that the bank, it's current customers, and future customers would be proud of.

On its 63rd anniversary, in October 1971, the bank opened its doors for business in the new building, housing some of Denver's most experienced bankers. The new 26-story Colorado State Bank Building was the beginning of downtown Denver's building boom and was the only locally-owned, new high rise. Over the years, Colorado State Bank has earned the reputation as being one of the soundest banks in the industry. This is attributed to the bank's prudent, steady growth, far-sighted leadership, and steadfast adherence to remain independent and locally owned.

In 1996, Colorado State Bank celebrated its 88th year of sound banking at the same location at 16th and Broadway. The bank offers a complete complement of consumer and business financial products, including a well-rounded and diversified trust department. A full service brokerage firm, CSB Investments Co., began operations in 1994 as a subsidiary of the bank.

Colorado State Bank has come a long way since the early years of the Twentieth Century and looks forward to serving the community into the next century. With innovative leadership tempered by careful growth, Colorado State Bank enters the Twenty-first Century with financial strength, vigor, and confidence.

FOUNDERS ASSET MANAGEMENT

Denver is a recognized hub for one of the most rapidly growing industries in the country — the mutual fund industry.

This recognition has been driven by the success of a few key players. One of the most successful of these firms is Founders Asset Management, Inc., distributor of the Founders Funds.

Founders Funds has been a part of the Denver community since 1938 and provides investors across the country with growth-oriented, no-load equity mutual funds to help them pursue their financial goals.

Founders Funds has been a part of the Denver community since 1938 and provides investors across the country with growth-oriented, no-load equity mutual funds to help them pursue their financial goals.

Bjorn K. Borgen is Chairman, CEO and Chief Investment Advisor of Founders Asset Management.

The Founders Funds

In recent years, the investment community has recognized Founders Funds for its history of strong long-term performance — a discovery that has resulted in tremendous growth in assets for the firm.

Founders offers eleven no-load funds which span the investment spectrum. These range from aggressive growth funds, such as the Founders Discovery and Frontier Funds, to more conservative funds, such as the Founders Balanced and Blue Chip Funds.

Over the past several years, Founders has gained additional recognition for its international offerings — Founders Worldwide Growth, International Equity and Passport Funds.

The Founders Philosophy

Founders attributes its success to an unwavering commitment to a growth-style philosophy. This means that managers build equity portfolios one stock at a time, searching for companies with fundamental strengths — regardless of their sector — that give them the potential to provide superior earnings over time. These strengths include:

- Above-average prospects for earnings growth
- Growth in revenues
- Strong management
- Leading market positions
- Financial, marketing and operating strength

After all, regardless of market conditions, there are always good companies to invest in. The key is finding them.

To accomplish this task, Founders' portfolio managers spend a considerable amount of time meeting with companies and their managements — learning their industries, businesses and financial prospects. In a typical year, each manager may meet face to face with the representatives of more than 300 companies. On the international front, the investment team typically spends 15 weeks a year on the road visiting companies in more than 20 countries.

Founders digs deep during this process, meeting middle as well as upper management, sampling products, touring facilities and reviewing inventories. The firm may visit the company's suppliers, customers and even competitors to truly understand every aspect of its business and industry.

The Founders History

Founders' history in Denver dates back to 1938 and the establishment of Founders Mutual Fund, known today as the Blue Chip Fund. From the beginning, it was Founders' objective to help individuals plan for their financial goals by providing investment products that capitalize on the growth potential of the stock market.

After nearly 30 years of success with this flagship fund, Founders underwent rapid expansion in the

1960s when it acquired the assets of three Denver-based mutual funds — today known as the Founders Growth (mid- and large-cap), Special (capital appreciation) and Balanced (balanced) funds.

Realizing that a flexible and fee-based management system offered more growth potential than a static list of companies, Founders moved toward the concept of active management in the 1960s. The driving force behind these changes was Bjorn Borgen, currently the firm's Chairman, CEO and Chief Investment Officer, who joined Founders in 1966.

In 1979, Founders made another historic move when it realized the need to offer a low-cost product to investors and began to offer its funds without a sales charge.

HIGHER RISK	
HIGHER RETURN POTENTIAL	
Micro/Small Cap	Discovery Fund
Small Cap	Frontier Fund
International Small Cap	Passport Fund
Capital Appreciation	Special Fund
Core International	International Equity Fund
Global Equity	Worldwide Growth Fund
Mid/Large Cap	Growth Fund
	Blue Chip Fund
Growth and Income	Balanced Fund
Balanced	Government
Fixed Income	Securities Fund
Money Market	Money Market Fund
LOWER RISK	
LOWER RETURN POTENTIAL*	

The company followed this bold move into the no-load mutual funds arena with another burst of expansion in the 1980s. This time, unlike its expansion in the 1960s, Founders designed its own fund offerings, beginning in 1981 with Founders Money Market Fund.[1]

In 1987, Founders opened the Frontier Fund, its first true small-cap offering. The success of this fund prompted the establishment of a more aggressive alternative, Founders Discovery Fund, to pursue

capital appreciation through investments in "micro cap" companies.[2]

In 1988, the fund family totaled five stock funds and a money market fund. In order to help its clients diversify a portion of their portfolios into income producing securities, Founders Government Securities Fund[3] was added.

With the success of the firm's domestic funds, Founders believed it could apply the same growth investment philosophy around the globe. In 1989, the firm launched the Worldwide Growth Fund. In 1993, this fund inspired a more aggressive descendant — Founders Passport Fund — designed to pursue opportunities arising from small companies abroad. Investing exclusively in overseas companies, Passport was Founders' first purely international fund.[4]

Founders most recent expansion occurred in 1995, when the company created a less aggressive, purely international investment vehicle — Founders International Equity Fund.[4]

Founders has been a driving force in the Denver community and the mutual fund industry for more than half a century. The firm's unwavering philosophy of growth-oriented investing has been its key to providing shareholders with the time-tested performance of the Founders Funds.

The Rink at Founders Center offers outdoor ice skating each winter to the Denver community, with proceeds going to a charitable fund to assist disadvantaged youth.

LEFT: Founders offers eleven no-load funds which span the investment spectrum.

*The risk/reward spectrum is not indicative of the past or future performance of any particular Founders Fund. Positions of Funds on the spectrum are subject to change.

[1] An investment in Founders Money Market Fund is neither insured nor guaranteed by the U.S. Government. There can be no assurance that the Fund will be able to maintain a stable net asset value of $1.00 per share.

[2] Investments in small companies may pose greater risks and rewards through the volatility associated with such factors as limited market share and financial resources.

[3] Fund shares are not guaranteed by the U.S. Government or any of its agencies. Principal value will fluctuate

[4] Foreign investing may entail special risks generally not associated with domestic investing, such as currency, economic and political risks.

Past performance is no guarantee of future result. For more complete information about the Founders Funds, including management fees and expenses, call to request a current prospectus. Please read it carefully before you invest or send money.

Founders Funds is a registered trademark of Founders Asset Management, Inc. Founders Asset Management, Inc., Distributor.

MATRIX CAPITAL CORPORATION

Matrix Capital Corporation is a specialized financial services company which combines the expertise of its operating subsidiaries to create revenue-enhancing opportunities within the residential mortgage and financial services industries. By leveraging upon the synergies among its subsidiaries, Matrix Capital Corporation generates significant returns in ways not available to its competition.

Established in Denver in 1993 as a Colorado-based corporation, Matrix Capital Corporation went public in October 1996 through the issuance of 1,750,000 shares of common stock. The company employs 275 people through its subsidiaries, which include United Financial Inc., Matrix Financial Services Corporation, Matrix Capital Bank, First Matrix Investment Services Corporation, United Capital Markets, United Special Services and Sterling Trust Company.

United Financial Inc., established in 1989 and based in Denver, is a mortgage servicing brokerage firm specializing in providing portfolio valuations and consulting services to its customers. United Financial Inc.'s clients represent some of the largest financial institutions and mortgage banking firms in the country, including Banc One Mortgage, Chase Manhattan Mortgage and Mellon Mortgage Corporation.

In acting as broker, United Financial Inc. arranges for the sale of serving portfolios between parties in negotiated deals or in auction or sealed-bid situations. The company brokered in excess of $30 billion in servicing portfolios during 1996, placing it among the three largest servicing brokers in the country.

As a consultant, United Financial Inc. provides advice to other companies that originate and service residential mortgages. This advice includes determining the value of servicing portfolios, monitoring trends on pricing in the market, analyzing potential impairment of servicing assets and developing hedging strategies.

Because there is no centralized exchange for the trading of servicing portfolios, the market intelligence that United Financial Inc. supplies its clients is critical to their success. Likewise, Matrix Capital Corporation and its other operating subsidiaries profit greatly from utilizing United Financial Inc. as their "eye to the market."

Another subsidiary of Matrix Capital Corporation is Matrix Financial Services Corporation, established in 1990 as a full-service mortgage banking company that originates, purchases, services and sells residential mortgages and the servicing rights to residential mortgages. Matrix Financial Services Corporation is headquartered in Phoenix, Arizona, and maintains branch offices in Denver, Colorado, and Atlanta, Georgia.

Unlike typical mortgage banking companies, Matrix Financial Services Corporation focuses on acquiring bulk packages of seasoned, low-balance servicing portfolios with higher balances of custodial escrow deposits as compared with newly originated mortgage servicing acquired by most other mortgage bankers. By concentrating on this less competitive niche, Matrix Financial Services Corporation is typically able to acquire these portfolios at a lower purchase price, which provides enhanced returns.

By the end of the first quarter of 1997, Matrix Financial Services Corporation will be servicing in excess of 80,000 mortgage accounts with an aggregate balance of greater than $4 billion. These mortgage accounts are serviced for each of the government-sponsored agencies, including Ginnie Mae, Fannie Mae and Freddie Mac, as well as more than 250 other institutional investors.

As a function of owning and managing servicing portfolios, Matrix Financial Services Corporation collects payments from borrowers on a monthly basis, which are in turn remitted to investors and other entities on a monthly, quarterly or annual basis. All funds received from borrowers are held in custodial escrow accounts until remitted. The timing difference between receiving and remitting payments creates positive cash "float" for the company.

Matrix Financial Services Corporation is able to direct the placement of the custodial escrow accounts to any FDIC-insured financial institution. Because of the unique corporate structure of Matrix Capital Corporation, all accounts and resulting positive-float benefit are directed to Matrix Capital Bank.

Matrix Capital Bank, acquired by Matrix Capital Corporation in October of 1993, is a federally chartered savings institution with assets of approximately $180 million at the year-end 1996 and has branches located in New Mexico and Arizona.

Matrix Capital Bank benefits significantly from the synergies existing among Matrix Capital Corporation's subsidiaries. First, Matrix Capital Bank takes in no-cost or low-cost deposits from the other subsidiaries and invests them in residential mortgage loans, thereby generating a higher level of income than other financial institutions, which must rely on traditional higher cost liabilities.

Second, Matrix Capital Bank is able to acquire loan packages on a geographically diversified basis by relying on the servicing expertise of Matrix Financial Services Corporation, which services loans on a nationwide basis. This provides Matrix Capital Bank with the ability to diversify its risk to regional economic fluctuations.

Lastly, by again relying on Matrix Financial Services Corporation's servicing infrastructure to manage its loan portfolio, Matrix Capital Bank can significantly increase its asset base in residential mortgage loans. Matrix Capital Corporation anticipates that the bank can grow to an asset base of $500 million without a corresponding increase in overhead expense.

In 1995, Matrix Capital Corporation formed *United Special Services*. As with United Financial Inc., United Special Services' revenue is derived from fee income and is not subject to interest rate or credit risk. United Special Services provides residential asset valuations as well as foreclosure and loan disposition services to mortgage lending institutions such as mortgage companies, banks and thrifts, including Matrix Financial Services Corporation and Matrix Capital Bank.

United Special Services is one of the largest sources of appraisal information used by Freddie Mac. Some of its biggest clients include Mellon Bank Corporation, Comerica Inc., Chase Manhattan Corporation and Banc One Corporation.

In early 1997, Matrix Capital Corporation acquired The Vintage Group, headquartered in Waco, Texas, for $11.25 million in stock. The Vintage Group, through its subsidiary *Sterling Trust Company*, specializes in self-directed qualified retirement plans, individual retirement accounts, custodial and directed trust accounts. Sterling Trust Company administers approximately $1 billion of such assets.

With this acquisition, Matrix Capital Corporation hopes to repeat the success of its approach to mortgage banking in a new sector of the financial services industry. A key to this success will be the benefit derived from directing to Matrix Capital Bank approximately $60 million to $70 million of low-cost money market accounts directed into Sterling Trust Company. Additionally, Matrix Capital Corporation would expect to benefit from cross-selling products among several of its subsidiaries, including mortgage loan products, banking services and trust services.

Matrix Capital Corporation is certainly one of the most exciting companies in the specialty financial services industry. It has created or acquired a group of interrelated subsidiaries which are driven to enhance their profitability, and thus Matrix Capital Corporation's profitability, by leveraging on each other's strengths. No other publicly traded company found in this country combines the unique features of Matrix Capital Corporation.

MATRIX CAPITAL CORPORATION

- United Financial Inc.
- Matrix Financial Services Corporation
- Matrix Capital Bank
- United Special Services
- Sterling Trust Company
- First Matrix Investment Services Corporation
- United Capital Markets Inc.

NORWEST BANK COLORADO

For more than 110 years, the company now known as Norwest Bank Colorado has been an integral part of the Denver community and its economy. Through the years, Norwest has grown not only in size, but in services as the needs of the community have changed.

The story of Norwest in Colorado began in 1884 when the Denver National Bank opened. Founded by a group led by Denver pioneer Joseph Thatcher, the bank served individual customers as well as the Colorado mining and livestock industries. A glance at the early signature books of the bank shows that customers included companies like Stearns-Rogers and the Denver Dry Goods Company, and individuals like Buffalo Bill Cody and members of the Boettcher family.

Always on the cutting edge of customer service, Giles Foley, a Denver National employee, convinced the bank to start a Personal Loan Department in 1931, one of the first such departments in Denver. At the time, most commercial bankers regarded making loans to individuals as beneath their dignity. But the Denver National felt that banks should make more banking services available to more people. That com-

munity attitude was a key reason why Denver National also was one of the first Denver banks to make oil loans at a time when most oilmen had to go to banks outside of Colorado to get a loan.

Another key Norwest predecessor was the United States National Bank, which opened in 1904. The foundation for this bank was the Daniels Bank, founded in 1901 by William Daniels, to serve employees and customers of the Daniels and Fisher store, now known as Foley's.

Much of the bank's success can be attributed to its innovation. When the outlook appeared bleak in the 50s, U.S. National began to do things to attract new business that were unheard of in banking. It advertised. Officers made calls on customers — outside of the bank! People were invited to come into the lobby to see all kinds of exhibits — from flowers to oil derricks. This fourth largest downtown bank developed a reputation as an underdog that was challenging the way the bigger Seventeenth Street banks had done business for years.

Innovative marketing was one way the bank felt it could grow. Another way was to expand its services and facilities. In 1959, U.S. National Bank and the Denver National Bank merged. The banks were almost equal in size at the time of the merger, and together they created the second largest bank in the state known as Denver U.S. National Bank.

In the 1960s, the company moved strongly into the forefront of the financial industry. It again sought avenues of growth — to better serve shareholders, businesses and consumers in Colorado. More and more people were moving in to enjoy the Colorado lifestyle. New businesses opened creating new jobs. Downtown Denver became a financial center.

People, however, lived in the suburbs, and many even worked there. Participation in this growth was only possible for a downtown bank two ways — if it had suburban banks as correspondents, or if it joined

Denver National Bank opened for business in 1884 at the corner of 17th and Champa streets in downtown Denver.

Denver National started a Personal Loan Department in 1931, one of the first such departments in Denver.

RIGHT: Norwest CultureFest is just one of the many ways the bank contributes to the Denver community. On an annual basis, Norwest in Denver provides more than $1.5 million of support to local nonprofit organizations.

in a partnership with suburban banks in a bank holding company. This company took the bolder step! In 1964, a holding company was formed — one of the first in Colorado. Three banks made up Denver U.S. Bancorporation: Denver U.S. National Bank, Arapahoe County Bank in Littleton, and Bank of Aurora.

Denver U.S. Bancorporation continued to grow with Denver, and continued its commitment to making banking services accessible. In 1967, the company introduced the Guaranteed Check Card to help people cash checks. Then it helped bring Master Charge (now MasterCard) to Coloradans. In 1969, Personal Banking was introduced to the region — a new concept of one banker for all a person's financial needs.

The company grew to include more banks in areas of the state experiencing growth such as Boulder, Fort Collins, Grand Junction, Greeley, Lakewood and Pueblo. With this expansion, a new name and common identity was needed, and in 1970, the holding company became known as United Banks of Colorado, and each bank took the name United Bank.

Two years after the name change, United Banks had grown remarkably to 12 banks and more than $1 billion in assets. Banks were acquired in Colorado Springs, Longmont and Montrose. United Banks was operating its own data processing company, a mortgage company and two insurance subsidiaries. At one time, United Banks had the world's largest auto bank, constructed in 1964, and was the first to offer equity lines of credit.

Widely recognized as a leader in the banking industry, bankers from across the country came to United Bank in Denver to learn about such programs as Executive Banking, which served high net worth individuals, and the Women's Banking Center created to meet the needs of professional women.

The 1980s were difficult years for the Colorado economy. The dramatic downturn in the oil industry left Denver with high unemployment and vacant office space at a time when interest rates were soaring nationally and the Savings and Loan industry was in crisis. United Banks continued to grow, however, and by the end of the decade had assets of approximately $6 billion and owned 40 banks.

It was 1990 before the name Norwest began being seen and heard in Colorado. On July 25, 1990, United Banks of Colorado and Norwest Corporation signed a definitive agreement to merge. The merger was completed in April of 1991 and a year later, United Banks officially changed its name to Norwest Bank Colorado.

Norwest continues to abide by the philosophy of providing the most banking and investment services to the most people. The banking innovation that has been the hallmark of its predecessors remains true to Norwest. For example, the Urban Banking Group was formed to make Norwest accessible to customers living in all areas of the Denver community. Also, Norwest now offers its customers a complete range of financial services, including mortgages, insurance, and investment options through its brokerage and trust departments, in addition to traditional banking services.

Norwest's many achievements have not gone unnoticed. In 1996, Norwest was honored with the prestigious Colorado Business in Ethics award for its lending policies and community involvement. For the fourth straight year, Norwest was named the top lender by the Small Business Administration, and for an unprecedented third time in a row, Norwest received an "outstanding" rating for its Community Reinvestment Act (CRA) efforts.

Today Norwest is a network of community banks set up so each location can make decisions locally to best serve customers while drawing on the company's sizable resources. Norwest currently has nearly 50 stores in Denver and the surrounding suburbs, with 88 stores throughout the state. It is the largest bank in Colorado with more than $7 billion in assets.

LEFT: A long standing tradition, Norwest routinely invites customers and the community at large into its banks for exhibits and special celebrations. Here, Norwest customers commemorate the Chinese New Year in the Norwest atrium at 17th and Broadway in downtown Denver.

The 52-story One Norwest Center at 17th and Lincoln is a Denver landmark.

CAPITAL ASSOCIATES, INC.

Capital Associates, Inc., one of the largest independent equipment leasing companies, was established in 1976 to provide lease financing for well-run companies — both growing and established.

Capital Associates successfully completed a public offering in 1987 and consolidated its operations in the Denver metro area in 1989. The company has its headquarters in Lakewood and a warehouse in Englewood for the sale of previously leased equipment.

From offices throughout the United States, the company serves Fortune 1000 investment-grade and select middle-market companies. The company employs 100 people.

Capital Associates has been providing its national and international customers with innovative and flexible lease financing solutions for more than 20 years.

Capital Associates finances many kinds of equipment for Fortune 1000 investment-grade and select middle-market companies.

Capital Associates originates or acquires leases of all sizes — from $25,000 to $30 million.

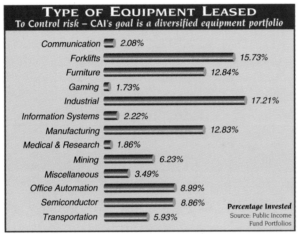

TYPE OF EQUIPMENT LEASED
To Control risk – CAI's goal is a diversified equipment portfolio

Type	Percentage
Communication	2.08%
Forklifts	15.73%
Furniture	12.84%
Gaming	1.73%
Industrial	17.21%
Information Systems	2.22%
Manufacturing	12.83%
Medical & Research	1.86%
Mining	6.23%
Miscellaneous	3.49%
Office Automation	8.99%
Semiconductor	8.86%
Transportation	5.93%

Percentage Invested
Source: Public Income Fund Portfolios

For many companies, leasing some or all of their equipment provides a significant advantage over purchasing it outright or using traditional bank loans. These advantages include equipment flexibility, financial reporting considerations, federal income tax benefits and cash management options.

Capital Associates has been providing its customers with innovative and flexible lease financing solutions for more than 20 years. The company originates or acquires leases of all sizes — from $25,000 to $30 million. Over its 20-year history, the company has arranged more than $3 billion in equipment financing.

Capital Associates professionals guide the company's customers every step of the way through the leasing process — from identifying a capital equipment need and selecting the best piece of equipment to disposing of aging pieces in a customer's equipment portfolio and maximizing its resale value.

The company's emphasis is on providing exceptional customer service coupled with innovative solutions for its customers' financing needs. Capital Associates has a variety of resources within the company ready to focus on customer needs. These resources include:

- A Financial Advisory Services Group that provides customers with value-added income tax, legal and accounting advisory services;
- On-staff professionals with more than 30 years industry experience as purchasing professionals, which they call upon to assist customers in the appropriation and procurement of capital equipment;
- Equipment specialists that can assist customers in all phases of the equipment selection process;
- Professionals that will act as lessee-advisors and develop cost-effective structures for large transactions; and
- A responsive, customer-oriented back office.

Capital Associates finances all types of equipment, with special expertise in material handing equipment; office furniture and store fixtures; electronic test, production and measurement equipment for the semiconductor and printed circuit board industries; and machine tool and factory automation equipment.

Capital Associates is a unique financial company. It is small enough to care about each of its customers and provide them with outstanding service. At the same time, it is large enough to get the job done quickly and efficiently.

YOUNG AMERICANS BANK

Young Americans Bank is the only bank in the United States dedicated to providing banking services and financial education to youth under the age of 22.

The mission of this unique bank, founded by Bill Daniels, is to help its customers become financially responsible adults by providing them with a hands-on learning experience in banking and personal finance.

The financial education of youth is a priority for Daniels, who is widely regarded as "the father of cable television." Inspired by his long-time belief in free enterprise, Daniels set out to open a bank dedicated to youth. After years of effort, Young Americans Bank opened its doors in 1987 in Cherry Creek North.

Young Americans Bank has served customers from all 50 states and a dozen foreign countries. The majority of its customers have savings accounts, but checking accounts, loans, credit cards, ATM cards and certificates of deposit are also offered. The bank staff turns every visit to the bank into an educational experience.

Daniels took his vision a step further in 1988 when he established Young Americans Education Foundation as a charitable organization dedicated to providing economic education for young people. By 1990, the foundation was approved as a non-profit bank holding company with Young Americans Bank as its flagship program.

Young Americans Education Foundation encompasses a wide array of financial literacy programs which complement the bank's philosophy of hands-on learning. Banking and finance, free enterprise, entrepreneurism and investing are the primary focus areas.

The foundation's free enterprise program, Young AmeriTowne, is a nationally recognized hands-on lesson in free enterprise that gives students the opportunity to run their own life-sized town. It consists of various shops and businesses, which are located on the second floor of the bank. Students apply and interview for jobs, elect a mayor and judge, manage bank accounts, act as producers and consumers, and view the effects of their decisions on the town economy.

The thousands of youth who have gained financial experience through Young Americans Bank and Education Foundation offer their sincere appreciation to Bill Daniels and the other sponsors who have made a commitment Denver's future generation.

The Future Begins Here

LEFT:
Young Americans Bank, founded by Bill Daniels, provides banking services and financial education to young people.

Staff at Young Americans Bank turn every visit into an educational experience.
Credit: Stephen M. Crain, Crain Photography

"Citizens" of Young AmeriTowne, a hands-on lesson in free enterprise, listen to a welcoming speech from their "mayor."
Credit: Stephen M. Crain, Crain Photography

National Factoring Services

Entrepreneurs face a wide variety of challenges as they attempt to get their fledgling businesses off the ground. One of the most vexing of these challenges is maintaining the cash flow needed to nourish a growing company.

Nobody understands this problem better than Gary Bryan, a Denver-area native and entrepreneur who has been involved in a variety of start-ups, including restaurants, retail, aviation and temporary employment services.

From his own experience, Bryan knows what it is like to go to the bank, hat in hand, only to be refused a traditional loan because of inadequate cash flow, track record or assets.

Gary Bryan, a Denver-area native and entrepreneur, established National Factoring Services in 1987 to provide reputable asset-based financing for start-up and growing companies. The company also offers a complete outsourced credit and accounts receivable department.
Credit: Alisa Becerra

From his own experience, Bryan knows that alternative sources of credit exist, but that they often have less-than-sterling reputations. The more Bryan researched this problem for his own endeavors, the more he felt convinced that there was a real market for a reputable, less restrictive credit alternative.

In 1987, Bryan established National Factoring Services. Factoring is an ancient but under-used kind of asset-based financing in which a company's accounts receivable are used as collateral for a loan.

Bryan's sense of the market was correct and, in just ten years, the firm's business has doubled annually and expanded to all 50 states — using mostly word-of-mouth marketing. The firm's clients range in size from $2,000-per-month to $5 million-per-month accounts. National Factoring Service has achieved this success by combining a thorough understanding of entrepreneurship with honesty and sound business practices.

Many factors will not finance receivables without an entrepreneur's personal guaranty. National Factoring Services, in contrast, bases its financing decisions on the quality of a business's products or services and the credit-worthiness of its client's customers.

In addition, National Factoring Services allows clients to "age" their receivables and to "deposit" receivables with the company, drawing funds as needed. Most factors require their clients to sign a long-term contract. National Factoring Services does not, and still enjoys productive, long-term relationships with its clients.

National Factoring Services also acts as a complete outsourced credit and accounts receivable department for its clients — even those who do not use its factoring services. Services include billing, credit enhancements, business consulting, Chapter 11 bankruptcy financing and escrow. The company employs 12 people at its Downtown Denver location.

With no formal background in finance, Gary Bryan has capitalized on his real-life experience to become a respected expert in the field of factoring. He has served as an arbitrator for the Denver Better Business Bureau and is active with the Boulder Technology Incubator, an organization that supports Colorado entrepreneurship.

Bryan's expertise has also been tapped by Coopers & Lybrand, which uses him as a regular source when calculating its quarterly TrendSetter Barometer for the financial media. Bryan provides his insights on the performance of national accounts receivable. He also serves as an expert witness in court cases involving factoring and as a consultant to the factoring industry.

In just ten years, National Factoring Services has emerged as a nationally respected credit alternative for small and rapidly growing businesses.

Denver is known as the
"Wall Street of the Rockies."
As of 1997 Colorado has more
venture capital available per
capita than any other state.

Partners in Denver

IN ADDITION TO PRODUCING EXCEPTIONAL GOODS FOR INDIVIDUALS AND INDUSTRY, DENVER'S

MANUFACTURING & MINING

MANUFACTURING AND MINING COMPANIES PROVIDE EMPLOYMENT FOR ITS RESIDENTS.

MAIL-WELL INC.

How This Company Came to Be

Mail-Well Inc. is a leading printer in the United States and Canada, specializing in high-impact color printing and customized envelopes. In 1996, *American Printer* magazine ranked Mail-Well as the 16th-largest and fastest growing printer in North America.

Headquartered in the Denver suburb of Englewood, Mail-Well operates 50 printing and envelope manu-

Gerald Mahoney (left) is chairman and chief executive officer of Mail-Well. Robert Terry is president and chief operating officer.

facturing plants and numerous sales offices throughout North America. Mail-Well employs 6,000 people and posted 1996 sales of nearly $800 million.

Mail-Well is a holding company with four significant subsidiaries — American Mail-Well Envelope, Supremex, Quality Park and Graphic Arts Center. American Mail-Well's envelope plant has been operating continuously in Denver for more than 75 years.

RIGHT: American Mail-Well Envelope is a direct descendent of the Rocky Mountain Envelope Company, founded in Denver in 1920. The name was shortened to Rockmont in the 1930s.

American Mail-Well Envelope is the largest printer of customized and specialty envelopes in the United States, where it holds a 20 percent share of a highly fragmented market. Thirty percent of the company's product consists of high-margin direct mail.

The envelopes manufactured by American Mail-Well Envelope are designed to appeal to consumers and often include vivid color graphics and interactive features like pull-tabs, scratch-offs, perforations and three-dimensional viewing devices.

Other specialty products manufactured by American Mail-Well Envelope include medical folders, packaging for customized tags, overnight courier envelopes, expanding envelopes, photofinishing packaging — and more. They range in size from the tiny envelopes that florists include with deliveries to the large envelopes healthcare institutions use to hold X-rays.

The Denver plant alone manufactures five million envelopes a day — 120 million a month — for distribution to an eight-state region. General Manager of the plant is Michael Carrender. At its Denver manufacturing plant and Englewood headquarters, American Mail-Well Envelope employs 280 people.

The Denver plant was founded in 1920 by Carl Tucker and Willet "Bill" Lake, who had arrived in Denver from Kansas City with a few envelope-making machines — and little else but their talent and their hopes. From the beginning, "Mail-Well" was the company's trademarked brand name. The company's original name, Rocky Mountain Envelope Company, was shorted to Rockmont in the 1930s.

In 1927, Bill Lake moved to Portland, Oregon, to open a second manufacturing facility to serve the West Coast market. Rockmont also established Pak-Well Paper Products in Portland, an affiliated company which manufactured specially designed paper bags for department stores and industry.

Eventually, Rockmont operated ten plants throughout the West. Although it kept a low profile in Denver, Rockmont was well known from coast to coast in its specialized field. The company also manufactured a

MAIL-WELL ENVELOPE CO.

line of low-cost stationery and school supplies. During World War II, the company manufactured the V-Mail envelopes used by military forces around the world and the light-weight Sky Mail package.

In the 1960s, Rockmont moved to a new manufacturing facility along the Platte River northwest of Downtown Denver — a site still occupied by American Mail-Well Envelope today. In 1975, Rockmont was purchased by paper manufacturer Great Northern Nekoosa. In 1990, Great Northern Nekoosa was acquired by Georgia Pacific.

Georgia Pacific put the envelope subsidiary on the market and, in 1994, it was purchased by a group of private investors known as The Sterling Group. At the same time, The Sterling Group purchased Pavey Envelope. Shortly thereafter, it purchased American Envelope. The three companies were merged into American Mail-Well Envelope, creating the largest envelope printer in the United States.

In 1995, the company continued to pursue its acquisition strategy to take advantage of the consolidation occurring in the envelope and commercial printing industries. Mail-Well purchased Supremex, the largest envelope printer in Canada, and added Pac National Group Products to the group giving it 50 percent of market share and 12 facilities.

Like American Mail-Well Envelope, Supremex concentrates on the specialty envelope segment of the market. Supremex holds a patent on the two-way return envelope, which it markets in both the United States and Canada. In 1996, Mail-Well acquired Quality Park, a manufacturer of envelopes for the wholesale market.

Shortly after acquiring Supremex, the company purchased Portland-based Graphic Arts Center. With this purchase, Mail-Well entered the new-but-related business of high-impact color printing. One of the largest of its kind in the highly fragmented United States printing market, GAC maintains technologically advanced printing facilities in Portland, Pasadena and San Francisco, as well as 12 regional sales offices.

Graphic Arts Center prints high quality promotional advertising literature for manufacturers, retailers, service organizations and advertising agencies, including brochures, leaflets, color folders, manuals and posters. Advertising literature accounts for about 70 percent of GAC's business.

The remainder is evenly divided between high-quality mail-order catalogs and annual reports. In 1995, GAC printed more than 15 million copies of annual reports, destined to be read by the shareholders of many leading corporations — including those in the Fortune 500.

In 1996, GAC acquired Shepard Poorman Communications, another high quality printer with sales of more than $50 million. With that addition, the company has further expanded its network of printing plants capable of serving the high-end commercial printing market.

To reduce debt and raise funds for additional acquisitions, Mail-Well Inc. went public in 1995 and traded on the Nasdaq national market. Late in 1996, the company's common stock was transferred to the New York Stock Exchange.

In 75 years, Mail-Well Inc. has grown from a rented loft on Arapahoe Street to the largest manufacturer and printer of customized envelopes in North America.

LEFT:
In the 1960s, Rockmont moved to a manufacturing facility along the Platte River near downtown Denver — a site still occupied by American Mail-Well Envelope today.

American Mail-Well Envelope is the largest printer of customized and specialty envelopes in the United States, where it holds a 20 percent share of a highly fragmented market.

GOLDEN STAR RESOURCES LTD.

From the tropical jungles of the Guiana Shield to the concrete jungles of the world's financial capitals, Golden Star Resources has been making quite a name for itself as one of North America's most successful exploration organizations.

LEFT: The Omai Mine in Guyana, Golden Star's first exploration project, is one of the most significant gold operations in South America.

....

BELOW: Haul trucks at work moving ore from the Fennell Pit, Omai's primary hardrock ore source, to the mill.

Golden Star is a focused mining exploration company that concentrates its efforts on searching for gold and diamonds — minerals with enduring popularity because they appeal, stereotypically, to "man's greed and woman's vanity."

Golden Star believes that the greatest "value-added" in the mining sector comes from the discovery of valuable deposits rather than from mine construction or operation.

Golden Star's business strategy is to find and develop world-class gold and diamond mines that are operated by others but in which the company continues to maintain a non-operating interest. Eventually, the company will hold a significant interest in a large number of substantial gold and diamond mines.

In contrast, many other mining companies are willing to sacrifice ongoing exploration on the altar of operations. When funds are tight, the exploration budget is the first to be cut and exploration geologists are the first to be laid off.

To help fund its exploration efforts and to actually build and operate gold and diamond mines, Golden Star establishes joint ventures with mining industry giants like ASARCO, Broken Hill Proprietary Co.,

Since commencing operations in 1993, the Omai Mine has produced more than 790,000 ounces of gold.

....

Cambior, Campanhia Vale do Rio Doce and LaSource Developpement.

Very few mining company's spend more on exploration than Golden Star. As recently as 1993, Golden Star's exploration expenditures were $16 million with no contribution by joint venture partners. During 1996, the company spent almost $35 million for exploration, with about $13 million of that amount subsidized by its new partners — a clear vote of confidence in the company's expertise.

With one mine in operation, another set to be built in 1997, and a number of others poised on the brink, Golden Star anticipates that, within five years, gold production of approximately 500,000 ounces will be credited to its account each year. These funds will be re-invested in the company's large exploration portfolio — and will reward the company's astute investors.

The operation of gold and diamond mines requires one set of skills; exploration for these mines requires another. By establishing its unique niche, Golden Star is able to focus exclusively on its core skills of gold and diamond exploration and property acquisition. As a result, Golden Star has become very good at what it does.

Because of its known commitment to exploration, Golden Star is able to recruit and keep the world's most talented, creative and adventuresome exploration geologists. The company currently employs 75

The intrusive bodies at St-Elie in French Guiana have produced a gold-bearing stockwork of quartz veining and well-developed sulfides. This hard rock mineralization at the bottom of the old Devis Pit displays quartz, pyrites and even visible gold.

The Brazilian technicians working for Golden Star play a key role in tropical gold reconnaissance exploration and can be as effective in identifying anomalous areas as modern geochemical sampling methods.

geologists and 700 support people around the world. A generous employee stock option program gives these workers an added investment in the company's success.

Golden Star has earned its reputation by being willing and able to explore in remote tropical regions of the world, by being reasonably risk-tolerant, and by persisting in the face of adversity.

The company offers exceptional expertise in exploring tropical Proterozoic greenstone regions like the Guiana Shield and the Brazilian Shield in South America and the similar greenstone belts in West and East Africa. "Greenstones" are ancient volcanic-sedimentary rocks known to host a significant portion of the world's gold deposits.

Golden Star was one of the first North American gold companies to become actively involved in the search for gold and diamonds in Guyana, Suriname and French Guiana in South America. It was also one of the first to explore on the Ivory Coast in Africa.

Competing with some of the largest and best exploration organizations in the world, the Golden Star group was one of the first foreign companies to be awarded exploration rights in Ethiopia and Eritrea. When Golden Star went into Eritrea in 1994, it was the only mining company there. In 1996 alone, nearly 30 other mining companies established offices in the capital city of Asmara.

Golden Star was also the first foreign company awarded the right to enter into a gold exploration and development joint venture with the government-owned Brazilian mining giant CVRD.

The company's first exploration project, for example, was in Guyana. In 1985, the company's critics said that there was no gold in Guyana. When Golden Star found gold, critics said a mine would never be built. When the mine was built, critics said that the Guyanese government would never let the company export gold. When the company began to export, with the blessings of the government, critics said it would never be profitable. In 1997, the Omai Mine is expected to produce and sell 340,000 ounces of gold — and Golden Star's critics are eating their words.

By being the first to explore in many countries, Golden Star often has been able to acquire promising land packages at minimal cost. The company works closely with local mining experts and maintains a strong presence in the local communities. Most of the company's charitable spending takes place in these countries, especially in the form of scholarships for the education of local geologists.

Exploration in remote areas combines the best of

A Golden Star mineralogist examines samples for the presence of diamond indicator minerals as part of the diamond exploration work carried out during the Guyana reconnaissance program.

The Devis Pit at St-Elie was the site of hydraulic mining operations from 1878 to 1956. Vegetation in the pit illustrates the power of renewal offered by the tropical environment.

traditional and modern mining techniques. Golden Star geologists still pan fragments out of streams, observe them with a hand lens and record the data in a field notebook. They also use cell phones, modems and computers to communicate with sophisticated labs in the outside world and to generate precise maps.

In 1997, Golden Star's exploration and development portfolio includes active projects in eleven countries on two continents.

The Omai Mine in Guyana is one of the most significant gold operations in South America. The mine is owned by Omai Gold Mines Limited, a Guyana company. Golden Star owns a 30-percent interest. Cambior, which built and operates the mine, owns a 65-percent interest. The government of Guyana holds a five-percent interest.

Since commencing operations in 1993, the Omai Mine has produced more than 790,000 ounces of gold. The mine has proven and probable reserves of

A mechanized deep augering program was conducted over the whole of the Didulafoundou project area in Mali in early 1996.

approximately 3.3 million ounces. A second mine, Gross Rosebel in Suriname, has proven and probable reserves of more than 2 million ounces of gold. The mine, in which Golden Star and Cambior each own a 50-percent interest, was acquired in 1992. Construction is scheduled for 1997 and production is expected to commence in 1998.

In 1996, Golden Star also announced probable reserves of 876,000 ounces of gold at the Yaou project in French Guiana. A significant diamond field was also discovered in French Guiana. In addition, the company's portfolio includes eight other advanced gold projects, 24 early-stage gold projects and 31 early-stage diamond projects.

Golden Star has adopted an environmental man-

agement system to establish consistent world-wide environmental procedures and monitor the company's activities in light of local environmental standards — or, where none exist, in light of North American standards.

In 1995, Golden Star survived an environmental nightmare when the tailings pond dam failed at the Omai Mine in Guyana, which is operated by its joint venture partner Cambior. The dam failure resulted in pollution of the Omai and Essequibo rivers, but at no

A worker at the Dul Project in Ethiopia washes ore in a water hole to recover free gold.

time were safe drinking water standards exceeded.

Mine personnel immediately advised employees, government officials and local residents along the rivers of the situation and contained the flow of effluent within 100 hours. An inquiry by the Guyanese government exonerated Omai Gold Mines Ltd. of responsibility for the accident and, after the situation was remedied, allowed the mine to not only resume but expand operations.

Golden Star is a Canadian company with its head office in Denver, Colorado. It is listed on The Toronto Stock Exchange (GSC) and the American Stock Exchange (GSR). In order to carry out its worldwide exploration activities, Golden Star has created two publicly traded subsidiaries and a wholly owned company.

Guyanor Ressources S.A., in which Golden Star has a 70-percent interest, was created to maximize the advantage of working in French Guiana as a French Company. It is listed on The Toronto Stock Exchange (GRL.B). Guyanor has six active projects in French Guiana: Yaou, Dorlin, St. Elie, Paul Isnard, Regina Est and Dachine. President of Guyanor Ressources is David Fennell.

Pan African Resources (PARC), in which Golden Star has a 60-percent interest, was created to establish exploration project across Africa. It is listed on the Canadian Dealing Network. President of PARC is Adrian Fleming.

The tropical rain forest environment in which much of Golden Star's activities are carried out is one of the most diverse ecosystems in the world. Golden Star is committed to sound environmental management of its activities, wherever they may be located.

PARC presently has rights to and is exploring promising properties in six African countries. In West Africa, PARC is active in Mali (Dioulafoundou and Melgue), Cote d'Ivoire (Comoe) and Gabon (Eteke and Kolissen). In East Africa, PARC is exploring mines in Ethiopia (Dul Mountain) and Eritrea (Galla Valley). Most recently, PARC has become involved in Kenya (Ndori).

Southern Star Resources, a wholly owned company, is pursuing opportunities in South America outside the Guiana Shield. Southern Star holds the company's Andorinhas and Abacaxis projects in Brazil and the San Simon and Sunsas projects in Bolivia. President of Southern Star Resources is Dr. Jeffrey Abbott.

Golden Star Resources was established in Edmonton in 1984 as Southern Star Resources and adopted its present name the following year. In 1992, the company amalgamated with South American Goldfields Inc. and relocated from Edmonton to Denver, helping to fuel Denver's reemergence as a North American mining center.

President and chief executive officer of Golden Star is David Fennell, one of the company's original founders. Fennell attended the University of North Dakota on a football scholarship and went on to play professional football for the Edmonton Eskimos — where he earned the nickname "Doctor Death" and won the Canadian Football League's Gray Cup for four of the eight years he played. Fennell holds a law degree and specialized in the area of resource law and the rights of indigenous peoples.

Adrian Fleming, a world-renowned geologist who is president and chief executive officer of PARC, is also executive vice president of Golden Star, where he oversees all exploration efforts. Chairman of the board is David Fagin, a 35-year veteran of the mining industry who has been president of both Homestake Mining and Rosario Resources.

Since its establishment in 1985, Golden Star Resources Ltd. has concentrated on developing its property portfolio, its joint venture relationships and its corporate structure. With these elements in place, Golden Star is now positioned to stand out as one of the most successful exploration organizations of the 1990s — and beyond.

Golden Star has earned its reputation by being willing and able to explore in remote tropical regions of the world, by being reasonably risk-tolerant and by persisting in the face of adversity. Pictured is the Gross Rosebel mine in Suriname.

ASARCO GLOBE PLANT

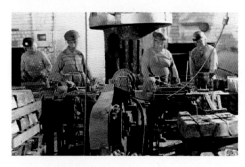

TOP: A lithograph depicts the Globe Smelting and Refining Company during its heyday of the late 1800s.

MIDDLE: Workers at the American Smelting and Refining Company take time out to pose for a picture in the early 1900s.

BOTTOM: In 1926, the Globe Plant began casting cadmium metal into various shapes including bars, rods and balls.

For more than 100 years, the Asarco Globe Plant has been a part of the north Denver neighborhood of Globeville. Located on 89 acres in the heart of the community, the plant has occupied the same site since 1886 when it began operations as the Holden Smelter. That name was later changed to the Globe Smelting and Refining Company to reflect the multi-ethnic population that made up the workforce.

These workers and their families, many of German, Polish and Russian descent, settled near the plant creating the town that became known as Globeville. Annexed by Denver in 1902, Globeville became one of the city's best known ethnic neighborhoods. Today's Globeville, with a largely Hispanic populace, continues to be recognized for its cultural diversity.

The history of the Globe Plant, like that of Colorado, is closely tied to the mining industry and the rail system. Construction of the original Globe Plant coincided with the advent of the railroad in Colorado, which made it economically feasible to transport ore from the state's numerous gold, silver, lead and copper mines in the mountains to the smelters in Denver. By 1890, smelting was the city's largest industry and the Globe Plant was processing ores from throughout North America. In the Globe Plant's heyday, more than 1000 people were employed at the facility; today there are fewer than 100.

The Globe Smelting and Refining Company was one of several plants consolidated in 1899 into the American Smelting and Refining Company, now known as ASARCO Incorporated. Asarco, headquartered in New York, is one of the world's leading producers of nonferrous metals, principally copper, lead, zinc, silver and molybdenum. Asarco also produces specialty chemicals and aggregates and provides environmental services.

The Globe Plant smelted lead from 1901 through 1919. In 1919, after 30 years as one of the country's largest smelters, the Globe Plant changed its focus. Lead smelting was replaced by the production of arsenic trioxide, a compound used in alloys, insecticides, medicines and glass.

In 1926, the Globe Plant ceased the production of arsenic trioxide and began producing cadmium, a metallic by-product of zinc and lead. Cadmium was vital during World War II, when it was used in the protective electroplating of iron and steel. Later, cadmium was also used in rechargeable nickel-cadmium batteries and paint pigments. Large scale cadmium metal production ceased in 1991; however, cadmium oxide and cadmium powder production continued until 1993.

Current Operations

For most of its 110 years, the Globe Plant has been closely linked with Colorado's mining industry. Current operations at the Asarco Globe Plant, however focus on the production of small quantities of high-purity metals and specialty chemicals used in a variety of industries.

The Globe Plant has been producing litharge (lead oxide) since the early 1900s and its Pueblo Brand litharge continues to be recognized around the world as the standard in the industry. Litharge, a specialty chemical produced through the interaction of molten lead and air, is used by chemists to determine the concentrations of precious metals in ore. This analytical technique is known as fire assaying. Test lead, a low-silver granular lead, is also used by chemists for fire assay purposes. Asarco's test lead can be found in oxygen sensors and as a standard for analytical work.

Although the Globe Plant ceased large-scale cadmium metal production in 1991, the plant continues to produce small quantities of cadmium sulfide and

Bismuth oxide is an environmentally friendly chemical used for a variety of purposes. It can be used as an alternative to litharge in fire assaying or to increase the weight of plastic resins. Bismuth oxide is used in the manufacture of ceramics and glass and to improve soldering and brazing processes, as well. Bismuth pellets and powder, the newest bismuth products at the Globe Plant, are used as metallurgical alloying agents.

cadmium telluride. These specialty chemicals are used in the manufacture of photovoltaic (solar) cells.

A number of high-purity metals and compounds are produced at the plant. These semiconductor-grade materials are used in many "high-tech" applications and are sold to companies located all over the world. For example, the metals bismuth, tellurium, antimony and selenium, all by-products of Asarco's worldwide copper and lead operations, are refined to +99.99 percent purity at the Globe Plant using metallurgical techniques that the company has developed over the past several decades.

These metals are used in the manufacture of thermoelectric modules or electronic coolers. Electronic coolers do not contain chlorofluorocarbons (CFCs) and are found in a multitude of consumer products ranging from portable "iceless" coolers to personal computers.

Recently, the plant has become involved in several innovative applications which utilize bismuth metal. Bismuth is widely used in pharmaceuticals, including a popular stomach medication. Because the physical properties of bismuth are similar to those of lead, bismuth is emerging as an important non-toxic lead substitute. For example, bismuth shot is being used successfully as a replacement for lead shot in waterfowl hunting.

In addition, bismuth selenide, a bismuth compound, shows promise as a substitute for lead in the machining of brass. Because lead in brass pipes and spigots is believed to impact drinking water quality, mandatory removal of lead from some plumbing fixtures is under consideration by manufacturers.

Environmental Commitment

In the late 1800s and early to mid-1900s, industries such as the Globe Plant operated before advances were made in emissions control technology and before environmental regulations were created. While the Globe Plant was built in the late 1800s when towering smokestacks represented prosperity and success to most people, the plant originally incorporated some of the most progressive technology of the day.

Dr. Malvern W. Iles, Globe's first superintendent and a well-respected and progressive metallurgist of that time, built one of the first baghouses at the Globe Plant for processing furnace gases. As pollution control technology developed over the years, Asarco continued to install numerous devices to reduce the impacts of plant operations on the environment. Even so, today the Globe Plant bears the environmental burdens of more than a century of smelting and refining activities.

With the advent of strict environmental regulations in the early 1980s, the Globe Plant came under scrutiny for pollution related to its historic operations, and in the mid-1980s was found responsible for impacts to soil and water on the plant and in the surrounding community. Asarco and the State of Colorado worked together to determine the extent of the environmental impacts and to develop an acceptable method of remediation.

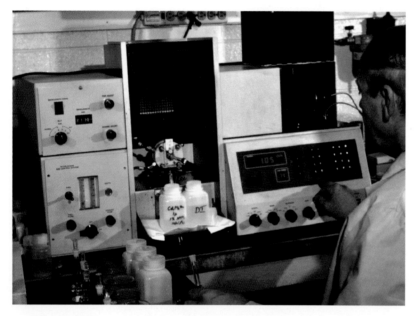

An Asarco chemist analyzes a sample of water treated at the Globe Plant's wastewater treatment plant to ensure the water meets permit discharge requirements.

The remediation plan, approved in 1993 with the majority of the project expected to be completed by the year 2000, includes conducting studies to determine potential health effects from exposure to lead, cadmium and arsenic, remediation of soils in the community and on the Globe Plant, and remediation of groundwater and surface water.

Today, to ensure the health and safety of Globeville residents, employees and the environment, the Asarco Globe Plant operates sophisticated emissions and wastewater control systems. Asarco uses baghouses and wet scrubbers on many of its operations to reduce emissions to the air and routinely monitors ambient air surrounding the plant. A 1990 study conducted by the State of Colorado found that the plant's emission control systems capture 99 percent of air-borne contaminants.

In 1986, the Globe Plant installed a new wastewater treatment plant using chemical precipitation technology to remove contaminants from the water. In 1994, the plant enhanced its wastewater treatment system by adding membrane media/biobead technology which reduces the amount of chemicals needed for water treatment and the amount of sludge produced during treatment.

These systems help ensure that the Asarco Globe Plant remains well within its emission limits established by a written agreement with the state, as well as within the emission and discharge limits set forth in federal, state and local environmental regulations. In addition, a biological monitoring program and state-of-the-art ventilation systems ensure a safe work environment for the company's employees.

Community Involvement

The employees at the Asarco Globe Plant make community involvement in historic Globeville a priority. Asarco opened the Globeville Information Center in the summer of 1993 to provide local residents with information about the remediation process and the many products manufactured at the plant.

The Globe Plant has sponsored community events such as picnics, a local health fair and a lecture series on various topics. Asarco employees participate in community cleanup days and serve on various boards and committees within the community. The Globe Plant takes a special interest in youth by regularly supporting youth programs and employing youth from the community during the summer in order to help them earn money for college.

The Globe Plant is committed to producing high-quality products, meeting the challenges of increasing environmental regulations and being a good neighbor in the Globeville community. The Globe Plant continues to strive for excellence in its industry and is looking forward to meeting the demands of another century.

MATERIALS HANDLING EQUIPMENT COMPANY

In 1952, contracts were consummated with a handshake, and you knew most everyone you met on your way to the bank. Businesses moved their goods by hand, around tiny warehouses and lots. It was then that engineer Asher Patten purchased a struggling equipment company for his son, Jack. The business was renamed Materials Handling Equipment Company (MHECO), and a Rocky Mountain legacy was born.

MHECO had meager beginnings. Jack had taken over a company which had little more than competitors. Shortly thereafter, Jack designed the familiar logo of an industrial worker handling materials.

When Jack's younger brother, Bob, entered the Army in 1956, Jack's attempt to run both Bob's Mercury Motor franchise and MHECO ended in the selling of Bob's franchise — an act known to thrust lesser siblings into combat. When Bob returned, the brothers became partners, and have remained best friends ever since.

Jack and Bob sold and serviced increasingly sophisticated material handling equipment, such as conveyors, pallet rack, loading dock equipment, and forklifts.

Over time, MHECO prospered with a solid foundation of good people and intense involvement with their national trade association. The Pattens, and a Utah engineer, designed and built an automated, floor-controlled, stacking and retrieval system in 1967. Ahead of it's time, most companies are just now installing these systems.

After two moves, their current 13th Avenue facility became home. With 17 employees, the business literally rattled in the former freight terminal. Today, over 100 employees and 150 state-of-the art product lines fill every nook and cranny.

Decades of sixteen hour days burned Jack out. Gary Moore was then hired as Sales Manager in 1976. Gary's vision and vitality made work fun again. Gary is now President, and the Pattens are passing the business torch to him.

Material handling distribution is a capital-intensive business, and as such, MHECO struggled with sudden 21% interest during the recession of the 1980's. It was a turn-back, but Denver's industries had grown confident in MHECO's abilities to recommend material handling systems and warehouse layouts that would improve their bottom line. MHECO purchased their first computer in 1980, and when the economy recovered, the company was ready.

Yesterday's slide rules and hand-drawn warehouse blueprints have given way to today's computer-driven layouts and technologies, but people remain crucial. MHECO's success is due, in large part, to their dedicated employees — some with 30 years tenure.

Over the decades, MHECO's focus shifted. Early emphasis remained on the equipment itself, but as customers' businesses accelerated, they demanded higher levels of service. MHECO established three

Materials Handling Equipment Company's shop, circa. 1960, in the old Mercury Outboard Motor building at 1795 Sheridan Blvd. **Credit: Bob Patten**

distinct service departments and an unprecedented customer service strategy — to focus on learning customer expectations, and exceeding them.

Industries continue to seek Denver's exciting environment, along with MHECO's warehouse layout, distribution, and material handling expertise. As the Pattens plan for retirement, Gary plans the company's future. MHECO has survived boom and bust, and though the company is technologically-driven, they're equally customer- and community-focused. After all, forty-five years of history doesn't mean a thing without a strategy for helping people tomorrow.

Colorado Container Corporation

At Colorado Container Corporation, designer and manufacturer of corrugated shipping containers, the strongly held ethical beliefs of the Kelley family are an integral part of doing business.

So integral, in fact, that this family-owned company was honored with a 1996 Colorado Ethics in Business Award. These awards showcase individuals and companies who have thoroughly integrated social, employee and environmental responsibilities into their corporate cultures.

Colorado Container has designed and manufactured corrugated shipping containers in Denver since 1963.

The Colorado Ethics in Business Award was sponsored by the DU Daniels College of Business, The Samaritan Institute, *Colorado Business* magazine, the Colorado Chapter of the American Society of CLU and ChFC and Rotary International. Colorado Container was specifically recognized for the breadth of its community involvement.

Colorado Container maintains these high standards while turning out a respected product and a respectable profit.

When the producers of *The Simpsons* television show tried to come up with the most boring destination possible for a school trip, they decided on a tour of a cardboard box factory. Despite this perception, a tour of Colorado Container is anything but boring.

High point of any tour is the company's massive corrugating machine, which is the length of a football

field. The corrugator allows Colorado Container to produce its own corrugated sheets rather than purchasing them from outside suppliers. The company can also supply corrugated sheets to other box manufacturers.

Colorado Container's customers are Front Range manufacturers of products that require special custom packaging. About 20 percent of these customers manufacture high-tech products like computers, communications equipment and medical equipment. Other market segments include food processors, growers, and furniture and equipment manufacturers.

Although most of its work is custom, the company also manufactures some standardized boxes. In order to control the timeliness of its deliveries, the company maintains its own fleet of trucks.

Colorado Container provides a positive work environment for its employees — one of the reasons that the company received a 1996 Colorado Ethics in Business Award.

Colorado Container Corporation was founded in 1963 by three men — Chick Smith, Myron Dragieff and Rollie Kelley — who had $3,000 in capital and 6,000 square feet of space. Smith and Dragieff were in sales. Kelley, a South Dakota native who had previously worked for a large packaging company in California, ran operations. Kelley eventually bought out his two partners.

Colorado Container Corporation is currently owned by the Kelley family. In 1996, Rollie Kelley is chairman and CEO. Three of his children are active in the company — Bruce Kelley as president, Barbara Kelley as an officer and Kathryn Huwaldt as a director.

In 1970, Colorado Container employed 20 people, occupied 29,000 square feet of space, and produced ten million square feet of corrugated annually. In 1996, the company has 125 employees, occupies 227,000 square feet of space, and produces more than 300 million square feet of corrugated. The company recently added $4 million in new equipment to further increase its capabilities.

In the early 1970s, when the box-making industry faced severe problems due to a shortage of raw material, Rollie Kelley was inspired to become a founding member of the Association of Independent Corrugated Convertors.

Over the years, the AICC has developed a health insurance program to provide superior benefits to employees and to control costs, both for the participating companies and for those who work there. Additionally, the AICC has initiated an extensive employee training program in the areas like sales, service, production and safety.

Colorado Container's generous profit sharing plan was established more than 30 years ago — far before profit sharing became a common concept. Each quarter, a percentage of profits is distributed to employees, with specific amounts dependent on base pay and years of service.

In addition, Colorado Container contributes the maximum amount allowed by law to a deferred profit-sharing plan for employees' retirement — 15 percent of each employee's salary per year. As might be expected with benefits such as these, employees have a unusual stake in the company's success and there is little employee turnover.

Over the years, Rollie Kelley has been a strong supporter of organizations like Civitan International, the YMCA, the Iliff School of Theology, Emmanuel United Methodist Church, Dakota Wesleyan University, Denver Urban Ministries and the Denver Zoological Foundation.

The company has hired handicapped and disadvantaged individuals through programs like Goodwill Industries' School-to-Work Transition Program.

Rollie Kelley recently established the Kelley Family Foundation, which will manage the company's contributions to local charities. Colorado Container has committed to contribute a percentage of its annual profits to the community through the foundation.

High point of any tour of Colorado Container is the company's massive corrugating machine, which is the length of a football field.

The company has also taken steps to preserve the environment, buying recycled paper stock when appropriate and recycling its own trim and scrap. The company has invested in equipment to purify its waste water in order to minimize environmental impact.

Over the years, Colorado Container has occupied four different sites in the Denver area. The company's current facility is located on nine acres of land near the former Stapleton Airport.

Colorado Container Corporation, recognized by the Denver business community for the way it conducts business, produces a quality product, emphasizes customer satisfaction and provides a positive work environment for its employees.

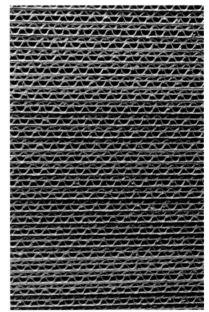

Colorado Container produces its own corrugated sheets rather than purchasing them from outside suppliers; it also supplies corrugated sheets to other box manufacturers. All *Photos*, Credit: Stephen M. Crain, Crain Photography

COORS BREWING COMPANY

The 124-year history of the Coors Brewing Company is a tale of pure Rocky Mountain spring water. It's also the story of an ambitious young German immigrant with a dream, a company with an uncompromising commitment to quality, and a product held dear in the hearts of beer lovers everywhere.

Adolph Coors, born in Prussia in 1847, was the son of a master flour miller. A brewery apprentice at 14, his life's ambition had been charted. A year later, Adolph's parents passed away. His job at the Prussian brewery went from a means of training to a means of survival. The young man worked nights as the brewery bookkeeper, earning extra money while adding to his passion of the trade.

This Coors beer label was used from 1936 to 1940. Credit: *Coors Brewing Company Archives.*

When war broke out in his homeland, Adolph left Dortmund as a stowaway on a ship headed for America. He had no money and no job, just dreams of a new country and a brewery all his own.

Adolph worked his way across America as a bricklayer, stonecutter, laborer, brewery foreman, and a railroad worker. He reached Denver in 1872. Within a month, he had a partnership in a bottling company, and, by year's end he was sole owner. This would have sufficed for most people, but Adolph had brewing in his blood.

Adolph found the prized ingredient for his perfect beer in the icy streams near Golden. At 26, Adolph dedicated his life savings, his expertise, and his enthusiasm with money put up by Jacob Schueler,

a bottling customer, to open 'The Golden Brewery.'

Adolph's beer was good. He shipped it by train, mule-drawn wagons, and boxcars to thirsty miners and early settlers. By 1880, the business was so successful that Adolph bought out his partner. Producing 17,600 barrels annually by 1890, Adolph's vision was firmly established.

Over several decades, the brewery thrived despite a national depression, a devastating flood, and Prohibition, which came to Colorado in 1916. The Coors family sustained the brewery during the eighteen dry years of Prohibition manufacturing malted milk, near-beer, pottery, and laboratory porcelain.

Adolph Sr. died in 1929, before the repeal of Prohibition. His son, Adolph Jr, took over the brewery and expanded its market to include ten Western states.

A 1916 Coors Malted Milk ad. Adolph's experience with malt led him to use the brewery's equipment to manufacture what would become America's second most popular brand of malted milk. Credit: *Coors Brewing Company Archives.*

During this time, the famous slogan, 'Brewed With Pure Rocky Mountain Spring Water,' was born.

The onset of World War II didn't slow Coors' progress. Important to the troops' morale, half of Coors' beer production was set aside for the military. By 1955, Coors was producing one million barrels of beer annually.

Coors experimented with packaging during the post war years, introducing the country's first all-aluminum beverage can in 1959. The recycling revolution started when Coors offered a penny for every can returned to the brewery.

The aluminum can increased demand for Coors beer. Under third-generation direction of William K. (Bill) Coors, technological brewing innovations fueled company growth. Up until the 1960's and the 1970's, Coors produced just one beer- the Original Coors Banquet brand. Limited distribution left eastern states clamoring to taste the 'Coors mystique.'

Meanwhile, monumental changes were transpiring in the brewing industry. Refrigerated marketing, increased distribution and advertising, new brands directed to specific market segments, and a growing interest in reduced-calorie beer all increased the demands of the marketplace. Coors responded with a new product- Coors Light- and a national expansion strategy that brought Coors products to all regions of the country. The 'Silver Bullet' is now one of the coun-

A Coors keg line worker bunging (racking) a keg of
beer, during the late 1930's or early 1940's.
Credit: *Coors Brewing Company Archives.*

try's best-selling beers. Growing demand led to a new packaging plant in 1985 in Virginia. Five years later, Coors purchased a brewery in Memphis and began brewing with the same Coors quality and tradition that consumers had grown to love.

Beneath the guidance of fourth-generation Peter H. Coors, the company has become the nation's third largest brewer, with products now sold in more than 30 foreign markets. Coors genetically-tailors barley for supreme enzymatic, malting and brewing characteristics. It is the only U.S. brewery to malt its own barley. Coors' brand portfolio now comprises twenty-four malt beverages and the company employs more than six thousand people worldwide.

Coors' brewery personnel take a beer break in the year 1894.
Credit: *Coors Brewing Company Archives.*

Coors gives back to the community by supporting educational programs that promote healthy lifestyles. Coors strongly advocates the prevention of alcohol abuse. The company supports environmental programs directed toward the most efficient use of resources, industrial recycling, and pollution prevention programs that reduce the brewery's impact on the environment. In addition, Coors contributes nearly $2.5 million annually to philanthropic causes. To the Mile High City's delight, Coors helped bring Major League Baseball to Denver with investments in the National League's Colorado Rockies and Coors Field.

It's hard to imagine that it all began with an ambitious young German immigrant who started from scratch, and built his brewery from the bottom up. The Coors family's Western spirit of sacrifice, hard work, and dedication to excellence is a tradition that keeps a Rocky Mountain dream alive and brewing.

HUNTER DOUGLAS WINDOW FASHIONS

When the energy crisis of the 1970s set motorists gnashing their teeth at gasoline shortages, it also put into action the creative juices of a dynamic entrepreneur, Richard Steele and a brilliant young inventor, Wendell Colson. The result: a window covering that excited and stimulated consumers, built a company and transformed an industry.

The Hunter Douglas Business Park in Broomfield, Colorado.

The germ of the idea began on a wintry night in a big, drafty Victorian house in Massachusetts, when Colson, fresh out of Princeton with an architecture degree, was shivering in bed. He said to himself, "There has to be a better way to cover those windows and keep the warm air in and the cold air out!" Then he noticed that a double curtain on one of the windows had come together in a series of folds that trapped air between them. It was a honeycomb-like configuration that created a thermal insulating effect.

Steele, head of Thermal Technology Corp., a small company based in Broomfield at the foot of the Rockies 15 miles northwest of Denver, believed in the idea and persuaded Colson to work with him to develop a product. They soon began manufacturing a pleated window shade in the shape of a honeycomb called "Thermocell" that was made of a polyester film with no visible holes or tapes to interfere with the look. However, Thermocell was designed primarily as a functional, energy-saving window covering and had limited decorative appeal for consumers. As a result, the company was running out of money and could not long survive on its own.

When the Duette® honeycomb shade was introduced in 1985, it created a revolution in the window coverings industry.

Another innovative Hunter Douglas product, Silhouette® window shadings is today the fastest-growing window covering on the market.

More than one leading window covering manufacturer turned down the opportunity to purchase Thermal Technology, until Jerry Fuchs, then president and now chairman of Hunter Douglas — the New Jersey-based company which had pioneered the first aluminum venetian blinds in the 1940s and 50s — saw the unique shade. He immediately recognized its potential, not just as a functional product, but as an exciting new decorative window fashion.

So, in 1985, Hunter Douglas purchased Thermal Technology and established the Hunter Douglas Window Fashions Division in Broomfield to manufacture and market this unique honeycomb shade — now made with soft, durable fabric in a selection of fashionable colors — and renamed the new product Duette®.

The Duette shade was not just a variation of an old theme. Under the leadership of Marv Hopkins — recruited by Fuchs to head the infant Window Fashions Division, and now President and CEO of Hunter Douglas North America — Duette achieved unprecedented success and renewed consumer interest in window coverings, an industry that hadn't had a significant new product introduction in decades. Retail sales soared to an estimated $300 million by 1988, and now the Duette honeycomb shade is the single most important brand in the entire custom window coverings market.

While highly functional and energy-efficient, Duette was successfully promoted as fashion for the home, something that was stylish and aesthetically appealing to the upscale consumer. This was a revolutionary step for the industry, which had previously marketed its products based almost exclusively on their functionality.

In 1987, Hunter Douglas launched the first in a series of successful national consumer ad campaigns in *Architectural Digest*, *Town & Country* and other prestigious publications. The company also provided a toll-free consumer "help line" which now yields over 100,000 calls annually to the Broomfield-based Customer Information Center. Extensive consumer advertising campaigns in magazines and on television continue to distinguish Hunter Douglas today.

But the revolution is never over at Hunter Douglas. In 1991 the company developed another unique proprietary fabric window covering with early and explosive sales — Silhouette® window shadings. Featuring soft fabric vanes suspended between sheer facings, Silhouette looks like a sheer curtain, rolls up like a shade and has vanes that rotate like a blind for light control. Like Duette, Silhouette has garnered top national design awards and is now the fastest-growing window fashion in North America.

In 1994 Hunter Douglas introduced yet another innovative new product: Vignette® window shadings, a unique and dramatically improved innovation on the traditional Roman shade with a soft, clean look appropriate for both casual and formal interiors. Vignette has already had a significant impact in the industry.

The latest chapter in the innovation story is Luminette® Privacy Sheers®, introduced in early 1997. It is the world's first window covering to offer a soft sheer with fabric vanes bonded to the rear of the sheer facing for light control and privacy. When the vanes are open, Luminette appears as soft, tailored sheers and when closed, the product is reminiscent of luxurious draperies.

Of course, more revolutionary new products are on the way, ensuring that Hunter Douglas will maintain its leadership in custom window fashions that marry high style with high-tech and offer superior craftsmanship and dependability.

To distribute its custom-made products, the company relies on a dedicated network of 35 fabrication operations across the United States and Canada, which provide outstanding service and quality directly to many thousands of window covering retailers. The company also distributes its products internationally to Asia, Australia, Latin America and Europe.

Hunter Douglas Window Fashions Division has come a long way since its beginnings in 1985, when a handful of employees and all manufacturing, warehousing and administrative operations were housed in one small plant. As a result of the success of its new products, the company now employs over 700 people in its own 43-acre, multi-facility business park located in the burgeoning town of Broomfield.

Today, Hunter Douglas is one of the largest employers in Boulder County and credits its strength in no small part to the people of the State of Colorado. The company gives back to the community as a major supporter of the Bal Swan Children's Center in Broomfield as well as many other charitable and civic organizations.

Suitable for French doors as well as a variety of window openings, Luminette® Privacy Sheers® — the newest Hunter Douglas innovation — is an entirely new concept in window coverings.

With its gently contoured fabric folds, Vignette® window shadings achieve a casual elegance.

KATZKE PAPER CO.

Sometimes the idea for a business is not as much inspired as it is driven by necessity. Such is the case for industrial packaging supplier Katzke Paper Co., which began as a way to make ends meet for two brothers struggling to make a success out of an auto repair shop.

Clarence G. and half-brother Robert (Bob) J. Katzke started the shop in the late 1940s when they moved from Chicago to Denver. Although their intentions were good, they found that their strength wasn't in the auto repair business, and they decided to supplement their income by buying and selling cardboard boxes out of their garage.

The brothers soon realized they were much more successful at selling boxes than at repairing broken-down cars. By the beginning of 1948 they abandoned their auto repair business, and with $3,600 borrowed from Clarence's soon-to-be wife, they established Katzke Brothers Paper Company. A logo of two cats, one playing with a dangling key, was adopted in 1949 to help customers pronounce the company's name. "Your Shipping Room Supply House," the company's slogan, also appeared during that time.

Katzke Brothers inhabited several temporary locations before settling at 2942 Zuni Street in 1949. Bob assumed overall management of the company while Clarence focused on sales. From their store-front location, they bought and sold the packaging materials of the time-corrugated boxes and rolls, twine, gummed paper tape, kraft wrapping paper, and other paper specialties. Times were lean, and Clarence actually lived at the store,

The Katzke Bros. Paper Company store front on Zuni Street. After inhabiting several temporary locations, the company settled here in 1949.

Katzke Paper Co. Warehouse Manager Taylor Snyder loads Katzke-brand paper tape into one of the company's trucks. The company private-labels a selection of products that meets Katzke Paper Co.'s level of quality.

folding up his rollaway bed every morning and storing it in the back room.

The brothers were dedicated to hard work and the business grew. By 1955 organizational charts were drawn up showing the company's various divisions. Also in

1955, the brothers bought 28,500 square feet of land at 2495 S. Delaware Street. On a lot that had been somewhat of a neighborhood dump, they built a 10,200-square-foot metal office and warehouse building, which, in expanded form, continues as the company's headquarters today.

In February 1957, Katzke Brothers underwent a significant change when Bob decided to leave the company. Clarence purchased Bob's interest; four years later the company was incorporated and renamed as Katzke Paper Co., Inc. Two expansions to the original building during the 1960s reflected the company's continuing growth and expanded the structure to 26,600 square feet. Other reflections of the company's growth during that time included the purchase of delivery trucks-up to then the company had hired outside trucks and drivers.

Like many small business owners, Clarence Katzke was conservative. His goal never was to be the biggest; instead, he focused on keeping his employees happy and on using existing resources fully. This philosophy

Katzke Paper Co. today occupies a 26,600 square-foot facility on Delaware Street. Seven company trucks deliver packaging products to a variety of Front Range industries.

paid off during the paper shortage that struck the industry in the early 1970s. Greg Katzke, Clarence's son and current president of the company, recalls that " ...there wasn't much to do but sweep the empty warehouse floors. No one could get any product to sell. They were lean times, but there was money to be made if you had any product at all."

At the end of the shortage, the warehouse was full of backordered product and the company returned to full profitability. Even still, Clarence Katzke remained conservative. "We kept growing and kept profitable, largely because of my father's attitude towards the business," Greg says. "He did everything himself, even cleaning the bathrooms."

Greg Katzke grew up watching his father tend the needs of his company, and in 1978 he assumed some of those responsibilities when he joined the company. Over the next few years, Greg focused on reshaping areas of the company to better meet the needs of its customers.

Late in the evening of April 1, 1984, Greg received a phone call that would strike fear in any business owner's heart. It was the company's controller, working late at the end of the fiscal year, calling to tell Greg she smelled fire. "I told her to grab Red, our cat (the company's other mascot, Blue, was at the veterinarian), to grab our computer tapes, and to get out," Greg recalls. The ensuing fire was a two-alarm blaze that necessitated 60 pieces of equipment to extinguish it.

After the fire was out, Greg picked through the charred ruins in hopes of finding the sheets detailing the company's year-end inventory count. If they had somehow survived, he would know exactly what was lost in the blaze. He found the desk where the records had been placed-fortunately, they had survived, saved by a piece of fallen insulation. With the help of its employees, neighbors and others in the industry, Katzke Paper was out of business only one day. It was the first of many times, Greg says, when he felt the company derived its strength from a source larger than itself.

Although Clarence retired soon after the fire, Katzke Paper still runs on the principles he instilled at its heart. Today, its 37 employees, many of them with the company since Clarence's time, serve the packaging needs of a wide variety of Front Range industries, regardless of size, offering free delivery and no minimum purchase.

In 1996, Katzke Paper was named one of the 150 fastest growing private companies by The Denver Business Journal. The honor pleases Greg Katzke but it's not the yardstick by which he measures the company's success. "I'm not here for the corporate stuff," Greg says. "I'm here for the people."

Katzke Paper will celebrate its 50th anniversary in 1998, and it's an occasion eagerly anticipated by its owner and its employees. "Being in business for a half-century is an incredible milestone," Greg Katzke says. "We're looking forward to celebrating that achievement with many of the people who made us successful, and we're looking forward to even bigger and better things in the years ahead."

Knights of Columbus Council 3340 in Littleton is one of several organizations and charities supported by Katzke Paper Co. Company employees annually help build the council's St. Patrick's Day parade float, which in 1997 featured a shamrock farm in keeping with the parade's theme, "Forty Shades of Green."

KEEBLER COMPANY

The catastrophic earthquake of 1906 was bad news for the residents of San Francisco. In Denver, it was good news for the founders of Merchants Biscuit Company, who got their first big break when the bakery received an emergency order to manufacture eight railcar loads of survival biscuits.

ABOVE: The Denver Bakery of Keebler Company can trace its heritage directly to Merchants Biscuit Company, founded in Denver on Market and Walnut Streets in 1906.

RIGHT: Merchants Biscuit Company was one of 16 family owned bakers that banded together in 1927 to form United Biscuit Company of America — the predecessor of Keebler Company.

Today, the Denver Bakery of Keebler Company can trace its 90-year heritage directly to Merchants Biscuit Company. The Denver bakery, which manufactures Keebler products for distribution throughout the West, employs 700 people and produces cookies and crackers with a production value of $183 million.

Merchants Biscuit Company was founded in Denver in April of 1906 by Clinton Bowman and two of his friends who had just relocated from the mining town of Silverton. The fledgling operation was located on the corner of Market and Walnut Streets.

The bakery's 15 employees produced soda crackers, hardtack, ginger snaps and sugar cookies using a second-hand reel oven and a used cracker-cutting machine. The bakery's products were packed in large barrels with glass tops for bulk display in area grocery stores. When the Cherry Creek flooded in 1913, the entire operation had to be rebuilt. The trade name "Supreme" was added in 1916.

During the 1930s, large band ovens with a baking capacity of two tons per hour replaced reel ovens and allowed the company to increase production and

serve a larger geographical area. The name of the company was changed to Bowman Biscuit Company in 1945, to commemorate the death of founder Clinton Bowman. He was succeeded as president by his son, J.C. (Clint) Bowman.

In 1961, Bowman Biscuit Company relocated to a modern new plant with four production lines on a 42-acre site at 5000 Osage. This ideal location, which today consists of 900,000 square feet, is just northwest of the intersection of I-70 and I-25 and adjacent to the primary switchyard of Southern Pacific, which facilitates the delivery of bulk syrups, oils and other raw materials. The bakery is also located less than ten minutes from its flour mills.

In 1927, in order to achieve economies of scale and distribution, Merchants Biscuit Company had been one of 16 family owned bakers that banded together to form United Biscuit Company of America. For nearly 40 years, each baker continued to use its own name and manufacture and package its own unique products.

In 1966, faced with competitive challenges, the remaining six bakeries carried their consolidation a step further by forming the Keebler Company and unifying their various product lines. The Keebler Company name came from the oldest of the bakeries, which had been founded in Pennsylvania in 1853 and had the best national name recognition (although it had never ventured west of the Rockies).

The newly formed Keebler Company, which was headquartered in the Chicago suburb of Elmhurst, Illinois, retained the Leo Burnette advertising agency to develop a brand recognition campaign. In 1969, the company introduced "Ernie the Elf — baking *uncommonly* good cookies and crackers with a magic oven in a hollow tree."

In 1974, Keebler Company became a wholly owned subsidiary of United Biscuit Co. Limited of England. The owner immediately made a strong capital investment in the Keebler/Denver Bakery, including a fifth oven connected to an automated packaging line and a 65,000-square-foot expansion of the shipping department. An automated 45,000-square-foot warehouse was added in 1992.

In 1995, United Biscuit Co. Limited of England sold the Keebler Company to INFLO, a private group of investors composed of INVUS (a Delaware Company that invests in the United States for the Artal family of France) and Flowers Biscuits (a United States Company.)

In 1996, INFLO purchased Sunshine Biscuits and is in the process of merging operations of the two companies, which include a total of ten bakeries The combined company will control about 25 percent of the United States market for cookies and crackers.

Employment at the Keebler/Denver Bakery reached an all-time high of 1000 in 1978, following the addition of the fifth oven, and remained at that level until 1985. Today, because of restructuring and automation, employment has leveled off at approximately

700. Because of automation, for example, eight people can now produce 36,000 boxes of crackers every eight hours.

Most of the bakery's highly experienced workforce has been employed there for more than ten years. Employees are represented by three labor unions: Bakery, Confectionery & Tobacco Workers, Local 26; Operating Engineers, Local 1; and Teamsters, Local 537.

Today, the Keebler/Denver Bakery maintains five "high altitude" production lines, all of them certified Kosher. Line one manufactures Fudge Shoppe and traditional cookies. Line two manufactures NutriGrain Bars. A third production line manufactures restaurant-pack Club Crackers and Cafe Crackers, as well as Cheeze-Its and Shuffles — new additions since the acquisition of Sunshine Biscuits.

Line four produces Zesta Saltine Crackers, Fat Free Zesta Saltine's and Sunshine's Fat Free Krispy Saltines. Line five is devoted to a full array of graham crackers — cinnamon, low fat, chocolate, regular and honey.

The Keebler/Denver Bakery is proud to celebrate 90 years of providing good jobs and quality products in Denver.

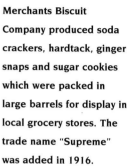

Merchants Biscuit Company produced soda crackers, hardtack, ginger snaps and sugar cookies which were packed in large barrels for display in local grocery stores. The trade name "Supreme" was added in 1916.

The Denver Bakery of Keebler Company employs 700 people and manufactures Keebler products for distribution throughout the West.

NORGREN

**Carl A. Norgren,
Innovator 1890-1968**

From humble beginnings in a Denver basement, Norgren has grown to be a worldwide leader in the development and manufacture of pneumatic products. The man behind the Norgren name is Carl A. Norgren, who believed in the ideals of America's free enterprise system. "I believe in the free enterprise system, the right of every individual to start on a shoestring or with an idea, and through conscientious endeavor, build that idea into a fortune." And that is what Carl Norgren did.

His rags-to-riches story began when Carl Norgren designed a new type of hose coupling and a fulflo air chuck for service stations in his Denver home in 1925. He then had the couplings and chucks manufactured in a local machine shop. With the addition of other types of couplings and fittings in 1926, his venture was organized as an operating partnership on March 1, 1926. Concurrent with the organization, came a move from his home to more spacious quarters in the Steel Building at 16th and Welton streets in Denver.

Seven months later, his organization became recognized as the C.A. Norgren Co. Hose clamps were added as a product line while Mr. Norgren also developed a line of oxyacetylene welding fittings. He also manufactured photo enlargers and small air compressors for beverage dispensers. While exploring an opportunity with General Motors in Detroit, Norgren learned GM engineers were having maintenance difficulties with air tools and air equipment. Norgren sketched an idea on the back of a GM interoffice memo that later became the "Norgren Automotive Sight Feed Airline Lubricator." This crudely sketched plan was designed to eliminate the high maintenance cost of air tools and air equipment, and was the forerunner of the now-famous Norgren Oil-Fog® Lubricator.

Norgren's involvement in World War II was extensive. The company supplied hose assemblies for the M-3 and M-4 60-ton military tanks, and Norgren lubricators were used in shipyards, aircraft plants, Army arsenals as well as other war production plants.

After World War II, in a significant business move, Norgren joined the international trade scene on a large scale. The company entered into an agreement with Rocky Mountain Export Company to handle its export business until Norgren created its own International Operations division in 1956. Soon, the firm strategically located manufacturing plants worldwide to best serve its growing European markets. Early agreements were established with England, Sweden, and Holland, and subsequent agreements were made with West Germany, Japan, Italy, India, Argentina, Mexico, and Brazil. Today, Norgren has distributors in over 70 countries, including 138 distributors in the U.S. alone.

In 1957, Norgren consolidated operations to a new facility, on 22 acres at South Delaware Street in Littleton, Colorado. This site remains Norgren's headquarters throughout the Americas. Further expansion continued when Norgren purchased the Hoffman Valve Company of Dayton, Ohio, and trans-

Norgren's first manufacturing site consisted of only 7875 square-feet, serving its needs until 1952.

ferred its machinery and inventory to Littleton. In 1965, Norgren-Detroit was established to promote Norgren products to the automotive industry.

In 1972, Norgren was acquired by IMI, one of Europe's foremost industrial companies. Based in Birmingham, England, the IMI Group, with revenues

Norgren distributors worldwide.

now over $2 billion, is quoted on the International Stock Exchange in London. IMI employs more than 17,300 people worldwide and has major plants in the United Kingdom, North and South America, Europe, and Australia. In addition to Fluid Power, IMI's other business operation areas include Building Products, Drinks Dispense, and Special Engineering.

Belonging to this new organizational structure fueled growth through innovation and acquisition. In 1988, Norgren acquired C&C Manufacturing in Rockford, Illinois. Mosier Industries, Dayton, Ohio, and ISI Automation, Detroit, Michigan, were 1996 additions to the company. Acquiring these significant industry leaders has enhanced and broadened the

existing services and products Norgren offered throughout the years.

Today, Norgren's product line is comprised of a broad, fully integrated selection of compressed air preparation components, directional control valves, versatile actuators, and fittings, flow controls, and other accessory items.

Norgren provides pneumatic solutions to automotive, pulp and paper, packaging, manufacturing, medical, and high-tech industries worldwide. The company's latest innovations reflect technological advances such as modular FRLs, electropneumatic equipment for precision automated manufacturing operations, fieldbus technologies, smart function fittings, and new innovations in using stronger, lightweight materials for extended life cycles and reduced cost.

Norgren's commitment to quality is reflected in certification to ISO 9001 standards, the highest level of certification worldwide. Globally, all of Norgren's manufacturing facilities conform to ISO 9000 Standards. It's just one of many direct benefits to the many thousands of companies worldwide that are Norgren customers.

Carl Norgren said, "Equality of opportunity is an experience not common to any other nation on earth. It is a facet of American life that must be defended at all costs." Today, Carl Norgren's philosophy of America's free enterprise system has expanded in Norgren's worldwide business endeavors.

Norgren's manufacturing site in Littleton, Colorado serves Norgren operations throughout the Americas.

DAKOTA MINING CORPORATION

Dakota Mining Corporation has demonstrated beyond a doubt that it is possible for a small mining company to be both successful and environmentally responsible.

Ten years after its founding, Dakota Mining Corporation is poised to join the ranks of gold companies that produce more than 100,000 ounces of gold per year.

Dakota Mining, which produced 49,000 ounces of gold in 1995, anticipates 1996 production of 75,000 ounces, 1997 production of 100,000 ounces, and 1998 production of 140,000 ounces.

Dakota Mining is a "junior" mining company primarily involved in the exploration, acquisition, development and operation of precious metal deposits in the United States. The company's current gold resource base is about 2.6 million ounces; 1.1 million of that amount is defined as proven/provable reserve.

With roots in Canada and a strong U.S. asset base, Dakota Mining chose Denver as its headquarters because of the city's prominence in the North American mining industry. Most of the company's 250 employees work at its mine sites.

Since 1988, Dakota Mining has produced more than 600,000 ounces of gold from two primary sources, the Gilt Edge Mine in South Dakota, and Stibnite Mine in Idaho. In addition, the company holds a 40 percent interest in the Golden Reward Mine in South Dakota.

Dakota Mining's success has not come easy. In 1992, the company's operations and cash flow were imperiled by a conflict with the Endangered Species Act and other complex mine-permitting issues. When faced with such challenges, small mining companies often lack the will and the resources to survive.

Operations at the company's Stibnite mine were suspended when the State of Idaho cited potential environmental impact on Chinook salmon, a protected species. For more than two years, the company worked closely with regulatory agencies to develop an alternative operating plan for the mine — a plan that would eventually satisfy even the most extreme environmental activists.

Most of Dakota Mining Corporation's 250 employees work at its mine sites in Idaho and South Dakota.

Due to extraordinary effort on the part of the company's current management team, headed by president and chief executive officer Alan Bell, Dakota Mining satisfied and exceeded all regulatory requirements and resumed production in 1995.

In addition, impressed with Dakota Mining's commitment to the environment, regulatory agencies of the State of South Dakota took the unprecedented step of approving the new Anchor Hill operations at the Gilt Edge Mine.

Dakota Mining emerged from its travails with healthy cash reserves and minimal debt. With permits in place, a healthy cash position, drilled-out reserves, established and paid-for mines, and stepped-up exploration programs, Dakota is definitely positioned for growth.

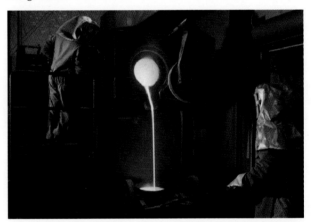

Dakota Mining Corporation is a "junior" mining company primarily involved in the exploration, acquisition, development and operation of precious metal deposits in the United States.

Through the development and operation of existing gold mines, exploration programs, joint ventures, mergers and acquisitions — including efforts outside of North America, the company plans to grow into the next tier of mining companies.

Dakota Mining Corporation has demonstrated beyond a doubt that it is possible for a small mining company to be both successful and environmentally responsible.

EAGLE DIRECT

With a firm foundation in Denver's past, Eagle Direct is striding at full speed into the future.

Eagle Direct has grown up with Denver. What began in the 1950s as a two-man 2,000 sq. ft. direct mail printing facility serving the greater Denver area is now a 125 person, 125,000 sq. ft. direct marketing organization with clients throughout the nation and the world. Like Denver, Eagle Direct has changed over the decades, re-positioning itself, re-inventing itself, in a never ending process of evolution.

One thing has not changed. Gerald V. Harris and his son, Howard Harris built Eagle Direct on the platform of customer service and measurable results. Eagle Direct's constant credo is "You can't manage what you can't measure."

Eagle Direct has always stressed innovation as a means of keeping their clients ahead of the pack. Not afraid to put new ideas into practice, they have pioneered many of the now-proven techniques commonly used today. Combining the emerging computer technologies of the 1970s with real world experience, Eagle became a forerunner in the development of marketing databases, helping client companies enhance marketing program performance, build customer loyalty, increase revenues, and reduce costs.

Eagle Direct is a full-service database marketing organization that provides a unique combination of strategic and implementation services, fully-integrated

under one roof. The core of most Eagle Direct projects is database management. A typical program will begin and end with a thorough understanding of the target market, closely aligned with segmentation, scoring and modeling to create a basis for campaign strategy, test marketing, and finally program roll out.

Eagle Direct's strength is in the integration of their services. Concept, creative and print production are tailored to a specific target audience, then mailed using the latest in automated insertion and addressing techniques. Response-driven fulfillment systems are orchestrated to provide follow-up material, and capture every detail available from the responder.

Eagle Direct has earned the respect of their peers throughout the country, with appointments to various boards and committees within the graphic arts industry. Both Howard and Gerald Harris have served on the board of the National Association of Printers and Lithographers, and Gerald Harris is the recipient of the Walter E. Soderstrom award, the graphic arts industry's highest award given to an individual in recognition of outstanding and sustained industry leadership.

Today, Eagle Direct continues to thrive because it views change as opportunity and is willing to take the risk to venture into uncharted territory. Now, as in their beginnings, Eagle continues to view the client relationship as a partnership, and they measure their success by their clients' success.

DREYER'S GRAND ICE CREAM, INC.

Dreyer's Grand Ice Cream, Inc., is the leading manufacturer, marketer and distributor of premium ice cream in the United States. In Denver, it enjoys a 30 percent share of the market.

T. Gary Rogers (left) and William F. Cronk purchased Dreyer's in 1977, growing the local operation to a regional and then a national company with 1995 sales of nearly $679 million.

Denver residents love Dreyer's Grand Ice Cream! In fact, almost 30 percent of all packaged ice cream sold in the Denver metropolitan area is Dreyer's Grand Ice Cream.

Many of these ice cream *afficionados* do not know that their favorite product is manufactured right here in Denver, and has been for nearly 20 years.

Since 1979, the company has been manufacturing ice cream in Denver for distribution throughout the Rocky Mountain region. Dreyer's has long recognized that a high-altitude manufacturing facility is imperative to a quality product. Through partnership agreements, the company also distributes Ben & Jerry's, Starbucks Ice Cream, Healthy Choice® and Nestlé USA ice cream novelties.

Dreyer's Grand Ice Cream, Inc. is the leading manufacturer, marketer and distributor of premium ice cream in the United States. The company's products are sold under the name "Dreyer's" in the western United States and "Edy's" in the East and Midwest. The company employs 2800 people and posted 1995 sales of nearly $679 million.

Dreyer's was founded in 1928 by William Dreyer, an ice cream maker, and Joseph Edy, a candy maker. The two combined their talents to open an ice cream store on Grand Avenue in Oakland, California. The "Grand" in the company's name refers to this early location, as well as the quality of the product.

One of Dreyer's and Edy's innovative formulations was Rocky Road, the first ice cream flavor to feature "mix-ins." Rocky Road, a combination of smooth chocolate ice cream, marshmallows and toasted almonds, debuted during the Great Depression with a name to match the times.

In 1977, the company was purchased by T. Gary Rogers and William F. Cronk. Rogers and Cronk developed and implemented a management philosophy called "The Grooves," which creates an environment where employees make decisions, solve problems,

take initiative, and are accountable for results. They turned Dreyer's Grand Ice Cream into a regional company by expanding first into Colorado and Arizona, and then throughout the West.

In 1995, when Dreyer's officially became the largest dollar-share ice cream company in the nation, all of its employees were flown to Oakland for a celebration bash dubbed MOAP (Mother of All Parties).

Dreyer's has been manufacturing ice cream in Denver since 1979 for distribution throughout the high-altitude Rocky Mountain region.

Dreyer's invests in the community through the Dreyer's Grand Ice Cream Charitable Foundation. The Foundation was established in 1987 to provide focused community support, particularly for youth and K-12 public education. Dreyer's sets aside two percent of pre-tax earnings for Foundation contributions.

In Denver, the Foundation makes countless donations of ice cream and gift certificates for non-profit special events, especially to Denver Children's Hospital, the Ronald McDonald House and the Denver Rescue Mission. Dreyer's was selected as official distributor of ice cream when Pope John Paul visited Denver in 1993. Each year, the company participates in events like The Taste of Colorado, the Parade of Homes and the International Golf Tournament.

In 1999, Dreyer's Grand Ice Cream will celebrate 20 years of manufacturing and distributing quality ice cream in Denver and throughout the Rocky Mountain Region.

THE GATES RUBBER COMPANY

When Charles Gates and his new bride, Hazel, bought The Colorado Tire and Leather Company in 1911, little did they know that their one-room shop on a dirt street in Denver would evolve into one of the world's largest rubber companies.

Colorado Tire and Leather made a single product, the Durable Tread, a steel-studded band of leather that motorists fastened to their flimsy car tires to increase mileage. Using an aggressive advertising campaign, Gates sold the tire covers to Eastern motorists.

Gates began making horse halters from leftover leather scraps. In 1912, he persuaded Buffalo Bill Cody to use the halters on the mustangs in his world-famous Wild West show. Buffalo Bill was so impressed, he appeared in Gates' advertisements promoting the "never break" halters.

In 1914, Gates introduced the Half Sole, a rubberized fabric cover cemented over worn tires. Its superiority and success convinced Gates to quit producing the leather Durable Tread and prompted a name change to the International Rubber Company.

Three years later the company set the automotive industry on its ear when John Gates, Charles' brother, invented the rubber and fabric V-belt. The first V-belts were crude, but far superior to the hemp ropes found in car engines at the time. Within a decade, Gates became the world's largest manufacturer of V-belts, a title it proudly holds today.

Gates changed the business name to The Gates Rubber Company in 1919 and the company grew and prospered in the 1920s and '30s.

World War II brought drastic changes to the rubber industry. With most of the world's natural rubber in short supply, allied rubber companies were struggling to meet the needs of the war effort. Gates entered into a joint venture with several other rubber companies and formed the Copolymer Corporation to develop methods to produce synthetic rubber from petroleum. The successful endeavor played a key role in supplying much-needed car, truck and aircraft parts to allied manufacturers.

In the prosperous years following the war, the company expanded from its Denver base to its first international facility in Brantford, Ontario, then into Mexico, along with factories and distribution centers throughout the United States.

Charles Gates Jr. took over in 1961 after his father's death. He oversaw the company's aggressive growth into Europe, South America and Asia. In 1974, Gates exited the tire business to focus on its core belt and hose products.

In 1996, the Rubber Company became a wholly-owned subsidiary of Tomkins PLC of London, England, ending 85 years of family ownership. At the time of the merger, Gates was the world's largest non-tire rubber company with 42 manufacturing facilities in 14 countries and 13,500 worldwide employees. Gates is one of only a handful of rubber companies with factories, distribution centers and sales offices in all of the world's major markets, including North America, Europe, Asia and Latin America.

A Gates Vulco Cord belt is used to lift this Ford Model T and four men in the early 1920s. Gates invented the V-belt in 1917, completely changing the power transmission industry. Today, Gates is the world's largest manufacturer of V-belts.

REGAL PLASTIC SUPPLY COMPANY

Edward F. Statter, Chairman and CEO of Regal Plastic Supply Company.

The Regal Plastic Supply Company was founded in Kansas City, Missouri, in the late 1940s as a retail outlet for a local plastics manufacturer. In 1954, it separated from the parent company and became an independent entity. Shortly thereafter, three additional locations were established. The Denver operation opened in 1956. The company's original products were acrylic and polycarbonate.

Regal Plastics now distributes all types and forms of brand name plastic materials manufactured by leading companies such as General Electric, Atohaas, DuPont, Cyro Industries and ICI Plastics — and many others. The company also offers its customers many value-added services such as thermoforming and custom fabrication.

Present-day manufacturing companies use large quantities of high-tech plastic materials. Regal Plastics is a preferred supplier of this material to a list of well-known Fortune 500 clients that includes Lockheed Martin, Boeing, McDonnell-Douglas, Hewlett Packard, Ford Motor Company, Chrysler Corporation and General Motors.

Regal Plastics also serves customers of all sizes in a broad range of businesses, including construction, medical, sign, glass and glazing contractors, exhibit and display manufacturers, and plastic fabricators.

Regal Plastics' growth in the West began when Edward F. Statter, who had been employed by the company in Kansas City, Missouri, as a fabricator, purchased an interest in the Denver operation in

Regal Plastic Supply Company Distribution Center

1958. In 1962, Mr. Statter acquired his partners' interests and became sole owner.

Shortly thereafter, Mr. Statter began to expand the Western region by opening a branch in Albuquerque, New Mexico. This was followed by additional branch offices in Colorado Springs, Colorado; El Paso, Texas; Phoenix, Arizona; and San Diego and Los Angeles, California. Recently, Regal Plastics expanded into Northern Mexico where it established a branch in Tijuana, followed by branches in Mexicali and Juarez.

In 1991, Regal Plastics consolidated all of its Denver area operations by moving the distribution center from Englewood to a 7.4 acre historical industrial site in Littleton, Colorado, where the fabrication facilities were located. The facility was renovated and now includes approximately 40,000 square feet of office, warehouse and fabricating space.

Ed and Beverly Statter are active members in the plastics industry and in the community. Mrs. Statter previously served on the boards of directors of the Swedish Medical Center and J.K. Mullen High School. She is presently involved with the Rocky Mountain Chapter of the Multiple Sclerosis Guild. Mr. Statter served on the boards of J.K. Mullen High School,

St. Mary's Academy, The United Bank of Littleton and The First Interstate Bank of Englewood. He is a past president of the International Association of Plastic Distributors, the Colorado Chapter of the Society of Plastics Engineers and the Littleton Kiwanis Club.

Regal Plastic Supply Company is proud to celebrate 40 years of doing business in Denver and the West.

EVERGREEN RESOURCES, INC.

During the energy boom of the 1970s and early 1980s, roughly 140 oil and gas companies were brought public via the Denver penny stock market. Fortunes were made by investors who sold their stock in many of the companies — in time. Fortunes were lost by many more investors who didn't get out before the bust of the mid-1980's — when oil and gas prices plummeted. Of the 140 original companies, only a handful survived and are still around today. Evergreen Resources, Inc., founded in 1981, and headquartered in Denver, is one of the survivors of what turned out to be the most prolonged slump in U.S. energy history.

Spurred by continued strong U.S. and world energy demand, oil and gas prices have rebounded and a leaner, tougher group of U.S. Independent oil and gas companies are now thriving. Armed with new technology, a more focused approach to their business and a sharp eye on the bottom line, these Independents have not just survived — they're now healthy growing enterprises.

After years of exploration and development activity throughout the Rockies and mid-Continent regions, Evergreen discovered a terrific application of improved technology just 200 miles south of Denver in the Raton Basin, near Trinidad, Colorado. The Raton Basin lies just east of the Sangre de Cristo mountain range. Since 1990, Evergreen has acquired leases over 120,000 generally contiguous acres, virtually all of which are prospective for developing coalbed methane gas production. Evergreen is using this relatively new technology — coalbed methane recovery — to revive the energy industry in the historic coal mining region of Southern Colorado in Las Animas County.

Coalbed methane requires very little treatment to be sold as natural gas in conventional natural gas pipelines. Starting in 1994, Evergreen has drilled and placed into production over 50 new wells. They plan to drill and hook-up 40 to 50 wells per year, and hope to develop over 500 new wells. Evergreen's successful drilling program has made them the largest natural gas producer in Las Animas County, and allowed the area to become a net energy exporter. Natural gas has taken the place of historic coal as the region's principal energy development and export.

Evergreen's most valuable resource is the talent of their technical staff, which they believe to be one of the most knowledgeable in the industry regarding coalbed methane extraction technology. They pay attention to a wide range of details — technology, operations, environmental impact and land use planning. Evergreen's management believes strongly that the land and environment should have minimal disturbance from resource development. Evergreen's activities in the Raton Basin have been planned to keep the natural landscaping intact and to be compatible with the increasing ranchette development in the area.

Evergreen's gas treating and compressor station in Burro Canyon, (Las Animas County, Colorado) was specifically designed and located to mitigate noise and visual impact to canyon residents.

Over 90 percent of the company's time, energy and capital expenditures are dedicated to this Raton Basin project, which could cause Evergreen to become a very large natural gas production company. They are developing and producing natural gas for a cost which represents roughly one-third of what they can sell it for. Evergreen has one of the lowest finding and development costs of any oil and gas producer in the U.S.

After many painful years, Evergreen is very well positioned for strong growth in a positive upward cycle for their Industry. Denver survived the energy bust of the mid-1980s, and is now thriving. The same thing is true of the oil and gas business . . . and Evergreen.

AB Hirschfeld Press, Inc.

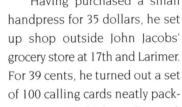

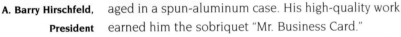

A. Barry Hirschfeld, President

In 1454, Johannes Gutenberg developed the miracle of movable type — the printing press. Four-hundred-fifty years later, AB Hirschfeld stepped off the train in Denver, a young, bustling town whose streets were covered in mud and manure. And that was just the beginning.

For three years, AB worked as a "printer's devil" and an apprentice typesetter until 1907, when he founded what has become the oldest family-owned printing company in Colorado — the AB Hirschfeld Press.

Having purchased a small handpress for 35 dollars, he set up shop outside John Jacobs' grocery store at 17th and Larimer. For 39 cents, he turned out a set of 100 calling cards neatly packaged in a spun-aluminum case. His high-quality work earned him the sobriquet "Mr. Business Card."

Business grew dynamically over the next decade-and-a-half. In 1923, the industrious AB moved the company to 1840 California Street, where he installed a phalanx of state-of-the-art equipment: a two-color Kidder press (for printing aluminum and glassine candy wrappers); and two-; three-; and four-color offset presses — all were the first of their kind to be employed in Denver.

During the Depression, AB sold his life insurance policy to keep the company solvent, but by World War II, deluged with government contracts to print war bonds and ration stamps, the company was squarely back on its feet.

An avid baseball fan, AB built the company's Speer Boulevard headquarters on the home of the former Denver Bears stadium — literally. AB welcomed his son, Ed, into the business with an office that sat over home plate. Today, the company is a big part of the home team, printing the programs for the Colorado Rockies.

AB said Ed was "programmed for sales from the day he was born." Teaming up together during the late '40s and '50s, this "one-two punch" landed major contracts with, among others, Coors, Samsonite, and Gates Rubber Company.

When Ed's son, Barry, joined the fold, he picked up where AB left off, exhibiting passion for technical details. He also brought with him a vital new approach to management. Today, the company boasts a progressive Quality Assurance program, and its 98-percent on-time performance leads the industry. Through aggressive recycling, the company recovers more than 2.2 million pounds of paper each year. And employees now have an unprecedented array of savings and retirement options.

When AB contributed $5.00 to National Jewish Hospital back in 1905, he engendered the spirit of corporate largesse that has permeated the firm ever since. Today, Barry sits on the board of directors of a dozen local and statewide civic and cultural organizations, including the Denver Area Council of the

Barry Hirschfeld and Hirschfeld's Baker-Perkins 8 unit Web Press.

Boy Scouts and the Denver Metro Convention and Visitors Bureau. The firm is also a major sponsor of the Cherry Creek Arts Festival.

In the mid-90s, the company purchased Second Nature, Ltd., a maker of greeting-cards. As the company looks for new ways to modernize and grow, it holds to the values instilled by its founder: honesty, integrity, and an unwavering attention to detail.

Partners in Denver

DENVER'S TRANSPORTATION, COMMUNICATIONS, AND ENERGY FIRMS KEEP PEOPLE, INFORMATION

NETWORKS

AND POWER CIRCULATING THROUGHOUT THE REGION.

CENTENNIAL AIRPORT

Centennial Airport's yesteryear is as soaring and full of promise as its future.

By the mid-1960's, Denver's burgeoning growth had put a strain on Stapleton International Airport, and on one man's nerves, in particular. Furious that his new car was scratched while parked downtown, engineer George Wallace set out to decentralize Denver. He purchased 40 acres of land southeast of downtown at about the time the Federal Aviation Administration proposed a general aviation reliever airport for Stapleton.

Looking west at Centennial Airport, with the majestic Rocky Mountains in the background.

On June 23rd, 1967, construction began on the Arapahoe County Public Airport. Situated where Arapahoe and Douglas Counties converge, the little 'airfield in the tumbleweeds' quickly landed its first fixed-base operator (FBO) when Clinton Aviation signed a 30-year lease. Wallace then opened the Denver Technological Center, soon to become it's own micro-metropolis.

Arapahoe County Airport officially opened for business May 12, 1968 with an Aviation Fair. Lear Jet, Hughes Helicopter, the FAA, the Antique Aircraft and the Experimental Aircraft Associations, the Civil Air Patrol, and numerous Colorado dignitaries participated in the event. By the end of its inaugural year, 98 aircraft were based at Arapahoe. Wallace pushed for the airport's expansion to help accommodate the many corporations that relocated to the southeast-corridor.

Within three years, aircraft parking aprons, connecting taxi ways, and two new runways were added to better serve tenant growth. To help battle Denver's unpredictable climate, the Airport's first snow removal equipment was purchased. In the ensuing years, snow removal personnel would twice be awarded the Colonel Bernt Balchen Award for Excellence in Airport Snow Removal and Ice Control.

In 1972, construction on the original control tower began. A short time later, DTC neighbor George Wallace became the head of the Arapahoe County Airport Executive Management Committee. The tower, dedicated in 1973, was selected as the FAA's Terminal Air Traffic Facility of the Year for the Rocky Mountain Region the following year. Arapahoe then added its second FBO — Colorado Flying Academy.

Land acquisitions, new features and lighting systems were added to enhance operations. During the 1970's, ten major federally funded projects were completed, totaling nearly $14 million.

As Denver's 'business connection,' Arapahoe Airport's general aviation amenities catered to air charter, air ambulance, law enforcement, agricultural applications, search and rescue, corporate aviation, wildlife management, flight training, and recreational flying.

The airport skyrocketed to the sixth busiest general aviation airport in the nation as the Control Tower became a 24-hour facility. The FAA's Denver Flight Service Station at the airport was dedicated, and the airport funded nearly $800,000 for rehabilitation, landscaping, street lighting and widening of S. Peoria Street.

In recognition of its continued growth, the airport's name changed to Centennial Airport in 1984. Ground broke for a new state-of-the-art control tower and administration complex, and Air Plaza 50 — a 90,000 sq. ft. hangar/office complex — was completed.

Shortly thereafter, Douglas County was given non-voting board representation by the Airport Authority due to the increasing operations' impact on Douglas County. Centennial then landed its third FBO, Beckett Aviation, which helped propel airport operations to over 350,000 by the end of 1985.

The airport's importance as a training base for student pilots cannot be overlooked, as training traffic accounts for almost 55 percent of the total air traffic at the airport. Denver is now home to nearly 10,000 active pilots, many of whom received training at Centennial.

Centennial Airport has always been concerned with its effect on neighbors. A Citizens Advisory Committee, consisting of airport and residential members, worked together to developvoluntary FAA-approved noise abatement measures that minimized aircraft noise impact on surrounding communities.

Meanwhile, the closure of Stapleton and the opening of Denver International Airport have had a significant impact on Centennial. Denver's air traffic flow was completely redistributed. Centennial, having served as a reliever airport for Stapleton for decades, immediately became a popular general aviation reliever airport for DIA. During any given week, hangars, taxi ways, and FBO ramps are increasingly crowded with a vast array of business jets, turboprops, and helicopters. Jet fuel sales increased dramatically, with nearly 7 million gallons pumped in 1996.

Hundreds of pilots bypass DIA weekly, flying in and out of Centennial for refueling. Centennial's award-winning 24-hour control tower, snow removal, top-flight, full-service fixed-base operators, heated corporate and private hangars, on-site Holiday Inn, restaurant and charter flight catering service, rental car, limousine, and shuttle service all fuel Centennial's superb reputation.

The commitment to excellence that keeps Centennial a top-flight general aviation airport is rewarded with occasional barnstorming. The airport has hosted numerous air shows, rendezvous and derbies over the years. Attractions have included the aeronautical talents of such groups as the Red Devil aerobatic teams, the Black Hawk demonstration team, the Northern Lights, the Army Golden Knights Skydiving team, the Confederate Air force, and the Navy Blue Angels.

And you won't find Centennial Airport in a holding pattern any time soon. Pilots will be ableto fly into Centennial's U.S. Customs Facility, which will accommodate jets coming in non-stop from places as far away as Japan. Future expansion will stay in step with the economic environment of Arapahoe County, Douglas County, and South Denver.

....

At 10,001 feet long, runway 17L/35R allows pilots to fly in to Centennial during all types of weather by using its ILS (Instrument Landing System).

Centennial is now one of the busiest general aviation airports in America. With over 650 based aircraft, a prime location, and hundreds of thousands of streamlined annual operations, Centennial Airport is setting the pace for general aviation airports across the nation.

DENVER INTERNATIONAL AIRPORT

Some airline passengers make the telephone call from their city of destination, while others are Denver-bound travelers dialing from their hotel room. And many visitors to the 2-year-old Denver International Airport are awaiting their connecting flight and feel compelled to call DIA's customer service via a paging phone.

They don't yell about lost luggage, moan about late departures or gripe about confusing directions to a terminal. Instead, visitors sing the praises of the Mile High City's 53-square-mile airport whose operating efficiency is reaching sky-high proportions.

The northwest corner of DIA's Jeppesen Terminal is equivalent in length to three football fields.

Twice the size of New York's Manhattan Island, DIA, the world's 10th-busiest airport, has become a model for future airports with its efficient layout, artistic flair and refreshing open-spaced ambiance. While passengers boast of DIA's friendly confines, airport and city officials brag about its superior efficiency. In 1996, the Federal Aviation Administration reported that of the nation's top 20 airports, DIA had the fewest delays — 0.19 percent of all flights. Its 1996 on-time arrival rate of 82.2 percent was ranked No. 2 by the U.S. Department of Transportation.

An average of 88,000 passengers arrive and depart daily via the airport's 21 airlines that include four foreign carriers and five regional commuters. Nonstop flights depart daily or weekly to eight international destinations — Amsterdam, Calgary, Los Cabos, Mazatlan, Toronto, Vancouver, Zacatecas, and Seoul.

Airport usage has paralleled the city's impressive growth as weekly nonstop international departing flights almost tripled during DIA's second year of operation.

Located 23 miles northeast of downtown Denver, the 34,000-acre airport services travelers to and from the metro area that Fortune magazine, in November 1995, ranked as the nation's third best city to conduct business in. Telecommunications and financial services were cited as economic strengths for the area, whose central geographic location has made it an attractive destination for communities throughout the Rocky Mountain region and a connecting hub for airline flights between the coasts and other major metropolitan areas. The magazine projected that by 2010, 90,000 jobs will have been created by the world's third-largest airport, which has the capacity to expand to handle up to 110 million passengers annually.

Most travelers pass through the 1.5 million square-foot Jeppesen Terminal that has captivated the world with its tent-shaped roof. The Teflon-coated fiberglass shell has become a signature statement for Denver — similar to Australia's Sydney Opera House or Paris' Eiffel Tower. Reflecting 90 percent of sunlight, the roof dually symbolizes Colorado's Rocky Mountains and its eastern plains. The floor of the 1,200-foot-long terminal, longer than Chicago's Sears Tower is tall, features a variety of granite from around the world that duplicates the roof design.

Overlooking the airport is the 33-story FAA control tower, the tallest in North America. From inside the tower, which is engineered to sway only one-half inch in an 86 mph wind, air-traffic controllers coordinate arriving and departing aircraft and have an unobstructed view of all five runways. DIA's design standards specify runways with a 40-year life span — more than double the life of most runways — and no runways cross, which boosts the level of safety. Depending upon wind direction, controllers can quickly shift traffic from

The Jeppesen Terminal silhouettes Pena Boulevard, the main entranceway into the DIA complex.

one runway to another with minimal delays or disruption of air traffic. Crucial wind shear information is provided by 29 sensors that transmit data to a centralized computer system via 152 miles of fiber optic cabling. All of the FAA's navigational, warning and controlling systems give DIA the most advanced aviation technology available.

Operators of the FAA's Terminal Radar Approach Control facility coordinate triple independent simultaneous landings at DIA, the first airport in the world to have such poor-weather capability. Equipped with cutting-edge technology, DIA's traffic efficiency rate and safety rating soared over its predecessor, Stapleton Airport. In 1996, the new airport's per-hour arrival capability was 35 percent higher than Stapleton's rate in good weather and 275 percent better in bad weather. Nationwide, in March 1996, a month with 16.4 inches of snow, Denver ranked first for on-time arrivals and was third best for on-time departures.

DIA, the first all-new major American airport built in the past 20 years, was designed to meet or exceed all environmental requirements. For instance, glycol used to deice planes is recaptured in detention ponds. About 90 percent of all airport fleet vehicles, plus rental car shuttles, run on natural gas, eliminating 52 tons of smog-causing chemicals annually. A cooperative effort has reduced noise pollution and the FAA has redrawn some flight paths to lower noise from DIA's 1,200 daily flights.

Future development includes a 72-acre mixed-use business park. The DIA Business Center, a $1 billion, 450-acre project, features a community of office buildings, light industry, stores, apartments, houses and hotels about six miles from the airport. The Denver Mayor's Office of Economic Development, the DIA Business Partnership, the Greater Metro Chamber of Commerce and the economic development councils in Adams County and Aurora are working with developers and interested businesses to help match future needs with opportunities.

As the Denver area continues to bustle, E-470, a toll-paid highway that eventually will connect the metropolitan area via a circular route encompassing the city, will provide quicker access to the airport for suburban residents. Also, the city is studying a public/private partnership to build an "air train" link from DIA to downtown Denver — just another way that DIA is contributing to the welfare of metro area residents and the controlled growth of the Queen City of the Rockies.

DENVER WATER

"Except for a few hoary cottonwoods and evergreen conifers, the trees which make an oasis of the city are imports: they and the lawns are kept alive only by faithful and ritualistic irrigation. The garden hose and lawn sprinkler deserve a place on the city seal along with the mountain skyline and soaring eagle."

Robert L. Perkin, The First Hundred Years,
Doubleday & Co., 1959

"Green oasis" is a term frequently used to describe the Mile High City. There is a pride found among Denver residents who have taken a hostile, dry prairie and converted it into one of America's most attractive cities. Explorers of the early 19th century had written off this place as "uninhabitable — unfit for cultivation." Settlers, early and late, have come from the water rich east, where an adequate water supply is taken for granted. Most major American cities developed in locations where water was plentiful. Denver's earliest supply was the south Platte River which, as early residents soon discovered, had the disconcerting habit of drying up in the fall and early winter as the last of the mountain snowmelt trickled downstream.

The first attempt to supply water to the city came in 1859 with the formation of the Capitol Hydraulic Company to dig a ditch from the South Platte, far south of Denver to "Browns's Bluff," now Capitol Hill.

It was followed by another ten corporations intending to supply water to the community. In 1870, with the arrival of the railroad and the beginning of a population explosion, the Denver Water Company built a pumping plant at 15th Street and the Platte River to supply a million gallons of water a day. It would be replaced by a still larger plant in 1880, now preserved at Denver Water's headquarters as the "Three Stone Buildings."

But pumping water from a river that would sometimes dry up did not appear as a long term solution to Walter S. Cheesman and David Moffat, who interested themselves in nearly all phases of life in this developing city. With uncanny skill, they consolidated a last remaining competing water system into their Denver Union Water Company in 1894 and began a tradition of long-range planning for Denver's water future. In 1905, they completed Cheesman Dam on the south Platte River more than 60 miles upstream of Denver. It was Denver's first mountain water storage facility.

But public dissatisfaction with Denver Union's political clout and ability to dictate franchise conditions and water rates led to voter approval of City Charter amendments in 1918 creating the Denver Water Board and the public purchase of Denver

Turn-of-the-century water company survey party. Finding water and ways to bring it to the city were essential to the survival of the community.

Union. For $14.2 million the people of Denver now owned their water system and had a "non-political" Board of Water Commissioners with "complete charge and control of a water works system and plant." Water Boards continued the long-range water supply planning initiated by Cheesman and Moffat.

Since 70% of Colorado's water resources are found on the western slope, these more abundant sources were tapped for a rapidly growing city. Water was brought through the pilot bore of the famous Moffat railroad tunnel in the mid 1930s. Shortly thereafter, work began on the Roberts Tunnel, a spectacular plan to bring water from the Blue River some 23 miles under the Continental Divide to the South Platte system and into the city. Dillon Reservoir in Summit County would store water to be sent through the tunnel to the city. The project was completed in 1964 and Dillon has become one of the state's top recreational attractions.

These bold and imaginative projects helped secure what the Daily Colorado Tribune had called for in 1866 — "a never failing supply of water" and they earned Denver's Water Boards a reputation for "foresight and vision" in making possible the development of a refined civilization on Colorado's high, dry plains.

As Denver approaches the dawn of the 21st century, new social, political and environmental circumstances face the community. What at the turn of the last century were scattered, sparsely settled communities outside of Denver are now rapidly growing suburbs. With a metropolitan area of more than 2,000,000 people, the city of Denver itself now accounts for only around 500,000 people, one-fourth of the area's population.

Today's Water Board is also looking ahead and planning to meet the needs of future decades. The emphasis however, now incorporates a stronger reliance on the conservation of existing water resources and other strategies to meet short term, (2013) and long term, (2030) needs. Colorado's economy, climate and environment still act as magnets — attracting scores of new residents every month. Preservation of features of the natural environment

are perceived as major priorities by those who are attracted to the Colorado lifestyle. These perceptions, and an explosion in federal regulatory requirements on natural resources development, constrain traditional methods of developing water supplies. A meticulous examination of all options, undertaken over the past three years, has led to the adoption of a Water Board policy outlining ways to make sure the million people relying on the Denver water system have a "never failing" supply of water. Recycling, smaller system modifications, and supply projects will play a role in Denver's water future.

For nearly 137 years, water has played a central role in the lifestyle of Denver. It is a key to the survival of the city in generations to come. The challenge of meeting the vital water needs of those relying on Denver's system will probably by greater than ever. Conservation programs requiring heightened public awareness of the value of water and asking for the cooperation of more than a million people will be a major focus of 21st century efforts. Partly due to the efforts of pioneers in developing a water supply for this city on "the great American desert," this valuable resource had often been taken for granted. The time for casual treatment of water is gone. The next century requires a careful stewardship of remaining supplies so the community's "green oasis" lifestyle can survive.

Xeriscaped lawn in Denver. Xeriscape is the use of low water consuming grasses and plants which can dramatically reduce the amount of water needed to maintain a green urban environment.

FRONTIER AIRLINES

Long-time Denver residents have fond memories of the original Frontier Airlines. From 1946 to 1986, it was the community's one-of-a-kind hometown carrier — known for its friendly, western-style hospitality and its outstanding service. Frontier's routes — flown by more than 87 million passengers over the years — linked Denver to 89 cities across the nation.

Frontier folded its wings in 1986 after its purchase by another airline. At the time, the carrier's top managers vowed that someday — somehow — they would bring it back.

The opportunity to resurrect Frontier Airlines came in 1993 and 1994, when Continental Airlines cut out all but a handful of its more than 200 flights a day from Denver to 55 desinations. The "new" Frontier was formed to fill selected gaps in those flight lines.

When Frontier took off in mid-1994, its product looked a lot like that of its predecessor — many of the same routes; the same type of Boeing 737 jets; extra

legroom; frequent flyer credits; and the same type of friendly, courteous service that had made a legend of the old Frontier.

There are also a number of important differences. The new Frontier offers the lowest fares in town — something that the old Frontier, saddled with much higher operating costs, could not do.

In addition, since today's Frontier Airlines is a totally new company, it offers a totally new look. This new look, "The Spirit of the West," is featured prominently on everything from the airline's logo to the paint scheme on its jets.

The "spirit" theme is further accented on the planes' tails, which sport huge decals of western animals, including a Bambi-like fawn, a wide-eyed raccoon, a galloping mustang, a soaring goose and Denver's own polar bear twins — Klondike and Snow. The animals vary from plane to plane and from one side of the tail to the other.

Many people are surprised to learn that the decals are not painted on. Instead, each one starts out as an actual photographic image on 35 millimeter film, which is computer-enlarged many thousands of times before it reaches its impressive 21-foot-tall size.

Passengers enjoy the convenience of boarding and deplaning Frontier's aircraft at gates located on the west side of Denver International Airport's close-in "A" concourse. Further, that concourse is the only one connected to the main terminal by a pedestrian bridge as an alternative to the increasingly crowded underground train system.

Including the security check at mid-point, it usually takes less than four minutes to walk across the bridge to the "A" concourse.

Visitors to DIA enjoy sampling the pedestrian bridge during Frontier's busy "bank" periods — morning, early afternoon and evening — when many of its animal-tailed planes are actually at the airport, allowing passengers to transfer from one plane to another.

....

Frontier Airlines, Denver's hometown airline, is proud to offer a low-price alternative to the city's residents and visitors.

JOHNSON STORAGE & MOVING COMPANY

In 1897 William Johnson settled his family on the second floor and opened his blacksmithing and wagon building shop on the first floor of a building at Second and Broadway. In 1900 William, concerned about the loss of two of his customers who had purchased automobiles, began draying baggage from Denver Union Station. This line of work also created storage and the Johnson Storage and Moving Company was established.

Nearly 100 years later, Johnson Storage & Moving Company operates twelve offices in seven states — storing clients' valuable belongings in secure environments or transporting them safely across the

....

Johnson Storage & Moving was founded in 1900 by William Johnson, a successful blacksmith and wagon builder.

In 1919, Johnson built a fully fireproof warehouse next to his blacksmith shop on Broadway — a site still occupied by Johnson Storage and Moving today.

street, throughout the nation or around the world. The company is still headquartered in Denver and is owned and operated by a fourth generation of the Johnson family. Principals of the company are Mark Johnson, president, and James Johnson, vice president — both great grandsons of the company's founder. Kenneth McKee is vice president, chief financial officer and general counsel.

In 1915, Johnson Storage & Moving retired its horses and wagons and made the transition to motorized truck transport. Before long, trucks had replaced railroad cars as the preferred vehicles for long-distance moves. This transition presented the nation's movers with a new problem. Once a truck reached its destination, it usually had to make the long return trip with no load.

To deal with this inefficiency, Johnson Storage & Moving and other movers banded together to form Allied Van Lines in 1928. The company remained affiliated with Allied until 1937, when it became a founding member of United Van Lines — today the nation's largest household goods carrier with more than 1,000 agencies around the world. Johnson Storage & Moving holds the unique distinction of having been a founding agent of two of the largest household goods movers in the world.

Today, Johnson Storage & Moving is the largest shareholder of UniGroup, headquartered near St. Louis, Missouri, which is the parent company of United Van Lines, Mayflower Transit, Vanliner Insurance Company, United Capital Services and United Leasing. UniGroup is owned and directed entirely by active United Van Lines agents. In 1996, UniGroup's gross revenue exceeded $1.6 billion.

Johnson Storage & Moving maintains a fleet of more than 425 Sanitized® treated trucks and trailers, which are air-ride equipped — a significant part of United Van Lines 6,000-truck domestic fleet. Many of Johnson Storage & Moving Co.'s trucks are equipped with VanStar, a satellite location and communication system that can pinpoint a truck's location at any given time anywhere in the United States or Canada.

In 1996, Johnson Storage & Moving served 25,000 families and posted revenues of $37 million. About 75 percent of the company's business consists of moving household goods within the United States, with more than half of that amount being corporate relocation work. The company also moves household goods for the U.S. government and military. The company employs between 300 and 450 people, depending on the season.

Johnson Storage & Moving operates several specialized groups to focus on clients' specific needs. These specialized groups include the Fine Art Services Division, the International Division, the Hotel and Restaurant Services Division, the Office and Industrial Division and the Small Package

Mark Johnson, great-grandson of the founder, is president of Johnson Storage & Moving.

The management team includes (left to right) Jim Johnson, vice president; Kenneth McKee, vice president, chief financial officer and general counsel; and Al Swanson, vice president for quality control.

Division. Johnson Storage & Moving Co. transports a wide variety of non-household goods ranging from Girl Scout cookies, to travelling stage shows, to pieces of equipment that now orbit in space.

Johnson Storage & Moving Company is developing a ten-acre facility in suburban Denver which will house the company's headquarters by the turn of the century — the beginning of the company's second century in business. The original warehouse on Broadway will remain in operation to serve the company's loyal customers, some of whom have maintained secure private vaults there for more than 50 years. Johnson Storage & Moving has a combined warehouse capacity of 425,000 square feet throughout the United States.

In 1995, the company established the Johnson Storage & Moving Company Foundation to support several causes which the company has become associated with over the years — Young AmeriTowne at Young Americans Bank, several Girl Scout Councils and The St. Joseph Hospital Foundation. The company also stores and transports the support materials for the popular Cherry Creek Arts Festival.

A visit to the Broadway warehouse of Johnson Storage & Moving today is an eclectic mix of old and new. State-of-the-art computer systems and satellite tracking equipment can be found next to the restored brick walls laid in 1919 by construction contractors and second generation family member Raymond Johnson. It is intriguing to step onto the dock, look across the lot — now filled with the latest in modern moving equipment — and imagine the days when the clap of hooves and the light crack of a whip signaled the beginning of another day at Johnson Storage & Moving Co.

Johnson Storage & Moving Company looks forward to a second century of providing friendly, caring, on-time solutions to the worldwide transportation challenges of its customers.

Johnson Storage & Moving is the largest shareholder of UniGroup, the parent company of United Van Lines and Mayflower Transit.

UNITED AIRLINES

It was a golden flight home.

Amy Van Dyken, the 1996 Summer Olympics' sweetheart who won four gold medals in swimming, returned to her home in the Denver area aboard a United Airlines flight from Atlanta, Georgia, host of the Olympics. Whether slicing through water or air, once again, Van Dyken was a winner.

Millions of passengers, athletes, business travelers and vacationers, but just one airline worthy of being the official airline sponsor of the 1996 U.S. Olympic team — United Airlines. UAL is the only air carrier to provide round-the-world service, making it the only

The United concourse at Denver International Airport.

true global carrier. It offers more than 2,200 flights a day to 139 destinations in 30 countries. Denver International Airport, which opened in 1995, serves as one of United's four U.S. hubs and leases half of its gates to the air carrier, which, in 1997, is celebrating 60 years of service to the Denver area.

UAL employs 8,200 Denverites and contributes more than $500 million annually to the local economy. The company has forged a long-term partnership with DIA and credits the country's second-largest and 10th-busiest airport for improving its bottom line. UAL officials have called DIA the most operationally efficient U.S. airport and, in turn, increased its daily-flight service in Denver from 238 to 300 from January 1994 to January 1997.

Founded in 1934 as a fusion of four of the first commercial air carriers — Boeing Air Transport, National Air Transport, Pacific Air Transport and Varney Airlines — UAL since has become the largest air carrier in the world. Four years earlier, Boeing made aviation history when eight stewardesses flew in a 12-passenger aircraft between San Francisco and Chicago via Cheyenne, becoming the skyway's first flight attendants. In Oakland, Calif., in 1936, United established the first airline flight kitchen for the preparation of inflight food. In 1955, its 8 3/4-hour nonstop flight from New York to San Francisco was an industry first. Then, in 1964, UAL became the first domestic carrier to install a fully automatic, all-weather landing system.

The company again stole business headlines when it became the largest employee-owned company in America. The July 1994 investment plan created majority stockholders out of three employee groups — pilots, machinists, and salaried and management personnel. This concept has boosted the employees' sense of participation and control, while escalating the level of customer service. A 1987 study backed United's business acumen by stating consumers prefer buying products and services from employee-owned companies.

UAL's steadfast determination to please its employees and customers again was apparent when it recently modernized its entire air and ground fleet by improving air fuel efficiency, extensively using electric vehicles to support ground operations and testing the use of compressed natural gas vehicles.

Some of the employee-run company's biggest growth has been in the international marketplace,

United Airlines flies
to 139 destinations
in 30 countries.

where UAL has doubled its capacity. In recent years, the airline carrier has concentrated on eliminating less-profitable routes, allowing it to maintain superior service to more popular destinations. Plus, to succeed in a new area of industry competitiveness, United instituted "short haul" routes in 1994 when it launched Shuttle by United.

UAL remains the largest carrier at each of its U.S. hubs including Denver, home of the company's only flight training center. The state-of-the-art, 100,000-square-foot center, completed in spring 1997, houses 10 full-flight simulator bays, space for fixed-base simulators, ground training classrooms and office space for simulator maintenance and for the subsidiary UAL Services. It supplements the existing facility, which holds 26 full-flight and five fixed-base simulators. Each simulator is an exact replica of an airline cockpit and is capable of duplicating virtually any hazardous condition of inflight emergency. The Denver Flight Center is visited for training at least once annually by each of the company's 8,500 flight officers and provides training for more than 130 domestic and international carriers such as Air Force 1, Continental Airlines, Hawaiian Airlines, NASA, Royal New Zealand Air Force and Western Pacific.

The facility's $100 million expansion at the old Stapleton Airport insures further development on the grounds of the former air field that is designed to become a successful new community. The economic support provided by UAL is expected to bring at least 100 new permanent jobs to the area and guarantees long-term support for Stapleton-area businesses that were financially affected by Stapleton Airport's closure.

United's presence is felt throughout the Mile High City area. At DIA, it leases 45 gates and has an option on 64 additional acres to expand its 500,000-square-foot maintenance center. United and United Express carry about 72.5 percent of all passengers in the city, some relaxing in the comforts of the carrier's new B-777s.

United's outreach program provides funds, resources and air transportation to organizations promoting education, the arts and public health. It proudly supports the National Jewish Medical Center, Colorado Uplift, Junior Achievement, the Denver Center for the Performing Arts and Colorado's Ocean Journey. For over 25 years, it's been the official airline of the Muscular Dystrophy Association and it operates the Friendly Skies program for children with serious medical illnesses.

Intermountain Jewish News

In 1943, the Central Jewish Council in Denver found its 30-year- old house organ to be a financial drain. Council leadership turned to Max Goldberg, a 32-year-old self-educated Denver native who had already managed one successful gubernatorial campaign and raised nearly $3 million in war bonds, a local record. Max Goldberg took over the reins of the **Intermountain Jewish News.** Thus was born the modern era of a unique, fully independent weekly newspaper that reported the Jewish community's interests in their larger political and philanthropic contexts.

and a doctorate in Near Eastern and Judaic Studies before becoming **IJN** executive editor in 1985. Miriam, an indefatigable and gracious publisher, is a member of the Colorado Women's Hall of Fame.

The partnership of mother and son has been fruitful. Since 1972, the **IJN** has added 12 annual special sections, ranging from health to literature to business, and begun the bi-annual **IJN** supplement, *L'Chaim Magazine*, which includes a comprehensive community directory.

The **IJN** treasures stability. A family-owned business for over 50-years, Editor and then Israel Corres-

Left to right:
Rabbi Hillel Goldberg,
Miriam Goldberg, and
(in picture) the late
Max Goldberg.

pondent Robert Gamzey worked for the **IJN** for 32 years, until his passing; Managing Editor Doris Sky worked for the **IJN** for 28 years, until her passing. As of 1997, Executive Editor Larry Hankin and Assistant Editor Chris Leppek have worked for the **IJN** for 21 years apiece, and Office Manager Judy Waldren for 14 years.

The **IJN** also treasures the next generation. The **IJN** sponsors a journalism student intern program each summer, and an annual, elementary school Chanukah coloring contest, which draws over 700 entires from around the intermountain region.

Max Goldberg went on to manage many more successful political and philanthropic campaigns, to bring the first national television outlet (ABC) to Denver, and to write bi-weekly for the *Denver Post*, all while publishing the **IJN.** His breadth of perspective made the **IJN** much more than an ethnic newspaper. It became a staple of Denver communal life.

When Max Goldberg died in 1972, his wife, Miriam Goldberg, became editor and publisher, and his son, Hillel, became Israel correspondent. Versatile and probing, Hillel went on to earn rabbinical ordination

In depth, the **IJN** covered the two momentous Jewish stories of the 20th century — the Holocaust and Israel — from their first moments. The newspaper looks to the 21st century with editorial and advertising staffs that possess dozens of national and statewide journalism awards — and with a third generation of Goldbergs trained in journalism school and newsrooms on two continents.

THE DENVER METRO CHAMBER

For more than a century, the pages of Denver's history have been filled with noteworthy events orchestrated by the business community and others. In 1860 the Denver Board of Trade (which became the Denver Metro Chamber of Commerce in 1884) ensured Denver's future as a western metropolis by coordinating private-sector funding to bring a rail spur down from Cheyenne. In 1908 the Chamber successfully raised funds that prevented the threatened closure of the Denver Museum of Natural History. And the launching of the ambitious Forward Metro Denver economic development program in the mid-1960s — which attracted 280,000 new jobs to the metropolitan area in 10 years — are just a few examples of events initiated by the Denver Metro Chamber of Commerce. For more than a century the Chamber has been an active participant in shaping metropolitan Denver's economic, civic, cultural, and political destiny.

The Denver Metro Chamber of Commerce continues to be a membership organization dedicated to meeting the identified needs of the metropolitan business community by fostering economic opportunity and a favorable business climate. The Chamber works aggressively for small business because more than half of the 3,300 member companies have 10 or fewer employees.

The Denver Metro Chamber provides leads connections, networking and referral opportunities as well as programs featuring an outside board of directors to advise small business. The diverse training programs provide innovative training seminars focused on managing people and technology, customer service, marketing, sales and personal development. In addition to the training and networking opportunities, the Chamber hosts the Business EXPO, the largest business trade show in the Rocky Mountain area, attracting more than 300 exhibitors and 20,000 people. The objective of the Chamber is to maintain a strong membership base, continue to provide tangible benefits to its members, and to constantly strive to better serve its members.

The Denver Metro Chamber of Commerce continues to be a vital organization within the metro area due to its members' active role in the community. The three areas of focus identified by members are: education, transportation and quality of life including issues such as arts and culture, health care and the environment. Through targeted educational programs, the Chamber has recognized the need to assume an active role in developing our future work force. The Chamber has mobilized coalitions to address the drastic need to improve Colorado's transportation infrastructure, while continuing to concentrate on environmental, health care, and economic development issues that directly affect the quality of life in Colorado and the metro area.

Historically, the Denver Metro Chamber of Commerce can be viewed as a catalyst for improvement and change within the metro area. The Chamber and its strong membership core have played major roles in projects like: Denver International Airport, the Colorado Convention Center, and many others that have directly enhanced Denver's quality of life. And today, the Denver Metro Chamber continues its commitment to the business community by identifying critical issues and taking a proactive role in determining solutions.

Building Business Success Since 1884

The Denver Metro Chamber of Commerce's Business EXPO is the largest of its kind in the Rocky Mountain region.

METROLIST

A *Partner in Real Estate Information*

Welcome to the information age. Today, business as usual in real estate means information on demand. The most successful companies and individuals are those who can best make use of the vast amount of information that is readily available to them. It matters little if one is a REALTOR® in ranch country, a broker in a big city, or an independent agent affiliated with a national franchise. Real estate professionals all need access to the same accurate, precise, immediate, enhanced property information in whatever form, format, quantity, and characteristic that best suits their needs.

In 1984, Metrolist, Inc. was formed by the six Realtor Associations from the Denver Metro area: Aurora, Denver, Douglas/Elbert, Jefferson, North Metro, and South Metro. Metrolist was designed by Realtors for Realtors and is directed by Realtors. Currently, it serves more than 3,336 offices with approximately 11,300 Realtors. Since its inception, Metrolist has produced more than 60,000 listing brochures, received in excess of 485,00 listings, and printed over 2.5 million MLS books.

For more than a decade, Metrolist has been providing MLS services in print and online for Metropolitan Denver. Through its affiliation with DATAQuick®, they can also supply property information nationwide. They are a multiple listing service, a property data center, technical support consultants, and a product services group. Look to Metrolist for state-wide listed property data, ownership data, new owner information, property history, builder data, mortgage and tax information, and much more.

RIGHT: Metrolist's temperature-controlled computer room features 220 phone lines, which access three, 64 bit Digital computers.

Metrolist's customer service personnel for tech and product support are available during and after business hours, including weekends.

Property Data Center (PDC) is the business-to-business subsidiary of Metrolist. PDC reaches into markets other than the Realtor community and makes selective property information available to businesses. Commercial enterprises, entrepreneurs, and government agencies rely on PDC for various types of property information. Currently, PDC has more than 1 million records economically available online through a PC or as list products.

Metrolist is the premier regional real estate database and its sole obligation is to the real estate community, providing it with comprehensive databases, superior service, and meaningful applications of technology. In its never-ending quest to deliver accurate, reliable information, Metrolist has developed Homer™ Real Estate Systems. Ten years in the developmental and refining stages, Homer is a bundle of twenty-five dynamic online real estate products and services that aids in property research, marketing, business development, real estate business operations, presentation packages, financial analysis, and much more. Homer is a professional's best friend for researching property data.

Metrolist has a track record for excellence because it is dedicated to accuracy, reliability, and timeliness (MLS is updated instantly, PDC — quarterly, Deed Data — biweekly, New Home Construction — weekly). Their superior data, service, and industry-based, practical technology marks them as a leader in supplying real estate data to professionals by pulling all facets of property information into one cohesive unit.

REGIONAL TRANSPORTATION DISTRICT: RTD

As the country constructs its proverbial bridge to the future, RTD will transport metro Denverites across that passageway.

The Regional Transportation District operates and maintains a mass transportation system for the burgeoning metropolitan area that's home to more than 2.3 million people in six counties. In 1996, its fleet of more than 1,000 buses, light rail cars and access-a-Ride vehicles carried over 70 million passengers — a landmark number that represents eight successive years of increased ridership.

To prepare for continued growth, the 27-year-old agency has developed a multi-tiered plan for the region's transportation projects. The strategy includes the creation of eight transit corridors designated for light rail, commuter rail or high-occupancy vehicle lanes; improvements on many of its 59 Park-n-Ride transfer facilities; neighborhood circulator service; and bus redeployment.

RTD's everyday, round-the-clock access covers a 2,406-square-mile area and caters to work commuters, event-goers, tourists, airport-bound travelers, bike riders, senior citizens, the physically disabled and youth.

Sharing the recent revitalization of downtown Denver is the Downtown Express, a 6.6-mile route in the middle of Interstate 25. Exclusively for buses, car-

pools and vanpools, these HOV lanes save up to 24 minutes round-trip for northern suburb residents who commute to downtown Denver.

Coors Field, situated in lower downtown, and Mile High Stadium, located near the bustling district, are home to the Colorado Rockies and Denver Broncos, respectively. RTD runs BroncoRide and RockiesRide from selected park-n-Ride locations. Whether seeking post-game entertainment or lunchtime fare, downtowners ride the free 16th Street Mall Shuttle across the 14-block-long pedestrian mall. Opened in 1982, the congestion-relieving Shuttle now has three peak periods for the 45,000 people who ride it daily.

Bus service features Route 15 along Colfax Avenue — the nation's seventh busiest route — and more than 150 other local, express and regional routes.

Introduced in 1994, RTD's Light Rail Transit runs along the 5.3-mile central Denver corridor. The increasingly popular transit mode services riders from the historic Five Points neighborhood through downtown Denver, past the Auraria Campus, then to I-25 and Broadway. Ridership sailed over the 15,000/day mark, 2,000 more than original projections. Future plans call for the extension of the route along the southwest corridor along Santa Fe Drive to Mineral Avenue in Littleton.

The skyRide transports commuters from 29 pickup points to Denver International Airport, about 20 miles east of the Mile High City. These routes have shown dramatically increased ridership since DIA opened in 1994.

RTD's mass transit system helps improve air quality, eases traffic congestion and reduces employees' and other residents' parking and commuting expenses. The company has a 95 percent on-time performance on its express and regional routes, and it received a safety award in 1996 from the American Public Transit Association — all the more reason why metro Denverites find RTD transit "The Ride Thing To Do."

As RTD passengers stroll by, a bus connects with a light rail car at the I-25 and Broadway Park-n-Ride.

An access-a-Ride bus picks up a passenger in front of the Colorado Convention Center.

Partners in Denver

ATTORNEYS, ACCOUNTANTS, ARCHITECTS, ENGINEERS AND ADVERTISING PROFESSIONALS PROVIDE

PROFESSIONS

ESSENTIAL SERVICES TO THE DENVER COMMUNITY.

BAKER & HOSTETLER LLP

Colorado, served as of counsel to the Firm. Raymond L. Sutton, Jr. succeeded Mr. Clark as the Denver office Managing Partner in 1995 and leads a full-service office of 40 lawyers practicing in core substantive groups of litigation, employment, business and tax.

Since Baker & Hostetlers founding more than 80 years ago, it has grown into a national law firm with nearly 500 lawyers and offices in 10 cities: Cincinnati, Cleveland and Columbus, Ohio; Denver, Colorado.; Houston, Texas; Long Beach, Los Angeles and Palo Alto, California.; Orlando, Florida.; and Washington D.C.

Baker & Hostetler's Denver office combines the myriad of resources of a national law firm with the personal contact traditionally found in a local firm.

Baker & Hostetler LLP, Counsellors at Law, was founded in 1916 in Cleveland, Ohio, by Newton D. Baker, who served as Secretary of War in President Woodrow Wilson's cabinet, and his contemporaries, Joseph C. Hostetler and Thomas L. Sidlo. The Denver office of Baker & Hostetler resulted from a 1980 merger with the local firm of Clark, Martin & Pringle. James A. Clark served as the first Denver office Managing Partner and Fred M. Winner, former chief judge of the United States District Court for the District of

"Our national scope enables us to provide to our local and regional clients the resources of one of the largest and finest law firms in the country," said Ray Sutton. "Access to these resources is essential to our mission of providing the highest quality of professional services to our clients in a courteous and cost-effective manner."

In 1994, Baker & Hostetler introduced national Industry Teams, which integrate attorneys from all of the offices to solve industry-common problems. From health care to high tech to hospitality, Baker & Hostetler's national Industry Teams address clients' needs, sharing skills and experiences across geographic boundaries.

BAKER & HOSTETLER PRACTICES IN MANY AREAS OF BUSINESS AND FINANCIAL LAW

Antitrust	Employment and Discrimination	Trade Names and Trademarks	RICO
Banking	Environmental	Labor Unions	Securities
Class Actions	ERISA	Mortgage Banking	Sexual Harassment
Condemnation	First Amendment (libel and slander)	Oil and Gas	Tax
Construction	Insurance	Products Liability	Telecommunications
Domestic	Intellectual Property	Real Estate	Water and Natural Resources

Litigation and Employment

The Denver Office Litigation and Employment practice groups are staffed with experienced litigation and trial attorneys who have guided clients through state and federal courts and administrative tribunals in the Rocky Mountain Region and throughout the country. They counsel clients on how to prevent litigation and when to consider alternative dispute resolution forums such as mediation and arbitration. The Litigation and Employment groups pride themselves on tailoring staff to the needs of the client, emphasizing streamlined staffing with a senior attorney assigned to all cases.

Business and Tax

The Denver Office Business and Tax groups work closely with clients in a broad range of commercial transactions, including public and private securities offerings; mergers and acquisitions; real estate acquisi-

---

By sharing information through our computer networks, multioffice teleconferences, and in face-to-face meetings, Baker & Hostetler's Denver attorneys stay on top of national, state and local legal issues affecting their clients, their businesses, and their industries.

tions and financings; foreign investments in the United States; start-up and venture capital financings; lending and borrowing; partnerships and other non-corporate structuring; general corporate counseling; regulatory compliance; commercial contracts; structured and project finance; intellectual property transfers and licenses; oil, gas and other natural resources transactions; bank and bank holding company activities; gaming and alcoholic beverage matters; and strategic partnerships/alliances.

The spirit of Baker & Hostetler's mission statement is a part of daily life in our Denver office. "...We take a personal interest in our clients and give them the service, value and attention we seek in our own relationships..."

They have built a reputation for solid, dependable counsel based on long-standing client relationships, commitment to the legal profession, and dedication to the communities in which their people live and work. In Denver, Baker & Hostetler and its people have actively supported the U.S. Olympic Ski Team, the Make-A-Wish Foundation, the Christmas Crusade for Children, the Colorado Children's Chorale, the Denver Rescue Mission, Colorado Uplift, Children's Hospital, The Cherry Creek Schools Foundation, and the Colorado Ballet.

BERENBAUM, WEINSHIENK & EASON, P.C.

"Founding Fathers" — Joseph Berenbaum and Richard L. Eason. *Credit: Russell M. Smoak*

Situated on the 26th floor of one of downtown Denver's premiere office buildings — an impressive space with a panoramic view of the Mile High City's distinctly modern skyline — Berenbaum, Weinshienk & Eason, P.C., has positioned itself as one the Rocky Mountain region's most prominent law firms.

Members of the firm have counseled businesses and individuals for over 50 years. The practice of Berenbaum & Berenbaum was founded in the late 1940s by Denver natives Joe Berenbaum and his brother Mandel. In 1982 they joined forces with fellow Denver lawyer Hugh Weinshienk and his partners,

and then in 1994 the firm merged with the firm of Eason, Sprague & Wilson to become Berenbaum, Weinshienk & Eason.

The firm currently has 35 lawyers, 5 paralegals, and 26 support staff.

Berenbaum, Weinshienk & Eason seeks to retain and recruit lawyers with experience in specialist areas, inasmuch as the diversity and complexity of modern law demands such an approach. Such a policy enables the firm to provide a broad range of sophisticated legal services, and assures client confidence in the legal work-product generated.

While the firm has always practiced in the real estate and commercial fields, its client base and practice has broadened to include bankruptcy, litigation, commercial lending, foreclosures, loan workouts, mergers and acquisitions, venture capital investment, securities offerings, tax and corporate planning, asset protection planning, intellectual property, environmental matters, labor law, and trusts and estates.

Clients of Berenbaum, Weinshienk & Eason range from individuals and start-up enterprises to leading Denver-area companies, large national corporations, and international firms doing business in the Rocky Mountain region.

The firm's clients include well-known banks and mortgage companies; real estate developers with projects located in Colorado and several other states; local and national real estate brokerage firms; a wide range of securities and venture capital firms, and industrial firms and businesses. Other increasingly important areas of the law with which the attorneys at Berenbaum, Weinshienk & Eason have had experience are environmental regulation and hazardous waste cleanup, as well as emerging fields such as telecommunications law and international commerce.

A large and indispensable area of the firm's work is litigation: the phrase "I'll see you in court" is heard more often in the United States than in any other country in the world. Litigation attorneys at Berenbaum, Weinshienk & Eason take a down-to-earth approach to their craft: represent aggressively the client's interests; keep legal costs to a minimum.

The firm's overall philosophy combines quality and professionalism with the development of personal relationships with its clients. Where necessary complimentary teams of lawyers are formed to best serve the client in any particular matter.

Berenbaum, Weinshienk & Eason recruits its professional staff from the nation's leading law schools. A mentor system ensures an emphasis on commitment to quality of work-product and a dedication to client satisfaction. Many of the firm's associates will go on to be shareholders in the firm.

Berenbaum, Weinshienk & Eason, P.C. exits the 20th Century proud of its record as a quality producer of legal services in the Denver area. It enters the new millennium with an assurance of excellence in legal practice. Such a commitment, the firm's attorneys agree, is what clients have every right to expect.

Some of the shareholders of Berenbaum, Weinshienk & Eason, P.C. at their Republic Plaza offices in downtown Denver.
Standing Right to Left: James A. Jacobson, Kenneth S. Kramer, Daniel S. Duggan, Charles A. Bewley, Richard L. Eason, Eugene M. Sprague, Keith M. Pockross, Isaac Kaiser, Liza Meyers. *Sitting Right to Left:* James Kurtz-Phelan, Barry Permut, Edward L. Sperry, Charles P. Leder, Robert G. Wilson, Jr., H. Michael Miller.

Brownstein Hyatt Farber & Strickland, P.C.

(From Left) Tom Strickland, Steve Farber and Norm Brownstein
have a well-deserved reputation for providing good advice
and excellent service to their clients.

When Denver natives Norman Brownstein, Jack Hyatt and Steve Farber met in 1951 as classmates at Colfax Elementary School, a relationship began that is still shaping the history of the highest state. The entrepreneurial trio, bonded by common interests and backgrounds, grew up in the same neighborhood, remaining friends through high school and college. After graduating together from the University of Colorado Law School in 1968, they founded a law firm focused on real estate, with offices located at the Capitol Life Center on 16th & Grant. To determine whose name came first on the door, the three chums sportingly drew straws.

Since then, Brownstein Hyatt Farber & Strickland, P.C. has developed into one of the most successful and influential law firms in the Rocky Mountain region, whose activities set a high standard for critical legal, political and business decisions in the community. Dynamic and result-oriented, the firm is national in scope, with a high profile client lineup that includes Ascent Entertainment, Inc. (Owner of The Denver Nuggets and The Colorado Avalanche), The Denver Broncos, Vail Associates, Ltd., Pfizer, Inc., United Airlines, Inc., Nomura Asset Capital Corporation, The Hertz Corporation, U.S. Home Corporation, Corporate Express, Inc., Renaissance Cosmetics, Inc., and SunAmerica Inc., plus a galaxy of other local, national and international companies, public bodies, not-for-profit organizations and individuals.

Over the years, Brownstein Hyatt Farber & Strickland, P.C. has grown to include 122 employees, 59 of whom are lawyers, making it the city's eighth largest law firm. For the past 18 years, they have been comfortably but unpretentiously quartered on 17th St. A second office was established in Washington D.C. in 1995.

The firm's services incorporate legal areas essential to business in both the private and public sector, with specialties in:
- banking and finance
- business, corporate and securities
- employment law
- environmental and land use
- litigation
- municipal and public finance
- real estate and lending
- regulatory, legislative and administrative law
- tax law
- water and public lands law

The success of Brownstein Hyatt Farber & Strickland, P.C. may be attributed to a well-deserved reputation for providing good advice and excellent service to their clients. The firm prides itself on bold thinking and solid reasoning, assembling top legal talent with broad-based expertise, graduates of the best law schools in the country. Their in-depth knowledge of legislative, regulatory, corporate and courtroom environments provides their clients with a definite advantage and results in an impressive success record for the firm.

Thirteen years ago, the partnership was joined by Tom Strickland, a venturesome former Texan who had served as Policy Director under Colorado Governor Richard Lamm and later as chair of the State Transportation Commission. Strickland was the key player in the development of E-470, a badly-needed new expressway that now connects Aurora and Denver International Airport with the southern and northern suburbs. Although a 1996 bid for the U.S. Senate resulted in a near-miss, Strickland remains heavily involved in state-wide community and political concerns, adding to the firm's active practice in public affairs.

Brownstein Hyatt Farber & Strickland, P.C. encourages their attorneys to become community leaders, participating fully in civic, political and charitable activities. Members of the firm serve on boards of colleges and universities, hospitals and innumerable charitable organizations, not only benefiting the community but bridging the gap between the public and private sector. Their support of charities is wide-spread, ranging from causes at CU's Denver and Boulder campuses, Health Sciences Center and the Law School to Brokers for Battered Kids, Food Bank of the Rockies, SafeHouse Denver, Inc., and Family Tree, Inc. Growing up in a poor community in a west Denver neighborhood, the founders realize the importance of sharing the rewards of their success with the community. The partners remain deeply involved with Jewish philanthropies both locally and nationally, including the Allied Jewish Federation, which Steve Farber has chaired, and AIPAC, which Norm Brownstein serves as Vice President.

While the firm relishes the new opportunities provided by their remarkable expansion, dedication to interests of Denver and the Rocky Mountain region remains paramount. Says managing partner Steve Farber, "We know where our roots lie, and we are committed to this community. Professionally, our goal is to provide top-notch legal services, but we have to enjoy our clients while providing these services."

Brownstein Hyatt Farber & Strickland, P.C. offices:

Comfortable but unpretentious

CRAIN PHOTOGRAPHY

In 1997, Crain has been in Denver three years (his wife is a fourth generation native). After having studios on both seaboards, Crain decided he could service clients better away from the bustle of the coasts. Located just three blocks north of the new Coors Field on Denargo Market, Crain not only takes advantage of his geographic location to provide access to clients, but he persuades clients to take advantage of the locations available in this region. Denver is also a great place to raise a family and be close to relatives.

Crain Photography is a unique business. The company produces not only the finest photography Denver has to offer but also advertising brochures and catalogs for clients. Crain foresaw future trends

Photographers march to a different drummer. In 1987, after almost ten years as a photographer, Stephen M. Crain, president of Crain Photography, left his business in Washington D.C. and headed to the West Coast to go back to school. To be the best in a highly technical medium, he had realized, he had to devote time to studying the science behind the art he loved.

Crain and his wife Linda drove across country to Santa Barbara, California, where he attended the famed Brooks Institute of Photography. After extensive research, the Crains realized that Brooks offered the ultimate education in photography and its underlying sciences. At Brooks, Crain became one of only a handful of photographers in the world to earn a Masters of Science Degree in Photographic Sciences. As a result of his comprehensive education, Crain has lectured at several universities and colleges and is a requested speaker for organizations and clubs.

and began producing full advertising pieces for clients with one-stop convenience. Crain Photography not only photographs a client's products but also writes, designs and lays out a client's advertising pieces in house. This concept-to-press service saves clients time as well as money — up to 50 percent.

Stephen Crain uses his talents in business, photography and advertising to help his small clients

garner more business for less advertising expense and to help his larger clients glean more from their advertising money. All of these clients get one of the hottest photography boutiques in the business. Consequently, Crain Photography enjoys an unusual mix of money-conscious smaller companies who want the best for less and market savvy high-end corporate clients who simply want the best.

Crain is also a consummate people photographer. Over the last ten years, he has photographed business executives, performers (Barbra Streisand, Peter Noone, Kenny G and Cheryl Ladd), politicians (George Bush and Robert Dole) and many others. He also did a stint with *Playboy* magazine and has photographed every major professional sporting event in Colorado for United Press International. Crain is also one of the premiere food photographers in the country.

Stephen Crain has also written, photographed and produced a book, recently released by Amherst Media.

"Lighting For People Photography" is the most comprehensive manual on the science of lighting for photography on the market. As a result of this project, one of the most sought after photographers in the business has also become a sought after writer. Who said perfectionism is not all that it's cracked up to be?

All photographs copyright of Crain Photography

HOLME ROBERTS & OWEN LLP

Holme Roberts & Owen is a law firm that embodies community. One of the Rocky Mountain region's oldest and largest law firms, it has 180 attorneys in seven offices serving the Rocky Mountain region, Europe and South America with its offices in Denver, Boulder, Colorado Springs, Salt Lake City, London, Moscow, Kiev, and a legal representative in Buenos Aires. Founded in Denver in 1898, exactly 40 years after the city was established, the firm has grown with Denver.

The Roberts Tunnel, named for the firm's Harold D. Roberts, carries water from the Dillon reservoir to Denver.

Then known as Dines & Whitted, after its founders Tyson S. Dines and Elmer E. Whitted, the firm began by representing railroads and local banks and, in 1908, was instrumental in forming the bank that grew to be Colorado's largest, now known as Norwest Bank Colorado. The firm still represents the bank today. At the same time, mining and railroading were big industries, and the firm expanded its emphasis to oil development and litigation when the great Salt Creek Field in Natrona County, Wyoming, came into prominence. The firm, known at this time as Dines, Dines & Holme, after the addition of attorneys Orville Dines and Peter Hagner Holme, represented many of the people and companies who developed Salt Creek including Verner Z. Reed and the companies that ultimately became Midwest Oil Corp., Argo Oil Corp., and Standard Oil Co. of Indiana.

In 1919, Harold D. Roberts joined the firm and became one of the most knowledgeable and expert oil lawyers in the West. He was one of the principal draftsmen of the Mineral Leasing Act of 1920, a foundation stone of modern oil and gas law. In addition, Mr. Roberts became an outstanding water lawyer and

under his direction the firm represented Denver's Board of Water Commissioners as special counsel for many years. Mr. Roberts dedicated his time and ultimately his life to the Blue River Tunnel Project which was developed to carry water from the Dillon Reservoir to Denver. According to a 1964 newspaper article in *The Denver Post*, "If Denver were to grow, it would need water — water in amounts quadruple the developed supply at that time." The tunnel solved Denver's development problem and was completed in

1962. Mr. Roberts did not live to see its completion, and the tunnel was renamed the "Roberts Tunnel" after his death to reflect the tremendous time and effort he gave to the project.

By 1926, Robert E. More, J. Churchill Owen and Milton J. Keegan had joined the firm and in 1950 the firm name was changed to Holme, Roberts, More, Owen and Keegan recognizing the most senior partners.

Both then and now through the efforts of the firm's attorneys, Holme Roberts & Owen, as it is known today, has involved itself in the local and national community in civic, charitable, educational and professional activities. These include memberships on College Boards of Trustees, Planning Commissions, the Colorado Commission on Higher Education, presidencies of Colorado and Denver Bar Associations, American Bar Association activities at a high level, Legal Aid, lending charitable drives, a membership on the Denver School Board, activity in continuing Legal Education and teaching courses at the law schools, involvement in Boys' Clubs and many other civic and charitable activities. In fact, one of J. Churchill Owen's greatest contributions to the community, aside from the numerous boards on which he served, was the establishment of the Boys Club of Metro Denver. According to a newspaper article in the *Rocky Mountain News* from 1989, "Owen gathered 30 friends, raised $28,000, and opened the first branch to serve boys in underprivileged neighborhoods. But his work didn't stop there. The club now has five branches and a foundation with more than $3 million in trust."

Other contributions to the community include the Robert E. More Evergreen Arboretum at City Park, the Keegan lilac collection, and the perennially popular and beautifully illustrated books of Harold and Rhoda Roberts on Colorado desert and alpine wild flowers.

The firm's significant *pro bono* contributions were recognized in 1994 when the firm received an award for the Outstanding Business in Philanthropy bestowed by the National Philanthropy Day in

Colorado Committee, in 1995 the firm received the Corporate Advocacy Award from the Colorado Women's Chamber of Commerce, and in 1996 the firm received an award from the Children's Legal Clinic in appreciation for its commitment to children.

**Harold D. Roberts, name partner of
Holme Roberts & Owen LLP.**

Today, the firm serves clients throughout the world, providing legal expertise in thirteen different practice areas, including commercial law and securities; community resources; environmental law; ERISA; federal income, state and local tax; individuals, trusts and family businesses; intellectual property; international law; labor and employment; litigation; natural resources; public law; and real estate. As Holme Roberts & Owen nears its 100th anniversary (in 1998), it looks forward to continuing to grow with Denver, the Rocky Mountain region and its international communities.

THE JOB STORE, INC.

The Job Store is locally owned and operated by the Grandbois family. From left to right: Dan Grandbois, company president Dorothy Grandbois, Julie DeGolier, and Alan Grandbois.

RIGHT:
The Job Store offers a PC-equipped training center and a training program for receptionists and customer-service representatives.

Not so long ago, a business employer called upon a temporary staffing agency to fill the occasional short-time gap in its work force. Each time the company hired a temp, it hurt the bottom line.

Today, business employers are increasingly relying on staffing agencies as strategic partners in the battle to match costly employment levels with fluctuating production schedules. These days, working with a good staffing agency actually strengthens a company's bottom line.

The Job Store, Inc. is a full-service provider of regular full-time and temporary staffing that works as a strategic partner with its clients to formulate creative solutions to a wide variety of staffing needs in the areas of office support, accounting, light industrial and technical work:

- Temporary
- Direct hire
- Project staffing
- Try Before You Hire
- On-site vendor partnerships

Project staffing allows employers to "staff up" for special assembly, telemarketing or customer service efforts. The "Try Before You Hire" concept gives an employer a 90-day "working interview" with a potential employee before making the decision to hire. An on-site vendor partnership allows an employer to benefit from The Job Store's recruitment and management expertise by using the company as an on-site extension of its human resources department.

Unlike many of its out-of-state competitors, The Job Store has been locally owned and operated for nearly 30 years and has a broad knowledge of the Denver metropolitan market. The company's clients range in size from small offices to Fortune 500 companies.

The Job Store is ranked among the top ten of the Denver metropolitan area's 250 staffing services. It is one of the area's top 25 woman-owned businesses and is listed among the top 100 fastest-growing private companies in the State of Colorado.

The Job Store did not achieve its impressive success overnight. The company got its start in Denver in 1973 when Dorothy and Alan Grandbois purchased a personnel agency franchise from a national chain. For the next five years, even though it was a start-up operation, the Grandbois' Denver office near Cinderella City led the company's 160 franchised offices in total number of placements.

In order to capitalize on their obvious talent, the Grandbois' bought out their franchise in 1978 and opened Job Store Staffing. In 1979, they incorporated at The Job Store, Inc., and added a temporary help component specializing in clerical and administrative support. Dorothy Grandbois was president of the new company and Alan Grandbois was secretary/treasurer.

A second office opened at I-25 and Hampden in 1979 and a third office in Aurora in 1981. During the 1984-85 economic downturn, operations were consolidated at I-25 and Hampden. The company credits its loyal clients with helping it survive this difficult time.

In 1987, The Job Store opened a PC-equipped training center that is used to evaluate a potential job

candidate's skills using the highly rated Qwiz system software. In 1996, in order to meet market demand for qualified workers, The Job Store added a training program for receptionists and customer-service representatives, who are also available for temporary

assignments. In addition to skills training, the program covers the essentials of time management, office dress and decorum, ergonomics and workplace safety.

In 1987, The Job Store was awarded membership in TempNet, an association of North America's top independent staffing agencies. Only one candidate is selected from each market. TempNet offers peer reviews and keeps its members informed of innovative staffing concepts and legal issues. Dorothy Grandbois has held a variety of elected offices with TempNet since 1992.

During the 1990s, fueled by new marketing ideas and the healthy Denver economy, The Job Store grew from a relatively small operation to the highly successful staffing agency it is today — quadrupling in size between 1992 and 1996. A second generation joined the company in 1991 when Julie DeGolier became vice president with responsibility for marketing and Dan Grandbois became secretary and risk control and operations manager. Alan Grandbois, who became co-owner and president of Lode Data Corporation in 1983, remains treasurer.

In 1992, The Job Store purchased its own headquarters building at 7100 East Hampden. A second office opened in Westminster in 1994 and a third in Aurora in early 1997. The company employs 26 people and interviews 800 to 900 job candidates each month.

Dorothy Grandbois is a native of Abbotsford, Wisconsin, where she grew up in a blended family with 16 children. The family was not wealthy, but her parents' work ethic was very strong and all of the children were honor students. She credits her upbringing for her own strong work ethic, pride in individual accomplishment in spite of adversity, and integrity — values she has embedded in her business.

In 1996, Dorothy Grandbois received a leadership award for contributions to her profession and community from BlueCross and BlueShield of Colorado

and the Colorado Chapter of the National Multiple Sclerosis Society. Award winners were challenged to raise money to fund research to find the cause and cure of multiple sclerosis.

The Job Store is committed to providing excellence in service to its customers, personal growth to its employees and a spirit of shared responsibility with the Denver community.

Unlike many of its out-of-state competitors, The Job Store has a broad knowledge of the Denver metropolitan market.

PATTON BOGGS, L.L.P.

Patton Boggs, L.L.P. is a Washington, D.C. Based law firm with six regional offices in: Baltimore, Maryland; Dallas, Texas; Denver, Colorado; Research Triangle Park and Greensboro, North Carolina; and Seattle, Washington. Their lawyers are also regularly on every continent handling the international needs of their clients. Founded in the nation's capital in 1962, Patton Boggs, L.L.P. has grown to nearly 300 attorneys today, providing the full spectrum of legal services. The firm is nationally recognized for its public policy, international, construction, and environmental practices and has an unparalleled reputation for solving challenging business and political problems in any arena, regulatory, legislative, or judicial.

Patton Boggs' Denver partners and of council include (from left) David M. French, J. Greg Whitehair, Carolyn L. Buchholz, Timothy D. Knaus and Mark K. Osbeck.

Established by partners with extensive experience in government service, the firm was among the first in the nation to recognize the emerging influence of international issues and to emphasize merging legislative, regulatory, and public policy expertise with more traditional legal practice. Consequently, they have a demonstrated track record of finding the right blend of strategies — litigation, legislation, negotiation — before courts, agencies, state legislatures and the Congress. Patton Boggs has developed into a full service law firm; their federal and state administrative and regulatory practices include work before the Environmental Protection Agency, the Food and Drug Administration, the Federal Trade Commission, the Federal Aviation Administration, the Occupational Safety and Health and the Mine Safety and Health

Boards, the Postal Service, the Department of Interior, the Department of Energy, the Department of Defense, Department of Agriculture, the Bureau of Land Management, and counterpart state agencies in more than two dozen states throughout the country. They have assisted numerous clients in developing internal training, compliance and self-audit programs to resolve complex managerial, economic, and enforcement issues. Regardless of the forum, Patton Boggs has the capability to guide their clients to straight forward, often creative, solutions.

Patton Boggs also has a long history of pro bono service. The pro bono efforts are varied, but include adoption of a school in the inner urban area of Washington D.C., providing a full gamut of legal assistance to the elderly, serving as lead counsel seeking to overturn a death sentence, and working with the primary legal service agencies in the Denver metropolitan area. In both 1995 and 1996, Patton Boggs has met the American Bar Association challenge by donating at least three percent of its total attorney time to pro bono representation.

The Denver office of Patton Boggs was started in 1990 with four attorneys. In seven years they have grown to twenty lawyers, the largest regional office in the Patton Boggs national system. The Denver office emphasizes litigation, environmental, public policy, procurement, OSHA/MSHA, Food and Drug, and trade practices.

Reflecting the broad scope of the Denver office practice, litigators represent the interest of clients concerning: regulatory compliance; commercial/transactional litigation (including white-collar criminal defense); technology and intellectual property, environmental matters, insurance coverage issues, and construction and design disputes. Attorneys in the Denver office utilize their underlying substantive expertise equally well in the courtroom. James R. Prochnow is a nationally recognized practitioner before the Food and Drug Administration, particularly regarding dietary supplements. Jim also assists his clients in the courtroom with respect to the safety and labeling of their products. Similarly, Carolyn Buchholz and Mike Hope, both formerly from the CERCLA Litigation Section of the Colorado Attorney General's office, apply their environmental law expertise to resolve private party disputes and regulatory enforcement matters in the courtroom.

Patton Boggs' construction and design lawyers have a pre-eminent national reputation. Their construction lawyers are experienced in litigation and every form of alternative dispute resolution. They can provide project administration, insurance and risk management, claims management, collections, and very sophisticated, efficient litigation services. Their projects, include hospitals, water transmission systems,oil drilling platforms, hotels, warehouses, and corporate office buildings.

Patton Boggs is experienced pursuing or defending often simultaneous proceedings with a sensitivity to how the result in one (e.g., a grand jury investigation) can affect another (e.g., a parallel civil suit). Patton Boggs' Denver office offers substantial "depth of bench" for any complex litigation matter. Senior litigators in Denver include J. Greg Whitehair, formerly an Assistant U. S. Attorney, Kevin Taylor, formerly from the Denver District Attorney's Office, and Mark K. Osbeck. Greg also utilizes his scientific training to help clients develop and implement systems to protect the technologies integral to their business and competitive advantage.

In representing their clients on public policy issues, Patton Boggs not only seeks to achieve clients' business objectives, but also endeavors to do so in a way that promotes each client's long range interests and reputation. Because today's "opponent" may be tomorrow's "ally," an important part of the task is to help clients develop positive relationships with decision-makers in Washington, with regulatory agencies, and in state capitals that will enhance their ability to achieve future legislative and regulatory solutions to their business and financial objectives. Michael J. Driver leads the Washington aspect of the Denver public policy practice. Timothy D. Knaus and Peg A. Brown

provide clients state legislative experience and representation. Each year they monitor the over 100,000 bills introduced in state legislatures around the nation.

For nearly 25 years, the Patton Boggs' environmental practice has combined creative thinking and innovation with practicality and good sense in helping its clients avoid unnecessary problems. The Denver office is fortunate to have the founder of Patton Boggs' environmental practice, who relocated from Washington D.C. Clients range from international corporations to individuals and municipalities. Carolyn Buchholz and Mike Hope were able to obtain an excellent result for the City and County of Denver in a major Superfund action, quantifying the City's liabilities and obtaining contribution settlements to pay for the effective management of the site now, and in the future. Patton Boggs' Denver environmental practitioners have the proven flexibility and ability to be comfortable in the appropriate forum — the courtroom, a state legislature, or before any state or federal agency — and the willingness to address the issues in practical and technical terms.

The two most recent members of the Patton Boggs Denver team, Ann M. Bormolini and Claude C. Wild III, join the private sector from prestigious government service. Ann served for nearly four years as Chief of Staff to Secretary of Transportation Federico Pena. Ann brings with her a wealth of knowledge about transportation policy, finance, and regulation. Claude Wild formerly served as the Regional Director of the Federal Trade Commission. Patton Boggs is pleased to offer Claude's national antitrust and trade regulation expertise to clients as the need for sophisticated legal expertise in this arena increases with Denver's emergence as one of our nation's major trade hubs.

From its beginnings in the gold rush era, Denver has held the promise of economic development, new horizons, and individual challenges. Patton Boggs reflects the western values of practicality, adventure, individualism, creativity, frugality, and integrity. Patton Boggs is proud to be a part of Denver and share in its rich history.

RAYTHEON ENGINEERS & CONSTRUCTORS

Raytheon Engineers & Constructors is proud of its historic roots in Denver and its contributions to the city's growth and success.

The company's Colorado heritage began in 1885 when Tom Stearns formed an engineering firm to design and manufacture specialized equipment for the local mining industry. One hundred years later, in 1986, the Stearns organization joined the Raytheon family of

RIGHT: (left-right)
John Rogers,
Tom Stearns
Stearns-Roger
Manufacturing
Company 1891

BELOW: Metallurgical mill
in Florence, Colorado 1897

companies, continuing to serve industry from Denver.

The Colorado company's early history was fueled by the mining boom. In 1891, Tom Stearns and John Rogers incorporated as Stearns-Roger Manufacturing Co., with an engineering office in Denver and a manufacturing facility in Pueblo.

Following the 1893 silver crash, Stearns-Roger diversified into power and food processing plants. In 1898, it designed and built Colorado's first central power station in Canon City.

In the 1920s, after a flood destroyed its Pueblo facility, Stearns-Roger and a consortium of other manufacturers banded together to form a Denver manufacturing and fabrication complex known as the General Iron Works Co., which became the largest custom fabricating shop in the West. Today, the company continues to provide dryers, coolers, granulators, lime slakers, kilns and crystallizers for industry.

In the 1950s and 1960s, General Iron Works also supplied nuclear fuel handing equipment to 75 of the 110 operating nuclear powered utility units in the U.S. and 20 international units. The spare parts and service work continues today through the Raytheon Nuclear unit.

Diversification Continues

In the 1920s, the company entered the gas processing business, pioneering many processes including high pressure absorption, recycling, dehydration, sweetening, propane and butane recovery, and helium production.

During World War II, Stearns-Roger designed and built the top-secret plant that refined uranium for the Manhattan Project. Starting in the 1950s, it began building missile and rocket launch facilities for defense and manned space flights.

Expanding its mining business in the late 1950s, the company designed and constructed the Sierrita complex near Tucson, Arizona, housing the largest copper-molybdenum concentrators ever built at one time. The firm also engineered a copper concentrator for Southern Peru Copper Corp. in the Peruvian Andes, 13,000 feet above sea level, and connected it by rail to a Stearns-Roger engineered smelter at sea level.

In the years following World War II, the firm designed and built facilities for a vast variety of ores, including vanadium, iron powder, sodium sulphate, uranium and copper. The firm also designed nearly 80 percent of the potash capacity in the Free World.

More recently, Raytheon formed an alliance with FMC Corp. to lower cost and improve productivity at FMC's Alkali Chemicals Division plant in Green River, Wyoming, and its Phosphorus Chemicals Division in Pocatello, Idaho.

Industrial Growth

In response to increasing energy demands of the 1970s, Stearns-Roger built 57 coal-fired power generating units in the U.S. In the early 1980s, the company engineered the first U.S. utility commercial-scale fluidized bed combustion unit at Nucla, Colorado.

During the oil boom of the 1970s and 1980s, the company designed and built oil shale retort facilities for Union Oil Co. at Parachute, Colorado. Stearns-Roger introduced the concept of modular plants to the petroleum industry and completed the first of several annual Kuparuk River Unit sealifts for oil production facility modules to Alaska's North Slope.

Gas processing plants were designed and built for Amoco and Exxon in the Wyoming Overthrust Belt. The Exxon plant remains one of the world's largest natural gas processing facilities.

Moving into the Nineties

In 1982, after almost a century of private ownership, Stearns-Roger was acquired by Air Products and Chemicals, Inc., and combined with Catalytic World Corporation, a company already owned by Air Products. In 1986, Stearns Catalytic World Corporation was acquired by United Engineers & Constructors, a sub-

sidiary of Raytheon Company. In 1993, Raytheon Engineers & Constructors was formed through the consolidation of various Raytheon-owned firms.

Today, the Denver operations office of Raytheon Engineers & Constructors, located in Greenwood Plaza, provides services to the U.S. Departments of Energy and Defense, and to the hydrocarbons, power, infrastructure, and metals and mining industries.

Raytheon Engineers & Constructors is a worldwide organization crafted to bring capital intensive projects of industry and government to reality. Raytheon ranks among the top engineering and construction companies in the world and, as part of the Raytheon family, shares fully in its preeminent reputation for quality, integrity and technical expertise.

Raytheon Company, headquartered in Lexington, Massachusetts, is a $12 billion international high-technology company operating in four business areas: commercial and defense electronics, aviation, major appliances, and engineering and construction.

Colorado Landmarks

Every day, Coloradans use structures and services that were, in whole or in part, projects of Raytheon Engineers & Constructors and its predecessor companies. These include the Eisenhower Tunnel, the University of Colorado Auraria Campus, the IMAX Theatre at the Museum of Natural History, and electricity from the Cherokee and Zuni plants in Denver.

The company has also provided engineering services in support of U.S. government operations in the region, such as the U.S. Postal facility, Buckley Air National Guard Base, Rocky Flats, Rocky Mountain Arsenal and NORAD Headquarters in Cheyenne Mountain.

Co-generation plants at Rifle and Brush, which Raytheon engineered and built, provide electricity and also supply steam for on-site tomato greenhouses — a source of year-round fresh produce throughout Colorado.

With more than 110 years of engineering tradition behind it, Raytheon's Denver operations office proudly serves industry and is poised to meet the challenges of the next century.

LEFT: Fluidized bed combustion unit at Nucla, Colorado

Kuparuk River Unit modules North Slope of Alaska

Co-generation plant and tomato greenhouses at Rifle, Colorado

THE ROYBAL CORPORATION

Creating the Developed Environment

Michael and Ronald Roybal of The Roybal Corporation personify the spirit of the Mile High City. Born and raised in Colorado, they have made their mark on the local community and established their business as one of the most successful architectural/engineering firms in the region.

The Roybal brothers know what it takes to succeed in Denver's dynamic economy: quality, determination, vision and diversification. Realizing that a variety of professional skills would bring opportunity and stability to their endeavors, the brothers expanded the services of the company into five divisions: Architectural, Environmental, Communications, Facility Management and Advanced Technology. This innovative approach has proven beneficial. Since its inception in 1981, The Roybal Corporation has grown from a small home office to its current status as one of the largest architectural/engineering firms in the Denver area.

As prominent members of the Denver Hispanic Community, the Roybals understand and value diversity in its many forms. Although the firm is international in scope, the brothers understand that business has a responsibility to the community. Both Ronald and Michael take their message of opportunity to area schools and speak with children about their heritage, business achievements and local upbringing. In addition, the Roybals participate in various charity and community events throughout the year.

Ronald Roybal, President

Michael Roybal, CEO

The Roybal Corporation headquarters in Denver illustrates the firm's attention to detail and sensitivity to space planning, aesthetics and functional usage.

Beyond their executive roles, Ronald and Michael are directly involved in the design-related divisions of The Roybal Corporation. Together, they have developed an impressive architectural portfolio and have a combined experience of more than 50 years. Their project experience is reflective of their belief in diversity and quality, and includes a balance of private and public sector clients. Contributions include numerous joint venture projects at the new Denver International Airport as well as projects at several metro area schools and for different branches of the Federal Government.

Learning from the past. Looking to the future. The Roybal Corporation contributed to planning efforts for Downtown Denver and other surrounding communities, including the Platte Valley Region.

In 1988, The Roybal Corporation introduced its Environmental Division — a natural outgrowth of the firm's existing architectural services. The new department was Roybal's response to rapid regional development, attempting to alleviate the effects of increased population and commerce in Colorado. While the local environment is still the focus of Roybal's efforts, the company's regional capabilities have allowed Roybal to expand its scope. Roybal has worked with many of the premier U.S. governmental agencies to protect precious natural resources throughout the country. In addition, Roybal has taken its experience abroad, providing environmental assistance in more than 65 countries. This national and international exposure has strengthened the firm's position and reinforced its reputation for quality.

The Roybal Corporation's Communications Division specializes in designing interpretive exhibits for recreational facilities. This unique group studies outdoor

In 1984, through a joint venture, Roybal completed an expansion of Concourse B at Denver's Stapleton International Airport.

spaces — including national parks — and creates museums and visitor centers that emphasize the importance and beauty of the environment. The firm has produced numerous exhibits such as the White River National Forest Exhibit in Vail, the Great Plains Nature Center in Kansas, the National Elk Refuge in Wyoming and the Golden Gate Canyon Visitor Center in Colorado.

Finally, the growing Advanced Technology and Facilities Management Divisions have allowed The Roybal Corporation to provide operational assistance, information systems support, database management and computer-aided design. Clients include the Southwestern Power Administration in Tulsa, Oklahoma, and the Federal Aviation Administration at Denver International Airport.

In today's volatile economy, an organization is only as successful as its leadership. The Roybal Corporation of Denver, Colorado, has found success because it is a direct reflection of its reputable ownership. Michael and Ronald Roybal have found "Creative Solutions to Complex Problems" in every segment of their work.

Throughout its history, Roybal has been instrumental in developing Denver's international reputation for efficient transportation facilities. In 1992, The Roybal Corporation completed numerous projects at Denver International Airport, including the design of two firestations for the FAA.

Balancing urban design with environmental sensitivity, The Roybal Corporation is leading Denver's progressive architectural/engineering firms towards the new millennium.

Growing up in the Mile High City, Ronald and Michael learned the value of diversity, stability and vision. They have incorporated those elements and established a prosperous business that continues to make a positive impact on Denver and its surrounding communities.

Preserving the Natural Environment

Thomas & Perkins Advertising

Few things reflect a city's true character more accurately than its advertising. Which is why Thomas & Perkins, Denver's largest full-service agency, is where you'll find some of the city's richest memories. Through the years, Thomas & Perkins has become a center for high-end creativity on both a local and national scale. Despite its growth, the agency has chosen to stay on historic Larimer Street in the delightfully hip lower downtown.

Now in its second century, the revamped LoDo district couldn't be a more appropriate home for the agency. At the heart of Denver's cultural scene, Larimer Square sports cozy cafes, stylish restaurants and a potpourri of fashion, art and music. Even during Oktoberfest, when the sunny street is closed to traffic, the square draws agency members out for a lunchtime bratwurst. There, they get a firsthand glimpse of the trends that shape the city.

Bryan Thomas started Thomas & Perkins in the summer of 1984 with the generous assistance of Manilla Perkins, a close family friend. Denver's housing industry had just begun to awaken from the recession due in part to a blossoming love affair with the high-tech industry. Thomas personally wrote and directed campaigns for Home Buyer's Warranty and Celebrity Homes. And it wasn't long before United Technologies tapped into Thomas' skills as well. Perhaps this high-tech dabbling was a foreshadowing of the future when the cable giant Tele-Communications Inc. (TCI) and its satellite television off-shoot, PRIMESTAR, chose Thomas & Perkins to reach consumers across the nation.

Meanwhile, across town, Thomas' future partners Herb Allison and David Schiedt were busy at *The Graphics Studio* with a variety of projects from all over the city. By integrating conceptual thinking, art direction, illustration and design they had become one of Denver's most valuable creative resources. But the abundance of work soon created the need for a savvy business partner. And it wasn't long before they decided Bryan Thomas was their man.

Together, the trio began making Denver advertising history. Their vibrant posters for the annual International Film Festival spurred a local interest in the magic of film making. With a bouncing ball and a parody

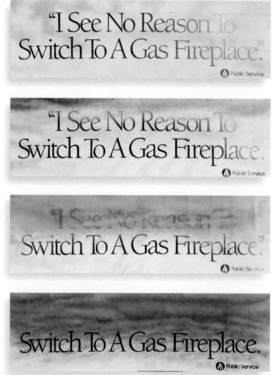

of the song *Deep in the Heart of Texas*, Thomas & Perkins helped keep the National Western Stock Show deep in the heart of Colorado, saving Denver's frontier heritage and $72 million in revenues.

In 1988, the agency succeeded in capturing two high-profile accounts: The Denver Post and Public Service Company of Colorado. With these wins, the creative work of Thomas & Perkins began to reflect the daily needs and concerns of Denver's population. An outdoor board with a vanishing headline addressed important pollution issues. In one of the country's most heated newspaper wars, the agency's attention-getting campaigns for The Denver Post gave citizens a multitude of reasons to choose their newspaper subscription carefully.

Perhaps even more than its business sense, Thomas & Perkins' fresh creativity is what kept the ball

rolling through the years. The agency leaders worked hard to keep those juices flowing. Rather than choosing a more corporate space to reflect their success, the environment mirrored employees' personalities. The result is neon lighting, brightly colored accent walls, eclectic artwork, aquariums of exotic reptiles and more. Outdoor spaces give these creative folks room to share afternoon barbeques and blow off steam with playful pranks. And it's not unusual to find the entire agency refilling their creative think-tanks with a company flight to Las Vegas or a bus ride to Steamboat Springs ski resort.

From ads proudly displayed on the walls to a cluster of industry awards absent-mindedly stacked in a corner, Thomas & Perkins' dedication to Denver's creative reputation is clear. Diamond Shamrock gasoline, Norwest Banks, Hinckley & Schmitt bottled water, King Soopers grocery stores, Scott's Liquid Gold, Tele-Communications Inc., PRIMESTAR By TCI, The Denver Broncos, MarkAir and even Larimer Square have all made their names in the Denver marketplace as clients of Thomas & Perkins. But some of the agency's most memorable work has been done for free. An emotional television spot, for example, tapped into Denver's hopefulness in support of the Mile High

United Way. And the agency resurrected the sixties hit, Hey, Hey, We're the Monkees, to trumpet the arrival of the Denver Zoo's new Primate Panorama exhibit.

Now 75 employees strong, Thomas & Perkins also boasts a group of interactive technologies experts who use their considerable talents to bring clients to the World Wide Web. Their award-winning Pentax and Bollé sites as well as high-energy web-sites for The Denver Broncos, EduSearch and StorageTek keep a reputation for leading-edge high-tech work in tact. The agency's direct marketing group uses the sciences of consumer research and database management to replace the inefficient mass mailings of the old days with highly relevant, personalized, integrated communications.

Every day outdoor boards, television and radio spots, print ads and personalized letters from Thomas & Perkins make Denver's citizens think harder, laugh louder, hope higher and dream more. "Advertising, like architecture, is reflective of the culture of a city. It's pop-culture — what's kicking, what's in vogue, the way people are feeling," says Bryan Thomas. As Denver saddles up for a wild ride into the twenty-first century, Thomas & Perkins will no doubt continue to profoundly shape the city's image.

LEFT: Newspaper Ad for The Denver Post.

CENTER: Poster for Central City Opera.

BELOW: Television stills for the National Western Stock Show, the Denver Zoo and Mile High United Way.

Don't lose the Stock Show to Texas.

BUCK CONSULTANTS, INC.

Buck Consultants is one of the world's leading employee benefit, actuarial and compensation consulting firms — serving clients in all 50 states and throughout the world.

Managing employee benefit programs is an increasingly complex, time-consuming and expensive function for plan sponsors. In today's business world, "change" is the only consistent theme employers face. Buck Consultants helps employers use change to their advantage. Buck prides itself on customizing its consulting services to design benefit programs that fit each client's unique business strategy and organization.

Buck Consultants, which is headquartered in New York City, opened a full-service office in Downtown Denver in 1987. The office's location in the Denver World Trade Center is appropriate, as Buck Consultants is (among other distinctions) the market leader in the design and administration of global employee stock ownership plans.

Services provided by the Denver office include:
- Actuarial Consulting
  - tax-qualified retirement plans
  - retiree medical and other post-retirement benefits
  - nonqualified plans for executives
- 401(k) and Defined Contribution Consulting and Administration
  - local service
  - periodic and daily valuation services
  - interactive voice response
  - complete customization and flexibility
- Health and Welfare Plan Consulting
  - managed care strategies
  - funding opportunities
  - plan design and cost sharing
  - provider consulting
  - claims analysis
  - flexible benefits design
- Employee Communications
  - investment education
  - surveys and focus groups
  - enrollment and SPD materials
  - campaigns to increase plan participation
  - Intranet applications and video
- Outsourcing
  - integrated defined benefit, defined contribution, and health and welfare administration
  - participant service center
  - interactive voice response
  - human resource functions
- Tax and Legal Consulting
- Strategic Human Resource Planning
- Investment Consulting
- Forecasting and Planning
- Compensation Consulting

With a consulting staff of 30, the Denver office meets its clients' needs with a solid base of local resources. In addition, the company's worldwide reach provides ready access to a wealth of national and international expertise.

Included in Buck's Denver office are three Fellows of the Society of Actuaries, six Enrolled Actuaries and two benefit lawyers, plus health and welfare and communications consultants.

Buck Consultants was founded in New York City in 1916 by George B. Buck, a consulting actuary. Mr. Buck worked with major cities and states in establishing funded retirement systems and was instrumental in promoting pension reform legislation that eventually brought about the Social Security Act of 1935.

Today, Buck's clients include some of the world's largest corporations, as well as small businesses, tax-exempt organizations, educational institutions and health care providers. The firm serves a large number of governmental retirement systems, as well as prestigious national and international quasi-governmental organizations.

Internationally, Buck provides comprehensive professional services to more than 5,000 clients. The company employs more than 2,500 people worldwide, including 250 senior consultants.

DESIGN WORKSHOP, INC.

Memorable landscapes around the world are a canvas for Design Workshop. Whether the task at hand is designing an intimate garden or developing a plan for regional tourism, the firm's landscape architecture and land planning services shape places that bring people and the environment together. These places span mountain, desert, coastal and urban settings worldwide, but much of Design Workshop's work is evident in the Denver area.

A recent example is Design Workshop's plan for the South Platte River greenway system. This plan creates the framework for Denver's $40 million effort to rescue more than 10 miles of the river for new parks, recreations trails and activities, and wildlife habitat. Also, Downtown Denver and surrounding neighborhoods will be enriched by the firm's plan for The Commons, a 65-acre urban neighborhood and park on former rail yards behind Union Station. On a 27-square-mile piece of land between Denver International Airport and Commerce City, the Rocky Mountain Arsenal is being transformed into an immense National Wildlife Refuge under a Design Workshop plan.

These efforts will enhance the Denver area by balancing the need for economic development with preservation of important natural landscapes. Other Design Workshop projects range from master plans for counties, new communities, urban centers and resorts, to detailed design for public parks, residences and roadways.

A quintessentially Western firm, Design Workshop was founded in 1969 by two friends and colleagues, Don Ensign and Joe Porter. One of their first big projects was to plan the 1,500-acre Owl Creek development near Aspen. In 1976, Ensign and Porter moved the firm permanently to Aspen and the Denver office was founded in 1984. Today, Design Workshop has nearly 100 employees; offices in Denver, Aspen, Vail, Phoenix, Albuquerque, Santa Fe, Jackson Hole, Lake Tahoe and São Paulo, Brazil; and more than 50 local and national awards to its name. The staff includes landscape architects, land planners, urban designers, market analysts and architects.

As the firm's name suggests, Design Workshop is a creative, solution-oriented company. Special teams are formed to meet the needs of each project and local citizens often play an important role. With inclusive public participation methods, the firm forges a common vision from diverse, even conflicting, priorities and sets the stage for long-term stewardship of the land.

In 1995, Design Workshop staff celebrated the firm's 25th anniversary by each donating 25 hours to environmental and community service. Efforts of the Denver staff included building recreation trails; participating in Governor Roy Romer's Smart Growth and Development Task Force; and designing a little-league baseball field. These activities were one reason Design Workshop was named Professional Services Company of the Year by *Colorado Business Magazine*, Coopers & Lybrand and the Colorado Association of Commerce and Industry in 1996.

By carefully balancing social, economic and environmental needs, Design Workshop brings people in harmony with landscapes in Denver and beyond.

Deer are among many species of wildlife already living at Rocky Mountain Arsenal National Wildlife Refuge.

Landscape design for KUSA Channel 9 broadcast facility was designed to blend with character of the surrounding neighborhood.

Children can pan for gold and enjoy other outdoor educational activities in revitalized parks along the Platte River. Credit: *Greenway Foundation*.

COCALLAS AND HOSKIN ARCHITECTS

**RIGHT: Carriage Row
Denver, Colorado**

The project began simply as a modest backyard deck designed by Cocallas and Hoskin Architects. The result produced a lucrative, multi-year relationship with Kaufman and Broad, the nation's second-largest homebuilder.

Cocallas and Hoskin, a 19-year-old architectural firm that supplies its clients with one-stop architectural needs, has its blueprints on several metro Denver projects, including historic preservation, affordable housing, custom homes, multi-family housing and commercial buildings.

"What distinguishes us is the breadth of our projects and the attention we pay to our clients," says Mark Hoskin, co-owner of the firm that designed the deck for a Kaufman and Broad principal in 1989. C&H's expertise and service-oriented dedication induced the goliath California-based homebuilder to hire the downtown Denver firm to provide a majority of the architectural process for its multi-family and production houses in five states.

**FAR RIGHT:
Elite Auto Glass
Arvada, Colorado**

Oftentimes, architects will design buildings, produce construction drawings and disappear from the construction process, says co-owner Chris Cocallas. But the firm's devotion to detail and customer satisfaction has created an architectural methodology that provides residential and commercial clients with a complete menu of services — project analysis, site planning, preliminary design, engineering production, budget review, construction administration and more.

The firm's mastery in designing production homes or multi-family homes is parallelled by its superiority in historic preservation and adaptive reuse. It successfully preserved such Denver landmarks as the Oxford and Burlington hotels, the Seattle Fish Building and Silver Square. It has converted mansions to office buildings and designed more than 100 LoDo rental lofts including the 33 residential units above Patagonia at the Studebaker Building.

"We take pride in changing a building from its original purpose, maintaining its historic character and putting a modern use into it," Cocallas says.

Hoskin adds: "We often work in the shadow of someone who was an accomplished architect in their time. We're respectful of other people's work and craftsmanship and integrate our work into theirs."

That same desire is manifested in their mission to satisfy their clients, who include many repeat customers and most prominent downtown Denver and inner-city developers. A growing part of their business is owner-occupied commercial pad buildings. The company just introduced two similar, non-competing businesses owners so to increase their presences in suburban shopping centers and cross-market each other's products.

"That's a long path from doing historic preservation," Hoskin says of his company's diversity and its ability to let creative solutions evolve from clients' needs. "Our company's style is dictated by our clients' wishes and constraints. We sell our creativity."

M+O+A ARCHITECTURAL PARTNERSHIP

Excellence in design and quality technical delivery have been the foundation of the services provided by M+O+A Architectural Partnership since the firm was established in 1981. This philosophy has resulted in numerous design awards and high accolades from clients, building tenants, and building contractors.

Communication is the cornerstone of M+O+A's creative process. An open, interactive approach is taken with every client and their program. This ensures that the design is responsive to the client's concerns and makes a unique aesthetic statement within the parameters of function, technical specifications, and economic reality.

The personal commitment of M+O+A's professional staff, along with computer technology, enhances the firm's ability to produce accurate technical documents and manage construction projects of diverse scope and schedules. With this attitude and technical tools, the building components and systems are thoroughly coordinated to ensure the economical and timely construction of each project.

The reputation of M+O+A has been founded on this ability to provide imaginative and technically responsive designs, resulting in distinctive, quality projects in a number of building types ranging from Municipal Buildings, Office Buildings, Industrial Buildings, Educational Facilities and Housing Facilities for the Elderly.

Above, from top to bottom: ACX Corporate Headquarters, Broomfield Municipal Center, Denver Business Center.

Below, clockwise from upper left: The Valley House, K N Energy Corporate Center, Pacifica Pointe.

CPC CORPORATE PLANNERS & COORDINATORS, INC.

When CPC Corporate Planners & Coordinators, Inc. was founded in 1971, its principals were already looking toward the future. As a pioneer in the field of tenant representation, CPC developed and refined a philosophy which remains true today — to provide a superior level of personal service, steadfast loyalty and dedication to its clients' best interests.

In 1987, the state of Colorado recognized the importance of having professional expertise and representation in the marketplace — representation that stands up to multiple levels of scrutiny, especially in

CPC Corporate Planners & Coordinators, Inc., represents tenants like the state of Colorado in their commercial real estate transactions. CPC is owned by David Freyer (left) and Bernie Martin.

a politically charged environment. For the first time in Colorado history, the state awarded an exclusive contract to a private sector firm, CPC, for commercial real estate representation, including leasing and acquisition services and financial and facility evaluation.

From the time of the intial contract and throughout the following years, nearly every major real estate brokerage firm in Denver has attempted to acquire this contract. Over time, none has been successful in meeting the high standards required to represent what is probably the largest single user of real estate

in the state. CPC has won the state award time and again, and it continues to save dollars for taxpayers by providing a wide range of quality real estate services.

Following its proven methodology, CPC carefully determines a client's space and location needs, completes market research, analyzes the options and provides detailed information to assist the decision maker — whether the choice be a lease renewal or new space. CPC works not only to secure the best rental rate/purchase price for its clients, but also addresses other pertinent issues such as term, expansion options, co-location rights, renewal and early termination options, and tenant finish allowance — to name a few.

CPC believes that it is difficult — if not impossible — for one firm to simultaneously serve the conflicting interests of both tenant and landlord. CPC represents only the interests of its clients, operating like a real estate partner and supporting its clients' operational and strategic goals. There is never a hint of conflict of interest or a question as to where CPC's loyalties lie.

Originally, CPC was a branch office of a larger firm headquartered in New York. Today, it is a private Colorado company representing private sector firms, locally and nationally, as well as the state of Colorado. CPC is owned by Bernie Martin and David Freyer. Martin has been with CPC since 1988 and Freyer since 1984.

The partners' business philosophy is to develop long term alliances with their clients — partnerships that are relationship-driven, not transaction-oriented. Nearly all of CPC's work comes from repeat business and through direct referrals. Martin and Freyer control growth by working with a select client base, which allows the firm to maintain its effective personalized service.

Commercial property owners and managers are well-qualified to defend their own interest at the bargaining table. CPC Corporate Planners and Coordinators, Inc. believes it is important for all tenants and buyers to engage a knowledgeable and experienced tenant representation firm to represent their interests.

Denver Physical Therapy — Downtown, P.C.

Denver Physical Therapy — Downtown offers high quality orthopedic and sports rehabilitation programs at two sites that are familiar to all discriminating Denver athletes.

The historically significant Denver Athletic Club, built of red sandstone and completed in 1892, is located at 13th and Glenarm. The International Wellness Center is located at Sixteenth and Welton,

directly off the Sixteenth Street Mall and Denver's light rail.

Denver Physical Therapy — Downtown is owned and operated by well-known Denver physical therapist Merry Lester, P.T., O.C.S.

Lester and her staff pride themselves in providing the highest quality personal service with "hands on" physical therapy techniques. "We don't schedule patients every 20 minutes and then push them out the door," said Lester. "We take time with our patients, who enjoy coming to see us. When they leave, we want them to feel better."

Because of the therapists' highly personalized approach and enviable success rate with difficult cases, word-of-mouth referrals account for more than 90 percent of the patients at Denver Physical Therapy — Downtown.

One of Lester's most unusual referrals occured a few years ago when she was called upon by the Denver Zoo to develop a therapeutic program for Snow, the weaker of the city's famous twin polar bear cubs.

Denver Physical Therapy — Downtown also offers seasonal sports fitness evaluation and conditioning programs designed to help athletes of any age and caliber improve their performance and avoid injury.

The practice's popular golf conditioning program teams licensed physical therapists with PGA and LPGA golf instructors in order to evaluate and improve the biomechanics of a client's golf swing.

Denver Physical Therapy — Downtown videotapes a client's golf swing; evaluates flexibility, strength, timing and skill; and develops a personalized training regime. One on one, a physical therapist treats a client's critical stress points and a golf professional addresses technique.

Also popular is Denver Physical Therapy — Downtown's "ski fit" evaluation program, which consists of a series of objective tests linking the demands of skiing — strength, balance, agility, coordination, endurance and flexibility — to a person's physical condition. After an assessment is made, a personalized series of conditioning exercises is recommended for each participant.

In fall 1996, Lester's program was prominently featured by *The Denver Post* in an article on the particular needs of female skiers.

Denver Physical Therapy — Downtown also offers popular lectures and programs on osteoporosis, workplace ergonomics, orthotics, racket sports conditioning, neck and back pain, arthritis and total joint replacement, spinal stabilization classes, and a specialized women's health program.

Rehabilitating an ailing golf game. Resuming normal physical activity after injury or surgery. Relieving chronic pain. Denver Physical Therapy — Downtown is dedicated to helping Denver residents return to good health — and good games — as soon as possible.

FAR LEFT: Merry Lester, P.T., O.C.S., owner and operator of Denver Physical Therapy — Downtown, offers high quality orthopedic and sports rehabilitation programs at two sites.

LEFT: Merry Lester and her staff pride themselves in providing old fashioned "hands on" physical therapy. Lester is shown working with prominent Denverite Norm Early.

BELOW: Merry Lester developed a therapeutic program for Snow, the weaker of the Denver Zoo's famous twin polar bear cubs.

OCCASIONS BY SANDY

Denver, a city known for its sense of hospitality and style and "party animals" has a population that thrives on magnificent galas and opulent corporate and private entertainment.

Award winning design for Best Off-Premise Catering for the National Tour Opening Gala for Sunset Boulevard.

RIGHT: An elegant setting by Occasions by Sandy.
Credit: Jerry Werth

Nationally and internationally, Occasions by Sandy's reputation has been indigenous with state of the art buffet creations, creative culinary presentations and unbeatable unobtrusive service staff. As a national award winner in the hospitality industry, Occasions by Sandy is often referred to as Denver's "Boutique Caterer."

Occasions by Sandy was founded in 1968 by the present owner, President Sandy Tenenbaum. In those days, the word "catering" had to be explained to people as the industry that brings food, kitchen, service equipment and staff to your location versus the common practice of using an "on premise" hotel or country club's facilities.

In 1980, Barry Tenenbaum joined his wife's flourishing catering business. With many years experience as one of Denver's leading restaurateurs, and with an established reputation of serving innovative, remarkably delicious menu selections and creative presentations, he brought his expertise and attention to consistency, quality and keen business sense to Occasions by Sandy.

Since the thriving oil and gas days of the 1980s, Occasions by Sandy has experienced remarkable growth and transformation. A household catering business, in its inception, evolved into Denver's foremost wedding and corporate caterers and event planners.

Occasions by Sandy at the present time has the capability of handling events of any size and stature. Their policy is to *listen to* the clients, evaluate their personal needs and subsequently transform their desires into a memorable event. "No party is too big or too small."

The staff is always so diversified and fun! On July 10, 1996 when they catered the National Tour Opening Gala for Sunset Boulevard at the Denver Performing Arts Complex, the orchestra played a newly popular visual dance piece. None of the cast, including the dancers, knew it or could participate until the Occasions' staff, exhausted from two full days of set up and serving at the event, gathered on the dance floor and taught everyone the "Macarena!"

Occasions by Sandy's motto is to make each host or hostess "A Star" and to "Always promise a lot but deliver much more!"

Occasions by Sandy is certainly excited about Denver's robust economy and population explosion and cherish all of their new and continued relationships. They operate with enthusiasm, unparalleled style and integrity to offer the most innovative, organized and creative parties in the world!

SINK COMBS DETHLEFS

Hockey. Basketball. Baseball. Football. People who live in Colorado love their sports — both as spectators and participants

Many of the state's finest sports, recreational and entertainment facilities were designed by the Denver architectural firm of Sink Combs Dethlefs — one of only a handful of architectural firms in the United States to specialize in this unique field.

Sink Combs Dethlefs has also designed such significant out-of-state facilities as the FargoDome, the Copps Coliseum in Ontario and the $130 million San Jose Arena — which has been described as the finest facility in the National Hockey League. About 50 percent of the firm's business is in Colorado and 50 percent elsewhere.

The firm has also designed many recreational, commercial, condominium, club-house and restaurant facilities. Sink Combs Dethlefs offers special expertise in designing for cost-effective construction in the mountains.

The firm was founded in 1962 by Charles Sink, a Harvard-educated architect who had relocated to Denver in 1950 because of his love of skiing. Prior to establishing his own firm, Sink was associated with

Front Range projects of the internationally known architect I.M. Pei.

One of Sink's first projects was the Vail clock tower, one of Colorado's most beloved and photographed structures. The firm went on to design base and summit facilities, restaurants and condominiums at Copper Mountain, Vail and Aspen. In the boom years of the 1970s early 1980s, the firm concentrated on the design of office buildings.

Following the oil bust, which led to the demise of 25 percent of the state's architectural firms, Sink Combs Dethlefs survived by expanding its involvement in the sports, recreational and entertainment niche, which it had entered with the design of McNichols Arena in 1975.

Principals of the firm, who are closely involved with each project, are Richard Combs, Donald Dethlefs Jr. and Andrew Barnard. Founder Charles Sink, who still contributes his seasoned perspective to the firm, is now principal emeritus. The firm occupies space in Downtown Denver and employs 25 people.

For 35 years, the success of Sink Combs Dethlefs has been closely linked to Colorado's unparalleled athletic lifestyle.

McNichols Sports Arena, Denver, Colorado

1900 Grant Street, Denver, Colorado

Beaver Creek Residence, Beaver Creek, Colorado

The Dal Ward Athletic Center, University of Colorado at Boulder

The San Jose Arena, San Jose, California

Some Representative Projects Designed By Sink Combs Dethlefs

COLORADO:
Auraria Science Center
Colorado State Fair Events Center
Colorado State University
    Recreation Center and Moby
    Gym Renovation
Copper Mountain Day Center
    and Mountain Restaurant
1900 Grant Street Building
Highlands Ranch Recreation Center
McNichols Arena and Additions
Mile High Stadium Improvements
Mountain State Employers
    Council
One Cheeseman Condominiums
SOCO Plaza
University of Colorado-Boulder
    Dal Ward Athletic Center
University of Colorado-Boulder
    Folsom Stadium Master Plan

University of Denver
    Wellness & Athletic Center
University of Northern Colorado-
    Greeley Recreation Center
University of Northern Colorado-
    Greeley Stadium
U.S. Air Force Academy
    Cadet Gymnasium

ELSEWHERE

CALIFORNIA:
National Orange Show Master Plan
San Diego State University
    Events Center
San Jose Arena

IOWA:
University of Iowa
    Recreation Building Addition

MANITOBA:
Manitoba Entertainment Complex/
    Arena

MICHIGAN:
The Palace at Auburn Hills

MONTANA:
Montana State University Arena

NEVADA:
University of Nevada-Los Vegas
    Thomas and Mack Center

NORTH DAKOTA:
Fargodome
Fargo Baseball Park

OKLAHOMA:
Oklahoma City Arena

OHIO:
Ohio State University Arena

ONTARIO:
Copps Coliseum
Metro Toronto Hockey League
    International Hockey Center

SOUTH DAKOTA:
South Dakota State University
    Wellness Center

WYOMING:
University of Wyoming North End
    Zone Athletic Complex

Parcel, Mauro, Hultin & Spaanstra, P.C.

In just ten years, Parcel, Mauro, Hultin & Spaanstra has become the fifth largest law firm in the Denver metropolitan area. Although the firm has grown rapidly, it has remained entrepreneurial — combining the responsiveness and personal attention of a moderate-size law firm with the experience and expertise of a large firm.

Founded in 1986 by the merger of two small firms and headquartered in downtown Denver, PMHS employs nearly 200 people, including 77 attorneys. The firm's practice groups specialize in litigation, labor and employment, natural resources, environmental law and business transactions.

Parcel, Mauro, Hultin & Spaanstra, the fifth-largest law firm in Denver, is managed by a three-person group of senior practicing attorneys. (Left to right) Marcus Squarrell, a litigator, is vice president for human resources and operations. Linda Rockwood, an environmental lawyer, is president. Mike Page, a real estate attorney, is vice president and chief financial officer.

The firm's litigation practice encompasses nationwide experience in commercial cases, including suits concerning product liability, contracts, franchises, antitrust, patents and unfair competition and securities. The firm serves as national trial counsel in major pattern litigation in the automotive, pharmaceutical, asbestos and household appliance industries.

The labor and employment practice provides administrative, litigation and counseling services to clients in matters relating to contracts and disputes between management and unions, employment practices and occupational safety and health.

Reflecting Denver's status as a major center of the mining industry, PMHS offers one of the broadest and most diverse natural resources practices in the United States, emphasizing both transactional work and litigation. This practice embraces mining, oil and gas, water rights and public lands law. The firm maintains offices in Santiago, Chile, to serve mining clients with activities in South America.

PMHS' environmental practice provides permitting, compliance and enforcement advice concerning a broad range of environmental laws and regulations, and emphasizes proactive representation to anticipate issues and avoid liability. The practice also offers substantial experience in the environmental litigation arena and in the application of environmental laws to commercial and real property transactions.

Specializing in corporate law, securities, taxation and real estate, business lawyers represent financial, manufacturing, telecommunications and other commercial enterprises both domestically and abroad. This practice group represents clients in mergers and acquisitions, business and financial restructurings, securities offerings, financings, real estate development and other commercial transactions.

PMHS also assists clients in resolving problems associated with interactions with local, state and federal government, particularly with respect to business, economic development and environmental matters. It refers to this practice area as "business-government solutions."

A variety of community activities are supported through volunteer and pro bono efforts. Attorneys serve on the boards of directors for educational, civic and charitable groups including the Rocky Mountain Mineral Law Foundation, the Metropolitan Denver YMCA, the Colorado School of Mines, the American Heart Association, the Rio Grande Compact Commission and the Hispanic Leadership Memorial Fund.

Believing that lawyers should spend their time and energies serving their clients, enhancing their specialties and enjoying the practice of law, the firm strives both to minimize administrative demands on its lawyers and to preserve a friendly, informal and non-bureaucratic atmosphere.

As Parcel, Mauro, Hultin & Spaanstra enters its second decade, it continues to build its reputation for providing the highest quality, most cost-effective and most responsive legal services for its clients in Colorado, the region and across the United States.

Townsend Consulting Group

The primary objective of the Townsend Consulting Group (TCG) is to help clients achieve success by developing and implementing support service strategies that enhance core competencies. Whether assessing performance, measuring capacities, facilitating change, implementing technology, simplifying procurement, improving supplier chains or providing outsourcing support, TCG strives to be a catalyst for world class performance.

The 30-person firm sees itself as a quality, client-focused, cost-effective alternative for senior level managers who do not have access to larger, more costly consulting firms. While no stranger to corporate America, TCG primarily assists public organizations and regulated industries facing privatization, restructuring, competitive or global forces that demand organizational change. This includes state and federal agencies, banks, utilities, communications and transportation organizations. In addition to the Denver market, TCG serves clients in a variety of locations including New York City, Washington D.C., Charleston, Phoenix and Los Angeles. Representative clients include the Philadelphia Electric Company, Intertech Manufacturing, Colorado Department of Transportation, Imperial Bank of California, the U.S. Earthquake Information Center, and the City of Aurora, Colorado.

When asked what influences have shaped TCG's development since its inception in 1987, Les Townsend, president and founder, cites three factors. First is the accelerating pace of change, which demands that TCG stay ahead of the marketplace power curve. "We must provide our clients with success solutions for today while accommodating an uncharted future."

Next is a requirement to provide total solutions. "From input to deliverable, from supplier to customer, clients rightfully expect us to provide comprehensive, end to end solutions that meet their highest expectations."

Last, says Townsend, is the changing nature of company operations. Today, TCG is as much a services firm as it is a consulting organization. "We started with a single focus — workload measurement. We have broadened our services to include endeavors ranging from reengineering and organizational transformation to accepting on-site outsourcing responsibilities.

This multifunctional capability is best illustrated by citing the firm's five most recent engagements:
- reengineered administrative processes for a state agency
- operated an electronic customer service center
- provided analytical support staffing for federal research programs
- developed community-based economic development plans for a city agency
- developed a cultural diversity program for an 1100-employee hotel

TCG is one of the few minority-owned consulting firms that work nationally with transformation issues such as streamlining, team-building, diversity and performance strategies to improve productivity, quality and customer service. The firm is an imaginative innovator in developing programs that transform processes and cultures, providing customizing solutions to meet clients' needs.

Another unusual aspect of TCG is a requirement that program and project managers must have practical experience as operating executives in addition to an advanced degree. The firm also takes great pride in providing highly qualified diverse project teams that offer clients a sensitivity and affinity rarely found in larger firms.

Because TCG teams work together and in collaboration with clients, there is a high degree of synergy and mutual respect for a job well done. This shared enthusiasm and commitment makes TCG a remarkable organization. The firm is confident that it will continue to play an important role in helping its clients meet the challenges of the future.

Les Townsend and members of the Group from left to right: Sam Richardson, Les, Mark Monk, Cheryl Wright, Jay Perez and Pam Benfield. *Credit: Stephen M. Crain, Crain Photography*

PETERSON CONSULTING L.L.C.

Peterson Consulting L.L.C. (Peterson Consulting), a national consulting firm, was founded in 1980. Peterson Consulting's professional team of experts advise clients in managing the economics of disputes, regulation, and change. These teams also provide their clients with objective analytical and information management expertise to understand and resolve claims, business disputes, and commercial litigation matters.

Peterson Consulting's downtown Denver office is one of more than 20 principal offices located in major U.S. cities. Peterson Consulting also provides consulting services in the United Kingdom. As the country's first full-service firm dedicated to providing objective, confidential fact-finding and analysis for business and legal matters, Peterson Consulting currently employs more than 500 consultants.

A cross section of disciplines provides a comprehensive base for the clients' various challenges. Peterson Consulting employs certified public accountants, financial analysts, and engineers, as well as information systems and document management experts.

Vice-Presidents of the Denver office (left to right): Joe Kellogg; John Farnan; Steve Holloway. Credit: Steven M. Crain, Crain Photography

Peterson Consulting has a diverse client base, which includes large and small companies, law firms, and governmental entities. Peterson's consultants work individually or as a team with their clients' representatives to analyze the accounting, financial, economic, engineering, computer, lending, investment, and information management aspects of businesses' problems. The analysis of the facts and Peterson's consultants' advice are used by decision-makers in both legal and business communities.

Representative types of projects on which Peterson

Consulting offers its expertise follow:
- Insurance and environmental
- Commercial litigation
- Construction and utilities
- Financial institutions
- Public contracts
- Health care

Project work at Peterson Consulting varies from one project to the next. One consultant may provide expertise for the entire project; however, other projects require a team of consultants to analyze its multifaceted issues.

When Peterson Consulting begins work on a client's project, a fact-finding period is commenced to accumulate and interpret the information obtained from extensive document reviews and interviews. Next, research allows investigation of relevant project issues. Various research methods are used such as interviewing client personnel and experienced firm members, and reviewing published materials and trade association publications. Additional research is obtained from various other sources as needed. The final step in the project is analysis. The analysis includes preparing and reviewing claims, counterclaims, and cost studies on the results of the fact-finding and research. Types of analysis specifically include lost profits determinations, time impact and schedule analyses, cost allocations, special-purpose reviews, and other valuations.

Peterson Consulting also provides special advice to attorneys by formulating or responding to information requests, preparing for the questioning and cross-examination of expert witnesses, preparing reports and exhibits for trial or settlement negotiations, and presenting expert testimony.

Information management is another area in which Peterson Consulting offers its expertise. In the ever-changing field of information management, consultants design and implement manual and computerized information management systems, including creating databases, document management applications, and allocation systems for the distribution of claim settlements.

SLATER-PAULL & ASSOCIATES, INC.

In 1997, Slater-Paull & Associates, Inc., celebrates 25 years of "architecture with integrity" in the City of Denver. This full-service architectural firm is consistently ranked among Denver's ten largest.

Slater-Paull's roots extend even further back into the city's history. Seymour Slater began his Denver career in 1951, working for well-known local architect Raymond Harry Ervin. Eventually, he and other Ervin protegees formed Piel, Slater, Small and Spenst. James Paull joined this firm in 1962 and, ten years later, Slater-Paull & Associates was born.

In its early years, Slater-Paull specialized in the design of shopping centers. More recently, the firm has built a strong reputation in the fields of educational and religious facilities. It has completed projects for ten Colorado school districts and facilities for many religious denominations.

Recent design projects include the Wheat Ridge Middle and Elementary School complex and Church of the Risen Christ Parish Center.

Slater-Paull also offers special expertise in architectural design for financial institutions, government agencies, community centers and communications facilities.

Since the early 1980s, Slater-Paull has become well-known for its building preservation projects, including historic East High School and Garden Place Academy. Other projects include restoration of Denver Academy; Mason, Foote, and Frontier Halls at the University of Denver; the US WEST Communications Center at 14th and Curtis; and the City and County Building for the City and County of Denver.

The firm's interior design projects range from high-end executive offices to economical school interiors, including projects for the State of Colorado, AT&T, Mountain Bell, and US WEST.

A good example of the firm's interior design work can be seen in its office at One Park Central in downtown Denver. The office demonstrates the principles of sustainable design and uses a wide variety of recycled and environmentally friendly materials. It was designed by an employee team in concert with management.

In 1985, the firm opened an office in Atlanta, Georgia, to serve its southeast regional clients.

Slater-Paull embraces a team approach to achieve its award-winning, cost-effective design solutions. A group of staff architects, interior designers, and CADD technicians, under the leadership of a principal architect, develops the best possible solution for client projects.

Principals of Slater-Paull in 1997 are James Paull, Gerhard Petri, James Pedler, Clayton Cole, Bruce Lott, and Richard Ricker. Associates are Adele Willson and Fred Baruchmann. The firm employs 35 people in Denver and 21 in Atlanta.

The firm credits its success to its integrity and the relationship it cultivates with its clients. More than 90 percent of the firm's satisfied clients have engaged it for multiple assignments over time.

It is Slater-Paull's philosophy that honesty, integrity and service are essential to success in today's complex building environment.

Slater-Paull & Associates, one of Denver's ten largest full-service architectural firms, has incorporated the principles of sustainable design in its downtown home office.

Slater-Paull & Associates has a strong reputation in the field of educational facilities, like the Wheat Ridge Middle and Elementary School complex.

Many of Denver's historic sites, like the City and County Building, have been restored by Slater-Paull & Associates.

HUMPHRIES**POLI**ARCHITECTS, P.C.

**Dennis Humphries
and Joseph Poli.**

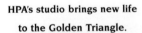

**HPA's studio brings new life
to the Golden Triangle.**

**Site Plan - Civic Center
Cultural Complex.**

For 25 years, architects Joe Poli and Dennis Humphries harbored the same dream. They wished to set up shop in a community they could call home, where they would become known as "neighborhood architects," as familiar and reassuring as the local grocer, butcher, or coffee house.

In Denver's Golden Triangle, the two architects found the ideal site. Through their "neo-traditionalist" approach to urban design, they would help reshape the Triangle — a neighborhood virtually abandoned — into an "urban village."

They formed Humphries**Poli**Architects in early 1994 and within months had moved to a former auto repair shop just around the corner from the Denver Public Library. As the Triangle's dismal parking lots and dilapidated buildings started giving way to an eclectic group of cultural and arts organizations, attractive residential dwellings, and small community-minded businesses, HPA found itself deeply entwined with one of the most exciting urban makeovers of the 20th century.

Since its founding, the energetic company has already designed four major Triangle projects — the Century and Grand Cherokee lofts, the Acoma Avenue of the Arts, and the Civic Center Cultural Complex parking lot, with its whimsical façade. HPA's renovation of its own offices garnered the coveted Design Award in 1995 from the Colorado chapter of the American Institute of Architects.

Today, the partners are among Denver's most ardent and articulate Triangle boosters. From serving on design review committees to conducting walking tours of the area, their community involvement takes many forms. They welcome the neighborhood association to hold its meetings in HPA's offices, and often hold their own meetings while strolling the area.

Elsewhere along the Front Range, the firm has reinvigorated several public buildings, most notably the historic East High School clock tower restoration and the bowling-alley-to-town-library conversion in Parker. In the summer of 1996, HPA transformed the Park Central Office Complex lobby from an aloof single-tenant foyer into an inviting multi-tenant arcade that opens onto the 16th Street Mall.

**Detail - Westminster City
Center Marketplace.**

**Reading Area - Parker
Public Library.**

In 1996, the firm completed the DUT Intermodal Feasibility Study. Commissioned jointly by the city, RTD, and Trillium Corporation, the study lays the groundwork for development of a regional transit hub situated in the Platte Valley. The coalition envisions extending the 16th Street Mall west to Wewatta Street; and combining centralized ticketing, baggage, and retail services in a new terminal for RTD, Amtrak, intercity buses, light rail, and the ski train. The project is designed to reduce commute times, improve air quality, and a create a more pedestrian-friendly downtown Denver — benefits that reflect the underlying values of the firm.

By late 1997, Humphries**Poli**Architects will have moved to its permanent home in the Triangle. There, the firm's gallery, which faces the historic Speer Boulevard Corridor, will house architectural drawings, fragments of former buildings, and computer-generated "fly-bys." The display will become part of HPA's ongoing effort to engage the public in an architectural discourse and will serve as a reminder that thoughtful design enhances the quality of our lives.

Professionals find creative ways to network in order to succeed in the vibrant business community.

Partners in Denver

MEDICAL, EDUCATIONAL, AND RELIGIOUS INSTITUTIONS, AS WELL AS RECREATION AND LEISURE ORIEN

QUALITY OF LIFE

Centura Health

More than a century ago, a group of German-speaking Franciscan nuns dedicated their hospital on the shores of Sloan Lake, just west of downtown Denver.

More than a century ago, a group of Seventh-day Adventists opened a sanitarium in the healthful climate of Boulder.

This century-plus of mission-based service is evoked by the name of the organization that manages the descendents of these two institutions today — Centura Health.

Centura Health was formed in 1995 as a not-for-profit operating company that oversees the operations of 75 Colorado health care facilities owned by two health care groups with strong Christian traditions — the Sisters of Charity Health Services Colorado and PorterCare Adventist Health System.

Now Colorado's largest health-delivery system, Centura Health employs more than 14,000 people and posted 1995 revenues of about $1.3 billion. The organization's facilities include ten general acute care hospitals and nine other hospital facilities that Centura Health manages under contract.

In late 1996, Centura Health announced that it also would affiliate with The Children's Hospital of Denver, giving the system improved access to Colorado's leading pediatric hospital.

In addition, Centura Health manages five senior care centers and several physician group management organizations. It also holds minority ownership of a managed care health plan. Facilities are located in Canon City, Colorado Springs, Denver, Florence, Frisco, Monument, Pueblo and Woodland Park.

Centura Health is more than a larger version of its affiliates. It is a new kind of health care organization — the only one of its kind in the United States — with a new vision for creating and sustaining healthier communities. It is not a hospital-based system. Rather, it is a pluralistic, integrated health delivery system.

After strategic meetings with its affiliates, Centura Health announced its new mission statement: "With the foundation and commitment of our Christian heritage and values, our mission is to promote the health and well-being of the people in the communities we serve through a comprehensive continuum of services provided in collaboration with partners who share the same vision and values."

Centura Health is making a fundamental and profound shift away from the old health care model of healing those who have become sick or injured to a new health care model that concentrates on preserving the health of people and communities so that they require fewer expensive health care services in the long run.

To this end, "healthier communities" teams have been formed to construct community health profiles — a first step toward improving local health standards. Two areas already identified for action are alcoholism (as a major contributor to trauma injuries) and teen pregnancy.

Another outcome of this affiliation is the creation of Centura Senior Care which provides a continuum of care ranging from senior health centers staffed by geriatric physicians, to inpatient acute and sub-acute care at the Centura Senior Life Center, to senior housing at the Villas at Sunny Acres, the Gardens at St. Elizabeth and PorterPlace.

Centura Health was created to streamline costs, making health care more affordable and accessible to residents throughout the state. Without affiliation and its attendant cost controls, many of these venerable Colorado hospitals could not survive into the next century.

The assets of Sisters of Charity Health Services Colorado and PorterCare Adventist Health System are affiliated, not merged, which means that ownership of those assets has not changed. The affiliate boards remain in place with full responsibility for maintaining the hospitals' historic missions and values. Also intact are the various facilities' foundations and volunteer efforts.

Partners in Centura Health have identified core values that will guide the organization's behavior and activities. They include:

- Preservation and enhancement of our Christian identity, heritage and mission;
- Unwavering dedication to delivering quality service everywhere we are and in everything we do;
- Values-oriented leadership and management committed to innovation and excellence in organizing and providing health services;
- Wise stewardship and respectful use of all resources: natural, human and financial;
- Respect for each person, with particular attention to the elderly, sick, poor and needy; and
- Consistent, enthusiastic and collaborative effort to improve the health and well-being of the people in the communities we serve.

Centura Health intends to be the preeminent health system serving the people of Colorado in the 21st century. While in pursuit of this goal, Centura Health — with more than 100 years of service to Denver and Colorado — is committed to respect all people and to be guided by its Christian values and heritage.

Centura Health Affiliates

CAÑON CITY
Progressive Care Center
St. Thomas More Hospital
Sister Judith Kuhn Outpatient
    Rehab Center

COLORADO SPRINGS
Namasté Alzheimer Center
Penrad Imaging
Penrose Community Hospital
Penrose Home Health
Penrose Hospital
Penrose-St. Francis Medical Group
ReadyCare North and South
St. Francis Health Center
Surgery Ltd.
The Medalions
Total Healthcare of Colorado
    Springs

DENVER METRO AREA
Avista Medical Associates
Centura Managed Health
    Organization
PorterCare Hospital
PorterCare Hospital Avista
PorterCare Hospital Littleton
Porter/Littleton Medical Group

PorterPlace
St. Anthony Health Services East
St. Anthony Hospital Central
St. Anthony Hospital North
Senior Life Center
SouthCare
The Villas at Sunny Acres
Team Care
The Gardens at St. Elizabeth

FLORENCE
ClearView of Colorado
St. Joseph Manor

FRISCO
Summit Medical Center
    Monument
Penrose-St. Francis Medical Center
    at Monument

PUEBLO
St. Mary-Corwin Medical Group
St. Mary-Corwin Regional Medical
    Center
Total Healthcare of Pueblo
Villa Pueblo

WOODLAND PARK
Langstaff-Brown Medical Center

Managed Health Care Facilities

BRIGHTON, COLORADO
Platte Valley Medical Center

COLORADO SPRINGS, COLORADO
The St. Francis Nursing Center at
    Mount St. Francis

DURANGO, COLORADO
Mercy Medical Center

GOODLAND, KANSAS
Goodland Regional Medical Center

JULESBURG, COLORADO
Sedgwick County Memorial
    Hospital

KREMMLING, COLORADO
Kremmling Memorial Hospital

LA JARA, COLORADO
Conejos County Hospital

LEADVILLE, COLORADO
St. Vincent Hospital

WALSENBURG, COLORADO
Huerfano County Medical Center

SISTERS OF CHARITY HEALTH SERVICES COLORADO

More than 100 years after its founding, St. Anthony Hospital Central is one of Denver's largest and most sophisticated hospitals.

RIGHT: St. Anthony Hospital was founded by an order of German-speaking Franciscan nuns who raised the necessary money by begging in saloons and mining camps.

An early operating room at St. Anthony Hospital.

St. Anthony Hospital Central, the oldest of the Centura Health affiliates, can trace its roots back to the rough-and-tumble days of early Denver. In 1884, seven nuns arrived to staff a 66-bed hospital that had been built by the Union Pacific Railroad.

These nursing nuns were members of the newly formed American branch of a Franciscan order that was headquartered in Lafayette, Indiana. The order's motherhouse was located in Olpe, Germany, and some of the new nuns spoke only German.

After six years, the sisters decided to build their own hospital — a mission that would require a great deal of money.

The intrepid sisters with their tin cups became a common sight in the most unlikely places. They begged outside the Union Pacific pay car. They begged inside barber shops and smoke-filled saloons. They begged in the primitive mining camps that dotted the Rockies, traveling by mule and camping in rugged conditions.

Thanks to the determination of these strong women, St. Anthony Hospital opened near Sloan Lake in 1892. Today, more than 100 years later, St. Anthony Hospital Central is one of Denver's largest

and most sophisticated hospitals — the cornerstone of Sisters of Charity Health Services Colorado.

In 1972, recognizing the need to stabilize trauma injuries at the scene and the remoteness of many Colorado accident locations, St. Anthony established

Flight For Life, a helicopter emergency service — the first such hospital-based service in the nation. Today, thanks to the support of many public and private contributors, Flight For Life serves more than 200 Colorado communities.

In the 1970s, St. Anthony became the first hospital in Colorado to create an operating room dedicated to trauma patients. In 1996, St. Anthony is the only private Level I trauma center in Colorado accredited by the American College of Surgeons and the only trauma center serving the western part of the metropolitan area. Each year, St. Anthony treats nearly 1500 victims of major trauma.

St. Anthony Hospital Central is also a leading center for the prevention and treatment of cardiovascular disease. For patients who need acute care services, St. Anthony offers chest pain emergency centers, (a successful concept that has been extended to all Centura Health hospitals), coronary intensive care units, telemetry units, new cardiovascular labs and

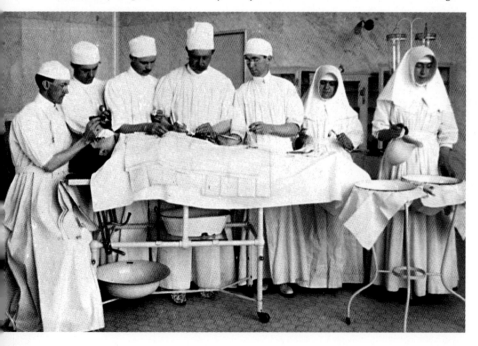

operating rooms staffed by cardiovascular specialists. St. Anthony also offers the leading nonsurgical coronary intervention program in Denver.

In addition, St. Anthony Hospital Central is home to the Rocky Mountain Gamma Knife Center, where neurosurgeons from all of Denver's major hospitals come to treat brain abnormalities using a noninvasive stereotactic radiosurgical instrument.

In 1971, St. Anthony Hospital Central opened a satellite campus, St. Anthony Hospital North, to serve Westminster and adjoining Adams County communities. Today, St. Anthony Hospital North is no longer a satellite but a health care facility in its own right.

St. Anthony Hospital North celebrated its 25th anniversary in 1996 by dedicating a new two-story addition that consists of an 81-bed medical-surgical unit with all private rooms, six pediatric beds and a 13-bed intensive care unit. Projects to expand the emergency department and to add a new labor and delivery facility are scheduled for completion in 1997.

Women's and children's services are an important component at both St. Anthony Hospitals. St. Anthony Hospital Central is equipped to handle the full range of obstetrical situations from routine delivery to obstetrical trauma patients. It is also a site for the Mother's Milk Bank program, the Women's Resource Center and the Shared Beginnings program for pregnant teens.

The St. Anthony Family Medicine Residency program, established in 1970, is one of the oldest programs of its kind in the nation. The program operates at both St. Anthony Hospitals.

In 1978, St. Anthony Hospital Central opened Summit Medical Center and, in 1991, opened a licensed outpatient surgery center to serve the residents and physicians of Summit County. In 1997, Summit Medical Center added a CT scanner and complete obstetrical services including two labor, delivery and recovery rooms.

In 1987, to pursue a shared health care ministry, the Sisters of St. Francis joined with the Sisters of Charity of Cincinnati to form Provenant Health

St. Anthony Hospital, served by horse-powered ambulances, opened its doors near Sloan Lake in 1892.

Partners. In 1995, the Sisters of Charity regionalized its 17 Colorado facilities under one corporation — Sisters of Charity Health Services Colorado. This group became a member of the Mountain Region of Catholic Health Initiatives.

In early 1996, SCHSC affiliated with PorterCare Adventist Health System to form Centura Health, a private, not-for-profit Christian health care organization.

Flight For Life, established by St. Anthony Hospital in 1972 to provide emergency treatment in Colorado's remote locations, today serves more than 200 Colorado communities.

PorterCare Adventist Health System

One hundred years ago, sanitariums were popular destinations for people in search of better health. One of the most famous of these was the Battle Creek Sanitarium in Michigan, established by John Harvey Kellogg — inventor of corn flakes.

In 1896, a sanitarium was dedicated on 90 acres of land in Boulder — a joint project of the General Conference of Seventh-day Adventists and Dr. Kellogg's International Medical Missionary and Benevolent Association. In 1919, the Adventist Church became the sole owner.

The PorterCare Hospitals are named after successful Denver entrepreneur Henry M. Porter and his daughter, Dora Porter Mason, who greatly admired the Seventh-day Adventists.

At the Boulder-Colorado Sanitarium, patients under the care of Adventist physicians received a variety of treatments that would help the body heal itself, aided by hydrotherapy, rest, proper diet, exercise and "the reform of injurious habits." Horseback riding, mountain climbing and hiking were included in the regimen inspired by the Adventists.

FAR RIGHT: In 1928, the Porter family donated the money to build Porter Sanitarium and Hospital along South Downing Street in Denver.

Almost 35 years later, during the Great Depression, a second Adventist institution — Porter Sanitarium and Hospital — opened in Denver. This 75-bed institution and 40 acres of land along South Downing Street were the gift of successful Denver entrepreneur Henry M. Porter and his daughter, Dora Porter Mason.

Mr. Porter's generosity was inspired by his positive experiences at other Adventist sanitariums where he had been delighted with the quality of care he received. At one site, he was impressed with an attendant's refusal to accept a tip. At another, he was amazed to receive a refund check for a 45-cent overcharge. Porter was determined to bring this caliber of health care to Denver.

In 1956, the Boulder-Colorado Sanitarium changed its name to the Boulder-Colorado Sanitarium and Hospital. The original building was razed and a new modern hospital erected in its place. In 1962, this institution became known as Boulder Memorial Hospital.

In Denver, Porter Sanitarium and Hospital continued to enjoy the generous support of the Porter family. Their gifts helped subsidize major additions and remodelings in the 1960s and, in 1963, the name of the institution was changed to Porter Memorial Hospital.

Today, the hospital is a 368-bed general, acute care facility offering a full range of health care services. It employs more than 1600 people. Special services

include cancer and heart centers, the Clyde G. Kissinger Center For Sight, the Centre for Behavioral Health, rehabilitation services including Independence Square (a simulated rehabilitation environment), The Birthplace and Level II nursery, a unique outpatient surgery facility, breast services, emergency services, and a kidney, kidney-pancreas, pancreas and liver transplant program.

In addition, PorterPlace, a retirement facility located on the hospital grounds, offers a unique lifestyle for active seniors complete with independent and assisted living services.

In 1989, in order to serve Douglas and southern Arapahoe Counties, Porter Memorial Hospital opened 105-bed Littleton Hospital.

Today, Littleton Hospital is a general, acute care facility with more than 400 employees. It provides a full range of general hospital services including a 24-hour emergency center with a Level III trauma designation, the Family Life Center, The Birthplace and Level II nursery, rehabilitation, pediatrics, surgery/ ICU, diagnostic services, cardiopulmonary medicine and radiology services.

In 1989, the struggling Boulder Memorial Hospital was sold to its competitor, Boulder Community Hospital, and the Mid-America Union Conference of Seventh-day Adventists used the proceeds to build a new facility in the rapidly growing city of Louisville. Avista Hospital opened in 1990 and employs nearly 250 people including many who had worked at Boulder Memorial.

The 58-bed facility features medical/surgical services, pediatrics, radiology, cardiopulmonary, rehabilitation and 24-hour emergency care. The New Life Center offers maternity and Level II nursery services.

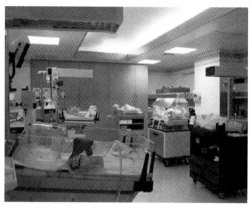

In 1995, the various Adventist facilities formed PorterCare Adventist Health System — one of nine divisions of the Adventist Healthcare Association of the Seventh-day Adventist Church. Consequently, the three facilities were renamed PorterCare Hospital, PorterCare Hospital Littleton and PorterCare Hospital Avista.

The organization's mission is to improve the physical, emotional and spiritual health of the individuals and communities it serves. In 1995, the PorterCare Hospitals treated more than 21,500 inpatients and nearly 194,000 outpatients — assisted by 640 dedicated volunteers.

All three PorterCare Hospitals offer The Birthplace and Level II nurseries.

All PorterCare Hospitals offer ASK-A-NURSE, a free 24-hour health information and physician referral service. In addition, ASK-A-NURSE is a well-known community health expert providing programs such as after-hours call for physicians, rural outreach, postpartum callback, emergency department callback and managed care contracting.

Adventist ownership has influenced certain operational practices at the PorterCare facilities which observe a smoke-free environment, a caffeine-free and vegetarian diet in cafeterias, respect for the Seventh-day Sabbath (from sundown Friday to sundown Saturday), and the encouragement of Christ-like speech and action. The facilities continue to promote healthier lifestyles and preventive care by offering a variety of ongoing health education classes for the public.

It is the mission of PorterCare hospitals to improve the physical, emotional and spiritual health of the individuals and communities they serve.

In early 1996, PorterCare Adventist Health System became PorterCare Hospitals and affiliated with Sisters of Charity Health Services Colorado to form Centura Health, a private, not-for-profit health care organization.

ELITCH GARDENS

**Mary Elitch with her
lion cubs, Ed & Kate**

*From our Beginnings
in 1890...*

Like so many who crowded into bustling 1880s Denver, John and Mary Elitch decided it was the place to seek their fortune. They opened a restaurant which soon proved so successful that the couple purchased Chilcott's Farm complete with orchards to supply the fresh produce they needed.

It wasn't long, however, before townspeople were urging them to turn the farm into a Park so all of Denver could enjoy their cool, green oasis.

**RIGHT, TOP TO
BOTTOM: From the
1890's, to the 1930's,
to the 1990's**

While Mary designed walkways, fountains, flower-beds and even a cafe on the grounds, John built a stage to indulge his first love, the theater. Through circus friends, they even acquired various zoo animals, and became one of the first zoos west of Chicago. On May 1st, 1890, Elitch's Zoological Gardens opened its gates to welcome guests.

Mary continued their dream after John's sudden death the next year, and successfully ran the growing amusement park until 1916 when ownership passed to John Mulvihill. Under his guidance, guests enjoyed Denver's first roller-coaster — the Wildcat, a chilling Haunted House, a hand-carved Carousel, afternoon band concerts amid lush flower gardens, nightly dances at the Trocadero Ballroom and first-class drama in the theater.

In 1930, the Leadership of Elitch Gardens came into the capable hands of Mulvihill's son-in-law, Arnold Gurtler. And in 1945, Arnold's two sons, Jack and Budd, returned from the War to help their father run the Park. They had worked at almost every job there since they were boys. Eventually, they took over the entire operation. The immensely popular Kiddie-Land was their first success, followed by the awesome 'Twister' rollercoaster and the 'Splinter' flume water ride. Budd Gurtler was also instrumental in establishing the Colorado Carnations Growers Association, and Elitch's vast greenhouses soon were the largest supplier of carnations in the country. The two brothers constantly sought out new rides and attractions, and adapted the Park's entertainment to the tempo of the times.

Sandy Gurtler, the fourth generation of the family, assumed the Presidency of Elitch Gardens in 1985. It was under his guidance that the move was made to the Platte River Valley in the heart of downtown Denver.

TOP LEFT:
Douglas Fairbanks
(1906)

BOTTOM LEFT:
Edward G. Robinson
(1922)

RIGHT: Grace Kelly
(1951)

The Oldest Summer Stock Theater in America

John Elitch was a great lover of the Arts and, himself, a sometime actor. In an effort to bring theater to Denver, he included a stage in his new amusement park design which would play host to actors, jugglers, dancers and musicians. Unfortunately, after his first successful season, he fell ill with pneumonia and died while on tour with a traveling theater troupe.

Tommy Dorsey

Lawrence Welk

Harry James

Les Brown

Mary Elitch continued her husband's dream, and by 1897 had replaced Vaudeville and Light Opera with Summer Stock Theater. Actors during these early years included Sarah Bernhardt, Douglas Fairbanks and a youthful Cecil B. DeMille. The next two decades brought such names as Harold Lloyd, George Brent, Edward G. Robinson and Frederic March to Elitch's stage. During the 1940s, '50s and '60s, the Theater was so popular that it was usually sold out for the entire season. Raymond Burr, Patricia Neal and a lovely, young ingenue named Grace Kelly were presented during this period. During the 1970s and '80s, summer stock gave way to limited engagement, Star-centered productions. Some of the more popular players to entertain Denver during these later years were Lana Turner, Mickey Rooney, Walter Pidgeon, Caesar Romero and Cloris Leachman.

The venerable, much-loved theater gave it's last performance at the close of the 1991 season, leaving the rich legacy of 100 years of quality entertainment for the people of Denver.

The Trocadero Ballroom — Summer Home of the Big Bands

The Trocadero Ballroom had a reputation almost as legendary as the beautiful Gardens in which it sat. Begun in 1917, it always maintained a strict dress and behavior code. In fact, one night a young Denver Belle was reprimanded for dancing cheek-to-cheek — she was Mamie Doud, who would later marry a West Point graduate named Dwight D. Eisenhower. Admission in those early years was five cents.

In the 1930s, the Big Band Era was approaching its zenith and the Trocadero's expansive layout and extravagant decor made it an ideal setting. Famous orchestras book into 'The Troc' included both Dorseys, Harry James, Gene Krupa, Wayne King, Lawrence Welk, Ozzie Nelson, Stan Kenton, Guy Lombardo, Eddy Howard, Les Brown, Bob Crosby and Dick Jurgens just to mention a few. Benny Goodman performed here but was fired when Denver audiences couldn't yet embrace his unique 'swing' sound and refused to dance.

Interior of the Trocadero Ballroom

The Trocadero was the 'in' place to go for a night on the town for years, and many romances took root on that famous dance floor. During the War years, uniformed GI's were always admitted free. The Ballroom was reluctantly demolished in 1975. But the music… and the memories live on.

. . . Into the 21st Century!

After 104 years of entertaining guests in its northwest Denver location, Elitch Gardens opened the 1995 season in the Central Platte River Valley in the heart of downtown Denver. The move took more than seven years of planning, a passage of the voter-approved $14 million bond issue and the development of a $95 million financing package, consisting of both public and private support. Elitch Gardens Denver's oldest and largest amusement park finally has a new home.

The new Park is nearly two and a half times larger than the old Elitch's, and features the best of the old Park along with spectacular attractions designed and built in the tradition of America's finest amusement parks.

One of the Park's premier rides is Twister II, built in the style and design of Elitch's original Twister. The Twister II is higher, faster and more exciting than any coaster in Elitch Gardens' history. The Park also features other premier rides, including the giant swing known as The Avalanche, a white water rafting ride called Disaster Canyon, and the Sidewinder, a steel coaster with an incredible, full 360 degree loop. Elitch Gardens also has the city's only observation deck at the top of the 250 foot high Total tower. Elitch's boasts of 38 rides, including an area for little adventurers called Kiddieland.

Keeping memories alive has been a primary goal for Elitch Gardens during the move to its new location. Part of this effort included the restoration of the magnificent, 1928 Carousel, which is the focal point of the Entry Pavilion at the new Park. It was made by the Philadelphia Toboggan Company, and took their master craftsmen three years to carve by hand. It con-

tains 67 horses, each one different, and two intricately carved chariots.

The new Park also features the beautiful gardens that made Elitch's famous. Under the direction of master gardener, Karyl Wilson, the new gardens have been designed to include the unique topiary carousel horses that have been intriguing and delighting Elitch's guests for many years. More than 50,000 flowers and 2,000 trees have been planted in the new gardens, and the famous Elitch floral clock now makes its home at the base of the Big Wheel near the front of the Park.

Elitch Gardens remains one of Denver's highlights. The new location in the Central Platte River Valley has helped to revitalize the lower downtown area, which continues to flourish. Elitch Gardens, which is already responsible for many of Denver's most treasured memories continues that tradition as it marches eagerly into its second hundred years offering a place where dreams come true — if only for a day.

Panorama of Elitch Park and the Denver skyline.

BONFILS BLOOD CENTER

A Community Center for Transfusion Medicine

Every day, more than 100 lives are saved, improved or extended thanks to the expertise of the Bonfils Blood Center and the generosity of its volunteer blood donors.

Bonfils is a priceless community resource, satisfying more than 70 percent of Colorado's blood-supply needs. Colorado residents trust Bonfils to make sure that the state's blood supply is sufficient, safe and available whenever and wherever it is needed.

To ensure sufficiency, Bonfils conducts regular well-publicized blood drives — and special appeals in times of shortage. Each week, Bonfils recruits, collects, tests, prepares and distributes more than 2,000 units of blood products — more than 100,000 units of whole blood a year. Blood is processed and tested 24 hours a day, seven days a week.

More than 1,000 Colorado businesses, churches, schools and community groups conduct volunteer blood drives in conjunction with Bonfils each year, generating half of the center's blood supply. Corporations such as Rocky Flats, Coors, Colorado State University, Kodak, the University of Colorado and AT&T also host major blood donation programs.

To ensure safety, Bonfils accepts only voluntary blood donations and enforces rigorous standards and procedures. A series of eleven tests is performed on every single unit of blood. Bonfils also offers the options of autologous blood donation, in which a person anticipating surgery can donate his or her own blood ahead of time, and directed donations, in which blood is donated to a specific patient.

In 1995, Bonfils was the first community blood

Bonfils initiated its mission to the community in 1943, when it was founded as the Belle Bonfils Memorial Blood Bank in donated space at Colorado General Hospital.

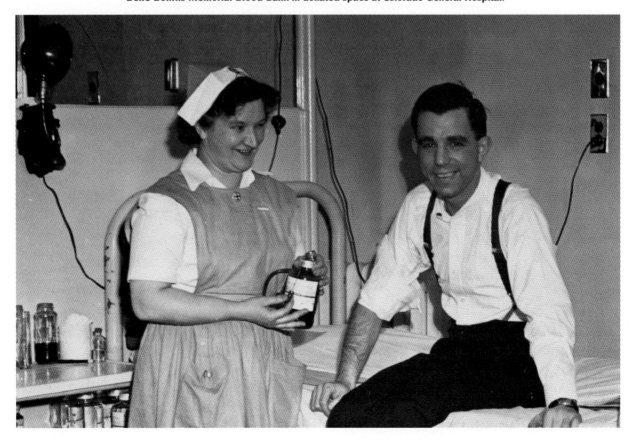

center in the country to receive accreditation by the Commission on Laboratory Accreditation of the College of American Pathologists.

To ensure access, Bonfils employs a computerized tracking system to make sure that small community hospitals in rural areas of the state enjoy the same access to blood products as major trauma centers in Denver. This system is so sophisticated that only one percent of the blood products collected by Bonfils goes unused.

Bonfils is the primary source of blood products for 89 hospitals and health-care facilities throughout the state. In addition, it supplies all Colorado hospitals on a supplemental, special need or emergency basis. It is also part of a national network that provides blood in case of national emergencies.

In recognition of its businesslike attention to detail, Bonfils was named 1995 Healthcare Company of the year by the Colorado Association of Commerce and Industry — the only non-profit organization to be recognized.

Bonfils Blood Center's mission centers on excellence in providing transfusion medicine services, research and education. Primary among its services, of course, is the provision of whole blood, platelets and plasma.

Platelets, which are needed for clotting, are frequently transfused to patients with cancer, leukemia and other life-threatening diseases. They are also needed by many patients undergoing chemotherapy and marrow transplants. In 1989, Bonfils became home to the Colorado Marrow Donor Program.

Plasma, which replaces lost body fluids and proteins, is frequently used to treat burn victims, patients requiring multiple transfusions and patients receiving organ transplants. Both platelets and plasma are collected via a special process called apheresis.

About 60 percent of Bonfils' blood products is used as an essential component of scheduled surgeries and therapies. The remaining 40 percent is used to save the lives of trauma victims.

The center offers a number of specialized services,

including the identification of specially-matched blood donors for Colorado's 300 sickle cell anemia patients. In addition, Bonfils operates one of only 54 reference laboratories certified by the American Association of Blood Banks, which enables the center to identify and provide rare blood units throughout the region.

In 1995, Bonfils consolidated its operations at a 150,000-square-foot state-of-the-art facility at the former Lowry Air Force Base.

Researchers at Bonfils are constantly developing new methods and treatments to expand the field of transfusion medicine. Current research efforts include the study of blood-organ compatibility and the development of new dosing standards that would take into account the differing needs of children, adults and the elderly.

Educational efforts include programs for the community and medical professionals as well as a patient/family advocacy program.

Bonfils Blood Center initiated its mission to the community in 1943, when it was founded as the Belle

Bonfils Memorial Blood Bank. It was sponsored by the Denver Medical Society, the University of Colorado Medical School, the American Red Cross, the city and state health departments, Denver hospitals and a group of community-minded citizens, including Helen G. Bonfils.

Helen Bonfils provided the first financial donation to fund the Blood Center, which was named in memory of her mother, Belle Bonfils. Helen Bonfils was the daughter of Frederick Bonfils, publisher of The Denver Post. Although the private, nonprofit center carries the

Bonfils is a priceless community resource, satisfying more than 70 percent of Colorado's blood-supply needs.

Bonfils name, it is not endowed by the Bonfils family or its foundation — although many people mistakenly think that it is.

The blood bank was originally located in donated space at Colorado General Hospital. In 1954, it relocated to the campus of the University of Colorado School of Medicine. In 1971, reflecting the growing role of transfusion medicine, the blood bank changed its name to the Belle Bonfils Memorial Blood Center.

By the mid-1990s, growing rapidly and pressed for space, Bonfils was operating from a variety of sites around the city. In 1995, Bonfils consolidated its operations at the former Lowry Air Force Base. The center had acquired the former commissary building, which it remodeled to house its new laboratories and headquarters.

Bonfils received the building and approximately 13 acres of land through a Public Benefit Conveyance from the U.S. Government. It undertook a fund-raising drive to pay for remodeling, assessments and capital improvements.

The end result of its effort is a 150,000-square-foot state-of-the-art blood center that reinforces Bonfils' vital role as a major community resource. Bonfils employs 280 people and benefits from the additional services of 52 reliable volunteers.

It is hoped that the new facility will serve as a magnet at Lowry for other biomedical companies and businesses. Bonfils, with its state-of-the-art laboratory capabilities, is considering joint ventures for the development of new blood products.

In 1996, Bonfils acquired Immunological Associates of Denver to build a regional resource for tranfusion medicine and transplantation. These testing capabilities are wide in scope and will further strengthen the position of Bonfils in the health care community.

Bonfils also operates five metropolitan area "walk-in" blood donation centers in the Denver metropolitan area. In addition, it maintains donor centers in Pueblo and Sterling and hosts periodic donor programs in 79 other communities throughout the state.

In 1996, Bonfils is Colorado's only community blood center and is one of 122 community blood centers in the country. A founding member of the American Association of Blood Banks, the Council of Community Blood Centers, and the South Central Association of Blood Banks, it is licensed by the Federal Food and Drug Administration.

Medical director, president and CEO of Bonfils Blood Center is William Dickey, M.D. Daniel Ambruso, M.D. is associate medical director and head of the research department. Thomas Puckett is the organization's administrator and chief operating officer.

In 1994, the Bonfils Blood Center Foundation was created to encourage and manage charitable contributions in support of programs, services, facilities, education and research in transfusion medicine. In addition, the foundation will assist in the promotion of the center's mission and the involvement of community leaders.

For more than half a century, Bonfils Blood Center has served as a responsible steward for Colorado's precious blood supply.

UNIVERSITY OF DENVER

The City of Denver and the University of Denver have literally grown up together. Founded in 1864 by territorial governor John Evans and other city leaders, the University counts more than 90,000 alumni. Today the oldest independent university in the Rocky Mountain West is focused on the future.

The future was on the mind of the University's second chancellor, Henry Buchtel, whose trademark red vest symbolized optimism and ambition at the turn of the century. Inspired by that tradition almost 100 years later, the University's sixteenth chancellor, Daniel L. Ritchie, is widely recognized for his leadership and extensive involvement in Denver's civic life. Like Buchtel, Ritchie wears his red vest to many events to celebrate the institution's progress.

Signs of that progress abound. The largest campaign in the institution's history has raised $127 million of its $150 million goal. A $100 million plan is under way to provide students with the best facilities anywhere. F.W. Olin Hall for undergraduate science education has been completed. Construction of the 400,000-square-foot Daniel L. Ritchie Sports & Wellness Center has begun, and ground will be broken soon for a new home for the Daniels College of Business, the nation's eighth oldest collegiate school of business.

A total renovation of University hall, DU's most historic structure, is finished. Two interconnected buildings will be renovated to house most humanities and social departments. Enrollments are growing. The University has announced its intent to return its Pioneer varsity athletics to NCAA Division I.

The University's size — about 8,700 students — provides a highly personalized education emphasizing values, leadership, a global perspective, and commitment to community through volunteerism. DU's 2,950 undergraduate students enjoy a 13 to 1 student/faculty ratio, one of the lowest in the West. Twelve percent of the undergraduates are international students.

Through special programs, undergraduates can complete both bachelor's and master's degrees in five years. Graduate and professional programs attract about 3,000 students, including those in the Graduate School of International Studies, the oldest such program between the two coast. The remaining 2,750 students are adults in master's degree and certificate programs.

Lifelong education is mores than a motto at DU. The Ricks Center enrolls about 275 gifted children through eighth grade. The University of Denver High School attract motivated students who prefer a small school setting and opportunities to take college courses. The Women's College, with nearly 500 adult women in weekend degree programs, is considered a model. University College has won scores of award for creating quality programs targeted to professional people seeking to improve or change careers.

The University's reputation for cutting-edge volunteer and community service is growing, thanks to the Community Action Program, Graduate School of Social Work, and others. Denver elementary schools, West High School, and children in public housing communities benefit from University students, faculty and staff who share their time and talents as mentors. Internationally, students have worked in rural Mexico, and DU is one of the few American universities to arrange volunteer projects in Croatia and Bosnia.

The future of the city of Denver and the University of Denver will be as intertwined as the past. John Evans and Henry Buchtel would have wanted it that way.

LEFT: Chancellor Daniel L. Ritchie wears the University's trademark red vest.

The Mary Reed Building, originally the University's library and now home to central administrative offices, is a signature building on campus representing a strong tradition in quality higher education.

THE CHILDREN'S HOSPITAL

The idea for a children's hospital in Denver blossomed in 1897, when Dr. Minnie C.T. Love opened a temporary summer tent hospital for infants and children at 18th & Gaylord. In response to the rapidly developing awareness of children's special medical needs, Dr. Love and several other prominent Denver women soon began planning for a permanent hospital. In 1908, supported by influential Denverites including

The Children's Hospital and Training School for nurses, 1910-1917

The Children's Hospital 1997

Thomas Patterson and future senator Lawrence Phipps, The Children's Hospital Association had raised $15,729 to purchase a house at 2221 Downing Street, which had formerly served as the Denver Maternity and Woman's Hospital.

Opened on August 11, 1910, The Children's Hospital was originally planned to serve the needs of 30 patients, with a staff largely comprised of specialists in children's diseases. The first superintendent was an especially talented nurse and administrator named Oca Cushman, who played a major role in the development of the hospital until she retired 45 years later. Mrs. Cushman kept order while allowing the children to be children, lifting their spirits with colorful toys and bright snips of paper that cheerfully decorated the wards. A wing of the hospital was dedicated to her in 1957.

With 291 patients treated during the first year, overcrowding soon became a problem. On February 12, 1917 a new and technically advanced building was constructed at Nineteenth and Downing. Every ward had sterilizing equipment, a kitchen with refrigeration, steam tables and gas for cooking, special bathing areas and steam blanket warmers. Combining a nurturing, sunny environment with the ideals of science and efficiency, The Children's Hospital was fast becoming a model for the future.

By 1920 the new hospital already needed a new wing. The primary benefactor was *The Denver Post* owner Harry C. Tammen, who handed his wife Agnes a check for $100,000 at Christmas for the new wing. Mrs. Tammen had requested this gift instead of the string of pearls Harry had originally intended for her. At the opening ceremony, Harry Tammen dedicated the Agnes Reid Tammen wing of the hospital "For A Child's Sake," which was the hospital's motto for some time. After Harry Tammen's death, Mrs. Tammen devoted much of her life to philanthropy for the hospital, leaving a substantial bequest upon her death which continues to help provide for today's patients.

As dramatic advances in pediatric medicine developed during the ensuing decades, Children's Hospital remained in the forefront. Pioneering efforts included the nation's first and largest outreach program for children with heart problems, the first newborn and pediatric transport system, and the first pediatric after hours triage system for community physicians.

The use of nitric oxide to save newborns with severe lung disorder originated at The Children's Hospital, as did the discovery of toxic shock syndrome.

Today, The Children's Hospital serves a vast geographic region, the only institution of its kind in the northern Rocky Mountain region devoted solely to caring for kids. U.S. *News and World Report* has rated Children's among the nation's top 10 pediatric health care institutions — the only such designation between Chicago and Los Angeles.

Staffed by some of the world's top pediatric specialists, The Children's Hospital has a multitude of achievements to its credit, including one of the largest and most successful pediatric and newborn heart transplant programs in the nation. Specializing in complex care, the hospital's surgical teams perform an average of 400 heart operations each year.

Children's is a national leader in many areas, boasting the region's only pediatric burn unit, Level I Pediatric Trauma Center, pediatric organ and bone marrow transplant program, sickle-cell anemia program, pediatric neurotrauma unit, and the only treatment center for pediatric HIV and Aids, among others. Children's Centers of Excellence care for the majority of the region's pediatric cardiology, surgery, oncology, hematology, neurology, psychiatry, otolaryngology and rehabilitation patients.

The Children's Hospital also oversees a major community outreach program, including school-based clinics, four community care centers, home care and home infusion therapies and a host of family resource information programs. Last year, the hospital recorded more than 200,000 outpatient visits for services such as emergency care, rehabilitation, psychiatry and dentistry.

To provide the best possible care, Children's Hospital has created linkages with primary care doctors, pediatric subspecialists, families and community hospitals. Through affiliation with the University of Colorado Health Sciences Center (UCHSC), the hospital has consolidated pediatric services, concentrated subspecialties, and enhanced teaching and

research. Children's also enjoys the status of serving as the pediatric arm of UCHSC.

The Children's Hospital also works very closely with local, regional and national managed care providers and other health care systems to allow widespread access to services, forging creative partnerships with health maintenance organizations such as Kaiser Permanente. The hospital also negotiates with national insurance carriers to secure specialized care for subscribers' children by competitively pricing health care to reflect the intensity of services. Through these efforts, the Hospital's expertise — both its pediatric specialists and its services — are readily available to primary care physicians and their pediatric patients.

"Improving the health of children through excellence in patient care, education, research and advocacy."

As Children's Hospital approaches its centennial the institution continues to be a strong advocate for children, with a growing focus on outreach and prevention. The hospital continues to be governed and supported by community leaders and partially supported by area citizens through their generous donations.

In today's competitive, profit-driven health care marketplace, the mission of Children's is and has always been to provide outstanding care to improve the health of our children. With continued community support, The Children's Hospital flourishes as a regional source of pride and a specialty center of excellence, delivering world-class health care to our children and their families.

National Jewish Medical and Research Center

In 1999, National Jewish Medical and Research Center will celebrate its centennial in Denver.

National Jewish, a local and national treasure, is the only medical center in the United States devoted entirely to the research and treatment of respiratory and immune system diseases.

National Jewish is the only medical and research center in the United States devoted entirely to respiratory, allergic and immune system diseases, including asthma, tuberculosis, emphysema, severe allergies, AIDS, cancer and auto-immune diseases such as lupus.

BELOW: Founded in 1899, National Jewish is a non-profit institution dedicated to enhancing prevention, treatment and cures through research, and to developing and providing innovative clinical programs for treating patients regardless of age, religion, race or ability to pay.

Science Watch magazine ranks National Jewish as the number one independent immunology research facility in the United States and one of the top ten independent biomedical research institutions in the world. *American Health* magazine lists National Jewish as among "The Best Hospitals in America."

National Jewish's sphere of influence extends far beyond its central Denver campus. Each year, patients come to Denver from all 50 states and many foreign countries. For many of these patients with serious chronic illness, National Jewish is a refuge of last resort.

About 200 physicians and scientists serve on the clinical and research faculty at National Jewish. Twenty-five percent of its clinical faculty was listed in *The Best Doctors in America*, compared with only two percent of practicing physicians nationwide.

In theory, the activities at National Jewish can be divided into the categories of patient care, research and education — although all three overlap in practice.

Each year, patients come to Denver from all 50 states and many foreign countries. For many of these patients, National Jewish is a refuge of last resort.

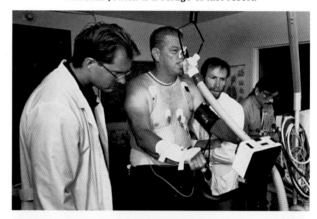

Dr. Robert Murphy, one of about 200 physicians and scientists who serve on the clinical and research faculty at National Jewish, works in the mass spectrometry lab.

National Jewish offers an intense program of disease education and self-management that addresses the medical, psychological, environmental, occupational and nutritional aspects of disease management. Thanks to this highly effective program, the health of these patients typically improves while their medical expenses decrease substantially in the years following their treatment.

In addition, National Jewish is the anchor institution of the National Asthma and Allergy System — a new and highly specialized independent physician association that allies the finest allergy practices in 50 cities for purposes of shared disease management programs, research and contracting with managed care organizations.

In 1995, National Jewish shifted its focus from inpatient to outpatient care. To provide inpatient care, the center has affiliated with Denver Children's Hospital and University Hospital.

The applications of research done at National Jewish are far-reaching. Each year, National Jewish invests $40 million in research that increases the world's knowledge of the genesis and treatment of respiratory and immune system diseases. About two-thirds of this amount comes from competitive research grants. The remainder comes from generous individuals, businesses and foundations.

One indicator of National Jewish's standing as a research facility is the fact that it receives 53 percent of the National Institutes of Health grants it applies for, compared with the 24-percent approval rate of other institutions. Other major supporters of National Jewish are the American Lung Association and the Howard Hughes Foundation.

Thanks to this continuing support over the years, researchers at National Jewish discovered the first effective drug to kill tuberculosis bacteria, the molecule that causes allergic responses, and the gene that causes lupus.

Researchers at National Jewish developed the aerosol bronchodilator for asthma and identified how HIV kills certain T cells. Current research, sponsored by the U.S. Department of Energy, addresses the detection and prevention of lung disease in radiation workers.

In 1995, two scientists from National Jewish were awarded Columbia University's coveted Louisa Gross Horwitz Prize for their research on the body's immune system. More than half of those who receive this prize go on to win the Nobel Prize.

The third facet of the mission at National Jewish is the education of physicians, patients and the general public.

By 1996, the center had trained nearly 500 postdoctoral fellows who went on to practice in 47 states and 17 foreign countries. In addition, the center has trained more than 4,400 other health professionals from throughout the world.

A large percentage of practicing allergists in the United States have been, and continue to be, trained at National Jewish. Also, thousands of physicians and allied health professionals from the United States and around the world participate each year in National Jewish's continuing medical education programs in lung, allergic and immune diseases.

Patient education is also a major component of the intense case management program offered by National Jewish. The education of adolescents, who are more likely to put their health at risk, is the focus of a whole new set of courses.

Also, nearly 100 children are enrolled in the state-funded Kunsberg School, which is located on the National Jewish campus. At the Kunsberg School, children learn to manage their respiratory or immune-system diseases while keeping up with their academics.

Community outreach includes LUNG LINE®, established in 1983, one of the ten best and one of the most popular health hotlines in the nation. National Jewish also offers a home page on the World Wide Web.

National Jewish Medical and Research Center has a long tradition of service to Denver, the nation and the world. With the continued support of its community, National Jewish is well-positioned for a second century of discovery and care.

In 1905, patients at National Jewish often slept outside to enjoy the benefits of fresh air at high altitude.

Columbia Colorado Division

Columbia/HCA Healthcare Corporation is the largest healthcare company in the nation — one that's making healthcare more accessible, efficient and accountable in all the communities it serves. Columbia's 342 hospitals, 570 home health locations and 148 surgery centers are located in Colorado, across the country and even beyond United States borders.

Columbia/HealthONE

Columbia Colorado Division took root in 1994 when Columbia's merger with Galen Health Care, Inc., added Aurora Regional Medical Center, in Aurora, and North Suburban Medical Center, in Thornton, to its growing number of hospitals, other healthcare facilities and services. Less than a year later, Rose Health Care System, including Rose Medical Center, joined the

BELOW: Columbia Rose Medical Center

Denver network. Then, in November 1995, Columbia and HealthONE announced a 50/50 joint venture. The agreement added Presbyterian/ St. Luke's Medical Center, Aurora Presbyterian Hospital and Swedish Medical Center, among other facilities, and allowed HealthONE to remain a not-for-profit entity.

Comprehensive Healthcare Services

Columbia in Colorado offers a comprehensive range of readily accessible healthcare services including five acute care and two specialty hospitals, two health-care plazas, 60 healthcare centers, mental health and rehabilitation services, five outpatient surgery centers, home health services and numerous affiliated programs including clinical outreach to rural areas in Colorado and surrounding states. More than 10,000 employees and some 3,000 affiliated physicians in Colorado are building a patient-oriented system. It blends the most advanced technology and information systems with education, research and compassion to deliver cost-effective, quality healthcare.

Clinical Expertise

The independent physicians associated with Columbia Colorado Division facilities represent all primary care, medical and surgical specialties. Many are involved in clinical research or developing processes to monitor quality. Others serve as faculty in our teaching hospitals, helping train tomorrow's physicians.

Community Service and Contributions

Columbia Colorado Division is responsible for contributing more than $1.4 billion in annual revenue to the state's economy. Columbia is also one of Colorado's largest employers with 10,000 employees. The Division pays some $22 million each year in taxes and earmarks approximately $47 million annually for uncompensated care. Additionally, Columbia Colorado Division provides more than $1 million annually in direct community contributions, supporting a variety of clinical services, not-for-profit organizations and charitable activities.

A New Kind of Healthcare

In Colorado and at Columbia facilities throughout the country, healthcare information is becoming more accessible so patients have the information they need to get well or stay well. Columbia offers national as well as local sites on the Internet; translation services; *One Source*, a free consumer healthcare magazine; and a 1-800-COLUMBIA phone number for physician referral and health services information.

Columbia works to make healthcare more efficient by reducing duplication, combining services and programs, benefiting from national vendor contracts, passing on cost savings to customers, and implementing systems like the Columbia Patient Care System. This computerized data base allows physicians ready access to patient records and links every Columbia facility so records can be transferred instantly to any location.

Columbia is also making healthcare more accountable — developing systems to track the effectiveness of treatment and continually monitoring patient satisfaction. In fact, their latest Joint Commission on Accreditation of Healthcare Organization (JCAHO) scores were 90 or better for all Columbia hospital facilities in Colorado. Additionally, we continue to search for ways to make healthcare more effective by sharing "best practice" administrative and clinical procedures across their local and national networks.

Columbia is making sure that each of their hospitals preserves its unique character and long-standing involvement in its community. For example, Columbia Medical Center of Aurora sponsors a mobile van supplying clinical services to areas of north Aurora. They're also one of the long-standing supporters of the Aurora Gang Task Force. At Columbia Swedish Medical Center, they've responded to gang activity by offering free laser removal of gang-related tattoos to

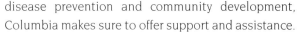

LEFT: Columbia Presbyterian/ St. Luke's Medical Center

BELOW: Columbia North Suburban Medical Center

individuals choosing to leave gangs. At Columbia Rose and Columbia Presbyterian/St. Luke's Medical Centers, they've respectively developed strong mentoring programs with Gove Community and Wyman Elementary Schools. And at Columbia North Suburban Medical Center, they support the Tri-County Health Department and Adams 12 Five Star Schools. From the youngest, oldest and most needy members of their community, to organizations involved with arts, education, sports, minorities, disease prevention and community development, Columbia makes sure to offer support and assistance.

Columbia /HealthONE has the determination and commitment to create a new kind of healthcare — responsive to the business and technological demands of a changing world, sensitive to the needs of individuals, and supportive of the community.

COLUMBIA COLORADO DIVISION — *an enterprise between an affiliate of Columbia/HCA Healthcare Corporation and HealthONE*

Columbia Medical Center of Aurora	Columbia Bethesda Behavioral Health	8 Columbia Senior Healthcare Centers
Columbia Presbyterian/St. Luke's Medical Center	Columbia Healthcare Plaza - Centennial	37 Columbia Neighborhood Healthcare Centers
Columbia Rose Medical Center	Columbia Healthcare Plaza - Highlands Ranch	21 Columbia Rehabilitation Centers
Columbia Swedish Medical Center	Columbia Homecare Colorado	
Columbia Spalding Rehabilitation Hospital	5 Columbia Surgery Centers	

THE DENVER BRONCOS FOOTBALL CLUB

How do you measure the soul of a city?

In Denver, for the better part of three decades, its been by the Broncos.

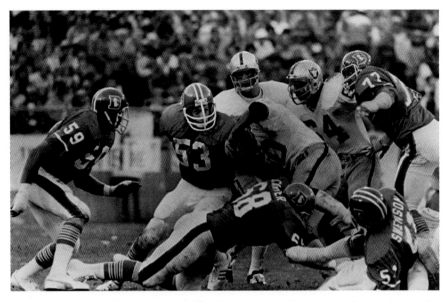

In 1977, the "Orange Crush" defense propelled the Denver Broncos to the team's first Super Bowl game.

From the first nationally televised Monday night game in 1973, through 20 post-season games that include four Super Bowl appearances, the Broncos arguably have provided the Mile High City's primary identity on a national level.

The attachment of Denver's fans with their football team stands out as unusual even in a city that has as strong an affinity for all its teams as does Denver — whether judged by 28 consecutive seasons of sellouts (with the last non-sellout being in 1969), by the highest local television ratings of any NFL city during that time frame, or just by the impact of Broncos wins and losses on Denver's collective Monday-morning psyche.

The term "Broncomania" was coined in response to the genuine fanaticism surrounding pro football in the Mile High City.

Denver's love affair for and support of the Broncos certainly helped spawn the eventual arrival of and fan loyalty to the other professional teams here, but the term "Broncomania" was born out of necessity as a response to the genuine fanaticism surrounding pro football in the Mile High City.

The nation's first truly regional sports franchise, the Broncos were the first major league team to call Denver home, beginning play as a charter member of the new American Football League, with its first sea-son being 1960. The next year, the team was sold to Rocky Mountain Empire Sports — a syndicate head-ed by Gerald and Allan Phipps. In 1965, the Phipps family became sole owner.

Ownership of the Denver Broncos passed to Edgar Kaiser in 1981 and, three years later, to current owner Pat Bowlen. Bowlen, a businessman with interests in oil, gas and real estate and an avid amateur athlete in his own right, is actively involved in the team's day-to-day operations as president and chief executive officer.

Widely praised throughout the National Football League as a dynamic chief executive, during his own-ership Bowlen has stamped the Broncos as a domi-nant team in the AFC West, posting more division titles (five), conference Championship Game appear-ances (four), and Super Bowl appearances (three) than any other division club from 1984-96.

The Denver Broncos have played in Mile High Stadium since their inception. The stadium was orig-inally built in 1948 with a capacity of 18,000 for the city's minor league baseball team, the Denver Bears. Capacity was doubled in 1960 for the Broncos' first season.

In 1967, the Denver Broncos faced a crisis when voters declined a bond issued to construct a new sta-dium. But local fans came to the rescue, forming a non-profit group called the "DOERS," and raising $1.8 million to purchase Bears Stadium from its private owners and present the deed to the city.

The following year, the addition of an upper deck increased capacity to 50,000 and the facility was re-named Denver Mile High Stadium. In 1971, voters approved a $25 million bond issue to expand the stadium to more than 75,000 seats. Now almost 50 years of age, it is the oldest sta-dium in the NFL.

The Denver Broncos played their first winning season in 1973, which was also the year of their first nationally televised game. Since then, the team has served as a lightning rod in helping to focus the attention of the nation and the world on Denver.

In fact, when it snows in Denver during a televised game, calls making reservations at the state's ski resorts go up 50 percent. Televised Bronco games from Denver offer the entire nation incredible vistas of the Rocky Mountains.

An internationally popular team, the Denver Broncos have represented the NFL, the city and the region in five American Bowl games since 1987 — playing in London, Berlin, Barcelona, and twice in Tokyo.

In 1977, a defense composed of five Pro Bowl Players known collectively as the "Orange Crush" propelled the Denver Broncos to the team's first Super Bowl game, validating the faith of the team's loyal and long-suffering fans. In 1983, legendary quarterback John Elway joined the team, the first player taken in that year's NFL draft.

During the 1980s, the Denver Broncos became the only American Football Conference club to appear in

three Super Bowls — 1986, 1987 and 1989. In all, the Broncos have won seven AFC Western Division titles, made five AFC Championship Game appearances, and played in Super Bowls XII, XXI, XXII and XXIV.

The team also earned wild-card playoff berths in 1979, 1983 and 1993.

With four full time staff in the Broncos Community Relations Department, the Broncos are able to extend the work which was started by the Broncos Youth Foundation in the early 1980s. Members of the Broncos staff spend hundreds of hours in the community speaking to area youth as well as bringing Broncos players and alumni to many of these events or school assemblies. In addition, Pat Bowlen has served as chairman for many non-profit events including Colorado Relay Classic which benefits St. Joseph Hospital Foundation. He served as honorary chairman for eleven year with Colorado Special Olympics and has served as a Denver University trustee since 1987.

In 1983, legendary quarterback John Elway joined the team, the first player taken in that year's NFL draft.

The Denver Broncos Football Club dramatically increased its financial impact on the community through the development of The Denver Broncos Charities Fund, a fund of the McCormick Tribune Foundation, in 1993. The Charities Fund enables the Broncos to raise and give away money to qualified non-profit organizations throughout Colorado. Each dollar raised by the Fund is matched by the McCormick Tribune Foundation greatly increasing the Broncos' ability to help the non-profit community. The Denver Broncos Charities Fund supports programs designed to positively impact disadvantaged and at-risk youth. The Fund also has an emphasis on programs devoted to physically or mentally challenged individuals and the hungry and homeless. To date, the Charities Fund has contributed almost $3 million to area non-profits.

Before the Nuggets, before the Rockies, before the Avalanche — the Denver Broncos Football Club was here, helping Denver make the transition from "cow town" to major metropolis.

Denver Broncos players and staff are active in communities throughout the state. Pictured is Terrell Davis.

The Denver Center for the Performing Arts

Denverites have flocked to entertainment extravaganzas since the city was a dusty mining camp on the banks of Cherry Creek. Vaudeville, melodrama, chautauquas and traveling circuses created much-needed diversions from the backbreaking labor that built a metropolis out of prairie mud.

More than a century later, the mud has sprouted a city on the move. Denver offers no apologies for its humble beginnings, embracing them with pride. Dusty wagon trails have given way to freeways, mom-and-pop

Denver Center Theatre Company production of "A Christmas Carol"

stores have been replaced by world-class shopping centers and sun-gilt skyscrapers dramatically complement the snow-capped peaks of the nearby Rockies.

But some things never change. The historic tree-lined banks of Cherry Creek, site of The Denver Center for the Performing Arts (DCPA), still resound with the theatrical fervor that made the city a Mecca for the arts and artists since its earliest days.

The DCPA is one of the largest and best-known arts organizations in the country. At home in the eight-theatre Denver Performing Arts Complex, it produces and presents live theatre, produces feature-length film and television programming, does scientific research on the voice and offers post-graduate theatre education as well as classes for the community.

In this melding of arts, science, technology, education and creativity, the DCPA stands alone among centers of culture.

It grew out of a small and much-loved community theatre — The Bonfils, now called the Lowenstein — at the corner of Elizabeth Street and Colfax Avenue. Helen Bonfils, producer and philanthropist, was a great believer in populist theatre. Many a Denver actor got his or her start at the beloved old Bonfils. Miss Helen, as she was known, was a producing partner with Donald R. Seawell, theatre lawyer, Broadway and London theatrical producer, publisher of *The Denver Post*. Together they embarked on many local, national and international producing ventures.

After Miss Helen's death in 1972, Seawell expanded her dream of a professional arts center in the heart of Denver. As he tells the story, he one day found himself at the corner of 14th and Curtis looking at the old Auditorium Theatre and the four dreary blocks surrounding it: an all-but-abandoned sports arena, a police headquarters in the process of relocating and acres of parking lots.

The arena and police building were scheduled for demolition. Seawell thought this would be an ideal spot for a major performing arts center that would also utilize the existing buildings. He sat on the curb and sketched the plan of what would become The Denver Center for the Performing Arts. Before the day was out, he had secured the approval of his fellow Trustees of the Helen G. Bonfils Foundation and then-Mayor William McNichols.

Today the DCPA, of which Seawell is the chairman, is unrivaled in the country for pushing the envelope of form and function with respect to cultural centers. It has three producing divisions: the Denver Center Theatre Company (DCTC), Denver Center Productions and the Wilbur James Gould Voice Research Center.

The Theatre Company is the largest resident, professional theatre company between Chicago and the West Coast. Under the leadership of Artistic Director Donovan Marley since 1984, the DCTC presents classical and contemporary drama and new plays, many developed in the DCTC's new play program. The Theatre Company houses the National Theatre Conservatory (NTC) — the country's only Congressionally-chartered acting school, which offers a graduate program for aspiring artists — and Denver Center Theatre Academy, an acting school for the community at large.

Denver Center Productions includes Denver Center Attractions (Executive Director Randy Weeks), which produces cabaret theatre and brings Broadway touring shows to Denver; Theatre Productions, which alone or in conjunction with other theatres, develops new productions with an eye to seeing them flourish on America's great stages — and Denver Center Media (Executive Director Dirk Olson), which produces feature films and television specials, commercials and documentaries.

The heartbeat of American theatre has always been its musicals. To ensure the future of this art form, Denver Center Productions has forged an alliance with The Directors Company of New York and its Harold Prince Musical Theatre Program to develop new musicals. Under the guidance of pre-eminent Broadway producer Harold Prince, new works are presented in workshop performances in New York. Subsequently, the most promising efforts are moved to Denver for further development in preparation, ultimately, for the Broadway stage.

Finally, the Wilbur James Gould Voice Research Center, named after the late prominent otolaryngologist, conducts voice workshops and does laboratory research on both the human and the synthetic voice.

But the DCPA is more than a world-class player in the arts and sciences. It is an organization that understands the significance of its role in an economically thriving community. The Center, along with its cultural colleagues in a six-county area, led the charge that established the Scientific and Cultural Facilities District (SCFD) in 1988. The SCFD is a voter-approved one-tenth of one percent of the sales tax that goes to support not-for-profit scientific and cultural facilities along the Front Range. Proceeds from this tax have created one of the liveliest and eco-nomically sound communities in the country.

The impact of the arts, both in terms of the economy and of quality of life issues, is a reality. In substantial and quantifiable ways, the arts in Colorado mean business.

The DCPA's outreach programs touch the lives of thousands of students each year by bringing students into the theatre, often for the first time. If students cannot come to the theatre, the theatre goes to them with annual high school and elementary school tours.

The DCPA also offers school residencies, free matinees of Theatre Company productions, internships, an ushers program and special programming for children and seniors. It relies on its hundreds of volunteers to take the story of the DCPA into the community, help out backstage and in fundraising efforts and to help move the DCPA toward its central goal: ongoing participation in a circle of give and take that con-

The Denver Performing Arts Complex

tributes to the vibrancy of the community and serves to raise the banner of human thought and expression through the arts.

Continuing the march into the 21st century, the DCPA's mission is to widen that circle. The tale of civilization is told in its art. As a new era dawns on the banks of Cherry Creek, the story continues.

DENVER HEALTH

A Public Health Care System Model for the Next Century

Founded on the banks of the Cherry Creek in 1860, Denver Health reflects the historical mission of our nation's medical safety nets. Denver Health meets:

- The special needs of the entire population with services such as trauma care;
- The needs of special populations such as the poor, chronically mentally ill, pregnant teens, persons addicted to alcohol and other substances, victims of violence, the homeless and those with AIDS.

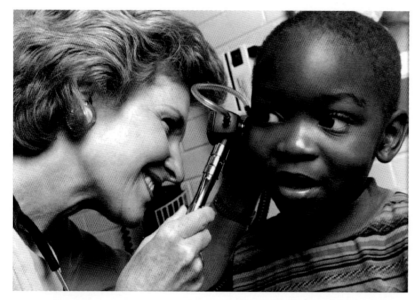

A DHMC pediatrician checks up on a young patient.

To meet these needs, Denver Health integrates acute hospital and emergency care with public and community health to deliver preventive, primary and acute care services. Denver Health owes its philosophy of integration to a former manager in the early 1950s, Dr. Florence Sabin, who is memorialized by a statue in our nation's Capitol.

Multiple components comprise the Denver Health system, which promotes delivery of health care in the least costly, most appropriate setting.

A major component of the Denver Health system is Denver Health Medical Center (DHMC). With 349 licensed beds, DHMC offers a range of inpatient medical and mental health services. DHMC is the location of the Rocky Mountain region's top trauma center for children and adults. It also operates Denver's emergency medical system, paramedic service and one of the nation's most competitive emergency residency training programs.

Community Health is the backbone of the Denver Health system, managing more than 400,000 outpatient visits and serving 20 percent of Denver's population annually. Women delivering babies at DHMC receive prenatal care through one of 11 family health centers — located throughout Denver's medically under-served neighborhoods — or the primary health clinic on the main campus. Adolescents reluctant to seek care in a traditional health center are reached through school-based health centers sponsored jointly by Denver Health, the Denver Public Schools and other agencies.

These primary care sites are linked to an ambulatory care center where hospital-based physicians offer a full array of subspecialty services. Individuals can access urgent care at the hospital's walk-in clinics,

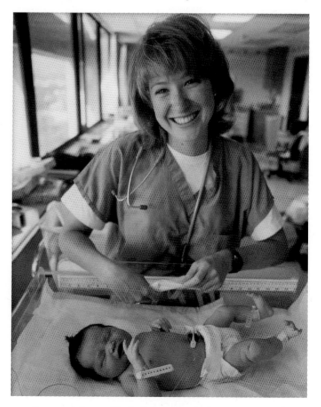

A nurse takes pride in helping a newborn get a good start on life at DHMC.

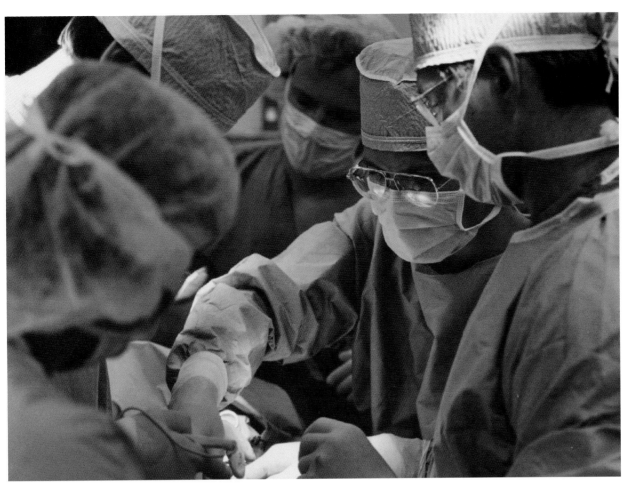

thus reserving the emergency room for more serious emergencies. Integration of these components permits a seamless movement of patients from primary care to specialty care to hospitalization and back to primary care.

Two Denver Health services offer alternatives to expensive emergency department visits or hospitalization. Denver CARES, a 100-bed non-medical facility, provides a safe setting for detoxifying chronic public inebriates. The 24-hour hotline at the Rocky Mountain Poison Center handles most poisoning emergencies by telephone. It also supplies toxicologists who attend to hospital patients and monitor the system's use of pharmaceuticals.

The Public Health Department carries out its traditional charge of monitoring disease. An integral part of Denver Health, this department uses the infrastructure of the hospital and community health system to accomplish disease prevention activities such as immunizations and HIV testing. And, infectious disease physicians in Public Health attend to hospital patients. Integration of these services improves care and lowers costs for serving certain populations of patients such as people living with HIV or AIDS.

The efficiencies derived from Denver Health's integration are matched by the organization and reimbursement of its physicians. Affiliation with the University of Colorado Medical School has ensured recruitment and retention of outstanding physicians, most of whom are faculty members of the medical school. Nearly all Denver Health medical staff trained in America, most are board certified in one discipline and one third of these are certified in more than one discipline. Denver Health has independent house staff programs in emergency and dental medicine and shares house staff with the medical school in all other disciplines.

Denver Health physicians are salaried employees who are highly involved in day-to-day operations. Their salaried status insulates physicians from financial incentives which encourage unnecessary or marginally beneficial services, as reflected in DHMC's low Cesarean section rate.

The integration Dr. Sabin envisioned in the 1950s, along with a high quality physician group, comprise the foundation on which Denver Health has launched strategic initiatives to secure the agency's ability to fulfill its mission well into the next century.

EMILY GRIFFITH OPPORTUNITY SCHOOL

In 1916, when Miss Emily Griffith stood by her roll-top desk on the opening day of her school, the last thing on her mind was becoming a legend. She just hoped some students would show up.

She needn't have worried.

From the day she told the elderly man who came in the door that she would teach him sign painting, even if it wasn't on the schedule, she began the journey that would end by touching the minds and hearts of millions. Her goal was simple — to help people help themselves.

Miss Emily Griffith

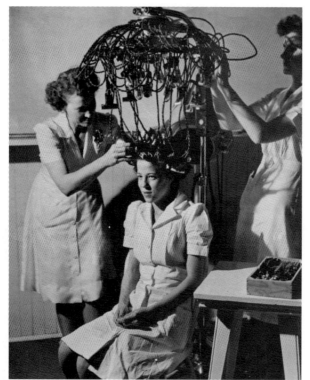

The original home of Emily Griffith Opportunity School was at the old Longfellow School at 13th and Welton Streets.

Early Machine Shop

Mid-century Chemistry

Cosmetology in the '40s

Women in Auto Mechanics during World War I.

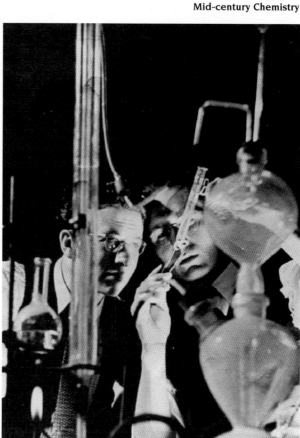

Aircraft Mechanics students keep
up with jet age transportation.

....

Second Chance students seize opportunity for success.

ABOVE: English as
a Second Language
continues to draw
students from
throughout the
world.

Computer training
prepares students
for 21st Century
jobs.

Today, more than 1.3 million students have attended Emily Griffith's school. Although the content of the courses has changed and sophisticated computers now occupy the desks, the philosophy of the school remains the same — to make it possible for people to obtain a quality education and become more productive citizens.

Opportunity School is meeting the challenges presented by the 21st century with the same dedication and enthusiasm for providing excellence in relevant education for Colorado citizens as it has from the beginning.

A significant factor in the development and maintenance of a strong state economy, Opportunity School provides a resource of workers to fill jobs, giving training and retraining in skills currently in demand by business and industry.

Throughout the next century and beyond, Opportunity School will continue as Colorado's benchmark for quality adult education, with Miss Griffith's goals firmly in mind:

....

"We will not accept failure. There is something useful in life that everyone can do if he or she can only find out what it is. The business of Opportunity School is to find that talent, help develop it and stand by until the pupil is safely launched."

Emily Griffith

GENASSIST INCORPORATED

Genassist Incorporated, an "Always Buy Colorado" woman owned and operated genetics company, was created like so many companies in Colorado… out of necessity. Prior to Genassist, the number of patients who had access to genetic information was severely limited. In addition, test results took weeks to return so that the information that the patient received was not timely. With a background in hospital administration, in 1983, Hildegarde S.

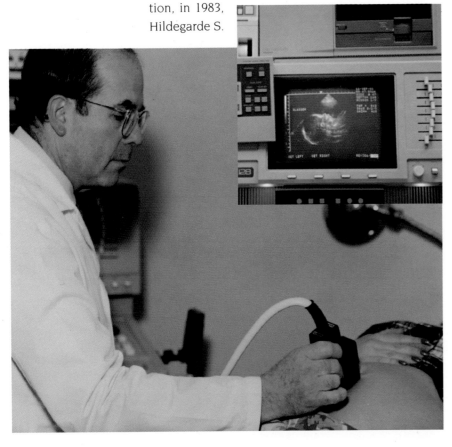

Wexler, the founder and owner, created Genassist Incorporated to ensure that any and all pregnant women in Colorado would be able to receive the necessary genetic services that they required in a reliable, cost-effective, and timely manner.

Since 1983, Genassist Incorporated has been an integral part of the Denver medical community. As the program grew in numbers and in acceptance, Hilde was joined by her husband, Paul Wexler, M.D., as Medical Director, who was already Board Certified in Obstetrics and Gynecology as well as having just completed post-Doctoral work in genetics.

Dr. Wexler has performed extensive work in the expanded applications of ultrasound studies in pregnant women and the use of diagnostic amniocentesis. While working in conjunction with the University of Colorado on pregnant women with Rh disease in the late 1960s, Dr. Wexler took over the amniocentesis portion of the prenatal genetic diagnosis program at the University of Colorado in 1974 and remained in that capacity until 1980 when he opened the Rose Medical Center Prenatal Diagnosis Program.

Dr. Wexler has published more than 30 papers in the field of obstetrics and gynecology. He also served as first author of five chapters and coeditor of a widely received textbook, *Medical Care of the Pregnant Patient.*

Genassist Incorporated provides a service that is designed to assist the patient and the physician to research, record, and review the patient's family history for inherited conditions. Genassist Incorporated's staff includes counselors, genetic associates, and certified technologists who work under Dr. Wexler's direct supervision. They also have access to specialists in all aspects of genetics. This approach allows the patient access to the latest genetic information and testing.

Genassist Incorporated works with hundreds of physicians and most hospitals throughout Colorado as well as hospitals and physicians from other parts of the U.S. and internationally. To help make genetic technology available to all patients, Genassist Incorporated has secured insurance contracts with more than 10,000 companies nationwide including Medicaid, Medicare, and most major HMOs, PPOs, EPOs, and Point of Service plans.

Genassist Incorporated provides a type of "one-stop" shopping for genetic services that patients can use for the following type of needs:
- Prenatal Genetics
- Cancer Genetics
- DNA Probe Genetics and other new genetic services

Within these three areas, specific services that Genassist Incorporated provides include the following:
- Amniocentesis and Early Amniocentesis
- Blood Chromosome Karyotyping
- Bone Marrow Karyotyping
- Female Cancer Evaluations/Surgery
- Chorionic Villus Sampling (CVS)
- DNA Studies
- Emergency Newborn Blood Karyotyping
- Genetic Consultation
- High Risk Pregnancy Evaluations
- Infertility Services
- Leukemic Blood Karyotyping
- Pediatric Genetic Evaluations
- Preconceptional Counseling
- Prenatal Diagnosis Counseling
- Publishing
- Tissue Karyotyping
- Ultrasound – High Level Evaluation

As well as providing these genetic testing services, Genassist Incorporated is a unique company in that they provide coordination for any and all genetic services that a patient may need. Genassist Incorporated uses a network of laboratories to provide the prompt service they feel a patient is entitled to. This unique approach saves the patient time and money while providing an atmosphere of safety during an uncertain time.

The wide breath of work in genetics makes the compilation and use of the emerging information by any single specialty difficult. With the rapid pace with which genetics continues to progress, advancements introduced in one area may not see introduction into other specialties for several years. Genassist Incorporated, with its extensive coordination efforts through the use of its own in-house laboratory as well as other specialty labs throughout the nation, attempts to shorten the lag between the development of newer approaches to medical problems and their applications to families at risk. Also, approaches that appear to have promise for the future and those that currently offer diagnostic and therapeutic options for families and physicians can be explored.

Private family ownership has allowed Genassist Incorporated to provide 1 to 2 percent of all the genetics work performed nationwide each year. Genassist's onsite laboratory is federally licensed and regulated, and is certified by C.A.P. (College of American Pathologists) and C.L.I.A. (Clinical Laboratory Improvement Act of 1988). Its 13-year commitment to zero defects, fastest turnaround times, and user-friendly atmosphere for both patients and doctors has made it an example for other programs to strive for and has

Michael E. Poile, Lab Supervisor, preparing a specimen for chromosome analysis. Credit: Steven M. Crain, Crain Photography

helped put Denver high on the genetics map both nationally and internationally.

The emerging area of family genetic history profiling is another service into which Genassist Incorporated plans to expand. As more people become aware of the role that genetics plays in their personal lives, such as the possibility of a patient or a patient's family member developing certain medical conditions, the need for accurate, cost-effective, and timely genetic services will grow.

St. Mary's Academy

St. Mary's Academy, one of the city's oldest institutions, has educated Denver since 1864.

The first high school diploma awarded in the Colorado Territory was issued in 1875 to a young woman who was graduated from St. Mary's Academy. She later earned a master's degree in an era when few women were college-educated.

Since then, St. Mary's Academy has educated many thousands of young women and men who have contributed to the Denver community in significant ways.

Few people realize that St. Mary's Academy, one of the city's most popular private schools, is also one of its oldest institutions. The school was founded by the Sisters of Loretto in 1864 — only five years after Denver became a city. From the start, St. Mary's Academy accepted students of all faiths and ethnic backgrounds.

Today, St. Mary's Academy is both Catholic and independent, operating in the Loretto tradition of providing an excellent education while fostering a sense of community and service. Through a challenging curriculum, students are encouraged to become life-long learners as well as persons who will make a difference in their communities.

About half of the school's approximately 900 students are Catholic; the remainder represent a variety of other faiths. Students come to St. Mary's Academy from as far south as Castle Rock, as far north as Longmont, as far east as Parker and as far west as Pine. The student population is almost 17 percent minority. Parental involvement is strong.

On the 24-acre University Boulevard campus, the Academy educates girls and boys from pre-kindergarten through grade eight and girls only in grades nine through twelve. An extended-day center offers before- and after-school activities.

St. Mary's Academy also operates an Early Learning Center on a satellite campus at the Denver Tech Center. Established in 1985, the Early Learning Center is among the three percent of Colorado programs accredited by the National Academy of Early Childhood Programs.

At St. Mary's Academy, a challenging academic program is offered in a nurturing atmosphere with emphasis on each individual child's needs. The curriculum includes comprehensive programs in religion and values, language arts, mathematics, social studies, science, foreign language, fine and performing arts, and physical education from the earliest grades. State-of-the-art technology is integrated throughout the curriculum.

At the high school level, St. Mary's Academy provides the state's oldest and largest single-sex program for girls, basing its approach on research which demonstrates that adolescent girls learn best in an environment that is free from distractions and supports their self-confidence. Graduates of SMA

BOTTOM LEFT: Foreign language studies, beginning in pre-kindergarten, give students at St. Mary's Academy an early start in speaking another language.

BOTTOM RIGHT: Performances, concerts and art shows are central to the St. Mary's Academy curriculum.

continue their education at the finest colleges and universities in the country.

With a student-to-faculty ratio of twelve-to-one, classes at St. Mary's Academy are small and personal. The Academy prides itself on the excellence of its teachers and places a high priority on faculty and staff professional development. Academy teachers are frequent presenters at workshops and conferences across the United States.

In a ceremony at the Rose Garden of the White House, St. Mary's Academy Lower School was named a "blue-ribbon" school by the U.S. Department of Education. This designation is intended to spotlight exceptional schools and encourage other schools to strive for similar excellence.

At St. Mary's Academy, spirituality and community are inextricably linked. Throughout the year, students donate their time to child care facilities, residences for the elderly, causes to benefit the homeless and soup kitchens. High school students complete at least 40 hours of community service.

The Academy is a member of the National Association of Independent Schools and is accredited by the Association of Colorado Independent Schools. The high school has been accredited by the North Central Association of Colleges and Schools since 1925.

St. Mary's Academy was founded in 1864 as a boarding and day school for girls by three Sisters of Loretto — Joanna Walsh, Ignatia Mora and Beatriz Maes-Torres — who had journeyed to Denver by mail coach from Santa Fe.

The three women had come to Denver at the invitation of Fr. Joseph Machebeuf, who had asked their order to establish a school that would provide an education-al opportunity for girls and perhaps temper some of the wild spirit of Denver in its post-gold-strike days.

St. Mary's Academy was originally located in a spacious frame house at the corner and 14th Street and California. Five years later, a three-story brick school building was built. By 1884, the school had 100 boarders, 125 day students and 25 teachers.

A new school — which neighbored the home of the legendary Molly Brown — was built at 14th Avenue and Pennsylvania in 1911. In 1952, after 88 years in Downtown Denver, St. Mary's Academy relocated as a day school to University Boulevard — the former estate of A. R. Hickerson, a prominent businessman.

In 1974, a lay board was instituted to govern the Academy while maintaining the spiritual tradition and values of the Sisters of Loretto. The 21-member board is composed of parents, alumnae, business people and members of the Loretto Community.

St. Mary's Academy on University Boulevard includes the lower school, built in 1952; the Hickerson home, which was built in 1947 and houses the middle school; Bonfils Hall, built in 1964 and housing the high school; and the Bishop Evans Sports Center, built in 1985. The campus also includes two playgrounds, a softball diamond, and a large field for soccer, field hockey and lacrosse.

Since 1864, St. Mary's Academy has taught the values of the Loretto tradition to the young people — and future leaders — of Denver.

UPPER LEFT: Girls at St. Mary's Academy High School excel in science and math because classes are designed to meet their particular learning styles.

UPPER RIGHT: From the earliest days of St. Mary's Academy, students took such non-traditional courses as physics, astronomy and moral philosophy.
Credit: Library of the State Historical Society of Colorado.

Children at the Early Learning Center begin the process of age-appropriate learning in a trusting and caring environment.

UNIVERSITY OF COLORADO HEALTH SCIENCES CENTER

Founded more than 100 years ago, the University of Colorado Health Sciences Center remains an active institution in Colorado, turning out accomplished scientists, physicians, nurses, dentists and pharmacists to serve in the world of health care. Each year, campus faculty conduct $160 million worth of research and treat hundreds of thousands of patients.

Since its beginning in 1883 on the University of Colorado Boulder campus, when it consisted of two medical students and two teachers, the CU-Health Sciences Center has grown into a bustling "city within a city" in the heart of Denver.

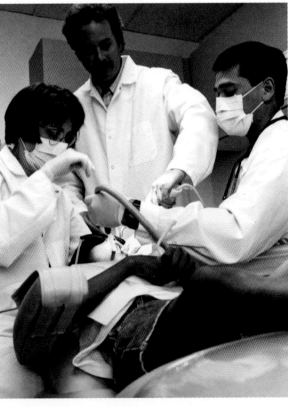

Students learn techniques from School of Dentistry faculty dentists in the Kids in Need of Dentistry (KIND) Clinic at the University of Colorado Health Sciences Center.

Early in the century, a new medical center was built on 17 acres of land located at East Ninth Avenue and Colorado Boulevard that had been donated by Frederick G. Bonfils, then-publisher of The Denver Post. The four-building campus, including Colorado General Hospital, was dedicated in 1925.

In 1975, the medical center became an autonomous campus of the University of Colorado. In 1979, its name was changed to the CU-Health Sciences Center and Colorado General Hospital was renamed University Hospital. In 1991, the hospital became the University of Colorado Hospital Authority.

One of four campuses of the University of Colorado system, the CU-Health Sciences Center today thrives as a $640 million economy which involves more than 10,000 people.

The CU-Health Sciences Center encompasses five schools — the School of Medicine, the School of Nursing, the School of Pharmacy, the School of Dentistry and the Graduate School — and two teaching hospitals, University Hospital and Colorado Psychiatric Hospital, as well as affiliations with numerous local research and treatment institutions.

In 1988, the University of Colorado Cancer Center, housed primarily within the CU School of Medicine, received National Cancer Institute designation. This prestigious research designation allows the CU-Health Sciences Center to undertake the most advanced cancer research and treatment in the Rocky Mountain region.

The educational, research and clinical activities of the state's only academic medical center have enormous value for the citizens of Denver and Colorado. The most critical function is the education of future health professionals in the context of patient care and discovery of new knowledge. However, the campus' contributions to the community extend far beyond this three-part mission of education, research and patient care.

Campus construction and external research funding, for example, annually create local employment opportunities for thousands of Coloradans. The CU-Health Sciences Center's community service programs offer free health-care education to both rural and urban citizens.

Just ten percent of the campus' annual budget comes from state funds. Of the approximately $165 million in construction projects during the past six years at University Hospital and the CU-Health Sciences Center, only six percent was funded by state

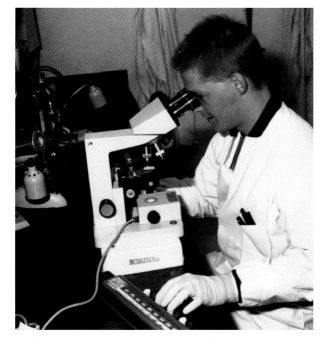

dollars. Yet campus construction has generated an estimated 15,000 jobs.

The CU-Health Sciences Center has a campus community of more than 10,000, including students, medical residents, patients and 5,000 employees of the Health Sciences Center and University Hospital. Payroll runs in excess of $264 million.

The campus also brings in millions of external dollars for research and training which, in turn, generate jobs. Sponsored programs and grants totaled $160 million in 1996. According to a recent U.S. Commerce Department study, 37.7 internal and external jobs are created for each $1 million in National Institutes of Health and National Science Foundation academic research funding. Using this formula to make a calculation, faculty research in 1996 will generate more than 5,000 Colorado jobs.

Since the end of World War II, when biomedical research became a priority of the federal government, the CU-Health Sciences Center has been a leader in advancing human health through research. Many important research discoveries have changed medical education and contributed to the on-going effort to conquer human disease.

Another important role fulfilled by the CU-Health Sciences Center is the treatment of people who become ill or are injured. University Hospital serves a regional population of some six million people. In 1997, about 325,000 visits are expected on an outpatient or emergency basis, and more than 14,000 hos-

pital admissions. Last year, University Hospital provided $55 million in uncompensated care to Coloradans without health insurance.

Providing community service and education to Colorado citizens is another major component of the mission of the CU-Health Sciences Center. Each year, the faculty, students and staff donate time to many programs that bring free medical and health-care information to the public.

In Denver, the CU-Health Sciences Center sponsors many health-related activities and community education lectures and events. The campus also has "adopted" Gove Middle School, its neighbor to the north, providing tutoring, assembly programs, scholarships and a shadowing program.

Particularly popular community education efforts are longevity lectures for older adults and the Mini Med School, a survey course on the sciences of medicine.

The CU-Health Sciences Center's community of doctors, nurses, educators and administrators also travels regularly into rural Colorado to conduct formal outreach programs as well as informal, smaller, individual contributions to patient care and community education.

Each year, this contribution amounts to millions of dollars in free community services, such as AIDS education, migrant health programs, school-based clinics, free dental care and more.

Education. Research. Patient Care. Community service. For more than 100 years, the University of Colorado Health Sciences Center has been serving this mission for Denver and the Rocky Mountain West.

The bridge crossing Ninth Avenue in Denver symbolizes the transfer of medical research from the science lab to the patient bedside at the region's only academic medical center.

VISITING NURSE ASSOCIATION

One hundred years ago, the Visiting Nurse Association was providing home health services to Denver's sick poor — with one nurse.

Today, more than 1,000 VNA employees and 1,000 VNA volunteers provide exceptional home health care and support services to individuals and families along the Front Range.

Unlike most home-healthcare providers in the state, VNA remains a non-profit organization that belongs to the community. Charity cases account for about ten percent of the organization's work; the rest is funded by Medicare, Medicaid, insurance companies, various grants and individual private payors.

The Denver VNA is accredited — with commendation — by the Joint Commission on Accreditation of Healthcare Organizations. Through a consortium of county nursing services and home health agencies, the VNA now serves the entire State of Colorado.

Modern technology and training have made sophisticated medical procedures much more portable. Patients who were once confined to hospitals or nursing homes can now be treated at home, much more economically and with greater peace of mind, with the support of regular visits from mobile healthcare providers.

Modern VNA nurses confidently perform complex procedures like IV insertion, intubation, and administration of drugs — even chemotherapy — all in the comfort of a patient's home. In fact, the VNA pioneered home IV care in Denver in 1975.

The VNA also provides in-home services — nursing, therapies, personal care and respite care — for adults and children living with AIDS. It offers the Prelude program to provide aggressive home treatment of patients with life-limiting illnesses. It also offers the Hospice-at-Home program, which has as its goal the comfort of terminally ill clients rather than aggressive treatment.

Today, new mothers and babies are routinely discharged from the hospital 48 hours after delivery. As a result, many insurance companies contract with VNA to provide post-discharge follow-up visits including, when necessary, phototherapy for jaundiced infants.

The VNA also offers home nursing for short-term, acute, and chronic illnesses; bone-marrow and organ transplant care; high-risk pregnancy support; in-home mental health services; medical social work services; durable medical equipment; rehabilitation therapies; pregnant teen support; the Health Watch personal response system; and personal care/homemaker assistance.

VNA outreach programs include "Serving Seniors" wellness clinics for older adults, occupational health services for business and industry, flu clinics for the general public and corporate employees, and physical exams for camp- and school-bound children.

The Denver VNA was founded by volunteers; volunteers continue to play an important role in the organization today, participating in friendly visiting, peer visiting, respite care, Hospice-at-Home care, telephone reassurance, clinic assistance, maternal outreach, AIDS project support, household chores,

More than 100 years ago, the Visiting Nurse Association was bringing comfort to the poor squatters who camped in tents and shanties along Cherry Creek and the Platte River.

Many of those who moved West in search of economic opportunity were indigent by the time they arrived in Denver. An early visiting nurse tends to the foot of an injured miner.

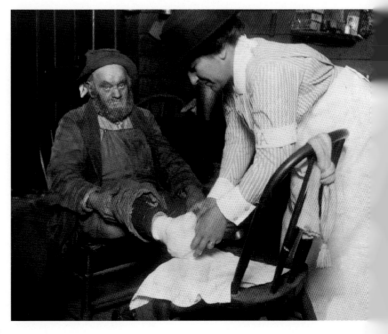

office and clerical work, and special projects. There is a special volunteer program for teens.

The VNA has survived for more than 100 years by adapting its practice to the constantly evolving health-care system. In the 1990s, this means working hand-in-hand with managed care organizations and federally funded health programs to provide the best possible patient service at the lowest possible cost.

Currently, about 50 percent of the VNA's $20.3 million in revenues comes from the work its does for managed care organizations.

Managed-care organizations contract with the VNA because of its exceptional customer service model, which includes around-the-clock availability, case evaluation and case management services, a mental health team and pay-source expertise.

The VNA can trace its history to 1889, when a group of wealthy Denver women established the Denver Flower Mission to bring comfort to the poor squatters who camped in unsanitary tents and shanties along Cherry Creek and the Platte River.

It soon became obvious that these indigent patients, many of whom had moved West in search of economic opportunity, needed much more than flowers, food baskets and religious tracts. In 1890, the Denver Flower Mission hired its first visiting nurse.

Soon thereafter, the group became a charter member of the Associated Charities (today known as the United Way) and reorganized itself as the Visiting Nurse Association — the fifth-oldest VNA in the United States. In 1902, service was broadened to include paying patients, who were charged 25 cents a visit.

Over the years, the VNA did much to improve the quality of life in Denver. In the late 1920s, when Denver had the nation's highest infant mortality rate, home-delivery and child immunization services were started. Nurses also became expert in treating the many tuberculosis patients who came to the city for its favorable climate.

During the Great Depression, the city began paying the VNA for some of its services. In 1948, the VNA and the City and County of Denver entered into an agreement that unified all public health nursing (except public schools) into one agency — the publicly subsidized Visiting Nurse Service. During this time, all visiting nurses were city employees. This relationship lasted until 1984.

In the early 1980s, the home-healthcare field changed dramatically when federal law for the first time allowed reimbursement of for-profit home-healthcare providers. In response, many new for-profit organizations were established and many hospitals established their own home-healthcare divisions. For the first time in its long history, the VNA had tough competition.

In the 1990s, the Denver VNA has successfully met this challenge by re-inventing itself to operate in the competitive environment of managed care — while maintaining its non-profit status and clearly defined community mission.

ABOVE:

Today, home-healthcare providers armed with the latest technology bring exceptional home health care and support services to individuals and families along the Front Range.

LEFT: A speech therapist works with a recovering patient in the comfort of his own home.

THE AURARIA HIGHER EDUCATION CENTER

Home of Community College of Denver, Metropolitan State College of Denver, and the University of Colorado at Denver

On a weekday afternoon at 5:00 pm, when many college campuses are winding down for the day, the Auraria Higher Education Center in downtown Denver starts picking up the pace. Students toting backpacks or briefcases scramble off to class — a downtown office worker taking night classes to get that promotion, a single mother trying to make a better life for her children, a recent high school graduate balancing education and a full time job. From 7 a.m. until 10 p.m. and even on weekends, this commuter campus pulsates with energy and a sense of purpose.

Auraria's non-traditional environment offers students many educational choices. Under a unique arrangement, three separate schools — Community College of Denver, Metropolitan State College of Denver, and the University of Colorado at Denver share space and centralized services on Auraria's 127-acre grounds. Their combined enrollment of more than 33,000 makes this the largest campus in the state.

The Auraria Campus was an urban renewal project that blossomed in the late 1960s on the site of Denver's oldest neighborhood. Blending the old and the new, Auraria reflects the ethnic diversity of the original neighborhood. A former Jewish synagogue, an Hispanic church and a German brewery converted into a student union are among historic

One of the most unusual student unions in the country is a former German brewery built in the 1870s. The Tivoli on the Auraria campus houses restaurants, shops, conference rooms and 12 movie theatres as well as student functions and administrative offices.
Credit: Michael Gamer

landmarks. Juxtaposed with modern buildings, they add architectural flavor, continuity and a visual link with the past.

Community College of Denver

Community College of Denver is the leading point of access for first-time college students from the city and county of Denver, open to all students over age 16 from all educational backgrounds. Many find CCD an advantageous starting point for college or career,

with small classes and an array of academic and personal support programs offered.

Approximately 36 percent of degree seeking students enroll in occupational programs leading to certificates or Associate degrees. More than 60 percent of CCD's Associate of Art and Science graduates transfer to a four-year college, a high percentage among the nation's community colleges. CCD has the highest minority graduation rate (47 percent) among all Colorado higher education institutions.

Metropolitan State College of Denver

Metropolitan State College of Denver is entirely a baccalaureate institution, the largest in the nation, offering majors in 49 fields of its three schools: Business, Professional Studies, and Letters Arts and Sciences. The emphasis at MSCD is on teaching and on meeting students at their level of readiness. The school is open to high school graduates and non-graduates with a GED certificate.

Metro State's classrooms are a rich mixture of age groups, socioeconomic classes, ethnic backgrounds and lifestyles. MSCD takes pride in programs leading to employment, placing considerable emphasis cooperative education and service learning, where students can combine employment or volunteer programs.

University of Colorado at Denver

CU-Denver offers extensive programs, including 29 undergraduate degrees, 43 masters and six doctoral degrees. Three dozen majors lead to baccalaureate degrees in the Colleges of Business and Administration, Engineering and Applied Science, and Liberal Arts and Sciences. The institution places relatively more emphasis on professional and advanced professional programs and upper division and graduate level studies.

Through its New Urban University initiative, CU-Denver views its location in downtown Denver as a fertile ground for free-flow of knowledge between the campus and the community. The institution seeks to link the teaching, research and service of its faculty to urban issues and needs of the state, the nation and the world.

THE UNIVERSITY OF COLORADO AT DENVER

In Colorado's mobile, footloose society, education is prized. Denver boasts the second highest educational level in the country. While the main campus of the University of Colordo has remained in Boulder, extension courses have been offered in Denver since 1912. This tiny Denver campus — run for years by a single full-time faculty member — became the Denver Center in 1957, with authority to grant undergraduate and some graduate degrees.

Full independence came in 1973, when the Denver Center became the Denver Campus of the University of Colorado. More than 10,000 students a year are enrolled at CU-Denver, confirming the need for the new campus.

Then and now the CU-Denver student tended to be unique. The average age is 30, 80 percent are employed, 55 percent are married. Over half the students and many of the faculty are part-time, enabling them to bring work experiences into the classroom.

Between 1973 and 1976, the state built the Auraria Higher Education Center on a downtown campus shared by the University of Colorado at Denver, Metropolitan State College of Denver and the Community College of Denver. Auraria — from the Latin word for gold — has evolved from a gold rush boom town to a booming

campus, the largest in the state with approximately 33,000 students. One out of every five Colorado college students is enrolled at Auraria.

The campus is a unique experiment in higher education; its shared facilities include a library, student center and recreation complex. Each institution maintains a different academic role; CU-Denver is charged with emphasizing upper division and graduate programs at the M.A. and Ph.D. levels.

CU — Denver Finds a Home

After 76 years in recycled downtown office buildings, CU-Denver in 1988 moved into its first, custom-made new home. This $28,000,000, 257,000-square-foot building occupies two full blocks between Speer Boulevard

and Twelfth Street, Larimer and Lawrence streets. Hoover, Berg, Desmond, a Denver architectural firm, designed this Postmodern brick structure with distinctive and generous glass wall atriums. From a five-story frontage facing downtown, the CU-Denver classroom, laboratory and office complex steps down to two stories facing the athletic facilities and library at the heart of the campus. In 1990, the fast-growing CU-Denver also acquired the CU-Denver Building at 14th and Larimer Streets, which houses the university's administrative offices.

CU-Denver offers 30 undergraduate programs, 43 master's degree programs, and five Ph.D. programs through the colleges of Architecture and Planning, Business and Administration, School of Education, Engineering and Applied Science, Liberal Arts and Sciences, and Graduate School of Public Affairs. Ninth Street Historic Park in the center of the campus survives as a reminder that CU-Denver occupies the creek bank where Denver — and Colorado — began. CU-Denver flourishes today on that Auraria site where prospectors found paydirt and founded what is now a metropolis of 2.2 million people. CU in the City welcomes your inquiries and hopes you will become one of the many graduates of Denver's user-friendly urban university.

COBE

A Company With Worldwide Operations

FAR RIGHT: GAMBRO Healthcare - Dialysis system with a patient.

A truly international company, COBE is a world leader in medical equipment systems and dialysis patient services, employing almost 6,000 people in more than twenty countries who work directly for the company to serve the global marketplace. The parent company, COBE Laboratories, Inc., is located in Denver, Colorado, USA and oversees the activities of the three COBE businesses.

Three Global Businesses in one Company

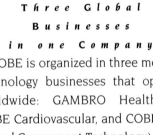

COBE is organized in three medical technology businesses that operate worldwide: GAMBRO Healthcare, COBE Cardiovascular, and COBE BCT (Blood Component Technology). Each business is responsible for conducting its own research, development, and manufacturing of products. Additionally, through its extensive network of clinics, GAMBRO Healthcare provides dialysis care to patients with end stage renal disease. Marketing, sales, and distribution of COBE products are carried out by COBE employees in the USA and through COBE subsidiaries and independent distributors worldwide.

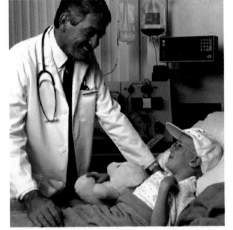

COBE BCT - Spectra™ apheresis system with a patient.

COBE'S Beginnings

COBE's beginnings in 1964 can best be described as humble — supplying custom heart lung tubing packs (used in open heart surgery) from a small garage. Over the years, a series of new product developments and acquisitions have dramatically expanded COBE's markets, products, and service areas.

The company has grown rapidly in global markets and has gained great recognition and respect for its innovative, high-quality, cost-effective products and services.

All of the most important COBE products — membrane oxygenators and heart lung packs for use in cardiovascular surgery, blood separators for blood banks and hospitals, blood salvage equipment, dialy-

COBE Cardiovascular - Integrated perfusion kit with oxygenator and heart lung pack.

sis machines and dialyzers — have been introduced throughout the world.

COBE Today

Today, COBE is active in more than 95 geographical markets and maintains a position at the forefront of medical technology in all businesses as well as delivery of quality dialysis patient care. COBE's operating philosophy is to allocate resources to the following areas:

- Advanced research
- Development of new products, from concept to market introduction
- Efficient manufacturing operations worldwide
- Direct marketing, sales, and distribution operations throughout the world
- Effective delivery of dialysis patient care

COBE provides patients and customers with a specialized blend of technical skills and knowledge. The company employs experts in the fields of clinical applied electronics; electrical, mechanical, and software engineering; chemistry; biology; plastics technology; nephrology; and many other areas of medicine. This expertise contributes to COBE's continuing leadership in medical technology research, development, and patient care.

COBE is committed to serving its customers by designing, manufacturing, and delivering high-quality, cost-effective medical products and dialysis patient services that meet customers' needs.

The COBE Team has been the driving force behind the company's success to date and will continue to guarantee COBE's excellence in the years to come.

Historic Denver, Inc.

If neighbors unite to entertain a group of people — say about 50,000 — protocol suggests a spirited sprucing up of the neighborhood.

When Coors Field opened for business in lower Downtown Denver, Historic Denver, Inc. teamed up with other community leaders to breathe life into the blighted district. HDI, a private organization whose mission is to preserve the city's historic fabric, participated in the stadium's design-review process to instill the old warehouse district's character into the new ballpark.

The 50,249-seat Coors Field, home to the Colorado Rockies Baseball Club, now joins the greatest collection of turn-of-the-century warehouses west of the Mississippi, supporting the resurgence of Lower Downtown (LoDo) and developing new interest in the emerging ballpark neighborhood to the north.

HDI, through its 1,500 members, 35 trustees and several hundred volunteers, serves as the community's voice for historic preservation, neighborhood revitalization and downtown redevelopment. For instance, historic houses in the Capitol Hill neighborhood that are shadowed by the Colorado Capitol once were threatened by commercial high-rises.

"Great mansions were being torn down and replaced with undistinguished apartment buildings," says HDI president Kathleen Brooker. "HDI fought for zoning changes so the houses could accommodate offices. Our supporters helped to save many of those homes."

The advocacy group's flagship landmark is the 107-year-old Molly Brown House Museum, at 13th Avenue and Pennsylvania Street, which hosts over 40,000 visitors annually. Other recent accomplishments include:

- restoration of Thomas Hornsby Ferril's Victorian home at 2123 Downing Street. Now owned by Colorado Center for the Book, the house supports the nonprofit agency's literacy mission. Ferril was Colorado's first poet laureate.
- assisting in the acquisition of a Masonic temple for the Eulipions, an African-American theater group formerly based in the Five Points neighborhood.

- designation of historic districts in LoDo, Larimer Square and 9th Street Historic Park on the Auraria Campus.
- an 11th-hour rescue of the Justina Ford House in Curtis Park. Now home to the Black-American West Museum, the house was facing demolition in 1970 when HDI trustees raised money within 24 hours to halt the wrecking ball. Ford was Colorado's first African-American physician.

Yet Historic Denver is more than bricks and mortar; the organization strives to maintain the integrity and quality of urban landscapes and promotes historic preservation through special events, publications, advocacy and more.

"Most people who live in Denver value its irreplaceable assets such as the beautiful parkways, landmarks and neighborhoods that we protect," Brooker says. "Residents feel strongly that we need to keep the city's character and identity intact. That's our mission at Historic Denver."

Lower Downtown Denver boasts a thriving nightlife and the greatest collection of turn-of-the-century warehouses west of the Mississippi.
Credit: Roger Whitacre

That passion has garnered over 30 awards and recognition as one of the nation's most effective preservation organizations.

"We try to popularize history and encourage people to see their communities with new eyes," Brooker says.

HDI will continue to step to the plate to preserve Denver's prominent legacy.

Fey Concerts

A history of rock music in Colorado and a history of Barry Fey are synonymous, for Barry Fey is rock music in Colorado. By opening The Family Dog, Denver's first and only psychedelic ballroom, Fey brought forth a tidal wave, welcomed by some, scorned by others, of underground music which changed not just the musical taste of Denver, but the lives of countless of her citizens.

Barry Fey in the '90s

Barry Fey and friend in the '70s

The Family Dog opened in September 1967 with Big Brother & The Holding Co. featuring Janis Joplin. In its first month, Denver experienced Big Brother, Quicksilver Messenger Service, The Grateful Dead and Fey's first concert under the banner of Feyline, The Doors with Jim Morrison.

On September 1, 1968, Fey brought his first concert to Red Rocks, Jimi Hendrix and Vanilla Fudge.

For three days in June of 1969, Fey produced Denver's first Pop Festival, featuring Jimi Hendrix, CCR & Iron Butterfly. The festival launched Fey's national reputation.

In November 1969, two acts would shape a good deal of Fey's and Colorado's musical destiny, The Rolling Stones and Crosby, Stills, Nash & Young. CSNY was also Fey's first concert in Salt Lake.

In June 1970, Fey brought what he says is the greatest single show he has ever seen to Mammoth Gardens; The Who.

In December 1970, Fey expanded to Kansas City and St. Louis promoting the Moody Blues.

In July 1971, Fey got a call to go to France to meet with the Stones to plan their 1972 tour. Consequently, in the summer of 1972, Fey did 17 dates with the Stones, followed by 3 shows in Hawaii, in January 1973.

In 1975, Feyline introduced the Red Rocks Summer of Stars. The first year there were six shows. In 1985, there were 55 shows. The Summer of Stars is now recognized as the top music series in the U.S. And Red Rocks is named the top amphitheatre year after year.

In 1978, 1979, and 1980, Fey was named "Promoter of the Year" by Billboard magazine.

In 1979, Fey opened the Rainbow Music Hall. It had 1430 seats with an unbelievable sound system. Acts such as U2, The Police, Van Halen, Tom Petty and John Cougar Mellencamp made their Denver debut on the Rainbow stage.

In 1982, Fey was the first to do a concert in a Third World country with the Jamaican World Music Festival in Montego Bay. It featured the Dead, Jimmy Cliff, Aretha Franklin and Jimmy Buffett.

In 1983, Fey was selected to book the talent for the US Festival in California. It drew 700,000 people. A week later, Fey co-produced the famous "Under A Blood Red Sky" video with U2 at Red Rocks.

In October 1983, Fey produced Denver's first Oldtimers Baseball Game at Mile High drawing 60,000 to see DiMaggio, Aaron, Mays, Mantle and other baseball greats.

In 1989, Fey saved the bankrupt Denver Symphony Orchestra and created the Colorado Symphony Orchestra which is now thriving, and in 1995, Fey Concert Company and partner MCA Concerts kept the wrecking ball from the Historic Paramount.

Today, Fey Concerts produces 250–300 concerts annually in the Southwest U.S. grossing as high as 60 million in one year.

ST. ANNE'S EPISCOPAL SCHOOL

In 1931, a group of Episcopal Sisters from the order of St. Anne, which had recently relocated in Denver from New England, started a convalescent home for children with polio, tuberculosis, and other long-term childhood diseases. The original property, once a farm, was given to the Sisters by the Junior League.

In the fall of 1950, a school was started by Sister Irene for children in need in the community, and by the end of the first year, there were over thirty students enrolled in the kindergarten. In the early years, the focus was on children with learning disabilities, yet by the middle for the 1970s, the school had become a mainstream, independent school. The Sisters remained active in the governance of the school, and a Board of Trustees of parents and local leaders was established.

In 1988, the Sisters deeded the pastoral campus near the corner of Yale and University to the school, thereby ensuring its independence and securing its future. Mother Irene, the school's founder, taught reading to small groups of children until she was ninety-three and read to many classes until she died in 1996 at the age of ninety-six.

The school has remained true to its mission of caring for children of many different talents and abilities. The legacy of doing good works for the community, which was the hallmark of the Order, is still strong and vital to the culture of the school.

Today St. Anne's has 420 students from Preschool through Grade Eight and a faculty and staff of sixty-eight. Its nine-acre campus is enhanced by innumerable gardens — another legacy of the Sisters. The academic program is indeed a rigorous one, yet the first goal in the school's mission is to ensure that its graduates are active, kind and compassionate citizens of the greater community.

Outreach efforts are plentiful, and the arts and athletic programs are crucial to the overall education received by the children. St. Anne's is committed to making this experience available to children from a wide variety of backgrounds. The school is accredited by the Association of Colorado Independent Schools and the National Association of Independent Schools, and is a member of the National Association of Episcopal Schools and the Educational Record Bureau.

Regis Jesuit High School

The student body of Regis Jesuit High School, rich in spirit and tradition, gather together for a pep-rally.

Regis Jesuit High School is a Catholic college preparatory high school for young men. The goal of Regis is to form "Men for Others": men of competence, conscience, and compassion. This educational community provides a student-centered environment in which each individual achieves academic excellence and develops social and cultural skills that are reflective of the world's cultural diversity. Moreover, Regis aims to form students who strive for excellence in all their endeavors and who are leaders in service, in imitation of Christ Jesus.

The chapel, which is the focal point of the campus, reflects the strong Jesuit and Catholic heritage of Regis.

Regis traces its origins to the College of the Sacred Heart, which was founded in 1877 in Las Vegas, New Mexico, by Jesuits from Naples, Italy. In 1884, the Jesuits opened a second school in Morrison, Colorado. Four years later, the Las Vegas and Morrison schools were merged into Regis College and moved to West 52nd and Lowell Boulevard in Denver. In 1921, the high school and college were formally separated into two distinct entities, and in 1979, they became separate corporations. With the completion of a new high school building on the college campus in 1984, Regis Jesuit High School moved out of the Regis University facilities. Regis was one of sixty-five private schools selected in a nationwide competition and the only senior high

school in Colorado to receive the Exemplary Private School Award in 1985. On September 16, 1989, the cornerstone was laid for the new campus in Aurora, and classes began in this location in September of 1990. In January 1997, Regis purchased thirty-five additional acres at this site to serve the growing needs of the school. Future plans include a fine arts center, additional classrooms, a swimming pool, and athletic fields.

Over ninety-eight percent of Regis graduates continue their education at leading colleges and universities across the nation. Regis has had over fifty National Merit Semifinalists and commended students in the last five years, and counts among its graduates men who are prominent in the fields of medicine, law, business, engineering, politics, the arts, and public service.

Education at Regis strives to develop the entire person — mind, spirit, and body. Thus, in addition to a challenging academic curriculum that includes col-

Regis students take active roles of planning and participating in all-school celebrations like this one held on the Regis Jesuit High School campus.

lege credit courses, Regis offers its students the opportunity to exercise and learn leadership, sportsmanship, loyalty, and self-discipline through participation in eleven interscholastic athletic programs and thirty-three student clubs. The pastoral and service programs aid students in their spiritual growth, as each student participates in a yearly retreat and service project.

Regis is proud of its alumni and their accomplishments, and is confident about graduating leaders for the future: "Tradition Touching Tomorrow!"

REGIS UNIVERSITY

Founded in 1877, Regis University is proud of the Jesuit roots which promote the mission of developing leaders in the service of others. Today Regis University LIVES its mission which states, in part, *"Regis University educates men and women of **all** ages to take leadership roles and to make a positive impact in a changing society ... We encourage the continual search for truth, values and a just existence. Throughout this process, we examine and attempt to answer the fundamental question: **'How ought we to live?'"***

Regis University is comprised of three schools: **Regis College**, the **School for Professional Studies** and the **School for Health Care Professions.**

- Regis College is a traditional liberal arts college, focusing on students 18 - 23 years old, and affording full campus life experiences. Thirty-two majors are available. Students may also design their own program through the interdisciplinary and flexible major plans.
- The School for Professional Studies is tailored to meet the needs of the working adult, offering Bachelor's or Master's Degrees through evening accelerated courses (five to eight weeks in length), guided independent study, or televised/video classes. Over 40 majors (including individualized courses of study) are available through the undergraduate program, and six graduate programs are offered.

- The School for Health Care Professions includes both undergraduate and graduate studies in Nursing, a Master's Degree in Physical Therapy, and Bachelor's Degrees in Health Information Management and Health Care Administration.

In addition, Regis has partnerships with corporations which afford employees a variety of certificate programs offered in the workplace environment. Prospective public school teachers may complete Colorado or Wyoming teacher licensure. The New Ventures Department has ten "partner schools" in the United States and Puerto Rico, each implementing an adult program fashioned after the Regis model.

Regis programs are accredited by the North Central Association of Colleges and Universities. The University serves approximately 10,000 students each year in its three schools.

The main campus of Regis University is located in North Denver on 90 rolling acres. The University also has twelve satellite campus sites throughout Colorado and Wyoming.

The Society of Jesus (Jesuits) is an international Roman Catholic order of priests and brothers known for its educational work. For four centuries, the Jesuit fathers have been perfecting an educational tradition of academic excellence, values-centered education and service to the community. Regis University is one of 28 Jesuit colleges and universities throughout the United States; it moves toward the next millenium as an innovative educational institution dedicated to meeting the needs of its students, its community and our global society.

U. S. *News & World Report* rates Regis as a Top Tier Western University.

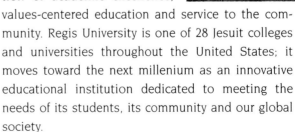

Colorado Brunswick Recreation Centers

The story of Brunswick in the Denver Metro area can first be traced back to John Brunswick, a Swiss immigrant who built his first billiard table in 1845. His legacy spans more than 150 years, from his small Cincinnati firm into today's multinational, diversified Brunswick Corporation.

The acquisition of Colorado bowling centers by Brunswick first occurred in the late 1960s when the bowling boom went bust. Circle lanes in Colorado Springs was the first Colorado bowling establishment operated by Brunswick in the late 1960s. Following Circle Lanes, Brunswick soon released Broadmoor Bowl, Hoffman Heights, and Elitch Lanes, all found within the Denver metropolitan area.

Brunswick Sierra Vista Lanes, located in Wheatridge, Colorado is one of three recreation centers built by BRC in June of 1982.
Credit: Steven Swenson

In the late 1970s, the Bowling Center Operations Division was reorganized into Brunswick Recreation Centers ("BRC"). After a decade of managing bowling centers, BRC decided to build them. In 1977 Brunswick built Heather Ridge Lanes, in Aurora Colorado. Rocky Mountain Lanes, in Westminster, was modeled after Heather Ridge Lanes and built in January of 1979. BRC built Sierra Vista in June of 1982. The three new centers offered state of the art equipment in big, bright, tastefully designed centers. They became the trend setters in the bowling industry.

Brunswick A-2 Pinsetters.
Credit: Steven Swenson

In February 1993, Green Mountain Lanes, in Lakewood Colorado, became a part of the Colorado Brunswick Recreation Centers. The latest acquisition occurred October 29, 1995 when Brunswick took over the lease of Superbowl Lanes, associated with Fun Plex in Littleton Colorado. Currently Brunswick owns and operates 288 lane beds in Colorado. Collectively, they employ more than 350 drug free employees in the Colorado Brunswick Centers.

The Brunswick bowling centers offers the community of Colorado a fun, safe, environment where families, neighbors, friends, newcomers and visitors to Colorado can socialize and bowl in a stress-free environment. Bowling today is for everyone.

As a sport, bowling can be serious or for fun. The recreation centers are places to make new friends. Bowling is fun and wholesome for the whole family. Senior citizens find bowling a relaxing social event, and juniors can earn college scholarships by participating in this sport.

Brunswick's corporate friends use bowling as a great way for their associates to interact, build morale, and have fun. Many companies sponsor employee bowling parties, company tournaments, and charity fund raisers. Bowling is the number one participation sport in the world!

Brunswick has recently added something new, Cosmic Bowling™! Cosmic bowling is a futuristic bowling experience that features a cosmic light show, laser, fog machines, great music, plus glow in the dark bowling lanes, pins and glowing balls! Cosmic Bowling is perfect for company-sponsored parties, organizations, schools and youth groups.

The Brunswick Recreation Centers in Colorado are committed to their communities. Each center is active in charitable fund raisers, such as MDA, the local fire fighter's association, Centikor, school fund raisers, St. Jude's Children Research Hospital, and many more.

Through the past thirty years of operation, Brunswick has developed some criteria for their recreation centers:

We will provide OUR CUSTOMERS courteous, prompt, friendly, high quality service. OUR FACILITIES will be the Cleanest! Our equipment will operate efficiently and reliably. OUR EMPLOYEES will be selected, trained and supported to provide quality customer service. OUR BUSINESS strategy will be to grow as a business. To build a strong organization based upon individual integrity, ultimate customer service and long term probability.

Denver's Emily Griffth Opportunity School offered free training to all who wished to learn,
attracting men, women and boys to this class in automobile repair.

Credit: Denver Public Library

Partners *in* Denver

A Diverse Group of Businesses Make Denver a Leader in Research, Development,

Telecommunications & Technology

Manufacturing and Employment of Technology and Telecommunications Products and Services.

U S WEST

It's a safe bet that Frederick Vaille had no idea of the world class business he was launching when he decided to build a telephone company in Denver.

He had no way of knowing a company offering information, entertainment and telecommunications services — local and long distance, wired and wireless — would grow from his simple idea. Or that the company would expand to create a nationwide and international presence.

In 1878, Henry Wolcott, an old college chum, urged Vaille to come check out Denver's potential as a place to start a business.

Four years out of Harvard, Vaille took up Wolcott's offer and rode the train to the Mile High City.

Denver was a conglomeration of smelter smoke and bright blue skies, outdoor toilets and a world-class opera house, shacks and mansions, unpaved streets and streetcars. Vaille decided a telephone company would fit right in.

Vaille partnered with Henry and Edward Wolcott to form the Denver Telephone Dispatch Company. Vaille returned to Boston to arrange a franchise from the American Bell Telephone Company after 161 adventuresome souls signed up for telephone service. Construction began, and the exchange opened on February 24, 1879, making it one of the world's first 25 exchanges.

This first step to becoming the world's telecommunications center didn't cause much of a stir in the local news media. The Feb. 23, 1879, edition of Denver's *Daily Tribune* described Denver's first telephones as "electrical Punch and Judys" and "galvanic muttering machines."

The American Bell Telephone Company had ultimate control of the Dispatch Company until 1881 when the Colorado Telephone Company was formed.

Henry Wolcott became the first president of Colorado Telephone, with Vaille staying on as general manager until 1884.

Early telephone transmitters shrieked and spewed unearthly sounds. Telephones had one handset that served as both transmitter and receiver, requiring the user to perform with amazing dexterity — alternately talking into and listening from the same device.

Mountain States Telephone & Telegraph Company headquarters building, 931 14th Street, 1929.

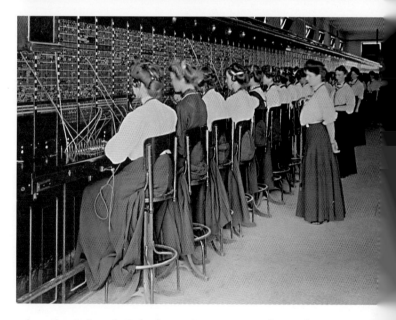

UPPER RIGHT: Mountain States Telephone's first truck, circa 1910. Only 200 Franklin trucks were manufactured and only one was a telephone truck.

LOWER RIGHT: Telephone operators at the Denver Main office in 1912.

Constant investment in better telephones, new switchboards, long-distance lines, and disaster repair took heaps of capital, which American Bell provided by purchasing the local company's stock. Eventually, American Bell and its successor, AT&T, owned the controlling interest in Colorado Telephone.

In 1907, financier J. P. Morgan gained control of AT&T and named Theodore Vail president. Vail is recognized as the father of today's telecommunications because of his extraordinary vision and management. He reorganized the cacophony of little AT&T-controlled telephone companies into the Bell System.

Thus, the Mountain States Telephone & Telegraph Company was born on July 17, 1911, combining Colorado Telephone, Tri-State Telephone and Rocky Mountain Bell Telephone.

A major transmission relay and control center on the nation's first transcontinental telephone line was based in Denver. Vail promised there would be a long-distance line from New York City to San Francisco when the Panama-Pacific Exposition opened in 1914.

Media Group's AirTouch Cellular customers enjoy leading edge wireless service.

The "Transcontinental" was operational on June 11, 1914, but the Exposition wasn't, so the line didn't officially open until Jan. 25, 1915.

In 1927, construction began on Mountain Bell's new dial switching center/corporate headquarters building at 931 14th Street.

U S WEST Dex introduced its White and Yellow Pages on the Internet in 1996.

Only Colorado's best was good enough for the headquarters building. It features 13 murals by Colorado's Allen True, pink granite and interior travertine quarried in Colorado, steel from Pueblo, and white terra cotta exterior cast and fired in Golden.

Denver's first dial service began on May 4, 1929, when 40,000 new "automatic" phones replaced manual phones.

Mountain Bell struggled through the depression with a minimum of layoffs and never missed a dividend. World War II brought labor and material shortages. Denver's operators had to turn in a stub to get a new pencil and telephone installers were required to pick up solder drippings for reuse.

After the war, Mountain Bell invested heavily in repairing and expanding service. In 1965, the Denver metro local calling area became the nation's largest.

On Nov. 20, 1974, the U. S. Department of Justice filed a civil antitrust suit against AT&T, charging the company was a monopoly. No one knew it then, but this was another step in making Denver a world player in telecommunications.

The antitrust case was settled on Jan. 8, 1982. AT&T agreed to divest its operating companies, including Mountain Bell. The Bell System had 18 months to decide the fate of one million employees, and the ownership of 24,000 major buildings, 177,000 motor vehicles, millions of switches and billions of miles of circuits. All without affecting customer service.

In spite of a labor strike, employees pulled it off *ahead of time and under budget.*

On Feb. 19, 1982, AT&T announced the 14-state region served by Mountain Bell, Northwestern Bell and Pacific Northwest Bell would be served by a new Regional Bell Operating Company temporarily called the "Mountain and Plains Company." Jack MacAllister, then president of Northwestern Bell, was named chief executive officer.

The corporation needed a name. Stat! Stock had to be marketed. Stat! A staff had to be assembled. Stat! A headquarters site had to be selected. Stat!

After choosing its name in April 1983, the company adopted a cowboy theme to represent U S WEST's individualistic, tough, hard-working personality. The image helped get its stock favorably considered by Wall Street.

Denver's central location, quality of life, climate, and highly skilled and educated work force combined to make it the perfect choice for U S WEST's new world headquarters.

U S WEST, Inc. was born and the Bell System died at 12:01 a.m., Jan. 1, 1984.

U S WEST began with $15 billion in assets, 73,000

With its local partners in Malaysia, Media Group offers customers telephone, cable tv, wireless and satellite services.

employees, nine million customers, and a service area covering 25 percent of the contiguous United States. Operating revenues were $7.4 billion, with a net income of nearly $950 million.

Just as Denver has grown from a frontier cowtown to a technologically sophisticated, high-growth metroplex, so U S WEST has grown to become a world leader in communications, including a powerful mixture of entertainment, data transmission, wireless services, fiber networks, Internet, telephone and directory services.

Richard McCormick, who became the company's chief executive officer after MacAllister's retirement in 1990, oversees U S WEST's two major units, U S WEST Media Group and U S WEST Communications, which have nearly equal revenue streams.

While the traditional voice traffic represents U S WEST Communications' mainstay, the data portion of this company's business is growing rapidly. Headquartered at 1801 California Street, the company has 11 percent of the nation's sophisticated data services market and plans to offer low-cost data services in 300 cities by year-end 1997.

Today's customers use services such as Caller ID and Voice Messaging to help them manage their lives. Many homes now have more than one phone line — with additional lines serving teenagers, fax machines, personal computers and home-based businesses.

In 1996, Congress passed the landmark Telecommunications Act. The law removed many of the barriers that had separated the telephone and cable television industries, as well as the 1984 court order's separation of local and long-distance services.

Meanwhile, U S WEST Media Group has become one of America's largest broadband communications companies, with domestic and international cable/telephony, wireless and directory and information services.

It probably didn't realize it at the time, but in Nov. 1996, Media Group returned to some of its earliest roots. That's when its subsidiary U S WEST Direct announced a new brand and company name, U S WEST Dex. Because the "Yellow Pages" name was generic, the new, distinctive brand name was developed to help solidify U S WEST's reputation for being "your directory expert" with the most accurate and complete directories.

The history? In 1881, the world's first **real** "yellow pages" directory was issued in Cheyenne by the Wyoming Telephone & Telegraph Company, an early U S WEST ancestor. It seems the printer only had yellow paper available.

U S WEST Dex now publishes directories for more than 300 communities in 14 states.

A 118-year collection of Denver telephone directories reflects Denver's economic and social trends. For example, the 1910 Denver directory contains headings for "Clairvoyants," "Carriage Repositories" and "Vaudeville," while the 1997 Denver book has listings for "Palmists," "Junk Dealers" and "Theaters-stage."

With its merger with Continental Cablevision on Nov. 15, 1996, U S WEST Media Group became the nation's third largest cable company. Through its Time Warner Entertainment alliance, MediaOne properties in Atlanta and its Continental Cablevision properties, Media Group's cable services are available to 26 million American homes in 60 top markets.

Media Group is upgrading its cable networks to offer ultra high-speed Internet access, additional video channels and competitive local phone service.

Under the AirTouch Cellular brand name, Media Group provides cellular telephone service to more than two million customers in Denver and 53 other markets. U S WEST was the first to bring cellular to Denver, the first to offer Denver digital services such as messaging and paging, and among the first to deploy CDMA digital technology, which provides greater call quality, additional privacy and greater network capacity.

On Nov. 13, 1996, Media Group, partnering with AirTouch, Bell Atlantic and NYNEX, introduced a new generation of digital wireless service in 16 major cities across the U.S. through PrimeCo Personal Communications.

Telewest's Network Operations Center employees monitor cable/telephony operations throughout the United Kingdom.

U S WEST International, a unit of the Media Group, has one of the largest cable/telephony and wireless footprints in the world. Its cable/telephony joint ventures have access to more than 20 million households and its wireless ventures hold licenses to reach nearly 200 million potential customers.

Its cable/telephony ventures are in the United Kingdom, the Netherlands, Belgium, the Czech Republic, Japan, Malaysia, Indonesia, Australia, Singapore and Argentina.

Media Group offers wireless communications in the United Kingdom, Hungary, the Czech Republic, Slovakia, Poland, Russia, India and Malaysia.

Thus, U S WEST, Inc.'s corporate staff oversees the operations of the Media Group with $8 billion in sales revenues around the world; and U S WEST Communications with $10 billion in operating revenues in its 14-state serving area. In metropolitan Denver alone, U S WEST entities employ more than 14,000 people.

Not bad for a little phone company from a mining town in the West.

COMMNET CELLULAR INC.

In the West, 90 percent of the population tends to live in about 30 percent of the geography — where the river is (or was), where the railroad is (or was) or where the interstate is.

Arnold C. Pohs

The wireless industry was still in its infancy when six independent telephone companies each invested $25,000 to bring cellular telephone service to some of the most spectacular — and remote — areas of the American West. From that initial $150,000 investment grew CommNet Cellular, one of the fastest growing public companies in the U.S. with $450 million in market capitalization.

The company got its start in 1983, when the government conducted lotteries to distribute the first cellular licenses. While all the hoopla and attention focused on the largest population centers in the country, CommNet's management realized that hundreds of small telephone companies operating in the

Arnold C. Pohs is chairman, president and chief executive officer of CommNet Cellular. Daniel P. Dwyer is executive vice president and chief financial officer.

rural West held valuable licenses but lacked the resources to finance, build and operate a cohesive cellular telephone system.

In fact, skeptics claimed it could not be done, for the challenge to bringing wireless telephone service to these rural communities lies not in countering the competition, but in conquering the terrain.

Incorporated as Colorado Cellular in 1983, the company began negotiating alliances with local telephone companies and erecting cell sites — the large towers that handle and route radio signals for cellular calls. It took three years before the first customer's call was activated in 1986.

Today, 16,000 miles of highway and 334 cell sites bear testimony to the viability of CommNet's managed network, which covers nearly 98 percent of the population in the markets it is licensed to serve. In addition, through its alliances with more than 120 independent telephone companies, CommNet owns interests and/or licenses to provide service in 10 MSA (urban) and 72 RSA (rural) markets.

In 55 of these markets, CommNet has established a contiguous service area in nine states — Colorado, Idaho, Iowa, Montana, New Mexico, North Dakota, South Dakota, Utah and Wyoming. This managed area represents the largest contiguous collection of cellular markets in the country, an ongoing strategy that provides significant economies of scale.

In 1986, the company went public as Cellular Inc., with the NASDAQ National Market symbol CELS. Arnold C. Pohs, previously a consultant to the company, became chief financial officer and subsequently chairman, president and chief executive officer — responsibilities he continues to hold. During its first decade as a public company, CommNet was listed by Inc Magazine as one of America's fastest growing public companies. For the past three years, it has been ranked in the top 15.

While CommNet has evolved and changed its name, its primary focus has remained the same. This constancy of purpose served it well, as the nation's rural areas currently are experiencing a renaissance, outstripping urban areas in both population and job growth.

Founded in 1983, CommNet is one of the nation's fastest growing public companies with $450 million in market capitalization.

Due to the nature of rural life, where work and recreation often puts people at a distance from telephone lines, rural cellular phone usage has skyrocketed. Rural residents routinely use their cellular phones more than their urban counterparts.

In February, 1997, CommNet had 230,000 managed market subscribers, having doubled its number of subscribers in less than two years, while the cellular industry as a whole grew by 40 percent. Customers can add service through CommNet's various sales channels — 32 company-owned stores, small locally owned retailers, large mass retailers such as Radio Shack and Wal-Mart, and a centrally operated telemarketing unit.

Today, CommNet employs more than 550 individuals in its nine-state region, with more than 300 employees at its corporate headquarters in the Denver Tech Center.

CommNet Cellular believes in contributing to the communities with which it does business and encourages its employees to do the same. In Denver, CommNet was the first corporate sponsor of the DTC chapter of Sertoma and is an active supporter of the American Diabetes Association.

Outside Denver, CommNet is involved in a variety of national projects that provide free cellular technology and airtime for public service organizations. The company has donated phones and airtime to the Communities on Phone Patrol and the Domestic Alert Alliance. It has also installed state-of-the-art wireless phone systems in one school in each of its nine states.

CommNet actively supports Native American communities, donating phones and laptop computers to the Tribal health and Addiction Program serving the Flathead Indian Reservation in western Montana and underwriting a new phone system for the Navajo Mountain Boarding School in the Navajo Nation.

Despite CommNet's relatively small size when compared with the nation's telecommunication giants, the company is very active in the Cellular Telecommunications Industry Trade Association. CommNet CEO Arnold C. Pohs, an acknowledged authority on issues facing the wireless industry, is 1997 CTIA chairman.

CommNet Cellular's focus, expertise and pioneer spirit make it ideally suited for continued growth in the coming millennium.

Consolidated Communications Directories

Our History

Shortly after the Civil War, a young man by the name of Iverson A. Lumpkin came to Central Illinois settling in an area that had only the beginnings of a community. He was one of the early pioneers who built homes, started schools, founded churches, and brought industry to the prairie.

Like all pioneers, Dr. Lumpkin, who was one of the areas first dentists, was a visionary. Technology had

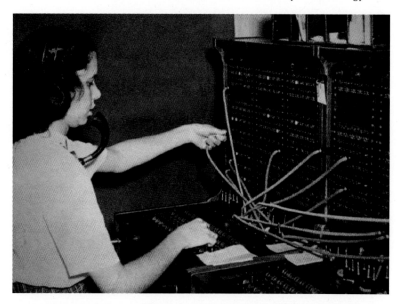

From 175 customers in 1895 to nearly 86,000 today, Illinois Consolidated Telephone Company serves as the foundation for Consolidated Communications Inc., a multi-faceted, highly-diversified telecommunications company which includes Consolidated Communications Directories.

always intrigued him, and he quickly recognized the potential in new inventions like the telephone and later, the automobile. He saw that a communications network encompassing both telephone lines and paved roads was vital to the growth of his community.

By 1894, Dr. Lumpkin was convinced that Alexander Graham Bell's little marvel, would play an important role in the future of Central Illinois and beyond.

On August 10, 1894 the Mattoon Telephone Company, (later to become Illinois Consolidated Telephone Company) was incorporated. A few months later, when the telephone company began service on

April 20, 1895, a total of 175 customers had signed up. To mark the event, Dr. Lumpkin chose 1-7-5 as his phone number.

Building the Foundation

Although a visionary, one wonders if Dr. Lumpkin could have possibly conceived what his small independent telephone company would later become.

In the early years, the company had it's share of struggles and successes as all businesses do. But the company — and it's people — persevered and continued to grow. From those first 175 customers in Mattoon, Illinois, to nearly 81,000 customers in 37 exchanges throughout the prairie state.

The foundation was built — and it was a solid one. This was important, because in 1984, monumental changes were happening throughout the telecommunications industry and the company.

This watershed year saw the break-up of the Bell system and the formation of Consolidated Communications Inc (CCI), with Richard A. Lumpkin as President. He was the fourth generation to join the business and serves as the corporations Chairman today.

With Illinois Consolidated Telephone Company at it's nucleus, CCI established a number of telecommunications subsidiaries, providing a range of products and services including: telemarketing, business systems, cellular phones, paging, operator services, long distance service, fiber optic networking, and telephone directory publishing.

Consolidated Communications Directories

From 4 directories in 1985 to nearly 400 directories today, Consolidated Communications Directories (CCD) is one of the fastest growing publishers in the industry, serving markets in 38 states and the U.S. Virgin Islands.

CCD's corporate offices are located at "the crossroads of America" near the intersect of I-57 and I-70 in Central Illinois. The heartland is the site of Consolidated's 42,000 square feet headquarters which houses all facets of the publishing process. This includes advertising sales to page design and layout. CCD also maintains regional offices in St. Louis, Missouri; Conroe, Texas; Charleston, Illinois; Fairview Heights, Illinois; as well as Denver, Colorado.

Although new to the Denver area, CCD brings with them a rich tradition of quality service and a dedication to excellence in all of its products. Their goal is to become a long-term, well-established business partner in this, their largest directory market. In fact, Denver is the largest independent directory market in the United States.

In 1996, CCD partnered with Centennial Media Corporation (CMC) to publish the 1997 Denver Directory. This new collaboration of efforts has provided Denver area advertisers with an affordable, effective directory advertising alternative, while consumers will see the difference in the quality and completeness of the new phone book. More than 885,000 copies are being printed for distribution in the greater Denver area.

The new directory boasts more than just white and Yellow Pages, however. CCD and CMC have included extensive community events information, full-color advertising options for businesses, and a complete audio information section which allows consumers to select from a variety of topics and receive information over the phone. The new audio information section will also be available via the Internet. More details are available in the front of the 1997 directory.

In addition to Denver, CCD is now the official publisher of the Boulder County Phone Book. A revised distribution area and value added directory features, make this an attractive advertising medium for area business — large or small. Both directories are supported with an extensive media and market development campaign.

Moreover, Consolidated Communications Directories gives back to the communities they serve. It's not enough to just publish a phone book. They get involved with local businesses, organizations, and civic clubs. CCD believes in their products and the people who use them. Their contributions to business and community endeavors echoes the philosophy on which the company was founded.

What's Next?

Consolidated Communications Directories is continually looking to the future, developing new and better ways to communicate the information needed by both business people and consumers. From our printed directories to the cyberspace of the Internet, CCD's quest to find a better way and make a difference never ends — In fact it's our mission.

All NHL logos and marks and all logos and marks of the Colorado AvalancheTM depicted herein are the property of the NHL and Colorado Avalanche and may not be reproduced without the prior written consent of NHL Enterprises, Inc. © 1996 NHL and the Colorado Avalanche, L.L.C.

The Denver Directory is CCD's largest publication and the largest independent directory in the United States.

Consolidated Communications Directories' corporate offices are located in the heart of Illinois in Effingham's high-tech business park; Network Centre.

Make A Difference! We are enterprising people with a youthful spirit building on established values, we seek new ideas to be the best at linking people with products and information. Find a Better Way!

DAVIS AUDIO-VISUAL, INC.

Davis Audio-Visual began in 1948 as a supplier of audio-visual programs for education. Over the past five decades, the company has grown to become a national provider of sophisticated presentation technology and one of Colorado's top 125 privately owned companies.

The company that Ainslee Davis started in the basement of his home now posts annual sales in excess of $17 million, has more than 100 employees and maintains branch offices in eight states throughout the Western United States to provide local support for its customers.

Audio-visual technology has changed dramatically over the years. The 16-mm film projector has been replaced by video projection. Typewritten overhead transparencies have been superseded by computer graphics. Multimedia, which once meant two slide projectors and a cassette tape, now refers to a CD-ROM based computer presentation with animated images and digital sound.

In addition, the Denver metropolitan area has emerged as an important regional center for high-tech businesses as well as the meeting and convention industry. Both of these market segments rely heavily on sophisticated data display and presentation technology. Davis Audio-Visual has capitalized on this trend to become one of the nation's top providers of sophisticated presentation systems.

The one thing that has remained constant over the years, however, is the need for quality audio-visual equipment and skilled professional technicians to support that equipment. Davis Audio-Visual has succeeded by providing a highly trained team of professionals who sell, install, rent and service the complete spectrum of audio-visual equipment.

The Systems Integration Group at Davis Audio-Visual is an exciting new division that designs and installs cutting-edge integrated audio-visual and data display systems for a list of high-profile clients that includes aerospace and defense contractors, military installations, telecommunication companies, government agencies, and industrial, corporate, medical and educational institutions. The Systems Integration Group services both the consultant-specified and the design-build markets.

In 1997, Davis Audio-Visual is working on an extensive presentation system for Lucent Technologies. In the past, the company has designed and installed such systems for AT&T Network Control Center West, Martin Marietta Astronautics Group, US West Communications Network Control Center, MCI, Time Warner

Davis Audio-Visual, now one of Colorado's top 125 privately owned companies, got its start 50 years ago as a supplier of audio-visual programs for education.

Davis Audio-Visual is one of the nation's top providers of sophisticated presentation systems for high-tech businesses and the meeting and convention industry.

Communications, TRACON (at DIA), Jeppesen Sanderson and Lockheed Martin.

Although the Systems Integration Group emphasizes command-and-control applications and presentation, training and corporate boardroom installations, the group is fully committed to a complete range of specialty and integrated systems, including conference rooms, video studios, learning laboratories and study carrels, closed circuit and surveillance systems, and public address systems.

Davis Audio-Visual also sells audio-visual equipment manufactured by more than 150 major brand names and is an authorized factory service center for more than 30 of those manufacturers. The service department includes highly trained and qualified technicians.

In addition to integrated systems and new equipment, Davis Audio-Visual offers an extensive rental division, including hotel services, convention and meeting services and special events.

The Hotel Services Division partners with prestigious hotels to establish, maintain and operate on-site audio-visual departments, providing advanced technology and the most skilled technicians available. The division's long list of clients includes, among others, the recently rebuilt and refurbished Adams Mark Hotel, the Westin Hotel Tabor Center Denver and Copper Mountain Resort.

The Convention and Meeting Services Division and the Special Events Division produce and stage audio-visual presentations for companies and organizations — from pre-show production to post-show finale. Depending on the client's needs, Davis Audio-Visual can produce a single event or design a customized ongoing relationship.

The company's long list of clients includes ABC Sports, NBC Sports, the National Western Stock Show, the City and County of Denver, the State of Colorado, all of Denver's professional sports teams, and a wide variety of country clubs, educational institutions and hospitals. Business clients include Artisoft, J.D. Edwards, Arthur Andersen & Company, AT&T and US West Communcations.

The rental division provides equipment and systems from a multi-million dollar inventory. An editing suite is available for post-production animation, 3D and character generation.

Davis Audio-Visual operates from its 27,000-square-foot Colorado headquarters near Mile High Stadium and maintains branch offices in Wyoming, Utah, Kansas, Texas, California, New Mexico and Arizona. In 1995, the company was purchased by Eric J. Golting, who is currently Chief Executive Officer.

Over the past 50 years, Davis Audio-Visual has grown from a one-man operation to a major regional provider of audio-visual systems, equipment and services. At the same time, the company has maintained lasting relationships with its clients based on quality service, mutual respect and competitive pricing.

IMPRIS

Mining For Gold In The Corporate Database

It's hard to believe that in just a hundred years Denver has gone from a dusty cowtown to a high-tech mecca. The high plains' wide open spaces have been superceded by cyberspace as the place where new frontiers are being explored. Today's cowboys are more likely to be riding 200Mhz multimedia workstations than quarterhorses.

Yes, Denver is once again a boom town. But the gold being mined and refined here in 1997 isn't gold at all. It's information. And nowhere is this historic evolution more apparent than in the virtual hallways of IMPRIS.

IMPRIS defined

We say, "virtual hallways" because IMPRIS is a combination of two well-established companies: Data National Corporation and Digital World, Inc. Data National is a database marketing firm with a 20-year record of delivering "technology-driven, customer-centric, marketing solutions" to Fortune 500 companies. Data National's expertise lies in analyzing a company's database and mining data to extract valuable marketing information. Once the information has been mined, Data National creates efficient, profitable and innovative marketing strategies designed to maintain the loyalty of existing customers and to attract whole legions of new ones.

"The customer database is a corporate asset of immense strategic value," says Don Warriner, CEO of Data National. "And yet, it is often under-utilized as a means of generating new business. We have very powerful analytical tools that help us discover the really valuable information and turn it into new profit centers and revenue streams for our clients."

What's really required, Warriner observes, is a fundamental change in the way a corporation thinks about information. "It's not just this huge, inert mass of stuff lying around on magnetic tapes and hard drives. It's a process that transcends geography and corporate hierarchy. Our job is to manage the process and make it work better."

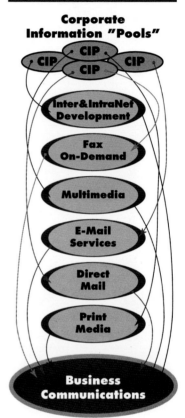

The "Old" Way

Corporate Information "Pools"

Information updates are duplicated; disjointed, unorganized and hard to find.

But one thing is still missing from the picture. *And that's the picture itself.*

Enter Digital World

Don Warriner will be the first to tell you, having the right tools and know-how to mine a customer database and develop innovative marketing solutions is only half of the story. The other, equally vital half has to do with bringing solutions to the market: creating the right communications vehicle, or combination of vehicles, and getting them in front of the right target audience at the right moment.

The IMPRIS Solution

- **Shared Corporate Information**
- **Inter&IntraNet Development**
- **Fax On-Demand**
- **Multimedia**
- **E-Mail Services**
- **Direct Mail**
- **Print Media**
- **Business Communications**

Information updates
are "on-the-fly."
Information posting
is automated,
complete and instant.

"That's where we come in," says Robert Vernon, president of Digital World, the other half of the IMPRIS equation. "Our expertise, as the name suggests, is digital media. And in today's world, that covers a lot of territory."

Print ads, brochures, reports, catalogs, direct mail pieces, multimedia (CD-ROM) programs, kiosk displays, web sites, flash faxes, on-demand faxes, e-mail... if it can be generated digitally (that is, on a computer screen), Robert Vernon's group can create it.

"We give color, shape, sound and dynamic presence to the marketing strategies of IMPRIS," says Vernon. "And, no matter what kind of communications vehicle

it is, we always make it interactive. Whether it's a state-of-the-art web site or a simple printed coupon, we build in a tangible benefit and an opportunity for the target audience to respond in some way. This is how we keep our clients' customers engaged, interested and loyal."

The Result: A New Model for Managing the Unmanageable

But, what happens when you have a rapidly changing database and multiple communications channels that must reflect those changes consistently? Certainly, the conventional model of database management seems inefficient and cumbersome to the task. Individual departments and work groups try to maintain and protect their own data, *and the result is chaos.*

"Usually what happens," says Vernon, "is that the new data is re-keyed every time it goes to a new department or application – like from an updated price bulletin into a new product catalog. Not only is this highly inefficient, it opens the door to countless errors."

What's needed is a new model for database management. Instead of multiple sources of shared information, there is one source. "A singular version of the truth," as Don Warriner describes it. Instead of multiple updates and entries for multiple applications, there is one update that automatically updates all relevant applications. Instead of waiting days or even weeks for new information to make it's way through conventional channels to the marketplace, e-mail and flash-faxes can get the word out in minutes. "For some of our clients," Warriner says, "that can mean the difference literally between success or failure."

Indeed, in the dynamic world of customer database management and communications, IMPRIS will mine your data and help you find the motherlode.

"Remember, there's gold in them thar databases."

....

"The customer database is a corporate asset of immense strategic value, and yet it is often under-utilized as a means of generating new business."

Don Warriner, CEO
Data National Corporation

INFORMATION HANDLING SERVICES GROUP INC.

IHS Group is one of the world's largest information database publishers and a pioneer in the electronic distribution of information. The Company generates more than 90% of its $350 million annual sales from

IHS Group's 150,000 square foot addition located in Inverness Business Park was completed in Spring, 1997.

subscriptions to its information products in electronic formats, ranging from CD-ROM to online access via the Internet.

IHS Group was originally founded to support the technical information needs of engineers. However, under the leadership of its Chairman and CEO,

Michael J. Timbers, the Company has grown from a small Colorado publishing company into a leading international technical, professional, business and consumer information group. Each IHS Group company produces value-added databases of focused information relevant to individual industries or business functions. These authoritative data collections represent timesaving tools that help customers overcome today's information overload.

Englewood, Colorado-based IHS Engineering Products Division, founded in 1959, is the world's largest supplier of engineering-related information. This includes information on all of the standards and specifications with which products must comply before being introduced into the United States and other world markets. Other IHS Engineering databases provide detailed information on industrial products, equipment and components. All databases incorporate vital information required by manufacturers and designers around the world.

Additional companies serving the engineering industry include IHS Group's main British subsidiary, Technical Indexes; Global Engineering Documents and DATA Business Publishing, both located in Englewood, Colorado; and IHS Publishing, based in Libertyville, Illinois.

A number of specialty companies within IHS Group's Regulatory Products Division produce comprehensive

IHS Group connects its customers to the information world with electronic products, solutions and services.

Michael J. Timbers, Chairman and CEO of IHS Group.

databases of laws, rules, and regulations relevant to highly-regulated and compliance-laden industries in both the United States and Europe. These provide senior managers with essential decision support tools in today's increasingly complicated and litigious business environments. This division has its headquarters in Greenwood Village, Colorado with offices located around the United States and in Britain.

Petroconsultants, a Swiss based subsidiary of IHS Group, is the world's leading supplier of information databases and related publications covering oil and gas exploration and production activities outside of the United States and Canada. Its products are used by oil and gas companies to identify attractive drilling locations in more than 200 countries, many of which represent the fastest growing exploration and production markets around the globe.

Another subsidiary of IHS Group, Beilstein Information Systems, based in Germany, maintains the world's largest database of information on organic chemical compounds — an essential reference tool for chemical and pharmaceutical research scientists. This database incorporates all information ever reported on an individual chemical compound's structure, its chemical and physical properties as well as its reactions with other chemicals.

Creative Multimedia Corporation, located in Portland, Oregon, represents IHS Group's only consumer-oriented company and is a leading publisher of multimedia consumer and business information products. Its specialty CD-ROM titles and Internet sites blend consumer and business reference information with related images, audio and video from a wide variety of sources, often matched to a familiar household brand name.

Almost 40 percent of IHS Group's revenues are generated outside of the United States. IHS Group maintains additional operating companies to those listed above in Canada, Mexico, France, Germany, Scandinavia, South Africa, the Middle East, Hong Kong and Australia, as well as a state-of-the-art electronic data conversion facility in India and a worldwide network of distributors.

Together, IHS Group companies employ 2,400 people worldwide. More than 1,000 of these highly qualified technical and professional employees are proud to call Colorado their home. IHS Group is one of Colorado's top 15 private companies and the largest private-sector employer in Douglas County. It is also a top-50 Colorado private-sector employer.

Michael Timbers is confident that IHS Group will continue to enjoy strong growth as a result of new product development, continued geographic expansion and an ongoing group-wide aggressive acquisition program.

The company is currently in the process of expanding its 40-acre main campus in Inverness Business Park. The addition of a new 115,000 square foot office and training facility reflects IHS Group's continuing growth and confidence in its Colorado home base.

IHS Regulatory's CD-ROM products include databases of rules, laws and regulations for specific industries.

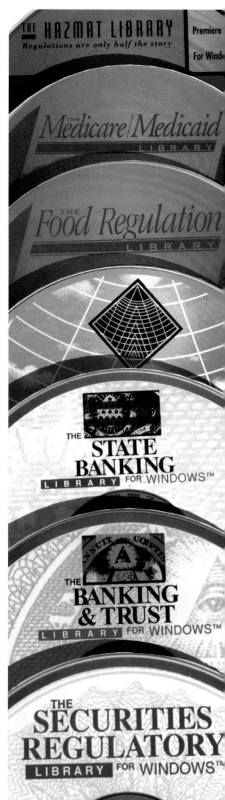

RMES Communications, Inc.

In a scant 20 years, Herman Malone has transformed RMES Communications from a one-man electrical supply company into one of the nation's largest and most respected African-American owned and operated telecommunications firm.

The company was founded in 1976 as Rocky Mountain Electrical Supply to provide electrical supplies to the construction industry. Malone kept the inventory in the garage of his northeast Denver home. After three years, he moved the company to the Denver Growth Center, the small-business "incubator" located in Curtis Park Community.

RMES Founder Herman Malone.
Credit: Michael Van Lowe

In the early '70s, African-American-owned electrical firms were, according to Malone, "totally unheard of." Equally unheard of was equal access to capital bank loans, and Malone was repeatedly thwarted in his numerous attempts to obtain business loans.

Nevertheless, the company moved steadily along until the mid-'80s, when it signed a multi-million dollar, multi-year contract with US West to provide PVC conduit throughout its 14-state Western region. The contract was awarded under its initial "Flagship Program," which was designed to foster links with minority businesses. At the time, the contract was the largest US West had ever awarded to a minority-owned firm.

The contract signaled a shift away from the electrical supply business. The newly-deregulated telecommunications industry was beckoning like a holy grail. In 1989, Malone added a computer division and changed the company's name to RMES Communications to reflect its new emphasis. Two years later, on the strength of its continued expansion and diversification, RMES purchased a 2-acre, 27,000-square-foot warehouse and office facility.

Despite a 3-year extension of the US West contract, RMES fell on hard times when, in 1993, the phone company took their contract elsewhere. RMES was forced to shed 39 of its 60 employees, and Malone endured "a lot of sleepless nights" deliberating over how to stay immune from the industry's volatility.

But RMES rebounded. In 1994, RMES teamed up again with US West, inking a 5-year deal to install and maintain the fiber-optic backbone at the new Denver International Airport (DIA). Everything from phone kiosks to control tower communications is covered in this comprehensive maintenance contract. Another partnership developed with MCI where RMES installed and maintains 310 payphones at DIA. Since 1994, that partnership has evolved to include pre-paid calling cards and more recently, a Mentor/Protégé relationship.

The passage of the Federal Acquisitions Streamlining Act in 1995 gave RMES another enormous boost. The Act mandates that, by the year 2000, the Federal government must conduct all purchases of less than $100,000 electronically, via Electronic Commerce. To streamline and standardize data transfer, and to ensure adequate security, the Department of Defense has certified a small number of value added networks, or VANs, to encrypt and funnel the mountains of data back and forth between hundreds of thousands of small businesses and the various government purchasing agencies.

RMES hired a Vice-President and Chief Operating Officer, Leonard Murray, to head up its newly-formed VAN subsidiary, FACNEX and to facilitate the company's growth and business development. Murray, a specialist in software and communications consulting and former president of the Opportunity Management Group, also supervises RMES' overall marketing efforts.

Today, as one of only 28 VANs in the nation, FAC-NEX is continuing its strong growth in the emerging market of Electronic Commerce/Electronic Data Interchange (EC/EDI) solutions. In addition to linking government buyers with small businesses, FACNEX conducts procurement workshops, and provides EDI-to-FAX services, Internet access and training, and complete EDI-integrated business systems.

In December 1996, RMES was awarded a General Services Administration contract to provide security monitoring services at the Federal Center in Lakewood. By the end of 1997, the scope of the project will be expanded to include electronic monitoring of all Federal buildings west of the Mississippi River. The "Mega Center" will act as the nerve center for the Oklahoma Bombing Trial and the Denver Summit of 8 in 1997.

Other recent contracts include projects with DOE's Western Area Power Administration, the National Park Service, and Eglin Air Force Base to provide video teleconferencing and PBX maintenance services.

Recently, RMES and MCI embarked on the Mentor/Protégé Program with the intent of expanding their network of payphones, and to roll out such contemporary telecommunications tools as pre-paid phone cards, videoconferencing, engineering services and a host of telecommunication applications.

These "enhanced services" also include tele-medicine, electronic security monitoring, inmate services (including, for instance, enabling officials to interrogate prisoners without having to transport them away from correctional facilities), and public phone kiosks featuring built-in PCs, modems, phone card dispensers, and touch-screen technology.

Permeating the company is the belief that creating a wealth of economic opportunities for minorities will reduce social unrest and improve the quality of life in minority communities. Accordingly, RMES contributes substantially to organizations that promote such economic empowerment or that are "entrepreneurially inclined." Its national beneficiaries include the NAACP, the Urban League, and the United Negro College Fund. Malone strongly believes in leading by example. He spends an enormous amount of personal time advising minority and women entrepreneurs and participates in numerous organizations that address the economic and political challenges confronting the African-American community.

In July 1996, Malone was elected Chairman of the 50,000-member National Black Chamber of Commerce, and is the Chairman Emeritus of the Colorado Black Chamber of Commerce. He sits on the boards of Porter Memorial Hospital, the Colorado Payphone Association, the State Financial Services Board, West High School Center for International Studies (CIS) Magnet Program, the Colorado 8(a) Association, and is a former board member of the Greater Denver Local Development Council, and the Colorado Association of Commerce and Industry. Malone has also received many awards over the years including the Martin Luther King "Social Responsibility Award," Colorado Gospel Music Academy's "Outstanding Achievement and Service Award," and the Juanita Ross Gray "Community Service Award."

Len Murray and Herman Malone

In late spring or early summer of 1997, RMES is scheduled to offer FACNEX training seminars for small businesses in more than 100 cities nationwide. Today, RMES stands as one of the nation's premier minority-owned-and-operated provider of value-added telecommunications equipment and service.

Denver Online

The Internet has emerged as an exciting and high-powered new communications medium for businesses interested in marketing themselves, their services and their products. Through the Internet, a small company can establish a global presence without incurring the expense of traditional sales and distribution channels.

Denver Online, owned by Amy and Jeff Luinstra, is a Denver-based Internet service provider that specializes in the design of Web sites and the local area hosting of Web sites for local businesses and community groups.

The Internet is also becoming a rich resource for consumers who see the benefits of electronic shopping and planning. This is especially true in Denver which has, compared with other major American cities, a very high percentage of people on the Internet.

Denver Online got its start as a local content site, serving as a resource for Denver-related issues and technical tips for computer and Internet users. Now, Denver Online is a Denver-based Internet service provider that specializes in the design of Web sites and the local area hosting of Web sites for local businesses and community groups.

By using the word "Denver" in its name, Denver Online attracts a wide range of potential customers who are using Internet search engines to look up information about the city and its many offerings. As a result, Denver Online has also attracted the atten-tion of businesses who want to advertise their products and services in the Denver metropolitan area via the Internet.

Denver Online specializes in the needs of local businesses seeking commercial hosting accounts on a secure server. A "secure" server is one that can safely handle credit-card transactions. Denver Online is also actively marketing its capabilities to businesses around the world that would benefit from advertising in the Denver area.

By offering a wealth of free information about the city in categories like Recreation, Community, Business and Computer, Denver Online attracts many consumer "hits" every day to the site and its advertisers — who can be found in the Denver Online retail sites, including the Online Mall, Classifieds and Newcomer Services.

Who would benefit from Denver Online? A family looking for a fun weekend getaway. A couple planning a visit to Denver for business or pleasure. A woman moving to Denver who needs a job and an apartment. A man who would like to collect more information about a product or service before actually venturing out to buy. A child working on a class project who needs technical help on the computer. Any business trying to reach any of these consumers.

Denver Online is locally owned and operated by Jeff and Amy Luinstra. Jeff had been the operations manager for Apartment Finders International, where he was responsible for coordinating AFI's presence on the Internet. After outsourcing this service for a while, Luinstra realized he could perform it better himself and for less cost to the company.

This site grew in popularity and, in 1996, the Luinstras created Denver Online with AFI as a major client. Although the future of the company is closely linked with Internet growth patterns, Denver Online has targeted other cities for the same kind of full-content hosting service.

Denver Online offers competitive products and services to clients interested in reaching a world-wide market through low-cost electronic communications.

ICG COMMUNICATIONS, INC.

Few who saw the trailer, portable satellite uplink dish and microwave tower back in the late 1980s knew it, but those three lonely structures on a vast open space in southeast Denver were symbolic of a new age in the telecommunications industry.

The site belonged to Teleport Denver Ltd. (TDL), which was constructing a satellite communications facility in Denver's Meridian Business Park that, due to its unique position on the 105th meridian, could reach five continents in a single satellite hop. When completed in 1987, the facility housed eight earth satellite stations.

Instead of leasing expensive circuits from the local exchange carrier serving the Denver area, TDL had decided to build its own fiber-optic connection, which later became the basis for the company's entry into the local exchange telephone network industry. That TDL could build such a network was the result of massive changes in the U.S. telecommunications industry occurring during the same period, which introduced a competitive long-distance industry and created a market for companies that could provide local connectivity.

Competition in the U.S. long-distance phone market proliferated in the mid-1980s, with the first competitors in the local exchange telephone market emerging in cities including New York, Chicago and Washington D.C. TDL management realized the same business opportunity existed in Denver, and in November 1990 began construction on fiber-optic rings along Denver's I-25 business corridor. TDL's Denver network was further aided by the acquisition of an eight-mile fiber network in the Inverness Office Park and the acquisition of Fiber Optics Technologies, Inc. (FOTI), a network systems integration company based in Englewood.

Renamed ICG Communications, Inc. (for IntelCom Group) in 1996, the company continues to take advantage of the ongoing changes in the telecommunications industry. Through expansion and acquisitions in key markets, ICG today offers a wide range of network communications systems, services, and satellite communications through three business units.

ICG Telecom is a leading competitive local exchange carrier serving targeted "cluster regions" in California, Colorado, Texas, the Ohio valley and other regions in the southeastern U.S. ICG also has moved into the burgeoning switched local telephone market created by the sweeping federal law signed in February 1996 that promotes competition and deregulation in every segment of the industry.

Through FOTI, its wholly-owned subsidiary, ICG is a leading supplier of information technology services, offering integrated cabling services for large networks, consulting engineering services for designing enterprise and local area networks, and the support to manage and maintain corporate information technology systems. ICG's Satellite Services division is the dominant provider of service to cruise ships, naval vessels, and private yachts.

The Denver network control center monitors the nationwide ICG network around the clock, assuring maximum "up time" for the network.

ICG's mission is to build a comprehensive telecommunications company that will become the new competitive telephone company in its target markets. Today it is moving forward aggressively to achieve that goal.

STRATICOMM

Creighton Bildstein, founder and President of Straticomm, was working for a small, used telephone equipment company back in 1988. He felt that the owners weren't focused on giving customers what they wanted — bench-tested telephone equipment with a near-new appearance and factory-like warranties at less cost. So, he formed Straticomm to fill that need.

Straticomm specializes in A T & T, Northern Telecom and Rolm brands of equipment because of their reputations for dependability, their large market shares, availability of parts and the large number of

Creighton and Julie Bildstein

technicians able to work on them. Straticomm has provided complete systems, as well as individual phone sets, circuit boards and voice mail systems to companies such as AAA, Barnes & Noble, Blue Cross and Blue Shield, Citicorp, Norwest Banks and Storage Technology.

Straticomm has found that many small- to medium-sized businesses spend unnecessarily on new telephone equipment, when reconditioned equipment is available at a substantial discount. Their exclusive and rigoruos telephone equipment testing

system, Rhino-Test, sets them apart from their competitors. Every piece of Straticomm equipment undergoes this extensive testing procedure, which includes a 48-hour burn-in, comprehensive diagnostics, an additional 24-hour burn-in and another round of tests. This process detects intermittent problems that otherwise are not found.

Straticomm repairs or replaces all damaged equipment. Each phone receives a complete disinfecting, new cords, new or buffed plastics, designation strips and is properly packaged for shipping anywhere in the U.S. or Canada.

Straticomm is a small, successful, family-owned and operated company. Creighton Bildstein is President; his wife, Julie, is Vice President; and Marge Nelson, Julie's mother, is Warehouse Manager. Their ten outstanding and knowledgeable employees are experienced telecommunications professionals committed to customer service through the buying, reconditioning and selling of top-quality telephone equipment. They are the force behind the success and the promise of the continued success of Straticomm.

Straticomm intends to keep up with future developments in the ever-changing telecommunications arena by offering Computer Telephony Integration components and more sophisticated voice mail products. Telecommunications is now changing at a pace commensurate with the computer industry. To keep up with new developments, Creighton Bildstein attends conferences, seminars, trade shows, reads industry periodicals, and networks with the Presidents and CEO's who are "in-the-know."

Straticomm plans future expansion into the area of providing reconditioning products, such as designation strips, handsets, cleaning materials, plastic tops and cords to other reconditioners. These products are expensive and in high demand. Straticomm has joined forces with an entity which produces high-quality reconditioning components at low prices. Offering these new products will require Straticomm to add more positions, which will ultimately benefit the Denver economy.

HI COUNTRY WIRE & TELEPHONE LTD.

The official "mascot" of Hi Country Wire & Telephone Ltd. is a cherry-red 1935 Chevrolet roadster — with a Corvette engine. This car is an appropriate symbol for a company that combines a "classic" approach to service with high-powered product and capabilities.

Prior to the historic break-up of the telephone company in 1983, Denver native Robert Whitfield Sr. was Mountain Bell's district manager in charge of installation and maintenance of business telephone systems and equipment. He had been with Mountain Bell for more than 30 years.

Seeing opportunity in the midst of a crisis, Whitfield, joining together with a few of his colleagues, founded Hi Country Wire & Telephone in 1984. By establishing their own company, these former telephone company employees knew that they could provide their long-time customers with a higher level of service at a lower cost.

All together, the company's 41 employees offer close to 500 years of experience in the telecommunication industry — experience that allows them to generate viable solutions for their customers' telecommunication problems. The company's growth has been fueled almost entirely by the recommendations of current clients.

Initially, Hi Country Wire & Telephone was a small operation composed of experienced workers who provided basic business systems and wiring services.

After a few years, the company welcomed a new wave of employees — including Whitfield's two sons — who guided its expansion into the installation and maintenance of a full range of modern telecommunication

systems of the kind needed by companies that rely on telecommunications for their livelihood.

Today, Hi Country Wire & Telephone is the metropolitan area's fourth-largest provider of telephone systems, equipment and services to business and government. The company posted 1995 sales of $11.5 million.

About three-fourths of the company's revenues come from the business sector; the remainder come from the public sector, including hospitals, school districts and government agencies.

Many of Hi Country Wire & Telephone's 450 clients are located in the northwestern part of metropolitan Denver, although it operates as far north as Wyoming. In addition to its Arvada headquarters, the company maintains offices in Longmont and Durango.

Hi Country Wire & Telephone has been an authorized agent for US West since 1987. It is also an authorized distributor for NorTel Communications and Lucent Technologies. In 1995, the company was recognized as Gold Distributor of the Year for NorTel's cutting-edge Meridian system.

Hi Country Wire & Telephone is active in the communities it serves. In fact, the company belongs to nine chambers of commerce. One of them, the Northwest Metro Chamber of Commerce, named Hi Country Wire & Telephone 1992 small business of the year. The company has supported the Northwest Family YMCA, the Arvada-Jefferson Kiwanis and the Jefferson County Child ID Program.

Hi Country Wire & Telephone is a "classic" telecommunication company that builds and maintains long-lasting relationships with its customers.

Hi Country Wire & Telephone combines a "classic" approach to service with high-powered product and capabilities.

INSTALLATION TELEPHONE SERVICES

Combine hands-on technological knowledge with a desire to provide superior customer service. Add a good dash of entrepreneurial spirit and you have the recipe for success that has made Denver-based Installation Telephone Services a dominant force in the communications systems industry.

It was in 1982 that President and Founder Robert Laureti started ITS in his Louisville, Colo. home. During his 14 years with New Jersey Bell, Mountain Bell, and US West, Laureti saw service for the end user decline. He envisioned a company that would provide better customer service as well as innovative solutions to communications needs.

From left: President, Robert Laureti; Secretary, Loren Laureti and General Manager, Howard Rafsky

Laureti assembled a crew of five installers, and together they sold and installed small telephone systems, wired new construction for telephone and cable TV jacks, and provided home security systems, primarily in the Boulder County area. Loren, his wife, typed invoices and answered phones.

ITS eventually sold its security systems division and moved to a small office in Louisville's Pine Street Plaza. There, the Lauretis concentrated on providing easy-to-use telephone systems and wiring for construction. They set themselves apart from the competition by offering personalized training and a high level of service and attention.

Today, as ITS enters its 15th year with corporate headquarters on Grape Street in Denver, it provides a full range of business communication services, including systems integration and design, voice and data communications products, network solutions, digital telephony products, and computer and cable system services. ITS boasts revenues in excess of $3 million with 19 employees.

In recent years, ITS clients have included the Cherry Creek Shopping Center, where the company installed over two miles of distribution cable in less than two weeks; the cities of Aurora and Northglenn, where ITS provided Fujitsu PBX telephone equipment; and Front Range Community College, where ITS linked several sites in different cities together in a seamless environment. Other projects have taken the ITS crew to various locations across the U.S., including National Parks offices in Michigan and Texas.

ITS's focus is on providing its clients with the best possible solution to address their needs. Its size and entrepreneurial spirit facilitate a "can do" attitude of doing business that projects a sense of flexibility and attention to detail.

"We provide our clients with the best possible choice for a high-quality, cost-effective solution, resulting in the highest degree of price performance," says Laureti. "Because of this, our clients are assured they will receive the very best communications products and services to meet their present and future needs."

With its motto of "Integrated solutions for voice and data communications," ITS enjoys a reputation as a progressive and knowledgeable interconnect company on the cutting edge of technology.

NetworksNOW, Inc.

When Denver area business owners want to diagnose and cure a mysterious disease that is infecting their computers and computer systems, they arrange a house call from "Doctor" Dutch Humbert, owner of NetworksNOW.

Dutch Humbert earned his nickname during his first career as an auto body technician. At that time, there was no damaged vehicle the "Doctor" could not restore to good health.

After putting in a full day at the auto body shop, Humbert taught himself — in the tradition of Lincoln, Edison and the Wright Brothers — everything that there is to know about computers and local area networks. In 1992, he founded NetworksNOW, which he operated for two years from the living room of his apartment.

In 1994, Humbert moved his successful young business into facilities on South Kalamath — where he quickly expanded from 1,000 to 4,000 square feet. Because Humbert and his employees spend so much time there, the company's offices and shop have a home-like feel — including a fully furnished "living room" and a pair of cats, one black and one white, that greet and inspect each visitor.

NetworksNOW — an authorized reseller of Intel products — repairs, upgrades and sells used computers. The company is a full-service tech shop that can perform repairs at the motherboard level.

In addition, the company designs and installs local area networks. NetworksNOW is an authorized and certified provider of POWERLan network software. Local area network computer systems allow a small business' computers to communicate with each other. Recently, the company added Novell and Windows NT software products.

NetworksNOW also offers remote access to the local area networks it designs, which allows off-site individuals to access their business computer system via modem. The company can also use this remote communications system to perform most repairs over the phone.

NetworksNOW offers service contracts to its customers, which range in size from 3- to 50-computer operations. The company is also expanding into the field of on-site computer system administration.

NetworksNOW was also one of the first company's in Denver to offer computer video conferencing, which allows clients to look at each other, talk to each other and exchange data simultaneously — a service made possible by Denver's impressive fiberoptic capabilities.

Dutch Humbert is a member of the West Chamber of Commerce — a group that generated so many leads for the company owner that he now claims to be too busy to attend the meetings.

For simple computer repairs or installation of sophisticated video conferencing capabilities, Denver businesses rely on the diagnostic and treatment skills of "Doctor" Dutch Humbert.

SuperNet, Inc.

The frontiers of Colorado and the West were founded on pioneer spirit of a few brave men and women. With that same pioneer spirit, SuperNet is establishing Colorado as a major outpost on the newest frontier, the Internet.

Colorado SuperNet, the parent organization of SuperNet, Inc., was founded as a non-profit organization formed by the Colorado Advanced Technology Institute (CATI) in 1986 with a mission of promoting use of the Internet for research, education, and economic growth.

In 1994, for-profit Internet service providers began competing for Colorado's lucrative commercial marketplace. The explosion of the Internet and World Wide Web gave Colorado SuperNet the chance to create a commercial, for-profit company known as SuperNet, Inc. This new status enabled SuperNet to compete for local, national and international Internet related business opportunities, while maintaining its "home-grown"

Established in 1986, SuperNet continues to thrive as Colorado's oldest and largest provider of Internet-based products and services. Credit: *Stephen M. Crain, Crain Photography*

Colorado roots. This for-profit corporation is owned by the non-profit parent, and ultimately, the citizens of Colorado.

Today, SuperNet, Inc. is a thriving company located in the heart of downtown Denver. In the last twelve months SuperNet experienced exceptional growth, nearly doubling in size from 40 to 79 employees. As facilities in the One Denver Place building became more crowded, SuperNet acquired additional space two blocks west in the Colorado National Bank building. The new facility has a 2,500 square foot, state-of-the-art machine room and absolutely spectacular views of the Rocky Mountains.

Remarkably, SuperNet has achieved this growth in a purely "bootstrapped" manner. As one of the few profitable Internet companies, SuperNet has expanded its offerings and infrastructure without going into debt. Visionary management and technical savvy have made the company as solid as it is today.

SuperNet offers the full range of advanced Internet services including site hosting and development, dedicated and dial-up connectivity, and Internet business system creation and integration services. SuperNet employs a dedicated Research & Development group charged with keeping the company and its clients abreast of the Internet's rapidly evolving technologies.

SuperNet's excellent reputation, technical experience, and financial stability has solidified its presence in the Internet marketplace, both locally and internationally. Recently, SuperNet entered into a joint partnership with QDATA, Ltd. one of the largest Information Technology firms in Africa to provide advanced Internet services to the African Continent. SuperNet is also performing consulting services in the Middle East and Europe.

As the Internet marketplace continues to mature and grow, opportunities abound. SuperNet is confident that the firm will play an important role in keeping Denver and Colorado at the forefront of the revolution.

SUMMIT CONSULTING GROUP, LTD.

Summit Consulting Group, Ltd. integrates custom programming, lan based and client server accounting software...the nuts and bolts of computer systems hardware...and advanced enterprise network technologies; to provide Colorado businesses with strategic information management systems.

A common element among these Colorado businesses is the necessity to conduct *transactions*. Before the computer age, companies used banks of accounting clerks — often in Bob Cratchit type conditions — to record these transactions in manual journals and ledgers. These were collectively known as "the books."

With the advent of computers, larger businesses quickly began to adopt the new technology to record these business transactions. Today, accounting technology has become one of the most important segments of the computer industry. However, the selection, implementation and integration of these systems are difficult, requiring skills in accounting, information technology and change management.

Imagine mastering not only the intricacies of accounting for business, but more specifically what each different business needs from its information systems and making those systems work for that business. This demands the understanding of a wide array of hardware and software products, as well as the knowledge of how to successfully mold systems to fit each client's specific business needs; deploying a system that will make each business more efficient and more, well, accountable.

Based on this complex, yet achievable, idea Summit Consulting was founded in 1992. Summit was formed by a group of local individuals from public accounting and management consulting backgrounds. Initially, Summit provided consulting services solely, assisting organizations in the selection and implementation of information technology. Soon, however, clients began requesting that Summit provide the software, hardware and operating systems as a full service technology firm.

There was a need for a dependable resource that could not only recommend and sell accounting software but could also design and provide a hardware configuration to suit multiple requirements, implement both the software and hardware, successfully program the software to meet specific needs, and train those who had purchased the software on its most efficient use. Summit grew rapidly to fill that need, recognized as the 3rd fastest growing company in Denver by the *Denver Business Journal* 1996. Summit is now poised to meet new technology needs of the marketplace, some of which businesses are not yet aware.

Morris S. Wiginton, President, (left) and Robert Bennett, Vice President

For example, today virtually zero transactions are entered into manual systems, and fewer and fewer transactions are entered by data entry clerks. How are these other transactions being recorded? From other computers! Computer to computer transactions, such as EDI (electronic data interchange), electronic banking, bar code scanning, electronic timeclocks and optical character recognition all use technology to replace direct human entry of data, thereby reducing costs and potential for errors.

Summit Consulting helps its clients deploy these technologies using state of the art Windows and client/server software architectures and advanced hardware technologies. As Summit looks forward to bringing business software and transactions to clients via the emerging global network, it is dedicated to helping Colorado's businesses use it to gain a competitive advantage.

Partners in Denver

DENVER'S RETAIL ESTABLISHMENTS, SERVICE INDUSTRIES AND LEISURE/CONVENTION FACILITIES

THE MARKETPLACE

OFFER AN IMPRESSIVE VARIETY OF CHOICES FOR DENVER RESIDENTS AND VISITORS ALIKE.

THE FORT

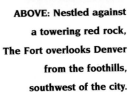

ABOVE: Nestled against a towering red rock, The Fort overlooks Denver from the foothills, southwest of the city.

TOP RIGHT: Preparation of The Fort site, in the summer of 1962, shows the location of a round tower.

LOWER RIGHT: Specialists in adobe from Taos, New Mexico, pour large adobe bricks for The Fort.

In 1961 while looking for ideas for a new house, Sam Arnold happened across a picture in a book in the Denver Public Library. The illustration, done in 1845 by Lieutenant James Abert, showed Bent's Fort, Colorado Territory's first fur trade fort. It was a two-story adobe fortress constructed around a courtyard, with two round bastions at opposite corners, a watch tower, and huge wood portals.

"It looked just like an adobe castle," remembers Arnold. "And I thought, 'wouldn't it be great to live in something like that?' So I built it." But because of the building's size, Arnold and his family lived on the second floor, and opened a 350-seat restaurant below. Thirty-five years later, The Fort has won the first Governor's Award for Excellence among Colorado restaurants, earned honors in the form of top awards by local newspapers, and enjoyed features in such publications as *The New York Times, Sunset, Bon Appetit, Gourmet, Wine and Food,* and *Modern Maturity.* Arnold and The Fort have been cited by the American Association for State and Local History, and the Western History Association.

It's easy to see why — no expense was spared in attention to authenticity. An expert on adobe architecture drew elevations and detailed plans from the Abert drawing, and construction began in 1961 in the foothills overlooking southwest Denver. To maintain the building standards of the early West, no plumb lines were used. A team of men from Taos puddled 80,000 adobe bricks on site, each over 40 pounds apiece, to build three sides of the citadel. The north side was bounded by a towering red rock. Still relatively undeveloped today, the area's deer, bear, raccoons, coyotes and mountain lions occasionally come to call (which is why Sam's wife Carrie always wears a hunting knife in a sheath behind her right hip).

The Fort owes much of its authenticity to research; Arnold studied western history at Denver University, where he pored over the journals of hundreds of nineteenth century trappers, traders, mountain men and frontier women. Working alongside Carrie, a respected historian and professional artist, Arnold created historically accurate decor, costumes, and

UPPER LEFT: A welcoming fire greets arriving guests nightly in The Fort courtyard. The round, outdoor oven is often used for baking. Traditional adobe fireplaces are throughout The Fort.

LOWER RIGHT: Besides premium beef and buffalo steaks, The Fort features unique selections including these roast buffalo marrow bones and buffalo sausage. Other fine game meats, such as elk, are featured on the menu with charbroiled salmon and other fresh fish.

menus. From the moment visitors enter the courtyard and smell the scent of smoke from the bonfire, they're drawn into the world of the 1840 American frontier.

High overhead on the red rock lurks a forty-foot long steel sculpture of a plumed serpent, symbolizing the Hopi water ceremonial. In summer, a large Cheyenne tipi and trade goods tent stand in the courtyard. Often a young woman in period dress bakes loaves of Pueblo Indian bread in the *horno*, the adobe beehive oven, and a welcome sign in Southern Cheyenne greets guests. In winter months, visitors first spot the glow of hundreds of *farolitos* (southwestern paper-bag lanterns) lining on the ramparts of the fort.

Inside, candlelit tables and beehive fireplaces abound; adobe walls are hung with fine art done in nineteenth century style and calico (to keep ladies' hoop-skirts clean!). Not a detail has been left unattended — from period Spanish doors and 1840s-style Padre Martinez style pine chairs carved by a master *madero* in New Mexico, to log beams and timbers stripped with drawknives and foot adzes. All machine-sawed surfaces were hand-planed to remove saw marks. Views extend to Pikes Peak in the south; to the east, the lights of the city suburbs spread out 900 feet below.

Seeking to keep the historic theme of early Colorado, Arnold sought out the foods the frontiersmen ate. Research into the fur trade period yielded a trove of recipes for buffalo and elk; mountain oysters; quail, lamb, pork, and trout. In the 1840s, Bent's Fort was an oasis of civilization in the Western wilderness; fine wines, elegant tablecloths, even oysters were

known to grace its tables. So it is at The Fort 150 years later, where the menu features "new foods of the Old West." Traditional, often long-forgotten ingredients of the Americas — such as Anasazi beans, purple potatoes, and a melange of chiles — are prepared and combined in contemporary ways on the cutting edge of cuisine. From certified Hereford beef, fresh fish, buffalo marrow and hump roasts, to selections such as ostrich, pintade guinea fowl, and Arctic musk ox, The Fort's customers enjoy a parade of delicious, uncommon foods. Menus change at least twice a year, with daily specials.

Visitors to a spring rendezvous gather in the Fort courtyard for feasting, trading, and enjoying the skills of the mountain men.

But the food synonymous with The Fort is bison — American buffalo. Since 1963, the restaurant has served over a million buffalo dinners, averaging over 50,000 a year. The modern buffalo industry grew up with The Fort. When Arnold began serving it in 1963, about 30,000 animals roamed the planet, up from only a few hundred in 1900. Most were in public herds in Wyoming and South Dakota. Only a few ranchers could supply enough high-quality bison meat for the restaurant's needs, and the public was skeptical for many years.

But that has changed. By 1996, bison numbered over a quarter of a million head, with ranches in all 50 states. As one of bison's leading exponents, The Fort has done much to educate people about its healthful qualities and fine taste.

Sam and Carrie Arnold are truly hands-on partner-

owners. An accomplished chef and author of three cookbooks, Arnold orchestrates the menu at The Fort with imagination and knowledge, including a drink menu offering historic pre-1850s libations. In order to stay at the forefront of the food frontier, both he and his wife attend cooking classes and food conferences around the world. Carrie's touches have helped to create a warm, friendly atmosphere in the huge building with its nine dining areas, and the two are often seen visiting guests' tables, checking on details and service. For guests from foreign countries, The restaurant staff includes several multilingual servers, and menus are available in English, Russian, German, French, Spanish and Japanese.

The Fort is much more than just a restaurant; for many, it is a way of life. In fact, buckskinning — practicing the survival skills of the mountain men — is the fastest growing outdoor sport in the nation. At no other time is this more evident than during The Fort's twice-yearly mountain man rendezvous.

A banquet set in
The Fort grill.

food is authentic early western fare — Sioux jerky stew, buffalo sausages, Indian fry bread and posole.

Throughout the year, The Fort hosts many other special events. Adults and children alike enjoy the ceremonial lighting of the farolitos, juried art exhibits, nineteenth-century military brass bands, and firing cannons on New Years and the Fourth of July.

Often, helicopters arrive at the heli-pad east of the patio, bringing guests to dinner. Many large corporations hold annual parties here, using the whole restaurant and often tenting the courtyard to accommodate more guests.

UPPER LEFT:
Bent's quarter, a private
dining area in The Fort.

LOWER LEFT:
The St. Vrain room
in The Fort.

One Sunday every spring and fall, the portals are thrown open at high noon to the tolling bells in the watchtower. The courtyard is transformed into a market where a passel of traders from near and far sell their period ware. Tinsmiths, blacksmiths, and silversmiths, gun and knife makers gather. Trade beads, shirts, coats, pants, jewelry, sculptures, furs and blankets are sold, all conforming to styles of the first half of the nineteenth century.

Over a hundred mountain men, women and children wear authentic 1840s garb such as hand-sewn buckskins. They engage in competitions for knife and tomahawk throwing, black powder long-gun shooting, and fire starting with flint and steel. Experts card wool and spin yarn while storytellers do much of the same. A phrenologist "reads" the character bumps on heads of paying clients. A military brass band with nineteenth century instruments plays, and two black-powder cannons are shot at the top of each hour. The

Every night, visitors hear Fort staff members use the mountain man term "Waugh!" meaning, "right on!" in Lakota Sioux as they assist guests celebrating special occasions. For the Fort staff, the real joy of being in the restaurant business comes when The Fort is able to lift the mantle of the world outside the adobe walls, to truly restore their guests, body and soul, in the old meaning of the word "restaurant." Having their guests experience "shinin' times" is their best pleasure.

Sam and Carrie Arnold
of The Fort.

BIG O TIRES

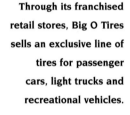

Big O Tires is one of the fastest-growing independent retail tire and auto service franchise networks in the United States.

Through its retail stores, the 35-year-old company sells Big O brand tires for passenger cars, light trucks and recreational vehicles — produced exclusively for the company's franchisees by some of the largest tire manufacturers in the world.

The company's retail outlets also carry other popular brand-name tires like Michelin, B.F. Goodrich and Uniroyal. Additional Big O Tires services include brake, alignment and front-end repair, as well as installation of shock absorbers and struts. The company uses ASE-certified technicians for most of this work.

Big O Tires currently offers its products through more than 400 franchised and company-owned retail stores in 18 states. In addition, the company has 40 associate dealers in British Columbia, Canada. The company, headquartered in Englewood, employs 200 people. Sales in 1995 exceeded $140 million.

The company's success has not gone unnoticed. In its 1996 "Franchise 500" special section, Entrepreneur magazine ranked Big O Tires as the country's top automotive franchise. Success magazine also ranked

the company number 26 in its "Franchise Gold 100" listing of the best franchise businesses in America.

In addition, the 1996 J.D. Power and Associates Replacement Tire Study ranked Big O Tires "best overall passenger car and compact van replacement tire" for the second year in a row — topping well-known brands like Michelin, Goodyear, Firestone and 15 others. J.D. Power and Associates is an international marketing information firm that measures and analyzes consumer opinion and behavior.

Big O Tires enjoys a special relationship with its franchisees, based on the company's four "Pillars of Strength" — exclusive market territory, exclusive Big O brand products and warranties, unique retail programs, and a system to encourage dealer participation in program formation and decision making.

Purchase of Big O brand tires includes the company's Premium Tire Service Policy, which offers consumers free tire mounting and balancing, free rotations and free flat repairs for the life of all tires. Premium Big O brand tires carry a unique lifetime-free-replacement road-hazard and materials-and-workmanship warranty.

The philosophy of "Big-Ology" and the company's retail programs are explained to new franchisees at an initial five-week training course offered at the Big O University in Denver. Franchisees learn personal

selling, product line, sales and marketing programs, personnel management, accounting, and most of the business skills and programs needed for a successful franchise operation.

Big O Tires democratic character can be traced to its origin as a tire-buying cooperative. Monthly regional owner meetings, national dealer board meetings, and an annual dealer convention provide constant franchisee input to company programs, especially in the areas of sales, product line and marketing.

The Big O Tires franchise support system also includes real estate development, merchandising and display assistance, operating store support programs, business systems, area management support and training, and product logistics support. A close relationship with various lenders to small business helps qualified prospective franchisees obtain Small Business Administration financing.

Big O Tires dealers are currently located in the 15 Western states plus Indiana, Kentucky and North Carolina. The company has plans for continued expansion. Dealers are served by three large distribution centers located in Boise, Idaho; Henderson, Nevada (Las Vegas area); and New Albany, Indiana (Louisville area).

Big O Tires was founded in 1962 when a small group of independent tire dealers banded together in order to consolidate their buying and advertising

power, thereby improving profitability. The group had broken off from O.K. Rubber Welders, which was at one time the largest passenger tire retreading company in the nation. The Big O name, which echoes the name of this early competitor, is an acronym for "Better Image — Greater Opportunity."

In 1965, Big O borrowed the basic premise of the drive-through car wash when it introduced the "speed lane" concept to the tire retailing industry. In 1967, the company introduced the nation's first free

Big O Tires outlets carry popular brand-name tires and ride-control products. They also provide brake, alignment and front-end repair.

replacement warranty on premium tires. In 1974, the company introduced its exclusive Big O brand of tires.

In 1984, Steven Cloward became president and CEO of Big O Tires and began an aggressive franchisee recruitment program that was aimed at doubling the company's size in ten years. The company's under-car program was expanded. In 1986, Big O Tires went public.

In 1994, Big O Tires began to explore a variety of value-enhancing alternatives. In July of 1996, Big O Tires was acquired by TBC Corporation of Memphis, Tennessee — a company with 1995 sales of $475 million. The new company expects annual sales of $700 million.

From its early years as a tire cooperative to its present status as the nation's top automotive franchise, Big O Tires has certainly earned the right to its motto: "A Reputation You Can Ride On."

THE BROWN PALACE HOTEL

For more than a century, The Brown Palace Hotel has reigned unchallenged as *the* monument to pleasure and commerce in downtown Denver. It is one of the West's truly great hotels.

The Brown Palace Hotel, completed in 1892, is constructed of Colorado red granite and Arizona sandstone.

When the luxurious Brown Palace was completed in 1892, it stood virtually alone on the edge of the city's rough-and-tumble downtown. Today, it stands at the center of Denver's business district, representing the best of both the old and the new.

The old West is evoked by The Brown Palace Hotel's stunning Italian Renaissance architecture, eight-story atrium lobby, white onyx walls, and time-honored commitment to full service. The new West is reflected in such new additions as the hotel's new high-tech telephone system, business center, and fitness room.

Architect Frank E. Edbrooke designed the nation's first atrium lobby for The Brown Palace Hotel.

In 1888, Denver was a bustling metropolis where vast fortunes had been made in gold, silver, and land. Real estate developer Henry Cordes Brown, who had come to Denver as a carpenter in 1860, thought that his city deserved a "palatial" hotel that would reflect its new status and properly impress potential investors.

Brown hired Denver architect Frank E. Edbrooke, who designed the nine-floor hotel to fit its unique triangular lot, using Colorado red granite and Arizona sandstone for the exterior. For the interior, Edbrooke designed the nation's first atrium lobby, crowned by a stained glass ceiling to provide natural light.

The architect imported 12,400 surface feet of white onyx from Mexico, which he used generously in the lobby and elsewhere throughout the hotel. With its floors and walls constructed of hollow blocks of porous terra-cotta, the Brown Palace was "fire proof" — the second such building in America. Two 720-foot-deep artesian wells provided all of the hotel's water — and continue to do so today.

After an expenditure of $2 million, the Brown Palace Hotel opened for business on August 12, 1892. The hotel has operated continuously ever since — day and night, seven days a week, through good times and bad — without ever once shutting its doors. It has been remodeled, updated and redecorated on an ongoing basis.

Shortly after The Brown Palace Hotel opened, the Silver Panic greatly reduced the fortunes of many Denver residents — including Brown. In 1907, he sold his hotel to W.S. Stratton, the "Cripple Creek Millionaire." During the Great Depression, the Boettcher family acquired the hotel and retained its interest for 50 years.

Today, The Brown Palace Hotel is an independent hotel managed by Quorum Hotels & Resorts. The Brown, along with its fine-dining restaurant, is the only downtown hotel consistently awarded Mobil Travel Guide's Four-Star designation — as well as many other industry awards and recognitions. Peter H. Aeby, a graduate of the Swiss Hotel School in

Lausaunne, Switzerland, has been managing director of The Brown Palace Hotel since 1987.

Over the years, the Brown Palace has hosted visiting presidents and celebrities. The hotel's two named suites — the Eisenhower suite and the Beatles suite — reflect some of these visitors. Today, the Brown Palace is primarily a business hotel, frequented by senior executives and boards of directors, although it is welcoming an steadily increasing number of tourists and their families.

The Brown Palace Hotel's three independently operated restaurants are a destination in themselves for long-time Denver residents. Recently redecorated, Ellyngton's is the preferred site for the city's power-breakfast-and-lunch crowd. On Sundays, Ellyngton's features a popular, jazz-accompanied Dom Perignon Brunch.

....

Recently redecorated, Ellyngton's Restaurant in The Brown Palace is the preferred site for a Denver business breakfast or lunch.

The Ship Tavern, which has operated since 1934, serves lunch and dinner — specializing in regional cuisine and microbrews — and offers a nautical decor. The Palace Arms, the hotel's Four-Star fine-dining restaurant, features Continental cuisine and an award-winning, 900-selection wine list. This elegant red-and-gold restaurant, operating since 1950, is home to a collection of fine Napoleonic antiques.

In addition to its restaurants, The Brown Palace Hotel recently opened The Churchill Bar, a sophisticated, book-lined retreat for the enjoyment of premium spirits, wines, and cigars. The private Brown Palace Club serves lunch and welcomes hotel guests

in addition to members. The spectacular hotel lobby offers a proper English afternoon tea service (booked solid for months in advance during the winter holiday season) and evening cocktails. The hotel's meeting rooms can accommodate groups ranging in size from 16 to 600.

The Churchill Bar is a sophisticated, book-lined retreat for the enjoyment of premium spirits, wines and cigars.

The Brown Palace Hotel prides itself on its long-standing tradition of exceptional service, offering full concierge, valet, and 24-hour room service. Each of the hotel's 430 employees receives two full days of hospitality training prior to assignment. Each year, all employees participate in a refresher course.

Tours are available of The Brown Palace Hotel, which is listed on the National Register of Historic Properties and is a registered Denver landmark. It is a member of the Historic Denver Centennial Ring and hosts Historic Denver's annual dinner each year.

For more than 100 years, The Brown Palace Hotel has defined elegance and hospitality in downtown Denver and the West.

THE BURNSLEY HOTEL

The Burnsley Hotel, situated on the northeast corner of Grant Street and 10th Avenue, began life as an apartment building in 1963. Shortly thereafter, it became The Hampshire House — a residential hotel owned by an investment group that included singer Ella Fitzgerald and actor Kirk Douglas.

In 1970, Denver business and civic maven Joy Burns, and her husband, distinguished real estate developer Franklin Burns, of The D. C. Burns Realty & Trust Company, acquired the hotel as an investment. The

....

The opulence of The Burnsley Hotel is evident as you step through the doors of the spacious lobby.

hotel continued operation as the Hampshire House for over a decade, while Joy and Franklin traveled together extensively on business ventures.

By the early 1980's, the hotel showed numerous signs of venerable deterioration. Joy found herself displeased with the hotel's old image. She entertained the notion of running the hotel herself, elevating its image to her personal standards of perfection. Joy's lack of hotel or restaurant expertise was no deterrent. On the contrary, she considered it to be a welcome challenge.

Joy, herself a discriminating, world-class traveler, wanted her hotel to be the embodiment of what she demanded in a first-class establishment. Armed with a staunch Texas business background, Joy commandeered the hotel's resurgence in 1983.

For two arduous years, Joy poured blood, sweat, tears, and long, exhausting hours into the hotel's renovation. She mastered crash courses in construction, interior design, and the hospitality trade. Joy also took the time to secure Mr. Karl Mehlmann, whose Brown Palace Hotel career ran the gamut from Bellman to General Manager over four decades, as her new Managing Director. The Brown Palace's front desk manager of twenty-five years soon followed, as did the Brown's maitre d', the coffee shop hostess, and some of the waiters. The Burnsley Hotel has been called 'the Little Brown,' which is no insult, by any means.

The renovation proved to be one of Joy's most difficult, demanding, and fun accomplishments. Literally devoid of any noteworthy architectural features, the aging high-rise graciously accepted her metamorphosis.

At the beginning, the 17-story structure's refurbishing focused on the first and second floors. The back walls of the recessed, uninviting entryway were knocked out to create a spacious atrium. The front lobby walls were extended almost to the curb. An imperial canopy cover was added to beckon guests inward.

Once inside, the drawing room-styled, two-story lobby relaxes in brass, polished Italian marble, oriental antiques, and original oil paintings. Richly textured furnishings embrace the classic melodies from a beautiful Steinway piano. Calm and soothing hues of burgundy, primrose, and teal resonate peacefully throughout the hotel.

The elegant mezzanine, embellished with lush carpeting, a charming period bar, and a game table, overlooks the lobby. It opens on to the adjoining poolside terrace. Two intimately personal private salons and a reception foyer accommodate special meetings and entertaining. A handsome Boardroom, with its own private patio for entertaining, is an attractive feature for executives.

Joy wanted a hotel with character, elegance, and a style of its own. Her painstaking efforts have resulted in the sophisticated aura of a small European-style hotel with the Texas accent of home.

On January 1, 1985, the new Burnsley Hotel officially re-opened for business.

Discounting hotel industry superstition, Joy reinstated the thirteenth floor. Thirteen is her lucky number. She met Franklin on August 13, 1958, at the Cherry Hills Country Club. Putting the 13th floor back on the elevator panel between the 12th and 14th floors was, perhaps, the simplest task of the entire renovation.

All eighty-two of the guest suites were gutted and completely remodeled. Each suite has its own bedroom, living room, kitchen, dinette, and balcony. Solid wood was removed from the balconies and replaced with plexi-glass to lend an open, airy view that accommodates the sights of the Mile High City below.

A new hotel kitchen was installed. A master chef creates ambrosial breakfasts, luscious lunches, and delectable dinners. Sunday brunch is a festive occasion, warmed by the yesteryear sounds of a harp.

Nearly $5 million later, The Burnsley Hotel is in a class all its own. Joy has focused on the details of service and atmosphere that sets her 'labor of love' apart from all others in the Denver-metro area. The concierge, staff, and often Joy, herself, greet guests by name. Special attention is given to guests' preferences and needs, while every precaution is taken in recognizing the privilege of privacy.

On the weekends, The Burnsley Bar jazzes up with Denver's hottest jazz musicians. Ella Fitzgerald would relish The Burnsley's big band dance sounds reminiscent of the famous New York City St. Regis Hotel where jazz ruled. And if jazz isn't "up your alley," transportation is on perpetual standby to whisk guests off for an evening of theatre or the symphony.

Joy Burns, Owner/President, poses with Managing Director, Karl Mehlmann, for The Denver Post in December of 1984. Two weeks later, the renovation dust had settled and the luxurious hotel officially opened for business.

Joy was a proud founding member of the exclusive American hostelry properties called Small Luxury Hotels, Inc. — a rare collection of the nation's finest privately-owned luxury hotels.

Joy's distinctive character emanates from every little detail of The Burnsley Hotel. From her hand-selected staff — The Burnsley Family, as she calls them — to the monogrammed terry robes, imported toiletries, and impeccably attentive service, Joy's namesake hotel has become a cherished and affordable sanctuary of respite in Denver in this increasingly rapid and mobile world.

BUSINESS INTERIORS

Business Interiors sells and installs office furniture along Colorado's Front Range, but the company is not in the office furniture business. Instead, Business Interiors is in the problem solving business.

How to design new office space? Which product lines best meet a company's needs? How to manage installation? Who is to handle maintenance? How to reconfigure existing space? How to refurbish existing furniture? Is leasing a cost-effective alternative? How to manage a move? How to pay for any of these many options?

These are some of the problems solved for numerous commercial and government clients by Business Interiors, one of Denver's largest full-service contract furniture dealerships.

At Business Interiors, it is understood that there are no excuses for not solving a customer's problem. From account representatives to designers to installers, everyone at Business Interiors is in the business of providing exceptional service — quality product, prompt follow-through and timely performance at a fair price.

A wall in the company's showroom displays scores of commendatory letters from satisfied customers, but the letter most valued by company founder and owner James Walters comes from a truck driver who praises the extraordinary cooperation of the company's crew. "Letters from satisfied customers are almost expected," said Walters, "but letters from satisfied truck drivers are extremely rare."

Major projects recently completed by Business Interiors include 3,500 workstations for StorageTek, 1,000 workstations for the Denver office of the federal General Services Administration, 525 workstations for Jeppesen Sanderson, 350 workstations for FHP Colorado (incorporating the existing systems of five different manufacturers) and 152 workstations for KUSA-Channel 9.

Most of Business Interiors' customers are located along the Front Range, but the company also does work outside the state — usually for customers headquartered in Colorado who are so impressed with the dealership's performance that they do not want to work with anyone else.

Business Interiors' capabilities range from complete interior architecture and project management to simply refurbishing or repairing a customer's aging office furniture. Customers are often so pleased with the company's ability to handle small orders that they later contract with Business Interiors for larger projects.

Business Interiors was founded in 1965 by Walters, who had previously sold office furniture for another company. "Someone forgot to tell me that, according to all the experts, I would never succeed," said Walters.

Business Interiors has installed 3,500 workstations for StorageTek, a client since 1989. Shown here are the conference room and the office of the president.

For years, Walters did most of the selling himself, using moonlighting Denver firefighters to make deliveries.

Today, Business Interiors is recognized as one of the region's best. The company's design department is directed by an AIA-licensed architect — a claim no other contract furniture dealer in Denver can make. Customers' project architects can be confident that someone at Business Interiors "talks their language."

Business Interiors architect oversees a staff of degree-holding interior designers. The entire design staff employs computer aided design and drafting with complete furniture software for all projects.

Business Interiors takes a team approach to solving its customers' problems. Each team, reporting to experienced and integrated management, includes an account representative, project expeditor, deliver and installation crews, and a maintenance expert. Each

team is dedicated to determining and satisfying a customer's objectives.

Business Interiors' list of vendors includes more than 200 manufacturers. Chief among those is Knoll, a top-of-the-line manufacturer with which Business Interiors has had a productive relationship for more than a quarter of a century.

Business Interiors displays its product lines at the 30,000-square-foot showroom, built in 1983, that it owns and occupies near the former Stapleton Airport. With no debt, the company maintains a strong credit line with office furniture manufacturers.

In order to insure quality control, Business Interiors maintains in-house installation, refurbishing and maintenance crews rather than subcontracting these services. The company's uniformed crews and chocolate brown trucks with the prominent BI logo are a familiar sight throughout the Denver area.

When a project is complete, Business Interiors seeks feedback to determine how the company's service can be continuously improved. Walters himself makes most of these calls.

Today, James Walters is still owner and president of Business Interiors, which has no desire to be the biggest contract furniture dealership in Denver — merely the best.

Business Interiors installed 525 Knoll open office stations at the new headquarters facility of Jeppesen Sanderson, increasing that company's occupancy beyond projected capacity.

Business Interiors is the best and most service-oriented commercial furniture dealership in the Rocky Mountain region — providing optimum value in product and price coupled with personal caring and responsive service. Business Interiors maintains offices in Denver, Fort Collins and Colorado Springs.

CHOICE TRAVEL SYSTEMS

While most travel agents are fast asleep, Choice Travel Systems' sophisticated computers are scanning the reservation systems of major airline carriers — tirelessly searching for the best ticket price.

A significant investment in this kind of cutting-edge travel automation technology — and in its employee-owners — has made Choice Travel one of Denver's most rapidly growing private companies, according to *The Denver Business Journal*.

Gary Buderus, president and CEO of Choice Travel Systems.
Credit: Pilon Studio

The company's gross sales nearly doubled from $21.7 million in 1994 to $43.1 million in 1995, making it the second-largest locally owned travel company in Denver. Gary Buderus, company president and CEO, predicts $50 million in revenues for 1996 and anticipates an annual 20-percent growth rate over the next five years.

Choice Travel specializes in corporate and incentive travel, which accounts for three-fourths of its business. The company also maintains a separate division dedicated to leisure travel.

Calling itself a travel management company rather than a travel agency, Choice Travel does more than merely book airline, rental car, and hotel reservations.

It also provides advanced management reporting, automated fare checking, meeting planning services, negotiation assistance and strong financial management.

The company prides itself on understanding and following its clients' internal policies for employee business travel. Whether a client's priority is controlling cost or minimizing time on the road, Choice Travel representatives are trained to come up with creative solutions that help its clients save money while they are spending money.

For some of its business clients, Choice Travel functions as a complete, out-sourced travel department. For others, it serves as a valuable adjunct to an in-house travel department. The company provides seminars for clients' travelers and travel coordinators.

In addition, Choice Travels sets up a travel advisory board with the owner and managers of each client company, meeting with this board at least once each quarter to discuss future travel needs, budgets, and any emerging problems.

Choice Travel's predecessor company was founded in 1966, but operated as a relatively small, family-owned concern. In 1991, the company reinvented itself — adopting its present name, starting to acquire other agencies, investing heavily in modern systems, and introducing an employee ownership plan. These changes have propelled the amazing growth of Choice Travel in the 1990s.

In 1996, Choice Travel expanded outside Colorado for the first time when it acquired a major travel agency in Ohio. The company currently operates offices in Boulder, Cleveland, Columbus, Colorado Springs, Denver, Fort Collins, Grand Junction, Loveland, and Steamboat Springs — allowing it to provide local, personal service.

These 12 offices (including four in Denver) support 17 satellite locations throughout the United States. Choice Travel, which currently represents a large number of oil and gas companies, is also considering numerous acquisitions in Texas and California.

Investment in top-of-the-line automated systems is central to Choice Travel's success. A data management system — MAX — provides clients with the information they need to track their travel expenses.

Choice Travel provides business owners with continuously updated, customized reports, accessible around the clock via a dial-in program.

The system also helps clients reconcile bills and forecast budgetary goals. Choice Travel's three-year data storage capacity provides effective tracking of company travel history and patterns.

A 24-hour automated quality control system — AQUA — monitors key travel issues for business clients, giving Choice Travel an important edge on the competition.

The "space buster" component of AQUA constantly scans the reservation systems of major airline carriers to look for opportunities and openings on special fares, promotions, or over-booked flights. These options may be originally sold out but later cleared and made available to savvy shoppers — sometimes at three in the morning.

The "fare buster" element continuously searches for changes in ticket prices and automatically initiates a new ticket purchase if a better fare is found. The "seat buster" searches for a better seat assignment right up until the moment a business traveler departs.

The "trip auditor" component of AQUA makes sure that the airline ticket is delivered to the traveler on time, electronically if necessary. It also guarantees rental cars at the destination and hotel reservations for the duration of the trip — all in compliance with the client-company's travel policies and regulations.

When travelers are en route, Choice Travel representatives are available, via a world-wide toll-free emergency number, at any hour of the day or night to make changes due to weather delays, missed connections, or unforeseen business developments.

High-tech systems, however, are only tools — only as effective as the people who make use of them. Choice Travel takes great pride in the personalized service provided by its dedicated, experienced agents. The company's employees are always willing to go the extra mile because, since 1991, everyone who has been with the company for at least five years is eligible to buy stock.

As employee-owners, Choice Travel representatives understand the importance of developing ongoing partnerships with their clients. Employee ownership has helped the company attract and keep a highly skilled and professional workforce.

The remarkable success of Choice Travel Systems is based on hiring talented individuals, providing them with the most advanced training and technology available, and encouraging them to build strong business partnerships with their clients.

Colorado Carphone

The new StarTAC™ Cellular Phone is the world's smallest and lightest at 3.1 ounces. Truly wearable, it features more talk-time options than any other cellular phone on the market.

For corporate clients operating a "fleet" of wireless communications tools, Colorado Carphone offers experienced sales consultants, a choice of quality equipment and accessories, the most appropriate air-time packages, and expert customer service after the sale. Colorado Carphone offers unparalleled technical support during business hours.

Film and television crews working on site in Colorado have come to depend on Colorado Carphone for reliable service. The company has provided wireless communications for many of the movies and made-for-TV movies recently filmed in the state.

As individual cell-phone users became more comfortable with wireless technology, the company opened retail stores to cater to this growing market. Cellular City retail stores are located in Denver, Boulder, Fort Collins, Greeley and Salt Lake City, Utah.

Denver area residents have become accustomed to the convenience of wireless communications — for the business person on the road, for the physician on call, and for the parents who want to keep in touch with the kids or the babysitter — or each other.

Only a short list of cellular phone companies can provide the kind of support and service today's "road warrior" requires — from pagers to carphones to pocket phones to the emerging PCS technology.

At the top of this list is Colorado Carphone and its six Cellular City retail locations which, as of 1996, have sold more than 35,000 cellular phones.

In fact, Colorado Carphone is a Motorola Signature dealer location, which grants it exclusive authorization to sell Motorola's highest technology products — like the new StarTAC™ wearable cellular phone.

Colorado Carphone got into the wireless communications business in the early 1980s, when cellular phones were carphones and had to be installed in automobiles. Those early carphones cost more than $3,000, and were initially sold with only the promise of a cellular communications system to support them.

When cellular service became available in 1984,

Colorado Carphone was one of the first companies to meet rigorous standards in order to become a Master Agent for US West Cellular. Today, Colorado Carphone is the only Master Agent still serving this system — now known as AirTouch Cellular.

Colorado Carphone was founded by A. Barry Hirschfeld, a well-known Denver businessman who wanted to invest in the avant guard of wireless communications. With Hirschfeld's entrepreneurial spirit and Sheila Bugdanowitz' sales skills and integrity, the company did well from the start. Colorado Carphone is located in Denver's booming and historically significant Golden Triangle neighborhood.

In 1989, current company president G. David Epstein joined Colorado Carphone as a partner. Today, with 28 employees, Colorado Carphone is expanding its product lines to keep pace with the rapidly expanding world of wireless communications. The company's original product has been virtually replaced by the even-more-portable pocket phone.

Some of these new products are vastly improved personal wireless phones. The StarTAC™ Cellular Phone is the world's smallest and lightest at 3.1 ounces. Truly wearable, it features more talk-time options than any other cellular phone on the market.

Colorado Carphone carries a wide variety of cellular phone and accessory options — including Motorola, Nokia, Audiovox, Mitsubishi, Sony and Oki. The company's sales representatives specialize in matching each customer's individual need to the most appropriate hardware and air-time package.

Modern alphanumeric pagers, also offered by Colorado Carphone, feature multi-line screens that can display e-mail, allowing companies to e-mail their employees any place, any time. The newest models can even receive sports results from ESPN, news updates from CNN and stock market quotes.

Colorado Carphone also intends to be in the forefront when digitally based mobile-phone service debuts in the Denver area. In addition, the emerging PCS technology combines calling, paging and personal messaging services in a single, hand-held device. These devices will even be able to surf the Internet.

For customers frustrated by the cost of cable television, Colorado Carphone has added to its array of wireless products by offering the crystal-clear digital television signal of DishNetwork by EchoStar.

Colorado Carphone, a pioneer provider of wireless products and services in Denver, intends to increase its presence as the city's wireless communications superstore of the future.

Colorado Carphone and its six Cellular City retail locations can provide the kind of support and service today's "road warrior" requires — from pagers to carphones to pocket phones to the merging PCS technology.

COURTESY FORD

Courtesy Ford is the single largest retail Ford dealership in the Rocky Mountain region and the 19th-largest Ford dealership in the United States.

Since its inception in 1974, Courtesy Ford has grown to a world-class operation. Currently, it is the single largest retail Ford dealership in the Rocky Mountain region and the 19th-largest Ford dealership in the United States.

Between 1994 and 1996, Courtesy Ford captured three world records for largest volume retail sales for the Taurus SHO, the Bronco and the all-new Expedition. During 1996, Courtesy Ford sold more than 7,500 cars and trucks and posted sales of $162 million.

Being the largest has certain benefits, which Courtesy Ford is quick to pass on to its customers. It is the only dealership in Denver that offers a five-day money-back guarantee on all new vehicles sold. In addition, by buying in volume, the company is able to provide its customers with the best selection and unparalleled value.

These benefits also accrue to used car sales and service. Courtesy Ford is able to offer the same five-day money-back guarantee plus a 30-day powertrain warranty on all of the used cars and trucks it sells. Courtesy Ford also guarantees 100 percent satisfaction on any service work performed. These benefits are matched by few of the dealership's competitors.

It is the goal of Courtesy Ford to provide an exceptional sales and service experience to every customer, every time. To achieve this goal, every employee — sales representatives, service technicians, body shop technicians, lot technicians and office support — undergoes constant coaching in customer service.

Courtesy Ford operates by 14 Core Values, including these three:

Foster Integrity and Honesty — We are reliable, dependable and can be counted on to keep our promises. We make every effort to do what we say we will do within the promised time frame. We strive to be genuine, open and above-board in all relationships. We honestly and accurately report the facts.

Maintain a Customer Focus — We focus on customers and their needs, providing what they want rather than what we want to give them. We are committed to finding out what their needs are and then providing innovative, exceptional products and services to meet those needs.

Place Quality First — The quality of our work is paramount. We pursue technological advances to deliver responsible, cost-effective products and services. We are determined to eliminate inefficiency, complexity and barriers to delivering what our customers require.

Courtesy Ford was acquired in 1974 by William Beck. Beck had previously owned a dealership in Charlotte, North Carolina, also called Courtesy Ford. In 1957, Beck hired Terry Dixon, who was only 19 years old at the time, as a salesman.

By 1961, Dixon had worked himself up the ladder to become manager at Courtesy Ford in Charlotte. That year, he won a national Ford Truck sales contest and used his winnings to open an independent used car dealership. By 1969, Dixon had acquired three more new car dealerships in Charlotte.

In 1974, Beck had the opportunity to purchase Courtesy Ford in Littleton. Dixon, long desiring to obtain a Ford dealership in the Denver metropolitan area, sold his dealerships in Charlotte and moved to Denver to become Beck's partner in 1975.

In 1977, a 24-year-old Colorado native named Ron Boyer started working for Courtesy Ford as a sales representative. Two years later, Boyer was named sales manager and quickly moved on to become general sales manager and general manager. In 1990, Boyer became co-owner and managing partner of Courtesy Ford.

Today, Courtesy Ford's $12 million state-of-the-art facility at 8252 South Broadway is the flagship operation of the Courtesy Automotive Group.

With 1996 sales of $900 million and 1,400 employees in four states, privately owned Courtesy Automotive Group is Denver's largest automotive group. The Courtesy Automotive Group owns dealerships representing Acura, Isuzu, Saturn and Ford and sold more than 40,000 vehicles in 1996.

The Courtesy Automotive Group includes:
- Courtesy Ford — Denver
- Courtesy Acura — Denver
- Courtesy Isuzu — Denver
- Saturn North — Federal Heights
- Saturn of Aurora — Aurora
- Courtesy Ford — Portland
- Prestige Ford — Seattle
- Prestige Ford — Dallas
- Park Cities Ford — Dallas
- Prestige Ford — Houston

In addition, the Courtesy Automotive Group includes support companies like Courtesy Leasing Company, Heritage Acceptance Company, Automotive Computer Technology (which sells the group's proprietary software to dealerships nationwide) — all located in Denver — and numerous other automotive related companies.

The group plans to make acquisitions in large metropolitan markets and to diversify into other automotive related products and services. As more and more automobile manufacturers allow public ownership of automobile franchises, the Courtesy Automotive Group may someday become a public offering.

Courtesy Ford and Courtesy Automotive Group play an active role in the Denver community as a member of the Denver Better Business Bureau and the South Metro Chamber of Commerce and by supporting local schools, law enforcement and firefighters.

As it approaches its 25th anniversary in the Denver metropolitan area, Courtesy Ford remains keenly focused on the principles of customer satisfaction, organizational excellence, productivity improvement and market leadership that have served it so well in the past.

Courtesy Ford's state-of-the-art facility on South Broadway is the flagship operation of the Courtesy Automotive Group, Denver's largest automotive group with 1996 sales of $900 million.
Credit: Landiscor

ELCAR FENCE

No boundary can confine Elcar Fence's commitment to customer service in the Denver area. The 51-year-old fence dealership even eluded the Mile High City's elevation limits when it installed the fence around the rooftop tennis courts on the five-story historic Gart Bros. Sport Castle.

Mack Ellerby, president and owner of Elcar fence.
Credit: Paul Reide

"Usually all work is on the ground," said Mack Ellerby, president of Elcar Fence, Denver's oldest fence dealership. "That project was unique because it was on the edge of the building."

Mack's father, Alfred "Bud" Ellerby, and his fellow CF&I Steel colleague, Bill Carlisle, became familiar with fence products while selling metal and chain link for the steel company prior to World War II. Bud then noticed that his hometown of Denver lacked a specialized fence contracting company so the duo founded Elcar Fence — a word play from the partners' surnames. After the war, they used a Packard touring car to pull carts stacked with fencing materials through Denver neighborhoods. Now one of the country's largest independent fence companies, Elcar Fence has blossomed from its five-employee shop on West Colfax Avenue to its 6.5-acre site in south Denver.

Simple wood picket fences, installed by homebuilders, and ornamental iron fences adorned only a handful of houses in the post-war years. The compa-

RIGHT: Alfred "Bud" Ellerby, co-founder of Elcar fence, metro Denver's prominent fence dealership.

ny found a niche in metal fences, but also became Denver's primary installer of wood fences when, by the early 1960s, a demand for privacy swept over the residential industry.

"Chain link is certainly more homogeneous and dependable, but wood gave more diversity to the industry in this part of the country," Ellerby says. Wood comprises about 90 percent of the company's residential business.

Denver's fence-conscious society, along with other Western states, differs from Eastern U.S. tastes, which are dictated by huge lots and vast open space between neighbors. "I remember growing up in Denver and everyone knew their neighbors and mingled," Ellerby recalls. "But the need for security has changed that."

Although wood fences are the prominent backyard barrier, Ellerby says ornamental iron fences are staging a comeback that provide a throwback to his friendly childhood days. People want fenced-in yards, sans ultimate privacy, and don't covet the institutional look of chain link. "Ornamental iron, similar to that at the Governor's Mansion, is a good go-between," he says. "It's quite elegant, it keeps kids and dogs in and out, and it adds beauty to the household."

While the metro area's recent housing boom has intensified the company's business, many Denver homeowners — in the Park Hill, Hilltop, Washington Park and other older neighborhoods — are calling upon Elcar to replace weathered 30-year-old fences. The firm's reputation and commitment to excellence are fiercely recognized throughout the region and generations.

"Our name is such that when you see our signs, it's an immediate association with Denver. Especially if you were brought up here, Elcar is synonomous with fence," says Ellerby, who started at the company as a fence installer, became a salesman and, finally, took over the presidency in 1992. He says working through the ranks was instrumental in establishing a sense of credibility among employees and customers, both residential and commercial.

While several competitors market strictly to one consumer, Elcar caters to both types of clients, making it one of the heavy hitters among fence dealers. "Residentially, if people want to buy a Cadillac fence, we can do that," Ellerby says. "For industrial, we have the technical finesse as well."

The firm's biggest project was in 1969 on Guanella Pass above Georgetown. In four months, Elcar installed about 100,000 feet of fence for a Public Service Co. of Colorado's hydroelectric facility. Two lakes of differing elevations were fenced off at the plant in which centrifugal forces push up water.

Other projects included installing high-security fence around a nuclear testing site in Las Animas, N.M., in the late 1950s, and positioning fenceposts through a lake at the Denver Zoo while employees sat in a rowboat.

Along with New Mexico, Elcar markets to Wyoming, Nebraska and Kansas. In fact, the company's reputation almost trancended national borders. In the early 1960s, an Elcar crew installed circular fenced enclosures around 10 microwave satellite stations at 500-mile intervals from the Canadian border to Mexico. The company's regional reputation helped land the job.

That same notoriety has helped the company garner two Dealer of the Year awards from the International Fence Industry Association. The IFIA, which attempts to upgrade the industry's business practices and philosophies, offers the accolade to reputable, tightly-run businesses.

"Thousands of people have called us over the years after seeing a chain link fence and say, 'I want one of those Elcar fences,'" Ellerby notes. "They think chain link is synonomous with Elcar. We've put in that many fences in Denver."

Selling nearly 3,000 fences a year, grossing between $3 million to $5 million annually and employing about 80 employees, Elcar Fence is a landmark historic Denver company.

"Our name rings a bell among Denverites," he says. "We're part of Denver history."

Classics of the 1950s — an Edsel, a Chevy, a Ford, a Buick and Elcar Fence.

A post-World War II work crew poses in front of the company's original location on West Colfax in Lakewood.

THE EMBASSY SUITES HOTEL AT DENVER PLACE

Like all Embassy Suites, the Embassy Suites Hotel at Denver Place offers its guests the luxury of a spacious suite for the price of a standard hotel room — plus a free breakfast and cocktail reception.

Unlike most other Embassy Suites, the Embassy Suites Hotel at Denver Place is located in the heart of downtown, convenient to local business centers, entertainment, dining and sightseeing.

The 37-story building that houses Embassy Suites is part of Denver Place, the largest mixed-use development project in Colorado. Denver Place covers two square blocks and also includes high-rise apartments, an athletic club, three office towers, a retail mall, a child-care center and an outdoor plaza.

On the first 19 floors, Embassy Suites offers 337 guest suites with one or two bedrooms; a separate living room for working, entertaining, or relaxing; three televisions, a wet bar, coffeemaker, and refrigerator; and two telephones.

The top 18 floors house The Apartments at Denver Place, some of which are furnished and set aside for short-term corporate and individual rentals. These one- and two-bedroom units are popular with traveling consultants and relocating executives. The 193 apartments include six penthouses, which feature added amenities like fireplaces, washer/dryers and jacuzzis.

In addition to suites and apartments, Embassy Suites offers 8,000 square feet of meeting space — a preferred site for corporate meetings, parties, weddings and reunions. The Crystal Ballroom has 2,000 square feet of space and the Remington Ballroom has 3,000.

Unlike most other Embassy Suites, the Embassy Suites Hotel at Denver Place is located in the heart of downtown.

RIGHT: Because of its convenient location, its sophisticated decor and its reasonable cost, Embassy Suites at Denver Place has been named a preferred hotel by a large number of corporations.

Embassy Suites' famous free complete breakfast is served each morning in the Foothills Restaurant, which is decorated in an appropriately Western style. Open to the public for lunch and dinner, the restaurant specializes in regional cuisine — including trout, prime rib of beef, and buffalo. In addition to more standard fare, the Foothills Lounge offers a selection of regional beers.

In addition to its on-site amenities, Embassy Suites is located within walking distance of historic Larimer Square, Writer Square, The Shops at Tabor Center, the financial district, the art and theatre district, and the rejuvenated LoDo district adjacent to Coors Field — all with the backdrop of the magnificent Rocky Mountains.

Because of these amenities and its reasonable cost, Embassy Suites has been named a preferred hotel by a large number of corporations whose executives and managers must travel to Denver for business.

Embassy Suites is also popular with visiting entertainers, ranging from Michael Jackson to Sting to the stars of Opera Colorado. International business and tourist visits have also increased dramatically. To accommodate some of these guests, Embassy Suites offers a special Japanese breakfast daily.

Embassy Suites plays an active role in the downtown Denver community, participating in the Downtown Denver Partnership, the Denver Metro Convention and Visitors Bureau, the Metro Denver Chamber of Commerce, and various arts organizations.

To help preserve downtown air quality, all Embassy Suites' employees are offered an Eco-Pass, which allows them to ride RTD buses to and from work for free. The company also supports United Way, Family Tree, and Special Olympics, and "recycles" used furnishings to organizations that assist the homeless.

When it was announced that the Oklahoma City Bombing trial would be held at the Federal Court House in Denver, the families of many bombing victims protested that they could not afford to attend. In cooperation with the Convention and Visitors' Bureau, Embassy Suites made five suites available, free of charge, to victims' families for the duration of the trial.

Adjacent to Embassy Suites is the Athletic Club at Denver Place, available to hotel guests for a nominal fee. This 65,000-square-foot facility features the latest in health and fitness opportunities, including a 25-meter indoor swimming pool; racquetball, squash and basketball courts; the longest indoor running track in Denver; state-of-the-art cardiovascular equipment and a circuit training area; a variety of aerobic and conditioning classes, and a masseuse.

Denver place offers 1.3 million square feet of secure office space in three towers — North, South, and Plaza — as well as 1,600 spaces of underground parking. Ownership and management are on-site, assuring a hands-on, accessible management style.

Denver Place also includes 95,500 square feet of service and retail space housing coffee shops, restaurants, hair salon, dry cleaners, shoe repair, video rental, copy center, florist, jeweler, travel, financial and medical services. Popular among downtown workers is the Montessori at Denver Place child care center.

Denver Place was developed in the early 1980s, with the hotel and apartment tower opening in 1983. In 1985, the privately owned property was purchased by Amerimar Realty Company of Philadelphia. The hotel affiliated with Embassy Suites the following year. Managing director of the hotel and apartments is Ian van Riemsdyk. Executive vice president and general manager of Denver Place is Robert T. Flynn. Senior vice president is Garth Tait.

The Embassy Suites Hotel, the apartments, the athletic club, the office towers and the retail space at Denver Place have been unified into a single, smoothly functioning, 24-hour environment — committed to downtown Denver, to its guests and tenants, and to success.

Embassy Suites is part of Denver Place which is, at 1.3 million square feet, the largest mixed-use development project in Colorado.

EMBASSY SUITES DENVER INTERNATIONAL AIRPORT

In 1995, this convenient Embassy Suites hotel changed its location — from the west side to the east side of Denver's airport — without dislodging a single brick or even changing its address.

It was, of course, the airport that moved. When Stapleton Airport closed, the hotel changed its name to Embassy Suites Denver International Airport and re-doubled its efforts as the only full-service all-suite hotel convenient to the new airport.

Denver International Airport is located a mere 20 minutes to the northeast of the hotel via a direct shuttle that leaves the hotel and the airport every half hour between 5:10 a.m. and midnight.

Also close to Embassy Suites Denver International Airport are the Stapelton Renaissance Center, golf courses, the museum of natural history, the zoo, and the National Western Complex.

The 600,000-square-foot National Western Complex was designed as a venue for the National Western Stock Show, which is held there each year in January. Many stock show participants return to the nearby Embassy Suites year after year, filling the hotel to capacity with satisfied, familiar faces.

Within 20 minutes to the southeast of Embassy Suites Denver International Airport are the attractions of downtown Denver, including the convention center, LoDo, Mile High Stadium, Coors Field, McNichols Arena, the Sixteenth Street Mall, Elitch

Gardens, the theater and arts district, the financial district and the State Capitol.

Within an hour's drive of Embassy Suites Denver International Airport are the front-range cities of Colorado Springs, Golden, and Boulder. Also within an hour's drive are the delights of the Rocky Mountains — skiing, hiking, biking, rafting, camping, and gambling.

Embassy Suites Denver International Airport consists of 210 two-room suites that include a microwave, coffee maker and refrigerator. Each suite also includes two televisions and two telephones. Other amenities include free local phone calls, free parking, an indoor pool and exercise equipment, and an outdoor sundeck.

Embassy Suites offers a complimentary full breakfast served in the hotel's seven-story atrium — also the site of a complimentary cocktail reception each evening, popular brunches on Easter and Mother's Day, Christmas concerts by local school children, and an extravagant New Years Eve party. Giatti's Restaurant

and Lounge, including a popular luncheon buffet, is open daily for lunch and dinner.

Embassy Suites Denver International Airport is popular with air travelers who want to spend a few days in Denver — adjusting to the "mile-high" altitude and seeing the sights — before heading into the

RIGHT: The hotel's seven-story atrium, lush with greenery and anchored by a lovely fountain, is available for weddings, reunions and bar mitzvahs.

BELOW: Embassy Suites Denver International Airport is the only full-service all-suite hotel convenient to Denver's new airport.

mountains for skiing or recreation. Families and groups appreciate the extra room and amenities of a full-service, all-suite hotel.

Thanks to its "suite packages," Embassy Suites Denver International Airport has become a popular destination for Denver residents and regional travelers as well.

The "Kidnap Your Spouse" escape package includes champagne, chocolates, and a bubble bath in addition to the usual free cocktails and breakfast. "Family Night at the Movies" features a movie rental, pizzas, soda, cocktail reception and breakfast.

The "Home Run" package is a popular item with baseball fans from Kansas and Nebraska as well as out-state Colorado. The "Gamblers" package includes transportation to and from the Central City casinos.

Business travelers appreciate Embassy Suites Denver International Airport because of its convenience to the airport, downtown, the Denver Technical Center, and the Montbello Business Park. The hotel includes twelve executive meeting suites, including a galley bar and kitchen, that can accommodate up to eight people.

Available for events is the hotel's stunning seven-story atrium — lush with greenery and anchored, in the style of a Spanish courtyard, by a lovely fountain.

The 5152-square-foot grand ballroom can be configured into a wide variety of theater, classroom, conference, banquet, dinner dance, and reception settings.

The hotel's flexible facilities, central location and easy airport access make it a popular site for a variety of social events, including weddings, reunions, and bar mitzvahs.

Civil wedding ceremonies are often held in the atrium and receptions in the ballroom. The hotel offers floral services and a discounted room rate for family and friends. Also included is a complimentary VIP bridal suite for the wedding night — and the first anniversary.

Embassy Suites Denver International Airport is experienced in hosting all kinds of reunions — family, military, fraternal, tribal, religious, all cousins, twins, high school, adoption, best friend, athletic teams, summer camp, and heritage.

Every reunion booked with the hotel receives a complimentary welcome reception, a keepsake welcome banner, complimentary ballroom rental with a catered dinner, and a complimentary hospitality suite when more than 50 suites are booked.

Embassy Suites Denver International Airport is an active member of the business community, including the Aurora and the Denver Metro chambers of commerce, the Denver Metro Convention and Visitors Bureau, and the Northeast Metro Hotel Association. Each year, the hotel sponsors "Bikers for Babies," a fundraising event for the March of Dimes.

Embassy Suites Denver International Airport, built in 1985, is owned and managed by Houston-based Westmont Hospitality Group.

ABOVE: Each year, Embassy Suites Denver International Airport sponsors a fundraising event for the March of Dimes, like Bikers for babies and Walk America.
Credit: Bettinger Photography

LEFT: Thanks to its "Suite Packages" promotion, Embassy Suites Denver International Airport has become a popular weekend destination for local and regional residents.

Inverness Hotel & Golf Club

The Zagat Survey cited first-rate service, excellent restaurants and well-appointed rooms when it selected Inverness Hotel & Golf Club as Denver's best overall hotel.

In addition, Inverness Hotel & Golf Club has received AAA's prestigious Four Diamond Award for five consecutive years.

The Inverness Hotel and Golf Club's unique status as a resort hotel plus sophisticated executive conference center makes it a preferred destination for all kinds of business events.

Now, with the opening of the neighboring Park Meadows shopping center, featuring the finest in Front Range shopping opportunities, Denver's best has gotten even better.

The Conference Center at Inverness is currently the only facility in Colorado certified by the International Association of Conference Centers.

Inverness Hotel & Golf Club's unique status as a resort hotel plus sophisticated executive conference center makes it a preferred destination for all kinds of business events.

In fact, 80 percent of Inverness Hotel's business is conference business. The facility attracts Fortune 500 companies from cities like New York, Chicago, San Francisco and Dallas.

The Conference Center at Inverness houses a 60,000 square-foot conference center. The center offers 33 rooms of dedicated meeting space, including auditoriums, conference rooms, board rooms and break-out rooms. There is also a 5,500-square-foot banquet room that seats 800 and an outdoor terrace and garden area.

The Conference Center at Inverness includes a full production studio offering complete on-site video production, high-tech computer graphics capabilities and photography services. It is currently the only facility in Colorado currently certified by the International Association of Conference Centers.

Each conference group benefits from the expertise of a personal conference services manager who assists with planning, development, theme and format of the meeting program and provides in-meeting services. Refreshments are available throughout the meeting day.

A variety of "Getaway Weekend" packages are also making the Inverness Hotel a popular destination for Denver metropolitan residents as well. Packages include attractively priced golf, dining, and Park Meadows shopping options.

Denver residents also flock to the award winning Swan restaurant at the Inverness Hotel, recipient of AAA's coveted Four Diamond Award, for fine international cuisine in a relaxed but elegant atmosphere.

Inverness Hotel & Golf Club is located in bustling south metro Denver, home to the Denver Technological Center, Inverness Business Park, Centennial Airport (the nation's 14th busiest airport) and the spectacular new $164 million Park Meadows shopping center.

The Inverness, the only resort hotel in the Denver area, is a short 25-minute ride from either downtown Denver or Denver International Airport. Door-to-door airport shuttle service is available. The hotel's 13 acres include an 18-hole champion golf course with a view of the majestic Rocky Mountains. The property also includes tennis courts, indoor and outdoor pools, whirlpools, jogging trails and a full-service fitness center.

The Inverness Golf Club is host to the annual FDC Colorado Open, featuring top golfers from around the country — one of the largest state golf tournaments in the United States. All proceeds go to fund cancer research at the University of Colorado.

Colorado Golfer magazine lists the par-70 championship PGA course as one of the top ten private courses in the state. On a 1996 campaign swing through Colorado, President Bill Clinton made time in his hectic schedule to play the course.

Inverness Golf Club offers a variety of levels of play that will challenge both pros and beginners. Because of Denver's exceptional 300 days of sunshine per year, the course is almost always playable.

The Inverness Hotel's 302 luxury guest rooms are spacious and include views of either the Rocky Mountains or the golf course. All rooms include two telephones, computer hook-up capability, a good-sized desk and a mini-bar.

In addition to The Swan restaurant, Inverness Hotel houses The Garden Terrace, which provides elaborate meals and buffets, including the ever-popular Friday- and Saturday-night seafood buffets and Sunday brunch; The Columbine Room, dedicated to conference attendees; and The Golf Grille, which appeals to hotel golf guests and members of the Inverness Golf Club.

The Columbine Room is also available for events like wedding receptions and anniversary celebrations. The Fireside Lounge, located in the hotel's lobby, offers premium cocktails as well as specialty coffees, fresh juices and pastries. The Pub, located on the lower level, offers a variety of microbrewed beers as well as complimentary foosball and pool tables.

To provide the freshest in bakery and floral arrangements, the Inverness Hotel & Golf Club maintains its own on-site bakery and florist. To provide superior service, the Inverness Hotel & Golf Club employs almost 500 people.

The facility, constructed in 1989, was purchased in 1995 by Los Angeles-based Lowe Enterprises and turned it over to its wholly owned subsidiary, Destination Hotels & Resorts, for management. Destination Hotels is headquartered in Englewood, Colorado.

In 1996, Destination Hotels commenced a massive refurbishing project of the Inverness Hotel & Golf Club at a cost of $3.5 million, giving the entire facility a warmer, more elegant appearance.

Destination Hotels & Resorts manages 25 facilities throughout the United States. Operations include condominium resort hotels, golf clubs, tennis clubs, conference centers and ski resorts.

A sophisticated business conference with the added lure of fine dining and exceptional golf. A getaway weekend of shopping and romance. The Inverness Hotel & Golf Club can meet your needs.

LEFT: The Conference Center at Inverness offers 33 dedicated meeting rooms, including auditoriums, conference rooms, board rooms and break-out rooms.

The Conference Center at Inverness includes a full production studio offering complete on-site video production, high-tech computer graphics capabilities and photography services.

King Soopers

In 1997, King Soopers celebrates a half-century of service to Denver and the Front Range. In that time, the company has grown from a single 3,000-square-foot store in Arvada to 70 stores along the Front Range. The company's territory extends from Pueblo to Fort Collins and from Bergen Park to Parker. With 14,000 employees, King Soopers is easily Colorado's largest private-sector employer.

The Denver metropolitan market has changed dramatically over the years — and King Soopers has survived and thrived by changing with it. Today's time-challenged shoppers are working and playing harder than ever before. They demand the kind of "one stop shopping" that offers them a wide choice of quality products at one convenient, pleasant location.

Today's shopper wants to be able to buy high-quality angus beef steaks for a dinner party, sushi for an appetizer, a deli-prepared vegetable salad for the side, bakery for desert, flowers for the centerpiece — and a video to keep the kids occupied while they get everything ready. This shopper also wants to be able to pick up a pre-scription, a good book or magazine, a bus pass or lift ticket, a card for a relative's birthday — and some cash.

To meet this need, King Soopers is now building "combination" superstores of 60,000 square feet and larger. The company also continues to continuously improve and refurbish its small and medium-sized locations.

In the early 1940s, Denver native Lloyd King was already an experienced grocer and entrepreneur with an interest in five grocery stores — an interest he sold when he joined the Navy. After the war was over, he opened a small meat market in Arvada, which he expanded into the first King Soopers store in 1947.

In this first store, King introduced the first of many consumer innovations — the self-service meat department. In 1951, King Soopers became the first store in the Denver area to offer trading stamps — an innovation that caused sales to increase dramatically. The company offered trading stamps until 1968.

By 1957, there were ten King Soopers stores in the Denver area. That year, to gain access to the capital needed for growth and expansion, Lloyd King merged his company with the Dillon Companies of Hutchinson, Kansas. This step allowed the company to add a warehouse in 1957, a central bakery in 1959, and a produce and frozen food warehouse and deli kitchen in 1963.

In 1997, King Soopers celebrates a half-century of service to Denver and the Front Range. Company founder Lloyd King still attends each store grand opening.

Lloyd King brought many innovations to Denver, including the first self-service meat department and the first trading stamps. King Soopers continues this tradition of innovation today.

After World War II, Lloyd King opened a small meat market in Arvada, which he expanded into the first King Soopers store in 1947.

In 1968, King Soopers closed all of its stores for a while, marked down all prices, and reopened its door as the region's first discount grocery retailer. Before the competition had time to react, King Soopers had established a new image as the area's low-price leader.

Fueled by this success, King Soopers added 23 new stores, a variety of warehouses, a bakery plant, a meat processing facility, a photo finishing plant and a complete dairy operation during the 1970s.

Other King Soopers "firsts" included unit pricing, open-code dating, in-store pharmacies, prescription drug posting, the introduction of generic products, the nation's first in store recycling program for aluminum, glass and plastic drink containers and newspapers. The company was one of the first to introduce optical scanning.

In 1997, the King Soopers floral departments constitute one of the top users of the FTD floral service in the nation. The company's fast-growing pharmacies provide convenient access to prescription medications for customers while efficiently managing prescription benefits for hundreds of local and national organizations.

King was succeeded as president of the company by Ray Rose in 1972, Jim Baldwin in 1979 and Don Gallegos in 1990. Fresh out of college, Gallegos had joined King Soopers as a buyer in 1955. Soon after his arrival, Gallegos walked into King's office, looked around and announced his intention of eventually sitting behind the president's desk. Impressed with the young man's drive, King started him on a long journey up the corporate ladder — a journey that ended in that same office 35 years later.

In 1983, the Dillon Companies (and its King Soopers division) were acquired by the Kroger Companies in Cincinnati. The merger brought the best of both worlds — greater financial strength and geographic coverage, with no change in management or company name.

From the beginning, it was Lloyd King's philosophy to "sell the best products, at the lowest prices, and develop a positive relationship with the customer that surpasses every competitor." That philosophy continues to govern the company today, supplemented by King Soopers' familiar slogan: Our People Make the Difference.

King Soopers' commitment to Denver and the Front Range goes beyond filling its customers' shopping carts. For example, King Soopers sponsors a program called HOPE, in which King Soopers' employees volunteer with a wide variety of local projects, including working in local schools and shelters. In Denver, HOPE volunteers have "adopted" Fairview and Rosedale elementary schools.

King Soopers celebrates 50 years of operation in Denver by renewing its commitment to be the best — for its guests, its employees, its shareholders and its community.

The new King Soopers at Smokey Hill Road and Himalaya features such innovations as a pet center, the Sooper City snack aisle and an abundance of express check-out lanes.

THE MORELAND AUTOMOTIVE GROUP

Dealin' Doug dressed as superman (offering a "super" deal). Dealin' Doug dressed as a pilgrim (refusing to sell any turkeys). Dealin' Doug dressed as Abraham Lincoln (as honest as they come.) Who knows what will be next?

Since he began producing his trademark Dodge commercials in 1980, Dealin' Doug and his show-manship — "I'll never lose a deal over price" and "Nobody beats a Dealin' Doug deal. Nobody!" — have become a local advertising legend.

Doug Moreland has also become a local business legend, growing a small dealership on South Havana into the largest Dodge dealership in the Rocky Mountain region and one of the top 25 Dodge dealerships in the United States.

Doug Moreland is founder of The Moreland Automotive Group, which owns franchises in five states and posted revenues of more than $450 million in 1996.

Despite his "down home" image, Moreland has demonstrated sophisticated business savvy in turning this one dealership into The Moreland Automotive Group, which owns a variety of franchises in five states and posted revenues of more than $450 million in 1996. The Moreland Automotive Group employs approximately 1,400 people in five states.

Dealin' Doug's commercials set the tone for buying a new or used vehicle at Cherry Creek Dodge or any of his other dealerships. Moreland realizes that buying a new or used car makes many people uncomfortable. For many customers, it is an expense second only to buying a home.

Injecting an element of wheeling and dealing into the process helps people relax and enjoy spending their money. Today, almost every purchase involves a take-it-or-leave-it price. Who can imagine taking a cart of groceries to the cashier and trying to negotiate the price? The only purchases left open to negotiation are a car and real estate.

Moreland cites research that says two-thirds of auto-buying customers feel better about buying a car when they are able to negotiate in a friendly, stress-free environment As a result, Dealin' Doug has accepted jewelry, property, recreational vehicles, vending machines and even a set of Clydesdale Horses in exchange for a car. He's even flipped a coin to settle a $50 difference.

Few customers walk away from a Dealin' Doug dealership over price or terms. The company deals with more than 50 financing and leasing sources to serve all types of customers with the best financial package available — from second chance to short term to an extended lease program. The group owns Brandon Financial, which offers second chance used car financing.

Doug Moreland got his start selling cars in 1969 when he was a college student at the University of Nevada in Reno. He worked for his future father-in-law, who owned a Dodge dealership. Reno is also where Dealin' Doug got his start doing "over-the-top" television commercials.

In 1980, Moreland came to Denver to become general manager of Cherry Creek Dodge, which was in such bad shape that he almost gave up and returned to Reno. With strong entrepreneurial drive, the support of his family and the financial backing of the out-of-state owner and the Chrysler Corporation, Moreland turned the operation around so quickly that, in 1981, it became the number one Dodge dealer in the Rocky Mountain region — a position it has held ever since. Moreland became sole owner of Cherry Creek Dodge in 1985.

The domestic automobile industry went through tough times in the early 1980s when Moreland was getting his start. Economic conditions were bad, gasoline was scarce, interest rates were high and the competition got tougher as the market was being inundated with thousands of unsold new cars.

Moreland survived these years and used this experience to design his approach to selling automobiles in the 1990s and beyond. To protect against the cyclic

nature of the economy, he diversified into additional new-car product lines, used car sales and financing, and like-new car sales and financing.

Moreland acquired his second dealership in Fort Collins in 1985. In 1997, The Moreland Automotive Group owns 13 new car dealerships, nine in Colorado and one each in Chicago, Phoenix, Reno and Sacramento. The groups holds franchises to sell the products of Dodge, Chrysler, Plymouth, Jeep, Eagle, Pontiac, Buick, GMC, Mitsubishi, Volkswagon, Suzuki, Subaru, Hundai, Honda, Toyota and Kia.

The Moreland Automotive Group has also purchased the franchise rights to 17 J.D. Byrider used car stores in Colorado and the rights to develop additional stores in Albuquerque, Reno and Las Vegas. To provide affordable financing and help customers rebuild their credit, the group has established a second financing entity, CNAC Financial.

The Moreland Automotive Group has also opened four Factory Car Outlets in Colorado to offer like-new cars with new-car financing. Eventually, The Moreland Automotive Group would like to own 50 car dealerships, roughly divided among these various components that serve every level of the new and used car market.

In Colorado, The Moreland Automotive Group supports a wide variety of organizations like Cystic Fibrosis, the Make-A-Wish Foundation, Cancer League of Colorado, Children's Hospital and DARE Colorado. In 1995, Moreland was recognized as Man

True to his words, Dealin' Doug has been known to accept jewelry, property, recreational vehicles, vending machines and even livestock in exhange for a new or used car.

of the Year for his support of DARE Colorado. The group also sponsors DECA scholarships at Smokey Hill and Cherry Creek High Schools.

In remembrance of Jennifer Moreland, Moreland's sister who died of cancer, The Moreland Automotive Group is a major sponsor of Cancer League of Colorado. The group also sponsors a scholarship at Eaglecrest High School in Aurora, where Jennifer Moreland had been a physical education teacher and girls' baseball coach.

Since 1980, "Dealin' Doug" Moreland has demonstrated to Denver that it is possible to have a good time, run a successful business and contribute to the community — all at the same time.

Since its introduction in 1980, Moreland's "Dealin' Doug" persona has become a local television advertising legend.

RICKENBAUGH CADILLAC/VOLVO

Rickenbaugh Cadillac/Volvo is located at the intersection of Speer Boulevard and Broadway — the apex of Denver's historic Golden Triangle Neighborhood.

For more than 50 years, Rickenbaugh has been locally owned and operated by one family. The dealership has earned a reputation for quality products and trustworthy service as well as for being a member of the Denver community. The Rickenbaugh family has had much at stake, because many of the company's customers over the years are friends, neighbors and business associates.

Rickenbaugh's organization chart proudly features its customers at the top and indicates three departments: sales, service and the Rickenbaugh Collision Repair Center. As a result of the Rickenbaugh Excellence Program, the company has won practically every award for sales, service and parts management offered by Cadillac and Volvo over the years.

Director of sales for both the Cadillac and Volvo product lines is Jack Gilman, who has been with the company for eleven years. The dealership is a member of the exclusive Cadillac Master Dealer Hall of Fame as well as a Volvo Dealer of Excellence. The dealership sells and leases new Cadillacs and Volvos as well as quality used cars of all makes.

James Shelton, who has been with the company 16 years, is director of customer service. The company, which features factory-trained master mechanics and technicians, has earned the highest Customer Satisfaction Index in the area for both Cadillac and Volvo.

In 1995, the company opened the 80,000-square-foot state-of-the-art Rickenbaugh Collision Repair Center at 444 Kalamath Street. The ultra-modern facility repairs all makes of vehicles at competitive insurance rates. The Collision Repair Center has established a Preferred Service Relationship with a number of automobile insurance companies. The facility was designed to turn out the highest quality work in the most efficient time frame while providing for the comfort and safety of its employees. The director of the Collision Repair Center is Amy Leidich, who has been with the company for seven years.

Rickenbaugh Collision Repair Center is located in a part of the city where the streets carry the names of Native American peoples. In recognition of this tradition, the company commissioned a 50-foot wood totem pole for the front of the building.

Rickenbaugh Cadillac/Volvo traces its history to 1944, when R.L. and Hilda VH. Rickenbaugh purchased the Cadillac distributorship located at 945 Broadway from the estate of R.R. Hall. Hall had held the franchise since 1906. Rick Rickenbaugh had worked for Cadillac Motor Car Division in Detroit since 1929. In 1950, the company moved two blocks south to its present location at 777 Broadway.

World War II was not the best time to be operating a new car dealership. Cadillac was manufacturing tanks for the war effort, not luxury automobiles for civilians. In addition, since used cars were in such great demand, they commanded a handsome street price and rarely made it to dealerships. Spare parts were hard to come by; the service department had to manufacture many pieces by hand.

When the war drew to a close, there was an incredible demand for new cars. People stood in line to sign orders for cars, price unknown, with delivery delays of up to 36 months. At this time, Rickenbaugh was also a wholesale distributor to more than 50 Cadillac dealers in Colorado, Wyoming, Nebraska and New Mexico. Cadillac took this function in-house in 1965.

In 1989, Rickenbaugh added the Volvo product line, giving Denver motorists a choice of luxury products at the same central location. Within its first year of operation, Rickenbaugh became the area's largest Volvo dealership.

The president of Rickenbaugh Cadillac/Volvo is Kent L. Rickenbaugh, son of the original owners, who has worked at the company in various capacities since he was twelve years old. In 1996, Mary Pacifico-Valley became Rickenbaugh's partner. She had joined the service department in 1976, went to night school to complete college and get her accounting degree, and worked her way up to her current position of vice president and executive manager.

Over the years, Rickenbaugh has accumulated more than four acres of space bounded by Speer Boulevard, Broadway and West 8th Avenue — only five minutes away from either downtown Denver or the Cherry Creek Mall. It features indoor shopping for new cars in the largest showrooms in the West, which hold more than 100 new cars ready for immediate delivery.

The company has grown to have more than 140 loyal employees. Fifty-three people have been with Rickenbaugh for more than five years. Twenty-six employees have more than ten years of service.

Rickenbaugh Cadillac/Volvo is a member of the Denver Metro Chamber of Commerce and the Better Business Bureau. The company belongs to Denver's Two Percent Club, a group of businesses that contribute a minimum of two percent of their profits to nonprofit organizations in the community.

As its embarks upon its second half-century of business in Denver, Rickenbaugh Cadillac/Volvo pledges to continue its efforts to be "Number One in the West" through providing innovative support and service to its highly valued customers and community.

Rickenbaugh features the largest indoor showrooms in the West, which hold more than 100 new cars ready for immediate delivery.

SEATTLE FISH COMPANY

"If it swims, we have it."

In 1918, when Mose Iacino opened his fish market in downtown Denver, it took a week for salmon and halibut to make the long trip from Seattle by railroad. The highly perishable product was packed in ice that had to be replenished at each stop along the way.

Today, fresh and frozen seafood is flown into Denver International Airport each day from both coasts as well as from other port cities around the world. The product travels in special, climate controlled compartments that maintain it in peak condition.

In the old days, Seattle Fish Market sold its fish to customers who visited its retail outlet and to Denver's finest restaurants and hotels.

Today, Seattle Fish Company provides fresh fish to many of these same establishments — and to many others throughout the West. The company also distributes fresh and frozen seafood to all of the region's major supermarket chains.

Seattle Fish Company is one of the largest wholesale distributors of fresh and frozen seafood west of the Mississippi. The company distributes to fine restaurants and supermarkets.

Seattle Fish Company is one of the largest wholesale distributors of fresh and frozen seafood west of the Mississippi. The company distributes to Colorado, Kansas and Wyoming out of the Colorado office, which employs 80 people. Seattle Fish Company of New Mexico, a sister operation established in the mid-1980s, distributes to New Mexico and Texas.

In 1998, Seattle Fish Company will celebrate 80 years of doing business in Denver. For all of that time, it has been owned and operated by the Iacino family.

Seattle Fish Company has succeeded because of good business practices and an enduring commitment to product quality and safety.

Even though the United States does not have a mandatory inspection program for the seafood industry, Seattle Fish Company has voluntarily adopted the federal government's strict HACCP program, which features on-premises supervision by quality control technicians and by U.S. Department of Commerce inspectors. Seattle Fish sells to all of the region's sushi restaurants, where quality and freshness are imperative.

Mose Iacino, who was destined to become a well-known and well-loved Denver personality, was born in Grimaldi, Italy, in 1902. At the age of four, he was sent to Denver to join his three older brothers, who operated the Diamond A meat market at 15th and Lawrence. After only a few years of formal schooling, Iacino got his start in the seafood business when be began selling oysters in a corner of the family store.

In 1918, at the age of 16, Iacino set off on his own pursuit of the American Dream when he opened the Seattle Fish Market in Lower Downtown Denver. For nearly three-quarters of a century, Seattle Fish would be his life. He set an example for his employees by regularly working 70 hours per week, and continued to report to the office until his 90th birthday. He died in 1995 at age 92.

In the company's early years, Iacino also sold rabbits — "Good choice rabbits — $1.75 per dozen" — as well as fish. He had two slogans: "If it swims, we have it," which is still the company's slogan today, and "Get the habit, eat more rabbit."

During the Great Depression, fish and rabbit provided an inexpensive main course for many a Denver family, and Seattle Fish began to grow. The company also sold a lot of fish to the city's Roman Catholics, many of them recent immigrants, who were proscribed from eating meat on Fridays. The city's plentiful Greek restaurants were also valued customers. In 1935, Iacino moved his retail store and warehouse into larger quarters at 1537 Market Street that the company would occupy for nearly 50 years.

In 1998, Seattle Fish Company celebrates 80 years of doing business in Denver. For all of that time, it has been owned and operated by the Iacino family. For 50 years, it operated from this site on Market Street. The building features the company's famous logo, which was designed in the 1920s.

During the 1930s, Iacino traveled to Washington State and Alaska to establish a personal relationship with the many seafood suppliers in those areas. Soon, he was traveling all around the world in search of the finest products for his Denver market. He was the first to import to Denver such luxury items as Icelandic lobster dainties, Spanish red shrimp and Australian lobster tails.

Although he was never a pilot himself, Iacino developed a deep love of flying. In 1937, he married Jeannie Bungee in an airplane one mile above the Mile-High City. The couple then traveled around the world by plane on a six-month honeymoon.

Iacino made many friends in the course of his travels, including Will Rogers. Iacino ate dinner with Rogers in Alaska just hours before the famed cowboy-philosopher was killed in a plane crash. Iacino also collected the Western art of Robert Lindeneux; his collection is on display at the Buffalo Bill Cody Museum on Lookout Mountain.

The 1980s brought a number of changes that dramatically expanded Seattle Fish Company's scope of operations. Young, well-educated and health-conscious immigrants from the coasts moved to Denver, bringing with them a taste for fresh fish. At the same time, air transportation made it possible to deliver truly fresh fish to the hotels, restaurants and grocery stores of the Rocky Mountain West. People began to buy less beef and more seafood.

At the same time, Seattle Fish Company benefited from the energy of a second generation as Edward Iacino took over operation of the company. In 1982,

From the beginning, Seattle Fish Company adopted the slogan, "If it swims, we have it."

he moved Seattle Fish from antiquated facilities downtown into a new $5 million state-of-the-art facility near Stapleton Airport. Iacino is also expanding the company's product line into quality canned goods and delicatessen products.

For nearly 80 years, Seattle Fish Company has provided quality seafood to the restaurants, hotels and supermarkets of Denver and the Rocky Mountain West.

THE SNYDER GROUP/ RED ROBIN INTERNATIONAL

The Snyder Group, and its principal interest — Red Robin Restaurants, is an engaging entrepreneurial chronicle that binds Denver to the Pacific Northwest through two brothers who brought their family's business code of honor, integrity, and compassion to the Mile High City.

At age 29, Horace Snyder founded Snyder's Bakeries in 1929 in Washington State. The small, wholesale bakery emerged from the depression one of the largest, privately-owned wholesale bakeries in the country.

When Horace's sons, Jim and Bud, were old enough to join in the trade, they successfully drove Snyder's Bakeries into head-on competition with industry giants like ITT Continental. Despite stiff competition, Snyder's garnered 80% of the market in their locales, due to their notorious delivery service.

The familiar "glass block" Red Robin Restaurant in Lakewood was Colorado's first. It opened in 1981.

Jim's sons, Mike and Steve Snyder, have been in the food service business their entire lives. They were born into the family of master bakers in the 1950s, in Yakima, Washington.

At age 7, Mike swept out the flour rooms of his family's bakeries. He spent Saturdays sacking crou-

tons for stuffing by hand. Steve, two years younger, soon followed in the family baking operations.

It was an innocent era. Drive-ins, restaurants, and grocery stores sprang up everywhere. Throughout the Northwest, it was known that if a Snyder customer ran out of buns or bread, and they couldn't find their route salesman, they could call a Snyder at home, and get product delivered swiftly, even though Snyder's Bakeries is a big operation covering several states. Jim often left the dinner table if an Oregon drive-in needed a tray of buns, or a small Idaho grocer needed more rolls for the holidays.

Word of Snyder's dedicated service spread rapidly. Soon, Snyder's Bakeries were servicing accounts that weren't even theirs, promptly winning them over. Jim was delighted when Mike and Steve got their driver's licenses, and later their pilot's licenses, to help with impromptu deliveries.

After Mike graduated from college, he returned to the family business. A new bun-packaging system, purchased to better service McDonald's and other customers in the Northwest, became Mike's first lesson in workplace compassion.

Mike worked the machine for months, learning its operation. Certain he'd mastered the machine, Mike went to his dad with visions of moving up the 'dough hooks' of the family business. Jim made Mike stay with the bun machine. This exchange took place again months later. Finally, when the machine's manufacturer wanted Mike to sell the machines because of his expertise, he confronted his dad again. Jim explained that until Mike knew what it was like to look forward to working on that bun machine for years, like all the great people in production in the bakeries who had done just that, until he understood how those people felt emotionally, Mike would stay with the bun machine. It was a compassionate lesson, indeed.

Like their granddad before them, Mike and Steve set sights on a business of their own. They contacted a Seattle man who owned a tavern-like hang-out called Red Robin. On a smile and a handshake, the man agreed to "pretend" he was a franchisor by letting Mike and Steve "pretend" to be franchisees. With money borrowed from Dad, the brothers opened their first Red Robin in Yakima, Washington, in 1979.

The "franchise" succeeded in spite of the brothers' lack of restaurant experience. Their "franchisor" enjoyed getting monthly royalty checks, and continued to find other "franchisee" groups in other parts of the U.S. Mike and Steve finally documented the franchisor/franchise agreement by borrowing a friend's Kentucky Fried Chicken franchise contract agreement, and tailoring it to their new business.

Mike and Steve opened more Red Robins in Washington, but Colorado's allure beckoned them to the Mile High City. Denver was a huge Yakima, with four distinct seasons and mountain skiing. The first Colorado Red Robin opened in Lakewood in 1981, with nine more in Colorado to follow.

In 1985, the original "franchisor" that Mike and Steve had shaken hands with sold his business to a large Japanese food service company. Mike contacted his old associate a decade later, and in March of 1996, the two travelled to Tokyo and bought the company back.

Granddad and Dad unwittingly planted in the young minds of Mike and Steve the tireless service mentality and deep-seated compassion that the brothers would ultimately lend to their increasingly successful management firm, and their popular franchises — Red Robin Restaurants. Headquartered in the Denver Tech Center, The Snyder Group operates as a Red Robin franchisee, while Mike wears two hats, both as a Red Robin International franchisor and a franchisee. There are about 148 Red Robins in the U.S. and Canada. Red Robin employs approximately 1,000 people in Colorado alone.

Today, Mike and Steve stand proud on their breadboxes, quick to point out that while they were fortunate to have a father who believed enough in his boys to invest in their dream, equally important were the inherent traits of commendable work ethics and a dedicated, service mentality.

Snyder's Bakeries, Inc. has since merged into a suc-

Today's contemporary Red Robins, such as this new one in Littleton, feed and entertain large, hungry crowds seven days a week.

cessfully prominent national conglomerate. Granddad Horace passed away; and Jim, now retired, enjoys traveling. Jim may be one of a handful of American fathers whose kids borrowed money and actually repaid it. Mike and Steve repaid their dad nearly $3 million within the first decade of their venture.

Mike and Steve consider themselves employees of the thousands and thousands of great people working diligently in Red Robins, creating happy guests. The Snyders whole-heartedly support their winning efforts.

The Snyder Group and Red Robin International anticipates $400 million in sales by the turn of the century, with aspirations of continued growth in Colorado, the United States, and internationally.

Food service is embedded in the family's history. Time, alone, will tell if Mike and/or Steve's sons will continue the family's legacy. However, many Red Robin restaurants carry the poster of an intuitive quote from Mike's son, Graham, delivered at the cosmopolitan age of 11, during a questionable dining experience.

"You know, Dad, it's the little things that make a restaurant big."

WYNKOOP BREWING COMPANY

The Wynkoop Brewing Company was the first brew-pub in the Rocky Mountain Region. Established in 1988, Wynkoop was also the first new brewery in Denver in more than 50 years.

The Wynkoop Brewing Company is located in the historic J.S. Brown Mercantile Building, which was constructed in 1899. The structure features an exterior of red pressed brick on a foundation of granite

blocks. On the main floor, owners of the Wynkoop restored woodwork of Oregon pine and oak and 15 foot ceilings covered with pressed tin. The building has been placed on the U.S. Department of the Interior's National Register of Historic Places.

Converting the handsome-although-neglected warehouse into a modern microbrewery and restaurant was an ambitious project, which was undertaken with the utmost respect for the building's history and integrity.

Founder John Hickenlooper, a Philadelphia native and ex-geologist, found himself jobless after Denver's Oil Crash of 1986. Using his severance pay and a

$125,000 loan from the Mayor's Office of Economic Development, Hickenlooper also raised funds from friends, family and acquaintances to build this brewpub.

The Wynkoop sells more than one million pints of beer annually, amounting to a production of more than 5,000 barrels. The Wynkoop is now the largest brewpub in the world in terms of beer produced and sold in its 30,000-square-foot facility. The company's signature beer, Railyard Ale, is also brewed and bottled at the Broadway Brewing Company, of which Wynkoop owns 50 percent. Railyard is distributed in eight states outside of Colorado.

The Wynkoop has earned a national reputation for its pub cuisine, banquet facilities and 26-table billiard parlor, including two private pool rooms. In addition, the Wynkoop played an instrumental role in the renaissance of Lower Downtown, which has been converted from an area once deserted after dark into a major destination for metro Denver residents and tourists.

Employing 185 people, the Wynkoop has become a notable fixture in Lodo. There are now seven other brewpubs and four micro-breweries within a one-mile radius of the Wynkoop, and more than 100 such establishments in Colorado.

Six of the Wynkoop's brews are always on tap, supplemented with seasonal and specialty beers. The Wynkoop also produces meads, hard ciders, barley wine and a non-alcoholic root beer. The reasonably priced menu features beer as a recurring ingredient in

The exterior of the Wynkoop Brewing Company taken at dusk shows the fine pressed brickwork on the building which was constructed in 1899.

The facade of the Wynkoop before renovation began in 1988.

some of the Wynkoop's dishes and baked goods.

Named in part after its location at 18th and Wynkoop Streets, across from Denver's Union Station, and in part after Edward W. Wynkoop, Denver's first sheriff and one of its founding fathers, the brewpub has a long tradition of community involvement.

Special beers are brewed and labeled to be sold as fund-raising tools for local philanthropic organizations such as the Denver Museum of Natural History, the Denver Zoological Gardens and the Denver Art Museum.

Two "volumes" of Denver Public Libation Ale, each volume consisting of short stories and poems by authors like Dave Barry, Clive Cussler and Kurt Vonnegut, have been produced. The company annually donates beverages valued at more than $50,000 to community events and non-profit organizations.

When Denver International Airport finally opened, the Wynkoop produced Denver International Ale — "The Beer Worth Waiting For." Recently, Light Rail Ale was introduced in honor of Denver's light rail system.

To celebrate its anniversary, the Wynkoop holds the "Running of the Pigs™ — Pamplona on the Platte," using pigs instead of bulls. This event allows local reporters to attempt their best Hemingway impersonations. A Pig Iron Stout is also produced at this time.

Due to its success in Denver, the Wynkoop has expanded its operations. In 1993, Phantom Canyon

Brewing Company opened in Colorado Springs. This brewpub is located in the historic Cheyenne Hotel Building, which had been scheduled for demolition prior to Wynkoop's involvement with the project. The building renovation has won two historic preservation awards.

The fabulous 26 table billiard parlor on the second floor of the Wynkoop Brewing Company.

In 1994, Wynkoop and the Flying Dog Brewery in Aspen became co-founders of Broadway Brewing Company. Broadway has a capacity of 22,000 barrels per year, the equivalent of 297,000 cases of beer. Broadway brews signature beers of both establishments for bottling and distribution across the country.

Nail City Brewing Company in Wheeling, West Virginia, opened in July of 1996 in the renovated Artisan's Center Building, which was constructed in 1869. Upstream Brewing Company in Omaha, Nebraska, opened its doors in September of 1996 and is located in one of Omaha's original fire stations, built in 1903 and completely restored. Titletown Brewing Company opened in Green Bay, Wisconsin, in November of 1996 in a restored train station built in the Romanesque style which was popular at the turn of the century.

The Wynkoop continues to work on new projects through the United states, pursuing its ongoing mission — to create locally owned and operated brewpubs in buildings with historic significance and landmark qualities, while maintaining the highest standards of quality beers and cuisine.

ABOVE: An evening view of Wynkoop's successful subsidiary in Colorado Springs, Phantom Canyon Brewing Company.

LEFT: For one of its may charitable brews, the Wynkoop "published" the pictured Volume One of Denver Public Libation Ale in 1995.

THE AVENUE GRILL

The private Eldorado Room of The Avenue Grill can accommodate up to 40 people for a sit-down dinner or up to 100 for a cocktail party.

The Avenue Grill is located in a restored turn-of-the-century building in the historic Uptown neighborhood, just a few minutes east of downtown Denver.

RIGHT: The Avenue Grill offers fine continental cuisine in the timeless atmosphere of a San Francisco-style bar and grill.

The lady sipping a perfect martini — stirred not shaken. The gentleman nestling a single malt scotch and smoking a fine cigar. The couple enjoying fine continental cuisine in the timeless atmosphere of a San Francisco-style bar and grill. In Denver, all of these people are likely to be found at The Avenue Grill.

The Avenue Grill is located in a restored turn-of-the-century building in Denver's historic Uptown neighborhood, just a few minutes east of Downtown Denver. Uptown is the site of Restaurant Row and some of Denver's finest dining establishments.

The tavern-like decor of The Avenue Grill includes natural wood, marbled columns, tall ceilings, antique fixtures and a fabulous 18-person vintage bar — offering what one local restaurant critic called "the best bar seat in Denver." During the day, when The Avenue Grill is popular with the lunch crowd, this cozy decor is brightly illuminated by a continuous bank of floor-to-ceiling windows.

Another critic has credited The Avenue Grill with "the best martini in Denver." In fact, The Avenue Grill serves ten varieties of martini — ranging from the classic to the trendy. It hosts a daily martini happy hour, a martini club, martini dinners and martini tastings.

Connoisseurs of single malt scotch, limited edition bourbon, sipping tequila, and fine port and cognac will find an excellent selection at The Avenue Grill. The Avenue Grill, which maintains a fully stocked humidor, is also one of Denver's few "cigar friendly" establishments. Each month, The Avenue Grill hosts a cigar and spirits party.

The dining room at The Avenue Grill specializes in fresh seafood, grill cuisine and pasta. Specialties of the house include appetizers like Dungeness crab cakes and wild mushroom strudel, entrees like herb-crusted salmon and blackened porterhouse pork chops, and signature items like southwestern Caesar salad and cioppino. Freshness is such a priority that The Avenue Grill grows its own herbs.

For those interested in lighter fare, The Avenue Grill offers entree salads and heart-healthy preparations. The wine list includes 30 wines by the glass and more than 70 bottled wines — both domestic and imported. The Avenue Grill offers a wide variety of specialty beers, and plans to establish an on-site microbrewery.

The restaurant seats 125 people. The private Eldorado Room of The Avenue Grill can accommodate up to 40 people for a sit-down dinner or up to 100 for a cocktail party. Valet parking is available.

The Avenue Grill is owned and operated by Basic Food Group, which also owns The Great Northern Tavern & Brewery located in Keystone and the Denver Tech Center. Owners of Basic Food Group, which maintains its headquarters above The Avenue Grill, are Bill Ferguson and Craig Camozzi.

The Avenue Grill is an active member of Capital Hill United Neighbors, an alliance of neighborhood businesses and residents, and often hosts the group's meetings. The Avenue Grill also donates meals to charitable groups holding fundraising auctions.

The Avenue Grill offers a true San Francisco-style bar-and-grill experience for Denver residents and visitors.

THE CAMBRIDGE HOTEL

An intimate, quiet, European-style, luxury boutique hotel experience awaits those who visit The Cambridge in Denver's historic Capitol Hill neighborhood.

As the neighborhood's name suggests, The Cambridge is just steps away from the Colorado State Capitol. Also convenient to The Cambridge are the Colorado State History Museum, the Denver Art Museum, the Western Art Museum — and the new architecturally brilliant Denver Public Library.

....

The personal size of The Cambridge Hotel immediately sets it apart from other downtown lodging facilities.

For shopping enthusiasts, the exciting outdoor Sixteenth Street Mall offers a myriad of cafes, restaurants and exclusive shops.

The personal size of The Cambridge immediately sets it apart from other downtown lodging facilities. After registering at the concierge desk, guests may enjoy the nearby lobby, which includes a marble fireplace, wing-back chairs and floral-upholstered sofas.

A complimentary continental breakfast is served each morning in the breakfast lounge, located right off the lobby. The adjoining Profile Restaurant and Lounge is a four-star restaurant that has been serving guests for more than 40 years in a rustic old world atmosphere. Room service is available through the Profile during the lunch and evening hours.

Elegantly designed, The Cambridge's Executive Boardroom is professionally furnished with a solid cherry table and plush black leather chairs. The boardroom is an ideal professional meeting suite and can easily accommodate up to 18 people.

The hotel's "Romance Rediscovered" package has become a popular get-away for many Denver couples. Welcoming them to their suite, guests will find a chilled bottle of champagne, engraved champagne glass souvenirs and a gift basket. "Romance" couples also receive complimentary valet parking and a refreshing late check out.

In a quaint, elegant style, The Cambridge features 39 spacious and distinctive suites. It is decorated in a fine European motif and each suite has its own personal charm. The hotel is distinguished by its exclusive atmosphere and unparalleled service. A stay at The Cambridge is always a memorable experience.

The Cambridge Hotel is a quaint, elegant building featuring 39 spacious and distinctive suites, each decorated in a fine European motif.

BISCUITS & BERRIES

As big as an extravagant sit-down dinner for thousands. As small as an intimate dinner for two. Whatever a client's catering expectations, they can be met and exceeded by Biscuits & Berries: The Catering Company.

Unparalleled quality and service have brought Biscuits & Berries a long way since Micki Neely

Biscuits & Berries specializes in the French Country presentation promoted in its slogan — "A Feast for Eye & Palate."

....

became sole owner in 1993. When Neely joined the struggling company, it had $100,000 in annual sales.

In 1996, Biscuits & Berries will post sales of $1.5 million — which makes it one of the Denver metropolitan area's largest caters.

Biscuits & Berries specializes in the French Country presentation promoted in its slogan — "A Feast for Eye & Palate " The company caters both social and corporate events and offers its clients a 20-page menu. Popular are the company's elegant, butler-passed hors d'oeuvres and French table-side service. All items are freshly prepared; there are always "heart healthy" choices.

Aggressive and creative marketing is responsible for much of Biscuits & Berries' success. On Neely's first Valentine's Day with the company, she baked beautiful rose-decorated tarts, placed them in florists' boxes, and delivered them to five potential clients. That same afternoon, she was asked to cater breakfast for 150 — the next morning. Neely and her crew stayed up all night.

Today, Biscuits & Berries is sole caterer for the Denver headquarters of this large regional company — among many others.

Neely credits Biscuits & Berries' success to a team of employees that exhibits thorough dedication and professionalism. "No one person could ever be responsible for the remarkable success story of Biscuits & Berries," said Neely. "It is our unity, our synergy, and our dedication to quality that have made the company what it is today."

Biscuits & Berries operates from a 4,000-square-foot facility in the Denver metropolitan area and employs about 40 people. The company also operates on-site delicatessens for a number of corporate clients.

Neely came to catering with 20-years' experience in the restaurant business. "My time in restaurants taught me to recognize the best," said Neely, "and I have staffed my company with people who can produce the best. This concept permeates Biscuits & Berries. The name of my corporation, as a matter of fact, is 'No Ka Oi, Inc.,' which is Hawaiian for 'We are the best.'"

DIXON PAPER COMPANY

At home and at work, Denver residents read magazines, annual reports and catalogs. They send and receive correspondence. They review and approve documents. A good portion of these materials are printed on paper distributed by Dixon Paper Company.

Chances are, these materials were also printed using electronic pre-press equipment and graphic supplies sold by Dixon. Some products may have been delivered in packaging designed and packaged.by industrial equipment and supplies distributed by Dixon.

Dixon Paper Company is the largest distributor of printing papers, graphic arts equipment and supplies, and industrial packaging equipment and supplies in the Rocky Mountain region.

Dixon Paper Company was founded in 1911 by T.A. Dixon. From the company's very beginning, it supplied paper to local printing companies like Frederic Printing and A.B. Hirschfeld Press. More than 85 years later, these Denver printers are still loyal customers of Dixon — a strong testimony to the company's long-time commitment to customer service.

In 1990, after a long history of independent operation, Dixon Paper Company was purchased by International Paper. With 1996 annual sales of $20 billion, International Paper is a worldwide manufacturer and distributor of paper, packaging and forest products. Dixon's 12 warehouses throughout the West became an important part of the parent company's distribution organization — ResourceNet International. ResourceNet International's West Region is also headquartered in Denver.

From its Denver Division, Dixon has linked customers in the Rocky Mountain Region with leading manufacturers of paper, industrial and graphics products whose standards of performance match its own. For the company's customers, this means quality products, consistent innovation and reliability. Altogether, Dixon distributes more than 30,000 different products from its 180,000-square-foot warehouse and employs 220 people.

Dixon Delivers

Dixon Paper Company is the largest distributor of printing papers, electronic pre-press equipment and supplies, and industrial packaging equipment and supplies in the Rocky Mountain region.

The printing paper department offers the finest selection of business premium coated and uncoated papers along with a wide variety of offset and copy papers. The printing paper department represents the highest quality manufacturers of these printing grades.

Dixon's graphics department represents electronic pre-press equipment, traditional graphics equipment and supplies to support Denver's dynamic graphic arts community.

The industrial department represents a vast array of products including industrial packaging equipment, custom-designed packaging applications and industrial supplies.

Dixon is a preferred supplier to wholesale customers that range in size from small start-up operations to huge Fortune 500 companies. The company also supplies products to Dixon Express retail outlets in Arvada, Aurora, Boulder, Colorado Springs and Denver.

The Rocky Mountain region has relied upon Dixon Paper Company as a source for printing paper, industrial and graphics products for more than 85 years.

Dixon Paper Company was founded in 1911 by T.A. Dixon. In 1990, the company became part of International Paper's ResourceNet International distribution system.

More than 30,000 different products are distributed from Dixon's 182,000-square-foot warehouse. The company employs 220 people.

BOISE CASCADE OFFICE PRODUCTS

Consider It Done.

Boise Cascade Office Products Corp. is one of the largest U.S. distributors of office supplies, furniture and computer products. Boise distributes directly to corporate, government and other offices through its contract stationer business, and to home offices and small- and medium-size businesses through Reliable, its direct-mail operation.

Boise's product line features a full range of office supplies from paper clips and pens to copy paper. It also carries office furniture including desks, chairs, filing cabinets and ergonomic accessories. Additionally, in conjunction with Boise Technology, they offer a full range of computer hardware, software, peripherals and accessories.

Thanks to its national buying power, Boise carries the best brand names in the business — Hewlett-Packard, 3M, HON, Avery and ACCO, to name a few. Also, private label items allow customers to trim costs without trimming quality.

Since the early 1960s, Boise has offered customers consistent national capabilities and highly personalized local service. Today, that philosophy remains unchanged. In fact, a recent customer satisfaction study found that ·96 percent of Boise customers rated Boise's overall quality "good" to "excellent." The company also maintains a steadfast commitment to work in conjunction with firms owned and operated by minorities (MBE), women (WBE) and persons with physical and developmental challenges (PC).

The world-class Boise sales force of more than 800 representatives nationwide ensures that superb service complements outstanding product selection. Sales representatives work closely with customers and in-house specialists in furniture and computer supplies to create customized solutions. Moreover, Boise offers the SAVE cost containment program to help customers streamline costs and improve ordering efficiency. In addition to its outstanding product selection and customer service, Boise makes ordering easy. Not only does the company provide user-friendly catalogs, dedicated fax order lines and a toll-free number, it also offers BC Connect electronic ordering options, including a CD-Rom catalog, Internet ordering and electronic data interchange (EDI) capabilities.

The company's centralized ordering process benefits customers big and small. A single computer system links all Boise locations, so clients receive national purchasing power while maintaining localized service and delivery. No matter where they're located, Boise's national account customers receive consistent product, pricing, services and reporting. And, with an integrated network of more than 40 distribution centers in the U.S., Canada and Australia, Boise can deliver your supplies whenever you need them.

DARDANO'S FLOWERLAND

In 1996, Dardano's Flowerland observed a bitter-sweet year. It was the year that the company celebrated 50 years of doing business in the same neighborhood on the south side of Denver. It was also the year that Frank Dardano died.

Frank Dardano was born in Denver in 1921 and grew up on the family farm on South Galapago Street near the South Platte River. His father, who had immigrated from Italy earlier in the century, was known throughout the region for his prize-winning celery.

When World War II broke out, Frank Dardano served proudly in both the Merchant Marines and the U.S. Army. When he returned to Denver in 1946, he married Arlene Garramone, the daughter of another well-known Denver farmer. Not surprisingly, the young couple started their own truck farm business.

Frank Dardano grew tomatoes, peppers, celery and other vegetables which he sold at farmers' markets. He also sold some of the young plants wholesale. Dardano's Flowerland can trace its history as a retail operation to the day when Arlene Dardano began selling a few bedding plants to passers-by.

Each year, Arlene sold a few more varieties of vegetables. Soon, the Dardanos were selling petunias and pansies as well — twelve plants in a handmade wooden box. In 1965, Frank Dardano purchased a two-acre piece of land across the street from his farm on which he built a 30,000-square-foot greenhouse and a 100-car parking lot.

When Dardano's Flowerland opened on April 25, 1965, its was the first "supermarket" for bedding plants west of the Mississippi. Opening day was successful beyond the couple's wildest dreams, with cars lined up on Evans Street waiting for a parking spot.

Just two months later, bad weather and the collapse of several dams in the mountains combined to send a 12-foot wall of water down the South Platte River — destroying not only the new Flowerland but Frank Dardano's wholesale operations as well. The total loss — uninsured — was more than $950,000.

Thanks to a determined effort and the support of family and friends, Dandano's Flowerland reopened in 1966. Growing operations were expanded to include award-winning carnations, leaf lettuce for restaurants and poinsettias. A 10,000-square-foot addition was made in 1977 and the entire greenhouse was remodeled in 1992.

Frank Dardano was the first in Denver to advertise bedding plants on billboards and on television and to sponsor a television show on gardening. He was a pioneer in using disease-resistant mixtures to grow his plants. In 1980, Frank Dardano received the grower of the year award from the Colorado Bedding and Pot Plant Association.

In 1984, Frank and Arlene Dardano moved to Arizona for health reasons, leaving Dardano's Flowerland in the capable hands of their daughter, Loretta Dardano. Together with Denver Children's Hospital, the Osmund

Frank Dardano (1921-1996), shown here with his daughter Loretta, established Dardano's Flowerland in 1946. Dardano's celebrated its 50th anniversary in 1996.

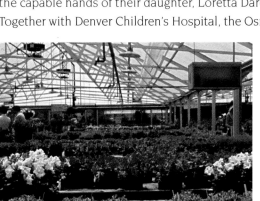

Foundation and Channel 4, Dardano's Flowerland created the Children's Miracle Rose in 1987.

Today, Dardano's Flowerland has expanded its offerings to include a full service flower shop that provides local and worldwide delivery of floral arrangements for all occasions. Arlene Dardano has returned to Denver and has joined Loretta Dardano and Frank Dardano, Jr., in keeping the tradition of Dardano's Flowerland alive.

The seed planted 50 years ago by Frank Dardano continues flowering today through his family and his family business.

Dardano's Flowerland offers bedding plants and a full-service flower shop that provides local and worldwide delivery of floral arrangements for all occasions.

Canino's Sausage Company

Sausage's history is as colorful as the Italian enclave that flourished north of downtown, in an area called 'Little Italy.' Little Italy wrapped around Our Lady Of Mount Carmel, a Roman Catholic church built for Italian immigrants. The Caninos, and their hand-crafted sausage, remain integral to Little Italy's history.

Lena "Grandma" Canino displays her hand-crafted, Old World recipe sausage in front of the family market at 35th and Navajo. Circa 1969.
Credit: Bill Peery

In 1897, 9-month-old Lena Pagliano came to America. She wed Joseph J. Canino the day after Christmas, 1917. Eight years later, the couple established the Navajo Meat Market, on the corner of 35th and Navajo. The site is now a Denver landmark.

Joseph's mother, Assunta, gave the newlyweds her Old World sausage recipe, brought to America from Calabria, Italy — the 'toe' of Italy's 'boot.' The rest is sausage-making history.

For hours, Joseph cut pork. Lena's strong hands measured, mixed, kneaded, and stuffed five hundred pounds of meat daily. Lena made light the task by singing beloved Italian songs; her five children often at her side.

Times were tough. Families had little money for food or rent. Lena let no one go empty-handed, including the down-trodden and homeless of nearby rail yards. At Lena's rosary in 1975, a clean-shaven, raggedy clothed hobo touchingly bid a final farewell to the kind 'lady in the store.'

During World War II, the government's meat restrictions never hampered the sausage making due to the devotion the meat salesmen had for Lena.

In 1957, the Navajo Meat Market became Canino's Italian Sausage Company. Son Louie, and son-in-law, Tony Tarantino, helped out. Joseph passed away in 1969, and the company was reluctantly sold to Lena's grandson, Joe Tarantino, in 1970.

Joe and school chum, Mike Payne, worked diligently for eighteen years developing new sausages. Joe ultimately sold Canino's to Mike in 1988. The company was incorporated, and the name changed to Canino's Sausage Company to accommodate the many sausage varieties. Tragically, Mike died the following year.

Diana Payne, Mike's widow, retained the company. With the love and support of family, she kept it going. Over the years, many of Mike and Diana's family members worked at Canino's. Loyal to the Canino family, Diana still uses the recipe that the Canino's carried from Italy.

In 1992, Diana's high school classmate, Lou Nowakowski, became a partner. Today, one mile north of the original location, Canino's Sausage Company processes nearly five thousand pounds of fresh meat daily into the highest caliber sausages available. Hand-stuffing has been replaced by today's state-of-the-art, stainless steel, V-neck stuffers. Production temperatures stay in the low 40's, and the process now involves ice, which improves shelf life and enhances color, flavor, and texture.

The savory aroma of fennel, paprika, chili carribe, and garlic waft nostalgically from the spice room, soon to be mixed into Canino's famous hot and mild Italian, German, Polish, Mexican, Bratwurst, and Italian turkey sausage.

Family strength and determination, original recipes, natural casings, low fat content, and no preservatives or artificial color makes Canino's sausages a perennial favorite in a city that appreciates heritage — a legacy "Grandma Canino" could be proud of.

PARK MEADOWS

Park Meadows, Colorado's only retail resort, has been carefully designed as a tribute to the state's unique image and lifestyle.

You are greeted with the relaxing sound of water rushing over the nearby falls as warm sunshine splashes across comfortably carpeted oak and marble floors at your feet. You sink into a soft leather couch and gaze up at the magnificent beamed ceiling overhead. The delicious smells of carefully prepared cuisine waft by as you catch sight of a friend and wave hello. This wonderful place has the feel of your favorite mountain resort — but it is more. Welcome to Park Meadows.

TrizecHahn Centers is pleased to introduce Park Meadows, Colorado's newest and only retail resort. Conveniently located at the northwest quadrant of I-25 and C-470 in Douglas County, this 1.5 million square foot, $164 million retail shopping center has been carefully designed as a tribute to Colorado's unique image and lifestyle.

Park Meadows' interior design incorporates indigenous building materials, native Colorado artwork and locally crafted furnishings into a hospitable and user-friendly shopping environment. It offers the local, regional and international shopper a warm and welcoming ambiance amid the nation's leading retail shops and restaurants.

Four distinct retail districts make Park Meadows an exciting departure from conventional shopping center design.

The Lifestyle District, centered around the Majestic Court, pays tribute to the extraordinary Colorado landscape and lifestyle. This environment features native rock, warm wood surfaces and a cascading red rock waterfall encircled by the moving words to Katharine Lee Bates' poem, *America the Beautiful*. Retailers located in the Majestic Court are dedicated to lifestyle merchandise.

The Fashion District, featuring Nordstrom, is dedicated exclusively to fashion for individuals and their homes. The Chalet Court, featuring a 66-foot-tall limestone and granite fireplace, is surrounded by plush, handcrafted leather furniture, lodge-style lighting fixtures and commissioned artwork from regional artists. The hospitable ambiance of the Chalet Court is designed for socializing and relaxing.

The Family District, featuring Dillard's, evokes the wonder of childhood and the family lifestyle around the Centennial Ranch Court. The decor is inspired by the romance of ranch life. A playful atmosphere is encouraged here with hanging mobiles of native Colorado wildlife and overstuffed leather animals designed for active children's play.

The Entertainment District, centered around a towering 87-foot sandstone fireplace, welcomes Park Meadows' guests into the Grand Dining Hall. In an atmosphere that resembles a ranch dining hall, guests will find wooden tables inlaid with a Native American motif, mission-style chairs and chandeliers that resemble upside-down open umbrellas in a columbine bloom and pine cone print. The Grand Dining Hall is Park Meadows' center of entertainment with seating for 800 guests surrounded by 12 food venues.

Included in the Grand Dining Hall is the United Artists' Theater Starport, a total entertainment destination including a movie theater and virtual reality experiences like *Showscan*, a motion simulation theater; *Virtual Hanglider*, the thrill of hangliding without the risk; and *Amazing Space*, offering games for younger children.

The Chalet Court, featuring a 66-foot-tall limestone and granite fireplace, anchors Park Meadows' Lifestyle District.

DENVER MERCHANDISE MART

Denver is well-known as the retail hub of the Rocky Mountain West. The Denver Merchandise Mart, in turn, is well-known as the retailers' source for a wide range of gifts, souvenirs, apparel and Western wear and equipment.

Built in 1965, the Denver Merchandise Mart has grown into the largest privately owned showroom and trade show complex in the region. Convenient to Downtown Denver as well as the interstate system, the Mart comprises three connected buildings plus an on-site hotel. Parking is plentiful and free.

The Mart Building contains 500 permanent showrooms leased by sales representatives and manufacturers — featuring a broad assortment of Western apparel, boots, jewelry and accessories, for which the Mart is internationally famous. In addition, these showrooms offer non-Western apparel and shoes for men, women and children; skiwear and activewear; gourmet food items; souvenirs, gifts and tableware; and decorative items and furnishings for the home.

The Mart Building also includes the Terrace Gardens, a four-story skylighted atrium that features 12,000 square feet of open space for receptions, dinners, dances, speeches, shows and other special events.

The Expo Building and the Pavilion offer flexible space for regional, national and international trade and consumer shows. Regular exhibitors include food wholesalers, antique dealers, doll collectors, gun collectors, associations, businesses and corporations — even modern-day prospectors who still pan for gold! The Mart's service and success can be measured by its 30-year-plus history of repeat business.

Two major shows held regularly at the Mart are among the foremost in their respective industries. The Denver International Western & English Apparel & Equipment Market, held each January, attracts buyers from around the world.

The Denver Merchandise Mart Gift, Jewelry and Resort Show, held twice a year, is a premier show in the gift and resort industry. The Mart also attracts the region's retailers and interior designers with the Denver Apparel and Accessory Market, Super Market Mondays, the Design Showcase and Design Open House.

The Expo Building offers 85,000 square feet of exhibit and display space and the Pavilion offers 65,000 square feet. The Pavilion's 20-foot open-beam ceiling makes it ideal for shows involving construction equipment, heavy machinery, and cars and trucks, as well as food distributors and jewelry exhibitors.

The Mart's full-service package of on-site services includes catering, security, loading dock, drayage, show set-up and housekeeping. The food service department provides daily service for permanent tenants as well as banquet service for as many as 3,000 people and buffet service for 6,500.

The Denver Merchandise Mart, a valuable resource for wholesalers and retailers for more than 30 years, ranks as one of the major show facilities in the Rocky Mountain West.

ABOVE: With 500 permanent showrooms, The Denver Merchandise Mart is a retailers' resource for a wide range of gifts, souvenirs, apparel and Western wear and equipment.

FAR RIGHT: The Denver Merchandise Mart is the largest privately owned showroom and trade show complex in the Rocky Mountain region.

LOWER RIGHT: The Terrace Gardens is an ideal site for receptions, dinners, dances, speeches, shows and other special events.

TATTERED COVER BOOK STORE

It all began twenty-three years ago, when Joyce Meskis purchased a small bookshop in Denver's Cherry Creek district. Measuring only 950 square feet it offered an eclectic selection of books, a cozy atmosphere, and good old-fashioned customer service. All this because Joyce furnished the shop with overstuffed antique chairs and stocked the shelves until they were overflowing with volumes and periodicals, many of which couldn't be found anywhere else in the city. The Tattered Cover soon became a "home away from home" for readers of all ages.

As requests for titles grew, Joyce began to push back the walls to make room for more books, expanding several times over twelve years; first opening up a second floor, then moving into a larger shop across the street. Finally, in 1986, the Tattered Cover moved just two blocks from the original bookshop into a vacant four-story building at the corner of First Avenue and Milwaukee Street. Many of Joyce's customers volunteered to help and the entire stock was relocated in a single day. With 40,000 square feet on four floors, the already phenomenal selection of titles soon redoubled.

Today the Tattered Cover at Cherry Creek houses a vast inventory of books as well as one of the best selections of magazines and periodicals in the city. With an espresso bar on the ground floor and The Fourth Story

Restaurant on the top, browsers can find sustenance in a uniquely literary setting. The entrance to the fashionable Cherry Creek mall is only steps away from the Tattered Cover's front door, directly across First Avenue.

In 1994 a second Tattered Cover opened in Denver's oldest district — historic Lower Downtown. The bookstore resides in the Morey Mercantile building, constructed in 1884 for a wholesale grocer named C.S. Morey. Located at the corner of Wynkoop and 16th Streets, the building was designed by the illustrious firm of Gove & Walsh, architects of Denver's landmark Union Station. According to historians, the Morey Mercantile Company, manufacturers of Solitaire brand coffee and food products, became the largest, most elegant operation of its kind in the west. Now fully restored to its original condition, the Morey building houses 35,000 square feet of books on three floors. Several cozy fireplaces, a spacious parlor for author readings and autographings, an abundance of comfortable antique furniture, and the smell of espresso all enhance the experience of shopping at the LoDo store. As a tribute to the building's origins, Joyce has placed a portrait of C.S. Morey over the largest fireplace in the shop.

Inside the Cherry Creek bookstore.

Historic LoDo bookstore.

Between Cherry Creek and LoDo, the Tattered Cover offers over half a million books, more than 150,000 titles, and a busy schedule of author appearances. Still, Joyce operates as only a local proprietor can — with an ear to the needs of the community and an emphasis on hospitality and personal service. Lots of nooks and crannies offer the intimacy of a smaller bookshop, while ample sofas and chairs make readers feel at home. Above all, browsers are encouraged to linger for as long as they like.

DENVER METRO CONVENTION & VISITORS BUREAU

Denver, with its rich heritage, pristine setting, and wealth of activities and events, has been a favorite travel destination for many years, largely due to the efforts of the Denver Metro Convention & Visitors Bureau, which for the past 88 years has worked with area businesses to promote the Mile High City as a vacation and convention destination to potential visitors across the United States and around the world.

The private, not-for-profit organization is the largest travel marketing organization in the state with almost 1,300 business members, 48 full-time employees, over 50 part-time employees and a team of 100 volunteers. Funding comes from its business members and a portion of the lodger's tax collected in the City and County of Denver, supporting a variety of services and programs designed not only to "get the word out" on Denver as a great destination, but also to help Bureau members tap into the billions spent in metro Denver every year by out-of-town visitors.

With offices in Denver, Washington D.C. and

Chicago, the Bureau's Convention Department promotes metro Denver as a destination for meetings and conventions and works with meeting planners to help with all their local needs. Convincing tour operators to include Denver in their itineraries is the focus of the Bureau's Tourism Department, which contacts hundreds of travel agents and group tour operators annually, both domestically and internationally. An Internet home page, interactive E-mail and a state-of-the-art CD ROM sales presentation are just a few of the ways the Bureau is using the latest technology to market Denver as a destination for conventions and vacation travel.

Millions of potential visitors annually are introduced to Denver through the efforts of the Bureau's Marketing Department, which coordinates all advertising, public relations, information centers and membership services. Ads in national publications generate hundreds of thousands of inquiries for Denver tourism information, and public relations efforts generate nearly $3 million in travel stories about Denver in major newspapers and magazines.

Almost a half-million individuals annually access tourism information at information centers located at Denver International Airport, in downtown Denver and the State Capitol; a new Event Marketing Department promotes Denver as a site for sporting and non-sporting events, ranging from the U.S. Olympic Festival to the International Golf Tournament.

The Bureau's efforts support an estimated $4.1 billion tourism industry in the Denver area, providing a number of opportunities for businesses to increase their bottom lines. Members of the Bureau, however, receive an edge in marketing to this community through a number of benefits, including sales leads, bi-monthly newsletters, educational marketing seminars, research reports, free listings in Bureau publications, lists of upcoming events with contact names, and free brochure display space at information centers. It's an investment, they believe, that pays off — not only for themselves, but for visitors to Denver as well.

Colorado Convention Center.
Credit: Denver Metro Convention and Visitors Bureau

GUMP GLASS

What do Currigan Hall, the Brown Palace Hotel and the chapel at the U.S. Air Force Academy have in common? They all sport windows and other glass installations by Gump Glass, a Denver-area leader in glass, mirror, and door installations for 73 years.

Tudor Gump began the company that would bear his name in 1924. Like most glass shops of the time, paint was also a significant component of the business and for a period of time the company was known as Gump Glass and Paint Co. From that time, the company has changed location twice, now occupying sales and showroom facilities at 1265 South Broadway, just south of downtown Denver.

Ownership of the company, like its location, has changed only twice in the firm's history, passing from one family to another when the Gump family sold the business to the Sigman family in 1968. Noted for their long history in Colorado's meat packing industry, the Sigmans owned and operated Gump Glass for 23 years, selling it in 1991 to Minnesota-based Harmon Glass, a subsidiary of Apogee Enterprises.

When the purchase was completed, the Harmon organization believed the local feel and family structure of the business should remain intact as much as possible. Today, Gump Glass continues to be managed by a member of the Sigman family while operating as one of eight regional shops in Harmon Inc.'s Full Service Division.

In this day and age of high specialization, Gump Glass takes great pride in maintaining a strong presence as a true full-service company. Its prime location and expansive showroom attract a strong walk-in trade. No fewer than four full-time inside customer service representatives assist the many customers who stop by or call in.

Commercial and residential glass repair and replacement is Gump Glass's primary business focus. The company also enjoys a strong reputation as a subcontractor, performing installations of storefront windows, exterior curtainwalls, skylights and entrances on new commercial structures and buildings undergoing remodel or renovation. In addition to installa-

tions for some of the Front Range's most noted structures, Gump Glass also has completed many hundreds of windowall scopes on various hotels, hospitals, schools and office buildings throughout the metro Denver area and in Summit County.

A custom-designed mirror from Gump Glass graces a Denver residence. Credit: Joel Eden

Gump Glass is also well known for its beautiful design work and installation of custom mirrored walls and for resilvering antique and heirloom mirrors. The company's specialty glass etching and sandblasting services are used to create products ranging from custom decorations to corporate recognition awards and plaques.

Few closely held and managed companies are able to prosper in any given local market for three quarters of a century. Gump Glass is extremely proud of this milestone and looks ahead to its next 75 years.

J.W. BREWER TIRE COMPANY

Brewer Tire sells after-market tires, retreading and service to customers who maintain fleets of commercial, heavy service truck, industrial and off-highway vehicles.

Brewer Tire's service fleet consists of 87 delivery and service vehicles — including specialized off-the-road service vehicles for tough locations.

J.W. Tire Company is one of the largest commercial tire dealerships in North America. It is also one of those rare private companies that have been in the same family for more than 75 years.

Brewer Tire sells aftermarket tires, retreading and services to customers who maintain fleets of commercial, heavy service truck, industrial and off-highway vehicles.

In addition to new tires, the company offers its clients retreads and service — including balancing and alignment for everything from passenger cars and pick-up trucks to semis and earth-movers.

In addition to the trucking industry, Brewer Tire's commercial accounts include small contractors, highway and mining contractors, fixed mine locations, equipment dealers, auction companies and utility companies.

Brewer Tire, headquartered in the Denver suburb of Wheat Ridge, does business in the Western states of Colorado, Nevada, New Mexico, South Dakota, Utah and Wyoming. The company maintains 20 locations, including four in the Denver Metropolitan area. Thirteen of these have adjoining Bandag retreading shops.

All of these locations put into practice the company motto: "Sell the Very Best and Replace the Rest". The company's service fleet consists of 87 delivery and service vehicles, including specialized off-the-road service vehicles for tough locations such as construction, sand and gravel, paving, mining and oil drilling sites. The company employs 350 people — about one-fourth of them selling to the company's commercial accounts.

In 1996, Brewer Tire is approaching $100 million in annual sales. About 60 percent of these revenues come from new-tire sales, 20 percent from retreads, and 20 percent from service.

The company was founded by Joseph W. Brewer in 1921, who opened Joe's Tire Shop in a corner of his father's dairy supply store in the small town of Ogden, Utah. In 1927, the company sold $50,000 worth of tires and changed its name to J.W. Brewer Tire Company.

Alex Brewer started working for his father part time in the 1950s and full time in the 1960s. One of his first jobs was selling a brand new product line — Michelin radial ply tires. Today, 75 percent of the company's business is with Michelin. At the request of Michelin, Brewer Tire expanded to Denver and Colorado in 1965. Eventually, the company's headquarters moved to Denver.

J.W. Brewer died in 1971 and Alex Brewer succeeded him as president — a position he held until 1996.

....

J.W. Brewer Tire Company, one of the largest commercial tire dealerships in North America with nearly $100 million in annual sales, has been owned and operated by the same family for 75 years. Alex Brewer is surrounded by his four sons (left to right) Eric, Chuck, Greg and Lex.

At that time, Alex Brewer became the company's chief executive officer and his son, Lex Brewer, succeeded him as president. Three other sons — Greg, Chuck and Eric — are actively involved with Brewer Tire as vice presidents.

In order to formalize its support of Denver charities, the company is in the process of establishing the Alex Brewer Family Foundation.

For more than 75 years, J.W. Brewer Tire Co. has grown steadily by following the Brewer family's principles of hard work, quality products and good service.

Garvin's Sewer Service Inc.

Garvin's Sewer Service, established as a franchise in 1940, has always operated in Denver's historic golden triangle neighborhood.

In 1990, Garvin's Sewer Service celebrated its golden anniversary — 50 years of operations, 50 years of integrity, 50 years in Denver's historic Golden Triangle neighborhood.

The following year, company founder Russell Garvin died at age 86.

Today, Garvin's Sewer Service is an independent company owned and operated by Garvin's nephew, K.C. Aston, who places top priority on maintaining his uncle's reputation for integrity.

When Garvin's Sewer Service was established in 1940, the company was one of the first franchises of a large national company whose name would soon become synonymous with sewer cleaning. Garvin maintained that relationship for half a century, going independent only in 1990 when he thought franchise fees had soared too high.

A third generation of Denver area residents is now growing up with Garvin's Sewer Service listed in the family address book. In fact, 80 percent of the company's business is repeat business — a sure sign of satisfied customers.

Multiple generations and extended families are also common in the company's 21-person workforce, which has an exceptionally low rate of turnover. Over the years, the company has operated from four differ-

ent sites, but always within the same Golden Triangle neighborhood, located just south of Downtown Denver.

Garvin's Sewer Service operates by the motto, "We clean drains, not bank accounts!" In fact, the company services the drain cleaning needs — routine and specialized — of residential and commercial markets all along the front range. The company's business is about 80 percent residential and 20 percent commercial.

Today, Garvin's Sewer Services is an independent company owned and operated by Garvin's nephew, K.C. Aston.

The company can clean drains from as small as one-quarter inch to as large as six feet in diameter. To provide this service, the company operates main line rodding equipment, drag line bucket machines, a high-pressure jet water system and video camera inspection.

With more than 55 years of operation, Garvin's Sewer Service continues to abide by its founder's business philosophy:

"The mission of Garvin's Sewer Service is to provide a service that is fair and honest. We believe that customers have the right to expect fast, efficient service; that our service will be done by employees who are knowledgeable, polite and neat.

"We treat our customers with respect in order to achieve a long and productive service relationship upon which they can rely. We are dedicated to maintaining the integrity of the Garvin's name."

Company founder Russell Garvin owned and operated Garvin's Sewer Service for more than 50 years.

HOLTZE EXECUTIVE PLACE

When Holtze Executive Place opened for business, an important piece of Downtown Denver's history was restored to the city.

A $21 million restoration has transformed a long-vacant eyesore along "Wall Street West" into stylish new downtown lodging — the first new hotel to open downtown in more than a decade.

Holtze Executive Place provides a convenient home-away-from-home environment for the extended-stay business traveler. The hotel includes 119 luxury "apartments," each of which contains a living room, fully equipped kitchen, spacious bedroom and deluxe bathroom with an oversized circular tub. Many of the units feature gas fireplaces.

Holtze Executive Place provides a convenient home-away-from-home environment for the extended-stay business traveler.

Adjoining each suite is a spacious guest room that can be "annexed" to create a two-bedroom two-bathroom suite — perfect for weekend visits from the family. Guest rooms are also available as traditional hotel rooms, giving Holtze Executive Place a maximum of 246 units.

The lower level of Holtze Executive Place houses the Executive Club, built with native Colorado materials and furnished in a classic-yet-comfortable style. The Executive Club, which serves as the hotel's "living room," includes an open atrium with a rock-and-water feature that evokes a running mountain stream.

Holtze Executive Place combines the convenience of a modern luxury apartment with a truly classic setting in Downtown Denver.

Each morning, Holtze Executive Place offers a complimentary breakfast in the Executive Club. Each evening, there is a guest reception. Game tables are available. The adjoining library offers space for quiet reading or research. For more structured business meetings, private rooms are available.

Holtze Executive Place is located in the heart of the

downtown business district, right on the light-rail line and one block from the 16th Street Pedestrian Mall and its free shuttle. The hotel also offers its guests free transportation within a three-mile radius. For guests with their own cars, on-site parking is available.

The historic building that houses Holtze Executive Place was originally designed for First National Bank by well-known Denver architect Frank Edbrooke, who also designed the Brown Palace.

When the First National Bank building opened for business in 1911, it was the city's tallest structure and helped secure 17th Street's reputation as the financial epicenter of Denver and the Rocky Mountain West. It later housed American National Bank.

The years, however, had not been kind. A 1950s "renovation" had removed the bank building's decorative cornice and covered its classic facade with a pre-cast concrete screen. When Stevens Holtze Corp. commenced its two-year renovation project in 1993, the building had been vacant for almost eight years.

Since it opened, Holtze Executive Place has been recognized with a Downtown Denver Award by the Denver Downtown Partnership, Inc., and by a Stephen H. Hart Award by the Colorado Historical Society.

Stevens Holtze Corp. also owns two other extended-stay facilities in the metropolitan area, Holtze Executive Village-Southeast, in Aurora, and Holtze Executive Village-Denver Tech Center.

Holtze Executive Place combines the convenience of a modern luxury apartment with a truly classic setting in Downtown Denver — for a day, a week or even a year.

THE WARWICK HOTEL

The Warwick Hotel in Downtown Denver is a member of the prestigious Warwick International Hotels group — one of only four hotels the group owns and operates in the United States. The group, founded in 1980 and headquartered in Paris, is named after its flagship hotel, the New York Warwick.

The Warwick Hotel's rooftop swimming pool offers a spectacular view of downtown Denver and the mountains beyond.

The Warwick International Hotels group owns hotels in Paris, Cannes, Lyon, St. Remy-de-Provence, Poitiers, Brussels, Genval, Rixensart, Waterloo and Geneva. When the Warwick Hotel in Denver calls itself a European-style hotel, it makes this claim with solid credentials.

In keeping with this theme, The Warwick Hotel is a major sponsor of the Denver International Film Festival.

The Warwick Hotel is a unique property located in the heart of Denver, within walking distance of the city's financial district. As a result, it is a very popular destination among business travelers who like to avoid the impersonal sameness of chain hotels. Eighty-five percent of the Warwick Hotel's guests are business travelers — either in groups or as individuals.

The Warwick Hotel offers personalized service to the small meetings market, specializing in groups of fewer than 100 people. The hotel offers 9,100 square feet of meeting space, including a flexibly configured ballroom and a variety of tastefully appointed meeting rooms, to meet a variety of needs. This space is also available for weddings and other social occasions.

Almost all of The Warwick Hotel's individual non-business guests are foreign travelers who have come to trust the Warwick name and the gracious international style it represents.

The 15-story Warwick Hotel offers 191 oversized, deluxe guest rooms — including 49 suites and four luxury suites. Each room is decorated in the classic "English hunt" style with fine Thomasville furnishings. Complimentary with all rooms is a European-style breakfast buffet.

Most rooms offer wet bars, refrigerators, dining tables and private balconies. All feature telephones equipped with data ports, voice mail and two incoming telephone lines. The hotel's rooftop swimming pool, open as weather permits, offers a spectacular view of downtown Denver and the mountains beyond.

The Liaison Restaurant features a full breakfast menu plus continental cuisine for lunch and dinner. During the cocktail hour, the Liaison Lounge presents each guest with complimentary hors d'oeuvres and drink specials. A town car provides free transportation around downtown Denver, the Cherry Creek shopping district and the museum area.

On weekends, The Warwick Hotel offers special packages featuring various combinations of accommodations, meals and downtown activities.

Activities can include Elitch Gardens amusement park, the Children's Museum, the Denver Museum of Natural History, the Denver Art Museum, rafting on the Platte River or a Colorado Rockies baseball game — or simply a quiet weekend alone.

The Warwick Hotel offers European-style accommodations in downtown Denver to business and individual travelers.

The Symphony Suite at the European-style Warwick Hotel, a member of the prestigious Warwick International Hotels group.

Paradise Cleaners and Shirt Laundry

When Denver residents invest in high quality clothes, they patronize the city's vast array of upscale stores and boutiques. When they want to safely clean those clothes, they patronize Paradise Cleaners and Shirt Laundry.

For almost 75 years, Paradise Cleaners has been providing Denver residents with high quality cleaning service.

And the tradition continues. Repeatedly, Paradise Cleaners has been named "Denver's Best" in the "Readers' Choice" competition sponsored by the *Rocky Mountain News*.

Paradise Cleaners is the chosen quality cleaner in the Denver area authorized to use Aqua-Clean, a patented "wet clean" process that is approved by the Environmental Protection Agency and cleans delicate fabrics thoroughly and safely using only special soaps and water.

This process allows Paradise Cleaners to accept such previously non-dry-cleanable items as sequined gowns and jackets, wedding dresses, delicate buttons, hand-painted fabrics and high-tech fabrics. Aqua-Clean offers an environmentally friendly alternative to dry cleaning.

Paradise Cleaners has also been recognized by the EPA for the way it handles its traditional dry cleaning chemicals. By consolidating all cleaning operations at one master plant, Paradise Cleaners can strictly monitor the proper use and disposal of these chemicals.

For many years, Paradise Cleaners has promised its customers odorless dry cleaning. Even though it takes longer, Paradise Cleaners gently tumbles clothes in the company's patented dry cleaning machines until all of the chemicals — and odors — have completely dissipated.

In addition, Paradise Cleaners hand finishes all garments — including the crease on the sleeves of men's dress shirts that is impossible to achieve by machine. Conversely, the company will dry clean blue jeans without the infamous crease. All of this attention to detail costs more, which is why Paradise Cleaners is a cut above its less particular competitors.

Paradise Cleaners, originally located on South Broadway, was established in 1924. Twenty years later, the company moved to East Colfax Avenue, where it continues to occupy Denver's largest self-contained master dry cleaning and laundering facility.

In 1958, Paradise Cleaners introduced the city's first drive-through service. In 1975, the company began to selectively franchise the company to qualified entrepreneurs. In 1997, the company has 12 retail outlets — located primarily on the city's southeast side.

Every two hours, six days a week, clothes are picked up and dropped off at each retail store and transported to the master plant for careful cleaning. The company's trucks, hand painted in a blue-sky-and-cloud motif that evokes "paradise," are a familiar sight around Denver. The company also offers home pick up and delivery.

Nearly 75 years and 50 million garments after its beginning, Paradise Cleaners and Shirt Laundry remains the cleaning service of choice for Denver's high quality garments.

CASTLE MARNE

Small wonder that *County Inn Magazine* ranked Castle Marne one of the top twelve B & Bs in America. Guests at this exquisite inn are pampered with extravagant breakfasts and afternoon tea, a high tech business office and an old fashioned library, a billiard room and a Victorian garden.

Wibur S. Raymond built the mansion in 1889 as one of the finest Romanesque Revival residences by celebrated Denver residential architect William Lang. Raymond wanted his house, with its soaring stone tower, turret and clustered chimneys as a showhome for the Wyman Addition. His family had purchased this northeast parcel of Denver's mansion-studded Capitol Hill neighborhood from John S. Wyman, who platted it in 1882 as an addition to Denver.

During the early 1900s, the Raymond House sank into slow decline. The Wyman Addition, a onetime enclave of the wealthy became noted for cheap apartments in subdivided, tumble-down mansions. The Raymond House became the Marne Apartments, then a processing center for parolees, then stood empty and derelict, occupied only by vagrants, pigeons and rodents.

This crumbling castle needed some magic when Jim and Diane Peiker fell in love with it. In 1988, they bought and restored it to glory with help from daughter Melissa and her husband Louis as well as their son Riley, who conducts neighborhood tours in an antique tour bus.

"When we told bankers we wanted to make this a hotel," Jim Peiker recalls, "their eyes would roll back into their heads. They just didn't understand the vibrancy, the excitement of a culturally diverse neighborhood. It took months to find financing. Finally Representative Pat Schroeder hand carried our Small Business Administration Loan application to that office and enabled us to open in 1989."

The Peikers persisted, restoring not only their own castle but helping to transform the 1500 block of Race Street as a splendid collection of restored Neoclassical, Four Square, Queen Anne and Romanesque style gems. The Peikers and their neighbors also spruced up the entire Wyman Addition, stretching roughly from York Street to Franklin Street between East 13th and East 17th Avenues. Revitalization was rewarded in 1993 with designation of the entire area as a Denver Historic District.

Castle Marne, which is also listed on the National Register of Historic Places, remains a centerpiece for this elegant, tree-shaded neighborhood whose sandstone sidewalks lead to both downtown and City Park, home of the Denver Zoo and Denver Museum of Natural History. The castle is a three-story monument of pink and grey rusticated lava stone embellished by flowery stone detailing. Exquisite stonework characterizes even the multiple stone chimneys and rough hewn stone balustrades crowning the porch and corner tower. Note the three porch column capitals hand carved with a series of budding, blossoming, and flourishing lotus plants.

Woodwork inside is as extravagant as the exterior stonework. Warm golden oak adorned with rosettes and garlands encloses the staircase. High ceilings and large windows make Castle Marne an unusually bright and airy Victorian. The nine bedrooms combine modern comforts with antique charm. Castle Marne is a spectacular, easy to find landmark, but a hard place to leave.

LEFT: The original fireplace still warms the formal parlor of Castle Marne.

When the snow melts, guests enjoy the beauty and serenity of Castle Marne's English Garden.
Credit: **T. Noel**

PEPSI-COLA BOTTLING COMPANY OF DENVER

Some 38 years after Pepsi-Cola was originally formulated by Caleb D. Bradham in the basement of his North Carolina pharmacy, the increasingly popular drink found its way to Denver. In 1936, James (Bert) Gooding Sr. put Pepsi on the map in Denver by purchasing a Pepsi franchise for $500. The production

and distribution of Pepsi in Colorado on 17th Street began on a shoestring and has grown along with Pepsi's phenomenal growth. And grow they have, at an average rate of 15 percent per year, doubling their business every five years. To illustrate this phenomenal growth, PepsiCo now sells more in one week than they did their entire first year.

In 1947, Bert Gooding became Chairman of the Board and his son, Jim Gooding, was named President and General Manager. A reminder of the Gooding family's beginnings in Pepsi are shown in

the 1936 Ford, a replica of the company car Gooding used to make his first sales call, which was the first thing a person is apt to see upon entering the plant. This reminder of Pepsi's more humble beginnings in Denver goes hand in hand with the employee-oriented atmosphere PepsiCo provides its employees. Incentives and company-sponsored family "fun days"

such as trips to the Denver Zoo, Elitch Gardens, Water World, and family carnivals to name a few, offer the Denver Pepsi Bottling Company a way to reward its employees for a job well done. Quality has been a key word at Pepsi from the beginning — quality in its products, its service, its employees, and the lives of those employees.

Because of the growth Pepsi experienced, a new 32,500-square-foot plant was built on Brighton Boulevard. Pepsi moved into the new plant in April 1951. By 1951, the Denver Pepsi employees had grown in number from four to 44. In 1962, Bert Gooding passed away after having seen his $500 investment and years of work grow into one of the largest operations in Denver.

In 1967, a new office building was completed freeing up the space from the old building for the building of a new facility for the can line. Technology and advancements through the years provided Pepsi with increasingly efficient operations. Distribution facilities were also added in the Colorado mountains in Kremmling and in Fort Collins. The existing Pepsi-Cola Bottling Company of Denver became fully operational in early 1975. Its expansive size and automated technology provide one of the most efficient bottling plants in PepsiCo's enterprise. Production from Denver's facility supplies six warehouses along the Front Range. In 1977, Jim Gooding's son and Bert Gooding's grandson, Richard Gooding, became Executive Vice President in charge of Personnel, Advertising, and Public and Governmental Relations. At age 62, Jim Gooding passed away in 1980, but his lifelong commitment to Pepsi's excellence lives on today.

PepsiCo was formed through the 1965 merger of the Pepsi-Cola Company and Frito-Lay, Inc. In 1988, the Gooding family sold the Denver franchise back to PepsiCo. PepsiCo operates on a worldwide basis within three industry segments: beverages, snack foods, and restaurants.

PepsiCo's stock is traded principally on the New York Stock Exchange and is also listed on the Amsterdam, Chicago, Swiss, and Tokyo stock exchanges.

Before Coloradans enacted statewide Prohibition in 1916, a dozen different breweries quenched the high, dry city. The Beer Depot at 2433 16th Street housed the Union Brewing Company, a boarding house, a restaurant and a saloon before its 1901 merger with the Tivoli Brewery. *Credit: Denver Public Library*

DENVER: AN ANNOTATED BIBLIOGRAPHY

General Works

Arps, Louisa Ward. *Denver in Slices*. Denver: Sage Books, 1959 (1983 reprint by Swallow Press) 263 pp., illus., notes, index.
Delicious slices of Denver's past including the two gold mints, drinking water, City Ditch, Cherry Creek, the South Platte, Tabor ghosts, the Windsor Hotel, the Baron of Montclair, Overland Park, Buffalo Bill, Elitch Gardens and Eugene Field. A delightfully written and diligently researched appetizer.

Denver Municipal Facts. City and County of Denver, 1909-1931. (Initially a weekly, then a monthly magazine.)
A house organ begun by Mayor Speer to publicize Denver's improvements at a time when newspapers seemed to focus only on his corruption and the city's problems. Many illustrations. A first-rate source for research on the city.

The Denver Westerners. Monthly Roundup. Denver: Denver Posse of Westerners, 1944-present. Brandbook. Annual 1946-77 & 1995.
A mother lode of original research on many aspects of Denver, Colorado, and Western history. You are welcome to join this group which meets monthly for dinner and a talk on local history.

Dorsett, Lyle W. and G. Michael McCarthy. *Queen City: A History of Denver.*. Boulder: Pruett Pub. Co., 1976, rev. ed. 1986. 382p. illus., bib., index.
A valuable overview focusing on the power elite and the quality of life for ordinary Denverites.

Ferril, T. H. *Thomas Hornsby Ferril & the American West* ed. by Robert C. Baron, Stephen J. Leonard & Thomas J. Noel (Golden: Fulcrum Pub. Co., 1996). 166 pp.
Colorado's greatest poet, in nationally acclaimed words, often focused on change in Denver and Colorado. This anthology contains his best poetry, prose, and commentary on his life and work.

Leonard, Stephen J. & Thomas J. Noel. *Denver: From Mining Camp to Metropolis* Niwot: University Press of Colorado, 1990, 1994 paperback. 544 pp. illus., notes, index, map, appendices.
The most comprehensive modern history with separate chapters on the suburban counties, automobilization and aviation. Over two- thirds of the book is devoted to the 20th-century metropolis.

Mehls, Steven, Drake, J. & James E. Fell. *Aurora: Gateway to the Rockies.* Denver: Cordillera Press, 1985. 243 pp. index, bib, endnotes, illus.
A sound survey of Denver's largest suburb and emerging rival. This is a model for suburban histories yet to be written.

Mumey, Nolie. *History of the Early Settlements of Denver, 1859-1860; with Reproductions of the First City Directory, the 1859 map, the First Issue of The Rocky Mountain News and the Rare Cherry Creek Pioneer.* Glendale, Calif: Arthur H. Clark, 1942, 213 pp., illus., notes, bib., index.
Dr. Mumey, a physician, calculated that human beings need only four hours of sleep a day. With all his spare time, he produced this and many other books on Denver and Colorado.

Noel, Thomas J. *Denver: Rocky Mountain Gold.* Tulsa, Okla: Continental Heritage Press, 1980, 256 pp., illus., maps, bib.,index.
A lavishly illustrated look at Denver, written in a rosy style during a boom era. Includes brief histories of leading businesses and institutions.

Pyle, Robert Mitchell. *The Thunder Tree: Lessons from an Urban Wildlife.* N.Y.: Houghton Mifflin Co, 1993. 220 p., sources, map.
Eloquent reminiscences of an ecologist who found the High Line Canal a great escape from the proliferating suburbs of Aurora, Colorado's largest city in terms of square miles and third largest in terms of population.

Sinclair, Upton. *Mountain City.* N.Y.: Albert T. Charles Boni,1930, 399 pp.
Denver inspired one of Sinclair's worst novels, but his worst is still one of the best novels so far about our town.

Smiley, Jerome C. *History of Denver.* Denver: Western Pub. Co., 1978, (Reprint of original 1901 edition), 1,115 p.,illus., index.
Centuries from now Smiley will probably still be the definitive and the longest-winded biographer of 19th-century Denver. A booster history written with amazing grace, wit, and intelligence. Crackerjack 37-page index.

Spencer, Elma Dill Russell. *Green Russell and Gold.* Austin: University of Texas Press, 1966, 239 pp., illus., bib.,index.
A descendant's biography of the Georgian whose gold discovery in the summer of 1858 gave birth to Auraria and Denver.

Vickers, W. B. *History of the City of Denver.* Chicago: O.L. Baskin, 1880, 652 p., illus., index in the DAR reprint.
A lavish booster history written when Denver was a 22-two-year-old adolescent. Wonderful drawings of bushy-bearded pioneers and their prickly Victorian homes.

Wharton, Junius E.& David O.Wilhelm. *History of the City of Denver from Its Earliest Settlement... To Which Is Added A Full Complete Business Directory of the City.* Denver: Byers & Dailey, 1866. 184 pp., illus., (1901 reprint by D.O. Wilhelm).
Invaluable first history of Denver with the best 1860s city directory to boot. A rare find in used bookstores and a closely-guarded rarity in libraries.

Wilcox, Patricia, ed. *Lakewood-Colorado: An Illustrated Biography.* Lakewood: Lakewood 25th Birthday Commission, 1994. 316 p., endnotes, illus., maps.
A good overview of Colorado's fourth largest—and youngest—city.

Art, Architecture & Tours

Bakke, Diane & Jackie Davis. *Places Around the Bases: A Historic Tour of the Coors Field Neighborhood.* Englewood: Westcliffe Publishers, Inc., 1995. 176 p.,index, photos, map.

Ballast, David Kent. *Denver's Civic Center: A Walking Tour.* Denver: City Pub. Company, 1977. 30 pp., illus., maps.
Elegant photographs and works on the park-like center of city and stage government.

Barney, Libeus. *Letters of the Pike's Peak Gold Rush.* San Jose: The Talisman Press, 1959, 97 pp., map. Intro. by Thomas Hornsby Ferril.
Witty letters portraying Denver at the age of one, by the '59er whose saloon hall—the Apollo—housed the Queen City's first attempts at self-government, theater, and church-going.

Bradley, Jeff, Jane Fudge, Jennifer Heath & Marilynne S. Mason. *Denver: Confluence of the Arts.* Denver: Meridian International, Inc., 1995. 176 p., index, illus.

Brettell, Richard B. *Historic Denver: The Architects and the Architecture, 1858-1893.* Historic Denver, Inc., 1973, 240 pp., illus., notes, bib., index.
A gorgeously illustrated coffeetable tribute to the brick and brownstone city now bowing to glass, steel, cement, and asphalt. The fine, brief overview of nineteenth-century Denver is followed by a critical look at its leading architects, Frank E. Edbrooke, William Lang, and Robert Roeschlaub.

Dallas, Sandra. *Cherry Creek Gothic: Victorian Architecture in Denver.* Norman: University of Oklahoma Press, 1971, 292 p.,illus., bib., index.
Intriguingly illustrated and written with a much broader historical value than the title suggests.

Davis, Sally & Betty Baldwin. *Denver Dwellings and Descendants.* Denver: Sage Books, 1963, 250 pp., illus., bib., index.
Many photographs and informative text on leading families and their mansions.

Etter, Carolyn & Don. *The Denver Zoo: A Centennial History.* Niwot: The Denver Zoological Foundation & Roberts Rinehart Publishing Co., 1996. 237 p., index, bib., color photos.

Etter, Don D. *Auraria: Where Denver Began.* Boulder: Colorado Associated University Press, 1972, illus.

Etter, Don D. *Denver Going Modern: A Photographic Essay on the Imprint of the International Style On Denver Residential Architecture.* Denver: Graphic Impressions, Inc., 1977, 132 pp., illus., index.

Etter, Don D. *University Park: Four Walking Tours.* Denver: Graphic Impressions, Inc., 1974, 55 pp., illus.

Etter, Don, D. and William D. West. *Curtis Park: A Denver Neighborhood.* Boulder: Colorado Associated University Press, 1980, illus.
Four photographic studies by Etter, an Historic Denver, Inc. activist instrumental in preserving Auraria's Ninth Street Park and the Curtis Park Neighborhood. The Curtis Park book has prose by West, a UCD English professor whose interest in all things Victorian prompted him to spearhead the renaissance of Denver's oldest intact Victorian neighborhood.

Goodstein, Phil. *Denver's Capitol Hill.* Denver: Life Publications, 1988. 182 p., index, note on sources, illus. Intro. by T.J. Noel.

Goodstein, Phil. *Denver Streets: Names, Numbers, Locations, Logic.* Denver: New Social Publications, 1994. 144 p., index, sources, illus., maps.

Historic Denver, Inc. *Historic Denver News.* Monthly. 1971-present.
Join Historic Denver, Inc. and get a free copy every month. Back files feature Denver's rapidly vanishing landmarks and the struggle to save some of them.

Kohl, Edith E. *Denver's Historic Mansions: Citadels to the Empire Builders.* Denver: Sage Books, 1957, 268 pp., illus.
Photographs and descriptions of 31 mansions, many now gone.

Murphy, Jack A. *Geology Tour of Denver's Buildings and Monuments.* Denver: Historic Denver, Inc & Denver Museum of Natural History, 1995. 96 p., index, bib., photos, drawings.
The erudite curator of Geology at the Natural History Museum has produced a path-breaking look at the stones (and source quarries) used in notable downtown structures.

Noel, Thomas J. *Denver's Landmarks & Historic Districts: A Pictorial Guide.* Foreword by Mayor Wellington Webb. Niwot: University Press of Colorado, 1996. 162 p., index, bib., appendices, photos, maps.
Illustrated, brief sketches of some 160 individual designated landmarks and 28 historic districts.

Noel, Thomas J. *Richthofen's Montclair: A Pioneer Denver Suburb: A Brief History Illustrated Walking Tour and Research Guide To Denver Houses and Neighborhood History.* Boulder: Pruett Publishing Co., 1976, 116 pp., illus., maps, bib., index.

Noel, Thomas J. and Barbara S.Norgren. *Denver :The City Beautiful and Its Architects* (Denver: Historic Denver, Inc., 1987/1993 reprint). 248 pp., index, 400 illus., bib., illustrated glossary of architectural terms, biographical dictionary of architects.

Peters, Bette D. *Denver's City Park* (First Ed. UCD Historical Studies Journal, 1985; Second rev. ed. Boulder: Johnson Pub. Co., 1986). 67 p., index, notes, illus., maps.

Sagstetter, Beth. *Side by Side: A History of Denver's Witter Cofield Historic District.* Denver: Witter Cofield Historic District, 1995. 231 p., index, bib., illus, maps.
A grass roots history of the vintage neighborhood bordered by Federal Blvd. and Irving St. between W. 20th and 25th aves.

Van Wyke, Millie. *The Town of South Denver: Its People, Neighborhoods and Events Since 1858.* Boulder: Pruett Pub. Co., 1991. 150 p., index, bib., endnotes, photos, drawings, maps.

Wiberg, Ruth Eloise. *Rediscovering Northwest Denver: Its History, Its People, Its Landmarks.* Boulder: Pruett Publishing Co., 1976, 1995 paperback reprint by Univ. Press of Colorado. 212 pp., illus., notes, bib., index.
Northwest Denver is a fascinating, neglected quadrant of the Queen City. This readable, highly informative book collects in words and numerous illustrations the forgotten history and charm of Highlands, Argo, West Colfax, and Berkeley.

Wilk, Diane. *A Guide to Denver's Architectural Styles and Terms.* Denver: Historic Denver, Inc & Denver Museum of Natural History, 1995. 96 p., index, bib., photos, drawings.

Communications

Denver Chamber of Commerce. *Distinctive Denver: The Romance of An American Capital.* Denver: Chamber of Commerce, 1926, 63 pp., illus.
An example of many booster publications on the Queen City by the Chamber of Commerce since its 1884 organization.

Fowler, Eugene. *Timber Line: A Story of Bonfils and Tammen.* N.Y.: Covici, Friede, 1933. (many reprints) 480 pp.
A gossipy, not always true, account of the adolescence of The Denver Post, written with as much zest and a shade more accuracy than the former con-man and bartender ever mustered for their outrageously sensational (and profitable) newspaper.

Fowler, Eugene. *A Solo in Tom-Toms.* N.Y.: The Viking Press, 1946, 390 p.
Heart-warming, rib-tickling reminiscence of Fowler's puppyhood in Denver.

Hackenburg, Herbert J., Jr. *Muttering Machines to Laser Beams* (Denver: Mountain Bell, 1986) 365 + p., index, bib. illus.
A most lavish corporate history.

Hosokawa,Bill.*Thunder in the Rockies: The Incredible Denver Post.* N.Y.: William Morrow and Co., 1976, 447 pp., illus., index.
A candid, insider's peek at the paper that has done so much to shape 20th century Denver. A sequel and reliable antidote to Fowler's Timberline.

Culture, Education, Religion

Bleumel, Elinor. *The Golden Opportunity: The Story of the Unique Emily Griffith Opportunity School of Denver.* Boulder: Johnson Pub. Co., 1965, 198 pp., bib.,index.
Elinor Bleumel has also written Dr. Florence Sabin and Colorado Women of the Century.

Fallis, Edwinia H. *When Denver and I Were Young.* Denver: Big Mountain Press, 1956, 198 pp., illus.
Childhood memories of a schoolmarm born in Denver in 1876.

Noel, Thomas J. Colorado *Catholicism and The Archdiocese of Denver*, 1857-1989 Niwot: University Press of Colorado, 1989. 468 pp., index, bib., illus, maps.

Whitacre, Christine. *Molly Brown: Denver's Unsinkable Lady*. Denver: Historic Denver, Inc., 1984. 84 p., illus. Foreword by Tammy Grimes. Introduction by Debbie Reynolds.
The best book so far on Mollie attempts to unravel multiple layers of folklore shrouding Denver's most remarkable women—an early day feminist, suffragist and historic preservationist.

Economic History

Bean, Geraldine. *Charles Boettcher: A Study on Pioneer-—Western Enterprise*. Boulder: Westview Press, 1976, 220 pp., illus., notes, bib.
Biography of the co-founder of Great Western Sugar Company, Ideal Basic Cement Company, Capital Life Insurance Company, and numerous other entrepreneurial activities as well as Colorado's greatest philanthropic foundation.

Breck, Allen D. *John Evans of Denver: Portrait of a Twentieth Century Banker*. Boulder: Pruett Pub. Co., 1972, 249 pp., illus., notes, bib., index.

Breck, Allen D. *William Gray Evans: Portrait of a Western Executive*. Denver: The University of Denver, 1964, 290 pp., illus., notes, bib., index.
Biographies of Governor John Evans' son (William) and grandson (John) who continued with some of his many city-shaping enterprises. These are the definite accounts by the longtime chairman of the University of Denver History Department.

Brundage, David. *The Making of Western Labor Radicalism: Denver's Organized Workers, 1879-1905*. Urbana & Chicago: Univ. of Illinois Press, 1994. 207 p., index, endnotes.
A well-written overview of the labor movement, emphasizing the evolution of radical unions such as the WFM and IWW.

Foster, Mark S. *Henry M. Porter: Rocky Mountain Empire Builder*. Niwot: Univ. Press of Colorado, 1991. 184 p., index, notes, illus.

Noel, Thomas J. *Growing Through History...The Colorado National Banks, 1862-1987* Denver: CU-Denver Colorado Studies Center, 1987. 160 pp., illus., index, bib.

Smith, Duane A. *Horace Tabor: His Life and the Legend*. Boulder: Colorado Associated University Press, 1973. 1990 reprint. 395 pp., illus., notes, bib., index.
The best account of Tabor's personal, business, and political life by the much published professor at Fort Lewis College. A superb attempt to sort out facts from folklore.

Ethnic Groups

Coel, Margaret. *Chief Left Hand: Southern Arapaho*. Norman: University of Oklahoma Press, 1981, 338 pp., illus., maps, notes, bib., index.
A fascinating, sad look at one of the original Denver natives.

Dunning, John. *Denver*. N.Y.: Times Books, 1980, 407 pp.
A lusty historical novel that vividly portrays Denver journalism, politics, and the Ku Klux Klan in the 1920s.

Uchill, Ida Libert. *Pioneers, Peddlers and Tsadikim*. Denver: Sage Books, 1957, 327 pp., notes, bib., index.
Splendid history of Jews in Colorado.

Government & Politics

League of Women Voters of Denver. *Know Your Denver Government*. Denver: L.W.V., 1979, 1989, 1996. 80 pp., illus.
This booklet outlines everything from Denver history to the water system, from the tennis courts to the judicial system, from public housing to population trends. Wonderfully concise and systematic coverage of the myriad arms of city government. Fifteen maps and charts help make this an invaluable handbook for every Denverite. The League also publishes neighborhood guides in connection with their annual tours of Denver neighborhoods.

Johnson, Charles A. *Denver's Mayor Speer*. Denver: Green Mountain Press, 1969. 255 pp., illus., bib., index.
A eulogy to Denver's greatest mayor and city boss who converted a drab, dusty frontier town to a city beautiful.

Kelly, George V. *The Old Gray Mayors of Denver*. Boulder: Pruett Publishing Co., 1976, 266 pp., illus., index.
An insider describes the mayoral regimes of Stapleton, Newton, Nicholson, Batterton, Currigan, and McNichols in one of the few books on 20th century Denver.

Kelsey, Henry, Jr. *Frontier Capitalist: The Life of John Evans*. Boulder: Pruett Publishing Co. and Colorado Historical Society, 1969, 372 pp., index, illus., notes, bib.
Definitive portrait of the key man in 19th-century Denver.

King, Clyde I. *The History of the Government of Denver with Special References to Its Relations with Public Service Corporations.* Denver: Fisher Book Co., 1911, 322 pp., notes, index.
A progressive reformer attempts to document the sometimes shady development of Denver's municipal government and public utilities.

Larimer, William H. H. *Reminiscences of General William Larimer and of His Son, William H. H. Larimer,* ed. by Herman S. Davis. Lancaster, Pa.: The New Era Printing Co., 1918, 256 pp., illus., notes, index.
Entertaining recollections of the claim jumpers who founded Denver and proclaimed, "I am Denver City."

Larsen, Charles. *The Good Fight: The Life and Times of Ben B. Lindsey.* Chicago: Quadrangle Books, 1972, 307 pp., bib., index.
Good biography of Colorado's greatest reformer who was run out of state in the 1920s.

Lindsey, Benjamin Barr & Harvey J. O'Higgins. *The Beast.* Garden City: Doubleday, 1911. 340 p.
Chilling exposé by the celebrated Juvenile Court judge and muckraking reformer who blackens Denver's power elite—Evans, Moffat, Hughes, Cheesman, Buchtel—sparing not even the clergy. The trail of the Beast in Denver led, according to the Judge, "step by step, from the dives to the police board, from the police board to the lower courts, from the courts to the political leaders to the corporation magnates who ruled all. The trail leads from the offices of the corporations to the doors of the Capitol, it ascends the steps of the State House; it enters the sacred precinct of the Supreme Court itself." A fast cure for any nostalgic soul hungry for the good old days when politicians were supposedly honest and democracy supposedly pure.

Noel, Thomas J. *Denver's Larimer Street: Main Street, Skid Row, and Urban Renaissance.* Denver: Historic Denver, Inc., 1981, 1983. 195 pp., illus., maps, index.

Parks, Planning, Recreation & Sports

Foster, Mark and Irv Moss. *Home Run in the Rockies: The History of Baseball in Colorado.* Denver: A.B. Hirschfeld Press, 1994. 144 p., illus. Company, 1983).
Foster, a star of the Denver Bluestockings Vintage Baseball team, also booked the Denver Bears.

Noel, Thomas J. *The Denver Athletic Club, 1884-1984.* Denver: D.A.C., 1983, 106 p. illus., index.

Parkhill, Forbes. *The Wildest of the West.* N.Y.: Henry Holt and Co., 1951, 310 pp., index, bib.
Parkhill pulls the sheets off Denver's 19th-century demi-monde.

Parkhill, Forbes, *Mister Barney Ford: A Portrait in Bistre.* Denver: Sage Books, 1963, 218 p., illus., bib., index.
Another of Parkhill's half-dozen books on Denver, this one focuses on Denver's leading black entrepreneur.

Perkin, Robert L. *The First Years: An Informal History of Denver and the Rocky Mountain News,1859-1959.* N.Y.: Doubleday, 1959, 624 p., illus., notes, bib., index.
This witty, highly readable account of the Rocky Mountain News and Denver is a splendid complement to the less reliable Timberline by Gene Fowler, who wrote the introduction for this treasure chest of knowledge and trivia.

Reps, John W. *Cities of the American West: A History of Frontier Urban Planning.* Princeton: Princeton University Press, 1979, 827 pp., illus., notes, bib., index.
A monumental, lavishly illustrated 8.5 pound grand tour of the grid towns sprinkled across the West by town boomers.

Social History

Casey, Lee, ed. *Denver Murders.* N.Y. Duell, Sloan & Pearce, 1946, 217 pp.
Eight writers report on eight different and spectacular homicides from the Gordon case of 1860 to the Spider Man in 1942.

Cook, David J. *Hands Up: A Condensed Criminal History of the Far West.* Denver: Republican Pub. Co., 1882, 285 pp., illus. (Several reprints).
Harem-scarum war stories of Denver's most famous detective.

Halaas, David F. *Fairmount & Historic Colorado.* Denver: Fairmount Cemetery Association, 1976, 104 pp., illus.
Dr. Halaas has made this potentially morbid tale an engrossing history not only of Fairmount, but of other early boneyards and the city on which they have thrived.

Noel, Thomas J. *The City and the Saloon: Denver, 1858-1916.* Lincoln: University of Nebraska Press, 1982; Univ. of Colorado Press reprint, 1996. 148 pp., illus., maps, notes, bib., index.
A liquid history of Denver's founding, politics, ethnic groups, and social fragmentation.

Van Cise, Philip S. *Fighting the Underworld.* Boston: Houghton Mifflin, 1936, 369 pp., illus., index.
An exposé of Denver during the Prohibition period by the district attorney who finally nailed underworld czar Lou Blonger.

Transportation

Athearn, Robert G. *Rebel of the Rockies: A History of the Denver and Rio Grande and Western Railroad.* New Haven: Yale University Press, 1952. 395 pp., illus., notes, bib., index.
Of 100 Colorado railroads, this gritty narrow gauge incorporated in 1870 is the only Denver based survivor. Professor Athearn eloquently and authoritatively traces the D&RGW's long uphill route to profits, independence and fame through Rocky Mountain scenery still enjoyed by passengers on the Durango-Silverton, Cumbres-Toltec, and Rio Grande Zephyr.

Forrest, Kenton & Charles Albi. *Denver's Railroads: The Story of Union Station and the Railroads of Denver.* Golden: Colorado Railroad Museum, 1981, 244 pp., illus., maps, index.

Miller, Jeff. *Stapleton International Airport: The First Fifty Years.* Boulder: Pruett Pub. Co., 1983, 160 pp., illus., bib., index.

Jones, William C. & F. Hol Wagner, Jr. *Mile-High Trolleys.* Boulder: Pruett Pub. Co., 1974, 120 pp., rev. ed. of a 1955 work, over 200 photos, drawings, timetables, and maps.

Women

Bluemel, Elinor. *Florence Sabin: Colorado Woman of the Century* Boulder: Univ. Press of Colorado, 1959. 238 pp., index, bib.

French, Emily. *Emily: The Diary of A Hard-Worked Woman.* ed. by Janet Lecompte. Lincoln: Univ. of Nebraska Press, 1987, 199p., index, epilogue, notes. *A painfully detailed look at a year in the life of a washerwoman. The best insight we have on the life of a woman bearing the stigma of a divorce and "working out."*

Mazzulla, Fred (with Max Miller, Jo Mazzula and Margaret Miller). *Holladay Street.* N. Y.: Ballantine Books, 1962, 224 pp., illus., index. *A titillating tour of Denver's red light district that has since been cleaned up and renamed Market Street.*

Sanford, Mollie Dorsey. *Mollie: The Journal of Mollie Dorsey Sanford...* Intro. and notes by Donald F. Danker. Lincoln: Univ. of Nebraska Press, 1959. 201 p.

Secrest, Clark. *Helle's Belles: Denver's Brides of the Multitudes with attention to Various Gamblers, Scoundrels, and Mountebanks and a Biography of Sam Howe, Frontier Lawman.* Aurora: Hindsight Historical Publications, 1996. 348 p., index, bib, endnotes, photos, drawings, appendices.

Beaton, Gail. *Denver's Women's Clubs.* Univ. of Colorado, Denver. M.A. History Thesis, 1987.

Goldstein, Marcia T. *Breaking Down Barriers: Black and White Women's Vision of Integration.* Univ. of Colorado, Denver. M.A. History Thesis, 1995.

CHAPTER BIBLIOGRAPHY

Chapter One

Afton, Jean, David F., Halaas & Andrew E. Masich. *Cheyenne Dog Soldiers: A Ledgerbook History.* Niwot: University Press of Colorado, 1997.

Blue, Daniel, *"Statement of Daniel Blue, late of Clyde Township, Whiteside Co. Ill., made on the 12th day of May, 1859, at the office of the Leavenworth and Pike's Peak Express Company, in the City of Denver,"* reprinted in The Colorado Magazine, VII (November, 1931), p.232-233.

Cassells, E. Steve. *The Archaeology of Colorado.* Boulder: Johnson Books, 1984.

Coel, Margaret. *Chief Left Hand: Southern Arapaho.* Norman: University of Oklahoma Press, 1981.

Conard, Howard Louis. *"Uncle Dick" Wootton: The Pioneer Frontiersman of the Rocky Mountain Region...* With an intro. by Major Joseph Kirkland. Chicago: W.E. Dibble, 1890.

Larimer, William Henry Harrison. *Reminiscences of General William Larimer and of His Son William H.H. Larimer, Two of the Founders of Denver City.* Comp. from letters and from notes written by the late William H.H. Larimer... by Herman S. Davis. Lancaster, Pa.: New Era Printing Co., 1918.

Smiley, Jerome Constant. *History of Denver, with Outlines of the Earlier History of the Rocky Mountain Country.* Denver: Denver Times, Times-Sun Pub. Co., 1901.

Spring, Agnes Wright. *"Rush to the Rockies, 1859."* Colorado Magazine, vol. 36, April, 1959, p. 97.

Trenholm, Virginia Cole. *The Arapahoes, Our People.* Norman, OK: University of Oklahoma Press, 1970.

U.S. Bureau of Indian Affairs. *Letters Received by the Office [later Bureau] of Indian Affairs, 1824-1881,* Upper Arkansas Agency, 1855-1874., National Archives and Federal Records Center, Denver.

White, John. *Sketches from America.* London: Sampson, Low, Son and Marston, 1870.

Chapter Two

Arps, Louisa Ward. *Denver in Slices.* Athens, Ohio: Swallow Press, 1983.

Demas Barnes. *From the Atlantic to the Pacific Overland....* (N.Y.: D. Van Nostrand, 1866)

Denver, People's Government. *Minutes of the Meetings of the People's Government of the City of Denver, October 8, 1860-November 19, 1861.* Coe Collection, Beinecke Library, Yale University, New Haven, Connecticut.

Hill, Agnes (Leonard) Scanland. *The Colorado Blue Book.* Denver: James R. Ives, Pub., 1892. 237p.

Kingsley, Rose Georgiana. *South by West: Or, Winter in the Rocky Mountains and Spring in Mexico.* London: W. Isbister & Co., 1874.

Moynihan, Betty. *Augusta Tabor: A Pioneering Woman.* Evergreen, Cordillera Press, 1988.

Noel, Thomas J. *Denver: The City & The Saloon, 1858-1916.* Lincoln: Univ. of Nebraska Press, 1982/ University Press of Colorado reprint, 1996.

Noel, Thomas J. *Growing Through History with Colorado: The Colorado National Banks; The First 125 Years, 1862-1987.* Denver: Colorado National Banks & The Colorado Studies Center, Univ. of Colorado at Denver.

Smith, Duane A. *Horace Tabor: His Life and the Legend.* Boulder: University Press of Colorado, 1973.

Chapter Three

Breck, Allen D. *The Centennial History of the Jews of Colorado, 1859-1959.* Denver: The University of Denver & Hirschfeld Press, 1960.

Karnes, Thomas L. *William Gilpin: Western Nationalist.* Austin: University of Texas Press, 1970.

Kelsey, Harry E. Jr., *Frontier Capitalist: The Life of John Evans.* Boulder: Colorado Historical Society & Pruett Publishing Co., 1969.

Lovelace, Walter B. and Walter S. *Jesse Shwayder and the Golden Rule: First Fifty Years of Shwayder Bros., Inc., 1910-1960.* Chicago: The Lakeside Press, 1960.

Noel, Thomas J. *Colorado Catholicism and the Archdiocese of Denver, 1857-1989.* Niwot: University Press of Colorado, 1989.

Noel, Thomas J. *"All Hail The Denver Pacific: Denver's First Railroad,"* The Colorado Magazine , Spring, 1973 (L, 3), p. 91-116.

Perkin, Robert L. *The First Years: An Informal History of Denver and the Rocky Mountain News,1859-1959.* N.Y.: Doubleday, 1959.

Chapter Four

Arps, Louisa. *Denver in Slices.* Denver: Sage Books, 1959 (1983 reprint)

Converey, William. *John Kernan Mullen.* CU-Denver in-process M.A. History Thesis, 1997.

DeRose, Christine, *"Inside Little Italy: Italian Immigrants in Denver,"* Colorado Magazine, LIV (Summer, 1977), p. 277-293.

Dorsett, Lyle W., *"The Ordeal of Colorado's Germans During World War I,"* Colorado Magazine, LI (Fall, 1974), p. 277-293.

Historical Journal of the Denver Turnverein, 1865-1965. Denver: Denver Turnverein, 1965.

Leonard, Stephen J. *Denver's Foreign Born Immigrants, 1859-1900.* Claremont, California: Claremont Graduate School History Ph.D. Dissertation, 1971.

MacArthur, Mildred Sherwood. *History of the German Element in the State of Colorado.* Chicago: German-American Historical Society of Illinois, 1917.

Noel, Thomas J. *Denver: The City & The Saloon, 1858-1916.* Lincoln: University of Nebraska Press, 1982 (1996 reprint: University Press of Colorado).

Perelli, Giovanni. *Colorado and the Italians in Colorado.* Denver: Smith-Brooks Press, 1922.

Spence, Clark. *British Investments and the American Mining Frontier, 1860-1901.* Ithaca: Cornell Univ. Press, 1958.

Townshend, Richard B. *A Tenderfoot In Colorado.* London: John Lane and Bodley Head, 1923.

Vickers, William B. *History of the City of Denver.* Chicago: O.O. Baskin, 1880.

Wahlberg, Edgar M. *Voices in the Darkness: A Memoir.* Boulder: Roberts Rinehart, 1983.

Chapter Five

Bowles, Samuel. *The Switzerland of America: A Summer Vacation in the Parks and Mountains of Colorado.* Springfield, Mass.: Samuel Bowles & Co., 1869.

Ekstrand, Margaret E. & Thomas J. Noel. *The University Club of Denver: The First Hundred Years.* Denver: The University Club of Denver, 1991.

Gauge, Emma Abbott, *Western Wanderings and Summer Sauntering Through Picturesque Colorado.* Baltimore: The Lord Baltimore Press, 1900.

Hunt, Corinne. *The Brown Palace Story.* Denver: Rocky Mountain Writers Guild, 1982.

Noel, Thomas J. *The Denver Athletic Club, 1884-1984.* Denver: The Denver Athletic Club, 1983.

Simms, Willard E. *Ten Days Every January: A History of the National Western Stock Show.* Denver: The Western Stock Show Association, 1980.

Thompson, Phyllis T. *The Use of Mountain Recreation Resources: A Comparison of Recreation and Tourism in the Colorado Rockies and The Swiss Alps.* Boulder: University of Colorado Ph.D. Dissertation, 1970.

Whitacre, Christine. *The Denver Club.* Denver: University of Colorado at Denver M.A. History Thesis, 1994.

Chapter Six

Denver Municipal Facts. *City and County of Denver,* 1909-1931.

Larsen, Charles. *The Good Fight: The Remarkable Life and Times of Judge Ben Lindsey.* Chicago: Quadrangle Books, 1972.

Noel, Thomas J. and Barbara S. Norgren. *Denver: The City Beautiful and Its Architects.* Denver: Historic Denver, Inc., 1987/1993 reprint.

Reese, Carol McMichael. *The Politician and the City: Urban Form and City Beautiful Rhetoric in Progressive Era Denver*. Austin: University of Texas, 1992 Ph.D dissertation.

Russell, Don. *The Lives and Legends of Buffalo Bill*. Norman: Univ. of Oklahoma Press, 1960.

Wilson, William H. *The City Beautiful Movement*. Baltimore: The Johns Hopkins University Press, 1989.

Chapter Seven

Bluemel, Elinor. *Florence Sabin: Colorado Woman of the Century*. Boulder: University of Colorado Press, 1959.

Etter, Carolyn & Don. *The Denver Zoo: A Centennial History*. Niwot: The Denver Zoological Foundation & Roberts Rinehart Publishing Co., 1996.

Leonard, Stephen J. *Trails and Triumphs: A Colorado Portrait of the Great Depression, with FSA Photographs*. Niwot: Univ. Press of Colorado, 1993.

Miller, Jeff. *Stapleton International Airport: The First Fifty Years*. Boulder: Pruett Pub. Co., 1983.

Roundtree, Russ. *Western Oil Reporter's Rocky Mountain Oil History*. Denver: Hart Publications, 1984.

Wickens, James Frederick. *Colorado in the Great Depression*. Denver: University of Denver Ph.D. History Dissertation, 1964.

Chapter Eight

Bakke, Diane & Jackie Davis. *Places Around the Bases: A Historic Tour of the Coors Field Neighborhood*. Englewood: Westcliffe Publishers, Inc., 1995.

Gibson, Barbara. *The Lower Downtown Historic District*. Denver: Historic Denver, Inc. & Denver Museum of Natural History, 1995.

Etter, Don D. *Auraria: Where Denver Began*. Boulder: Colorado   Associated University Press, 1972.

Goldstein, Marcia Tremmel. *Breaking Down Barriers: Black and White Women's Visions of Integration: The Young Women's Christian Association in Denver and the Phyllis Wheatley Branch, 1915-1964*. Denver: Univ. of Colorado at Denver History M.A. Thesis, 1995.

Ferril, T. H. Thomas *Hornsby Ferril and the American West* ed. by Robert C. Baron, Stephen J. Leonard & Thomas J. Noel. Golden: Fulcrum Publishing Company, 1996.

Noel, Thomas J. *Denver's Landmarks & Historic Districts: A Pictorial Guide*. Foreword by Mayor Wellington Webb. Niwot: University Press of Colorado, 1996.

Noel, Thomas J. *Denver's Larimer Street: Main Street, Skid Row, and Urban Renaissance*. Denver: Historic Denver, Inc., 1981, 1983.

West, William D. *Curtis Park: A Denver Neighborhood*. Photos by Don D. Etter. Boulder: Colorado Associated University Press, 1980.

Chapter Nine

Arps, Louisa Ward. *Cemetery to Conservatory and A Jubilee History of Denver Botanic Gardens, 1951-1976 by Bernice E. Peters*. Denver: Denver Botanic Gardens, Inc., 1980.

Bradley, Jeff, Jane Fudge, et. al. *Denver: Confluence of the Arts*. Denver: Meridian International, Inc. & Hirschfeld Press, 1995.

Chandler, Roger A. *Fentress Bradburn Architects*. Washington, D.C.: Studio Press, 1995.

Denver Planning Office. 1989 *City of Denver Comprehensive Plan*.

Hornby, William J. *Eye on the Horizon: The Greater Denver Corporation, 1987-1995*. Denver: Denver Metro Chamber of Commerce, 1995.

Morley, Judy. *Oasis in the City: The History of Denver Botanic Gardens*. Denver: M.A. History Thesis University of Colorado at Denver, 1995.

Noel, Thomas J. *Denver's Larimer Street: Main Street, Skid Row, and Urban Renaissance*. Denver: Historic Denver, Inc., 1981, 1983.

Noel, Thomas J. "Unexplored Western Skies: Denver International Airport," Journal of the West, XXX, 1 (January, 1991), pp. 90-100.

Chapter Ten

The Denver Art Museum: The First Hundred Years. Denver: Denver Art Museum, 1996.

James, Franklin J. *"Patterns of Homelessness in the Denver Metropolitan Area."* Denver: University of Colorado at Denver, 1995.

Mehls, Steven, Drake, J. & James E. Fell. *Aurora: Gateway to the Rockies.* Denver: Cordillera Press, 1985.

Pettem, Silvia. *Boulder: Evolution of A City.* Foreword by Liston Leyendecker. Niwot: University Press of Colorado, 1994.

Smith, Marion. *Westminster Then and Now.* Westminster: City of Westminster, 1976.

Smith, Phyllis. A *Look at Boulder: From Settlement to City.* Boulder: Pruett Publishing Company, 1981.

Tucker, Deborah. *To Make A Mayor.* Lanham, Maryland: University Press of America, 1995.

Wilcox, Patricia, ed. *Lakewood-Colorado: An Illustrated Biography.* Lakewood: Lakewood 25th Birthday Commission, 1994. 316 p., endnotes, illus., maps.

INDEX

Partners In Denver Index

Photo Credits

Endsheets
In this painting of Denver's first year, the Arapaho welcome newcomers to their camp along Cherry Creek. Log cabins of Green Russell, William McGaa, Charles Blake, and other pioneers lined Wewatta Street before it turned into Ferry (now 11th) Street where wagons were ferried across the South Platte. *Credit: Denver Public Library*

Building a Greater Denver
Pages 200-205
Background art based on photo by Thomas J. Noel

Business and Finance
Pages 264-265
Background art based on photo by Thomas J. Noel

Manufacturing and Mining
Pages 286-287
Background art based on photo by Thomas J. Noel

Networks
Pages 318-319
Background art based on photo by Thomas J. Noel

Professions
Pages 336-337
Background art based on photo by Thomas J. Noel

Quality of Life
Pages 372-373
Background art based on photo by Thomas J. Noel

Telecommunications and Technology
Pages 420-421
Background art based on photo by Thomas J. Noel

The Marketplace
Pages 446-447
Background art based on photo by Thomas J. Noel